TRADITIONS OF ELOQUENCE

TRADITIONS OF ELOQUENCE

The Jesuits and Modern Rhetorical Studies

CINTHIA GANNETT AND

JOHN C. BRERETON, EDITORS

FORDHAM UNIVERSITY PRESS

New York   2016

Fordham University Press has no responsibility for the persistence or accuracy of URLs for external or third-party Internet websites referred to in this publication and does not guarantee that any content on such websites is, or will remain, accurate or appropriate.

Fordham University Press also publishes its books in a variety of electronic formats. Some content that appears in print may not be available in electronic books.

Visit us online at www.fordhampress.com.

Library of Congress Cataloging-in-Publication Data

Traditions of eloquence : the Jesuits and modern rhetorical studies / edited by Cinthia Gannett and John Brereton. — First edition.
        pages cm
    Includes bibliographical references and index.
    ISBN 978-0-8232-6452-0 (cloth : alk. paper) — ISBN 978-0-8232-6453-7 (pbk. : alk. paper)
    1. Rhetoric—Study and teaching (Higher) 2. Jesuits—Education (Higher)   I. Gannett, Cinthia, 1959–, editor.   II. Brereton, John, 1943– editor.
    P53.27.T728 2015
    808.0088'27153—dc23
                                    2015018253

Printed in the United States of America

18 17 16   5 4 3 2 1

First edition

CONTENTS

FOREWORD

John O'Malley, S.J.

When the Society of Jesus was founded in 1540, Europe was already engaged in a life–death confrontation known as the Reformation and Counter-Reformation. This confrontation dominates history textbooks dealing with the era. When the Thirty Years' War ended in 1648, the last great religious conflict of the early modern period, not only had nations and territories become permanently identified with specific religious confessions, but they had at the same time appropriated cultural configurations distinctively Lutheran, Calvinist, Anglican, or Catholic. Europe was divided culturally as well as religiously.

That is the scenario with which we are all familiar. Into it the Jesuits fit neatly not only as the premier "agents of the Counter-Reformation" but as propagators of a Catholic culture marked by baroque painting and architecture, elaborate civic and religious festivities that might go on for days or weeks, and a rhythm of feast and fast distinctively Catholic. Their churches were filled with images of Christ and the saints, and their exploits in Japan, China, New France, and other exotic places thrilled their supporters back home. There was little or nothing like this in Protestant cultures.

The scenario is correct but woefully incomplete. Yes, certainly, on a deep level Europe was culturally divided, but on an equally deep level it was not. The latter story is rarely told, even though over thirty years ago Marc Fumaroli issued its manifesto in his classic study, *L'Âge de l'éloquence*. Fumaroli's point, and the point of all those who seriously study the history of the rhetorical tradition, is that by the late sixteenth century the literate of every religious confession were products of the Renaissance revival of the *studia humanitatis*, in which rhetoric was the configuring discipline. They had appropriated and internalized a cultural ideal that cut across national and religious divides. The Renaissance and the humanism at its core did not die with the outbreak of the Reformation, as textbooks generally imply, but was just getting launched on a triumphant conquest of minds and hearts, which was accomplished primarily by school systems based on the humanistic program.

In the middle of the nineteenth century Ernest Renan delivered a powerful and influential address to the Académie français in which he denounced rhetoric as "the only error of the Greeks," and he held the Jesuits principally responsible for foisting this aberration onto the public. Within a decade the French government suppressed the teaching of rhetoric in public lycées. The rhetorical tradition began to suffer similar attacks elsewhere.

Nonetheless, despite the blows now directed against it, the "age of eloquence," though weakening in its influence, was still strong. In roughly the same period when Renan spoke, for instance, Harvard College built Memorial Hall as its tribute to those from the Union side who had fallen in combat during the Civil War. The Hall, still standing today and a major landmark, is in essence a Neo-Gothic temple to rhetoric: running around the outside wall in a series of niches are the busts of great orators—Demosthenes, Chrysostom, Pitt, Cicero, Bossuet, Burke, and Daniel Webster.

For at least four centuries, therefore, everyone who had a "proper education" had a rhetorical education. It was, like every educational system, not without its weaknesses, but it had some splendid strengths, not the least of which was a fully articulated philosophy, whose rudiments go all the way back to Isocrates, Plato's younger contemporary. That philosophy, further developed in the Renaissance by such humanists as Erasmus, was radically student-centered. It looked to the physical, social, emotional, and especially ethical development of the student qua human person.

Literature in all its forms—poetry, drama, history, and so forth—constituted the core of the curriculum. The humanists saw these "humane letters" as crucial to true education because they treated questions pertinent to human life—questions of life and death, of virtue and vice, of greed and redemption, and of the ambiguities of human decision-making. They dealt with these questions not so much through abstract principles as through stories and historical examples that illuminated moral alternatives and, supposedly, inspired students to make choices leading to a satisfying human life.

In this tradition a satisfying human life was not self-enclosed and self-absorbed but directed, at least in some measure, to the common weal. Cicero put it succinctly in his *De officiis*: "We are not born for ourselves alone . . . but for the sake of other human beings, that we might be able mutually to help one another." That finality, which is what made the tradition appealing to the Jesuits, was imposed on the system by rhetoric, the culminating and defining discipline in the curriculum. The rhetor was a certain kind of person.

For Renaissance educators, as for their forebears in antiquity such as Cicero and Quintilian, rhetoric meant primarily the speech act. Although it included effective communication in all forms, it looked first and foremost to speech-making. Rhetoric and oratory were virtually synonymous. Speeches take place in public spaces with audiences present, awaiting the message. In such situations, the speaker's whole person and personality are on exhibition and play into the effectiveness of the words he utters. As the old saying goes, what you are thunders so loud I can't hear what you say.

Rhetors were by definition, therefore, public persons. They addressed their fellow citizens with the hope of persuading them to certain courses of action. Great responsibilities thus rested upon their shoulders. They had been taught that in the murky darkness of human motivation and decision-making one must often surrender the ideal of "the best course of action" for the more modest "better course." In the rhetorical tradition "humane letters" were supposed to sharpen students' aesthetic sensibilities but, more to the point, through their depictions of characters and situations they mirrored the ambiguities of our own life experiences and invited reflection upon them. Isocrates and others stressed that rhetors must speak appropriately for the occasion, for the *kairos*, which meant adaptation and accommodation to the situation as they found it, not as it was supposed to be. "Less" was sometimes the best that could be achieved.

The tradition nurtured what Henri Marrou many decades ago, borrowing from Pascal, called the "spirit of finesse," to be distinguished from the "geometric spirit." The virtue the tradition especially wanted to cultivate, therefore, was prudence—that is, good judgment, the wisdom that characterizes ideal leaders and makes them sensitive in assessing the relative merits of competing probabilities in the conflicts of human situations. Prudence is the virtue of making appropriate and humane decisions, the virtue of the wise person, who is the very opposite of the technocrat, the bureaucrat, and the zealot. The very opposite of somebody whose decisions are governed by "the geometric spirit."

Such talk of virtue leads to an altogether radical question: Is it too much to speak of a "rhetorical philosophy of life"? I am inclined to think that it is not. Rhetoric in the humanistic tradition was not simply a discipline, not simply the culminating discipline, but the discipline that imbued the whole system with its finality and gave it a life-shaping force. I repeat: The rhetor was a certain kind of person.

After Plato's scathing criticism of the sophists' indifference to ethical questions, theorists of rhetoric beginning with Isocrates have through the ages insisted that the good speaker, the good practitioner of rhetoric, the good leader had to be a good person. Quintilian defined the rhetor succinctly as "a *good* person, skilled in effective communication"—*vir bonus, dicendi peritus*. Almost from its inception, the rhetorical tradition had a moral center.

The program of student formation in this tradition began, however, not with the study of oratory but with other forms of literature. It aimed at developing in the students a high standard of excellence in written and oral expression, which was honed by paying attention to words and to their effective use. It was directed, that is to say, to the cultivation of eloquence. The ideal: to mean what you say and to say what you mean—and to say it with grace, accuracy, and force. No one put the issue better than Mark Twain, who said that the difference between the right word and the almost right word is the difference between a lightning bolt and a lightning bug. Eloquence consists in choosing the lightning bolt.

Furthermore, theorists in the rhetorical tradition realized, at least implicitly, that thought and finding the right word to express it were not two acts but one. Luther did not really know the truth his mind had been dancing around until his eureka experience gave him the words to express it, "justification by faith alone!" Without the right word, the theorists knew, we do not have the thought but a musing or a rumination. "Ya know what I mean" means you do not know what you mean because you cannot express it. At the very headwaters of the rhetorical tradition, Isocrates himself said, "The proper use of language is the surest index of sound understanding."

It should not therefore be difficult to understand why the *studia humanitatis* with rhetoric at its core would appeal to the Jesuits and make them such enthusiastic promoters of it. The finality of contributing to the common good and being of service to others, expressed so eloquently by Cicero, their favorite author, correlated well with the gospel injunction to love one's neighbors and be of service to them. But that is just the beginning of the story.

From their earliest days the Jesuits defined themselves as "ministers of the Word." In their foundational documents, preaching is the ministry that holds pride of place. No wonder that they pounced on classical rhetoric as holding the key to make them effective communicators of the Word of God. They produced books, "ecclesiastical rhetorics," that adapted rhetorical principles to the Christian pulpit. The study of rhetoric taught them that a sermon—that is, a "sacred oration"—is not a lecture and, further, that to be effective preachers they had to employ the right words and not the almost right words.

They undertook the laborious labor of operating schools in the humanistic tradition because of the type of person they promised to produce. I call attention to the fifteen goals for Jesuit schools that Juan Alfonso de Polanco, St. Ignatius's brilliant secretary, provided for members of the Society of Jesus just a few years after the Jesuits opened their first school in Messina, Sicily. The list could have been written by Erasmus himself. The last goal sums up the rest: "Those who are now only students will grow up to be pastors, civic officials, administrators of justice, and will fill other important posts to everybody's profit and advantage."

On a more profound and pervasive level, the rhetorical tradition's impact on the Jesuits was to incline them—or at least many of them—to a certain mind-set, to a certain "spirit of finesse" that became their hallmark. Their well-known "accommodation strategy" in the missions of Japan, China, Vietnam, and other places instantiated the flexibility and sensitivity to concrete situations characteristic of the ideal rhetor. Such flexibility is anathema to the zealot and all those whose decisions are made under the influence of the rigidity of the "geometric spirit."

Nowhere was "the spirit of finesse" more operative among the Jesuits than in their adoption of probabilism as their preferred system of ethical decision-making. In his *Provincial Letters*, Pascal's smear campaign against them on this score gave not only probabilism but casuistry itself a bad name that is with us still. But the system does not deserve Pascal's scorn, for, while upholding moral principles, it tried to accommodate them to the times, places, and circumstances in which we live our lives. It recognized that in moral decision-making we rarely face black-and-white choices but must, instead, often contend with issues where good arguments can be made on both sides.

In conclusion, I refer again to Marc Fumaroli. He made the crucial point about the Jesuits when he said that for them rhetoric was not "a trite technique of manipulation" but "the creative driving force of their ethics, spirituality, exegesis, anthropology, and theology." I have tried to suggest just why this was so and to provide a few examples of it. I have thus tried to anticipate in some small way the contributions that follow in this rich volume and to provide a certain context for them.

PREFACE

Traditions of Eloquence explores the important contributions that Jesuit rhetorical traditions have made—and continue to make—to higher education and to rhetorical theory, scholarship, practice, and pedagogy as a transdisciplinary project central to the humanities over nearly five centuries. We use the verb *explore* deliberately, because much of this history has been lost, effaced, or dispersed, and we see the book as a series of forays into unfamiliar territories. Indeed, what is now this collection started out several years ago as a process of self-education by teacher/scholar/administrators at Jesuit schools, trying to recover, from occasional, scattered, and often oblique references, the elusive notion of *eloquentia perfecta*, and of how it might be put to use once again, both as a signature project rooted in the Jesuit educational mission and as a project readily deployable everywhere for the current educational moment. As we undertook our work, writing for ourselves and giving papers on the subject at national and international conferences, we found that many others were intrigued by our investigations: scholars and teachers of rhetoric generally, those interested in Jesuit education nationally and internationally, those in schools that take their missions seriously, and those who regard American higher education as in need of greater intellectual and psychosocial integration. We believe that our inquiries into this often occluded but living set of rhetorical traditions, four hundred fifty years old, have much to say to each of these separate audiences.

However, apart from the three Jesuit contributors, we lay scholars are glad we knew so little when we started, or we might not have undertaken such a complex and ambitious task, and we acknowledge that our efforts are provisional—first maps of this huge intellectual geography, relying on disparate accounts and inquiries and our own novice observations. Asking top scholars to write outside their comfort zones, we came to rely on some of the often-invoked Jesuit educational values we have come to honor throughout the book's arduous creation, using terms that call up the Jesuit heritage in its own special language. The first is *accompaniment*, or *nuestro modo de proceder* (our way of proceeding)—working together to share resources and call on each other's drafts throughout the extended process. The second is *cura personalis*—supporting each other as "whole people" with demanding work and home lives, which took the form of offering regular encouragement or negotiating additional time to complete some chapters through the many-layered revision process. And, finally, *magis* (the more)—striving to work beyond our traditional areas of expertise in the service of this collective project. Of course, we have aimed for *eloquentia perfecta* in all our imperfect ways.

Given the multiple kinds of audiences, who may have quite different purposes for reading, however, we appreciate that some parts of the collection will be more interesting than others, according to one's expertise and point of entry. (We know this because each of our excellent reviewers liked the manuscript a great deal, but each one thought it should focus much more on one area that another reviewer felt already received far too much attention, and each suggested the chapters be reordered in quite different, even contradictory ways.) We have also tried to leave some contextual redundancies within various chapters, as authors used their own treatments of historical trends and insights to mark the development of their specific claims. The additional context means that essays can be better read as standalone works, as we know that readers of collections like this tend to sample and read according to individual principles of selection and not the order in which the chapters were placed. Also, we have prepared introductions to each of the three main parts as readerly guides to the sets of topics and claims addressed therein.

The Jesuits, the Roman Catholic order of men founded by St. Ignatius Loyola in the 1540s, in the midst of great intellectual and cultural growth and great religious conflict, have been alternately revered and reviled, honored and suppressed. Even as their fortunes waxed and waned in various countries and regions, they became known for the enduring system of schooling they developed. The first Catholic order to commit to teaching both religious and lay students as a formal ministry, by 1773 the Jesuits were operating over eight hundred schools and colleges around the world, the largest international educational system ever known. For centuries, the Jesuits were regarded as the schoolmasters of Europe and beyond, educating powerful religious and secular leaders in politics, arts, and the sciences. However, the Jesuits made powerful enemies during the Enlightenment; from 1773 to 1814 they were suppressed by the pope, their schools closed, their libraries dispersed, their members exiled.

"Contemplatives in action," the early Jesuits were consummate scholars and rhetors, employing all the intellectual and language arts for preaching and undertaking missionary, educational, and other charitable works in the world. The study, pedagogy, and practice of classical grammar and rhetoric, adapted to Christian humanism, naturally provided a central focus of this powerful educational system as part of the Jesuit commitment to "the ministries of the Word." The result was a distinctive, dynamic set of traditions that at its best integrated the spiritual, intellectual, and civic uses of language, *eloquentia perfecta*.

Traditions of Eloquence traces the development of Jesuit rhetorical practice and pedagogy in Renaissance Europe, follows the expansion of Jesuit education in the United States, with its attendant opportunities and many challenges and limitations, and documents the reemergence of interest in a newly reimagined *eloquentia perfecta* on campuses and in scholarly discussion across

America in the twenty-first century. Most Western education was rhetorically based for centuries, of course, but the Jesuits maintained a commitment to their distinct humanistic curriculum and approach even as educational and social cultures changed and the primacy of oral rhetoric was increasingly displaced by written discourse.

Indeed, in the later nineteenth century, while American higher education moved away from the classics and the broad humanities toward the German academic model, with departments, majors, and a focus on research, Jesuit colleges responded in complex ways, sometimes accommodating, more often resisting these shifts. Gradually responding to criticism that their curriculum was obsolete, mid-twentieth-century American Jesuit colleges slowly and often reluctantly reduced their multiyear classical humanities and rhetoric-based curriculum, branching out to include courses in philosophy and theology and with studies more closely aligned with modern careers.

Paradoxically, just as Jesuit colleges were jettisoning the final remnants of their extensive, integrated classical curriculum, America witnessed a remarkable revival of interest in classical rhetorical scholarship and pedagogy, spurred in significant ways by such Jesuits as Walter Ong and by such Jesuit-influenced lay scholars as Edward P. J. Corbett. Today lay scholars and teachers at a variety of Jesuit colleges are recovering and reimagining the role and place of *eloquentia perfecta* at their Jesuit colleges and universities and elsewhere.

Our book argues that rhetoric, what the Jesuits termed *eloquentia perfecta*, offers a means of overcoming the scattered, dispersed curriculum that characterizes so much contemporary higher education. Rhetoric never was *only* a discipline: It can act as a *transdiscipline*, a means of paying close attention to language, to making meaning, to connecting ideas with words across academic and social contexts. For centuries the study of the classical languages, texts, and their rhetorical uses and effects weren't a part of the curriculum, they *were the heart of the curriculum.* Though we cannot, nor would we want to, recapture the specific kind of integrated rhetorical curricula of earlier times, we may be able to consider how rhetoric and composition courses, well-developed communication-across-the-curriculum and writing-in-the-disciplines programs, along with capstone writing projects, might be brought to the service of this integrative aim, along with reconnecting many of the now dispersed sites of *eloquentia perfecta* across the whole educational culture of the university. As Part III of the book explains, some Jesuit colleges are already moving in this promising direction. We invite scholars from all colleges, secular as well as religious, to consider this type of model of curricular integration.

The book has multiple purposes: to understand better the past, present, and future of Jesuit traditions and institutions themselves, and to delineate some of the ongoing, if rarely visible, roles that Jesuit rhetoric has had in shaping contemporary rhetorical scholarship, pedagogy, and practice in many sites and forms. For scholars and practitioners alike, the recovery and revitalization of rhetorical work can have profound and productive consequences. In a period of increasing laicization of faculty at Jesuit institutions and of ongoing reformulations of Jesuit educational mission and identity, this collection can help provide needed historical context, a sense of continuity in current practice, and a platform for creating future curricula and pedagogy. Thus, it will also be a valuable resource for faculty, staff, and administrators at Jesuit, faith-based, or mission-based colleges and universities wishing to understand a core premise of our educational heritage—that studying language in all its forms and uses teaches us to know ourselves, others, the Word, and the world, and know to how to use this great human gift for the greater good. *Traditions of Eloquence* is, then, the first book to address the long and significant history—and future—of Jesuit rhetoric as the core of a liberal-arts education. We know it will not be the last.

TRADITIONS OF ELOQUENCE

INTRODUCTION: THE JESUITS AND RHETORICAL STUDIES—LOOKING BACKWARD, MOVING FORWARD

Cinthia Gannett and John C. Brereton

> I exhort you, then, as I am bound to do for the greater glory of God, our Lord, and I beg of you by his love and reverence to improve your writing, and to conceive some appreciation for it, as well as a desire to edify your brethren and your neighbor by your letters.
> —Ignatius de Loyola, Letters

> A detailed study of Jesuit influence in rhetoric has yet to be written.
> —Thomas Conley

Traditions of Eloquence offers a series of perspectives on the distinctive centuries-long Jesuit enterprise of what they called "ministries of the word," particularly as these have been practiced and taught as rhetoric. Indeed, for centuries Jesuits offered a curriculum in humanistic rhetoric in hundreds of schools and colleges across the globe. Calling on multiple Renaissance versions of classical traditions as well as new modes of spiritual discourse, this set of dynamic rhetorical traditions has played a significant—though poorly understood—role in shaping discursive Jesuit education across the centuries, culminating in a rich revival in twentieth-century America. This understudied strand of rhetorical history addresses the long living (if sometimes frayed or torn) traditions of Jesuit rhetoric and rhetorical education and their continued reanimation across all the language arts, from their extraordinary guide to the curriculum, the *Ratio Studiorum* (1599), to the very recent work on the Jesuit rhetorician Walter Ong and media ecology (Farrell and Soukup, 2012). We claim that Jesuit rhetorics have had a significant influence on American rhetoric, composition, and communication studies in the twentieth century, and that some of their principles and practices can still serve as an integrative force in humanities higher education for the twenty-first century.

WHO ARE THE JESUITS?

The Jesuits are an order of male clergy, founded by Ignatius of Loyola (1491–1556), a Basque hidalgo who, after being wounded in battle, turned to a life of religious service and decided to join the learned clergy. After trying the University of

Alcala, and then Salamanca, he attended the University of Paris, where he and his companions bound themselves to be a company of religious together. They became an order of priests, the Society of Jesus, in 1540, one of many sixteenth-century reform efforts within the Catholic Church. Their first aims were winning souls for Christ as preachers and missionaries and improving the quality of the priesthood, but they quickly turned to educational work, flourishing in the seventeenth century, and becoming famous for their colleges. As a result of complex political and cultural forces, they were universally suppressed by the pope in 1773, their colleges and educational work nearly completely destroyed. Revived in 1814, they reestablished their colleges throughout the world but found perhaps their greatest success in the rapidly growing missionary territory of the United States, where they now operate twenty-eight colleges and universities.

As John O'Malley, S.J., explains in the foreword and Patricia Bizzell details in her chapter, the Society of Jesus held the rhetorical and discursive arts at its heart.[1] From the founding of the order, the Jesuits' own training was saturated with rhetoric, aiming at mastery of both theory and practice, and the Jesuits have always been identified as being, and creating, powerful rhetors across sacred and secular domains: preaching, teaching, writing—in fact, every form of communication. Indeed, the whole order can be seen as a "rhetorical system." O'Malley explains this key feature of Jesuit identity in *The First Jesuits*:

> Beginning with the *Exercises* [Loyola's devotional guide] themselves, the Jesuits were constantly advised to adapt what they said and did to times, circumstances, and persons. The rhetorical dimension of Jesuit ministry in this sense transcended the preaching and lecturing in which they were engaged and even the rhetorical foundation of the casuistry they practiced— it was a basic principle in all their ministries, even if they did not explicitly identify it as rhetorical.
>
> —O'Malley, *The First Jesuits*, 255

This flexible, accommodative stance would become a hallmark for what the Jesuits called their "way of proceeding."

One striking characteristic of the Jesuits has always been their well-deserved reputation for intellectualism, derived in large part from their lengthy training and expertise in erudition and the rhetorical arts, or *eloquentia perfecta*. All of the early Jesuits, the international group that joined with Ignatius to establish their original Company at the University of Paris—Jerónimo Nadal (1507–80), Peter Faber (1506–46), Juan Alfonso de Polanco (1517–76), Diego Lainez (1512–65), Francis Xavier (1506–52), Alfonso Salmerón (1515–85), and Nicolas Bobadilla (1511–90)—were themselves highly educated orators, preachers, confessors, writers, and teachers.

Interestingly, Loyola may have been the Jesuits' founder, but as a latecomer to education, starting to learn Latin grammar only at thirty-three, Loyola never attained the elegant humanistic Latin style his order so prized in its pedagogy (Codina, *Modus Parisiensis,* 41; Munitiz and Endean, 113–14; O'Malley, *The First Jesuits,* 13–14). Instead, when in need of the finest Latin, Loyola called on his companions, particularly his secretary Polanco, whose eloquent style contrasted starkly with his own less polished, more direct way with words.

This is not to say that Loyola's own literacies were not important (Deans, Fitzsimmons, Part I). Loyola himself drafted the enormously influential *Spiritual Exercises,* a guide to the inner dialogue and spiritual conversation that leads to what Jesuits call "discernment" and a conversion to a deeper religious attitude toward life. And over a period of twenty years, he worked personally on the order's founding document, the *Constitutions,* and oversaw the composition of the largest extant collection of Renaissance letters—nearly seven thousand, which he carefully revised and used to administer a huge and far-flung educational network[2]—as he and the rest of the Company carried out their own developing vision of humanistic education for *Ad maiorem Dei gloriam,* "the greater glory of God."

The Jesuits' accommodative stance can also be seen in the composition of the early Jesuits themselves. Some of the early important Jesuits (Nadal, Lainez, and Polanco, among others) were New Catholics, Christians of Jewish ancestry whose forebears converted when the Spanish authorities expelled all Jews in 1492. These were talented, humanistically trained speakers and writers with ties to the Jewish intellectual tradition.[3] In fact, Loyola himself stated that he wished he were a Jew, with the blood of Christ in his veins. As recounted by an early Jesuit, Pedro de Ribadeneyra (1527–1611), himself a *conversio,* "Father Ignatius told me that he would count it as a favor of God to have been born of this [Jewish] lineage" (cited in Reites, 17). At a time of heightened European anti-Semitism and poorly educated Catholic priests, the Jesuits started out as a company of tolerant, well-educated, and rhetorically astute members from multiple intellectual traditions.

Choosing to accommodate to the varied social scenes of the larger world, the Jesuits joined sacred rhetoric with civic rhetoric and action for the public good, which suited their distinctive characteristic of being "contemplatives in action." Accordingly, they deliberately chose to become associated with cities—seats of power and traditional sites of public rhetoric.[4] Unlike the more contemplative, older Catholic orders (e.g., the Franciscans and Benedictines), which had tended to establish their monasteries at rural sites and to restrict their engagements with the larger world, the Jesuits relished the urban milieu and a wider scope for their "ministries of the word."

As further signs of their rhetorical accommodation, the Jesuits eschewed the distinctive habits that characterized priests of other orders, preferring the relative anonymity of standard priestly garb, as a means of fitting in, of accommodating. Also, unlike other orders, they were released from the obligation to chant the hours together or observe all the daily religious rituals (though they made regular time for prayer and confession), in order to "find God in all things" and focus outward on the world in flexible and responsive ways rather than living in a closed and fixed society.

CONTRADICTIONS AND COMPLEXITIES

We are particularly aware of the contradictions and complexities that have marked the Jesuit project throughout its long history, partly because it *is* a long and complicated story. From the very beginning the Jesuits were a truly international order, and had to negotiate across their own local, regional, and national identities and conflicted allegiances during periods of great regional, cultural, and religious strife. This was the only order in which individual priests made a vow of obedience directly to the pope, promising to go anywhere and everywhere in the world at the behest of the superior general in Rome. This stance often put them in the uncomfortable position of being considered ultramontane, of belonging not to their country of residence but owing ultimate allegiance to the Vatican, beyond the mountains—i.e., the Alps—and provided a ready rationale for countries to expel the Jesuits on the slightest of pretexts.[5]

The Jesuits have always been regarded as highly intellectual, powerful in secular domains, and fully active in the world, yet they dedicate themselves to an inner life of contemplation and reflection. They have contributed the wonderful legacy of deep discernment, the *Spiritual Exercises*, but they have at times engaged in fierce polemics, and have been characterized as worldly dissimulators and schemers. They have been both praised and condemned at times for being too politically astute, or not politically astute enough. For centuries, they were aligned with the powerful, acting as ambassadors, counselors, and confessors to cardinals, nobles, and kings, and yet their ministries also focused equally on serving the poor, the sick, and oppressed groups. While the Jesuits were slaveholders in Maryland, they resisted the enslavement of Christianized indigenous communities in South America, even at their own peril.

Early Jesuit schools have sometimes been characterized as rigid and elitist, specializing in the Greek and Roman literary classics. However, their curriculum also accommodated to time and place, welcomed theater and dance, and was offered free to students of all stations. Their humanistic education was intended to create productive Christians, but also produced many cutting-edge intellectuals and scientists, with varying degrees of spirituality.

Another tension relates to gender: The Jesuits were—and are—an all-male order with no corresponding women's order. While Loyola himself and the early Jesuits depended on the support of many women, and there is evidence that early on there were a few actual women Jesuits, throughout their history many Jesuits strongly resisted allowing women to be educated in their schools, some holding out until the late twentieth century (along with, it should be said, many other elite American colleges and universities). Even so, closer examination shows a richer and more complicated set of relationships with women in a host of spiritual, social, and educational domains. Taking all these contradictions into account, John O'Malley, S.J., has entitled his new book about the Jesuits *Saints or Devils Incarnate?* Suffice it to say here that the Jesuit legacy is complicated, and we can examine only a small portion of it in this volume.

Founding humanistic schools and colleges would become the best-known aspect of the Jesuits' apostolic work, but that was far from the only project of the early Jesuits.[6] Local preaching and international missionary work were priorities from the very beginning, often mixed with the educational enterprises.

PREACHING AND DEVOTIONAL PRACTICES

The Jesuits' early "ministries of the word" were made manifest most powerfully in preaching, sacred orations, devotional practices, spiritual conversation, confession, and teaching catechism (O'Malley, *The First Jesuits*, 91–133). Whereas much medieval preaching was highly formulaic and narrowly didactic, Jesuit preachers were encouraged to *move* their audiences through emotional and imaginative appeals suited to the specific moment and occasion. Jesuit-trained orators including François de Sales (see Thomas Worcester's chapter on de Sales) and Jacques-Bénigne Bossuet as well as Jesuits including Louis Bourdaloue and Peter Canisius became renowned throughout Europe for their style and their ability to create appropriate orations for important civic occasions.[7] Preaching like that is a lost art for Catholics in the twenty-first century, but it stood at the center of European religious, educational, and civic life for centuries. For example, orations by Bossuet were for a long time a significant part of the standard literature curriculum taught in French schools (Jey, 17–23), and his statue stands outside Memorial Hall at Harvard.

At the same time, there have always been other dimensions to the Jesuits' spiritual rhetorics, especially quieter, more contemplative discursive practices, rooted in Loyola's *Spiritual Exercises* and other devotional books, emphasizing reflection and inner dialogue and saving one's soul, rather than highly public persuasive preaching on grand occasions or on winning arguments against Protestant adversaries. These more personal rhetorics are rooted in Loyola's own early experience of being educated by God and, later, in his interest in "helping souls," an impulse that accompanied Loyola throughout his life, with links to the "devotio moderna," the popular Northern European spiritual movement of the fifteenth and sixteenth centuries intended to sponsor a more affective and intimate spiritual life (McGinn). To this day such individual rhetorical practice remains a strong part of the spirituality of the Jesuits, reminding us what Loyola shared with his great Spanish mystic contemporaries Teresa of Ávila and Juan de la Cruz. Loyola himself employed the term *conversatio* to characterize this approach to rhetoric. It involves both talking to others in an attentive and mindful way as well as facilitating inner conversations, first formulated in the *Exercises*—which predates the foundation of schools and still forms a core experience for Jesuits.

Moral values were cultivated through attendance at daily and weekly religious services and occasional retreats for students and non-students alike, through sodalities and associated extracurricular organizations. These spiritual conversations were intended to foster a *rhetorica sacra*—one that seems very different from the confrontational, argumentative rhetoric sometimes associated with the Jesuits' public face. It's the difference between a simple room set aside for silent prayer or intimate conversation and the large hall set aside for public debate. And the Jesuits inhabited them both with ease. Indeed, updated versions of the *Spiritual Exercises* have again become popular around the world, and have been taken up by a variety of denominational groups.

MISSIONARY RHETORIC: ACCOMMODATION AND EXCHANGE

The Jesuits were founded in the Age of Discovery, and not surprisingly, members of the order were prominent in carrying the Christian message (accompanied by the inevitable colonial entanglements, of course) to newly discovered lands far from Europe. Francis Xavier, one of Loyola's original companions, did early missionary work in the 1550s in Goa, India, where he also headed a college. Portuguese Jesuits in the 1560s were the first to settle São Paulo, Brazil, where they also opened a college. Jesuit missionaries became explorers in North America, among them Jacques Marquette in the seventeenth century. These early Jesuits started a college in Quebec in 1635, a year before Harvard was founded.

In South America the Jesuits oversaw large settlements (termed "reductions") where Christianized natives were taught religion and useful skills, using their native languages. (In these reductions the Jesuits, unlike other Spanish and Portuguese colonizers, promoted greater amounts of freedom, cultural and otherwise, another sign of the Jesuits' characteristic accommodationism.) In North America the missionary efforts of the French Jesuit "blackrobes" ended with the cession of New France to the British.[8] To aid their missionary work, however, early Jesuits undertook an endeavor for which they became famous, compiling dictionaries of Amerindian and Asian languages and creating the first translations of sacred works into them. True scholars of the word, their scholarship was practical, at the service of their larger mission, to help souls. If most non-Europeans first encountered the Jesuits through missionary activities, many Europeans first met them (and the larger worlds they traveled to) through the descriptive treatises, translations and dictionaries from faraway places they compiled with so much skill and dedication.

One famous example of the Jesuits' internationalism occurred in seventeenth-century China, where Italian-born Jesuit missionaries Matteo Ricci (1552–1610) and Michele Ruggieri (1543–1607) practiced accommodationism by speaking and writing in Mandarin and dressing in Chinese garb, at first Buddhist and then Confucian. (The pope, responding to complaints from rival Dominican and Franciscan missionaries, would eventually criticize these Jesuits in the "Chinese rites controversy" for being too willing to adopt Chinese customs and ideas, such as Confucianism and ancestor worship. For instance, Ricci's exposition of Christianity in his Mandarin book *The True Meaning of the Lord of Heaven* accommodates to Chinese conceptual and religious sensibilities by taking the dramatic step of omitting all mention of Christ's Passion and Crucifixion.)[9]

As another example, during the nineteenth century, Jesuit-run schools for Indians in the American West readily accommodated their teaching to the particular needs of their students, siting their schools near the reservations (as opposed to the Protestant missionaries' desire to remove the students far from their native soil, on the model of the Carlisle Indian School in Pennsylvania, founded in 1879). The Jesuits also learned and gave instruction in the students' native languages, despite pressure from the federal government to confine all instruction to English (McKevitt, 385). Finally, the Jesuits focused their instruction of Indian students on practical subjects, not the classical languages for which they had became famous.[10]

One final illustration of the international reach of the early Jesuit missionaries is the New World rhetor Antonio Vieira (1608–97), born in Lisbon to a mulatto mother. Vieira spent his life in Portugal, in Rome, and for the most part in Brazil, where he died. His complex, distinguished global career involved him preaching eloquent orations to protect the Indians of Brazil from enslavement by rapacious Portuguese plantation owners as well as arguing strenuously against restrictions on Jews and New Catholics, both perfect illustrations of Jesuit rhetoric applied directly to issues of social justice. He also visited England and France as an envoy from the Portuguese king, and served in Rome as the confessor to the exiled Catholic convert Queen Christina of Sweden, who had been the patron of Descartes and Bernini. Vieira's collected works (including many orations) form one of the glories of Portuguese prose; in Brazil he is commemorated through the "platforma Vieira" (www.letras.ufmg.br/vieira), part of the website of the Sociedade Brasileira de Retórica (SBR).[11]

SOURCES AND SIGNATURES OF JESUIT RHETORICAL EDUCATION

While the Jesuits initially aspired to become a preaching and missionary order, their high level of education rendered them attractive as faculty, first to teach Jesuit novices and then lay students. The Council of Trent (1545–63), the ecumenical council called by the pope partly to respond to Protestant advances in Europe, at which the Jesuits Lainez and Salmerón played important advisory roles, recognized the need for a better-educated clergy, a need that Jesuits quickly began to supply across Europe. At a time when tremendous religious ferment led to the violent splintering of the Catholic Church into a variety of reform movements, the Jesuits became the first Catholic order to commit itself to teaching both religious and lay students as part of a formal ministry to reform the Church.

Codina (49) claims that "the Jesuits were not very original" in their pedagogy. For example, they adapted many of their practices from Quintilian, and they were preceded in the sixteenth century by the Brethren of the Common Life, the Northern European group that had educated Erasmus and Luther. What distinguished the Jesuits' educational project was their systematic, carefully worked-out application of classical educational practices to a wide variety of international settings (Scaglione, 54–55).

Based on the successful experience that Loyola and his companions had at the Sorbonne, at the very time that scholastic education was being challenged by humanism,[12] Jesuit colleges adapted what came to be called the *modus parisiensis*. Its success lay in both the coordination and the coherence of the curriculum along with a well-theorized and progressive active learning approach. In this model, courses followed each other developmentally and in a clear sequence organized by the faculty, rather than being open to all comers at any level, as was the practice in Italy and Spain (the *modus Italicus*).

The developmental focus is also clear in the progress of students through the courses of study. Rather than having students move through the full-year course of study for each subject as a group, professors scheduled examinations at regular intervals across the year, so students could pass into the next class as soon as they could demonstrate mastery, a practice that permitted students to learn at different paces. This practice also fostered competition, which was seen as a spur to learning. Competition, *emulatio*, a striving for excellence, was, indeed, encouraged in several ways. For classroom work it was common for the Jesuits to divide large classes into groups of ten (a *decuria*) and to appoint a student to lead and monitor other students' performance.[13] Interestingly, unlike many educational institutions during the Renaissance (and a good deal afterward), the early Jesuits preferred emulation to punition as a prompt for active learning, and they awarded prizes through an series of intense competitions. One result of the *decuriae* was that the opportunities for awarding prizes increased dramatically, spreading the competition among groups of students rather than restricting awards to the same few. The *Ratio Studiorum* devoted an entire separate section to "Laws for Prizes" (59–62). Contrast this positive attitude to the much more common practice of beating recalcitrant students. (Serious offenders were still beaten, of course, but the *Ratio* urged the hiring of non-Jesuit specialists ["correctors," in Farrell's translation, 55] to inflict corporal punishment.)[14]

Both the teacher and the students had active roles in the teaching-learning encounter. One important feature common to many medieval and humanistic schools, including Jesuit schools, was *prelection*, which involved the teacher's declaiming or reading the passage aloud and then explaining key elements of meaning, structure, and style in class before students read it (rather than having students struggle through a passage on their own for the first time in homework).[15]

But the students were also asked to participate actively in the classes. Importantly, Jesuits taught students to achieve speaking competence in Latin, not just reading skill, using an early version of whole-language immersion, and since they had their students for seven years, they could move slowly, step by step, with plenty of active learning techniques: drills, carefully graded exercises, writing assignments of many kinds, and constant oral work (double translation, competitions, debates, declamations, and other verbal performances). Loyola himself endorsed this kind of rich, active learning process as learning with much exercise, "*con mucho ejercicio.*" Jesuit rhetorical education placed a great deal of emphasis on style, using Cicero as a touchstone (along with many other models in different settings), whereas today's rhetoric curriculum pays much less attention to style than did the Renaissance, though there are signs that an interest in style is once again coming into favor.[16] The many years of extremely close attention to analysis and production of language gave Jesuit education a distinct flavor.

The Jesuits evolved their approach to teaching over many years through intense experimentation and discussion, working extremely hard to develop the most suitable pedagogical methods for teaching grammar, humanities, and rhetoric. After much trial and error, they encapsulated their approach in the *Ratio Studiorum*, the remarkably detailed document that laid down educational practices for all Jesuit colleges. The distinctive nature of Jesuit schooling is summed up neatly by Vincent J. Duminuco, S.J.:

> The success of the Jesuits' efficient and carefully organized educational code, embodied in the Ratio of 1599, can best be explained by acknowledging that they did not merely resurrect and restore the modus Parisiensus or principles of Quintilian, but they impregnated them with their own distinctive spirit, purpose, and worldview, subjected them to prolonged tests in many different countries, and then shared their results after practical experience.
>
> —Duminuco, 149

At the college level, the guiding aim was *eloquentia perfecta,* which had its roots in the classicism of Cicero and Quintilian. To be sure, Cicero and Quintilian (and certainly "eloquence") were not the exclusive property of the Jesuits. In fact, Cicero had been an animating figure of the Italian Renaissance long before the Jesuits were founded in the 1540s. Many of Cicero's works had influenced the early Italian humanists, and after a full manuscript of Quintilian was discovered in 1415 by Poggio Bracciolini, he too became a key influence on pedagogy. This influence extended to Protestants as well as to Catholics during the Reformation. As James Murphy writes, "Martin Luther declared that he preferred Quintilian to almost all other authorities on education, 'for while he teaches he gives us a model of eloquence. He teaches by a happy combination of theory and practice'" (Murphy, Quintilian, xlv). As contemporaries of Erasmus, Vives, Ramus, and other major Renaissance rhetors, the early Jesuits were full participants in the rich conversations and debates that centered on the principles, uses, and practices of these newly rediscovered classical literary and rhetorical texts in a Christian humanistic context.[17]

Thus, the Jesuits, in centering their pedagogy on Cicero and Quintilian, were simply following good Renaissance practice. Still, it is hard to imagine a more language- and literature-rich environment than a seventeenth- or eighteenth-century Jesuit college. Every Jesuit student was first immersed in the close study of Latin and Greek grammar, and then was carefully taught classical literary works, word by word, since great Greek and Latin literature was regarded as a prime source of moral instruction as well as full of examples of the style that the Renaissance valued above all else. As Robert Maryks details in his chapter, Cicero served as the embodiment of the Jesuit ideal; he was a supreme stylist, whose facility with language they regarded as perfect, and his life provided an example of a public rhetor whose broad range of writings served as a basis for emulation.[18] For the Jesuits, then, *eloquentia perfecta* came to be understood as the joining of "erudition" (knowledge, wisdom) with "virtue" and "eloquence."

As Patricia Bizzell's chapter recounts, the colleges served young men from their early teens to about age nineteen or twenty, covering what we might now think of as secondary schooling and the first few years of tertiary education. The college was a full course of study in itself; only the tiniest minority went on to what we now consider university studies, which were limited to professional training in law, medicine, and theology. The small number of Jesuit universities in the Renaissance concentrated on law and theology, never medicine.[19]

The Jesuit colleges grew rapidly, from 35 at Loyola's death in 1556 to 150 in 1581, and then to 245 in 1599; by 1773, the year of their suppression, they were, as O'Malley states, "operating more than eight hundred universities, seminaries, and especially secondary schools across the globe. The world had never seen before nor has it seen since such an immense network of educational institutions operating on an international basis" (*The First Jesuits*, 16). Their rapid success quickly made them a model for Catholic and Protestant educators alike, though no other group was able to equal their success.[20]

For well over two hundred years, then, the Jesuits acted as the "schoolmasters of Europe" (Padberg, viii) and beyond, educating powerful religious and secular leaders in politics, arts, and the sciences. The Jesuits quickly gained a reputation as excellent teachers whose tuition-free colleges produced superb students. They even attracted the sons of Protestants, thanks to the free tuition and the Jesuits' successful pedagogy (Conley, 152). The Jesuits' principled decision not to charge tuition would, however, have serious consequences. Free tuition attracted many students from all segments of society but at the same time made the Jesuits dependent on wealthy benefactors, beginning the entwinement of the Jesuits with the nobility, which was to haunt them for centuries. Their classical curriculum was often considered elite,[21] as were their associations with the wealthy and influential, acting as confessors to the monarchs of France, Spain, and Portugal. Their priests were perceived as intellectuals, the stirring baroque architecture of their renowned churches as the site of pomp and noble ceremony.[22] So free tuition and the Jesuits' devotion to excellence—starting from a good impulse—was a double-edged sword.

The educational legacy of the early Jesuits was enormous. Many of the great intellectual figures of Renaissance and Enlightenment Europe, including some who later rejected their Catholic backgrounds, were educated at Jesuit colleges and universities. Among students of Jesuits in France alone were great preacher-orators: de Sales (see Worcester's chapter), Bossuet, Camus, and Bourdaloue; and such thinkers and writers as Descartes, Bayle, Voltaire, Diderot, Corneille, and Moliere. Even the Scottish philosopher David Hume spent time at La Flèche, the great Jesuit college at Anjou, where Descartes had earlier been educated. Other European students of the Jesuits included the Italian playwright Goldoni, the Spanish playwrights Calderon and Lope de Vega, the Italian poet Tasso, the Italian philosopher Vico, and the German Jesuit polymath Athanasius Kircher.

Among the most prominent Jesuits were rhetoricians: the Spaniard Cypriano Soarez (1524–93) served as the official rhetor of the early Jesuits; his *De arte rhetorica* became the standard textbook for all Jesuit colleges and went through some three hundred editions from 1560 to 1800.[23] Others included Pedro Perpiñan (1530–66), who edited and extended Soarez's book and whom Robert Maryks examines in his chapter, and Manoel Álvares (1526–82), whose Latin grammar appeared in over four hundred editions. In France the Jesuits were particularly active in writing rhetoric texts. Nicolas Caussin (1583–1681) was not only a famous preacher and confessor to Louis XIII, he was also the author of *De Eloquentiae Sacrae et Humana* (1619), an exhaustive and erudite treatment of all varieties of sacred and human rhetoric, focusing on the role of affect in moving an audience (Conley 155–56; Mack, 198–207). Later, Joseph Jouvancey (1643–1719) wrote books that went through many editions and translations all over Europe; other French rhetoricians included Claude Buffier (1661–1737), Dominique Bouhours (1628–1702), and René Rapin (1621–87), author of *Réflexions sur l'usage de l'éloquence de ce temps* (Paris, 1672). They also produced a wide array of textbooks, editions, and translations of Greek and Latin classics, many of them expurgated, to supplement their teaching activities (Taneja, Burke). As Thomas Conley writes, "So large is the number of [rhetoric] textbooks written by Jesuits, and so large the population reached by them, that it is difficult to arrive at any precise estimate of the total number of such books and of the extent of the Jesuit influence. But even a cursory glance at the available bibliographies shows the numbers to have been gigantic and the influence correspondingly great" (153). By the seventeenth century, according to Conley, "the most significant influence on the history of rhetoric . . . was that exercised by the Society of Jesus, the Jesuits" (152).

JESUIT COLLEGES AS CULTURAL CENTERS

In their urban settings, the Jesuit colleges became the site of "a set of amazingly elaborate and extensive programs in the arts" (Giard, 16). In effect, each Jesuit college served as a source of culture, particularly rhetorical culture, primarily for its students, but extending to their parents and to the surrounding community. Colleges, employing student actors as well as professional musicians and designers, staged elaborate public performances, including Greek tragedies and elevated scenes from classical history as well as biblical scenes, always with a moral purpose. Productions were in Greek, Latin, and often in the vernacular as well. Students were prepared for them by their teachers; the Jesuits involved many more of their students than in today's college dramatic performances by, typically, a small coterie of a school's student body. The Jesuits made the performances an integral part of the college curriculum.

Indeed, these rhetorical performances were a part of the characteristic Jesuit emphasis on stimulating all the senses to promote active learning,[24] which in France extended to ballet, a rhetoric of the body (which Judith Rock has ably chronicled). Jesuit students were regarded not simply as audiences for this rich artistic legacy but as actual participants.[25] This emphasis on theatrical performances stood in sharp contrast to the stricter Protestant sects, which deplored the theater as immoral. In contrast, the Jesuits saw the right kind of theater as part of the moral instruction of students and audiences alike. As the French rhetorician Jouvancey wrote,

> A serious play in which the morals are well regulated . . . produces an unbelievable result among the spectators, and often even counts for more to conduct them toward religion than the sermons of the greatest preachers.
> —Quoted in Dainville, 478; authors' translation

Instead of being ashamed of their enthusiasm for the theater, the Jesuits often reveled in it. Education through action was their specialty.

The colleges also served as centers of a whole web of rhetoric-intensive extracurricular sodalities and confraternities open to non-students and graduates alike. These organizations represented a way to encourage devotion as well as learning among Catholics who were no longer of student age, or as extracurricular organizations for students at Jesuit colleges. Judi Loach provides an excellent description of one confraternity run by a Jesuit, Claude-François

Menestrier, in Lyon during the seventeenth century. It's a richly rhetorical adult education, mostly in French, not Latin, aimed at a broad spectrum of artisans, small-business owners, and townspeople. Loach writes, "By thus targeting devout men so that they would enjoy a privileged position in determining civic affairs, the Jesuits literally brought about a cultural revolution" (78). The extent of this aspect of Jesuit education is impressive; in some settings, members in these extracurricular organizations outnumbered actual students enrolled in Jesuit schools and colleges. O'Malley describes the preexisting confraternities as well as the distinctive Marian confraternities that the Jesuits themselves founded (192–99, with a rich bibliography at 416–17).

The Jesuits also developed and practiced their rhetorical and cultural educational-arts outreach programs across the sixteenth and seventeenth centuries through the popular venue of emblem books, which connected to their interests in visual rhetoric and could reach larger and more distant audiences. Each book included an elaborate series of illustrations with accompanying text in Latin or the vernacular, most commonly with a moral aim, often drawn from sacred scripture. The Jesuits enthusiastically adopted this medium, producing, according to Richard Dimler, S.J., "more books in this genre than did any other identifiable group of writers" (22). What Dimler calls "the most Jesuit of all emblem books," with one hundred twenty-six images, *Imago Primi Saeculi,* was produced in 1640 to commemorate the centenary of the order's founding (22). The powerful rhetoric of emblems is discussed by Nienke Tjoelker in "Jesuit Image Rhetoric in Latin and the Vernacular: The Latin and Dutch Emblems of the *Imago Primi Saeculi,*" which provides an excellent bibliography of this important but often overlooked area of Jesuit rhetoric (Tjoelker, 113–15).

JESUIT EDUCATION UNDER ATTACK

Of course, assembling great educational and rhetorical power had its costs, and the Jesuits frequently paid a high price. As many of the chapters below make clear, their educational systems were criticized at various points as too formalistic and elitist and, at other times, as too flexible and progressive. During the turbulent eras of religious conflict that afflicted Europe during the Reformation and what has been traditionally called the Counter-Reformation, and for long afterward, the Jesuits were repeatedly condemned and attacked—on occasion with reason—by Catholics as well as Protestants, for wielding too much discursive power in both religious and temporal affairs. Their morality was also criticized as too flexible by Pascal in his *Lettres provinciales*, in which he attacked Jesuit casuistry, the practice of arguing morality from individual cases rather than from fundamental, invariable principles. The Jesuits were vulnerable also because, as an international order, under direct orders from the pope, they were often seen as foreigners wherever they were sent or settled; thus they were always in danger of expulsion by regional or national authorities, and expelled they were, over and over, especially in the eighteenth and nineteenth centuries. Some critics, frightened by the Jesuits' rhetorical power, accused them of practicing a kind of language alchemy or witchcraft. Indeed, the pejorative adjective *jesuitical* was coined by the Jesuits' detractors to refer to rhetorical manipulation or sophistry.[26]

Ultimately, a variety of turbulent religious and geopolitical events resulted in a series of suppressions, e.g., in Portugal in 1759, in France in 1764, and then in Spain in 1767 (Wright, 263–77). Eventually a weak Pope Clement XIV ordered a near-total, violent suppression of the Society in 1773, dismantling most of its global educational project for several decades. During this period, nearly all of their eight hundred schools worldwide were closed or appropriated by others, their properties confiscated, their libraries looted and dispersed, their members exiled or worse.[27] When they were revived in 1814, there was only a single Jesuit in France to lead the rebuilding (Padberg, 1): no libraries or laboratories, no schoolrooms, little beyond a dim memory of what had been.

One powerful way of thinking about the larger context surrounding the suppression of the Jesuits is suggested by Stephen Schloesser, S.J., who argues, following Toulmin's *Cosmopolis*, that Renaissance humanism was followed by a "post-1650 paradigm of 'objectivity' forged in response to the devastation of the Thirty Years' War—an epistemic shift to the universal, general, and timeless," which replaced the Jesuits' "rhetorical flexibility" and emphasis on accommodation, the contingent, and the particular. According to Schlosser, "if this narrative is true, then the images we have of Jesuits being forcibly evicted from houses, schools, kingdoms, and empires represent a deeper yet invisible cultural conflict: the repression of an earlier Renaissance version of modernity by a later counter-Renaissance" (350–51).

JESUIT EDUCATION RESTORED

The Jesuits would never again achieve the educational ascendancy of their first two and a half centuries, but on their revival in the early nineteenth century they quickly refashioned institutions that would begin to exert significant influence once more, especially establishing new schools and universities in the Americas (where their "blackrobes" had first carried on missionary work in French Canada in the early seventeenth century and where Spanish Jesuits had devoted themselves to exploration, conversion, and teaching in Jesuit colleges in Peru and Mexico, as did Portuguese Jesuits in Brazil), India (where the Jesuit Francis Xavier had established a mission and run a college in the 1540s), and China (where the Jesuit Matteo Ricci had worked in the seventeenth century) in the nineteenth and twentieth centuries.

In the post-suppression era, the Society of Jesus achieved some of its most spectacular growth in the United States, where it now operates twenty-eight colleges and universities; it runs many hundreds of educational sites in over twenty-seven countries worldwide (see the Association of Jesuit Colleges and Universities, www.ajcunet.edu). There are over 200,000 students attending American Jesuit colleges (one fifth of the nearly 950,000 students at all 240 or so U.S. Roman Catholic colleges). All twenty-eight of the U.S. Jesuit colleges and universities were listed in their appropriate categories as among the best by *U.S. News and World Report* for 2012.

Jesuit institutions have changed greatly in the four hundred fifty years since their founding, and much of their initial impulse has been transformed. The Jesuits' rhetorical legacy is one of the critical sites of simultaneous loss, erosion, preservation, accommodation, hybridization, and reanimation. Clearly, the Jesuits' traditional focus on explicit rhetorical training, historically accomplished through extensive study of classical and vernacular languages and literature, oral and written performances, theater, dance, and visual rhetorics, has been to varying degrees displaced or revised over time.[28]

Yet as the essays in this collection demonstrate, a curriculum rich in rhetoric and language-and-literature intensive has endured and flourished in many American Jesuit colleges and universities, albeit partially obscured or as a tacit part of the educational culture rather than an explicit center for the curriculum. Even today, for example, to be a "Jesuit-trained" public figure (someone with a public discursive role or facility and skill in speaking or argumentation) is considered a newsworthy attribute. A recent survey on the makeup of the 114th Congress notes that over fifty of its members, or 9 percent, were Jesuit-educated. Examples of Jesuit-trained figures prominent in recent American life abound, including writers and commentators Billy Collins, Ron Hansen, Sandra Cisneros, William Bennett, Charles Osgood, Tim Russert, John McLaughlin, Chris Matthews, Daniel Berrigan, Garry Wills, and Elmore Leonard; educators Ernest Boyer, Kathleen Hall Jamison, and Parker Palmer; politicians and judges Bill Clinton, Antonin Scalia, Clarence Thomas, Tom Foley, Dick Durbin, Robert Drinan, Barbara Mikulski, Steny Hoyer, Tip O'Neill, and John Boehner; and many international figures, including Pierre Trudeau, Michel de Certeau, Jacques Lacan, Henri de Lubac, Teilhard de Chardin, Michel Foucault, and now the Argentine pope, Francis, renowned for his irenic rhetorical prowess.

Additionally, the Jesuits seem to have a peculiar hold on the American popular imagination. Frequently on television or in a story, a role that simply calls for a Catholic parish priest will be filled by an actor billed as a Jesuit, and Jesuits are often called on to explain some matter of faith or ethics on television panels. Jesuits too have made many an appearance in literature, sometimes as caricatures, from Stephen Dedalus's teachers in James Joyce's *A Portrait of the Artist as a Young Man* to Leo Naptha in Thomas Mann's *The Magic Mountain* to Father Rothschild at the opening of Evelyn Waugh's *Vile Bodies* to Fathers

Pertuso and Bergamaschi in Umberto Eco's *The Prague Cemetery*.[29] And interestingly, if one googles the phrase "Jesuit-trained," one finds references to a whole host of bizarre conspiracy theories, while *The Jesuit Guide to (Almost) Everything* by James Martin, S.J., has been a *New York Times* bestseller.

JESUIT INVISIBILITY IN RHETORIC AND COMPOSITION STUDIES

Despite the Jesuits' rise to something approaching prominence in current American life, to date there has been little systematic effort to explore the enduring and complex interchange between Jesuit rhetorical and educational traditions, particularly the teaching of writing, communications, and language arts for an American audience. There *are* several resources that address Jesuit rhetoric and education, especially from the sixteenth through the eighteenth centuries, in specialized histories of European rhetorical traditions and in Jesuit studies, but those for the most part have not entered the mainstream of American rhetoric-composition or communications disciplinary literatures.[30] One obstacle is that few American rhetoric and composition scholars have had the wide-ranging language facility to handle the documents that would shed light on historical developments, particularly among the early Jesuits, who after all were, in their earliest generations in America, non-English-speaking European transplants. Rhetoric and composition research and instruction have been carried on in English departments, traditionally unilingual enclaves impervious to foreign influence. Rhetoric in departments of communication was somewhat better off, but only a few faculty at most were competent in Latin and Greek or any of the other languages in which such scholarship often appeared.

In addition, there are many books written about Jesuit educational history, often directed primarily to Catholic audiences, that have not been well integrated in "larger" educational studies that frame rhetorical histories.[31] Some of the American works, particularly those written early in the twentieth century by Jesuit apologists, make for somewhat uncomfortable reading today; they are full of defensive arguments, written as they were with a genuinely hostile audience in mind. The tone of these early works is a useful reminder that, despite their early eminence in the Renaissance, in the nineteenth and early twentieth centuries the Jesuits were marginalized, in Europe and particularly in North America.

Even so, one has to ask why the rich literature on Jesuit rhetoric has failed to penetrate the mainstream of communication, rhetoric, and composition studies. There are many answers.

Since Catholics were a small minority in American life until the nineteenth century, it is quite understandable that their European-centered educational theories and procedures were relatively unknown. Similarly, in terms of rhetorical history and systems of transmission, in the eighteenth century when the rhetoric curriculum reigned supreme in North American colleges, Jesuits were under threat of suppression in their home, Europe, and not positioned to make significant contributions to rhetorical thinking. Instead, the main historical influences on American rhetoric come from the Anglo-British traditions, influenced by Erasmus and Ramus (who was stridently opposed to the Jesuits), and can be traced to sixteenth-century figures—such as Leonard Cox, Richard Sherry, and Thomas Wilson—writing in English. And the familiar trio of Blair, Whately, and Campbell, seen as the immediate progenitors of American rhetoric and composition, were all mainline-Protestant ministers.

The later omissions of the Jesuits are due, in large part, to the nineteenth- and early-twentieth-century marginalization of Catholics and Catholic education by mainstream Protestant intellectual culture and cultural institutions in the United States. To be sure, the Jesuits themselves felt the need to develop a separate liberal-arts educational system, originally created for immigrant Catholic populations, and to maintain their Catholic identity, distinct from, against, and yet within the larger classical tradition (see Mahoney, *Catholic Higher Education in Protestant America*).

Recently, however, superb scholarly work by Winifred Horner, Roxanne Mountford, Vicki Tolar Burton, and Thomas Miller (among others) has uncovered another important strand of influence on rhetoric and writing instruction, the British dissenting academies dating back to the seventeenth century. And recently the work of Barbara Warnick and Thomas Conley has also uncovered previously unknown French Jesuit influences on Blair and Campbell, among others.[32] This seems highly important if as yet little understood: The Protestant divines from established churches who wrote some of the most influential rhetorical works of the eighteenth century learned a great deal from European Jesuits. And, despite recent attention to alternative histories, there has been surprisingly little work by communications or rhetoric and composition scholars on the development of American Catholic and Jesuit educational and rhetorical traditions during the nineteenth and early twentieth centuries, when Jesuit secondary schools, colleges, and universities were growing in number and significance.

Another critical reason for the absence of knowledge about Jesuit influence comes from the fact that historical scholarship in composition and rhetoric has traditionally tended to devalue the knowledge found in textbooks. This despite the fact that the focus of some of the key scholarly works—Kitzhaber; Carr, Carr, and Schultz; and Connors—has been on textbooks. Berlin's books have concentrated more on articles than on textbooks, as have Susan Miller's and those of a host of other scholars. This kind of imbalance has often reduced the focus on contributions from rhetoricians, whose major publication (until Perelman and Toulmin, at least) has often been the textbook. North's *The Making of Knowledge in Composition* furthered this practice in the 1970s, and it seems likely to continue.

Two slight references to Jesuit rhetorics are Kitzhaber's history, which makes a few, mostly critical, citations of the rhetoric textbook by the Jesuit Charles Coppens, and Wozniak's volume on the nineteenth-century writing curriculum, which does mention a few developments at Georgetown and Fordham. Lately, welcome scholarly attention has been brought to the Jesuits, with scholarly essays such as Kristine Johnson's and Paul Lynch's "*Ad perfectum eloquentiam*: The 'Spoils of Egypt' in Jesuit Renaissance Rhetoric" (2012).

CHANGES IN AMERICAN HIGHER EDUCATION

In the last quarter of the nineteenth century, the traditional classical educational system with its rhetorical center, which both Protestant and Catholic educational projects had previously shared, was transformed: Industrialization, the rise of the research university, the development of new kinds of disciplinary specializations (including literature-based language departments in France, Germany, Spain, Italy, and the United States), and new technologies that promoted written over oral rhetorics resulted in the reduction of the scope of rhetoric and its splintering into many subdisciplines (see Brereton, *Origins*; Mailloux, *Disciplinary Identities*; and Veysey).

This broad trend toward specialization and fragmentation of disciplines would inevitably undermine the integrative impulse of a rhetoric-centered curriculum. Jesuit colleges and universities, which tried to negotiate these radical changes while stubbornly clinging to their emphasis on classical language and rhetorical training as a crucial element of their cherished educational heritage, were often seen, if visible at all, as obsolete and anachronistic. The eventual effacement and dispersal of the traditional Jesuit classical curriculum has prevented contemporary scholars from seeing how much of their own work has common roots, and has obscured the strong historical connections between what are now seen as separate disciplines. Contemporary scholars of communications, rhetoric, and composition are still not aware of the conflict faced by early-twentieth-century Jesuit institutions as they tried to keep their four-hundred-year-old unified curriculum intact.

During the first half of the twentieth century the American Jesuits, prodded by accrediting agencies and student demands for practicality, gradually moved away from their traditional concentration on classical studies and rhetoric, on fostering eloquence, which pervaded the *Ratio Studiorum*, their foundational educational document for over four hundred years. Over the years, many Jesuits came to feel that the *Ratio* was out of date, though it was never officially replaced. (In 1832 an updated draft with modest revisions was circulated but never adopted.) Over the course of the twentieth century many Jesuit conferences and meetings wrestled with the issue of developing a new, integrative curriculum (Gleason, (250–56). Only in the late twentieth century did the Jesuits supplant the *Ratio* with a "new" pedagogy based on the earlier *Spiritual Exercises*, in which the Jesuits claimed to discern the wellsprings for their newly invigorated educational philosophy. In doing so they had to move from the *Ratio's* extremely detailed prescriptions (which were no longer being followed) for schools to a more generalized attitude toward learning that did not focus on the minutiae of educational practice.

THE REVIVAL OF RHETORIC

The gaps in our knowledge of Jesuit rhetoric are not simply a matter of older historical misunderstanding. The effect of the complex circulation of Jesuit rhetorical scholarship and practice on contemporary scholars and practitioners of communications, composition, and rhetoric has also been nearly invisible, even though many Jesuit high schools, colleges, and universities have by now clearly become part of the rich fabric of American education. Scholars have yet to seriously examine the interesting phenomenon that many important late-twentieth-century American theorists and scholars of communications, rhetoric, and writing studies were trained by, connected to, or taught at Jesuit institutions and were touched, directly and indirectly, by their Jesuit schooling or teaching experiences.

Recent years have seen a reemergence of attention to rhetoric within composition studies; in communications it has formed an identifiable if modest part from the very beginning of the field in the early twentieth century. Since the 1960s there has been an explosion of interest in the ways rhetoric has influenced and shaped human consciousness, resulting in hundreds of books and articles, the founding of the Rhetoric Society of America in 1968 and of the International Society for the History of Rhetoric in 1977, and the inauguration of journals including *Rhetoric Review, Rhetoric Society Quarterly, Philosophy and Rhetoric, Rhetoric and Public Affairs,* and *Rhetorica.*

A rich historiography has developed in collections such as Vitanza's *Writing Histories of Rhetoric*; Graff, Walzer, and Atwill's *The Viability of the Rhetorical Tradition*; and, most recently, Ballif's *Theorizing Histories of Rhetoric.* As part of this new work, the traditional American picture of composition's rise and rhetoric's decline across the nineteenth century has undergone significant changes. The first generation of historical scholars examining the rise of writing instruction and the eclipse of rhetoric in the nineteenth century focused on the major institutions: Harvard and other selective colleges and the largest, most prominent land-grant universities. More recently, scholars have expanded their purview to include different sites of rhetorical development: normal schools, women's colleges, historically black colleges, American Indian schools, Latino/a education, and nonacademic settings, all involving distinctive rhetorical spaces and stances. Some scholars have even begun to ask whether the long run of rhetorical instruction aiming at the goal of civic humanism has reached its end, given the way the world has changed and the increasing irrelevance of the classical norms.[33]

We are of course aware that studying the Jesuits has its complexities with regard to gender. For one thing, an all-male, distinctly hierarchical organization relying on a heritage of classical rhetoric can come in for serious criticism from feminists as patriarchal, agonistic, and exclusionary. Recently, though, the powerful work of feminist scholars including Cheryl Glenn, Susan Jarratt, Kathleen Welch, Jan Swearingen, Janet Atwill, and Krista Ratcliffe, among many others, has begun to revise and reclaim various aspects of classical rhetoric and its treatments (Agnew, 12–14). Of course the Jesuits, like so many other cultural elites, have had a well-deserved reputation for gender-based discrimination and exclusion. American Jesuits, sometimes reluctantly, admitted women students to their colleges over the twentieth century, beginning with programs at Marquette in 1909.

Nowadays in their American colleges more than half the students are female, and it seems right to highlight some of the relatively unknown connections between Jesuits and women's concerns. Carol Mattingly's important chapter (see Part I) about the practically unknown early historical interaction between the Jesuits and female religious orders provides a genuine breakthrough in expanding our understanding of Jesuit history, as does Boryzcka and Petrino's volume *Jesuit and Feminist Education,* which offers multiple feminist perspectives on Jesuit education and the Ignatian pedagogical paradigm. Rosemary A. DeJulio writes that "there is evidence, although not abundant, to support the fact that women in history were inspired to become the *patrons, pupils,* and *partners* of Ignatius and his followers" (emphasis in original, 107). (As an aside: Boston's Isabella Stewart Gardner Museum contains a portrait of Donna Juana of Austria [1545–73], sister of Philip II of Spain, one of the few women formally, if secretly, admitted into the Jesuit order.[34])

There is actually a long history of interchange between the Jesuits and women's religious orders, beginning in the sixteenth century, when almost all women religious were confined to the cloister. Elizabeth Rhodes ably chronicles the connections between Spanish women and the early Jesuits, and Margaret Gorman has written of the many links between Ignatian spirituality and women's teaching orders in the United States. Gorman administered a questionnaire to over one hundred fifty women's congregations and found that over half were influenced by Ignatian spirituality, largely through retreats given by Jesuits, and 26 percent said that their educational mission was influenced by the Jesuit philosophy of education. Twenty-five percent of the congregations said that their constitutions were based on Jesuit spirituality (187). Gorman also analyzes the specific Jesuit links to the Urusulines, Mary Ward and the Institute of the Blessed Virgin Mary, the Sisters of St. Joseph (themselves founded by a Jesuit, Jean-Pierre Médaille), the Society of the Sacred Heart, the

Sisters of Mercy, and the Religious of the Holy Child Jesus, all of which have been heavily influenced by the Jesuits (190–99).

Finally, there has been more-recent research on the fascinating issue of the Jesuits' connections to women's education, including Carol Mattingly's "Uncovering Forgotten Habits: Anti-Catholic Rhetoric and Nineteenth-Century American Women's Literacy" (2006) and Nan Johnson's and Elizabethada Wright's recent work.[35] Beth Ann Rothermel's comparison (2006) of two western Massachusetts institutions, Westfield State Normal School and Our Lady of the Elms College, contains tantalizing hints that the sisters at Elms may well have based some of their rich rhetorical curriculum on the liberal arts they took at Boston College and Fordham.[36] There is no doubt that some Jesuit colleges served as models for some women's institutions, but a definitive history of the interchange has yet to be written, especially in regard to rhetorical education. Then too, the half-century-long transformation of all Jesuit colleges from all-male to fully coeducational has yet to receive adequate scholarly treatment (but neither has the corresponding transformation of elite secular all-male colleges).[37]

Some of the most exciting recent scholarship in rhetoric and communications investigates the nexus of languages, cultures, and power, as well as questions of translation and globalization, issues of interest for the Jesuits for hundreds of years. Now is a useful time to examine the distinctive traditions at Catholic colleges and universities, especially Jesuit institutions, with their five-century legacy of rhetorical arts and instruction, and their American efflorescence across the nineteenth and twentieth centuries. The Jesuit way with rhetoric has represented a fully theorized approach to the subject, one with rich international connections and a lengthy intellectual background from its birth in the Renaissance.

Indeed, new scholarly attention *is* being devoted to the relationships among rhetoric, religion, and religiously affiliated institutions. New special-interest groups on religion and rhetoric have been founded within the Conference on College Composition and Communication. Other signs include the recent *College Composition and Communication* issue on Jewish rhetorics (2010); Andrea Greenbaum and Deborah Holdstein's important collection, *Judaic Perspectives in Rhetoric and Composition* (2008); Vicki Tolar Burton's *Spiritual Literacy in John Wesley's Methodism* (Baylor, 2008), and Michael Bernard-Donals's *The Practice of Theory: Rhetoric, Knowledge, and Pedagogy in the Academy* (1998), and DePalma and Ringer's *Mapping Christian Rhetorics* (2015).[38]

At the same time, interest has revived in the educational projects of the Jesuits, including several reconsiderations of the importance of the *Ratio Studiorum*, as seen in the new translation *The Ratio Studiorum: The Official Plan for Jesuit Education* (Claude Pavur, 2005); *Jesuit Education and the Classics* (Cambridge Scholars Press, 2009); *The Jesuit Ratio Studiorum: 400th Anniversary Perspectives* (Fordham University Press, 2000); *The* Ratio Studiorum

(Institute of Jesuit Sources, 2005); *A Jesuit Education Reader* (Loyola Press, 2008); *Jesuit and Feminist Education* (Fordham University Press, 2011), and Robert Maryks's *Saint Cicero and the Jesuits* (Ashgate, 2008), along with the many works by John O'Malley. Clearly, the time is right for a collection that brings the new historical work in all of these areas into dialogue.

DESCRIPTION OF THE COLLECTION

This volume takes a broadly chronological approach, organizing its essays in three major parts, roughly following what William B. Neenan, S.J., has identified as three broad periods in Jesuit history, the Age of Discovery (1548–1773), the Restoration of the Society of Jesus (1814–1960), and the Age of Globalization (1960–present). Our first part considers the continental origins and development of Jesuit rhetorical practices and formal pedagogies from the beginnings of the Society through their broad circulation over time and across multiple continents. Patricia Bizzell examines the founding of the order and the development of schools and curriculum and considers that legacy for the historical, present-day, and future Holy Cross as well as its current international Jesuit partners, including Sogang University in South Korea.

In related essays that focus on Loyola's own development, Thomas Deans first takes up the key early literacy experiences and the role of reading and writing in shaping and transforming the life and perspectives of Ignatius Loyola, while Maureen Fitzsimmons focuses on Loyola's particular spiritual development and orientation as they are enacted in his influential work on spiritual discernment, *The Spiritual Exercises.*

The broad, rhetorically centered intellectual milieu of the early Jesuit order, based on Ciceronian probabilism, is explored by Robert Maryks, who traces its expression in the Jesuit approach to confessional and devotional practices and in the development of "cases of conscience"—what would become the whole practice of "casuistry" and the field of moral theology. Thomas Worcester, S.J., addresses another incarnation of the Jesuits' "ministries of the Word," treating the influence of Jesuit rhetorical education on Renaissance epistolary, preaching, and peacemaking traditions, using the powerful example of St. Francis de Sales, the bishop of Geneva, who was educated by the Jesuits.

Carol Mattingly's essay details part of the rich, complex, and often productive relationship between the Jesuits and early women's religious orders, such as the Ursulines, particularly in the sphere of education for girls and young women. This first section concludes with the profile that David Leigh, S.J., draws of the continuity and diversity of Jesuit rhetorical education, through three separate scenes of Jesuit schooling: sixteenth-century Italy, eighteenth-century France, and the mid-twentieth-century United States at Marquette University.

Part II moves the scene to focus on nineteenth- and twentieth-century America, with an introduction charting the development of American Jesuit education, and individual chapters addressing particular aspects of Jesuit rhetoric. Steven Mailloux details the influence of understudied late-nineteenth-century Jesuit rhetoricians and popular educators. Katherine Adams describes how early in the twentieth century the Jesuits evolved a distinctive approach to professional communication. Janice Lauer Rice, who has herself greatly influenced writing studies, provides a portrait of her teacher Walter Ong, the highly influential Jesuit scholar of rhetoric and communication. Paula Mathieu probes some of the potential connections of the famous Jesuit philosopher and theologian Bernard Lonergan to rhetorical scholarship. Gerald Nelms addresses the important career of Edward P. J. Corbett, who studied and worked at Jesuit schools and helped shape American rhetorical education in the second half of the twentieth century. Thomas Pace and Gina Merys examine the career of Paulo Freire, the Brazilian educator who continues to exert great influence on literacy education in America, from the perspective of his Jesuit connections, which have gone mostly unremarked. Freire also illustrates the international reach of the Jesuits; he was influenced by them in his native Brazil; in return he influenced Jesuit thinking when he lectured in America; and his legacy lives on in Jesuit-sponsored international literacy centers, and in the ways his pedagogical project of *conscientizao* lives on in liberatory education.

Part II concludes with reflective essays by several important Jesuit-trained rhetoricians who treat their own encounters with Jesuit education: Frank D'Angelo, Michael Halloran, Gerard Hauser, Paul Rainieri, and Mike Rose all demonstrate how their Jesuit training shaped them as teachers at secular universities and as scholars in the fields of rhetoric, composition, and communication more broadly. Like Corbett's, these scholars' Jesuit backgrounds have not been seriously studied (or in some cases even acknowledged) to date. This small sample of Jesuit-trained scholars, working across many educational settings, secular and religious alike, demonstrates the subtle but significant influence of Jesuit rhetorical traditions on American higher education today.

Part III is devoted to understanding current and future forms of Jesuit and rhetorical education and the potential and challenges of the emerging *eloquentia perfecta* initiative. Its essays highlight the work of scholar-practitioners educated or teaching at Jesuit institutions who are connecting their research, scholarship, and programmatic and pedagogical interests with various facets of Jesuit educational rhetorical principles more broadly. Chapters by Anne Fernald and Kate Nash of Fordham University, K. J. Peters of Loyola Marymount University, and John C. Bean, Larry C. Nichols, and Jeffrey Philpott of Seattle University provide firsthand accounts of how the traditional Jesuit notion of *eloquentia perfecta* is being adapted and reimagined as a formative feature of general education, core curricula, writing across the curriculum, and other specific initiatives at Jesuit colleges and universities.

Two essays take up the relationships between various notions of Jesuit rhetoric and what is called the Ignatian pedagogical paradigm (IPP), the newly reconstructed set of educational principles, based on *The Spiritual Exercises*, that has become very influential at Jesuit schools today. Ann Green of Saint Joseph's University uses concepts from Ignatian pedagogy to support her service-learning writing and rhetoric course, and Karen Paley reports on her ethnographic study of the rhetorical and reflective assignments that fostered students' understanding of the Jesuit notion of *cura personalis* (care for the whole person) in two different courses at Loyola Marymount University.

In the spirit of the Jesuit interest in—and caution about—new media genres and modes of communication, Vincent Casaregola of Saint Louis University discusses ways to reintroduce rich rhetorical thinking, especially listening, to students who seem to be under the spell of social media and electronic communication. Offering a complementary perspective, Jenn Fishman and Rebecca Nowacek explore the possibilities of joining digital and Jesuit rhetorical principles in two non-curricular projects at Marquette University. Rhetorician and past president of the Rhetoric Society of America Krista Ratcliffe offers a final reflection in which she explores the ways her teacher Edward P. J. Corbett and her experience at a Jesuit university, Marquette, inform her perspectives, practices, and pedagogies in critical ways.

In the afterword, Joseph Janangelo of Loyola University of Chicago provides a thoughtful and challenging peroration that examines the limitations and possibilities of Jesuit principles of rhetorical pedagogy.

AN UNFINISHED TASK

We compiled this collection for those historians and educators interested in the Jesuits' mission-based educational institutions as well as to introduce members of the American rhetoric, composition, and communications communities to the work of a whole series of Jesuit and Jesuit-trained thinkers who played a fascinating set of roles in rhetorical history and in developing modern forms of rhetorical theory and practice. We try to move beyond hagiography or vilification to generate a more complex history, a more visible and textured present, and richer possibilities for the future of rhetorical study and pedagogy. By examining the visible and buried legacies of Jesuit rhetoric and pedagogy, we try to offer possibilities for the ongoing renewal of integrative mission-based pedagogical practices. The collection recuperates and interrogates some significant roles the Jesuits have played in the theorizing, studying, practicing, and teaching of rhetoric and eloquence—and, correspondingly, the roles that various forms of rhetorical work have played in defining and shaping Jesuit rhetorical and educational identity.

We are quite aware that our study is only a start on an extremely complex subject, one that touches on an enormous bibliography compiled over some four hundred fifty years, mostly by the Jesuits themselves, who have been extremely concerned with their own history. They have produced the *Monumenta*

Historica Societatis Iesu, numbering over one hundred fifty volumes in Latin, published from 1892 to the present, including volumes of Loyola's letters, early reports from the field, and editions of the major documents associated with the founding of the order, and including the *Monumenta Paedagogica Societatus Iesu,* which contains some ten volumes dealing directly with early efforts of Jesuit education. This is supplemented by the fifty-four volumes of the *Bibliotheca Instituti Historici Societatis Iesu,* along with an enormous outpouring of books and articles in French, Spanish, German, Italian, and English, published from 1550 to the present. The standard bibliography, C. Sommervogel's *Bibliotheque de la Compagnie de Jesus* (Brussels, 1897; 7 vols.), lists some 13,000 Jesuit authors in almost every area of scholarship. Though we have read some of this rich storehouse, we are the first to admit that we have not mastered all this material, and frankly, we wonder if anyone can.

But there are other places that remind us of our single volume's inevitable limitations. We primarily address matters from an American standpoint, while the Jesuits, the ultimate ultramontanists, have always operated internationally. We have endeavored to include material on sixteenth- and seventeenth-century France, twentieth-century Brazil and Canada, and twenty-first century South Korea, but in the main we have concentrated on the Jesuit experience in the United States. (We also know that we omit many salient examples of how Jesuit rhetoric figured largely in European intellectual life: Vico—Jesuit-trained— taught rhetoric courses at Naples and wrote a rhetoric, the *Institutiones Oratoriae* of 1711; Heidegger spent a brief time at a Jesuit seminary.)[39] But we also know that even our picture of American Jesuit education and rhetoric remains incomplete. We concentrate on colleges and universities, not the many Jesuit high schools that form a vital part of the Jesuit tradition and seem eminently worthy of a separate study of their own. The Jesuit educational and rhetorical enterprise is so rich that a single volume cannot hope to encompass its totality.

Even so, this is the first collection to bring together historical and contemporary work on Jesuit rhetorical practice and pedagogy as it pertains to the rhetoric-centric and language-arts-intensive legacies available to Jesuit higher education. In sum, it begins the exploration of what it has meant to enact, and now to reimagine, the aim of *eloquentia perfecta,* the central aim of a Jesuit liberal-arts education for hundreds of years, in the twenty-first century.

NOTES

1. There are many possible definitions of the term *rhetoric,* and the essays in this collection will call on definitions and models offered by specific figures and schools, such as Cicero's own definitions, or Ciceronian rhetoric more broadly understood. We see at least three domains in which the term can be invoked, using Andrea Lunsford's claim that "rhetoric is the art, practice, and study of human communication"

(http://davidbeard.efoliomn.com). *Traditions of Eloquence* concentrates on both rhetorical theory and rhetorical pedagogy.

2. Dalmases describes the "meticulous care" that Loyola exercised over his letters (281–82).

3. The Jewish origins of early Jesuits have been studied recently by Mark Rastoin, in *Du même sang que notre Seigneur*, and by Robert Maryks, in *The Jesuit Order as a Synagogue of Jews*.

4. See Luce Girard's excellent overview of the Jesuits' preference for urban sites, 3–6, and of the uses they made of them, 13–16.

5. *Ultramontanism*—literally, "beyond the mountains"—refers specifically to the source of the Jesuits' authority, Rome. Opposed to it in France was Gallicanism, referring to the source of authority within France itself, the king and, later, the French state. Each European country had to work out its own relationship with the Jesuits' strong Rome-centered version of internationalism.

6. Historians have tended to give greater weight to the Jesuits' educational achievements, even though they acknowledge their other accomplishments, including diplomacy, preaching, parish work, and devotion to missions.

7. For more comprehensive treatments of French preaching, see Peter Bayley, *French Pulpit Oratory, 1598–1650*, and Marc Fumaroli, *L'âge de l'éloquence*.

8. The Jesuit encounter with the native peoples of North America has spawned a rich literature, from the *Jesuit Relations* to many recent books and articles. For a useful bibliography, see Worcester, *Cambridge Companion*. See also Nicholas P. Cushner, *Soldiers of God: The Jesuits in Colonial America, 1565–1767* (Buffalo, N.Y.: Language Communications, 2002), and Joseph A. Gagliano and Charles E. Ronan, eds., *Jesuit Encounters in the New World: Jesuit Chroniclers, Geographers, Educators and Missionaries in the Americas, 1549–1767*. Rome: Institutum Historicum Societatis Iesu, 1997.

9. See Jonathan Spence's excellent *The Memory Palace of Matteo Ricci*.

10. Teaching the classical curriculum in schools was the most prominent Jesuit ministry but by no means the only one. Others included mission work (among native peoples, especially in the Americas and in Asia), preaching, and publishing (*America* magazine, university presses, and the Institute of Jesuit Sources in the United States and devotional manuals everywhere). All these ministries relied heavily on rhetorical skills, of course. Today, Jesuit colleges in India, Japan, Latin America, and Korea, like those in the United States, do not require Latin and Greek of their students, even those planning to become Jesuits. Many Jesuit universities (e.g., Sogang in Korea, Pontificia Universidad Javeriana in Colombia) do not even offer coursework in Latin. It's a mistake to conflate Jesuit education exclusively with the classics. The Jesuits from their beginnings taught the most common subjects available: In Europe and the American colonies it was the Renaissance humanism that was universal, and Loyola, though not a specialist in the humanities, devoted all of the Jesuits' efforts to their spread. In other parts of the globe, the classical humanities currently have no such sway, and so the Jesuits do not insist on teaching them.

11. Another illustration of the Jesuits' global educational mission in the Americas is illustrated in the lives of four prominent Spanish members of the order: José de Acosta (1540–1600) visited Panama, Peru, and Mexico and was a pioneer writer on the natural history of the Americas; José de Arriaga (1564–1622), rector of the College of San Martin

at Lima, wrote a key rhetorical treatise. Both traveled back and forth between Spain and the New World, and Arriaga actually died at sea on his way back to his homeland. Besides Arriaga, at least two other Mexican Jesuits produced rhetorical treatises, Domingo Velasquez and Tomás González (Kennedy, 254). See Abbott, *Rhetoric in the New World,* and Joseph A. Gagliano and Charles E. Ronan, eds., *Jesuit Encounters in the New World: Jesuit Chroniclers, Geographers, Educators, and Missionaries in the Americas, 1549–1767.*

12. For a good account of the transition from scholasticism to humanism, see Hendrickson, 128–42.

13. This practice, begun elsewhere, was imposed because of the enormous success of Jesuit colleges, outrunning the number of Jesuits available to teach each student. Naturally, the *decuriae* and the system of student monitoring attracted the notice of Foucault—himself educated by Jesuits—in *Discipline and Punish.* Scaglione (73–74) downplays the importance of the *decuriae* to the Jesuit system, but McDonough notes its persistence into the 1930s (422), at least in Jesuit high schools.

14. See Ong, "Latin as a Puberty Rite," for a description of the rigors of Latin instruction among the Jesuits. By the late nineteenth century, the Jesuits were depicted as having assumed the role of beaters themselves; witness the fictional Father Dolan in *A Portrait of the Artist as a Young Man.* This is perhaps a sign of how the Jesuits had lost touch with the *Ratio Studiorum,* which cautioned against beating and urged instead positive reinforcements such as contests and prizes. Codina also discusses corporal punishment among the Jesuits, 35. The humanities seem always to have been taught to young people through threats of physical punishment. Before the Jesuits were formed, Erasmus described the Parisian College de Montaigu, where Loyola would later study, as a "torture chamber" filled with "rods, switches, and straps," where students were punished for every "mispronunciation or mistake in grammar" (79).

15. Schwickerath (457–93) gives extended examples of prelection, based on the work of the French Jesuit rhetorician Jouvancey. A version of prelection persisted well into the twentieth century. Something like prelection appeared at Oxford when J. R. R. Tolkien began his series of lectures on *Beowulf*:

> He would come silently into the room, fix the audience with his gaze, and suddenly begin to declaim in a resounding voice the opening lines of the poem in the original Anglo-Saxon, commencing with a great cry of *Hwæt!* (The first word of this and several other Old English poems), which some undergraduates took to be 'Quiet!' It was not so much a recitation as a dramatic performance, an impersonation of an Anglo-Saxon bard in a mead hall, and it impressed generations of students because it brought home to them that *Beowulf* was not just a set text to be read for the purposes of examination, but a powerful piece of dramatic poetry.
>
> —Carpenter, 133

Decades later, W. H. Auden wrote to his former professor, "I don't think that I have ever told you what an unforgettable experience it was for me as an undergraduate, hearing you recite *Beowulf.* The voice was the voice of Gandalf" (Carpenter, 133). For another example of prelection, see Rose in Part II.

16. Three examples, among many, will suffice: the continuing popularity of *Style,* the textbook begun by Joseph Williams and now continued in its eleventh edition by Joseph Bizup; and two recent collections, Butler's *Style in Rhetoric and Composition* and Johnson and Pace's *Refiguring Prose Style.*

17. See Murphy, Conley, Mack, Kennedy, Fumaroli, O'Malley for varied treatments of Jesuit rhetorical practices and figures.

18. Robert Maryks's *Saint Cicero and the Jesuits* captures the way that Cicero's rhetoric connected closely to Jesuit conceptions of morality.

19. The word *college* still in rare instances covers both secondary and, more commonly, tertiary education; witness Eton College in Britain, Baltimore City College, and the Jesuits' own Gonzaga College High School in Washington, D.C.

20. The Protestant pedagogue Joannes Sturm (1507–89), Ramus's teacher, claimed that the Jesuits borrowed their approach from his school, but there is little evidence to support that claim. See McGucken, 23.

21. In contrast to the Jesuits, in the seventeenth century the French priest who established the Brothers of the Christian Schools with the explicit purpose of teaching the poor insisted that his order eschew Latin completely. According to Andrea Miller:

> When John Baptist de La Salle wrote the Rule (the set of directives for a religious community) for the new Institute, he was explicit about prohibiting Brothers from teaching or studying Latin. The reasons for excluding Latin were sound. In 17th-century France, education was a prerogative of the wealthy and was largely carried out in Latin to prepare students for advanced studies in the university or for careers in the Church. For the poor whom de La Salle sought to serve, neither a university education nor an ecclesiastical career was in prospect, and for them Latin had no useful purpose. He also feared that the Brothers themselves would drift away from the Institute's aim of serving the disadvantaged, possibly lured by the prestige of teaching the upper classes or called to a priestly vocation which required Latin. (Miller, 6)

22. Jesuit rhetoric extended to a rich variety of the arts, including theater, ballet, painting, and architecture (see O'Malley, ed., *The Jesuits and the Arts*).

23. See Jean Dietz Moss and William A. Wallace, "Cipriano Soarez's *Art of Rhetoric*," in *Rhetoric and Dialectic in the Time of Galileo* (111–86); Lawrence J. Flynn, "The *De Arte Rhetorica* (1568) by Cyprian Soarez, S.J.: A Translation with Introduction and Notes," unpublished dissertation (University of Florida, 1955); Lawrence J. Flynn, "The *De Arte Rhetorica* of Cyprian Soarez, S.J.," *Quarterly Journal of Soeech* 42 (1956) 367–74; and Lawrence J. Flynn, "Sources and Influence of Soarez' *De Arte Rhetorica*," *Quarterly Journal of Speech* 43 (1957): 257–64.

24. In Germany, Austria, and France, the Jesuits created a unique type of theatrical performance, now called Jesuit drama, usually in Latin but sometimes in the vernacular. Each college presented a play every year, with student actors and the public from surrounding areas invited to attend. For fictional treatments of Jesuit dramas at Paris's Louis le Grand, see Judith Rock's *The Rhetoric of Death* and *The Eloquence of Blood*. The Jesuit rhetorician Jouvancey is a character in both.

25. For an in-depth study of Jesuit dance in seventeenth-century France, see Judith Rock's highly original *Terpsichore at Louis-le-Grand*.

26. Experts in rhetoric are frequently regarded as wizards with language but essentially fraudulent. Plato's depiction of a rhetorician in his *Gorgias* is an early example.

27. The Jesuit facilities in Russia survived, thanks to Catherine the Great, who refused to publish the pope's suppression letter. She was mainly concerned with her Catholic subjects in the Polish provinces, then a part of Russia. For an overview of the

suppression, see Thomas Rochford, "Pain of Suppression Gives Way to Hope of Restoration," http://jesuitscentralsouthern.org .

28. One principal example of this displacement has been the fate of the *Ratio Studiorum*. Much of the curriculum, methods, and organization of rhetorical education set out in the *Ratio Studiorum* (1599), the comprehensive plan of education followed for hundreds of years across the globe, came increasingly to be regarded as obsolete, particularly after the suppression, rather than seen as a prospect for updating, or *aggiornamento*. Several efforts were made to revise the *Ratio*, but they were never formally accepted. And with the gradual move away from the *Ratio*, the explicit language-arts core of the curriculum was rendered increasingly opaque. Few Jesuits at the turn of the twentieth century were familiar with it. In the last few years, however, interest in the *Ratio* has been revived.

29. On the first page of *Vile Bodies*, Waugh depicts a nice caricature of a Jesuit, from his elite Jewish origins to his poverty to his disguises to his impressive intellectualism:

> With Asiatic resignation Father Rothschild S.J. put down his suitcase in the corner of the bar and went on deck. (It was a small suitcase of imitation crocodile hide. The initials stamped on it in Gothic characters were not Father Rothschild's, for he had borrowed it that morning from the *valet-de-chambre* of his hotel. It contained some rudimentary underclothes, six important new books in six languages, a false beard and a school atlas and gazetteer heavily annotated.) Standing on the deck Father Rothschild leant his elbow on the rail, rested his chin in his hands and surveyed the procession of passengers coming up the gangway, each face eloquent of polite misgiving.
>
> Very few of them were unknown to the Jesuit, for it was his happy knack to remember everything that could possibly be learned about anyone who could possibly be of any importance.

In 1930, when Waugh decided to convert to Catholicism, his command was "Find me a Jesuit." It was the well-known Martin D'Arcy, S.J., who received Waugh into the Church. http://magazine.nd.edu/news/14881-literary-scamp-evelyn-waugh/

30. See Brian Vickers, *In Defense of Rhetoric*; Thomas Conley, *Rhetoric in the European Tradition*; George Kennedy, *Classical Rhetoric and Its Christian and Secular Tradition from Ancient to Modern Times*; James J. Murphy, ed., *Renaissance Eloquence*; Wayne A. Rebhorn, *Renaissance Debates on Rhetoric*; Marc Fumaroli, *L'age de l'eloquence*; Robert Maryks, *Saint Cicero and the Jesuits*; J. Carlos Coupeau, *Beginning, Middle, and End: A Rhetorical Study of the Constitutions of the Society of Jesus as a Classic of Spirituality*; Alan P. Farrell, *The Jesuit Code of Liberal Education*; and Edward J. Lynch, "The Origin and Development of Rhetoric in the Plan of Studies of 1599 Ratio Studiorum of the Society of Jesus," along with many articles in English, French, German, Spanish, and Italian scholarly journals.

31. See John O'Malley, *The First Jesuits*; O'Malley et al., *The Jesuits: Cultures, Sciences, and the Arts, 1540–1773*; John W. O'Malley, "Five Missions of the Jesuit Charism," in *Studies in the Spirituality of Jesuits* (Winter 2006; St. Louis: Institute of Jesuit Sources, 2006); Gabriel Codina Mir, *Aux sources de la pédagogie des Jésuites: Le 'Modus Parisiensis'*; Christopher Chapple, *The Jesuit Tradition in Education and Missions*; William McGucken, *The Jesuits and Education*; François Charmot, *La Pédagogie des Jésuites*;

François de Dainville, *L'éducation des Jésuites*; John W. Padberg, *The Jesuit Schools in France from Revival to Suppression, 1815–1880*; Aldo Scaglione, *The Liberal Arts and the Jesuit College System*; Renaldo Bonachea, ed., *Jesuit Higher Education*; Robert Schwickerath, *Jesuit Education*; and Thomas Worcester, ed., *The Cambridge Companion to the Jesuits*.

32. See Conley (216–26) and Barbra Warnick, "Charles Rollin's Traité and the Rhetorical Theories of Smith, Campbell, and Blair," in *Rhetorica* 3 (1985): 45–65. Among the French influences on Scottish rhetoricians were two Jesuits, Claude Buffier (1661–1737) and Dominique Bouhours (1628–1702). See Conley (194–99).

33. Kinney and Miller, "Civic Humanism, a Postmortem?" in Graff, Walzer, and Atwill, *The Viability of the Rhetorical Tradition*. Kinney and Miller also cite Spellmeyer, Fusfield, and Bender and Wellbery's *The Ends of Rhetoric*.

34. See John Padberg, at http://jloughnan.tripod.com/femalej.htm.

35. Carol Mattingly, "Uncovering Forgotten Habits: Anti-Catholic Rhetoric and Nineteenth-Century American Women's Literacy," *College Composition and Communication* 58, no. 2 (2006). Johnson and Wright delivered important papers on American Catholic women's education at the 2014 Conference on College Composition and Communication): Elizabethada Wright, "'Without Schools, Religion Can Never Be Established': The 19th-Century Writing Curriculum at St. Mary's of Indiana," and Nan Johnson, "Rhetorical Education for Women of Conscience: Catholic Colleges for Women."

36. See Rothermel in Bizzell, ed. For an important contribution to an understanding of Catholic women's rhetorical education, see Suzanne Bordelon, Elizabethada A. Wright, and S. Michael Halloran, "From Rhetoric to Rhetorics: An Interim Report on the History of American Writing Instruction to 1900," in Murphy, *A Short History*, 208–31. The two presentations at the 2012 Conference on College Composition and Communication, by Wright and by Nan Johnson, also dealt with the subject.

37. Marquette was the first Jesuit college to admit women, in 1909. Holy Cross was the last to begin to do so, in 1972.

38. See also Elizabeth Vander Lei, Thomas Amorose, Beth Daniell, and Anne Ruggles Gere, eds., *Renovating Rhetoric in Christian Tradition* (Pittsburgh: University of Pittsburgh Press, 2014), and Roxanne Mountford, *The Gendered Pulpit: Preaching in American Protestant Spaces* (Cardondale: Southern Illinois University Press, 2003).

39. See the excellent discussion of Vico, with a fine bibliography, in Ferreira-Buckley's chapter "The Eighteenth Century," in Gaillett and Horner.

WORKS CITED

Abbott, Don Paul. *Rhetoric in the New World: Rhetorical Theory and Practice in Colonial Spanish America*. Columbia: University of South Carolina Press, 1996.

Agnew, Lois. "The Classical Period." In Gaillet and Horner, 7–25.

Association of Jesuit Colleges and Universities. http://www.ajcunet.edu/institutions.

Ballif, Michelle, ed. *Theorizing Histories of Rhetoric*. Carbondale: Southern Illinois University Press, 2013.

Bangert, William V. *A History of the Society of Jesus*. St. Louis: Institute of Jesuit Sources, 1972.

Bayley, Peter. *French Pulpit Oratory, 1598–1650.* Cambridge: Cambridge University Press, 1980.

Bernard-Donals, Michael. *The Practice of Theory: Rhetoric, Knowledge, and Pedagogy in the Academy.* Cambridge: Cambridge University Press, 1998

Bizzell, Patricia, ed. *Rhetorical Agendas: Political, Ethical, and Spiritual.* Mawah, N.J.: Lawrence Erlbaum Associates, 2006.

Boryczka, Joycelyn M., and Elizabeth A. Petrino, eds. *Jesuit and Feminist Education.* New York: Fordham University Press, 2011.

Burke, Peter. "The Jesuits and the Art of Translation in Early Modern Europe." In *The Jesuits II: Cultures, Sciences, and the Arts: 1540–1773,* ed. O'Malley et al.

Butler, Paul, ed. *Style in Rhetoric and Composition: A Critical Sourcebook.* Boston and New York: Bedford / St. Martin's, 2010.

Carpenter, Humphrey. *The Inklings: C. S. Lewis, J. R. R. Tolkien, Charles Williams, and Their Friends.* Boston: Houghton Mifflin, 1979.

Chapple, Christopher, ed. *Jesuit Tradition in Education: A 450-Year Perspective,* Scranton, Pa.: University of Scranton Press, 1993.

Codina, Gabriel. "The 'Modus Parisiensis.'" In *The Jesuit Ratio Studiorum: 400th Anniversary Perspectives,* ed. Duminuco.

Conley, Thomas. *Rhetoric in the European Tradition.* Chicago: University of Chicago Press, 1990.

Connors, Robert, Lisa Ede, and Andrea Lunsford, eds. *Essays on Classical and Modern Discourse.* Carbondale: Southern Illinois University Press, 1984.

Cueva, Edmund P., Shannon N. Byrne, and Frederick Benda, eds. *Jesuit Education and the Classics.* Newcastle upon Tyne: Cambridge Scholars Publishing, 2009.

Cushner, Nicholas P. *Soldiers of God: the Jesuits in Colonial America: 1565–1767.* Buffalo, N.Y.: Language Communications, 2002.

Dalmases, Candido. *Ignatius of Loyola, Founder of the Jesuits.* Translated by Jerome Aixalá. St. Louis: Institute of Jesuit Sources, 1985.

De Dainville, François. *L'education des jesuites.* Paris: Les Editions de Minuit, 1978.

DeJulio, Rosemary. 'Women's Ways of Knowing and Learning: The Response of Mary Ward and Madeline Sophie Barat to the *Ratio Studiorum.*" In *The Jesuit Ratio Studiorum: 400th Anniversary Perspectives,* ed., Duminuco.

DePalma, Michael-John and Jeffrey M. Ringer, eds. *Mapping Christian Rhetorics.* New York: Routledge, 2015.

Dimler, G. Richard. "Emblems." In *Ratio Studiorum: Jesuit Education, 1540–1773,* ed. John Attebury and John Russell. Boston: John J. Burns Library, Boston College, 1999. 20–23.

Duminuco, Vincent J., ed. *The Jesuit Ratio Studiorum: 400th Anniversary Perspectives.* New York: Fordham University Press, 2000.

Enos, Theresa, and Stuart Brown, eds. *Professing the New Rhetorics: A Sourcebook.* Englewood Cliffs, N.J.: Prentice Hall. 1994.

Erasmus, Desiderius. *The Praise of Folly.* Trans. Clarence H. Miller. New Haven: Yale University Press, 2003.

Farrell, Allan P. *The Jesuit Code of Liberal Education.* Milwaukee: Bruce Publishing Company, 1938.

Farrell, Allan P., trans. *The Jesuit Ratio Studiorum of 1559*. Washington, D.C.: Conference of the Major Superiors of Jesuits, 1970.

Farrell, Thomas J., and Paul A. Soukup, eds. *Of Ong and Media Ecology: Essays in Communication, Composition, and Literary Studies*. New York: Hampton Press, 2012.

Ferreira-Buckley, Linda. "The Eighteenth Century." In *The Present State of Scholarship in the History of Rhetoric: A Twenty-First-Century Guide*, ed. Gaillet and Horner.

Flynn, Lawrence J. "The *De Arte Rhetorica* of Cyprien Soarez, S.J.: A Translation with Introduction and Notes." PhD diss., University of Florida, 1955. Ann Arbor: UMI, 2001.

———. "The *De Arte Rhetorica* of Cyprien Soarez, S.J." *Quarterly Journal of Speech* 42 (1956): 367–74.

———. "Sources and Influence of Soarez' *De Arte Rhetorica*." *Quarterly Journal of Speech* 43 (1957): 257–65.

Foss, Sonja K., Karen A. Foss, and Robert Trapp, eds. *Contemporary Perspectives on Rhetoric*. Prospect Heights, Ill.: Waveland Press, 1985.

Fumaroli, Marc. *L'âge d'éloquence*. Geneva: Droz, 1990.

Gagliano, Joseph A., and Charles E. Ronan, eds. *Jesuit Encounters in the New World: Jesuit Chroniclers, Geographers, Educators, and Missionaries in the Americas, 1549–1767*. Rome: Institutum Historicum Societatis Iesu, 1997.

Gaillet, Lynée Lewis, and Winifred Bryan Horner, eds. *The Present State of Scholarship in the History of Rhetoric: A Twenty-First-Century Guide*. Columbia: University of Missouri Press, 2010.

Ganss, George. *St. Ignatius' Idea of a Jesuit University*. Milwaukee: Marquette University Press, 1956.

Giard, Luce. "The Jesuit College: A Center for Knowledge, Art, and Faith, 1548–1773," trans. Brian Van Hove. *Studies in the Spirituality of Jesuits* 40, no. 1 (Spring 2008).

Gorman, Margaret. "The Influence of Ignatian Spirituality on Women's Teaching Orders in the United States." In *Jesuit Tradition in Education: A 450-Year Perspective*, ed. Christopher Chapple. Scranton, Pa.: University of Scranton Press, 1993.

Graff, Richard, Arthur Walzer, and Janet M. Atwill, eds. *The Viability of the Rhetorical Tradition*. Albany: SUNY Press, 2005.

Greenbaum, Andrea, and Deborah Holdstein, eds. *Judaic Perspectives in Rhetoric and Composition*. New York: Hampton Press, 2008.

Hendrickson, Daniel Scott. "The Jesuit Imaginary: Higher Education in a Secular Age." PhD diss., Columbia University, 2012.

Horner, Winifred Bryan. *Nineteenth-Century Scottish Rhetoric: The American Connection*. Carbondale: Southern Illinois University Press: 1983.

Horner, Winifred Bryan, ed. *The Present State of Scholarship in Historical and Contemporary Rhetoric*. Rev. ed. Columbia: University of Missouri Press, 1990.

Jey, Martine. *La littérature au lycée: Invention d'une discipline (1880–1925)*. Paris: Klinksieck, 1998.

Johnson, Kristine, and Paul Lynch. "*Ad perfectum eloquentiam*: The 'Spoils of Egypt' in Jesuit Renaissance Rhetoric." *Rhetoric Review* 31, no. 2 (2012): 99–116.

Johnson, Nan. "Rhetorical Education for Women of Conscience: Catholic Colleges for Women." Conference paper, Conference on College Composition and Communication, 2012.

Johnson, T. R., and Thomas Pace, eds., *Refiguring Prose Style: Possibilities for Writing Pedagogy.* Logan: Utah State University Press: 2005.

Jones, Arthur. "Literary Scamp Evelyn Waugh." http://magazine.nd.edu/news/ 14881-literary-scamp-evelyn-waugh. Accessed November 6, 2013.

Kennedy, George A. *Classical Rhetoric and Its Christian and Secular Tradition.* 2nd ed. Chapel Hill: University of North Carolina Press, 1999.

Kitzhaber, Albert. *Rhetoric in American Colleges, 1850–1900.* Dallas: Southern Methodist University Press, 1990.

Leahy, William P. *Adapting to America: Catholics, Jesuits, and Higher Education in the Twentieth Century.* Washington, D.C.: Georgetown University Press, 1991.

Loach, Judi. "Revolutionary Pedagogues? How the Jesuits Used Education," 66–85. In *The Jesuits II: Cultures, Sciences, and the Arts, 1540–1773,* ed. O'Malley et al.

Lunsford, Andrea. http://davidbeard.efoliomn.com. Accessed July 5, 2014.

Lynch, Edward J. "The Origin and Development of Rhetoric in the Plan of Studies of 1599 of the Society of Jesus." PhD diss., Northwestern University, 1968.

MacCormack, Sabine. "Grammar and Virtue: The Program in Early Colonial Peru." In *The Jesuits II: Cultures, Sciences, and the Arts, 1540–1773,* ed. O'Malley et al.

MacDonough, Peter. *Men Astutely Trained: A History of the Jesuits in the American Century.* New York: Free Press, 1992.

Mack, Peter. *A History of Renaissance Rhetoric, 1300–1620.* Oxford: Oxford University Press, 2011.

Mahoney, Kathleen A. *Catholic Higher Education in Protestant America: The Jesuits and Harvard in the Age of the University.* Baltimore: Johns Hopkins University Press, 2003.

Mailloux, Steven. "Disciplinary Identities: On the Rhetorical Paths Between English and Communication Studies." *Rhetoric Society Quarterly* 30, no. 2, 5–29.

Maryks, Robert. *Saint Cicero and the Jesuits.* Aldershot, UK: Ashgate, 2008.

———. *The Jesuit Order as a Synagogue of Jews: Jesuits of Jewish Ancestry and Purity-of-Blood Laws in the Early Society of Jesus.* Leiden: Brill Academic, 2009.

Mattingly, Carol. "Uncovering Forgotten Habits: Anti-Catholic Rhetoric and Ninteenth-Century American Women's Literacy." *College Composition and Communication* 58, no. 2 (December 2006): 160–81.

McGinn, Bernard. *The Varieties of Vernacular Mysticism.* New York: Herder and Herder, 2012.

McGucken, William J. *The Jesuits and Education.* Milwaukee: Bruce, 1932. Reprint. Eugene, Ore.: Wipf and Stock, 2008.

Miller, Andrea. "New Century, New Challenges." www.delasalle.org/consumers /christian_schools/new_century03.pdf. Accessed September 14, 2013.

Miller, Thomas P. *The Formation of College English: Rhetoric and Belles Lettres in the British Cultural Provinces.* Pittsburgh: Pittsburgh University Press, 1997.

Moss, Jean Dietz, and William A. Wallace. *Rhetoric and Dialectic in the Time of Galileo.* Washington, D.C.: Catholic University of America Press, 2003.

Mountford, Roxanne. *The Gendered Pulpit: Preaching in American Protestant Spaces.* Carbondale: Southern Illinois University Press, 2005.

Munitiz, Joseph A., and Philip Endean, eds. *St. Ignatius of Loyola: Personal Writings.* London: Penguin Books, 1996.

Murphy, James J. *Quintilian on the Teaching of Speaking and Writing. Translations from Books One, Two, and Ten of the "Institutio Oratoria."* Carbondale: Southern Illinois University Press, 1987.

Murphy, James J., ed. *A Short History of Writing Instruction: From Ancient Greece to Contemporary America.* New York and London: Routledge, 2012.

Neenan, William B. "Jesuit International Education in History." http://eduignaciana .tripod.com/docum/je-int-ed.pdf. Accessed September 1, 2014.

O'Malley, John. *The First Jesuits.* Cambridge, Mass.: Harvard University Press, 1993.

———. "The Historiography of the Society of Jesus." In *The Jesuits II: Cultures, Sciences, and the Arts, 1540–1773,* ed. O'Malley et al.

———. *Saints or Devils Incarnate: Studies in Jesuit History.* Leiden: Brill, 2013.

O'Malley, John, Gauvin Alexander Bailey, and Steven J. Harris, eds. *The Jesuits: Cultures, Sciences, and the Arts, 1540–1773.* 2 vols. Toronto: University of Toronto Press, 1999, 2006.

O'Malley, John, and Gauvin Alexander Bailey, eds. *The Jesuits and the Arts, 1540–1773.* Philadelphia: Saint Joseph's University Press, 2005.

Ong, Walter J. "Latin Learning as a Renaissance Puberty Rite," 113–41. In *Rhetoric, Romance, and Technology: Studies in the Interaction of Expression and Culture.* Ithaca, N.Y.: Cornell University Press, 1971.

Padberg, John. *Colleges in Controversy: The Jesuit Schools in France from Revival to Suppression, 1815–1880.* Cambridge, Mass.: Harvard University Press, 1969.

Pavur, Claude, trans. *The Ratio Studiorum: The Official Plan for Jesuit Education.* St. Louis: Institute of Jesuit Sources, 2005.

Rastoin, Mark. *Du même sang que notre Seigneur: Juifs et jésuites aux débuts de la Compagnie.* Montrouge: Bayard, 2011.

Reites, James W. "St. Ignatius Loyola and the Jews." *Studies in the Spirituality of the Jesuits* 13, no. 4 (September, 1981). http://ejournals.bc.edu/ojs/index.php/Jesuit /article/viewFile/3714/3292. Accessed September 26, 2014.

Rochford, Thomas. "Pain of Suppression Gives Way to Hope of Restoration." http://jesuitscentralsouthern.org. Accessed September 7, 2014.

Rock, Judith. *Terpsichore at Louis-le-Grand: Baroque Dance on a Jesuit Stage in Paris.* St. Louis: Institute of Jesuit Sources, 1996.

Rothermel, Beth Ann. "Public Portals, Catholic Walls: Teacher Training and the Liberal Arts at Two Western Massachusetts Colleges for Women in the 1930s, the College of Our Lady of the Elms and the State Teachers College at Westfield." In *Rhetorical Agendas: Political, Ethical, and Spiritual,* ed. Bizzell.

Scaglione, Aldo. *The Liberal Arts and the Jesuit College System.* Amsterdam and Philadelphia: John Benjamins, 1986.

Schloesser, Steven. "Jesuit Rhetoric: Limit, Modesty, and Accomodation in Sixteenth-Century Modernism." http://www.schloesser_jesuit-rhetoric.pdf. Accessed February 13, 2012.

———. "Accommodation as a Rhetorical Principle: Twenty Years after John O'Malley's *The First Jesuits* (1993)." *Journal of Jesuit Studies* 1 (2014), 347–72.

Schroth, Raymond A. *The American Jesuits, A History.* New York: New York University Press, 2007.

Schwickerath, Robert. *Jesuit Education: Its History and Principles Viewed in the Light of Modern Educational Problems.* 2nd ed. St. Louis: B. Herder, 1903.

Sommervogel, Carlos. *Bibliothèque de la Compagnie de Jesus*. 7 vols. Bruxelles: O. Schepens, 1890–1900.

Spence, Jonathan. *The Memory Palace of Matteo Ricci*. New York: Penguin, 1985.

Taneja, Maneesha. "Translation as a Dialogue between Cultures: The Jesuit Experience." http://dadun.unav.edu/handle/10171/27928. Accessed October 13, 2013.

Tjoelker, Nienke, "Jesuit Image Rhetoric in Latin and the Vernacular: The Latin and Dutch Emblems of the *Imago Primi Saeculi*," *Renæssanceforum* 6 (2010). www.renæssanceforum.dk.

Tolar Burton, Vicki. *Spiritual Literacy in John Wesley's Methodism*. Waco, Texas: Baylor University Press, 2008.

Tripole, Martin, ed. *Promise Renewed: Jesuit Education for a New Millennium*. Chicago: Loyola Press, 1999.

Traub, George W., ed. *A Jesuit Education Reader*. Chicago: Loyola Press, 2008.

U.S. News and World Report. http://colleges.usnews.rankingsandreviews.com/best-colleges. Accessed December 10, 2011.

Vander Lei, Elizabeth, Thomas Amorose, Beth Daniell, and Anne Ruggles Gere, eds. *Renovating Rhetoric in Christian Tradition*. Pittsburgh: University of Pittsburgh Press, 2014.

Vitanza, Victor J., ed. *Writing Histories of Rhetoric*. Carbondale: Southern Illinois University Press, 1994.

Warnick, Barbara, *The Sixth Canon: Belletristic Rhetorical Theory and Its French Antecedents*. Columbia: University of South Carolina Press, 1993.

Welch, Kathleen E. *The Contemporary Reception of Classical Rhetoric: Appropriations of Ancient Discourse*. Hillsdale, N.J.: Lawrence Erlbaum Associates, 1990.

Williams, Joseph and Joseph Bizup. *Style: Lessons in Clarity and Grace*. 11th ed. New York: Longman, 2013.

Worcester, Thomas, ed. *The Cambridge Companion to the Jesuits*. Cambridge: Cambridge University Press, 2008.

Wozniak, John Michael. *English Composition in Eastern Colleges, 1850–1940*. Lanham, Md.: Rowman and Littlefield, 1978.

Wright, Jonathan. "The Suppression and Restoration." In Worcester, *Cambridge Companion*, 263–77.

U.S. News and World Report. http://colleges.usnews.rankingsandreviews.com/best-colleges. Accessed December 10, 2011.

PART I

HISTORICAL SITES AND SCENES OF JESUIT RHETORICAL PRACTICE, SCHOLARSHIP, AND PEDAGOGY

HISTORICAL NOTES ON RHETORIC IN JESUIT EDUCATION

Patricia Bizzell

In a focus group discussing new recruitment material for the College of the Holy Cross, I learned from admissions-office personnel that many students who are interested in our college seek excellent liberal-arts education but place little value on our affiliation with the Society of Jesus, little beyond a generalized feeling that Jesuit schools are "good." This vagueness about what constitutes Jesuit education may be due in part to the dwindling (though still significant) number of our students whose parents attended Holy Cross and who therefore have firsthand witnesses to inform them. But I dare say the vagueness is shared by many who are navigating the American academic scene. So what should these prospective students be looking for? Holy Cross has a robust sense of its Jesuit mission to educate the whole person, and this mission encompasses many components. But I will argue here that a major component of the Jesuit educational mission has been, and is, education in rhetoric and, often, more specifically, that blend of verbal facility and ethical action known in the tradition as *eloquentia perfecta* (see, in Part II, Brereton and Mailloux and, in Part III, Gannett and Fernald).

This focus was necessitated by the cultural milieu in which the order emerged, and it has significantly contributed to the Jesuit-educated becoming influential leaders throughout the world. As John O'Malley, S.J., points out in the foreword to this volume, the humanist rhetorical education of the Renaissance, which the Jesuits adopted, came to define "good education" for people of many different religious and cultural backgrounds. It can be argued, however—and indeed, the essays in this volume attest—that the Jesuits gave rhetorical education a particular ethical spin and held onto it through the centuries more tenaciously than did many others. Contemporary examples include the College of the Holy Cross, in Worcester, Massachusetts, and Sogang University, in Seoul, South Korea, where I was privileged to teach in 2011. The common denominator has always been to develop whatever language-using abilities are most needful for leadership in that time and place.

RHETORIC IN EARLY JESUIT EDUCATION

At the time of the founding of the Society of Jesus, which received papal approval in 1540, Europe was in the midst of violent cultural changes. Social classes were becoming more stratified, with greater concentrations of wealth above and poverty below; political upheavals and warfare were commonplace, as larger national entities were gradually hammered out; and explosive religious controversy had begun with the Reformation and the Roman Catholic Church's responses to it. It is easy to imagine how individuals in such a period would have difficulty finding their way. One such individual was Ignatius Loyola. Like many aristocratic young men of his day, he was proficient in arms, but while recovering at home from severe battle wounds, he experienced the religious revelation that set him on the path to founding the Jesuit order. (For more on his early spiritual development, see Deans, Part I.)

As Ignatius and his companions began to discern what their particular contribution to Christendom would be, "the basic impulse behind the new Order was missionary," as O'Malley has explained ("How," 60). The Jesuits were ready to travel anywhere in the world where they could serve "the good of souls" (60), and as is well known, early companion Francis Xavier set out for India, Japan, and China even before the order was formally approved. (I'll have more to say about Jesuits in Asia later.) O'Malley shows how the Jesuits evolved their program of helping souls from the spiritual development of Ignatius himself, characterized by "the primacy of personal spiritual experience" (61); "the conviction that God could be found in all things" (62), so that religion and secular learning need not be at odds; and the vision of "the Christian life as a call to be of help to others" (62).

Initially, the Jesuits aimed to enact this form of spirituality through pastoral care and preaching. O'Malley says that at first they explicitly ruled out education as part of their ministry (63). Indeed, no religious order had undertaken the education of laypeople as its principal mission, although some offered instruction to their younger members, as the Jesuits began to do. Nevertheless, as O'Malley has noted, Ignatius Loyola and his early companions were well equipped to become educators, as all were "from an academic elite" (*First*, 36). Having begun their education at universities in their native lands—Loyola's at the Spanish universities of Alcalá and Salamanca—they then traveled to the University of Paris, which for centuries had been the preeminent institution of higher learning in Europe. At Paris they completed their mastery of the classical languages, then the sine qua non of higher learning, as well as developing their own new emphases in theology, and when the companions then traveled to Rome, intent on offering their services to the pope, they entered the homeland of the humanist movement, of which rhetoric as exemplified in the classical texts was "the central discipline," as O'Malley says (253; for more on Loyola's rhetorical education, see Brereton in Part II, and Gannett in Part III). Italian humanist *pietas*, to be derived from classical learning, aimed to inculcate personal integrity and a commitment to public service, goals easily adapted to a more specifically Christian emphasis such as the Jesuits valued (see O'Malley, "How," 64). Indeed, Robert A. Maryks has argued that Ciceronian probabilistic argument provided the inspiration and model for the way the

Jesuits innovated in conducting the sacrament of confession (emphasizing individual conscience rather than strict legalism) (see Maryks, *Saint*, 97–101; and his chapter in Part I of this volume).

Combating Protestantism, as O'Malley emphasizes, was not an early motive for Jesuit missionizing activity (see "From," 135). Much of this activity took place in countries where Protestantism was not a great threat (e.g., Catholic European countries and "pagan" countries in Asia). But as Paul Grendler has explained, the early Jesuits believed that a new kind of schooling was necessary to prepare young men for the priesthood, and especially for membership in the Society of Jesus. O'Malley, who concurs, is worth quoting at length on the problem:

> The Jesuit educational venture originated with concern for the training of younger members of the Society, whose education the first companions hoped would be at least the equivalent of their own. Those companions must themselves be numbered among the clergy that benefited from the best their age had to offer. From their observations, however, and from many other sources as well, we know that the training of the diocesan clergy followed an extraordinarily haphazard pattern across Europe. Although a small percentage were well educated and devout, the seemingly vast majority were so ill-trained as to constitute a major scandal, and some were ignorant almost beyond description. It was almost inevitable that the Jesuits would be drawn into attempts to alleviate the situation.
> —John W. O'Malley, *The First* Jesuits, 232

Compounding the problem of inadequate training was misplaced fidelity to the cold logic of the medieval scholastic style of preaching, with its elaborately structured sermons of textual and doctrinal analysis. James J. Murphy gives detailed information on this *ars praedicandi*: in its ultimate form, circa 1200, the typical sermon consisted of a "'protheme' or 'antetheme' followed by a 'prayer' and then statement of 'theme' (Scriptural quotation) with 'division' and 'subdivision' of that quotation 'amplified' through a variety of modes" (331). Setting aside such elaborate schemes, the Jesuits introduced a new style of pulpit oratory that tried to reach people through arousing their emotions with both the religious sincerity of the speaker and his judicious use of rhetorical ornaments. Jesuit preaching concerned itself less with doctrinal niceties than with motivating people to love God and do God's will, even to the point of addressing "heretics" gently (see Worcester, Part I). To reach a wide variety of hearers, says O'Malley, "the Jesuits were constantly advised in all their ministries to adapt what they said and did to times, circumstances, and persons"— as O'Malley points out, a very rhetorical stance (255).

To provide better training for the clergy—and ultimately for the lay students they would educate in their schools—the Jesuits advocated that classical literature in Latin and Greek should be taught, as the Italian humanists had always promoted, but much more systematically (see Scaglione, 3ff.). Borrowing from the pedagogy they had experienced at Paris, the early Jesuits decided that humanist education needed to be organized in levels suited to the students' ability. Students would have to master the work at one level before proceeding to the next. Students also would have to be active learners, provided with many opportunities to use their classical-language skills in original compositions and oral presentations, including theatrical presentations, for which the Jesuit schools later became famous (see O'Malley, *First*, 223ff). Repetition, review, and drill would still be key aids to memory and mastery. Yet the students would need teachers who could motivate them with praise and friendly competition among them, rather than with the brutal forms of corporeal punishment employed elsewhere. Above all, if the students were to put their verbal skills to good use in the service of the Catholic Church, they would need teachers who could make them love doing God's will by the teachers' personal example rather than by exhortation and threat. (To glimpse a Jesuit classroom of the period, see Leigh, Part I).

Guidelines to this approach were eventually collected in the *Ratio Studiorum* of 1599. Many of its principles are widely accepted in secular education today, from the idea that students should be separated into classes according to ability level, to the liberal arts' educational goal of developing the students' psychological well-being and ethical sophistication as well as their intellectual competence. O'Malley contends that the Jesuits "saw a correlation between the *pietas* beloved of the humanists and the kind of personal conversion and transformation that were the traditional goals of Christian ministry" ("From," 135). Juan de Polanco, secretary to Ignatius, wrote an important letter on Jesuit education in 1547 that emphasized the contribution of humanistic learning to interpreting scripture, understanding philosophy, and fostering "the skills in verbal communication essential for the ministries in which the Jesuits engaged" (134). The ultimate goal, wrote Polanco, would be to create "pastors, civic officials, administrators of justice, and [those who] will fill other important posts to everybody's profit and advantage" (quoted in O'Malley, "From the 1599 *Ratio Studiorum* to the Present," 135). Surely the goal of creating effective civic leaders resonates with today's liberal-arts educators, especially rhetoricians. Moreover, having had his (or later, her) conscience developed by arguing cases of conscience according to Ciceronian probabilism, as Maryks explains, these leaders "would when necessary defy convention to follow what in these concrete circumstances was the better choice" (O'Malley, "From the 1599 *Ratio Studiorum* to the Present," 136).

The early Jesuits did not work out this educational philosophy in the abstract before they ever entered a classroom. But because they saw how better education could not only support their own mission but also improve the world in which they lived, they responded quickly to an invitation to open a school in the Sicilian town of Messina in 1548. It was at Messina that the rudiments of the Jesuit approach to education were worked out. Messina promised the Jesuits a school building and room and board for themselves, if they would agree to open a school in which any male student could be admitted free of charge. The Jesuits hoped—not without reason, as it turned out—that a significant number of the young men attending this school would choose a religious vocation or perhaps even seek membership in the Society of Jesus. But the Jesuits were quite willing to educate other students as well, who would enter secular life. Accepting such students was a condition of the town's support for the whole enterprise, but apparently the Jesuits did not resist the notion, because they believed that candidates for the clergy would be better educated if they studied in company with their lay peers—quite a new idea at the time.

The organization of this school responded in part to what the Jesuits found among the young students of Messina and in part to their own earlier educational experiences. These experiences convinced the Jesuits that the best way to create the accomplished rhetoricians they desired was to school the students in Latin and Greek grammar, composition, and literature. Most of the boys who came to the school were the sons of upper-middle-class merchants and wealthy aristocrats, but a few were sent by ambitious farmers and small tradesmen. These boys from the poorer social classes might not even be literate, and a few of them, at the young age of seven or so, were admitted to the school to learn their letters first. Most students, however, entered at around age ten, already possessing basic literacy, and began the first of three levels of classes in Latin. They then progressed to the "humanities" course, which focused on the appreciation of classical literature, and, finally, to the capstone "rhetoric" course, in which all the verbal skills they had learned so far in Latin, and to some extent also in Greek, were put to use in a variety of written and oral exercises. Students moved through these five levels at their own pace, with the more academically successful able to progress more quickly, but in general, young men completed the course when they were around the age of sixteen.

Latin classes focused on the work of Cicero and Vergil. The Jesuits used various manuals, especially one by the Italian humanist Guarino and one by the Jesuit Manoel Álvarez, but they also attempted to present students with complete classical texts, chosen to suit the class's ability level—what is nowadays called a "whole language" approach. The letters of Cicero were favored for this reason—they were relatively short—as well as for their ethical content. (For an extensive discussion of which Ciceronian texts were studied, see Maryks, *Saint*, 88–97; see also Scaglione, 85.) The humanities class (fourth level) continued to focus on Cicero but also read Sallust, Horace, and other Roman authors as well as, often, the *De Copia* and *De Conscribendis Epistolis* of Erasmus, as aids to developing Latin style. (The Jesuits received special permission to continue to use Erasmus even after his work was placed on the Index of forbidden books in 1559.) The study of Greek was begun in the humanities class as well, with readings in Aesop, Isocrates, Demosthenes, and others.

In the final, fifth-level rhetoric class, this study of Greek continued, and an intensive focus on the orations of Cicero was added, in addition to his dialogues on rhetoric. Aristotle's *Rhetoric* and *Poetics* were studied. Students might also read Quintilian—a major influence on the Jesuit educational approach, as Aldo Scaglione emphasizes—and the *Rhetorica ad Herennium* (still widely attributed to Cicero at that time) (see Scaglione, 84–85, and Grendler, 377–80). Very widely used, too, was a rhetoric manual written by a Jesuit, Cipriano Soares, first published in 1562 and running into more than 200 editions by the nineteenth century (for more information about this book, see Mailloux, Part II). Most of the early publications by Jesuits were textbooks in classical grammar, rhetoric, and literary appreciation (see O'Malley, *First*, 241). The Jesuit schools soon might claim to teach the most varied classical curriculum anywhere, since Protestant schools generally avoided pagan writers, and the Jesuits even bettered the secular Italian humanists in their teaching of Greek, according to both Grendler and O'Malley. A commitment to teaching languages, if not only classical languages, persists at Jesuit schools to this day; certainly it characterizes Holy Cross and Sogang, about which I will say more later in this chapter.

Most of the young men who graduated from the rhetoric class in the early Jesuit school received no further schooling. They returned to the lives their families had planned for them. Thus these early schools should not be considered as preparatory in the modern sense. But a few students, especially those intending to take holy orders, or to become lawyers or physicians, might then go on to university studies in philosophy, classical languages, mathematics, natural science, and the ultimate capstone course, theology. Scaglione has suggested that theology in the Jesuit system of education filled the place that philosophy held in Plato's thought (51–52). For the Jesuits, theology, as philosophy for Plato, would help students discover the eternal truths that they would convey through mastery of rhetoric. The Jesuits at Messina offered some university-level classes, but most students who sought further study went on to the secular universities in which Renaissance Europe was rich. Within a few years, however, the Jesuits had established universities of their own, notably at Rome, where young men could receive Jesuit education from the elementary level through their professional degrees. The inscription over the Roman university's door read "School of Grammar, Humanities, and Christian Doctrine, Free" (O'Malley, *First*, 205). Even after these universities were established, however, the self-contained curriculum of Messina, culminating in the rhetoric course, was the common focus of most of the Jesuit schools that sprang up quickly throughout Europe over the next fifty years.

The school at Messina was a great success, with over two hundred pupils in a year's time. Quickly, many other Italian towns requested Jesuit schools, and soon urgent calls came, too, from towns in the Protestant countries of northern Europe. Ignatius was persuaded to put the order's resources into this venture. O'Malley speculates that even at this early date, Ignatius realized that the project had profound implications for the larger Jesuit mission (see "How," 64–65). Grendler says that when the Jesuits set up a school in a town, they drew students away from the secular teachers by challenging them to a contest of oratory. Apparently the Jesuits almost always won! And they kept the rhetorical accomplishments of their form of schooling before the public eye by allowing their students to give speeches in Latin in the local church on religious holidays, to put on plays in Latin, Greek, or a vernacular language that were open to the public, and to give other kinds of public performances (377ff). In short, there was never any question that what the Jesuits were offering in their schools was advanced training in rhetoric.

For Ignatius, it was important that the schooling remain free and open to all. He saw it as an extension of the Jesuits' original missionary aim, since it was intended to strengthen the students' commitment to Catholicism and to make them more effective defenders of the faith, as well as of general benefit to the public good. Ironically, however, as Grendler explains, the decision to keep the schools free of charge meant that the Jesuits had to cultivate the wealthy and powerful who could support them (364). The order soon began to evince a preference for founding schools in larger towns, where the necessary financial support would be easier to obtain. At the same time, the rapid expansion of Jesuit schooling placed a severe strain on the order's manpower—there just were not enough qualified teachers to meet the demand (a problem that has persisted to this day). Reluctantly, the Jesuits decided to stop offering classes in basic literacy in their schools, in response to this manpower shortage, even though this change closed the doors to boys from the poorest backgrounds. The order also responded to pressure from parents and Catholic leaders in Protestant countries to board students, so as to take them out of a Protestant environment and immerse them in Catholic piety. Boarders, however, had to be charged something for their upkeep, hence once again creating a barrier for less wealthy students. Grendler believes that there was, at least at first, no deliberate strategy on the part of the Jesuits to become the schoolmasters of the rich and powerful; on the contrary, as I have noted, they at first provided some of the very few educational opportunities for boys from lower-class families. But circumstances gradually pushed them into that influential position. It was a position particularly congenial to the Jesuits' educational focus on rhetoric, perhaps, since the political, religious, and financial leaders of society, whom the Jesuits were eventually educating—in Catholic countries, almost all of these leaders—would be most favorably placed to use rhetoric effectively.

RHETORIC AT HOLY CROSS, THEN AND NOW

The Jesuit education I have been describing, centered on rhetoric, proved remarkably adaptable and durable. It was employed all over the world. It survived the period from 1773 to 1814 when the order was suppressed by the pope—and indeed, a major reason for the order's reinstatement was that the Jesuits were needed as teachers. The example of the College of the Holy Cross, where I teach, shows that it persisted virtually unchanged well into the nineteenth century. When Holy Cross was founded in 1843, the curriculum consisted of two introductory levels of Latin grammar; three levels of "Humanities," in which both Latin and Greek were studied; a class called "Poetry," where the focus was on the appreciation and imitation of classical literature; a class called "Rhetoric," where the focus was on composing and delivering orations in the classical languages and in English; and a class called "Philosophy," conducted in Latin and studying Christian doctrine. Boys came to the college at around age twelve. As had become the custom, no instruction in basic literacy was offered at Holy Cross.

Holy Cross did modify the tradition slightly. In traditional Jesuit education, the three beginning Latin classes typically occupied three years of study, and the humanities level two years. Here that sequence was modified, to give two years to Latin grammar and four to humanities, comprising the humanities and poetry classes. In traditional Jesuit education, the young men arrived at the rhetoric class at about the age of sixteen; here they were a year or two older. In traditional Jesuit education, university-level education began after the rhetoric class (if young men went on from the Jesuit school to a university), and that is how the curriculum was organized at Holy Cross as well: In addition to the philosophy class, corresponding to the capstone theology class in Renaissance universities, the young men specialized at this point in a series of electives designed to prepare them for careers in the Church (initially, the majority choice), law, or medicine (business was the career goal of only a few). Courses in mathematics, the sciences, English and other modern languages, history, and political economy were offered (see Kuzniewski, 179). Regardless of their specialization, however, the students were required to take both Latin and Greek as graduation requirements, and the college advertised its focus on classical studies as conducive to both eloquence and good Christian character, summed up as *eloquentia perfecta.*

Anthony Kuzniewski, S.J., has shown how reluctantly changes were made in this traditional curriculum (to compare how the Marquette curriculum evolved during the same era, see Leigh, Part I). Once again bowing to a manpower shortage, Holy Cross closed its preparatory branch in 1910, and by 1914, as already admitted students moved up, there were no more high-school-aged students at the college. All American Jesuit education soon separated itself into high school and college divisions such as we know today, in place of the six-to-seven-year continuous curriculum that had been in place for centuries. But even high schools run by the Society of Jesus could not, apparently, prepare students in Latin and Greek as well as Holy Cross teachers required, so in 1936, the college felt compelled to drop Greek as a degree requirement. During this same curriculum revision, the college also increased the number of electives and acknowledged that now the great majority of the graduates would be going into law, medicine, or business rather than holy orders. After a brief rise, the number of vocations dropped off even more dramatically after World War II, and Holy Cross became conscious that its graduates were not as well prepared as others for the rigors of contemporary professional schools. Accordingly, to make more room in the students' schedules for courses purveying modern academic knowledge, the degree requirement in Latin was finally dropped in 1959. It should be noted, however, that the Holy Cross classics department has remained one of the strongest among liberal-arts colleges to this day.

Further reform in 1963 for the first time removed formal reference to the *Ratio Studiorum* from the college catalog, and reduced students' training in the humanities and religion to a set of required courses: six semesters of philosophy, four semesters of theology, two to four semesters of classical or modern languages, two semesters of English and two of history, and one semester of natural science. This budget of required courses may sound rigorous today, but it represented quite a reduction from the traditional curriculum, in that the courses were not necessarily presented in sequence and guaranteed no mastery either of cultural content or of verbal skill. Indeed, a course in "composition" was added to this schedule almost as an afterthought, as a noncredit requirement. Within ten years, these requirements would be gone as well, and Holy Cross would resemble secular liberal-arts schools in being organized around academic majors. There has never been a required composition course for full credit at Holy Cross, nor is there now any single course that every student in the college is required to take.

Interestingly, according to Kuzniewski, reforming the structure of the curriculum proceeded in stages from the early 1950s to 1970 without serious controversy. Rather, conflict centered first in the emerging need to retire Jesuit teachers with inadequate professional training—President Swords removed five from the philosophy department in 1964 (Kuzniewski, 382)—and to hire laypeople with PhDs. The next flashpoint soon arose in Father Swords's determination to modernize the theology department by hiring two lay scholars with advanced degrees in biblical studies—neither of whom was a Roman Catholic (see Kuzniewski, 383ff.). Concern over whether the college was losing its essential Jesuit and Catholic identity concentrated, at that time, more on who was doing the teaching than on what was taught.

Nevertheless, when I arrived at Holy Cross in 1978, an elderly Jesuit then in the English department could still be heard lamenting the decline of humanities instruction at the college. He was convinced that student verbal skills were languishing owing to a neglect of the classics—even though at that time the English major required students to take two courses in the classics department. An idea of what rhetoric instruction at Holy Cross once was—the type of education my colleague lamented—can be gleaned from *Principles of Jesuit*

Education in Practice, by Francis P. Donnelly, S.J., published in 1934. Although the title refers to "Jesuit education" in general, the book addresses only instruction in rhetoric. Evidently Donnelly, a professor of rhetoric at Fordham, could take it for granted that his readers knew rhetoric to be the epitome of Jesuit education. The book is intended for teachers, and some clue as to its respected position at Holy Cross may be found in the fact that the college library has more copies of this book than of any other Jesuit work on education. Indeed, as Katherine Adams explains (Part II), Donnelly was a well-published and widely respected figure in Jesuit education nationwide.

Donnelly's philosophical statements and practical advice on teaching echo themes I have noted in my observations about Jesuit education since the Renaissance. He states that the ultimate goal of Jesuit education is "eloquence" (11). He considers the rhetoric class, which he has taught for thirty years to college sophomores, to be the real capstone of Jesuit education. Afterward, the young men disperse into their pre-professional studies (all men, in his day, but see Mattingly, in Part I, on Jesuit contributions to women's education). Similarly, in traditional Jesuit schooling, rhetoric was the last course young men took at their Jesuit school before either launching their adult lives or heading off to universities. Donnelly compares the rhetoric class to a studio art course: The focus should always be on practice and performance. He provides a list of nineteen specific goals for the course, which range from improved spelling of English words derived from Latin to the formation of good literary taste, refined style, and high moral character. Here is his general statement of pedagogical principles:

> To grasp fundamentals more clearly, to check the disintegration of classicism by a return to art appreciation and composition, to reinterpret traditional methods and apply them to the student's varied experience and in the student's own language, to have objectives and ideals crystallize sharply out of dimness, to feel that one's class is an imagining, realizing, judging, reasoning, hearing, questioning, seeing, writing and speaking thing and not simply a depository of facts, all these are advantages for a teacher.
>
> —Donnelly, 7

Donnelly expresses a traditional Jesuit fidelity to classical literature, and he clearly intends that students should learn to write correctly. But closest to the traditional spirit of Jesuit education are his references to the students' personal "varied experience" and "own language" as resources for composing, and his insistence on the students' imaginative and critical engagement with course material. They are not to be mere "depositor[ies] of facts," a value that chimes with progressive goals for education to this day in, for example, Paulo Freire's well-known condemnation of what he calls "the banking model of education," in which deposits of facts are made in hapless students. Indeed, Freire, Catholic-educated and active in radical Catholic social-action groups, probably borrowed his metaphor from a traditional Jesuit way of talking about educational ideals (see Pace and Merys, Part II).

Donnelly defends instruction in Latin and Greek as the best pathway to eloquence. The Latin and Greek authors raise literary art to the highest level it has ever achieved, he believes. Moreover, he says, the difficulty of the languages is actually an aid to appreciating their beauties, because it requires one to read slowly and puzzle out the details of style and structure (54ff). A central method of proceeding with these texts is the "prelection," which is found in Donnelly virtually unchanged not only from Renaissance times but from its earlier medieval avatars. Donnelly attributes the method to Quintilian. What he recommends is that the teacher and students read a given text slowly together, together pointing out whatever they can notice of its stylistic and structural features, identifying historical and mythological allusions, and noting evidences of the author's good character (59ff). This method is one progenitor of the famous New Critical close reading that is still a basic technique in literary study.

Don't let this work go on too long, though, Donnelly cautions teachers. Students must spend more time doing their own writing and speaking: imitating the authors they've analyzed on topics of interest to them, for example; translating back and forth among Greek, Latin, and English; performing classical plays and writing new ones; staging debates; and more (113ff). Donnelly recommends using friendly competition among the students to encourage application and excellence, just as Jesuits had done since the Renaissance. For instance, he cites a literary challenge issued by his Fordham sophomores to the students at other Jesuit colleges on the occasion of Vergil's bimillennium: They were to submit compositions in eighteen categories—that is, in either English, Latin, or Greek in each of six genres: an informal essay, a sonnet, a song, a one-act play, a short story, and a five-minute speech. The competition was judged by the school deans, since, Donnelly says sadly, not all the teachers of the three languages had sufficient competence in all three to serve that function (125).

The level of student competence implied by this competition is awe-inspiring. Here's another example, a question from one of Donnelly's final exams:

> With the subject: Who is the better model for a lawyer today, Demosthenes or Cicero, Burke or Macaulay, Webster or Phillips? Take one couple; state your audience and proposition and prove it, a. by an epichirema [sic]; b. by a dilemma; c. by induction; d. by analogy; e. by a collection. Only one page for each proof and spend about ten or twelve minutes answering each. The style should be oratorical.
>
> —Donnelly, 198

This is presumably a closed-book examination, and it is to be written in Latin. Donnelly evidently is able to assume that his students know enough about the six orators named to discuss them intelligently, as well as knowing rhetorical terminology such as *epicheireme*, *analogy*, and so on. As contemporary composition studies avers, writing is a process, and Donnelly shows some awareness of this by suggesting a format and time limit for students' work on each part of the question. As for student motivation, he probably knew that many of his students intended to become lawyers (as do many of mine at Holy Cross today).

Given the level of classical learning assumed by the influential Donnelly, it should come as no surprise that the man primarily responsible for introducing classical rhetoric to modern composition studies was a product of Jesuit education: Edward P. J. Corbett. Corbett attended Marquette University High School, took his PhD from Loyola of Chicago, and taught first at Creighton— all Jesuit schools. He was also influenced by the attention to rhetoric in the work of Walter Ong, S.J., according to Janice Lauer Rice (Part II). Admittedly, Corbett was not the first modern compositionist to show interest in classical rhetoric, as Gerald Nelms explains (Part II). Richard Weaver infused a classical spirit into the composition program at the University of Chicago, where Corbett took a master's degree in English, and Weaver even coauthored an article in 1953 for *College Composition and Communication*, recommending the use of classical *topoi* in the first-year writing course. Nelms reports that Corbett recalled little contact with the classicized composition program at Chicago, however. He remembered discovering classical rhetoric at Creighton. In any case, the results were spectacular. First published in 1965 and now gone posthumously into a fourth edition, Corbett's first-year composition textbook *Classical Rhetoric for the Modern Student* went far to convince the contemporary field of composition studies that the classical tradition has something to offer us.

Despite the continuities I have traced between Renaissance Jesuit education and Donnelly's widespread approach, many discontinuities could be found with how rhetoric is taught in Jesuit schools today. Many contemporary composition teachers might argue against making students learn rhetorical terminology, as Donnelly did. Some might disagree, too, that students need to know about Demosthenes, Burke, and Webster, or indeed about any great orators of the past. Moreover, few contemporary teachers would accept Donnelly's insistence that only Latin and Greek, not any other languages, foster excellence in written and oral expression. Indeed, a Jesuit colleague at Holy Cross tells me that Jesuits-in-training in the United States (and likely, around the world) are no longer required to master Latin and Greek; in the United States, the language that's pushed on native English speakers is Spanish.

Perhaps Donnelly swims most vigorously against the tide of contemporary educational trends, however, when he argues that the entire curriculum must be organized to produce the level of eloquence he desires. The idea that it could be developed in one or two first-year courses in English composition, as is usually assumed now in most American Jesuit schools, would be laughable to him. In naming his enemies, Donnelly says that "research usurps the place of creativity" in the modern curriculum (33). He deplores the division of the modern university into academic departments. This structure, he says, is favorable to imparting scientific knowledge but not to developing the creative powers that the humanities and arts aim to foster. He complains that this structure pushes students too early into specialized studies where they are occupied with "minute research" issues more appropriate to graduate school. Unfortunately, says Donnelly, students do little "original writing" outside the rhetoric course, and composition is not stressed in their other classes (for more on Donnelly's critical perspective, see Adams, Part II).

Writing-across-the-curriculum programs might have offered Donnelly a compromise, but one he would probably have rejected, because even though such programs evince some sort of commitment to developing verbal abilities throughout the curriculum, the writing in such programs is located in academic departments, including the natural and social sciences, and much of it is not what he would consider "creative." In many of those courses, the main focus will naturally remain on teaching disciplinary content, not fostering eloquence. When Holy Cross had such a program (which I directed), writing-intensive courses were offered in biology, economics, history, mathematics, psychology, sociology, Spanish (in Spanish), religious studies, and visual arts. At that time, the focus was on writing only, not the full range of rhetorical activities, and primarily academic discourse. It would be interesting to find out whether such programs persist at Jesuit schools in higher numbers, or with a more explicitly rhetorical focus, than elsewhere.

At Holy Cross, the formal writing-across-the-curriculum program was suspended in the late 1990s. Fifteen years later, resurgent faculty concern about students' writing ability provided one motive for the creation of Montserrat, a first-year seminar program in which courses that are supposed to be "rhetoric-intensive," adding instruction in speaking to instruction in writing, are taught by faculty from all the academic departments. Montserrat also draws inspiration from an earlier first-year elective program with an avowed goal of character formation, which remains a goal of Montserrat as well. The new program is named for the mountain monastery where Ignatius laid his sword at the feet of a famous Madonna icon and vowed to enter religious life. Montserrat course content varies widely, since faculty are encouraged to develop material from their own disciplines, if they wish, so long as the general goals of rhetorical and ethical development are addressed. Students pre-select several seminars whose topics appeal to them, and they are required to take the two of these into which they are placed by their class dean (fall and spring semester seminars are linked thematically although not always taught by the same professor). Having served on the committee that designed the program, I know that one of the original intentions was to revivify the college's commitment to rhetoric instruction without requiring a specific rhetoric or composition course, which we do not have the staffing to teach. Montserrat is only a few years old now, and it remains to be seen whether the seminars will be able to consistently deliver the full-bodied rhetoric instruction that was envisioned.

Holy Cross does have a first-year elective in composition, which I regularly teach, and my usual approach reflects a growing trend in American composition instruction, "translingualism," which might have been more to Donnelly's liking (see Horner et al.). Even though a translingual approach does not necessarily valorize fluency in Greek and Latin, as Donnelly would prefer, certainly it promotes an idea he would approve of, that valuing students' linguistic resources enriches composing in English, including languages other than English and dialects other than the standard. Arguably, doing so extends the Jesuit tradition of working with the students' "own language," as Donnelly advocates, or, more properly now, "languages." Translingual pedagogies may still center on English as the common language of American academic work, but they also encourage students to write and speak their other languages as well, and develop more opportunities for them to do so, as I do in my course that focuses on global Englishes (Bizzell). It would be interesting to find out whether translingual pedagogies have more traction at American Jesuit schools than elsewhere.

A key insight of translingualism is that the world's linguistic environment is becoming much more complex. Once upon a time, it seemed fairly simple to differentiate among monolingual, bilingual, and trilingual people. The monolingual knows only one language as a native speaker, while the bilingual and trilingual have native fluency in two or three languages. Nowadays, though, there are increasing numbers of people who have some knowledge, even if not native-speaker fluency, in two or three languages other than their native tongues, often at least well enough to get by in daily life, while there are few utter monolinguals anywhere. Even a person who has native fluency in only one language most likely comes in contact with at least one other language, and probably more than one, and has some knowledge of these other tongues. Holy Cross requires all students to achieve knowledge of a language other than their native one to the equivalent of two years of college-level study—certainly not native-speaker fluency but good earnest of the college's taking languages seriously. And even American students who don't have to satisfy such requirements may live in a region in which they read Spanish on street signs or sing along with Korean pop music.

Moreover, the advent of translingualism is not due simply to people around the world having English forced on them in colonial fashion—that is, the versions of English that prevail in so-called inner-circle countries where it is the native tongue (see Pennycook). As English goes global, ownership of the language is passing from the hands of its traditional masters to other peoples who use it for their own purposes. I participated in one of these transfer processes while teaching English composition and American literature at Sogang University, a Jesuit school in Seoul, South Korea, in the summer and fall of 2011, where, I can say, Koreans are very much in charge of how they learn and use English. At Sogang, rising to the level of fluency in English replaces the past emphasis on Latin and Greek, but still aims to give the native Korean-speaking students a sort of eloquence most useful in the modern globalized world, where English is the premier global language.

RHETORIC AT SOGANG, NOW AND FOR THE FUTURE

Founded by Theodor Geppert, a German Jesuit, in 1960, Sogang is one of the newer Jesuit schools worldwide, but Roman Catholicism has been on the Korean peninsula much longer. Indeed, as I mentioned earlier, Jesuit missions to Asia were launched even before the order was formally approved by the pope. Although Francis Xavier was the first to come, arguably the most successful was Matteo Ricci, who arrived in China in 1577 and became a trusted advisor to the Ming emperor. He gained entrée owing to his ability to teach upper-class children mnemonic devices learned in his study of Soares's rhetoric text, which they needed for the grueling Chinese civil-service exams (Spence, 4–5).

Although plans were made, no Jesuit missionary ever made it to Korea in the sixteenth century. Two Jesuit chaplains accompanied the troops of a Christian daimyo who joined the invasion forces of Toyotomi Hideyoshi in 1594, but James Huntley Grayson contends that they never had contact with the native population (140). Nevertheless, Korea was influenced by Chinese culture for centuries, and so, when Christianity came into vogue in the Ming court, a Korean diplomat brought back to his homeland devotional and scientific books that Ricci had provided. As Grayson explains, Catholicism in Korea was entirely a "self-evangelized church" until the late eighteenth century, when the first missionary, Father Chou Wen-Mu (not a Jesuit), arrived from China (142). Somehow, the faith spread, especially among the lower social classes, appealing with its message of equality before God, which helps to explain why it was periodically and violently suppressed by Korean rulers until the modern period. Protestantism did not arrive until the late nineteenth century. Today, about 25 percent of the population is Christian, and about half that number are Roman Catholics, although the Church is growing vigorously in the region and may soon be the majority denomination (see Grayson, 173ff). Sogang's current Jesuit president is Korean.

Sogang, the only Jesuit university on the peninsula, is now one of the highest-ranked institutions in South Korea, known for its academic rigor. It is also known for its commitment to develop excellent English language abilities for its graduates, a noteworthy distinction even though all of the top Korean universities emphasize English. At Sogang, there is a rigorous three-course English-language requirement for all students, and about one third of all classes are taught in English; many courses, especially in the natural sciences and engineering, use textbooks written in English even if the class is conducted in Korean. At the same time, Sogang boasts a strong department of Korean literature and one of the best programs anywhere for teaching the Korean language to non-native speakers, so it cannot be said that Sogang's emphasis on English represents merely a capitulation to cultural imperialism.

The English emphasis certainly could be seen as in line with the traditional Jesuit valuation of language study. But my perusal of scholarship on English in Korea as well as my conversations with Sogang colleagues and students all suggest to me that Koreans are not aiming to gain humanistic cultivation by their study of English. At least, I saw little evidence of explicit focus on the character formation that has traditionally been a goal of *eloquentia perfecta*. Rather, they see the language as a practical necessity for becoming leaders in the international academic community and global business (see Collins). Indeed, Koreans are so avid to learn the language that this national preoccupation has been termed "English fever," and parents go to great lengths to support their children's English-language learning (see Park). It would be interesting to explore the question of whether this more practical motive for language learning characterizes many Jesuit schools outside Europe and the United States.

For many Sogang students, the English they learn is a specialized vocabulary related to their majors in, for example, engineering or the natural sciences. Sogang also has departments of English literature and American studies, and a quick look at Sogang's English-language website reveals a curriculum in these departments that is virtually indistinguishable from comparable departments in American schools. I taught a course at Sogang on American novels featuring the theme of learning to perform one's gender. The majors in these English-based departments often have lived in English-speaking countries and may even belong to families who bilocate, traveling frequently between relatives' homes in South Korea and the United States. Many aim for careers in international industry or diplomacy, in which English will be a useful language even if they never live in an "inner circle" country. For example, my student Seoyoung (not her real name) was majoring in English, so she told me, in order to prepare for a career in hotel management—in Shanghai. Another student told me that his businessman father, as he hopes to do, uses English to communicate with his firm's factory managers in India.

I taught first-year students at Sogang who were not majoring in English and also juniors and seniors who were. I found that their abilities in English varied widely. All of them were able to put together coherent English sentences, and none made so many errors in English that their writing was incomprehensible. Some could write as well as my Holy Cross native English-speaking students. One significant difference from my Holy Cross students was the Koreans' general reluctance to speak in English. But Korean education in general does not encourage oral work, not even in Korean, or so I was told; my insistence that students make oral presentations was regarded as a novelty, unpleasant for some. To say in Korean that you are "taking" a course, you say that you are "listening to it": "Hi I'm Jae, listening to your course on American novels," a student might begin an email. Moreover, my students told me that they were accustomed to getting comments on their English writing that only corrected errors; my comments relating to their ideas and argument structure were rare and much appreciated. Overall, the emphasis at Sogang seems to be more on grammar than on rhetoric, although literature students analyze literary language in sophisticated ways and attempt to understand its cultural provenance.

However, Sogang has recently launched a writing-across-the-curriculum program and opened a writing center for one-on-one tutoring, projects I helped to develop while I was there. These initiatives suggest a broadening of the goals for rhetoric instruction at Sogang. The Writing Center, which opened on December 27, 2011, is a beautiful facility, well funded, with state-of-the-art technology, and housed in a centrally located building along with the Center for Teaching and Learning (faculty development) and the Center for Educating the Whole Person (Jesuit mission). Stacking these three facilities on three floors of the same building may represent Sogang's educational philosophy, and the Writing Center is literally on the ground floor. But I did not encounter any specific discussion of how these new writing initiatives might foster humanistic goals for rhetoric similar to those that were traditional in Jesuit education. Indeed, although "the question of writing has become topical recently for Korean intellectuals with the crisis of human sciences" (328), something like a Western "rhetorical consciousness" (317) is not widely shared either in academe or among the general public, as Jon Sung-Gi explains, while tracing historical disagreements over what term is best used to translate the word *rhetoric* into Korean. The top candidates are derived from Japanese or Chinese.

Sogang's Writing Center will accommodate the different levels of English ability that I noted among my students (the center will provide tutoring in Korean writing as well). In supporting it, then, Sogang Univerrsity at least enacts the original Jesuit intention to offer educational opportunities to all, regardless of economic background. This is because the ability to learn English in Korea is distributed to some degree according to families' financial resources. The least adequate English-language instruction is offered in the public schools, where it is a compulsory subject from third grade on up. Families who can afford to do so also send their children to after-hours cram schools in English (the Korean term is *hakwan*). The even more affluent send them to so-called international schools in Seoul (in which the entire curriculum is taught in English and a few of their children's fellow students will be expats from native-English-speaking countries), or even to English-language prep schools abroad.

I have noted that while the original Jesuit admissions policy was remarkably egalitarian for its time, Jesuit schooling quickly became the province of the socially privileged, for the most part. To what extent is that still true? As an elite university, Sogang is considered to be relatively expensive by Korean standards, though not by American (engineering, the most expensive under-graduate program, cost the equivalent in Korean won of about $13,400 for tuition and room and board in 2011). I do not know how much of a barrier cost is to the Korean students, but many spoke about working to help pay for school, and most live off campus. Most students at Holy Cross live on campus, pay-ing about $55,000 for a year's tuition and room and board as of 2011, and many of them receive no financial aid whatsoever. Of course many of them do receive aid. The college's stated policy is to meet the full financial needs of students admitted need-blind, but diversifying the school as to social class is probably the most challenging issue facing Holy Cross in regard to the makeup of the student body—at this point, possibly more difficult to achieve than racial diversity.

ASPIRATIONS

As we have seen, Jesuits got into education to train their recruits but responded to calls for better Roman Catholic schooling for many, first at Messina, soon throughout Europe, and, before long, throughout the world. From the begin-ning, Jesuit education concentrated on the study of classical languages and their use in literary analysis, composition, and performance, both oratorical and dramatic, thereby developing a constellation of abilities that conduced to rhe-torical fluency and skill. Liam Matthew Brockey notes that a major asset in Jesuits' evangelism worldwide was their classical-language training, not be-cause they would use Latin or Greek to proselytize in India or Japan but because this training facilitated their learning the native languages of wherever their mission led them (214–15). At the same time, the Jesuits' attention to developing the whole student, spiritually as well as intellectually, worked to increase the likelihood that the leaders they trained would serve the civic good.

Holy Cross and Sogang in the twenty-first century differ in many ways, of course, from Messina in the sixteenth, yet there are enduring themes. We see a focus on language education, although Latin and Greek form only two of the nine languages, including American Sign Language, in which Holy Cross stu-dents may satisfy the college's language study requirement, and at Sogang, the principal second language studied is English, though Chinese, Japanese, French, and German are also taught. Furthermore, both schools invest resources in developing students' language abilities throughout the curriculum, via a first-year seminar program at Holy Cross and a writing-across-the-curriculum program at Sogang. Both schools also support a number of student clubs and other co-curricular programs that provide opportunities for oratorical and the-atrical performance. I think it's fair to say that both schools are developing their students' rhetorical abilities.

Both Holy Cross and Sogang also aspire to produce leaders who will use these abilities for the common good. At Holy Cross, Montserrat encourages reflection on current social problems and enduring human questions. The mission statement affirms the Jesuit and Catholic value of creating "men and women for others." Very few Jesuits remain on campus to provide role models, as the early Jesuits aimed to do in their schools, but that the overwhelming majority of the student body is Roman Catholic infuses the place with a Catholic spirit, perhaps the more noticeable to me because I am Jewish, and the chaplains' office provides a wide range of activities to help develop the spiritual lives of all students, whether Catholic or not. My brief sojourn at Sogang left me less familiar with the university's efforts at character formation, but their Center for Educating the Whole Person is centrally located on campus, in an attractive new building, and seems quite active. Sogang's mission statement strongly resembles that of Holy Cross in its commitment to Jesuit and Catholic values—and is perhaps even more explicit concerning the aim to develop students' faith and civic usefulness (see www.sogang.ac.kr/english), even though the majority of students there are not Catholic. Why come to Sogang, then? Because it is one of the strongest Korean universities academically.

To provide such rigorous higher education is a socially progressive goal in and of itself, arguably, in a country that is only relatively recently recovered from decades of colonial exploitation and devastating war. Perhaps a Jesuit school can become a "university for social change" in a variety of ways (Beirne, 3); that's the epithet with which the Jesuit University of Central America in El Salvador has been tagged by its historian and faculty member, Charles J. Beirne, S.J., in recounting the tragedy there: Apparently the school was perceived by the ruling class to be so threatening to its power that it ordered the murder of six Jesuits who taught there, along with their cook and her daughter (November 16, 1989). Let us hope that this price will not have to be paid very often as Jesuit schools aspire to serve the common good throughout the world. From both history and current manifestations, I think it is reasonable to hope that they will have success.

APPENDIX: DONNELLY'S NINETEEN "OBJECTIVES" FOR JESUIT EDUCATION

From *Principles of Jesuit Education in Practice* (1934), by Francis P. Donnelly, 25–27.

Ability to read Latin after the formal study of the language in the school or college has ceased. 2. The ability to understand Latin quotations, proverbs and mottoes occurring in English literature and increased ability to understand Latin words, phrases, and abbreviations found in books and current publications. 3. Increased ability to understand the exact meaning of English words derived directly or indirectly from Latin and increased accuracy in their use. 4. Increased ability to read English with correct understanding. 5. Increased development of the power of thinking and expressing thought through the process of translating Latin into adequate English. 6. Increased ability to spell English words of Latin derivation. 7. Increased knowledge of the principles of English grammar, and an increased ability to speak and write English correctly. 8. An elementary knowledge of the general principles of language structure as exhibited in the Indo-European languages. 9. Increased ability to master the technical and semi-technical terms of Latin origin employed in other school subjects, and in the professions and vocations. 10. Increased ability to master other foreign languages. 11. An increased knowledge of the facts relating to the life, history, institutions, mythology and religion of the Romans, and of the influence of their civilization on the course of Western civilization. 12. The development of emotional attitudes (ideals) toward social situations (e.g., patriotism, honor, service, self-sacrifice, etc.), including a broader understanding of governmental and social problems. 13. A first-hand acquaintance through the study of their writings with some of the chief personal characteristics of the authors read. 14. The development of appreciation of the literary quality of the Latin authors read, and the development of general capacity for such appreciation. 15. A greater appreciation of the elements of literary style employed in English prose and poetry. 16. Improvement of the quality of the literary taste and style of the pupil's written English. 17. Increased ability to understand and appreciate references and allusions in English literature and current publications to the mythology, traditions, and history of the Greeks and Romans. 18. The development of generalized habits (e.g., sustained attention, accurate, orderly procedure, thoroughness, neatness, perseverance, etc.). 19. Increased capacity for abstract reasoning.

WORKS CITED

Beirne, Charles J. *Jesuit Education and Social Change in El Salvador*. New York: Garland, 1996.

Bizzell, Patricia. "Toward 'Transcultural Literacy' at a Liberal Arts College." In *Working English in Rhetoric and Composition: Global/Local Contexts, Commitments, Consequences*, ed. Bruce Horner and Karen Kopelson. Carbondale: Southern Illinois University Press, forthcoming.

Brockey, Liam Matthew. *Journey to the East: The Jesuit Mission to China, 1579–1724*. Cambridge: Harvard University Press, 2007.

College of the Holy Cross. www.holycross.edu. Accessed August 7, 2012

Collins, Samuel Gerald. "'Who's This *Tong-il*?' English, Culture, and Ambivalence in South Korea." *Changing English* 12, no. 3 (December 2005): 417–29.

Corbett, Edward P. J. *Classical Rhetoric for the Modern Student*. 1st ed. 1965; 4th ed., with Robert J. Connors. New York: Oxford University Press, 1999.

Donnelly, Francis P. *Principles of Jesuit Education in Practice*. New York: P. J. Kenedy and Sons, 1934.

Duminuco, Vincent J., ed. *The Jesuit Ratio Studiorum: 400th Anniversary Perspectives*. New York: Fordham University Press, 2000.

Freire, Paulo. *Pedagogy of the Oppressed.* 1968. Translated by Myra Bergman Ramos, 1970. Reprint, New York: Continuum, 2000.

Grayson, James Huntley. *Korea: A Religious History.* 1989. Revised ed., London: Routledge Curzon, 2002.

Grendler, Paul F. *Schooling in Renaissance Italy: Literacy and Learning, 1300–1600.* Baltimore: Johns Hopkins University Press, 1989.

Horner, Bruce, Min-Zhan Lu, Jacqueline Jones Royster, and John Trimbur. "Language Difference in Writing: Toward a Translingual Approach." *College English* 73, no. 3 (2011): 303–21.

Jon, Sung-Gi. "Towards a Rhetoric of Communication, with Special Reference to the History of Korean Rhetoric." *Rhetorica* 28, no. 3 (Summer 2010): 313–29.

Kuzniewski, Anthony. *Thy Honored Name: A History of the College of the Holy Cross, 1843–1994.* Washington D.C.: Catholic University of America Press, 1999.

Maryks, Robert Aleksander. *Saint Cicero and the Jesuits.* Burlington, Vt.: Ashgate, 2008.

Murphy, James J. *Rhetoric in the Middle Ages.* Berkeley: University of California Press, 1974.

O'Malley, John W. *The First Jesuits.* Cambridge: Harvard University Press, 1993.

———. "From the 1599 *Ratio Studiorum* to the Present: A Humanistic Tradition?" In Duminuco.

———. "How the First Jesuits Became Involved in Education." In *The Jesuit Ratio Studiorum,* ed. Duminuco.

Park, Jin-Kyu. " 'English Fever' in South Korea: Its History and Symptoms." *English Today* 97, no. 25 (March 2009): 50–57.

Pennycook, Alastair. *Global Englishes and Transcultural Flows.* London: Routledge, 2007.

Scaglione, Aldo. *The Liberal Arts and the Jesuit College System.* Amsterdam and Philadelphia: John Benjamins, 1986.

Sogang University. www.sogang.ac.kr (English). Accessed August 7, 2012.

Spence, Jonathan D. *The Memory Palace of Matteo Ricci.* New York: Viking Penguin, 1984.

RHETORICAL VERI-SIMILITUDO: CICERO, PROBABILISM, AND JESUIT CASUISTRY

Robert A. Maryks

In recent publications and conference papers,[1] I have suggested that the Jesuits experienced a radical transition between two different ethical systems they employed when confronting a doubtful moral issue: They moved from traditional tutiorism, which they inherited from medieval times (defined as for the sake of being on the safer side—Latin *tutior*—to achieve eternal salvation, one should follow the external law rather than the choice of conscience) to early modern probabilism (defined as "the moral freedom of a conscience to follow even the less plausible—Lat. *probabilis*—of two probable ethical opinions"). I argued that this transition seemed to have been the result of the Jesuits' own redefinition, occurring only after they dedicated themselves to a new ministry, or apostolate, of educating youth. In the aftermath of the Renaissance, by which the Jesuit had been influenced, this kind of ministry, which was not original to the Jesuit program approved by the pope in 1540, required from Jesuit teachers a deeper and more systematic engagement with Greco-Roman culture, called in the Jesuit *Constitutions* "spoils of Egypt." In it, they found important elements akin to their own spirituality, especially Ciceronian humanism (*humanitas*) and civic—i.e., urban—engagement (*civiltà*), along with the anthropologically founded rhetorical principle of accommodation to particular circumstances of places and peoples, so dear to their entire apostolic vision.

The new pastoral commitment soon sparked a fascination with the classics of antiquity, similar to the one that characterized earlier Renaissance humanists. "Nothing so marked the difference between the Middle Ages and the Renaissance as the revival of classical rhetoric," as Paul Grendler evocatively pointed out. "Medieval scholars had placed grammar and logic at the center of learning and expression. They had little interest in the whole of classical Latin rhetoric and ignored its cultural associations" (205). A revolutionary shift in Jesuit ministry of education could occur, for the Jesuits understood well these cultural associations of rhetoric. This can be seen especially in the association of rhetoric with casuistry in Jesuit educational practice. The weekly practice of discussing doubtful moral cases, which was introduced in Jesuit colleges from the very beginning, was an exercise of students' rhetorical ability to apply general rules to specific circumstances of moral cases they were asked to solve by discussing less and more probable opinions to persuasively support their argument.

Both Renaissance and Jesuit humanists were particularly captivated by Cicero—the beauty of his Latin prose and the sociocultural aspect of his rhetoric (which was not a mere intellectual system but part of the political formation of the citizen)—and so eagerly promoted his imitation, which often approached worship of him. Indeed, Ignatius of Loyola's secretary, Polanco, argued for founding Jesuit schools by highlighting this formation: "Those who are now only students will grow up to be pastors, civic officials, administrators of justice, and will fill other important posts to everybody's profit and advantage" (O'Malley, 213). Thus, when the Jesuits opened their school in Tivoli (1550), they gave reason for it by saying they did so "for the advantage of the city" (*ad civitatis utilitatem*). The same motivation was advanced in the founding of the college in Murcia five years later (O'Malley, 210–11). In his dedication to *Tullianarum Quaestionum de Instauranda Ciceronis Imitatione*, the Jesuit humanist André Schott (1552–1629) wrote to his compatriot senators that there are two valuable things in a republic—a good education of youth and eloquence, because "without that early education no one can become an orator in order to appease the civil discords, reunite the separated, and narrate the glory of the fathers." Finally, the Jesuit Cypriano Soarez praised Cicero's writings for their "solicitude, smoothness, grace, and learning that not even among Greeks is the art of speaking fitted out with more or finer precepts" (Flynn, 105).

Not surprisingly, we read in the official Jesuit pedagogical program, *Ratio Studiorum* (1599), that the main authors recommended for the classes of rhetoric are Cicero and Aristotle: "Cicero is to be the one model of style, though the best historians and poets are to be sampled. All Cicero's works are appropriate models of style. . . . Only Cicero is to be taken for orations, and both Cicero and Aristotle for the precepts of rhetoric" (1.2). The special role of Cicero is also patent in the humanities classes: "Knowledge of the language involves correctness of expression and ample vocabulary, and these are to be developed in *daily* readings in the works of Cicero, especially those that contain *reflections on the standards of right living*" (4; my emphasis). The *Ratio* advises the master of humanities that "the pupils have to spend their time in such exercises, choosing phrases from previously read passages and expressing them in different ways, reconstructing a passage from Cicero that had been disarranged for this purpose" (1.4). The familiarity with Cicero continued in the highest grammar class, where "the reading matter in prose in the first semester will be taken from the more important of Cicero's letters: *Ad Familiares, Ad Atticum, Ad Quintum Fratrem*, and in the second semester, his *De Amicitia, De Senectute, Paradoxa*, and the like" (Grendler, 217–22). In this class, the written exercises in the rules of syntax must be based also on Cicero's texts. Cicero's letters *Ad Familiares* are prescribed for the middle grammar class as well. The students of the lowest grammar class must start their school day by reciting by heart parts of Cicero's easiest letters.[2]

The organization of the Jesuit curriculum and the predilection for Cicero in the *Ratio* echo the tradition of Renaissance and Jesuit moderate Ciceronianism—the leading Jesuit humanists emphasized the preeminence, but not exclusiveness, of Cicero in the classroom (Fumaroli, 162–202). It is reasonable, therefore, to infer that the Jesuit professors and their lay students, who were trained in Ciceronian eloquence, found Cicero's texts inspiring not only in their grammar and rhetoric classes but also in their weekly conferences on cases of conscience (*lectiones casuum*), or casuistry, which would gradually develop into a new academic discipline of moral theology.

Given the scope of this volume, I shall focus in this chapter on just one aspect of potential Ciceronian influence—his epistemic notion of probability, which became the intellectual framework for the Jesuit transition from tutiorism to probabilism. Before I do so, let me provide a context for the Jesuits' embrace of probabilism, which is connected to the development of their ministerial identity.

Ministry is the key word for understanding who the first Jesuits were. Contrary to ungrounded ideas circulating among scholars and in many college textbooks, the Society of Jesus was founded to perform a defined list of consuetudinary ministries (*consueta ministeria*), such as ministries of the word of God and works of mercy, not to engage in academic education ("education of children and unlettered persons in Christianity" was quite different and reserved to the Jesuit elite, or *professi*) or to counter Protestantism, which did become part of the Jesuit agenda, but only a decade after the order's foundation in 1540. Even then, those consuetudinary ministries continued to be pivotal and at the core of the Jesuit self-understanding. As Loyola's close associate Jerónimo Nadal (1507–80) argued authoritatively, the Jesuit consuetudinary ministries did not evolve *after* the Society was founded but rather determined its vocation and goal already at the Society's inception.[3]

When the Jesuits shifted their ministerial focus to the education of youth after the opening of their first school in Messina (1548), the traditional ministries included in their foundational document, *Formula Instituti,* did not exhaust their list of priorities. To the contrary, schools and their environment provided new and numerous "souls" to be exercised in the new sacramental practices. One of the first reports from Messina was to inform the Roman headquarters that the population of the Sicilian city was so impelled by the Jesuit sermons as to confess frequently and that the fathers could not provide an appropriate response to the demand, even though they were confessing incessantly from early morning to late in the night.[4] Messina's students were required to examine their consciences daily and to confess every month.[5] Some college founders, including King John III of Portugal, saw the frequent confession so beneficial to the pious life of youth that they required students to confess even every eighth day.[6] The importance of sacramental confession required an appropriate instruction of both the confessor and the penitent, and hence the necessity of producing manuals.

Between 1554 (when the first Jesuit manual for confessors was published) and 1650 (when, approximately, the Jansenists began their campaign against Jesuit probabilism), thirty-nine Jesuit authors wrote fifty-eight different works on sacramental confession, resulting in at least 763 editions altogether. This significant Jesuit production of penitential books indicates the importance that the Society of Jesus gave to the ministry of confession and to the study of cases of conscience. Strikingly, most of the authors of these works were professors of the Collegio Romano, where the Jesuit pedagogical code was being simultaneously elaborated throughout the second half of the sixteenth century. The code highlighted the pivotal role of rhetoric and classes on cases of conscience in its humanistic curriculum.

Among professors of the exemplary Jesuit college in Rome was Cypriano Soarez (1524–93), a Spaniard who entered the Portuguese province of the Jesuits because of his Jewish background (whence a different spelling of his family name), which resulted in problems for some Jesuit promoters of purity of blood. He was related to the converso clan of the Suárez from Toledo, which included Francisco Soarez, a famous Jesuit casuist, and the latter's uncle Cardinal Francisco de Toledo, the Jesuit author of an influential manual for confessors, *Instructio Sacerdotum* (1596).

Whether echoing or not rabbinical ethical reasoning, Soarez's exposition of rhetorical invention in *De Arte Rhetorica* (1562), his standard textbook for the Jesuit schools, highlighted the interdependence between not only rhetoric and logical reasoning but also between rhetoric and casuistical reasoning, an association that became highly characteristic of the Jesuit pedagogical system. The aim of the orator, who for Cicero was at the same time a rhetorician and a statesman, was to devise a plausible cause by employing true or *very probable* arguments, which could serve to establish confidence in a doubtful case.[7] In the context of the Jesuit college, this sort of rhetorical language was applied to discussing moral cases during the Saturday conferences on cases.

The arguments, Soarez suggested, can be intrinsic or extrinsic:

Some arguments are inherent in the very nature of the subject under discussion; wherefore, they are termed intrinsic. Others, brought in from outside the subject, are called extrinsic because they are removed and widely separated from the subject being discussed. For example, if you say that eloquence is the art of speaking well, the reason is intrinsic to the subject, for eloquence is the art of speaking well. But if you say that eloquence should be sought because Aristotle, Cicero, or Plato thought so, the reason will be extrinsic, for the authority of these men is not contained in the very nature of eloquence which should be desired for its own sake without their recommendation.

—Soarez, trans. Flynn, 141–42

Cicero collected the extrinsic arguments in his *Topica* under the term *testimony*—"everything that is drawn from an extrinsic source to persuade" (164).[8] This collection of arguments cannot be used, however, without discrimination,

> for decisive proof does not always or in all cases come from the same sources. The prudent man will use discretion, then, and he will not only discover what to say but will weigh it. There is nothing more fertile than minds, particularly those which have been cultivated by training. But as fruitful and fertile fields bring forth not only useful crops but also weeds most harmful to these crops, so now and then frivolous or irrelevant, or useless arguments rise from those topics. . . . We must bear in mind that material is sought from these topics for convincing audiences and for arousing their emotions.
>
> —Soarez, trans. Flynn, 164

As Prentice A. Meador Jr. has aptly shown, the clue to understanding Cicero is his concern with living the good life, the root of which is the question "Are men always able to act on the basis of complete knowledge and truth or should they sometimes act on the basis of *probability* and expediency?" (340–41). In his *Academica,* Cicero stated—following Philo and, with him, the Carneadean tradition influenced by Pyrrhonistic skepticism—that probability is an alternative basis for practical conduct.[9] Meador concludes, then, that Cicero's theory of probability is "one of the greatest watersheds of classical thought" (341).

Indeed, both Jesuit rhetoricians and casuists would wholeheartedly subscribe to Cicero's description of the Academy: "We are the men who wish to discover the truth and our discussion has no other purpose than to force to the surface the truth or what *most nearly* approaches it" (Cicero, quoted by Meador, 348). Whence it can be inferred that Cicero understood probability as resemblance to the truth—*veri-similitudo*—as did Socrates, according to Plato's *Phaedrus* (273a). Contrasting his view with that of the dogmatists (who happened to have the same features of medieval and early Jesuit tutiorists), who maintained that to deny certainty in knowledge destroys all activity of life, Cicero stated that "the lack of a probable would rather be the destruction of all life (*eversio omnis vitae*), but the wise man accepts what seems probable, providing nothing appears contradictory to the probability, and so keeps in a straight course his whole life" (Meador, 348).

Cicero's acceptance of epistemological probability had direct implications for his theory of rhetoric. It became socially necessary as an instrument by which man admits propositions as true when arguments or proofs persuade him to receive them as true, *without certain knowledge* that it is so (Meador, 349). To Cicero, rhetorical argument is "a plausible (*probabile*) device to obtain belief" (351). Rhetorical principles lack universality because the rhetorical act is circumstantially conditioned: "Probabilities are obtained from the parts or members of the statement; these deal with persons, places, times, actions, occurrences–the natures of the actual facts and transactions" (351). This rhetorical accommodation to circumstances would be echoed in both Jesuit foundational writings, such as the *Spiritual Exercises* and the *Constitutions,* and in Jesuit texts for confessors and students of moral theology, which highlights again the close relationship between rhetoric and casuistry in Jesuit practice.

Douglas F. Threet went even further in arguing that probability, although a philosophical notion, was placed by Cicero as "the foundation for an interlinking relationship of the orator-message-audience" in his rhetorical system (309–21). Ciceronian probability, as Threet has shown, is not constrained to his few philosophical works—namely, *De natura deorum* and *Academica,* which Meador had already analyzed from this perspective—but permeates other Cicero's writings "as a virile and germane philosophical concept," for the Roman rhetorician naturally unifies rhetoric, civil duties, and philosophy. Cicero's orator is a "composite of the philosopher-statesman-orator" (309, 312, 314), who cannot act from knowledge of infallible truth. He has to make wise decisions guided by probabilities, which "in some cases carry their own weight intrinsically, and in others even if they seem to be slight in themselves nevertheless go a long way when combined together" (Cicero, *De partitione oratoria,* 9.40, quoted by Threet, 314). Cicero's civic experience led him to conclude that

> for all of the issues disputed among men, whether the matter is criminal, as a charge of outrage, or a civil proceeding, as one relating to an inheritance, or a discussion of policy, as one touching a war, or of a personal kind as a panegyric, or a philosophical debate, as on the way to live, there is not one of which the point is not either what has been done, or what is being done, or going to be done, or as to the nature or description of something.
> —*De oratore,* 2.24.104; quoted by Threet, 315

The source of probabilities by which the Ciceronian orator should convince the audience is to be sought in the opinions, customs, and ordinary beliefs of mankind: "That is probable which for the most part usually comes to pass or which contains in itself some resemblance to these qualities whether such resemblance be true or false" (*De inventione,* 1.46, quoted by Threet, 318). However, this way of approaching reality is not, in Cicero's view, restricted to the orator's duties. It should be characteristic of any wise and reasonable man. That idea clearly emanates from *De officiis,* one of Cicero's most influential works, which was highly regarded by the Jesuits:

> Can you imagine the sort of mind a man would have, or rather the sort of life he would lead, if he were completely debarred from rational discussion and a rational way of life? There are those who say that some things are certain and others uncertain. I disagree with them: I would say that some things are probable and others improbable. Is there anything, then, to prevent me

from pursuing what seems probable and rejecting the reverse? Surely by avoiding over-bold assertion one reduces the risk of being irrational, which is the very negation of philosophy. The very reason why we Academics question the certainty of everything is that the probability, which I have mentioned, could not come to light except from a comparative analysis of the arguments on both sides

—*De officiis*, 2.7–8; quoted by Threet, 320

Late sixteenth-century Jesuits—the early modern neo-Academics—took one step further with respect to Cicero, not only by denying the over-bold certainty of medieval tutiorism of the first Jesuit generation and embracing the Ciceronian notion of probability but also by following the founder of early modern probabilism, the Dominican Bartolomé de Medina, who allowed the penitent to choose even a less plausible of two probable opinions. In late seventeenth century, some Jesuits, after the turmoil of the tutioristic Jansenists, would make a step back to probabil*ior*ism (following the *more* plausible of two probable opinions), but they would never go back to the tutioristic position of the first Jesuit generation.

What cannot pass unnoticed here is the striking resemblance of Cicero's instruction on how the orator should proceed (present the case and use probable opinions to persuade the audience) with how the Jesuit *Ratio* lays out the procedure for lecturing on cases of conscience in Jesuit schools. A specific confirmation of the influence of the Ciceronian employment of probability in classes of rhetoric can be found in the unpublished lecture notes of Pedro Juan Perpiñan (1530–66), a leading professor of rhetoric at the Jesuit Collegio Romano and a colleague of Soarez.

Although "early death did him an injury," Perpiñan's voice can be considered authoritative for many reasons. He was considered one of the most illustrious humanists of the early Society of Jesus. Born in Valencia, he was trained at its academy, renowned for the famed humanist Pedro Juan Núñez (1522–1602). Perpiñan entered the Society in 1551 and became professor of rhetoric at the Jesuit college in Lisbon only two years later, where his colleague was Soarez, whose *De Arte Rhetorica* he later edited for its second publication (Velez, 595). In 1555 he moved to the newly established College of Coimbra, where, at its inauguration, he delivered an oration on the aim of Jesuit education. After his apparently successful oration at the funeral of Prince Luis in 1555—perhaps the first Jesuit humanistic oration that reflected Jesuit ties to the Renaissance—he was appointed in 1557 a court preacher to Queen Elisabeth, whom he lauded in his orations that he used to deliver on the occasion of Queen's birthdays. All this time he was teaching humanities at Coimbra. In 1561, Perpiñan was recruited to the Collegio Romano, where he taught rhetoric for four years.

During his Roman years, he participated in the discussions on the *Ratio Studiorum*, the codification of the Jesuit education system, with his other confrères: Manuel Sá (author of the probabilistic guide to confessors, *Aphorismi*),[10] Francisco de Toledo (author of *Instructio Sacerdotum*, the most popular Jesuit manual for confessors), and Diego Ledesma (who wrote *De Ratione et Ordine Studiorum Collegii Romani*, a preliminary version of the *Ratio*). Perpiñan's most relevant contribution to the *Ratio* was the set of rules for the distribution of scholastic awards. He moved to Lyons in 1565, and then to Paris, where he participated in the heated discussion with the French Parliament and the University of Paris over the presence of the Jesuits at the Jesuit College of Clermont. On this occasion, he confronted the famous French humanist Ramus, whose anti-Ciceronian rhetoric the Jesuits vigorously opposed. As the ashes of the anti-Jesuit dispute were still burning, he died at the age of thirty-six.

Despite his young age, Perpiñan was famous not only as a teacher of rhetoric but also as one of the most accomplished European orators. Besides his famous orations in Portugal, he drew attention to his talent in the orations delivered at the Collegio Romano: *De Arte Rhetorica Discenda* (1561), *De Officio Christiani Doctoris* (1562), and others. In his *Variae Lectiones,* the *arbiter elegantiarum* of neo-Latin Roman prose, Marc-Antoine Muret—a friend of Perpiñan and the master of another Jesuit humanist, Francesco Benci at the Roman university La Sapienza—compared the Jesuit orator to Homer's Nestor: "For I have never heard anybody, and I think you will not even hear one to whom the famous epithet of Nestor better applies: 'From whose mouth used to flow words sweeter than honey.'" No wonder, then, that a collection of Perpiñan's twenty-two orations was published not long after his death.[11] In its preface, his Jesuit confrère Benci declared Perpiñan the precursor of a Christian literary Renaissance. The fame of the first Jesuit humanistic orator remained was still vivid in the next Jesuit generations of literati, as the *Palatium Rhetoricae* by the Jesuit Michael Denis (1729–1800) shows. In it, at the beginning of his training in rhetoric an adolescent is guided in his dream by Cicero and encounters, among other famous classic and contemporary orators, our Perpiñan.[12]

During his sojourn in Rome, Perpiñan probably also composed a treatise on rhetoric, *De Oratore*, a manuscript of which was consulted by his biographer Bernard Gaudeau. Unfortunately, it is no longer available. Its content, which Gaudeau analyzed, can, however, be compared with another manuscript that has been attributed to Perpiñan and was the subject of an article by Jean Dietz Moss in 1986.[13] According to Moss, Perpiñan's *De Arte Rhetorica* (FC 1563) is likely a collection of lecture notes on Soarez's rhetoric textbook. A comparison of this manuscript with another one (APUG 1179), preserved in the same archives of the Gregorian University and containing almost the same text, sheds more light on the manuscript under discussion. The quality of Latin betrays a student's hand, and its content suggests that it consists notes on lectures given by a professor of rhetoric in 1563, most likely Perpiñan himself, as the secondhand inscription reads on the front page of both manuscripts.

The manuscript FC 1563 contains three marked chapters: (1) *De arte rhetorica* (On the art of rhetoric); (2) *De oratore* (On the orator); and (3) *Quibus rebus comparetur eloquentia* (To what eloquence can be compared). Each chapter corresponds to a different part of the course of rhetoric.

From the introduction to the first chapter, we learn that the chapter is divided in seven sections: (1) *De nomine artis rhetoricae* (On the name of the art of rhetoric); (2) *De origine et progressu rhetoricae ac eloquentiae* (On the origin and progress of rhetoric and eloquence); (3) *Quid sit rhetorica* (What is rhetoric?) (4) *De materia, fine et officio rhetoricae* (On the matter, end, and employment of rhetoric); (5) *An rhetorica sit ars, an scientia, an virtus* (Whether rhetoric is an art, a science, or virtue?); (6) *Similitudines et dissimilitudines logicae atque rhetoricae* (Similarities and dissimilarities between logic and rhetoric); and (7) *De utilitate artis rhetoricae* (On the usefulness of rhetoric).

The order of the notes themselves is slightly changed from the order in the introduction, however. In the notes, the last two chapters are subsumed under chapter 5 and their order is switched. In the introduction, the professor informs students that he had previously lectured them on the dignity and necessity of rhetoric and that this part of the course is indispensable to learn the precepts of rhetoric contained in Cicero's *Partitiones oratoriae*, which students would analyze immediately after this introductory part. The content of this section corresponds partially to Soarez's *De Arte Rhetorica*, published just one year earlier and edited by Perpiñan for its second publication in 1565, but the organization of the material here is different. The professor does not quote Soarez's text in his lecture, as he does the primary sources, including Cicero's *De finibus, Partitiones oratoriae, Brutus, De inventione, Ad Herennium, De oratore,* Quintilian's *Institutiones*, Vergil's *Georgics*, Livy's *Ab urbe condita*, Aristotle's *Rhetoric, Ethics, and Metaphysics*, and Alexander of Afrodisias's *Topicos*.

A synoptic look at both manuscripts (FC 1563 and APUG 1179) betrays, however, other circumstances, in which *Similitudines et dissimilitudines* from the introductory part of *De arte rhetorica* and the other two chapters may have been explained. The latter manuscript has an additional title that the former lacks: *Perpiniani in Tertium M. T. Ciceronis Librum De Oratore Annotationes*. This information fits perfectly the program of the Jesuit studies of rhetoric that were used in various colleges and have been studied by Paul Grendler: After the *Partitiones oratoriae*, Jesuit students would analyze one of Cicero's orations.

Of special interest here is the chapter *Similitudines et dissimilitudines logicae atque rhetoricae*, which was not developed in Soarez's *De Arte Rhetorica*, as noted above. In the text, Perpiñan begins his exposition by saying that

the aim of both rhetoric and dialectic [logic] is persuasion, which produces not a true science but creates faith and generates opinion. Both employ probable arguments and judgments, not the qualities of things and principles of sciences but certain assumptions found in daily life and in human opinion.[14]

The professor of rhetoric stresses the differences between the two. While logicians employ more general and common rules, orators accommodate their orations to concrete places, times, and persons.[15] Rhetoric should not use probable opinions, unless they are apt to persuade many.[16] Indeed, Cicero stressed in his *Partitiones* that "the statement will be probable if the facts narrated are in accordance with the persons, the times, and the places; if the causes of every action and occurrence are set out; if they appear to be based on evidence and to be in agreement with the judgment of mankind, and with law and custom and religion."[17]

As observed earlier, the manuscript under analysis may have been used either as an introduction to Cicero's *Partitiones oratoriae* (FC 1563) or as an explanation of Cicero's third part of *De oratore* (APUG 1179). At any rate, both manuscripts refer directly to Cicero's rhetorical corpus and confirm the influence, at the exemplary college of the Jesuit educational system, that the Ciceronian notion of probability had on the teaching of rhetoric and on its use in discussing cases of conscience. The Aristotelian distinction between art and sciences is here clearly evidenced, but filtered through Cicero. Indeed, Jesuit professors preferred to teach rhetoric on the basis of Tullius's texts, probably because Cicero—rather than Aristotle—represented to the Jesuit program of civic education a more holistic approach, in which rhetoric and casuistry were closely related. Francesco Benci explained it explicitly in his speech on Cicero's *Pro P. Sextio*. Asked why he preferred Cicero over Aristotle, Benci compared the former to the sun of the rhetorical universe. A few lines below, Benci quoted as an example of Ciceronian preeminence our Perpiñan, whose "eloquence was very close to that of Cicero" (166–69).

The analysis conducted in this paper shows that the leading Jesuit teachers of rhetoric and their students at the Collegio Romano—the alma mater of the Jesuit international web of education—were aware, since at least the 1560s, that at the very base of Ciceronian rhetorical construction was the epistemic theory of probability. The Jesuits employed Ciceronian probability in weekly conferences on cases of conscience, necessary for their own and others' training in the preeminent ministry of sacramental confession. The emphasis on rhetoric may have catalyzed the revolutionary transition from tutiorism to probabilism, from a medieval to a modern mindset, in the Jesuit approach to solving cases of conscience. When Bartolomé de Medina expressly formulated the doctrine of modern probabilism in 1577, the leading Jesuit minds found it akin to the way of reasoning that they had been already employing in their teaching of rhetoric and cases of conscience. Furthermore, they found themselves well prepared not only to adopt it, enthusiastically, but also progressively to adapt it. Initiating this process were two Jesuit academics from Spain, Gabriel Vázquez and Francisco Suárez (1548–1617),[18] and it was continued by almost all the authors of manuals for Jesuit confessors during the period between 1600 and 1630, when the production of such manuals boomed. For better or worse, the Jesuit infatuation with Cicero that led them to embrace probabilism in their confessional practice led in future generations, of Blaise Pascal and then of Fyodor Dostoyevsky, a profound scorn for Jesuit casuistry. Unaware of its Ciceronian and Renaissance roots, they unfairly turned it into popular proverbial Jesuitism—a mix of hypocrisy, laxism, and dissimulation. But this is already another chapter of the story.

NOTES

1. See especially my *Saint Cicero and the Jesuits: The Influence of the Liberal Arts on the Adoption of Moral Probabalism* (Aldershot, Hampshire: Ashgate, 2008).

2. See *Ratio,* "Rules of the Teacher of the Highest Grammar Class," 1, 4, 6; "Rules of the Teacher of the Middle Grammar Class," 1–2, 6–7, 10; "Rules of the Teacher of the Lowest Grammar Class," 1–2.

3. "Accidentalia et Societati adventitia, sed tamquam substantialia et cum ipsa Societate nata, sine quibus [ministeriis] nec finis nec vocatio nec institutum constare potest." *Mon Nadal,* 5:823.

4. "Populus autem excitatus concionibus, tam frequens ad sacramentum Confesisionis accedebat, ut iam confessarii nostri tam amplae messi colligendae non sufficerent, quamvis aliquando a primo mane usque ad multam noctem in ea functione desudarent." *Chron.,* 1:285, § 244.

5. *Chron.,* 1:368, § 414.

6. "Quos octavo quoque die veneris confiteri volebat, ut aetate crescentes, bonam pie vivendi consuetudinem retinerent." *Chron.,* 1:87, § 22.

7. See Soarez, *De Arte Rhetorica:* "Inventio est excogitatio rerum verarum, aut verisimilium, quae quaestionem probabilem reddant" (1:7). "Argumentum est probabile inventum ad faciendam fidem, vel aliter, est ratio rei dubiae faciens fidem" (1:13).

8. Soarez, *De Arte Rhetorica,* 1:164.

9. "Carneades (214–129/8 B.C.E.) was a member and eventually scholarch or head of the Academy, the philosophical school founded by Plato, for part of its skeptical phase. He is credited by ancient tradition with founding the New or Third Academy and defended a form of probabilism in epistemology." *Stanford Encyclopedia of Philosophy.* http://plato.stanford.edu/entries/carneades. Accessed January 26, 2015.

"Pyrrho was the starting-point for a philosophical movement known as Pyrrhonism that flourished several centuries after his own time. This later Pyrrhonism was one of the two major traditions of sceptical thought in the Greco-Roman world (the other being located in Plato's Academy during much of the Hellenistic period). Perhaps the central question about Pyrrho is whether or to what extent he himself was a sceptic in the later Pyrrhonist mold. The later Pyrrhonists claimed inspiration from him; and, as we shall see, there is undeniably some basis for this. But it does not follow that Pyrrho's philosophy was identical to that of this later movement, or even that the later Pyrrhonists thought that it was identical; the claims of indebtedness that are expressed by or attributed to members of the later Pyrrhonist tradition are broad and general in character (and in Sextus Empiricus' case notably cautious—see *Outlines of Pyrrhonism* 1.7), and do not in themselves point to any particular reconstruction of Pyrrho's thought. It is necessary, therefore, to focus on the meager evidence bearing explicitly upon Pyrrho's own ideas and attitudes. How we read this evidence will also, of course, affect our conception of Pyrrho's relations with his philosophical contemporaries and predecessors." *Stanford Encyclopedia of Philosophy*. http://plato.stanford.edu/entries/pyrrho. Accessed January 26, 2015.

10. Sá's *Aphorismi Confessariorum*, although the smallest in size, was the third-most published among the Jesuit manuals for confessors, reaching at least eighty editions. It had pan-European circulation: It was printed in Lyon and Cologne (eleven editions in each), Rome (ten), Brescia (nine), Douai (eight), Venice (seven), Antwerp (five), Paris (fice), Madrid, Rouen, Tarvisio, and Turin (two), and Alcalá, Bacelona, Pamplona, and Valladolid (one). After having composed the census, I learned about the Japanese translation of Sá's work: It was published in Nagasaki in 1605.

11. *Petri Joanni Perpiniani Orationes Duodeviginti juxta Exemplar Romae Editum* (Paris, 1588). The collection was reprinted, for example, in Lyon (1594), Douvai (1598, 1608), Lyon (1603, 1606, 1622), and Rouen (1611).

12. See Michael Denis, *Carmina Quaedam* (Wien: Ignaz Albert, 1794).

13. See Jean Dietz Moss, "The Rhetoric Course at the Collegio Romano in the Latter Half of the Sixteenth Century," *Rhetorica* 4, no. 2 (Spring 1986).

14. See the archives of the Pontifical Gregorian University, FC 1563 f. 31^v-32^r and APUG 37^v-38^r.

15. See *ivi*: "Itaque logici communioribus et latius patentibus pronuntiatis utuntur, oratores autem, quia ad loca, ad tempora, ad personas accomodant orationes, quae orationes rerum singularium sunt augustioribus."

16. See *ivi*: "Cum rhetorica non utatur probabilibus, nisi quia eadem apta sunt ad persuasionem popularem conficiendam."

17. See Cicero, *Partitiones Oratoriae*, 9.32.

18. Gabriel Vázquez (1549–1604) studied philosophy at the University of Alcalá under Bañez (1565–69), where he later also taught (1579–84). In 1585 he was called to Rome to replace Suárez.

WORKS CITED

Benci, Francesco. *Orationes & carmina: quae partim nvnqvam antehac, partim in Germania nunc primum in lucem prodierunt: orationvm singvlarvm argumentum, pagina quae primam orationem antecedit proxime, indicabit: his demum subiuncta est eiusdem de stylo & scriptione disputatio*. Ingolstadii, 1592.

Denis, Michael, *Carmina Quaedam*. Vienna: Ignaz Albert, 1794.

Fumaroli, Marc. *L'âge de l'Éloquence: Rhétorique et "res literaria" de la Renaissance au seuil de l'époque classique*. Geneva: Droz, 1980.

Grendler, Paul F. *Schooling in Renaissance Italy: Literacy and Learning, 1300–1600*. Baltimore: Johns Hopkins University Press, 1989.

Maryks, Robert A. *Saint Cicero and the Jesuits: The Influence of the Liberal Arts on the Adoption of Moral Probabalism*. Aldershot, Hampshire, England: Ashgate, 2008.

Meador, Prentice A. "Skeptic Theory of Perception: A Philosophical Antecedent of Ciceronian Probability." *Quarterly Journal of Speech* 54 (1968): 340–41.

Moss, Jean Dietz, "The Rhetoric Course at the Collegio Romano in the Latter Half of the Sixteenth Century." *Rhetorica*, 4, no. 2 (Spring 1986).

O'Malley, John. *The First Jesuits*. Cambridge, Mass.: Harvard University Press, 1993.

Schott, André. *Tullianarum Quaestionum de Instauranda Ciceronis Imitatione*. 1610.

Soarez, Cypriano. "Three Books on the Art of Rhetoric Taken Especially from Aristotle, Cicero, and Quintilian." Translated by Lawrence J. Flynn. PhD diss., University of Florida, Gainesville, 1955.

Threet, Douglas F., "Rhetorical Function of Ciceronian Probability." *Southern Speech Communication Journal* 39 (Summer 1974): 309–21.

Vélez, Iosephus M., ed. *Vita Ignatii Loiolae et rerum Societatis Jesu historia auctore Joanne Alphonso de Polanco ejusdem Societatis sacerdote*. Vol. 1, 1491–1549. Vol. 5, Madrid: Typographorum Societas, 1894.

LOYOLA'S LITERACY NARRATIVE: WRITING AND RHETORIC IN *THE AUTOBIOGRAPHY OF SAINT IGNATIUS LOYOLA*

Thomas Deans

Writing has a vexed relationship with *The Autobiography of Saint Ignatius Loyola* because Ignatius—despite being a prolific composer of personal notes and reflections, formal and informal letters, spiritual instructions and exercises, organizational plans and documents—did not write it. In fact, he resisted the whole project. His fellow Jesuits wanted an origin story, aware that St. Dominic and St. Francis had rendered their testaments, but Ignatius rebuffed their initial requests, hemmed and hawed, delayed.[1] Ultimately he gave in and narrated the story orally in several sittings to his Jesuit colleague Luis Goncalves da Camera, who listened and later wrote up notes from memory, then still later elaborated on them and dictated his account to a scribe.

Despite Ignatius's resistance to sharing his story and whatever alterations were made to the testimonial on its way from initial telling to final manuscript, the autobiography has become one of the essential documents for understanding the Jesuit tradition. In this essay I draw out the literacy narrative embedded in the autobiography to show how Loyola's literacy and spirituality develop in tandem toward a virtuosity of the sort celebrated by Renaissance humanism, albeit a version strongly conditioned by the Jesuit "way of proceeding."[2] The first image of writing that appears in the text is of Inigo carefully copying passages from a devotional book, proud of his penmanship. In the middle sections we glimpse emergent practices of reading, writing, speaking, and listening, each intriguing on its own but more so when examined in relation to Ignatius's broader development and cultural context. By the end we see a versatile rhetor using both private and public writing to serve at once an inward, increasingly contemplative relationship with God, and an outward, increasingly active engagement with the world.

The Autobiography of Saint Ignatius Loyola is intended as a spiritual testament—it concentrates on Ignatius's emergence as a religious exemplar, not as a writer or rhetor—so any interpretation that foregrounds literacy will be incomplete and selective. Further, the narrative itself is limited because it covers only seventeen years—from 1521, shortly before Ignatius committed to a devout life, to 1538, shortly after he and his companions arrived in Rome to offer their services to the pope.[3] Given those limits and the biases inherent to autobiography, readers seeking a comprehensive accounting of Ignatius's life would be better served by the biographies of him that draw on the full range of available sources. In this essay I will focus on the autobiography as we inherit it—that is, as a stylized self-representation filtered through memory, transmitted through collaborators and translators, and shaped by the generic conventions of medieval and early modern spiritual autobiography.[4] We should also keep in mind that the text is informed by later experience. Ignatius is telling his story near the end of his life, after he has established schooling systems and assumed leadership of a complex, rapidly expanding, worldwide organization. More important for this study is that he has already gone through his own experiential development—both a formal process of education and an intellectual enculturation, *rhetorica humana,* and an inward process of discernment and prayer (ultimately codified in the *Spiritual Exercises*), *rhetorica divina* (Fumaroli). While the core of this essay is a close reading of how writing and rhetoric function within the context of the autobiography, along the way I occasionally widen the lens to discuss how those literate practices resonate with not only the spiritual, intellectual, and rhetorical commitments of that later Ignatius but also with the prevailing intellectual currents of his early modern culture.

READING LOYOLA READING

The autobiography opens by recalling Inigo as the heroic soldier at a battle against the French in Pamplona, where his legs are injured severely and his health quickly deteriorates to the point that he anticipates death and receives the last sacraments. He recovers, except for lasting injuries to one leg, and is soon taken to Loyola castle to convalesce, where he tells the story—here and throughout the autobiography, in the third person—of how reading takes a central place in his conversion:

> He was healthy in every respect except that he could not readily stand on that leg, and he was thus forced to remain in bed. Since he was an avid reader of books of worldly fiction, commonly called chivalric romances, and since he was feeling quite well, he asked for some such books to pass the time. In that house, however, they found none of the type he was used to reading, and so they brought him *The Life of Christ* and a book on the lives of the saints in Spanish. By frequent reading of these books he grew somewhat fond of what he found written therein. Setting his reading aside, he sometimes paused to think about the things he read, and at other times he thought of the worldly things that had formerly occupied his mind.
>
> —Ignatius Loyola, *Autobiography,* 45

Reading is the pivot on which Loyola's conversion turns, and no representation of literacy in the autobiography figures quite as prominently and self-consciously as this one. Ignatius's reading habits will grow more sophisticated over time, but the basic notion persists that reading—especially comparative reading across the secular and the sacred—can spark internal dialogue on both the nature of

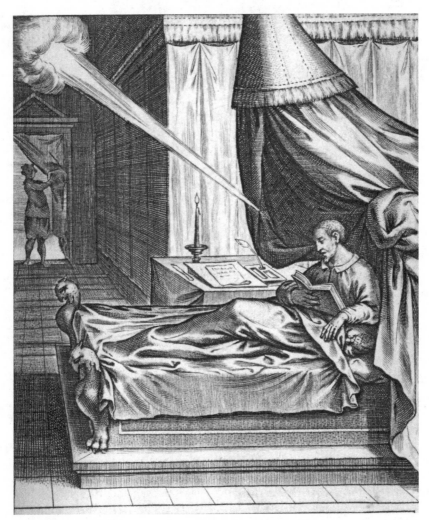

An engraving that depicts the conversion of Ignatius. From *Vita beati P. Ignatii Loiolae, Societatis Iesu fundatoris* (Life of the Blessed Father Ignatius Loyola, Founder of the Society of Jesus), commissioned by the Society of Jesus in 1605/1606 and published in Rome in 1609. The Institute of Jesuit Sources, copyright © 2000 by The Jesuits of the Missouri Province.

man and the nature of God, leading to changes of mind and heart. Reading cannot do it alone—prayerful contemplation and divine intervention are also essential—but here books open even the resistant reader to conversion.

What follows in the wake of this episode of reading is a sort of morality play of the mind in which the ideals of secular chivalry and Christian piety—images of both coming to Loyola directly from books—contend for his loyalty. He daydreams of himself as the knight errant enraptured with an unattainable lady, and these thoughts compete with others that arise from his current reading, supplemented by divine intervention: "Our Lord, nevertheless, came to his aid, bringing it about that these thoughts were followed by others arising from his reading. While reading the life of our Lord and those of the saints, he used to pause and meditate, reasoning with himself: 'What if I were to do what Saint Francis did, or to do what Saint Dominic did?'" (47). He goes on to ruminate more about how he might imitate those and other saints, especially their austerities. Indeed the desire to imitate, born of reading but extending into contemplation and prayer, is the catalyst for his conversion: "It was at this time that the desire to imitate the saints came to him, and without giving any consideration to his present circumstances, he promised to do, with God's grace, what they had done. His great desire, after regaining his health, was to go to Jerusalem" (49). This desire for pilgrimage is likewise bookish in origin: It comes not only from reading the saints lives, as Ignatius declares, but also from the introduction to Ludolph of Saxony's *The Life of Christ*, which valorizes traveling to the Holy Land.

These reading experiences early in the autobiography affirm Loyola's inclination to identity with and imitate textual subjects. They also reveal germinal spiritual practices such as visualization, which becomes a key tool of the *Spiritual Exercises*, and discernment, which is even more central to Ignatian spirituality.[5] In fact, as Inigo continues to toggle between the worldly temptations exemplified in chivalric romances and the ascetic models exemplified in religious books, we hear a stylized origin story for Ignatian discernment:

> When he thought of worldly matters, he found much delight; but after growing weary and dismissing them, he found that he was dry and unhappy. But when he thought of going barefoot to Jerusalem and eating nothing but herbs and of imitating the saints in all the austerities they practiced, he not only found consolation in these thoughts, but even after they had left him he felt happy and joyful. He did not consider nor did he stop to examine this difference until one day his eyes were partially opened, and he began to wonder at this difference and to reflect upon it. From experience he knew that some thoughts left him sad while others made him happy, and little by little he came to perceive the different spirits that were moving him; one coming from the Devil and the other coming from God.
>
> —Ignatius Loyola, *Autobiography*, 48

Here the practice of discernment extends beyond the bookish oscillation between chivalric and saintly texts into a reading of oneself, in particular one's own consolations and disconsolations. But that personal and spiritual process, at least in this paradigmatic case, owes its genesis to books, and in particular to a mode of reading that puts the sacred and the secular into vigorous conversation and drives toward the end of understanding God's will for oneself.

READING LOYOLA WRITING

Less dramatic but in many ways more interesting are representations of writing in the autobiography. Shortly after the discernment episode, Inigo decisively turns away from "all his past life" (49) and commits himself to pilgrimage, which is followed immediately by an impulse to write:

> He greatly enjoyed his books, and the idea struck him to copy down, in abridged form, the more important items in the life of Christ and of the saints. . . . He set about writing these things in a book, taking great care and using red ink for Christ's words and blue for those of our Lady. He used polished and lined paper and wrote in a good hand since he had an attractive penmanship.
>
> —Ignatius Loyola, *Autobiography*, 50

Here we witness a shift from reading to writing, and that writing is among the first outward manifestations of Ignatius's conversion. Yet as with his initial reading, his initial writing is imitative, here limited to copying. Ignatius seems to be self-consciously casting his earlier self—even when a battle-tested man of thirty—as childlike in religious sensibilities, just starting to find his way. Moreover, just as in his spiritual struggles at this moment in his development he is preoccupied with the body—recoiling at "motions of the flesh" as loathsome, yearning for austerely physical forms of penance, committing himself to an arduous pilgrimage—he is likewise obsessively attentive to the tactile physicality of writing: the type of paper, color of ink, and quality of penmanship. At this early stage, Inigo seems more scribe than rhetor. He not only copies lines from *The Life of Christ* but also follows Ludolph's practice of penning Jesus' words in red. For Mary's words, however, he opts for blue, a departure from Ludolph. Why does he volunteer that detail? It may be simply to signal his devotion to Mary; yet it also suggests, I think, an inkling of personal agency emerging in a process of otherwise deferential imitation.

Ignatius will never leave imitation behind—indeed it is a vital practice in his own spiritual and intellectual development, as it was a signature pedagogical practice in early modern humanism. But this early, mechanical manner of imitation we see in Ignatius's writing will give way to more flexible, dialogic modes of imitation. After this episode sets up Ignatius as devout in an earnest but rote way, he pivots to describing his prayer habits: "He spent some time in writing and some in prayer" (50). For now we don't get further details on how he toggles between prayer and writing, only that he does so, but by the close of the autobiography we will see the relationship between those activities become much more integrated, intimate, and intense.

PRIVATE WRITING IN THE BOOK HE GUARDEDLY
CARRIED WITH HIM

Writing next enters the autobiography not as a means of copying lines from a source but instead as a medium for recording the contents of one's own conscience. Inigo sets out from Loyola, eager to make a pilgrimage to Jerusalem, and at his first stop, Montserrat, he "made a general confession in writing, which lasted three days" under the direction of a Benedictine monk (61). According to historian John O'Malley, "These actions at Montserrat ritualized the definitive closing of the door on his past" (24). Just as writing starts to play a role in Ignatius's prayer and sacramental practice, it proves likewise instrumental in shedding his past. Even at this early stage in his pilgrimage we are starting to see writing serve multiple complementary purposes.

When describing his departure from Montserrat, the first stop on his pilgrimage, Ignatius mentions "jot[ting] down a few items in the book that he guardedly carried with him and that afforded him much consolation" (63). He has just given away his sword and dagger and all his clothing except for a pilgrim's tunic—yet he retains a book that we might label a journal, diary, notebook, or commonplace book. As he moves from Montserrat to Manresa, where he spends nearly a year doing works of charity and praying intensively, he uses a heavy-handed schooling metaphor when recalling his experience there. He says that he was being "taught by God" and lists his lessons by number like a schoolboy. While he frames himself as the young student, he has at least traveled some distance from Loyola castle and is already doing more than copying out lines from an authoritative book. He is instead jotting his own lines in his own book. And even if he is not yet sharing them with anyone but himself and his confessor, this personal writing is noteworthy. Private writing is a tool Ignatius uses not only for inward-directed devotion and decision-making but also, as we will learn, for invention and drafting of what will ultimately become public documents, including the *Spiritual Exercises* and the *Constitutions*.

Unfortunately the notebook that Ignatius refers to does not survive, although we do have access to one from much later, 1544–45, usually labeled his *Spiritual Diary*.[6] Written in Ignatius's own hand, this journal begins six years after the autobiography ends and features just over three months of daily entries (February–May 1544), most between one and five paragraphs; then it shifts abruptly to very brief daily entries—most just a single phrase of four or five words that logs whether he experienced tears or not before, during, and after daily Mass—that run for an additional eight months (June 1544–February 1545). Even though this spiritual diary sits outside the timeframe of the autobiography, from it we can learn something of Ignatius's private writing habits that we can use to speculate about what "the book that he guardedly carried with him and that afforded him much consolation" might mean for the younger Inigo.

The spiritual diary we have for March–May 1544 is a curious collection of fragments that do one or a combination of the following: register Ignatius's state of mind and emotions during morning prayers, at Mass, and/or at night; relate the frequency and nature his insights and visions, including his accounts of being visited in prayer by Jesus, the Father, or Mary; reflect on theological concepts such as the Trinity; and announce his state of mind on an important ethical and practical decision facing Ignatius in 1544—how the Society should handle income and poverty. This defies what we typically expect to find in self-sponsored private writing: either a detailed record of daily life, which we associate with a diary, or a therapeutic processing of anxieties, unconscious desires, experiences, and aspirations, which we associate with keeping a personal journal. Ignatius's sixteenth-century context makes such contemporary associations of writing with psychological and therapeutic purposes anachronistic, but more importantly the actual entries in the *Spiritual Diary* frustrate such expectations.

Joseph A. Munitiz, S.J., argues—rightly, I think—that the *Spiritual Exercises* are the key to understanding the diary. What we see unfolding in the entries is a case study in the method of discernment outlined in the *Exercises*. Munitiz writes that the diary "is not a mere collection of thoughts; it is kept with a definite end in view: the recording of consolations and desolations experienced in the course of reaching a decision about poverty" (14). This process plays itself out over months, with swings in several different directions on the question at hand, and with Ignatius intent on attending to the movements of grace within his mind and heart. Munitiz sees the notebook as not expressive but instrumental: Ignatius is using it to make a decision of great practical consequence for the Society, one that must ultimately be articulated in the *Constitutions,* which he is drafting at this time. In this case, private writing is party to a process of extended discernment, and ultimately that private writing will facilitate not only decision-making but also public writing. The diary gives us a glimpse of the inward-looking rhetoric of discernment as it unfolds over months; but all those fragments feed a process of invention that will, in due time, result in choices that must be articulated in the outward-looking rhetoric of the *Constitutions.* This is not the only thing going on in the diary—even during this later phase in his life Ignatius is still fashioning new ideas, especially about the Trinity (Munitiz 14); that is, he is still occasionally writing to learn. However, the dominant mode of writing in the diary is neither expressive nor epistemic but instead instrumental: This is private writing to make an important decision the Ignatian way.

So what might this mean for the notebook mentioned early in the autobiography? As he departs Montserrat and moves on to Manresa, Ignatius may have been struggling to figure out how to live up to the ideals of his recent conversion, but he was not wrestling with an important decision. However, historians and biographers agree that during this period—and for months, probably years afterward—he was drafting, testing, and revising the *Spiritual Exercises*. Ignatius corroborates this later in the autobiography when he tells Goncalves da Camera that "he had not composed the Exercises all at one time, but perceiving certain things happening in his soul, and finding them helpful, thought that they might be helpful to others, and so he set them down in writing" (186). We can thus speculate that if Ignatius employed a relentlessly instrumental mode of private writing in his later spiritual diary, he probably did the same with his earlier notebook, albeit with a different purpose: to work out his emerging methods of prayer, discernment, and devotion, methods that would ultimately be codified in the *Spiritual Exercises*. Here again we see private writing participating in a process of internal invention that will, in time, produce shared, deliberative rhetoric that will fundamentally shape the emergent Society of Jesus—in the case of the earlier notebook, the *Spiritual Exercises,* and in the case of the later diary, the *Constitutions*.

In these glimpses of Ignatius's private writing we might recognize a kinship with one of the signature literacy practices of Renaissance humanism: the commonplace book. Commonplacing was an important pedagogical practice but was also popular among striving middle class citizens. The commonplace book was a tablet or notebook in which to gather passages (aphorisms, proverbs, key quotes, facts, authoritative statements, snippets of wisdom and wit) culled from various sources—usually of cultural or literary importance, often classical—and sorted into categories under topic headings. Just as important as this gathering and sorting was the way humanists used the books: with the instrumental intent of weaving those commonplaces—judiciously and strategically—into their future writing and speaking, usually to garner authority or demonstrate cultural literacy (see Moss; Crane). The technology of commonplacing therefore introduced new ways of organizing knowledge, new habits of mind, and new ways of composing texts. The practice of copying out quotes from sources owed much to humanist imitation, but the commonplace habit of mind ultimately emphasized "reframing" or "recycling" (Crane) the inherited textual fragments, making them one's own by creatively integrating them with one's own discourse.

This resonates in some ways with what we see in Ignatius's private writing; yet he departs in several key ways from typical modes of commonplacing. Early on we see him copying out Ludolph's *The Life of Christ,* doing so sequentially with care, as if trying to imprint the text on his mind and soul. This is consistent with the commonplace tradition, both in the concrete sense that he is transcribing authoritative passages and in the conceptual sense that Ignatius is writing the passages out to make them more his own, to better lodge them in his memory and imprint them in his heart. However, in this case Ignatius does not seem to be culling fragments with an intent to recruit them for any potential future oral or written rhetorical performance. And we don't know if he similarly copies out other passages from other sources, although Broderick speculates that he does so in Montserrat: "The matters which he desired to write down in his big notebook may well have been remembered passages from the *Ejercitatorio* of Abbot Cisneros, and also probably extracts from some *Confesionionale*, or devout manual in vernacular, meant to help penitents with their annual or more frequent confessions" (85–86; see also Fitzsimmons, Part I).[7] In the spiritual diary of 1544 we don't see Ignatius recording any quotes from sources; his only sources are supernatural and personal, divine revelations and movements of his own soul and conscience. So when it comes to collecting notable and quotable passages from authoritative sources, we cannot claim that Ignatius follows that humanist practice in the conventional way. Nor does he seem to revel in language. As Munitz remarks, "The author of the Diary is not a lover of words; he treats them roughly, now sparingly, now in wanton excess; they are seized and hammered into place" (7). Still, what *does* seem evident in his private writing process (although it could simply be something he picks up from his cultural milieu) is the commonplace-like habit of recording fragments in a notebook less for psychological venting or spiritual solace than for instrumental purposes, whether that purpose is making a difficult decision or gathering bits of text to use as the basis for future texts—in this case the *Spiritual Exercises*.[8] The commonplace book, much more so than the personal diary or journal, is a genre oriented to *invention* and *action*, for gathering pieces into public performances. Ignatius's private writing seems complicit in that humanist orientation, even if he bends it toward his distinctive way of proceeding.

Although we can presume that Ignatius continues to write in his notebook—recording, reordering, and reframing the fragments that will ultimately become the *Spiritual Exercises*—explicit references to reading and writing disappear from the autobiography as he describes his stay in Manresa, where he spends nearly a year in an austere regimen of prayer, penance, and charity before continuing his pilgrimage to Jerusalem via Italy. The one exception is a brief reference to writing letters to spiritual persons in Barcelona during this period.

IGNATIUS AT UNIVERSITY

By this stage in the autobiography a pattern starts to emerge more clearly. When Ignatius is on the move, there is little talk of texts and more of travel, breakthroughs in prayer, and episodes of revelation. But when he settles in one place, literacy comes to the fore. One such time is when Inigo enters university. After all, writing is almost always a concern when a student—especially a nontraditional student—enters higher education.

Upon his return to Spain from his pilgrimage to Jerusalem, Ignatius enters the University of Barcelona, getting a late start on his formal education. As a thirty-four year old among teenage boys, he struggles to memorize Latin grammar, the prerequisite for further studies (he blames evil spirits for distracting him). Still, he makes progress and after two years is ready to move on to more advanced studies at the University of Alcala. There he remains hungry for knowledge and deferential to university authorities, but outside of university walls we start to see him pivot from student to teacher: "While in Alcala he engaged in giving the Spiritual Exercises and in explaining Christian doctrine" (113). That evangelizing work in the streets and his strange manner of dress make the Inquisition nervous and land Inigo in prison, although after a few weeks he is exonerated and released.

In 1527, at the prompting of an archbishop, Ignatius moves on to study at the University of Salamanca, where he runs into similar albeit more serious trouble. Dominican friars at Salamanca challenge the informal teaching that Ignatius and his companions are doing. They probe whether Loyola is under the sway of humanists like Erasmus, or otherwise straying from Church orthodoxy, and Ignatius recognizes the danger: "The pilgrim was now on his guard, for this way of arguing did not seem good to him" (127). He shifts between answering deferentially, acknowledging his lack of education, and questioning whether he is indeed doing anything wrong; then he resorts to silence and invites his questioner to consult his superiors. This soon leads to a formal trial before four judges who are interested in not just the street preaching but also the text of his *Spiritual Exercises*. Standing toe to toe with scholars while grilled about his street activity, theology, and writing, Inigo displays growing skills in forensic rhetoric, shuttling between strategic deference ("he always prefaced his remarks by saying that he did not know what the learned doctors held on these points" [131]) and strategic excess: "Then they ordered him to explain the First Commandment as he usually explained it. This he started to do, and did it in so great detail, saying so many things about the First Commandment that they no longer had any desire to ask anything more of him" (131). Ironically enough, to exhaust his inquisitors, Ignatius employs one of Erasmus's favorite rhetorical strategies, *copia*—a practice likewise associated with commonplace books.

After twenty-two more days in prison awaiting judgment, Ignatius and his colleagues are exonerated, except that they are banned from speaking publicly on how to distinguish venial from mortal sins until completing their university degrees. In recalling the event, Ignatius can't help but express a degree of impatience and self-righteousness:

> The pilgrim said that he would fulfill all that the sentence ordered, but that he did not agree with it, for though not condemning him on any single point, they were forcing his mouth closed so as to keep him from helping others in the way that he could. . . . The pilgrim said nothing else except that as long as he remained within the jurisdiction of Salamanca, he would do as had been ordered.
>
> —Ignatius Loyola, *Autobiography*, 133

While ever compliant to Church authorities, the rhetor's growing skill, swagger, and sense of purpose are on more and more on public display.

The autobiography then recounts Inigo's move to continue his studies in Paris (the transfer student, now on his third university). After taking the entrance exam there he discovers, as he did at Barcelona, that he is academically underprepared and needs to take foundational classes with boys. He also continues to have similar troubles concentrating on his studies. In Paris, Ignatius's ascetic practices, commitment to the poor, and informal teaching prove persuasive with his peers, inspiring some to quit their studies and enter his circle, which again raises concerns among Church inquisitors—some of whom accuse him of being "a seducer of students" (143). This time, instead of waiting for Church or university authorities to summon him, Ignatius takes the lead: "He went to the inquisitor, telling him that he had heard that he had been looking for him and that he was ready for whatever he might wish" (147). The matter ended there, although Ignatius opted to study more, proselytize less—at least until his courses were over.

Although Ignatius does not mention this detail in his autobiography, a year after he arrived in Paris he switched colleges from Montaigu to Sainte-Barbe, the school from which he received his master's degree. Sainte-Barbe was more liberal than Montaigu and "a crossroads in Paris at the time for the two prevalent intellectual currents—the scholastic and the humanistic" (Olin, 78n9). Residues of scholasticism never leave Ignatius, but during this pivotal moment in European culture and his own life, he engages more and more with humanistic practices such as imitation, commonplace writing, and rhetorical performance, albeit versions always tempered by resolute obedience to Church doctrine. As for direct references to reading and writing during the Paris section of the autobiography, he mentions writing letters—a favorite genre of European humanists—to his growing international network of friends and followers.

In Paris, Ignatius starts to build the core of his society, and by the time he leaves in 1535 for Spain—he had not been home for thirteen years, seven of them in Paris—he is credentialed with baccalaureate and master's degrees. Moreover, he and his companions have made a pact to go on pilgrimage to Jerusalem. Right before leaving, he hears rumors of another inquiry by inquisitors, and again goes proactively to the Church authorities and demands judgment. The inquisitor drops the case and even asks for a copy of the *Spiritual Exercises*. No longer just the deferential reader and private writer, Loyola is, with his university degrees and *Exercises* in hand, a confident and versatile rhetor. At the same time, writing never seems to get easier for him, because both the challenges facing him and the standards to which he holds himself keep rising.

COMPOSING IN ROME

While describing his travels with companions through Spain and Italy toward (they hoped) the Holy Land, Ignatius mentions little of reading and writing.

Along the way he is begging, performing charity, and offering his distinctive method of Christian instruction. He and several colleagues get ordained as priests in Venice and await passage to Jerusalem, but their pilgrimage is frustrated by political unrest in the Middle East, so instead they set off for Rome.

At this point the narrative starts to feel hurried, as if Goncalves da Camera is trying to fit in as much as he can before Ignatius's patience with the autobiography runs out. The troubles that Ignatius and his companions experienced in Rome are recounted, but then Goncalves da Camera breaks the into the narrative: "I asked the pilgrim on October 20, about the Exercises and the Constitutions, because I wanted to know how he had written them" (186). Ignatius explains how he composed the *Exercises* piecemeal as he perceived "things happening in his soul" (186). Then he gets especially self-conscious about his ethos, assuring Goncalves da Camera that "his intention had been sincere in all that he related" during their sessions (187). In the closing paragraphs the chronology jumps forward and Goncalves da Camera describes Ignatius's current work on the *Constitutions*, which gives us a window on Loyola's mature composing process:

> When he celebrated Mass he also had many visions, and when he was writing the Constitutions he had them quite frequently. This he can prove very easily because every day he noted what was taking place in his soul and all this is found written down. He then showed me a rather large packet of writing, and from these he read to me a sizable amount. For the most part they were visions that he had had confirming certain points of the Constitutions. Sometimes he saw God the Father, at other times all three Persons of the Trinity, and at other times our Lady, who was at times interceding for him and at times strengthening him. He especially spoke to me about certain items under deliberation and for which he celebrated Mass every day for forty days and daily had shed many tears. The question was whether a church should have any income, and if the Society should make use of that income. The method he followed when writing the Constitutions was to celebrate Mass every day and present the point under consideration to God and pray over it.
>
> —Ignatius Loyola, *Autobiography*, 187–88

Here we near end of Ignatius's autobiography, one in which we have witnessed his uses of writing and rhetoric growing more intense and sophisticated, although branching in two different (if ultimately complementary) directions: inward, increasingly unmediated by any source other than God; and outward, increasingly engaged in public deliberations and documents necessary to guide his growing Society. Toward contemplation through writing; toward action through writing.

By Rome, the rhetoric of contemplation has become more intimate than we have seen earlier in the autobiography, emphasizing the immediacy of Ignatius's relationship with God. Right before describing his mature writing process (quoted at length above), Ignatius mentions how now "whatever time or hour he wanted to find God, he found him," and how during this period "visions came to him as collaborations" (187). This is consistent with the rhetoric of the *Spiritual Exercises*, which, according to O'Malley, are grounded in the "fundamental premise" of the "immediate action of God on the individual" (43). A similar phenomenon is happening with the writing of the *Constitutions*—prayer and writing have by this point become so enmeshed that just as Ignatius' visions are now "as collaborations," so too are his invention and writing processes collaborations with the divine.

The complementary rhetoric of action through writing is more implied than described: The *Constitutions* were, of course, high-stakes documents needed to govern the expanding Society of Jesus, texts of deliberative rhetoric guiding social action on complex organizational matters. While the *Constitutions* were born of the internal rhetorics of contemplation and ultimately divine collaboration, they had to function politically and persuasively in Ignatius's complex, volatile, sixteenth-century world.

AN ABRUPT ENDING

Over the course of the autobiography we can trace Ignatius's progression from imitation to agency, from the careful copying of lines from *The Life of Christ* and zealous imitation of saints' lives in *The Golden Legend* to a mature and versatile—yet ever intense—rhetorical agency plied both inwardly or outwardly. By the closing scenes in Rome, Ignatius is no longer using writing to copy out the lives of saints; instead he is exercising writing to live the life of a saint.

It is a bit jarring, then, when the autobiography ends on a note of refusal. Goncalves da Camera reports, "I wanted to see all these papers on the Constitutions and asked him to let me have them for a while, but he would not" (188). Just as he resisted engaging in the autobiography initially, Ignatius is still hardly inclined to self-disclosure, especially when it seems—despite Goncalves da Camera's well-meaning intentions—driven by a kind of a celebrity curiosity. Loyola agreed to the autobiography only after being convinced of its instrumental purpose—to deliver a testament that would serve the future of his Society. Similarly, he engaged in private writing to the degree that it served the instrumental purposes of making decisions or helping to compose future documents. Like Goncalves da Camera in this final scene, we may want, out of curiosity, more access to how Ignatius composed the *Constitutions*, but he doesn't seem persuaded that sharing the details of his writing process has a compelling enough spiritual or institutional purpose. In his refusal to grant access to his papers, Ignatius seems to be saying that rather than talk about himself and his composing process, he ought instead to just move forward in the pragmatic work of writing the *Constitutions*.

NOTES

1. In his original preface to the autobiography Jeronimo Nadal writes, "Since I knew that the holy father-founders of monastic communities had been accustomed to leave their sons some admonition, as a testament, to help them grow in virtue, I waited for the opportune moment to ask the same of Father Ignatius" (189). There is also no authoritative title for the autobiography. The original title is *Acta Patris Ignatii*, and while the most popular English translation is *The Autobiography of Saint Ignatius Loyola*, several editors have preferred other versions: *The Testament of Ignatius Loyola, Inigo: Original Testament, A Pilgrim's Testament: The Memoirs of Ignatius of Loyola, St. Ignatius' Own Story*, and, most recently, *A Pilgrim's Journey: The Autobiography of Ignatius of Loyola*, which is the version that I am relying on for this essay (rev. ed., trans. Joseph N. Tylenda [San Francisco: Ignatius Press, 2001]). English versions published before 1950 were based on Annibal du Coudret's sixteenth-century Latin translation of the original manuscript; most editions published after 1950 work directly from the Spanish-Italian manuscript.

2. O'Malley discusses the importance of this phrase for early Jesuits.

3. Ignatius apparently recounted his early life in his oral narrative, but that part of the story is missing, probably because Goncalves da Camera never included it (O'Malley, 8). Broderick speculates that Goncalves da Camera did this intentionally, that he "kept to himself from mistaken reverence the details given him of Inigo's disorderly years" (43).

4. Marjorie O'Rourke Boyle shows how the narrative depends not just on the generic conventions of spiritual autobiography but also on familiar scripts of chivalry, asceticism, mysticism, and pilgrimage. She argues that the text is less the recounting of a unique life story than an assemblage of cultural commonplaces circulating in Ignatius's sixteenth-century world, and that ultimately the work is not autobiography in the contemporary sense of that term but instead a performance of epideictic rhetoric in praise of God, with Augustine's *Confessions* the exemplar of that genre.

5. While these practices can now be labeled Ignatian, he borrowed as much as he innovated. See Brou, i–6 on medieval precedents for Ignatian prayer; see Boyle for how Ignatius's autobiography is reflecting, consciously and not, a wide range of inheritances from his cultural-historical context; see Van Engen and Von Habsburg on how imitation, visualization, and similar practices fit into cultural and religious traditions that precede Ignatius; see Fitzsimmons, Part I, on the more immediate influence of Cisernos.

6. Joseph A. Munitiz's translation, which I relied on, adopts a dual title: *Inigo: Discernment Log-Book: The Spiritual Diary of Saint Ignatius Loyola*.

7. Broderick claims that Ignatius brings a "big notebook" with him on his journey from Loyola castle, the same one in which he earlier copied out *The Life of Christ*, and that he acquires a separate smaller notebook at Manresa to record his own thoughts, this latter becoming the basis for the *Spiritual Exercises*.

8. An intriguing coda to the melding of commonplace-book habits with Ignatian spiritual practices is the case of the French Jesuit teacher Claude-Francois Menestrier, who offered a course to adults in Lyon in 1658. Menestrier not only expected his students to keep commonplace books of a traditional sort (gathering and ordering passages from a wide range of secular and sacred texts) but also remarked on how the Jesuit cus-

tom of a bedtime examination of conscience "provides an opportunity for catching up on one's commonplace book" (Loach 83, note 76). In this case, keeping a commonplace book reinforces the discernment process.

WORKS CITED

Boyle, Marjorie O'Rourke. *Loyola's Acts: The Rhetoric of the Self.* Berkeley: University of California Press, 1997.

Broderick, James. *Saint Ignatius Loyola: The Pilgrim Years, 1491–1538.* San Francisco: Ignatius Press, 1998.

Brou, Alexandre. *Ignatian Methods of Prayer.* Translated by William J. Young. Milwaukee: Bruce, 1949.

Crane, Mary Thomas. *Framing Authority: Sayings, Self, and Society in Sixteenth-Century England.* Princeton: Princeton University Press, 1993.

Fumaroli, Marc. "The Fertility and Shortcomings of Renaissance Rhetoric: The Case of the Jesuits," 90–106. In *The Jesuits II: Cultures, Sciences, and the Arts, 1540–1773,* ed. John O'Malley, Gauvin Alexander Bailey, Steven J. Harris, and T. Frank Kennedy. Toronto: University of Toronto Press, 1999.

Ignatius of Loyola. *Inigo: Discernment Log-Book: The Spiritual Diary of Saint Ignatius Loyola.* Edited and translated by Joseph A. Munitiz. London: Inigo Enterprises, 1987.

———. *A Pilgrim's Journey: The Autobiography of Ignatius of Loyola.* Revised ed. Translated by Joseph N. Tylenda. San Francisco: Ignatius Press, 2001.

Loach, Judi. "Revolutionary Pedagogues? How Jesuits Used Education to Change Society," 66–85. In *The Jesuits II: Cultures, Sciences, and the Arts, 1540–1773,* ed. John O'Malley, Gauvin Alexander Bailey, Steven J. Harris, and T. Frank Kennedy. Toronto: University of Toronto Press, 2006.

Moss, Ann, ed. *Printed Commonplace-Books and the Structuring of Renaissance Thought.* Oxford: Clarendon Press, 1996.

Munitiz, Joseph A. Introduction to *Inigo: Discernment Log-Book. The Spiritual Diary of Saint Ignatius Loyola,* 3–18. Edited and translated by Joseph A. Munitiz. London: Inigo Enterprises, 1987.

Nadal, Jeronimo, Preface to *A Pilgrim's Journey: The Autobiography of Ignatius of Loyola,* 189–91. Revised ed. Translated by Joseph N. Tylenda. San Francisco: Ignatius Press, 2001.

Olin, John C. Notes to *The Autobiography of St. Ignatius Loyola, with Related Documents.* New York: Harper and Row, 1974.

O'Malley, John. *The First Jesuits.* Cambridge: Harvard University Press, 1993.

Van Engen, John. *Sisters and Brothers of the Common Life: The Devotio Moderna and the World of the Later Middle Ages.* Philadelphia: University of Pennsylvania Press, 2008.

Von Habsburg, Maximilian. *Catholic and Protestant Translations of the Imitatio Christi, 1425–1650: From Late Medieval Classic to Early Modern Bestseller.* Surrey, U.K.: Ashgate, 2011.

A PILGRIM'S STAFF VERSUS A LADDER OF CONTEMPLATION: THE RHETORIC OF AGENCY AND EMOTIONAL ELOQUENCE IN ST. IGNATIUS'S *SPIRITUAL EXERCISES*

Maureen A. J. Fitzsimmons

> Under the name of Spiritual Exercises is understood every method of examination of conscience, of meditation, of contemplation, of vocal and mental prayer, and of other spiritual operations . . . disposing the soul to rid itself of all inordinate affections, and, after it has rid itself of them, to seek and to find the divine will in the ordering of one's life with a view to the salvation of one's soul.
> —Ignatius of Loyola, *Spiritual Exercises*

Since the sixteenth century, members of the Society of Jesus have made the *Spiritual Exercises*, an extended series of meditations crafted by Ignatius of Loyola, available to men and women worldwide. Over the centuries, the brief, script-like text has been published more than forty-five hundred times (Ganss, 54), has remained central to Jesuit spiritual practices, and has also been adopted by several other institutions. Its powerful dialogic methods and rich rhetorical engagements have also been called on to serve as the foundation for what Jesuit educators refer to as Ignatian pedagogy, or the Ignatian pedagogical paradigm, which is an approach to teaching that developed in the 1980s and that fosters intellectual activity through the invocation of context, experience, action, and reflection in dynamic recursivity (Duminuco, 158ff.).

As popular as the *Spiritual Exercises* have become, they created problems for Loyola with the religious hierarchy of the premodern era; in fact, largely because Ignatius, as a guide, shared his meditative process with others seeking to move beyond their "inordinate affections" and toward an ability to make decisions that were not a result of "some disordered attachment" (Ganss, 51), he was called in front of the Spanish Inquisition three separate times, was jailed as part of those procedures for sixty-four days, and, although never found guilty of being anti-authoritarian, was compelled to leave two cities in order to circumvent the favorable but restrictive rulings of his inquisitors and continue his ministry.[1] What was so unusual about Ignatius's own practice of rhetoric that the meditations of an itinerant preacher (who was not yet a priest) would engender so much attention (both negative and positive) in sixteenth-century Europe and so much interest in the twenty-first century? How did Ignatius adopt and adapt the traditional Renaissance genres of the spiritual guide and devotional text to his own particular ends, joining emotion, imagination, and individual agency to create a distinctive text and rhetorical enactment of spiritual growth that has spoken to countless generations? How did Ignatius use the rhetoric of emotion to incorporate personal affections as useful instead of obstructive to the meditative process? How novel was Ignatius's rhetoric of individual agency in the *Spiritual Exercises* to the premodern powers that be? And how was that rhetorical agency built into both the actual form and practice of the *Exercises* as well as into the uses for which they were intended? To address these questions I will offer an historical-contextual rhetorical analysis to compare two very popular meditation texts and programs, one by the apostolic (meaning: out in the world) pilgrim, Loyola, the other by his countryman and predecessor, García de Cisneros, the abbot of the Benedictine monastery at Montserrat, and representative of the cenobitic, or monastic (meaning: withdrawn from the world) religious society, each possessing distinctly different cultural conventions and rhetorical purposes.

While the two texts draw on a common set of spiritual guides and practices, a comparison of them makes apparent that the latitude for individual imagination and agency afforded in each meditation is substantially different. As Daniel M. Gross asserts, "when we understand how the rhetoric of a particular social reality is put together, it becomes all the more clear how things might be different" (160). While the structure of the two guides and the discursive practices they invoke can be seen as parallel, the different rhetorical "social reality" that each is situated within constructs significant differences in the specific rhetorical situation of the authors, their texts, and their possible enactments. I will sketch the common historical setting for the two works as well as the context for each, including Ignatius's reading of Cisneros's text, which Ignatius encountered at Montserrat through the agency of his confessor, Fr. Chanones (Ignatius, *Ignatius*, 26), and then I shall offer point-to-point comparisons of how each author represents various facets of human agency and emotion in their texts and of the practice of multiple sets of meditational prompts.

Of Europe's substantial religious, political, and social upheavals during the fourteenth through sixteenth centuries, a few are worth highlighting to help focus this discussion. In the first several centuries of the Church, meditation was practiced as part of religious life; whole passages of scripture would be repeated, consequently becoming part of the memory of the monks. Although not strictly an imaginative act, this practice "did shape the imagination of monastics by implanting in them sacred images" (Studzinski, 124). By the later Middle Ages, it was not uncommon for meditations to include imaginative processes that conjured biblical scenes that promoted deep emotional reactions, even while the renderings of the scenes were not necessarily true to the original narratives (176).

The "affective mode" in spiritual practice, a contemplative style that focused largely on the Passion of Christ, emerged; texts for this type of prayer evolved from simple devotions in the eleventh century to more complex meditations by the fifteenth century. Sarah McNamer explains that "affective meditations on the Passion are richly emotional, script-like texts that ask their readers to imagine themselves present at scenes of Christ's suffering and to perform compassion for that suffering victim in a private drama of the heart" (1). In her work exploring medieval compassion, McNamer explains that these meditations were "widely copied and translated in the fourteenth century and exerted a profound influence on devotional art, practices, literature, and drama, effecting a shift to a more compassionate sensibility in late medieval religion" (17–18). Specifically, affective meditations on the subject of the Passion of Christ gain credibility before Ignatius's birth (ca. 1491) and during his lifetime (McNamer, 15–21).

Devotio Moderna, a movement from the Netherlands that reached much of Europe, had by the beginning of the sixteenth century developed a method of meditation. Participating members, both men and women, were deeply committed to living faithful lives but did not take vows within the Church. Instead, they "filled their day with spiritual exercises . . . . Their exercises, though widely varying, turn[ed] the day's structure into a personal plan" (Van Engen, 297–98). Drawing from surviving documents, Van Engen quotes Zerbolt and explains: " 'Truly and spiritually to be converted is to convert, reduce and reform the affections and powers of the soul . . . to their rightful state.' The return was ultimately to a state of inner tranquility (*statui illi tranquillitatis interne*), but it came only with a struggle" (78). The experience of meditation has gone from that of absence of emotion to one that addresses the management of affections. In fact, Thomas M. Gannon, S.J., and George W. Traub, S.J., consider Ignatius's work to have an "immediate link" with the Devotio Moderna movement (177).[2] Later, Loyola's spiritual exercises would join this growing genre of affective meditation in multiple scenarios, using the body and all of its senses and, thereby, invite engagement of the whole person.[3]

The early sixteenth century is also a time of Church reform, including a movement that begins in the fifteenth century, affecting most of the monasteries of Spain (Peers 7). García de Cisneros was a monk at Valladolid. Abbot Louis Barbo, of St. Justina at Padua, had drafted *Method of Meditation* as a means of reform; it included advice on administering meditations, along with some potential meditations, and made its way to Valladolid (Sitwell 137). In 1493, with Ferdinand of Spain "taking warmly to heart the work of restoring the Benedictine Order" (Speco, iv), Cisneros assumed the position of Abbot at Montserrat and successfully conducted a "striking resuscitation of spirituality" (Peers, 7) at the four-hundred-year-old Benedictine institution (Sagarra, 13). Apparently continuing Barbo's approach, Cisneros around 1500 wrote a text available to monks and penitents in Latin and Spanish outlining the steps in an extended meditation titled *Ejercitatorio de la vida espiritual,* or *Exercises for the Spiritual Life.*[4] Perhaps inspired by Barbo's belief in the power of meditation, Cisneros in his text focused on meditations and organized the experience of meditation into three traditional, successive stages, or "ways": the purgative way, the illuminative way, and the unitive way (discussed later in this chapter) (Sitwell, 137). In addition to prescribing his course on meditations, Cisneros also wrote a great deal about contemplation, a nod to the practices of the early Middle Ages (Sitwell, 138).

It is useful to compare Cisneros's text to Ignatius's *Ejercicios espirituales,* or *Spiritual Exercises,* for various reasons.[5] The first is that the Benedictine exercises were an important product of the movement toward religious reform, making them useful for identifying one style of sacred rhetoric in the early sixteenth century. In fact, the structure, if not the content, of Cisneros's exercises and of Loyola's exercises are consonant.

The second compelling aspect to this comparison is that Ignatius had access to Cisneros's work, albeit for a brief time, just before he started drafting his own spiritual exercises in earnest, suggesting the possibility that Ignatius's work was influenced by Cisneros's.[6] This brief exposure to the Benedictine work has engaged the imagination of many scholars, but for this study we'll note just a few historical details. Ignatius's path from courtier to the Benedictine monastery at Montserrat is well chronicled. And, as Gannon and Traub observe, "by the year 1500, God and his Church had become much smaller and man and his universe much larger" (153). In 1522, at the age of 31, recuperating from a serious wound received at the battle of Pamplona in 1521, Inigo (as he was known then) underwent a great deal of self-reflection and ultimately made a commitment to serve God. Ignatius traveled to the abbey at Montserrat to make his general confession and start his new religious life. The monastery at Montserrat, named after the "mountain [that] rises almost vertically from the valley below, in the geographical heart of Catalonia," served as a popular destination for pilgrimages (Boix, 7). While at Montserrat, Loyola was lent a copy of Cisneros's spiritual exercises as he prepared for his own general confession. Ignatius was at Montserrat for only three days and, though how much of Cisneros's exercises he read is unsubstantiated, it is known that he was in the habit of carrying a copybook in which he would take notes on texts that interested him.[7] So, during those three days, Ignatius could well have taken notes on Cisneros's meditations, or perhaps been influenced by aspects of Cisneros's rhetoric.

After Ignatius's general confession, he sat a prayerful night, for which he changed from his nobleman's clothes into pilgrim's robes and took up a pilgrim's staff. Ignatius was now formally dedicated to serving God (Ganss, 26), and his new vocation was symbolized by the pilgrim's clothes that he would wear throughout this part of his life.[8]

In 1523, while offering his service to the poor and otherwise largely in isolation in the valley near Manresa, Ignatius meditated on his own future spiritual path. During this year of service and meditation he came to reconsider an idea that he had once embraced—that he was a lone traveler—rejecting the company of first his brother and then travel companions, for fear that he would gain comfort from their unity, a comfort that was antithetical to his idea of living a saintly life. He set aside the idea of being a "solitary pilgrim . . . imitating the saints in prayer and penance" and realized that instead he was meant "to labor with Christ, amongst people, for the salvation of others." This movement away from the solitary influenced his manner of being in the world in many ways (Ganss, 31).

These meditations would be founded in the actual images and narratives of the Bible, not in fanciful elaborations of biblical themes. Also, "application of the will *and* affections" (my emphasis) would be acknowledged and engaged (Tugwell, 110). Ignatius brought to his work another aspect of meditation that was important to his beliefs; until now, contemplation was often considered the state of being close to God, while its apparent antithesis, being in the world, was considered a state of being removed from God. "For Ignatius, however, contemplation and action were to penetrate one another to perfect unity so that apostolic work for the salvation and sanctification of others was the informing principle of one's life and, consequently, the principle of one's striving for Christian perfection," Thoms M. Gannon and George W. Traub write. "Ignatius saw clearly the need for human experience in the world as the ground not only of knowledge but of that spontaneous affection without which any 'spiritual' love becomes thin and unsubstantial" (Gannon, 161). For Ignatius, action, which includes those activities of the apostolic life, are one means of achieving union with God (159).[9]

At Manresa, Ignatius was examining more than the efficacy of the life of a sole pilgrim; he had had experience sorting out, or discerning, good and bad spirits, "or sources from which the consolations and desolations had originated," and was now conceiving them as two paths, one of following Christ and one of following Satan—not as two different states of being, either good or evil. Ignatius's inclination to visualize a metaphor that allows movement (along a path—as is available to the pilgrim) and his preference for that over imagery involving two fixed conditions (the immovable poles of good and evil) is an early indication of his idea of agency. Instead of imitating Christ, as many of the saints had done, Ignatius was now seeing Christ as "the inspiring King sent by his Father on a mission to conquer the world, in order to win all humankind to faith and salvation; and calling for cooperators who would volunteer for this enterprise" (Ganss, 33).[10] "Conquer," "win," and "volunteer"; these are words of physical action and personal volition. This is the rhetoric of individual agency. In fact, fifty years later Robert Southwell, S.J., an English "martyr-saint" (Monta, 260), would write regarding the effect of the *Spiritual Exercises*: "I beeinge a Christain not onely my fayth and all mye actions proper there-unto ought to be different from the fayth and actions of infidels: But even mye vearye ordinarye actions of eating drinking, playeinge, wokreinge, & such like ought to have a marke & bagge [badge] of Christianity" (260). Very early in the disseminated, international life of the exercises, both affections and actions were considered aspects "of Christianity."

During this time, Loyola's thoughts shifted from entering a monastery to pursuing an apostolic mission—or becoming one who works within and among laypeople—and this is where things start to become sticky for him. In 1526, after a failed attempt to conduct his apostolic work in Jerusalem, Ignatius, at age thirty-five, decided to begin his formal education in order to become a priest. He learned Latin with young schoolboys in Barcelona and then attended the University of Alcalá in Spain. His preaching attracted a small group of people who became loyal to his teachings, some of whom would later become priests in the Society of Jesus. From this point on, Ignatius would involve other people in his ministrations. His orientation was becoming one of physical interaction untethered to a fixed location. His work, which included engaging people in religious conversation and directing them through early iterations of the *Spiritual Exercises*, gained the attention of the Spanish Inquisition, which was looking for those who were, among other things, antiauthoritarian. In his first appearance before Inquisitors, Ignatius defended himself and his spiritual exercises and was, as in two subsequent investigations, released.

One key to comparing the texts of Cisneros's *Exercises for the Spiritual Life* with Ignatius's *Spiritual Exercises* is the type of religious vocation each author embraced. Cisneros's approach is consonant with a popular image of the time, an image the author used in his text, that of the ladder of contemplation (64)—that is, an object that is man-made and must be maintained to be functional, that can be used only when stationary, and that facilitates movement that is only up or down. Cisneros's spiritual ambition is vertical and facilitates the path to heaven—an otherworldly goal not attainable by the physical body. On the other hand, the metaphor used by Ignatius in his autobiography is that of the pilgrim's staff (15); a staff can be sourced from the meanest of materials, must be easily mobile to be useful, and broadens rather than narrows one's directional options. Ignatius's rhetoric is earthbound and tailored to the exigencies of human agency. Later in life Ignatius would assert that "the workers of the Society should have only one foot touching the earth, the other always raised to begin a journey" (O'Malley, 19).

Between the uses of the two texts, there are some general parallels and divergences worth noting. Both the Benedictine exercises and the Ignatian exercises encourage the use of affective prayer. For example, each invokes the Passion as part of the last stages of meditation, asking the meditator to feel as well as witness the events (Cisneros, 34; Ignatius, 6). Each uses the same three-tiered structure of advancing through the purgative stage, the illuminative stage, and the unitive stage (Cisneros, 18; Ignatius, 10). In terms of differences, Cisneros's sequence was meant to take at least six weeks, though it may take longer, whereas Ignatius's program typically lasted four weeks, though the duration could be shortened or lengthened (Cisneros, 100; Ignatius, 10). The Benedictine program was designed to be used many times throughout a person's life, while Ignatius's process was conceived for a single use with subsequent daily practices.[11]

Cisneros, as a highly placed cleric, relied on extensive historical lineage in his writing. Like Ignatius, he opened his text with a prologue containing information on how the meditations would proceed. Unlike Ignatius, he supported his approach with references to the works of many other figures, including "the prophet David," the apostles "as a whole," St. Peter, St. Paul, St. Mark, St. Timothy, St. Augustine, St. Ambrose, the "holy youth Maurus," St. Benedict, St. Bernard, the "holy abbot Stephen of the monastery of Citeaux," choosing to stop short of listing "many more examples . . . to avoid prolixity" (22–23). He thereby established that he was a writer well acquainted with Church tradition. All of these references are cited in one and three-quarters pages. Subsequent chapters follow in this pattern.

Ignatius did cite Church and biblical sources but did so to a much lesser degree than did Cisneros. This could be a consequence of Ignatius's limited education at the time he first crafted the *Spiritual Exercises*—his rudimentary Latin could certainly have inhibited his access to extensive reading of Church documents—but over the eighteen years that elapsed between Manresa and his receiving papal support for the *Spiritual Exercises*, Ignatius gained access to exceptional academic and religious resources. At some point, the lack of extensive biblical or ecclesiastical references by Ignatius is probably the result of choice rather than circumstance.

The rhetorical processes that Cisneros and Ignatius invite their exercitants to engage in reflect and perpetuate the authors' different vocational stances and purposes. While Cisneros's authority is drawn from the ranks of the learned and lauded, Ignatius's authority is more basic and much less dependent on academic references. In fact, in the second point that Ignatius makes in his introduction to the *Exercises*, he concludes that "it is not abundance of knowledge that fills and satisfies the soul, but to feel and taste the matters interiorly" (7).[12] Cisneros's style is that of the well-placed contemplative; Ignatius's, of the itinerant pilgrim.

It is this kind of difference that yields an opportunity to engage in the analysis of rhetoric as "an embedded cultural practice and an inventive attitude which allows us to reflect critically upon those very same cultural practices" (Gross, 10). This is apparent in textual comparisons in which the use of rhetoric of emotion is markedly different. Cisneros does not completely refrain from invoking emotion and the senses when urging the reader to "feel thyself wounded by fear" (66) and to hear the "songs of sweetest melody" (150), but he does not regularly refer to the emotions or senses or make them an integral part of his process. However, Ignatius's goal is inextricably linked to emotion;

Ignatius "does not speak here of sins, nor of sinful affections, but of affections which are merely inordinate, because if these are got rid of . . . *a fortiori* sins themselves will be destroyed" (5). Using the senses to conjure and enrich an image during meditation is fundamental to the Ignatian process—it is through fully realizing emotion, or affection, that a retreatant is "prepared and disposed" during the exercises and through "daily exercises afterwards . . . to be secured and carried forward" (6). Each author acknowledges the retreatant's individuality; for Cisneros, that agency is, at best, a threat to the process, whereas for Ignatius that agency is the means to a fruitful retreat and a successful future.

For Ignatius, all five senses are tools of imaginative advancement—a protocol that is within the expression of the affective mode—and are referred to most expressly during the meditative exercise of composition of place (the culmination of each day's meditative work), wherein the exercitant conjures a specific location. If the place cannot be envisioned, as in the case of meditating on one's sins, Ignatius manages to maintain the theme of physicality through instructions to picture "that my soul is imprisoned in this corruptible body, and . . . in exile amongst brute beasts; I see my whole self, composed of soul and body" (53). Whether using the senses to enhance the realism of an imagined scene or to amplify the pains of a corruptible body, Ignatius encourages the greatest physical and emotional engagement available to the imagination. It is both a mental exercise that engages the person's body and a primer for entering into the world by every means possible. Through employment of the senses, the Ignatian process broadens the means by which a retreatant might successfully achieve this engagement.

For these two writers, how the meditator is allowed to engage the text is also indicative of how much personal volition is permitted. For Cisneros, the meditative process follows the protocol of the book of meditations as he has written it; the agenda of the exercitant, even under advisement by a director, is to begin at the beginning of the text and work through each point until the end, without varying the sequence (31). In Ignatius's exercises, which are also conducted under the supervision of a director, latitude is offered at every turn. For Ignatius, the written text is kept "breviter," as the exercises are "intended to be amplified by word of mouth," or through discussion with one's meditation director, and pursued by the individual in a sequence tailored to his or her particular style (Longridge, iii). Although later a type of instruction manual for the director of a retreatant is written and accepted by Ignatius, it is kept separate from the exercises, keeping the elliptical style of the *Spiritual Exercises* intact and easier to accommodate to individuals and circumstances. While both writers encourage prayer and meditation, one promotes following the written rules, the other following the tradition as it is understood at the time and between two people—in fact, the subtitle of Ignatius's work specifies that it is to "help who [it] is to give [the director], as of him who [it] is to receive [the retreatant]"

(3). For Ignatius, part of the nature of this individual journey is that it is not taken in complete isolation; this is the dialogue of a traveler and his or her companion, not a recluse.

Tropes, powerful rhetorical tools, are used differently by each writer. At the end of a day's meditations, Cisneros advises one to adopt the persona of "a slave that has offended his lord," as a precursor to a prayer that ends the day's work with begging for mercy (80). Ignatius also has his retreatant take on a subservient role, as a "servant to his master." Although the relationship between the servant and master is undeniably unequal, for Ignatius it occurs within the context of a colloquy, or conversation with God, toward the end of each meditation session, during which the person is advised, as part of the exercise, to seek "counsel" concerning his sins (58). Cisneros's construct and Ignatius's construct rely on substantively different relationships between the exercitant and God. In the former, the person's agency is limited to begging; in the latter, although the seekers are still in an inferior position, they are expected to make their concerns known to God in dialogue, an event drafted by the exercitants themselves, not by the director. Although God is the only path to the remediation of sins, Loyola leaves to the individual how one dialogues with God.

Of course, agency is made manifest not only in this dialogic process. In the Benedictine process, the tropes of the beloved and betrothal evolve as the person advances through the three stages of meditation. In the first stage, referred to as purgative, the exercitant is to achieve "an awareness of . . . sins, sorrow for the past, and a desire to expiate the offenses against God" (Hardon, 453). Once completed, the soul is like a mirror that was clouded and now is able "at last to see and know his Beloved, God" (Cisneros, 112). The person then advances through the "intermediary stage between purification and union," the illuminative phase, through which he or she seeks the "enlightenment of the mind in the ways of God and a clear understanding of His will in one's state of life" (Hardon, 265). Once retreatants achieve the final, unitive stage, where they experience a "more or less constant awareness of God's presence, and a habitual disposition of conformity to the will of God" (553), they can then seek the "Beloved" and take "his affection from creature love and turn it to love of the Creator" (Cisneros, 141). In other words, the process takes the individual from a state of not being able to see God clearly to one of directing love to Him. In fact, Cisneros in his opening and intermediary passages implies that the ultimate goal of the meditations is a state of being "made one with the blessed Spouse" (46). While this idea of union implies a great deal of parity, even in sixteenth-century terms, as compared with other possible imagery, there is one significant stumbling block; this moment comes with the successful completion of the three stages and, to quote Cisneros, "in this life we can never have full perfection in any of the three ways" (171). This union, the union of marriage, is ultimately unattainable.[13]

Ignatius's rhetoric casts a different conception of God's relationship to humans. Loyola is not inclined to use marriage imagery liberally or to associate certain phases of the meditations with different qualities of interaction with God. In fact, he segregates his recommendations regarding God's love from the three-stage process by positioning a meditative exercise on the topic at the conclusion of the four weeks of spiritual exercises (although, by convention, the meditation is often also worked into subsequent retreats) (Ivens, 169). Before launching into the details of the particular meditation, Ignatius asks that two things be noted: "The first is that love ought to manifest itself in deeds rather than in words. The second, that love consists in mutual interchange on either side" (154). While Cisneros's highest union with God, achieved through love, results in awaiting happiness, Ignatius has the exercitant compose a place where he or she stands before God, the angels, and his or her intercessory saints and, after reviewing God's gifts, offers all that God has given humans back to God, saying, "Give me Thy love and Thy grace, for this is enough for me" (155). This process ends, as in each part of the *Spiritual Exercises*, with a colloquy and an Our Father. While clearly the exercitant is supplicant and subordinate in this relationship to God, the level of agency necessary for a "mutual interchange," for colloquy (or familiar conversation) is greater than for a person who, as in Cisneros's text, celebrates that God has "drawn me from the world . . . giving me time for repentance" (118).

Agency is a seminal issue also in terms of the meditative process itself. Each work acknowledges that progress may be difficult or even thwarted at different points. For Cisneros, if our hearts are not moved to "contrition and devotion," we should "pray and sigh" (76). If that doesn't change things, we should not meddle with the meditations or the specified forms for enacting the exercises. Instead, we should consider that the difficulty may be a trial from God, who is administering "greater sorrow for sins which have been committed" (68). In the *Spiritual Exercises*, if there is no "interior movement" or "consolations or desolations"—that is, emotional engagement in the experience—then the exercitant is guided by the director through a series of questions and suggestions (called the "Additions") which advise on useful techniques for meditation (11). The section in which the Additions appear is subtitled "For the purpose of helping the exercitant to make the Exercises better, and to find more surely what he desires" (69). The Additions themselves, however, offer a great deal of latitude. They suggest tinkering with the amount of sleep, the type of food, and even the amount and source of ambient light during prayer to find a level in accord with the needs of the person (75). In Ignatius's world, obstacles to discovering God's will are often created by the individual, not by God, and are solvable by the individual with God's blessing; if a scenario exists that is not in the service of God, then it is up to the soul of the person to "to stir itself up and employ all its forces to arrive at the contrary of that to which it is wrongly affected" (16). For each author, the solution to problems within the meditations is within the power of the exercitant; however, Cisneros in his analysis makes those problems a test by God, while Ignatius makes them simple happenstance and manageable through human effort. For Loyola, the problems are much more human, more down to earth, more practical.

Of course, it is incumbent on each writer to define success. And, although we have not discussed in detail who would have taken these retreats, other than that they were available to both men and women, religious and laity, the idea of success would presumably have some importance to the Benedictine monks following Cisneros's text and to the Jesuit brothers and priests using the Ignatian method. Once again, each definition is consonant with the priorities of the authors, one from a relatively stable, monastic environment in which collective consensus and hierarchical authority are necessary, and the other from a more itinerant and mobile apostolic environment, which engages many kinds of individuals in the larger world. For Cisneros, each stage has its indications of completion—success at the purgative stage, for example, is indicated by achieving "fortitude, against all negligence; severity against concupiscence; and benignity against malice" (101)—and he warns at times that persons can lose what they have gained in one stage, which would thwart their advancement to the next stage. While it is unclear whether it is the exercitant, the director, or a combination of both who determine when a stage is successfully completed, it is still the case that advancing from one level to the next depends on achieving certain goals.

For the person pursuing the Ignatian exercises, there are no specified ends. In fact, when giving latitude in the second week to combine the meditations in a way that is comfortable for the retreatant, the instructions advise that the experience is "intended only to give an introduction and method, in order afterwards [for the exercitant] to contemplate better and more completely" (Ignatius, *Counsels*, 118). The goal is to provide practices that can facilitate a person's continual immersion in the meditative practices over a lifetime—a commitment that is ultimately self-defined and self-enforcing.

For Cisneros, "the contemplative is in general more perfect than the active" life and "the love of God should be such as to make a man despise the world entirely, and forget it completely" (194). Ignatius encourages "people to find God in all their activities, and he considered this preferable to long meditations" (Tugwell, 110). In fact, consonant with the mission of the pilgrim, Ignatius promoted the idea that "love ought to manifest itself in deeds rather than in words" (154). *Via contemplativa* versus *via activa*.

Both works are explicit about their goals. For Cisneros's reader—a Benedictine monk or a visitor to the abbey—the "desired end . . . is the union of the soul with God" (46). While he could mean a union that takes place after death, he exhorts the person to achieve the unitive stage, "which unites the soul with God and makes it perfect" (140); one aspect of of this phase is "withdrawing himself from all vanities and all things created" (141), making it seem that the union can be enjoyed in life. Although this union does not prohibit activity, there is a fixed quality to it, albeit of a sublime nature. Where do you go from perfect? In fact, there is no physicality to his image of culmination—it is the union of the soul and God. The life of the monastery can be in harmony with this goal—this is the world of the ladder of contemplation.

In Ignatius's exercises, the goal for a nascent member of the Society of Jesus or for a lay pilgrim is to "find the divine will in the ordering of one's life with a view to the salvation of one's soul" (4). Ignatius recognizes that that ordering occurs "always considering differing persons, places and times."[14] Ignatius does not propose that perfection is achieved, just that we can clear away our impediments to finding God's wishes for our lives. These are language exercises that support the process of finding God's path; these are a traveler's rhetorical tools (sacred and human) offered for a lifelong journey, not a destination in itself. Practitioners are set at the beginning of a course of action when they have deeply engaged these extended conversations between the individual and the divine. This is the material and the spiritual world open to exploration through individual agency, through the imagination, through the language of discernment, and with the pilgrim's staff in hand.

NOTES

1. See Ignatius, *Pilgrim's Testament* (often referred to as Ignatius's *Autobiography*).

2. Gannon and Traub also identify Thomas à Kempis and Bernardine of Siena as significant.

3. By the 1560s, outside of Belgium, which continued to accommodate Devotio Moderna practices for two hundred more years, Protestant and Catholic monarchs had quashed the movement (Van Engen, 194–95).

4. For more details, see the introductions to both Cisneros translations listed in "Works Cited" below.

5. For biographical information see, Ganss's *Ignatius of Loyola: Spiritual Exercises and Selected Works.*

6. St. Ignatius's text of *The Spiritual Exercises* was "revised and recast . . . until its printing in 1548" (Ganss, 33).

7. See Thomas Deans's essay in Part I of this volume.

8. St. Ignatius and the Jesuits would later become associated with the specific vocation of education, but Ignatius's primary work on the *Spiritual Exercises* predates that occurrence.

9. For other analyses of specifically Ignatian spirituality as understood through the *Spiritual Exercises*, see Gannon and Traub.

10. For more information about discernment, see Michael Ivens, *Understanding the Spiritual Exercises: Text and Commentary: A Handbook for Retreat Directors.*

11. See Cisneros (trans. Peers, 93) and Ignatius (trans. Longridge, 6). For more information about the daily practice of Examen, see Michael Ivens.

12. Unless otherwise noted, quotes from the *Spiritual Exercises* are from the Longridge translation.

13. In the closing paragraph of his *Exercises*, Cisneros, apparently contradicting a previous assertion, states that, if one follows the meditations diligently, one will be "united with Him by fervent love, and in that state he may most surely await the happiness which is to come" (333). How often this particular set of spiritual exercises might be conducted within one lifetime is unclear.

14. O'Malley, 18.

WORKS CITED

Bireley, Robert. *The Refashioning of Catholicism, 1450–1700: A Reassessment of the Counter Reformation.* Washington, D.C.: The Catholic University of America Press, 1999.

Boix, Maur M., and Kenneth Lyons. *What Is Montserrat: A Mountain, a Sanctuary, a Monastery, a Spiritual Community.* 3rd ed. Montserrat: L'Abadia de Montserrat, 1963.

Cisneros, García de. *Book of Exercises for the Spiritual Life.* Translated by and E A. Peers. Montserrat: Monastery of Montserrat, 1929.

———. *A Book of Spiritual Exercises, and a Directory for the Canonical Hours.* Translated by a monk of St. Augustine's Monastery, Ramsgate, U.K. Translator's preface, iii–ix. London: Burns and Oates, 1876.

Duminuco, Vincent J., ed. *The Jesuit Ratio Studiorum: 400th Anniversary Perspectives.* New York: Fordham University Press, 2000.

Gallagher, Lowell, ed. *Redrawing the Map of Early Modern English Catholicism.* Toronto: University of Toronto Press, 2012.

Gannon, Thomas M., and George W. Traub. *The Desert and the City: An Interpretation of the History of Christian Spirituality.* New York: Macmillan, 1969.

Gross, Daniel M. *The Secret History of Emotion: From Aristotle's Rhetoric to Modern Brain Science.* Chicago: University of Chicago Press, 2006.

Hardon, John A. *Modern Catholic Dictionary.* Garden City, N.Y.: Doubleday, 1980.

Ignatius of Loyola. *Counsels for Jesuits: Selected Letters and Instructions of Saint Ignatius Loyola.* Edited by and Joseph N. Tylenda. Chicago: Loyola University Press, 1985.

———. *Ignatius of Loyola: The Spiritual Exercises and Selected Works.* Edited by George Ganss. New York: Paulist Press, 1991.

———. "A Pilgrim's Testament: The Memoirs of St. Ignatius of Loyola As transcribed by Luis Gonçalves da Câmara," trans. Parmandanda R. Divarkar. In *The Writings of Saint Ignatius of Loyola.* St. Louis: Institute of Jesuit Sources, 2000.

———. *The Spiritual Exercises of St. Ignatius of Loyola.* Translated by W. H. Longridge. London: Mowbray, 1930.

———. *The Spiritual Exercises of Saint Ignatius: A Translation and Commentary.* Edited by George Ganss. Chicago: Loyola Press, 1992.

Ivens, Michael, and Ignatius. *Understanding the Spiritual Exercises: Text and Commentary: A Handbook for Retreat Directors.* Leominster: Gracewing, 1998.

Monta, Susannah. "Uncommon Prayer? Robert Southwell's Short Rule for a Good Life and Catholic Domestic Devition in Post-Reformation England," 245–71. In *Redrawing the Map of Early Modern English Catholicism*, ed. Gallagher.

McNamer, Sarah. *Affective Meditation and the Invention of Medieval Compassion.* Philadelphia: University of Pennsylvania Press, 2010.

O'Malley, William J. *The Fifth Week*. Chicago: Loyola University Press, 1976.

Sagarra, Josep M. *The Montserrat*. Barcelona: Editorial Noguer, 1954.

Sitwell, Gerard. *Medieval Spiritual Writers*. London: Burns and oates, 1961.

Studzinski, Raymond. *Reading to Live: The Evolving Practice of Lectio Divina*. Trappist, Ky.: Cistercian Publications, 2009.

Tugwell, Simon. *Ways of Imperfection: An Exploration of Christian Spirituality*. Springfield, Ill.: Templegate, 1984.

Van Engen, John. *Sisters and Brothers of the Common Life: The Devotio Moderna and the World of the Later Middle Ages*. Philadelphia: University of Pennsylvania Press.

ST. FRANCIS DE SALES AND JESUIT RHETORICAL EDUCATION

Thomas Worcester, S.J.

The extant letters of Ignatius of Loyola total nearly some seven thousand, most of them from his years as superior general of the Jesuits, 1541–56.[1] The letter, as an instrument of governance, and as a medium for exchange of information, played no small role in the nascent Society of Jesus. The letter was also a literary genre at the center of sixteenth-century humanist practices, practices that informed and were promoted by Jesuit schools. This essay will examine a single letter, but a lengthy one, by one of the best-known alumni of Jesuit colleges in the first century of Jesuit existence: Francis de Sales (1567–1622), bishop of Geneva, preacher, author of the bestselling *Introduction to the Devout Life*, and eventually a canonized saint.

Scholarship in recent decades has demonstrated how at least some French Catholic preachers of the late sixteenth century used the pulpit to exhort their hearers to violence. For example, in her work *Beneath the Cross: Catholics and Huguenots in Sixteenth-Century Paris,* Barbara Diefendorf explores how Simon Vigor and other Parisian preachers urged extermination of heretics. For these orators, Protestants were a cancer, a gangrene, eating away at the Church, the body of Christ, and indeed at the social and political "body" that was Catholic France. Nothing less than survival was said to be at stake. Those who attended sermons were told, Destroy the heretics, "wild boars" in God's vineyard, or they will destroy us; tolerate the evil they do, and God will punish us all (145–48). This was preaching as Counter-Reformation activity of the most virulent and violent kind. In a similar vein, in her book *The Politics of Piety: Franciscan Preachers during the Wars of Religion, 1560–1600,* Megan Armstrong shows how the Franciscan friars used the pulpit to advocate for radical policies in support of the Catholic League and its crusade against Protestants and Protestant sympathizers and any toleration of them.

Diefendorf is especially concerned to elucidate the mentality or "mental framework" that allowed the St. Bartholomew's Day massacre of 1572 to take place (177). Though this was an exceptionally bloody event—at least in number of persons killed—in France in the period of the Wars of Religion, those wars in fact continued well into the 1590s, if not beyond. Mack Holt's contribution to the Cambridge University Press series "New Approaches to European History" is *The French Wars of Religion, 1562–1629.* There Holt shows how the wars did continue, even beyond Henry IV's 1598 Edict of Nantes (which granted a limited measure of toleration to Huguenots), until Louis XIII and his minister Cardinal Richelieu had eliminated any military threat posed by French Protestants.

One question not discussed by Diefendorf is this: Were there preachers of moderation and at least some degree of toleration in late sixteenth-century Paris, or indeed elsewhere in France? From Diefendorf's book one could draw the conclusion that all French Catholic preaching in that period was an incitement to violence. How fair or accurate would such a conclusion be? While Diefendorf and Armstrong examine preachers who were members of some religious orders or, in Diefendorf's case, also some secular clergy, the question of preaching by bishops is not their focus, nor is preaching by Jesuits their concern.

This essay examines a 1604 letter of Bishop Francis de Sales on how to preach, a letter that I examine both as an case study of how a prominent alumnus of a Jesuit college promoted eloquence in the pulpit and as a significant piece of evidence for an agenda of pacification of French pulpit oratory in the early seventeenth century. A Savoyard, Francis de Sales had studied at the Collège de Clermont, the Jesuit college in Paris, from 1581 to 1588 (Ravier, 23–24). The report of Fr. Lorenzo Maggio, sent as an official visitor to the college in 1587, offers some insights into what this school was like in the time of Francis de Sales. With some fifteen hundred students, Clermont was divided into classes of grammar, humanities, philosophy, and theology; the later latter two were reserved largely to young Jesuit scholastics pursing the studies necessary for ordination. Not counting those Jesuit students, there were nearly some three hundred boarding students, though the majority of the lay students were day students.[2] According to Maggio there were then some eighty Jesuits at Clermont, priests, scholastics, brothers, and novices among them. Maggio encouraged and confirmed various practices extant in the Jesuit community, including what was known as distribution of saints of the month. Every month each Jesuit would pull from a container a slip of paper bearing the name of a saint. Throughout the month the Jesuit was to honor this saint by taking him as model and patron (Fouqueray II, 186–88).

The experiences of Francis de Sales in Paris would likely have exposed him, directly and at length, to the incendiary discourses Diefendorf has studied. But from his Jesuit teachers in those years he would have received other messages, other instructions, and been given other models to follow. The Jesuits would have given him a thorough training in classical languages, literature, oratory, and eloquence; as for pulpit oratory, it is very likely that panegyric of the saints played a major role in the Jesuit preaching he heard. A. Lynn Martin, in his book on Jesuit mentalities in early modern France, asserts that "Jesuits were extremely conscious of the important educational potential of the sermon" (Martin, 69). Preaching was the most "obvious" pastoral activity for Jesuit teachers in colleges, and such teacher-preachers strove to "overcome" ignorance and to teach people how to serve God (Martin, 69–70).

De Sales would also have been exposed to the *Spiritual Exercises* of Ignatius of Loyola, with their carefully constructed series of meditations designed to help those doing these "exercises" to make good decisions about the direction of their lives, and to live a life of gratitude in response to God's grace. The *Spiritual Exercises* were intended not only for clergy or members of religious orders but for all persons, of either gender, whether single or married. For an example of the writings of Francis de Sales wherein the influence of the *Spiritual Exercises* is obvious and abundant, the *Introduction to the Devout Life*, first published in 1609, stands out. It soon became a bestseller, in many languages.[3] In the *Spiritual Exercises*, Ignatius makes very few recommendations of reading, but one he does make is of the *Imitation of Christ*, an early fifteenth-century work attributed to Thomas à Kempis; at the same time, Ignatius recommends reading the gospels and lives of the saints (*Spiritual Exercises*, 100).[4] Two recent studies show the extraordinarily wide distribution of the *Imitation*, second only to the Bible in number of printings in early modern Europe (Delaveau and Sordet; Habsburg). It is safe to say that Francis de Sales had read the *Imitation* when he wrote his *Introduction*, whether he did so in response to Ignatius's recommendation or otherwise, for many of the *Imitation*'s themes are present in the *Introduction*.

After his years in Paris, Francis de Sales went to Padua to study law, 1588–91. While there, he took as his spiritual director, Antonio Possevino, S.J. (Ravier, 30). By then Possevino (ca. 1533–1611) was well known as a preacher and as a spiritual director. He had lots of other experience as well: He had founded the Jesuit college at Avignon, he had been the secretary to Jesuit superior general Everard Mercurian, he had been a papal diplomat in several countries (Boswell, 249). Possevino could number among his accomplishments mastery of the French language, unlike many other foreign Jesuits who spent time in France but did not do so well with the language (Martin, 56). In 1593 Possevino published in Rome an encyclopedic work on what Jesuit teachers needed to know; called *Bibliotheca Selecta*, it was a work that included detailed instructions on how to write letters (Boswell, 249–50).

The complete works of Francis de Sales include many letters, in several languages, with some of these letters of an administrative variety, many others more spiritual in nature, among them what one might call letters of spiritual direction. Viviane Mellinghoff-Bourgerie has argued that where the influence on Francis de Sales of Possevino's *Bibliotheca Selecta*, and of its recommended epistolary models and instructions, is most evident is in de Sales's Latin letters, letters between de Sales and Possevino among these (157).

A priest from 1593, the young Francis de Sales became an itinerant preacher in his native Savoy, especially in the duchy of Chablais, urging Protestants to return to the Roman Catholic Church (Fehleison, 53–99). Bishop of Geneva from 1602, he resided in Savoy, at Annecy, but also traveled frequently in the kingdom of France, and indeed part of his diocese was within France. In 1604 he preached a series of Lenten sermons in Dijon and met, in that context, Jeanne Frémyot de Chantal, with whom he would later found the Order of Visitation (Ravier, 119–29, 169–79). In 1604, Jeanne's brother, André, had recently been named archbishop of Bourges. In a letter dated 5 October 1604, the bishop of Geneva advised the archbishop of Bourges on how and what to preach (Francis de Sales, *Les epistres*, 12:299–325). It may be useful to recall here that the Council of Trent (1545–63) had identified preaching as central to the work of a bishop (Council of Trent, session 24, Reform decree, chapter 4). Many sixteenth-century bishops had not preached at all, so Trent's prioritization of preaching as an episcopal duty was no small reform effort.

Trent also insisted that bishops reside in and visit their dioceses. Visitation of the diocese was imagined, among other things, as a way to root out and correct failures of the parish clergy in particular. In his own actions as a bishop, visiting his diocese, Francis de Sales apparently did more than that; he also acted as a peacemaker, in a variety of ways. The English historian John Bossy in his fascinating study *Peace in the Post-Reformation* has shown how what he terms the "moral tradition" did and/or did not prosper in late sixteenth- and seventeenth-century Italy, France, Germany, and England. By the "moral tradition" he designates peacemaking efforts not between states or institutions but between feuding individuals and families. Bossy shows how some clergy, Francis de Sales among them, helped to bring such persons to reconciliation and peace (36–38). Bossy's study makes clear the not too surprising fact that peacemaking efforts were often met with considerable resistance. Love could conquer hatred, but hatred could be very tenacious indeed.

Bishop de Sales sent his 1604 letter on preaching to a newly named French archbishop of Bourges. Bourges was one of a dozen cities that, along with Paris, had participated in the St. Bartholomew's Day Massacre of Huguenots in August 1572 (Holt, 90–91). Thus sixteenth-century Bourges would seem to have been one of the hotbeds of fanatical anti-Protestant hatred. In the 1560s the Huguenots had for a time taken control of the town; though Catholics quickly regained control, hostility and tension lasted longer (Holt, 92). After King Henry III had the leadership of the fanatical Catholic League assassinated in 1588, Bourges was among the cities that embraced the cause of the League (Holt, 134). In the 1580s and early 1590s, the League sought to eliminate Protestants in France, if necessary by extermination. The League also sought to prevent, by whatever means necessary, the Protestant Henry of Navarre from becoming the king of France (Holt, 121–52). A measure of peace began to return to France after 1593, with the conversion of Henry of Navarre to Catholicism, and with his concession, in the 1598 Edict of Nantes, of a degree of toleration to Huguenots in France. All this had taken place only a few years before Frémyot's nomination to Bourges. Moreover, many Catholics, in seventeenth-century France, continued to resist the idea of tolerating 'heretics' in any way whatsoever (Dompnier). Though Francis de Sales did not explicitly discuss the particular history of Bourges in his letter to Frémyot, his appeals for love of Huguenots and for words of reconciliation in the pulpit seem well suited indeed to such a context.

In 1665, Pope Alexander VII canonized Francis de Sales as a saint. In the more than three centuries since then, hagiography has provided many images and stories of St. Francis de Sales as gentle, and kind. The assignment of sainthood status to any historical figure has a tendency to separate that figure from a specific context and to make him or her function in a more universal way, as an exemplar of timeless virtue. Yet those considered to be saints lived, like everyone, in a specific time and place, in a particular cultural, political, and religious context. In this essay I suggest that, in his 1604 letter to André Frémyot, Francis de Sales attempted to make preaching an effective instrument in bringing peace and reconciliation to a war-weary France, the city of Bourges included. I am not, therefore, debunking as a pious fraud the notion that Francis was a paradigm of gentleness and compassion; nor am I going to reveal some recently discovered archive that shows how he was, in fact, a bellicose demagogue and unrepentant murderer. I seek, rather, to demonstrate that the much lauded gentleness of St. Francis de Sales was his response to a very particular situation, in French Catholicism, ca. 1600. Though gentleness may well be a virtue laudable in many contexts, his gentleness was a strategy developed, lived, promoted, and advocated in a very specific set of circumstances.

Nothing is impossible for love (*il n'est rien d'impossible a l'amour*): With this hopeful declaration Francis de Sales begins his letter on preaching to André Frémyot (12:299). Bishop de Sales first treats who should preach. Citing the Council of Trent on preaching as the principal duty of bishops, he seeks to assuage any doubts Frémyot may have about his own abilities; de Sales asserts that God gives the episcopate special assistance in the task of preaching (12:301). He also points to the example of two Italian preachers, characterizing them as not very learned and yet great preachers: Francis of Assisi and Charles Borromeo (12:301).

The rejection of Erasmus of Rotterdam, by both Protestant and Catholic reformers in the mid-sixteenth century and beyond, has often been noted (Ozment, 299), though perhaps it has been exaggerated; in fact, Francis de Sales cites Erasmus approvingly. Continuing to reassure Frémyot that he is adequately prepared to preach, the bishop of Geneva states that "a great man" of letters, Erasmus, said that the best way to learn and to become learned (*sçavant*) is by teaching; thus by preaching one becomes a preacher (12:301). It is not hard to see, moreover, how Francis de Sales would have been very approving of much about Erasmus, perhaps above all his irenic nature and his vigorous critique of warfare and call for Christian princes to go to war only as a very last resort, and in very restricted circumstances.[5]

De Sales insists that a bishop must preach by word but also by the example of his own life. Thus among the things he must avoid are hunting, and superfluous spending on food and clothing. Before preaching a sermon, he should go to confession, celebrate Mass, and receive the Eucharist (12:302–3). When people comment on the sermon, de Sales cautions, it is better if they say things like penance is so beautiful and God is good, rather than things like the orator was so learned and spoke so well (12:305).

Citing his namesake once again, Francis de Sales points out that he writes on the feast of St. Francis of Assisi (4 October), and that St. Francis, in his rule for his friars, ordered that preachers preach on virtues and vices (12:305). The bishop of Geneva insists that preachers should teach their hearers to love and practice the virtues and to hate and flee the vices. The preacher should help his audiences, enlightening their understanding and warming their will (12:304).

Protestant reformers had excoriated Catholic sermons for their lack of focus on Scripture. Clearly well aware of such criticism, Francis de Sales defends preaching that relies heavily on the Church Fathers or on the lives of the saints. What, he asks, is the doctrine of the Church Fathers but explanation of the gospel and exposition of holy Scripture? The difference between Scripture and the doctrine of the Fathers is like the difference between a whole almond and an almond broken open, or the difference between a loaf of bread and bread cut in pieces to be distributed. The Church Fathers are the "instruments" through which God has communicated to us the true sense of his Word. As for the lives of the saints, there is no more difference between them and the gospel text than there is between music noted and music sung. What else is the life of the saints than the gospel put into practice (12:305–06)? Using another food analogy, de Sales cautions against too much use of what he calls "profane" histories; these, he says, should be used sparingly, like mushrooms used only to awaken the appetite (*pour seulement resveiller l'appetit*) (12:306).

Yet even as he seems to take on, as it were, Protestant opponents to Catholic preaching, Bishop de Sales is cautious and nuanced. By no means does he disagree with a principle that makes exposition of Scripture the goal of pulpit oratory. On the contrary, he affirms such a principle, but insists that it may be put into practice very appropriately and effectively in sermons that give much attention to the saints and to the Church Fathers. Francis de Sales is also very careful to caution against disputation in the pulpit. Admitting that Church Fathers and doctors have at times disagreed about the meaning of various passages of Scripture, he asserts that one should avoid mentioning opinions to refute them. One ought not to enter the pulpit in to dispute against the Fathers and Doctors (12:309).

De Sales does not necessarily oppose diversity of interpretation of Scripture. Indeed, he affirms what he calls the four manners or senses of the ancients: the literal, allegorical, anagogical, and tropological meanings of Scripture.[6] For Francis de Sales, one may include in a sermon several different interpretations of a text, provided that one praises them all and shows the value of each

(12:308–9). The four senses of Scripture provide great and noble material for preaching (12:311).

Sensitive to the needs and capacities of audiences, the bishop of Geneva urges Frémyot to explain things clearly and to avoid saying too much or too little. Having cited texts in Latin, the preacher should translate them into French and then show their value, paraphrasing in a lively manner. To teach virtue, use examples and stories, but choose beautiful stories (*histoires belles*) and present them clearly and distinctly (*clairement et distinctement*). Such examples have a marvelous force and give a great taste (*un grand goust*) to the sermon. But do not be so brief that the example does not penetrate your hearers or so long that it bores them (12:312–13). De Sales criticizes ostentation and flattery in the pulpit: The preacher should not use the ostentation of Greek or Hebrew words, and no preacher, especially not a bishop, should flatter his audience, whether it includes kings, princes, or popes (12:322).

Francis de Sales continues his list of things to avoid and things to do in the pulpit:

> Avoid the long sentences, the gestures, the tricks of facial expression, and the postures of pedantic preachers: All that is the plague of preaching [*la peste de la prédication*]. . . . . Speak affectionately and devoutly, simply and candidly. . . . Our words must take their fire not from disordered shouts and actions, but from interior affection; they must come from the heart more than from the mouth. . . . Heart speaks to heart, and the tongue speaks but to ears.
>
> [One should avoid] . . . the rustic action of some who bang their fists, their feet, and their stomach against the pulpit, who shout and bellow in strange ways, often not on their topic [*hors propos*].[7]
>
> —*Les epistres*, 12:321

If advice such as this suggests that the bishop of Geneva promoted a gentle voice in the pulpit, he in fact goes on to make quite explicit the need for preachers to speak with love and compassion, even for Huguenots: "I like preaching that inclines more to love of neighbor than to indignation, even of Huguenots, whom we should treat with great compassion (*grande compassion*), not by flattering them, but by lamenting them (12:323).

Moreover, de Sales insists that the preacher should show no discontentment in the pulpit, and certainly no anger (12:323). For preaching is "publication and declaration of the will of God," in order to "instruct and move" people "to serve the divine Majesty in this world in order to be saved in the other" world (12:323).

A bishop's love for his flock is the final theme developed in this letter. De Sales cites the conversation of Jesus and St. Peter in chapter 21 of the gospel of John, in which Jesus asked Peter, Do you love me? Jesus then commanded Peter to feed his sheep. Taking up once again Frémyot's sense of lack of talent or preparation, Francis de Sales asserts that nothing is impossible for love (*il n'est rien d'impossible a l'amour*); it is sufficient to love well in order to speak well (*Il suffit de bien aymer pour bien dire*); St. John always said, love one another, and with this phrase he entered the pulpit. Love cannot be silent when the interests of the one one loves are at stake (*L'amour ne peut se taire ou il y va de l'interest de celuy qu'on ayme*) (12:324–25).

Francis de Sales concludes his letter to Frémyot with an allusion to St. Paul's second letter to the Corinthians, chapter 5, verse 19 (on God's reconciling the world to himself, and not holding sins against the sinners). De Sales tells Frémyot: In the pulpit, speak the word of reconciliation (12:325).[8]

One might ask, at this point, whether Bishop de Sales put his own principles into practice, in his own preaching. This is a difficult question to answer, as what we have for his sermons are texts published after his death, by his disciples. We may have more of what his followers think he must have said, or should have said, than what he actually said. Rather than examine these texts, I shall turn briefly to one of the most important of his disciples: Jean-Pierre Camus (1584–1652). Consecrated by Francis de Sales in 1609 as bishop of Belley, a diocese adjacent to that of Geneva, Camus quickly became a protégé of his older episcopal confrère. Bishop Camus was an exceedingly prolific writer and preacher; his books include a six-volume work, first published in 1639–41, on the spirit of Francis de Sales.[9] By this time de Sales was a candidate for beatification and eventual canonization as a saint; Camus writes more as a hagiographer than a historian. Still, it is interesting to note the prominence, in Camus's account of the life and "spirit" of his mentor, of themes of gentleness, forgiveness, and charity.

The bishop of Belley asserts that, for Francis de Sales, zeal was a suspect virtue. Francis said that zeal was ordinarily impetuous; a bitter and ferocious zeal that pardons nothing is like the bad physician making illnesses worse. According to Francis, a gentle and gracious zeal (*le zèle doux et gracieux*) is incomparably more efficacious than that that is turbulent and tempestuous (Camus 1:106–7). Camus adds that in his own experience, Bishop de Sales excelled in this latter form of zeal; "extreme gentleness," which everyone loved and admired in him, he knew how to mix in with correction of others (1:107).

Camus also recounts the effect of a sermon his mentor preached in Paris, before an audience that included several Protestants. An entire family was converted, though the sermon was not preached against heresy (Camus 3:475). Bishop Camus adds that, in his own experience as a bishop and preacher, sermons on moral themes are well received by such persons; they are edified and become docile; later, in conversation, one may speak with them of debated points (of doctrine) (3:475). Perhaps de Sales was familiar with the advice that Ignatius of Loyola had given to Jesuits serving as theological advisors at the Council of Trent: "In your sermons do not touch on subjects on which Catholics and Protestants are at variance, but simply exhort your audience to virtue.... Awaken in souls a thorough knowledge of themselves and a love of their Creator and Lord" (Ignatius of Loyola, *Counsels for Jesuits*, 11).

Preaching could be a time-consuming matter in the sixteenth and seventeenth centuries, for preachers and their hearers. Sermons were often delivered outside Mass, as a separate religious occasion, typically taking place on Sunday afternoon (Bayley, 14). Sermons were not merely a few minutes long, but could last an hour or more.

In the early seventeenth century there were several prominent francophone Jesuit preachers, and their way of preaching may also have influenced the preaching of Francis de Sales even as his preaching influenced theirs. One such Jesuit was Étienne Binet (1569–1639). Just two years younger than the future bishop of Geneva, Binet first met de Sales when they were both students in Paris (Champagne, 156n31). Binet was a preacher, teacher, administrator, and the author of some fifty books. Devotion to blesseds and to saints, and imitation of these models of holiness, stand out among the themes in these volumes, including a book on St. Denis, martyr and first bishop of Paris (*La vie apostolique de Sainct Denis*), and another on a young Jesuit who had died in Rome while caring for plague victims (*La vie du bienheureux Louis de Gonzague*). Binet's published pulpit oratory includes an oration on King Henry IV, preached in the cathedral of Troyes on May 14, 1611, a year after Henry's assassination (*Recueil des ouevres spirituelles*, 787–809). In both his lives of the saints, and in orations such as that for Henri IV, Binet privileges the genre of panegyric, a genre of praise—in Binet's case, praise for those who show us how to live good Christian lives.[10]

Another French Jesuit preacher and prolific writer of the early seventeenth century is Nicolas Caussin (1583–1651). His work *De Eloquentia Sacra et humana*, in sixteen books, went though many editions and was used in Jesuit schools in France and elsewhere (Bayley, 32). Describing this as "a massive attempt to raise Christian preaching to the status of pagan oratory," Peter Bayley (66–67) stresses that Caussin describes Christian preachers as comparable to the best of pagan orators. Caussin was also for a time confessor to King Louis XIII, but he is perhaps remembered above all for his multivolume work *La cour sainte*, in which he argues that it is possible to be royal or noble and be a saint. On the very first page of volume 1, Caussin asserts that the court and devotion are not incompatible, and he speaks of "persons of quality" embracing devotion. Lives of saints make up parts of *la cour sainte*; Caussin also authored other panegyrics of holy persons, such as his life of Isabelle, sister of St. Louis, i.e., King Louis IX of France (*La vie de Sainte Isabelle soeur du Roy Saint Louis*). In this work Caussin lauds Isabelle's holiness and her decision to neither marry nor enter a convent (Worcester, "Neither Married nor Cloistered").[11] For Caussin, just as Christian preaching is in no way incompatible with or inferior to pagan eloquence, so too Christian holiness is in no way inferior to or incompatible with royalty and nobility. Continuity, not discontinuity, between "human" and "sacred" eloquence is what Caussin promoted, and such eloquence concerned not only varieties of public speaking but also the epistolary and the written and published word. Caussin's Jesuit confrères Coton, Binet, and Possevino, did not disagree, nor did Francis de Sales.

In conclusion: The approach taken by Francis de Sales to preaching, in his 1604 letter to the newly named archbishop of Bourges, was dramatically different from that of a Simon Vigor, or of other fanatical preachers of the late sixteenth century. Though Bishop de Sales surely sought to convert the Huguenots to Catholicism, his method was a preaching on vices and virtues, and a panegyric discourse of praise for lives of holiness, a discourse that could appeal to Protestants as well as Catholics. Indeed, the oratorical ideal he proposed to Frémyot was one in which not only was there no talk of exterminating heretics but all disputation and anger were to be put aside, in favor of love. Even if the gentleness and compassion of Francis de Sales earned him eventual canonization as a saint, and thus a universalization of the memory of his virtues, in his own historical context that very gentleness was directed at pacification of some quite specific, virulent hatreds, prevalent among French Catholics, in Bourges and elsewhere in France, in the wake of the Wars of Religion. De Sales would have learned Latin rhetoric from his Jesuit teachers, in the era of the Wars of Religion, but as a bishop his approach to rhetoric was focused on the French language and on rhetoric as productive of peace, not as an instrument of war, verbal or otherwise.[12]

De Sales was hardly alone among early modern francophone writers in producing a large number of lengthy letters. And in the decades after his death the epistolary genre served as a device for some of the most significant religious and political writings in seventeenth- and eighteenth-century France: One may think of Blaise Pascal's *Provincial Letters*, Montesquieu's *Persian Letters*, and Voltaire's *Letters on England*. These were not necessarily aimed at peace; for example, Pascal's fictional letters were designed to mock and discredit the Jesuits.

In his book *Four Cultures of the West,* John O'Malley identifies epistolography as "a distinct humanist genre," a genre promoted by Renaissance humanists such as Petrarch, Erasmus, and others (152). Of the four cultures O'Malley identifies, "poetry, rhetoric, and the common good" is the one in which he places letter writing.[13] For Francis de Sales, pulpit oratory could serve both the individual and common good of its hearers, especially if preachers heeded the advice offered in his letter to Bishop Frémyot, a letter conveying a message that would also reach a larger audience of ecclesiastical orators. It was not long after the death of Bishop de Sales (in 1622) that editions of his letters began to be published. For example, the letter to Frémyot was included in a volume of letters edited by a relative, Louis de Sales (*Les epistres du bien-heureux messire François de Sales*, 66–91). There were many editions and printings of this volume, a book of more than a thousand pages.

Whether Francis de Sales can or should, even today, be a model for preachers, writers, bishops, Jesuits, and perhaps in some ways for all persons, is a complex question.[14] There are surely massive differences between his era and our own, but there may also be some similarities between his context of the early seventeenth century and our own of the early twenty-first century. Central to de Sales's recommendations for pulpit oratory is the privileging of models of holiness; in rhetorical terms, panegyric is the (pagan) genre the preacher is likely to employ most often in his pulpit discourses. Praise and celebration of examples of holiness could encourage others to follow suit in their own lives. Imitation of Christ, imitation of the saints: These were the ways Francis de Sales thought that people could embrace virtue and leave vice behind; to lead a good life meant to follow saintly examples, to follow a path that had been traveled before, at least in its basic direction and goals, if not necessarily in all its details. While formal pulpit oratory plays a much smaller role in our culture than it played four centuries ago, the hunger for role models among students in high schools, colleges, and universities, and also among many other persons, is not small; such a longing and such a need have not faded at all. The Internet, not the pulpit, is where many may seek inspiration and meaning in their lives, and models to follow in achieving this. Can electronic eloquence be today what oratorical eloquence was in an earlier age?

NOTES

Translations are my own unless otherwise indicated.

1. For a selection of some four hundred of his letters, see Ignatius, *Letters*.

2. For a summary of Maggio, see Fouqueray, 2:184–211.

3. On the many editions of this work, see the translator's introduction to Francis de Sales, *Introduction to the Devout Life*, trans. John K. Ryan, 17–20.

4. I use here the standard numbers for sections of the *Spiritual Exercises*.

5. This may be most explicit in Erasmus's treatise of advice for Charles V; see Erasmus, 102–10.

6. These four senses are not original to de Sales but had been debated and developed from the early Church through the medieval period. See Grand and Tracy, 85–91; on the Bible in the seventeenth century, see also Laplanche.

7. Plague invoked as a metaphor, and *plague* used as a term for whatever brings distress, decline, and death, was frequent in early modern Europe, where outbreaks of contagious disease were many. See Jones, 97–127.

8. On clergy as peacemakers in early modern Europe, see Bossy.

9. My citations are from a nineteenth-century edition; see Camus. On the preaching of Bishop Camus, see Worcester, *Seventeenth-Century Cultural Discourse*.

10. Binet also published a work on eloquence, entitled *Essay des merveilles de nature, et des plus nobles artifices: Piece tres necesssaire à tous ceux qui font profession d'eloquence*. This volume appeared in many editions; see the discussion by Marc Fumaroli in a preface to a 1987 reproduction of a 1627 edition of the *Essay des merveilles de nature*, 9–50. Fumaroli explains how the *merveille* that Binet celebrates and encourages is the French language.

11. On Caussin, see also Conte. Another French Jesuit preacher, writer, and royal confessor is Pierre Coton (1564–1626), very much a contemporary of Francis de Sales. For an example of his publications, see Coton.

12. On the history of the agonistic nature of rhetoric, see Ong.

13. Like Francis de Sales, the playwright Pierre Corneille (1606–84) attended a Jesuit college in France (in Rouen, in Corneille's case). The role of theater in Jesuit schools was considerable, and it was another way of placing good examples of virtuous lives, and bad examples of vice-ridden lives, before the eyes of students. So too poetry, and Corneille became not only a playwright but also a poet. He published a version of the *Imitation of Christ* that he had put into French verse; see Delaveau and Sordet, 135–41. Jesuit interest in and emphasis on the saints also manifested itself in scholarly agendas. The Bollandists were founded in the seventeenth century as a group of Jesuits devoted to rigorous historical research on the lives of the saints; see Godding.

14. On some of the ways in which Francis could be a model today, see also my essay, "Do Good Leaders Abound in the Catholic Church?" Huffington Post.com, August 29, 2011, http://www.huffingtonpost.com/thomas-worcester/catholic-church-leadership_b_937801.html. Accessed January 31, 2015.

WORKS CITED

Armstrong, Megan. *The Politics of Piety: Franciscan Preachers during the Wars of Religion 1560–1600*. Rochester: University of Rochester Press, 2004.

Bayley, Peter. *French Pulpit Oratory, 1598–1650: A Study in Themes and Styles, with a Descriptive Catalogue of Printed Texts*. Cambridge: Cambridge University Press, 1980.

Binet, Étienne. *Essay des merveilles de nature, et des plus nobles artifices: Piece tres necessaire à tous ceux qui font profession d'eloquence*. 9th ed. Rouen: Jean Osmont, 1632. Reprint, with preface by Marc Fumaroli. Evreux: Association du théâtre de la ville d'Evreux, 1987.

———. *Recueil des oeuvres spirituelles du R. P. Estienne Binet*. 2nd ed. Rouen: Richard L'Allemant, 1627.

———. *La vie apostolique de Sainct Denis Areopagite, Patron & Apostre de la France*. Paris: Sébastien Chappelet, 1624.

———. *La vie du bienheureux Louis de Gonzague*. Paris: Chappelet, 1622.

Bossy, John. *Peace in the Post Reformation*. Cambridge: Cambridge University Press, 1998.

Boswell, Grant. "Letter Writing among Jesuits: Antonio Possevino's Advice in the *Bibliotheca Selecta* (1593)." *Huntingdon Library Quarterly* 66 (2003): 247–62.

Camus, Jean-Pierre. *L'Esprit du Bienheureux François de Sales*. 3 vols. Paris: Gaume, 1840.

Champagne, René. *François de Sales ou la passion de l'autre*. Montreal: Médiaspaul, 1998.

Conte, Sophie, ed. *Nicolas Caussin: Rhétorique et spiritualité à l'époque de Louis XIII*. Berlin: Lit, 2007.

Coton, Pierre. *Sermons sur les principales et plus difficiles matieres de la foy.* Rouen: Iacques Besongne, 1626.

Delaveau, Martine, and Yann Sordet, eds. *Un succès de libraire européen: l'Imitatio Christi.* Paris: Editions des Cendres and Bibliothèque Mazarine, 2012.

de Sales, Francis. *Les epistres du bien-heureux messire François de Sales.* Lyons: Vincent de Coeursilly, 1626.

——. *Introduction to the Devout Life.* Translated by John K. Ryan. Garden City, N.Y.: Image Books, 1972.

Diefendorf, Barbara. *Beneath the Cross: Catholics and Huguenots in Sixteenth-Century Paris.* Oxford: Oxford University Press, 1991.

Erasmus, Desiderius. *The Education of a Christian Prince.* Edited by Lisa Jardine. Translated by Neil Cheshire and Michael Heath. Cambridge: Cambridge University Press, 1997.

Fehleison, Jill. *Boundaries of Faith: Catholics and Protestants in the Diocese of Geneva.* Kirksville, Mo.: Truman State University Press, 2010.

Fouqueray, Henri. *Histoire de la Compagnie de Jésus en France des origines à la suppression (1528–1762).* 5 vols. Paris: Picard, 1910–25.

Godding, Robert, et al. *Bollandistes, saints et légendes: Quatre siècles de recherche.* Brussels: Société des Bollandistes, 2007.

Grant, Robert, and Tracy, David. *A Short History of the Interpretation of the Bible.* Rev. ed. Philadelphia: Fortress, 1984.

Habsburg, Maximilian von. *Catholic and Protestant Translations of the "Imitatio Christi," 1425–1650: From Late Medieval Classic to Early Modern Bestseller.* Farnham: Ashgate, 2011.

Holt, Mack. *The French Wars of Religion 1562–1629.* Rev. ed. Cambridge: Cambridge University Press, 2005.

Ignatius of Loyola. *Counsels for Jesuits: Selected Letters and Instructions of St. Ignatius Loyola.* Edited by Joseph Tylenda. Translated by William Young. Chicago: Loyola University Press, 1985.

——. *Letters and Instructions.* Edited and translated by Martin E. Palmer, John W. Padberg, and John L. McCarthy. St. Louis: Institute of Jesuit Sources, 2006.

——. *The Spiritual Exercises of St. Ignatius: A Literal Translation and a Contemporary Reading.* St. Louis: Institute of Jesuit Sources, 1978.

Jones, Colin. "Plague and Its Metaphors in Early Modern France." *Representations* 53 (1996): 97–127.

Laplanche, François. *La Bible en France entre mythe et critique XVIe–XIXe siècles.* Paris: Albin Michel, 1994.

Martin, A. Lynn. *The Jesuit Mind: The Mentality of an Elite in Early Modern France.* Ithaca, N.Y.: Cornell University Press, 1988.

Mellinghoff-Bourgerie, Viviane. *François de Sales: Un homme de lettres spirituelles.* Geneva: Droz, 1999.

O'Malley, John W. *Four Cultures of the West.* Cambridge, Mass.: Harvard University Press, 2004.

Ong, Walter J. *Fighting for Life: Contest, Sexuality, and Consciousness.* Ithaca, N.Y.: Cornell University Press, 1981.

Ozment, Steven. *The Age of Reform 1250–1550: An Intellectual and Religious History of Late Medieval and Reformation Europe.* New Haven: Yale University Press, 1980.

Ravier, André. *Oeuvres*. 26 vols. Annecy: Niérat, 1892–1932.

———. *Un sage et un saint: François de Sales*. Paris: Nouvelle Cité, 1985.

Trent, Council of. *Canons and Decrees of the Council of Trent*. Translated by H. J. Schroeder. Rockford, Ill.: TAN Books, 1978.

Worcester, Thomas. "'Neither Married nor Cloistered': Blessed Isabelle in Catholic Reformation France." *Sixteenth Century Journal* 30, no. 2 (1999): 457–72.

———. *Seventeenth-Century Cultural Discourse: France and the Preaching of Bishop Camus*. Berlin: Mouton de Gruyter, 1997.

BLACK ROBES / GOOD HABITS: JESUITS AND EARLY WOMEN'S EDUCATION IN NORTH AMERICA

Carol Mattingly

Jesuit missionaries were instrumental in initiating and assuring the success of many of the earliest schools for girls and women in North America. Although histories of "American" women's education often cite early Protestant women as "pioneers" in this cause, crediting them with the initiation of women's education, the French created schools for girls and women in New France much earlier. Even in the early nineteenth-century United States, Protestant pioneers such as Mary Lyon and Catharine Beecher successfully raised money for their own schools because of fears surrounding the highly successful Catholic academies operated by nuns and sisters (see Mattingly, "Beyond" and "Uncovering"). This chapter will discuss some of the more obvious ways that members of the Jesuit order helped to create interest in and assistance in establishing early instances of women's education in the New World.

The earliest schools for girls in North America were established by French missionaries. The "Black Robes" had arrived in Quebec as early as 1610; Ursuline nuns joined them in 1639, establishing the first schools for girls and young women in the Americas. Jesuits were also instrumental in the first school for girls in what would become the United States, the Ursuline Academy in New Orleans, begun in 1727, and they influenced significantly many of the early nineteenth-century schools for girls and women in the young United States.

The interest of many early European nuns in devoting their lives to the education of women and girls in the New World grew largely out of their reading of *The Jesuit Relations (Les Relations de Jesuites de la Nouvelle-France)*, reports from Jesuit missionaries in New France to their superiors, and from hearing the stories of returned missionaries. The *Relations* were "popular in the court circles of France . . . and assisted greatly in creating and fostering the enthusiasm of pious philanthropists, who for many years substantially maintained the mission of New France" (Thwaits, li). The *Relations* became popular reading in the Ursuline monasteries as well, where they inspired the earliest missionary nuns to New France, including Marie Guyart (Mother Mary of the Incarnation), founder of the first American school for girls in Quebec, as well as Madame de la Petrie (Madeleine de Chauvigny) and Mlle. De la Troche (Marie de la Troche de St. Bernard), important financial contributors to the nuns' efforts there. The Ursulines maintained their fledgling community with the substantial monetary donations they received when, in the words of the *Relations,* the Jesuit "Fathers set forth the poverty of the little convent, and the good the nuns were doing" (Greer, 23).

Subsequently, as nuns' missionary letters circulated across France, the models created by such women as Guyart increasingly fueled wishes of other young women to follow in the missionary tradition of New France. Marie Tranchepain, who led twelve religious women in community to New Orleans, had been inspired by Guyart's letters (Clark, 8) and came to believe that God had promised that a Jesuit would guide her in missionary work "in a strange land" where she would establish a community of Ursulines. This prophecy was fulfilled in 1726 when Jesuit Father Nicolas Ignatius de Beaubois sought help at her Rouen convent in establishing a group of Ursulines in New Orleans (obituary letter, quoted in Clark, 110; see also the obituary letter of Sr. Cecile, 114).

Although public dissemination of the *Relations* was suspended in 1673, extant copies continued to circulate, and Jesuits' "lioniz[ation] by the French public for their heroic exploits among the Indians of New France" persisted (Clark 13). During the eighteenth century, returning Jesuit missionaries spoke in the churches and circulated through communities in an effort to raise money for the missions. Such activity assured the continuing interest of numerous young French women in becoming missionaries to the New World. For example, an important French community of women settled on the frontier of the young United States, arriving in Missouri in 1818. Its leader, Philippine Duchesne, had thrilled to accounts of heroism and martyrdom in Jesuit mission life, especially those of Father Jean-Baptiste Aubert, who had been in Louisiana and the Illinois country as a missionary to the French and the Indians (Callan, *Philippine*, 22). Duchesne wrote her French superior in 1818:

My enthusiasm for missionary life was roused by the tales of a good Jesuit Father who had been on the missions in Louisiana and who told us stories about the Indians. I was just eight or ten years old, but already I considered it a great privilege to be a missionary. I envied their labors without being frightened by the dangers to which they were exposed, for I was at this time reading stories of the martyrs, in which I was keenly interested. The same good Jesuit was extraordinary confessor at the convent in which I became a pupil. I went to confession to him several times, and I loved his simple, informal manner of speaking, a manner he had used with the savages. From that time the words *Propagation of the Faith* and *Foreign Missions* and the names of priests destined for them and of religious in far-away lands made my heart thrill.
— Duschene to Sr. Madeleine Sophie, 1818; quoted in Callan

COMMON PURPOSES, DOUBLED EFFORTS

Once in the New World, many women religious worked closely with Jesuits to further their common educational mission. In order to instruct the American

Indians in the Quebec area, the Ursuline nuns, and especially Guyart, learned the Indian languages with help from the French girls in their school, some of whom had gained a measure of facility with the Indian languages, but primarily from the Jesuits, who had acquired the languages during their earlier years of missionary work with the Indians (*Glimpses*, 19). The women religious learned to speak the languages of the Hurons and Algonquins, and Guyart composed "a sacred history in Algonquin, a dictionary in Algonquin, a catechism in Huron, another catechism and a prayer-book in Algonquin" for use in the schools (101, 77). The nuns took responsibility for educating a large number of female boarders, both French and Indian, as well as day students. Seminarists, the name given American Indian girls who boarded at the convent, numbered as many as eighty during some years of the first half of the eighteenth century, and the number of French children was even greater (41). The nuns and priests instructed large numbers of adult American Indians as well, both women and men. The religious groups extended into other parts of Canada, such as Three Rivers and Montreal, establishing strong traditions of education among women; many of the schools and academies continue to operate today.[1]

Jesuits often played important roles in the establishment of schools for girls and young women in the United States as well. While the earliest communities of Catholic nuns settled in Catholic-friendly areas controlled by the French, after the U.S. Constitution guaranteed religious freedom, American Catholic women in the young United States began forming religious communities with educational missions. These communities were usually encouraged and supported by priests in the area, who sought educational institutions for girls and young women to complement their own efforts on behalf of boys and young men.

For example, in Washington, D.C., Fr. Leonard Neale, president of Georgetown College, helped found the Visitandine sisters; at the death of founding member Sister Ignatia, their most capable teacher, the Visitandines struggled to maintain the quality and reputation of their academy and began to recover only when Fr. Joseph Clorivière and Jerusha Barber, who became a member of the community, devoted themselves to educating the younger members whom Sister Ignatia would have taught. Clorivière also taught French to the students in the sisters' academy and helped the sisters to acquire up-to-date scientific equipment. Clorivière helped to begin and Jesuit Father Michael Wheeler helped to complete an Odeum, a magnificent music hall that also functioned as a science lab. The "Philosophical and Chemical Apparatus" Wheeler ordered cost the sisters $2,448.32 in 1828, and allowed the sisters "to demonstrate the theories of many useful branches of natural philosophy—such as astronomy, pneumatics, electricity, Galvanism, chemistry, Chladni's Acoustic figures, etc." In addition, they gathered "an increasing collection of minerals and Hauy's Primitive Forms assisted in the study of crystallography" (Sullivan, 74).

Such high-profile, up-to-date equipment helped to make the Visitation Academy one of the leading schools for young women in the country—one to which children of Washington's elite political community sent their daughters. The sisters were able to advertise accordingly. Their prospectus for 1828 read:

The ladies of the Visitation, with proper counsel, have sent for *apparatus,* by which they will be assisted in imparting an elementary insight, in at least fourteen branches of modern science. They have completed an edifice, named from an extension of the classic term, ODEUM, adapted for its reception, and for the annual public Examination and Exhibition. Within its limits are also comprised an extensive hall for recreation, bath apartments, laboratory, and mantua-room. To the basic subjects previously taught will be gradually added Algebra, Versification and Poetic Composition, Female Elocution, Popular Astronomy with the assistance of the newly invented Geocyclic of Delamarche, Logic, Ethics, Metaphysics, Natural Philosophy in its various branches, Anthology, the Spanish, Italian, and Latin languages if required, Vocal Music, the Guitar, and Painting on Velvet.

—*Georgetown Directory, 1830*; quoted in Sullivan, 75

As Kim Tolley has demonstrated, nineteenth-century academies for girls emphasized science, and the Catholic academies were clearly among the earliest and most advanced in this regard, assisted by male clergy in gaining the necessary equipment and knowledge for teaching with it. When the ecclesiastical superior of the Sisters of Loretto visited Europe in 1816, he returned with maps, charts, globes, and "philosophical apparatus" for the sisters' academy (Kelly; Boas, 6; Carroll, 60–64). The Jesuit-affiliated president of nearby St. Mary's College, Fr. William Byrne, instructed the sisters in the classroom use of these materials.

In addition to his assistance to the Visitation sisters, Clorivière actively promoted women's education among African Americans. He "helped the [Oblate Sisters of Providence] become accomplished teachers" (Morrow 184). In 1829, two Baltimore women, Elizabeth Lange and Marie Balas, both immigrants who may have escaped the San Domingo Revolution of the 1790s, founded the Oblate Sisters of Providence, the first African-American Catholic teaching community in the United States. While the early sisters had attained a rather sophisticated education before emigrating, they were unpracticed in teaching and found the English language challenging; they found Clorivière's support crucial. Their teaching mission was furthered in 1831 when Ann Marie Becroft, an experienced teacher, joined the community. At the behest of Jesuit Father John Van Lommel, Becroft had begun a school for African Americans under the auspices of Holy Trinity Church in 1827; her experience was critical to the success of the Oblates (Marrow, 106).[2]

Initiation of Catholic schools for girls was equally significant in other areas of the country. Many women's religious communities were formed in frontier areas where formal educational institutions were rare or nonexistent, especially for women; therefore, many of the early members had limited education and experience for teaching, despite the educational missions of their communities, and received educational support from the highly educated men in neighboring institutions. In fact, the founder and first ecclesiastical director of the Sisters of Loretto in frontier Kentucky instructed the sisters to include in their schedule, in addition to teaching, review of their studies and "attendance at all the classes taught by the President and other gentlemen" from nearby St. Mary's College, a Jesuit institution (Kelly 17). The prospectuses of both Nazareth and Loretto academies in frontier Kentucky explicitly state their close affiliation with men's schools, proclaiming their schools to be "conducted on the principles similar to those of St. Joseph's College," a Sulpician facility in nearby Bardstown, Kentucky, "and St. Mary's college" (see, for example, "Nazareth Female Academy," "Loretto Literary and Benevolent Institution," "Female Academy of Nazareth," and "Loretto Female Academy.")[3]

ONGOING SUPPORT AND AFFILIATION

The women religious often reminisced with fondness about the close affiliation between communities. Philippine Duchesne remembered:

> My community was animated by the spirit of the Jesuits, from whose Constitution they boasted their own had been drawn. The library was enriched with nearly all the works of Jesuit authors, because at the time of the suppression of the Society of Jesus three of its members found a refuge in our convent. During two whole years of my novitiate I read only Rodriguez, without tiring of it; and when we assembled for Vespers, I used to relate to my Sisters the lives of nearly all the saints of the Company of Jesus. That of St. Francis Xavier appealed most strongly to me.... I loved his touching appeals to the European schools to send him missionaries. How often have I not said to him since then, in my impatience, "Great Saint, why do you not call me? I would respond at once." He is the saint of my heart.
>
> —Quoted in Callan, 34

Both the Ursulines and the Sisters of the Sacred Heart were closely affiliated with the Jesuits from their inception, developing deep friendships in their communal missionary purposes. In addition, many siblings became members of the affiliated institutions. For example, Madeleine Sophie Barat, founder of the Sisters of the Sacred Heart, was sister to Jesuit Louis Barat, who gave her a classical education. He was instrumental in her relationship with Fr. Joseph Varin, who "received a bequest of a plan for a society of women, to be devoted to the Sacred Heart and consecrated to the instruction of children" (Frances, 63); the two Jesuits supported her in the founding and development of the community. Louis Barat later assisted Duchesne and other members of the Sacred Heart community in their preparations for and travels to the United States. This pattern was not uncommon. Many devout families contributed numerous daughters and sons to religious communities, and the siblings were naturally drawn to religious orders with similar constitutions and close ties.

Some communities of women religious were indebted to the Jesuits for educational curricula and methodology. Both the Sacred Heart *Plans of Study* and the *Reglements des Ursulines de Paris* were modeled on the *Ratio Studiorum*: "It has often been said that the Ursulines of the first house of the Order at Paris received their method of education from the Jesuits. This is very probable since three Jesuits, John Gontery, Charles de la Tour, and Pierre Coton helped to prepare their Constitutions" (Martin, 285). Marie de Saint Jean Martin has outlined the comparable history of the Ursulines and Jesuits as well as the parallel between the Jesuit *Ratio Studiorum* and the Ursuline *Reglement* to convincingly demonstrate the close affiliation.

The support was ongoing for many communities, with Jesuit spiritual and educational experts conducting workshops and conferences for the nuns. American orders affiliated with French-based sisters, such as the Ursulines and the Sisters of the Sacred Heart, received transcripts of conferences held in France. For example, Fr. Bartholomew Jacquenot, S.J., gave a thirty-day retreat for the early Ursuline nuns, and another Jesuit, Fr. Charles de le Tour, became chaplain for their convent at the request of Mme. De Sainte-Beuve, head of the Paris Ursulines. This tradition continued as nuns sought the help of the Jesuits in assuring their currency in curricular matters. Fr. Julien Druilhet, who had served as rector of the College de Saint Acheul at Amiens, conducted a series of educational conferences for the Sisters of the Sacred Heart at their motherhouse. He also adapted some Jesuit works to the nuns' needs; among these was the *Instruction for Young Professors Who Teach the Humanities*, written by Fr. Judde, a learned eighteenth-century Jesuit (Callan, *Society*, 732). These materials were made available to the nuns in the United States.

CONCLUSION

I don't want to suggest that the influence and assistance extended in one direction only. The Jesuits, too, benefited from their associations with the women religious. They sought the help of the nuns to teach girls and young women in order to further their own missions, to complement their own educational institutions for boys and young men. In many locations, the American sisters reciprocated by helping the Belgian and French priests to improve their English. In some cases, they provided housekeeping, laundry, and nursing assistance to the young men in the Jesuit colleges. Occasionally, impoverished though they were, they assisted newly arrived and destitute Jesuits materially.

For example, for the Jesuit community who arrived in the St. Louis area after the arrival of the Sacred Heart nuns,

> the kindly attentions lavished by Venerable Mother Duchesne upon the Jesuits when they arrived in 1823 were continued as long as economic distress made the position of the newcomers a difficult one. In straightened circumstances herself, the devoted superior of the Society of the Sacred Heart still continued to secure substantial aid for her Jesuit neighbors. Kitchen utensils, blankets, linen, food were either begged from St. Louis friends or furnished out of her own meager store. A gift of fifty dollars which she received was quickly placed in Van Quickenborne's hands. When he went forth on his missionary excursions he found the single horse that the convent could boast placed at his disposal while the chapel outfit he brought along had been provided for him by the attentive nuns. From a contemporary notice we get an intimate picture of Mother Duchesne pursuing far into the night her self-imposed tasks of making or mending the soutanes and parti-colored stockings of the Jesuit community
>
> —Garraghan, 1:112–13

Fr. De Theux reported similar assistance: "Ladies of Sacred Heart make and repair clothing and linen" (Garraghan, 132). In addition the nuns sometimes helped in fundraising for churches the Jesuits were building (Garraghan, 199).

Additionally, Callan suggests that while "educational aims and methods of the Religious of the Sacred Heart followed in great part Jesuit inspiration and models" (*Society* 750), at least in one case the influence was reversed. Callan convincingly demonstrates that Father Van Quickenborne "borrowed rather generously" from the Sacred Heart *Reglements* in formulating the regulations for Saint Louis College (751–53).

Nor do I wish to suggest that collaboration was always rosy. Occasionally women religious found individual Jesuits difficult to work with; however, especially for European women's orders, admiration (adoration) of the Jesuits learned in their youth helped them to set aside such difficulties. Additionally, the nuns often found working with the Jesuits far easier than working with diocesan superiors, who often seemed not to understand or appreciate their educational mission as did the Jesuits. Members of religious communities with traditions of educational ministry, such as the Jesuits and Sulpicians, especially those involved with the colleges and universities, shared an interest and purpose that others sometimes callously ignored. The sympathy, encouragement, and variety of supportive efforts proved crucial to the success of the sisters' missions. A clearer understanding of the Catholic influence on women's education in North America helps to revise our understanding of both women's education, which is far broader and more complex than our histories suggest, and of the Jesuit tradition, which included more assistance for and by women than is generally acknowledged.

NOTES

1. The Jesuits and the Ursulines had a far more positive relationship with Indians in North America than did associations established later by nineteenth- and twentieth-century governmental and religious groups. The relationship between religious and Indians was not coercive; attendance at Jesuit and Ursuline churches and schools was voluntary. The food provided for children in boarding schools and to adults present for daily instruction was clearly an incentive, as attendance at the schools was lighter during summer months. Many Indians left for the hunt, often taking their children from the boarding schools to accompany them, and returned when food and warmth were scarce. However, the Indians were free to attend activities provided by the religious when they found it to their own benefit. The religious demonstrated respect for Indian culture by accepting their dress and many of their customs, and by learning their language.

2. Becroft had operated her own school for a time, prior to the request from Fr. Van Lommel.

3. The Jesuits were not alone in their support of women's education. Other male religious orders assisted the educational mission of women religious in the early United States, especially the Sulpicians.

WORKS CITED

Callan, Louise. *Philippine Duchesne: Frontier Missionary of the Sacred Heart, 1769–1852*. Westminster, Md.: Newman Press, 1957.

———. *The Society of the Sacred Heart in North America*. London: Longmans Green, and Company, 1937. Print

Clark, Emily. *Voices from an Early American Convent: Marie Madeleine Hachard and the New Orleans Ursulines, 1727–1760*. Baton Rouge: Louisana State University Press.

"Female Academy of Nazareth." *The United States Catholic Advocate; or, Laity's Directory for the Year 1833*. 94–95.

Frances, Catharine. "The Convent School of French Origin in the United States, 1727 to 1843." PhD diss., University of Pennsylvania, 1936. Print

Garraghan, Gilbert J. *The Jesuits of the Middle United States*. Vol. 1. New York: America Press. 1938.

Glimpses of the Monastery: Scenes from the History of the Ursulines of Quebec during Two Hundred Years, 1639–1839. 2nd edition. Quebec: L. J. Demers & Frere, 1807.

Greer, Allan, ed. *The Jesuit Relations: Natives and Missionaries in Seventeenth-Century North America*. Boston: Bedford / St. Martin's, 2000.

Kelly, Theodosia. *Annals*. Sisters of Loretto Archives, Nerinx, Ky.

Kenton, Edna, ed. *The Jesuit Relations and Allied Documents: Travels and Explorations of the Jesuit Missionaries in North America (1610–1791)*. New York: Albert and Charles Boni, 1923.

"Loretto Female Academy." *Catholic Advocate* 4, no. 52 (February 1, 1840): 416. SCN Archival Center, Nazareth, Ky.

"Loretto Literary and Benevolent Institution." *Catholic Advocate* 3, no. 29 (August 25, 1838): 231. SCN Archival Center, Nazareth, Ky.

Marrow, Gloria. "Ann Marie Becroft." In *Black Women in America: An Historical Encyclopedia*, ed. Darlene Clark Hine. 2 vols. Brooklyn, N.Y.: Carlson, 1995.

Mattingly, Carol. "Beyond the Protestant Literacy Myth." In *Literacy, Economy, and Power*, ed. Julie Cristoph, John Duffy, Eli Goldblatt, and Nelson Graff. Carbondale: Southern Illinois University Press, 2012.

———. "Uncovering Forgotten Habits: Anti-Catholic Rhetoric and Nineteenth-Century American Women's Literacy." *College Composition and Communication* 58, no. 2 (December 2006): 160–81.

Morrow, Diane Batts. *Persons of Color and Religious at the Same Time: The Oblate Sisters of Providence, 1828–1860*. Chapel Hill: University of North Carolina Press, 2002.

"Nazareth Female Academy." *Catholic Advocate* 5, no. 8 (June 6, 1840). SCN Archival Center, Nazareth, Ky.

Thwaits, Reuben Gold. Introduction to *The Jesuit Relations and Allied Documents: Travels and Explorations of the Jesuit Missionaries in North America, 1610–1791*. Cleveland: Burrows, 1896–1901, xix–liv.

Tolley, Kim. "Science for Ladies, Classics for Gentlemen: A Comparative Analysis of Scientific Subjects in the Curricula of Boys' and Girls' Secondary Schools in the United States, 1794–1650." *History of Education Quarterly* 26, no. 2 (Summer 1996): 129–53.

The United States Catholic Almanac; or, Laity's Directory for the Year 1833. Baltimore: James Myres. SCN Archival Center, Nazareth, Ky.

THE CHANGING PRACTICE OF LIBERAL EDUCATION AND RHETORIC IN JESUIT EDUCATION, 1600–2000

David Leigh, S.J.

When Jesuits are asked about liberal education, they often invoke the *Ratio Studiorum* of the late sixteenth century as the founding document of Jesuit education. And it certainly is. But too often both their listeners and Jesuits themselves seem to think that the vision of liberal education embodied in this document is the only permanent legacy of Jesuits to liberal education. In reality, the Jesuits colleges and later universities that emerged from this founding document went through several radical changes as Jesuits adapted their vision to the changing contexts from the late Renaissance to the Enlightenment to the early twentieth century. Today the vision of Jesuit education is once again changing to meet the new situation of the beginning of the twenty-first century. I would like to revisit with you three scenarios from the past: first, in Italy in the late sixteenth century, a classroom in a Jesuit college run by the strict principles of the *Ratio*; second, in a Jesuit college in France in the eighteenth century, a classroom struggling with the rationalists and Jansenists; third, a classroom in an American Jesuit university like Marquette in Milwaukee around 1950. From these visits to the past, we will reconstruct the developing vision of Jesuit liberal education in each context as it is expressed in the curriculum, the methods, and the assumptions of those eras. Perhaps this historical review will bring us back to the future with a new understanding of what is perennial and what is novel in our own efforts to reinvent liberal education for the next century within the Jesuit tradition.

SIXTEENTH-CENTURY JESUIT COLLEGES IN ITALY

As students of Ignatius Loyola know, he insisted that Jesuit colleges follow the model of the University of Paris, which he attended after dropping out of the disorganized universities in Salamanca and Alcala, with their smorgasbord curricula and unsystematic methods. Thus, in our visit to an Italian college of 1590 (as in Messina, Padua, Genoa, Bologna, or Ferrara), we notice that the students are studying a variety of subjects, from Cicero's speeches to Aristotle's *Metaphysics*, all in a step-by-step order from the age of twelve to twenty-one. The *Ratio Studiorum*, which grew out of Ignatius's vision but was not finally formulated until 1599, called for a five-year curriculum that combined the Renaissance focus on the classical humanities (Latin and Greek grammar, literature, and rhetoric) with some mathematics and history, all leading to several years of integrative study of science, logic, philosophy, and, at the Collegio Romano or other universities or seminaries in Europe, theology. This latter emphasis on philosophy and theology, with its basis in the Aristotelian and Thomistic tradition, showed that Jesuit liberal education tried to combine the best of the past medieval education with the best of the contemporary renaissance learning. This integration of past wisdom with new studies would become one of the perennial principles of Jesuit liberal education. As several educational historians have noted, this was the first fully organized system of higher education in the Western world (Bowen, 2:430; Bowen, 3:9; Donohue, 39; Good and Teller, 215; Wise, 221).

Along with its quality of organized integration of the best of the old with the best of the new went several methods prescribed by the *Ratio*. These were based on the principle that the best learning comes from active self-education by the students themselves. Thus, the *Ratio* calls for a variety of teaching and learning methods to be used as needed throughout the five-hour days of the early Jesuit colleges. These methods included the use of short *lectures* with careful note-taking, to be followed by class *discussion*, to lead into frequent review through *recitations and quizzes*, to be reinforced through *written exercises* (both in class and at home), to be reviewed by *questions-and-answer* periods (questioning both of students by teachers and, after class, of teachers by students), and finally ending with the *prelection* (the explicit preparation by the teacher of the readings and assignments for homework by the students for the next day). The prelection was to alert the student to new authors, ideas, or difficulties in the reading and writing for the next class (Farrell, 182–84). Outside class, the better students were also organized into teams of tutors and recitators to help the slower students learn the material. This highly organized system of Jesuit classical colleges in the late Renaissance soon became the primary model for high school and university education throughout Europe, producing such famous pupils as Descartes, Molière, and even Voltaire.

What were the assumptions and goals of these colleges? On the level of liberal education of the mind, their main goals were rarely made explicit, except in such formulae as *eloquentia perfecta*, "developing an eloquent and mature" student or forming a person with a fully developed mind, emotions, and ability to communicate. But the wider assumption and goal was that such education was for the whole person—to develop persons who are intellectually, morally, and religiously integrated and responsible to become public leaders in a well-governed state. One early Jesuit educationist, Diego Ledesma, wrote around 1570 that Jesuit education has four goals: the practical goal of preparing for significant work; the social and civic goal of preparing leaders for society; the liberal goal of preparing a well-integrated person of intelligence, feeling, and eloquence; and, most important, the moral and religious goal of preparing a person for a mature relationship to God and other persons (Farrell, 171, citing *Monumenta Paedegogica*, 345). Thus, liberal education in the late Renaissance Jesuit schools was part of a larger plan for education of the whole person for a life of service to society and Church. The carrying out of this plan in the first half-century of Jesuit colleges was achieved despite many great political, ecclesiastical, and cultural difficulties (Carlsmith).

In this early Jesuit school curriculum, the main transitional subject was *rhetoric*, which was studied as the culminating subject in the last year of the "five-year college" before the transition to university studies of *logic*. As John O'Malley has written, "the system taught eloquence, for rhetoric was at the center of the curriculum; that is, it taught oratory, the power to move others to action—action in a *good* cause" (*Jesuit Education Reader*, 56). The teaching of rhetoric included study of the orations of Cicero and the *Rhetoric* of Aristotle and Quintilian, and was applied to the writing of Latin, Greek, and vernacular persuasive speeches on classical and contemporary topics. Supplementary authors included Demosthenes, Plato, Thucydides, some Roman historians and poets, and major Fathers of the Church (Farrell, 344). Students were expected to translate, memorize, summarize, and imitate speeches of Greek and Roman orators and then create and deliver in public their own speeches, with a special focus on "the artistry of the prose," "the elegance and adornment of speech," "the compositional unity," and other traits of argumentative writing (*Ratio*, 378). Teachers of rhetoric were directed to help students learn to interpret great oratory by exploring "the whole plan of the construction (namely, of the invention, arrangement, and expression) . . . —how skillfully the orator works himself into our good graces, how appropriately he speaks; or from what *loci* he takes his arguments for persuading, for embellishing, for moving . . . ; how he incorporates a means for creating trust through his figures of thought, and again weaves those figures of thought with the figures of speech" (*Ratio*, 382). Every two weeks, students would deliver their speeches in assemblies of other students, and every month students would participate in public debates or declamations on a controversial topic (*Ratio*, 390–91). All of this was aimed at "an education in perfect eloquence" (375). This eloquence was expressed in a variety of styles adapted to the variety of sacred and secular audiences to be persuaded by the speakers. As one commentator has said, "Jesuit eloquence as defined in the most authoritative Roman circles . . . amounted to a secularization of sacred oratory, as it were, coupled with a moralization of profane oratory" (Scaglione, 109).

This study of rhetoric was the crowning achievement of the Renaissance curriculum developed by the Jesuits in their early colleges and summed up in the method and goals of the official *Ratio Studiorum* of 1599 (Lynch). In fact, rhetoric presupposed and drew on all that the student had learned in the humanities, in grammar, literature, history, geography, etc. It was also taught simultaneously with the study and writing of poetry in order to develop the students' erudition and creativity as they learned how to relate their eloquent speeches to the range of human emotions. As Cicero taught them in his writing on oratory, the foundation of rhetoric was knowledge of human nature, both in the speakers themselves and in their audiences (Charmot, 263–78). This rhetorical education was not left behind when students went on to university studies. In fact, the first classes in the university curriculum that confronted students were in classical logic, primarily that of Aristotle (summaries of the first two books of his *Peri Hermeneias*). Thus, the argumentative writing that students mastered in their final college classes in rhetoric prepared them for the logical exercises and essays they wrote in their first university classes. This course in logic also prepared students for study of mathematics, science, and philosophy in the "arts and philosophy" phase of the university curriculum. As Farrell has written, "the Jesuit tradition has always been to give secular youth a training not merely in the humanistic branches but also in the arts—philosophy, mathematics, science. Some of the smaller schools, it is true, offered only the Humanities, but many carried the full arts curriculum, and a few, chiefly universities, added the theological sciences" (Farrell 339, 343).[1]

EIGHTEENTH-CENTURY JESUIT COLLEGES IN FRANCE

As we travel through the next century and a half to a Jesuit college in France around 1700, we notice several changes in the curriculum. The students are still studying the Latin and Greek classics as their primary texts in the high-school years and Aristotelian logic and Thomistic philosophical and theological works in their later studies. But they are also now studying history books, working over experiments in science labs, practicing plays or ballets in theaters on the campus, and learning to read and write in imitation of the French neoclassical authors (Harney, 197–98). As the context of the Enlightenment emerged—with its emphasis on mathematics and science, on historical and geographical discoveries of various cultures, and its development of the fine arts—so Jesuit liberal education tried to integrate the best of these new disciplines into the curriculum. As a result, the study day became longer and the length of years required to reach the master's degree greater. The students in France were also struggling, as their Jesuit mentors struggled, to find ways to integrate the metaphysics of the Aristotelian-Thomistic tradition with the new philosophical and theological questions raised by the Cartesian method and mechanistic worldview, by the development of Newtonian science and deism, by the discoveries of non-Western cultures and religions, and by the religious criticism of both the rationalists and the Jansenists. Although these educational struggles were not very successful in the political sphere, leading to the suppression of the Jesuit order in the late eighteenth century, the struggles produced some of the great names in the history of science—particularly the Jesuit mathematicians and astronomers, including Clavius, Matteo Ricci, Scheiner, Kircher, and Boscovich. Similarly, the teaching of rhetoric itself shifted in some French Jesuit schools from its traditional emphasis on a "golden age," Ciceronian profuseness of style to an emphasis on a "silver age," Senecan terseness. This latter style was more in accord with that of the neoclassical French writers such as Bousset, Bourdaloue, Fontenelle, and Voltaire (Dainville, 199–208).

As we notice the broadening of the Jesuit curriculum to include history, science, fine arts, and vernacular literatures, and the deepening of the questions in philosophy and theology, we also notice that the methods of liberal education remain remarkably similar to the self-educating practices of the late Renaissance Jesuit schools. Teachers are still lecturing, questioning, leading discussion, giving quizzes, requiring frequent writing assignments, and calling for daily review and recitations; students are still taking notes, asking questions, writing exams, doing guided homework, and giving frequent accounts of themselves in public recitations and debates. But now they are also learning the empirical methods through science experiments in labs, practicing their eloquence in vernacular plays and speeches (Bangert, 216–17), writing essays comparing the history of modern Europe with the history of Rome and Greece, and debating and discussing the relative merits of the philosophical approaches of Descartes and Aristotle. Both Jesuit mentors and students are caught up in the controversy between the Ancients and the Moderns. And once again, the Jesuit liberal education tries to integrate the best of the old with the best of the new (Bangert, 304–9).

As in the late Renaissance schools of Italy, so too in the Enlightenment colleges of France, the assumptions and goals are surprisingly the same—to produce the student with an integration of mind, emotions, and eloquence to become an effective public leader within the Church and within a society that would soon undergo revolutionary change. The goals of Jesuit colleges in France of this period had mission statements remarkably similar to the following:

> The chief Thing that is aimed at in this College, is, to teach and engage the children to know God in Jesus Christ, and to love and serve him in all Sobriety, Godliness, and Richness of Life, with a perfect Heart and a willing Mind: to train them up in all virtuous Habits, and all such useful Knowledge as may render them creditable to their Families and Friends, Ornaments to their Country, and useful to the Public Weal in their generation.

However, this goal statement was not from a Jesuit college but for the opening of King's College, New York City, in 1754, the college later known as Columbia University (from the *New-York Gazette,* June 3, 1754, cited by Herbert and Carol Schneider, 4:222).

What may be most surprising in eighteenth-century Jesuit education is that the course in rhetoric remained at the center of the college curriculum as the apex of humanistic learning and as the preparation for university philosophical, scientific, and theological controversies. Despite the addition of other subjects and the subtraction of some emphasis on Greek literature and poetry, the year of rhetorical study remained at the center of the Jesuit curriculum in the eighteenth century. This centrality of rhetoric appeared again over a century later when the Jesuits were restored and began to rebuild their colleges in France according to the new *Ratio Studiorum* of 1832. As John Padberg, S.J., has shown, the Jesuit schools in France in the nineteenth century were pressured to add to their curriculum material that would prepare students for the national exams for the BA and BS degrees (152). These additions were primarily classical French vernacular literature, some history and geography, and an updating of the science from the eighteenth century.

Despite a brief decade in which a few Jesuit schools bifurcated their curriculum into a humanities and a science track, most Jesuit colleges retained a curriculum centered on the humanities climaxing in the study of classical and modern rhetoric. The overall Jesuit college curriculum was modified "without sacrificing rhetoric and literary studies" (Padberg, 159). Using the traditional Jesuit pedagogy that called for prelection, active student learning, frequent competition, and public speaking and debates, the Jesuit schools sometimes extended their college studies from five to six years to preserve the classical rhetorical curriculum while somewhat accommodating the demands of governmental examinations, especially the demand for fluency in French rhetoric and literature. As Padberg says, "rhetoric inculcated, not only in Latin and Greek but also in French, the classical precepts of literature and literary style" (178–79). Once again, the university curriculum retained the foundational courses in logic that complemented the college courses in rhetoric. Although the controversies discussed in the public rhetorical exercises sometimes included nineteenth-century topics, such as political liberalism, the rise of historical studies, and modern philosophical issues, the use of classical rhetoric and logic remained central to the writing and speaking by the students.

EARLY-TWENTIETH-CENTURY JESUIT UNIVERSITIES IN THE UNITED STATES

Only a few of us can recall the curriculum and context of Jesuit universities like Marquette University fifty years ago. As we walk into the administration building in 1956, we learn that the liberal-education curriculum for the BA or BS degree requires a large amount of humanities and science—12 credits of English, 6 credits of history, 15–30 credits of foreign-language studies, 8–14 credits of math and science. But the demand for philosophy and theology is even greater—15 credits of philosophy and 10 of theology. There is even a speech-rhetoric requirement! All this adds up to a total of 82 credits of liberal arts for the BA and 69 credits for the BS degree, two thirds of the graduation requirement of 128 credits. The demands of the Enlightenment college still are there, except that the study of the classics in the original Latin and Greek is gone from the science degree, though required by the arts degree.

What is new about mid-twentieth-century education in an American Jesuit liberal-arts college? Simply put—the *major discipline*. Although each student must still spend two thirds of college on liberal education, he or she must also focus one third on a major field. Some students select a deeper study of one of the liberal arts or sciences, but many prefer to enter a professional field—nursing, engineering, business, or education. Liberal education has now been integrated into the great American experiment of pre-professional undergraduate education. This is a major change, the replacement of a classical core education in Latin and Greek with a professional field, but one that American Jesuit education has adapted, however slowly, to its overall mission and methods. Within the large liberal-education requirements that remain, however, we still find the study of rhetoric and logic. The two semesters of writing required in 1956 built steadily toward the use of rhetoric in argumentative writing in weekly essays. Rhetoric was also at the core of the persuasive oratory called for by the speech course. Finally, the first philosophy course that students took after finishing their English and speech requirement was a course in logic. For many Marquette students from Jesuit and other Catholic high schools, this college rhetorical education built on secondary studies in the Latin and Greek classics, literature, speech, and debate. The tradition of rhetorical education was not extinguished.

Have the teaching methods changed? Are teachers at Marquette University in 1956 still demanding self-active education of their students? Are they still calling for a variety of methods of learning, from lectures to discussion to papers to exams to tutorials, and so on?

The best teachers seem to be doing so still, but some have lapsed into the tradition of the larger American universities that have substituted lectures to large classes and end-of-term exams for the more self-active methods of earlier Jesuit colleges. In the liberal arts and sciences, especially mathematics, foreign languages, science labs, some literature and history courses, many philosophy and some theology classes, these active learning methods persist. Jesuit graduates of this period report over and over that the greatest benefit they got from Jesuit education was that they "learned to think." When pressed on what that means, many graduates say that their logic and writing courses taught them how to ask questions and to pursue them through critical thinking and logical analysis. And this habit of "learning to think" came from the insistence by teachers that students be able to participate in debates, to argue effectively in a term paper, and to answer difficult thought questions both in class and on long essay questions in examinations.

What did the Jesuit college of 1950 say of itself? What were its goals? Let us listen to the "statement of objectives" of Marquette University's College of Liberal Arts from a catalogue in 1956:

The purpose of the method of instruction used by the Society of Jesus is to lay a solid substructure in the whole mind and the character for any super-structure of scientific or professional study, as well as for the upbuilding of moral, religious, and civic life. . . . As a Jesuit institution of higher learning . . . its *ultimate objective* . . . is "forming the supernatural man or woman, who thinks, judges, and acts constantly and consistently in accordance with right reason illumined by the supernatural light of the example and teaching of Christ." . . . Its *immediate purpose* . . . is to help its students to view Catholicism as a culture, and to learn and appreciate the part which it has played in the building of western civilization, past and present. . . . The *specific objective* [of the BA and BS programs] is to provide a balanced cultural education as a foundation for a full, rich Catholic life. . . . The entire curriculum is to be integrated by an acquaintance with the social and religious factors which have entered into the making of western civilization and which contribute to the solution of contemporary problems.

Notice in this statement of 1956 the perennial Jesuit emphasis on *integrated* learning, on *formation* of mind and character, and on bringing together the *old and the new*. The context for such a statement, of course, was that of the emerging Catholic immigrant communities of the first half of the twentieth century. Such communities sought to retain the moral, philosophical, and religious values of the Catholic tradition, but also to produce educated leaders, from all levels of society and all ethnic groups, who could work to transform a pluralistic nation and postwar world. In response, Jesuit education began to expand its student body and its lay faculties.

With the upheavals of Vatican II and major changes in the world of the 1960s, the rise of new media and technologies in the 1980s, and the influence of globalization and a new world order in the 1990s, the Jesuit order and its educational mission gradually began a new transformation. However reluctantly at first, Jesuit high schools and universities heard and answered the challenge of the Jesuit world congregations from 1975 to 1995 to create an education that would explicitly focus on preparing leaders to bring "a faith that does justice" to a globalized, multicultural, and interreligious world. This call moved Jesuit and lay educators in the United States to make painful changes in their curricula, educational methods, and student bodies. In response to conferences at Santa Clara University in 2000 and Creighton University in 2013, Jesuit high schools and colleges have begun to include service learning, immersion experiences in world cultures, and international internships in their curricula. The response to Fr. Adolfo Nicolás's address to Jesuit higher educators at Mexico City in 2010 has moved many to address the complexities of globalization and international educational cooperation. The examples of radical adaptations in the history of Jesuit education from 1600 to 2000 that we have learned from this brief overview should help the advance of these changes to continue throughout the twenty-first century.

LIBERAL EDUCATION IN A JESUIT UNIVERSITY
FOR THE TWENTY-FIRST CENTURY?

What have we learned from this brief historical excursion that might help us to formulate a plan for liberal education for the new millennium? We have learned that Jesuit education is not static, but always in a process of development. We have learned that it retains several essential traits but also modifies them to meet new contexts and challenges. Among these essential traits are:

An integrated curriculum with the best of the old and the best of the new of each era

The use of teaching/learning methods that incorporate the active self-education of the students

A foundation of liberal education with four student goals: preparation for significant work; leadership for a more just society; integration of intelligence, feeling, and eloquence; and maturity in spiritual and social responsibilities

Among the changes we have seen in Jesuit education since 1600 are a variety of expanding curricula, an enlargement of the college and university years of study, adaptation of the teaching methods to contemporary contexts, and the various uses of rhetoric to assist students in their communications with their world.

Let me conclude by summing up my own thinking about this Jesuit history of liberal education—first, by providing a descriptive definition of liberal education, then by suggesting its basis in Jesuit spirituality, and finally by offering a series of challenges that we in Jesuit education must meet in the next decade.

Our review of the history of Jesuit liberal education shows that liberal education consists of several components. First, it develops a way of thinking that approaches any problem from many dimensions in an orderly way through the use of at least *six basic disciplines* or *modes of knowing*: historical, aesthetic-literary, mathematical-scientific, social-scientific, philosophical-ethical, and theological. As new disciplines emerged, Jesuit schools integrated them into the curriculum. Thus, liberal education in its curriculum and methods remained organized, integrative, and interdisciplinary. Second, liberal education is not only a structure and a method but also a content. Although this content has shifted throughout the past four centuries, Jesuit liberal education has tried to unite the study of the best authors, issues, discoveries, and texts of *the past with those of the present*. Thus, the canon of readings in a Jesuit core curriculum has retained Aristotle, Cicero, Thomas Aquinas, Dante, and Shakespeare while adding Descartes, Marx, Einstein, Hannah Arendt, Lonergan, and Toni Morrison. Third, the most persistent aspect of Jesuit liberal education, perhaps, is its use of *active learning methods*. In all ages, Jesuit colleges have been famous for their demand for active self-appropriation of learning by their students.

Fourth, Jesuit education has retained at least the remnants of *rhetoric and logic* as central to its foundational courses in writing and thinking. Although other universities have lessened the emphasis on writing and thinking, some Jesuit universities have recaptured it by revising their introductory courses. For example, Gonzaga University in the 1980s revised its first-year requirements to call for a three-course cluster of argumentative writing, speech, and logic, prepared and taught simultaneously in what is called the "Thought and Expression Block." Similarly, in 1990, Seattle University revised its Core curriculum to require that all students take a course in college writing: inquiry and argument, followed by (or taken simultaneously with) a course in the introduction to philosophy and critical thinking. Such courses were prepared by teachers in the English and philosophy departments, and common generic syllabi were agreed on by meetings of the two departments. Workshops were held in both universities to update teachers on these efforts to make rhetoric and critical-logical thinking central to learning at a Jesuit university. Likewise, Seattle University called for writing and critical thinking in all fifteen Core courses. In more recent years, as Anne Fernald describes in Part III of this volume, Fordham University has revised its core curriculum by centering it on the goal of "perfect eloquence" as the chief outcome of its liberal-education courses. (Other essays in this collection discuss many of the successes and failures in the teaching of rhetoric in the midst of the recent "core-curriculum wars.")

The basis for this liberal education, of course, can be traced to several principles from the *Spiritual Exercises* of St. Ignatius Loyola and from Jesuit spirituality generally. Three of these principles call for an education that is incarnational, that is transforming, and that is socially and historically embedded. As *incarnational*, Jesuit spirituality believes in the entry of God into the human condition in Jesus Christ; such a belief leads to the study of "all things human" as the place of finding God. Thus, in Jesuit spirituality (and correlatively in Jesuit education), there is no human struggle that is not an opportunity for finding something that can lead a person toward divine compassion. Jesuit liberal education has taught its students that to develop their human talents is to develop the very image and likeness of God within them. As *transformative*, Jesuit spirituality calls not for a quietistic or private religious or philosophical life, but for an education that prepares students for responsible service of others to transform a broken world, to make it into the kingdom of God, a place of justice and peace. As we have noted, from the beginning, graduates of Jesuit colleges were expected to think critically and to speak with persuasion, thereby to become leaders of society for a more just world. Finally, as *histori-*

cally embedded, Jesuit spirituality calls for its followers to adapt to and critique the time, place, and culture in which they move. Thus, our visits to four centuries of Jesuit liberal education have shown us several different but related ways in which such an education is embedded in history. In each period, Jesuit educators have tried to adapt to and critique the culture through a curriculum that retains the best of the old and inserts the best of the new. In each century, Jesuit colleges and universities have retained rhetoric and logic as the linchpins of their curriculum. As Gilbert Highet noted in his book *The Art of Teaching*, Jesuit schools were famous for two paradoxical traits—for highly organized and integrated liberal curriculums, and for their flexibility and adaptability to the culture and students of each era of history.

CHALLENGES TO JESUIT HIGHER EDUCATION TODAY

With the recent challenges given to Jesuits and lay colleagues by Vatican II in 1965 and by recent international Jesuit congregations in the past three decades, let me close with a series of questions that might begin a mutually persuasive conversation on Jesuit liberal education for the coming century. If John O'Malley is correct in his claim that persuasive rhetoric was the new mode of communication in Vatican II (rather than doctrinal definitions as in previous councils), then our rhetoric in discussing these questions may be more important to the future of Jesuit higher education than it was even in the past:

> How can we retain the best of the of Jesuit education, with its integrated liberal arts and sciences, and help it prepare students to transform their own culture and dialogue with other cultures? In particular, how can we retain, in all the disciplines, the centrality of rhetoric in writing and speaking and of critical thinking?
>
> How can faculty members learn the tradition of Jesuit education, incorporate some common texts, and assimilate active methods of teaching and learning?
>
> How can we integrate within our liberal-arts Core curriculum the study of both Christianity and other religious traditions in an interfaith dialogue?
>
> How can we continue to infuse in our faculty and curriculum an understanding of the structures of injustice and a passion for the service of faith that includes the promotion of justice? What is the role of rhetoric, persuasion, and the new media in this enterprise?
>
> How can we retain the centrality of philosophical and theological reflection in Jesuit liberal education but ensure that such reflection is in continual dialogue with the discoveries of the humanities as well as with contemporary social and physical sciences?

How can we maintain the importance of educating the "whole person" in Jesuit universities through cooperative education by faculty, staff, and administrators of the intellectual, emotional, physical, and spiritual development of students?

NOTE

1. It is difficult to determine how many Jesuit "colleges" were humanities schools and how many included arts and sciences, including philosophy. In Italy, in 1556 there were 21 Jesuit colleges and one university, the Collegio Romano; in 1750, Italy had 125 colleges and several universities. In France, in 1679 there were 83 colleges, but Jesuits taught in few universities. However, in the Paris province in 1627, 20 to 30 percent of students in Jesuit colleges completed the humanities and went on to study logic and science in these colleges. In 1750 worldwide, Jesuits taught in 621 colleges, 24 universities, and 176 seminaries, many of the latter including theology (Bangert 105, 214–17; Dainville 207; Farrell 197; Harney 201–2).

WORKS CITED

Bangert, William. *A History of the Society of Jesus*. St. Louis: Institute of Jesuit Sources, 1986.

Bowen, James. *A History of Western Education*. 3 vols. New York: St. Martins Press, 1972–81.

Carlsmith, Christopher. "Struggling Toward Success: Jesuit Education in Italy, 1540–1600." *History of Education Quarterly* 42, no. 2 (Summer 2002): 215–46.

Charmot, F. *La Pedagogie des Jesuites: Ses Principles, Son Actualite*. Paris: Spes, 1943.

Conley, Thomas M. *Rhetoric in the European Tradition*. Chicago: University of Chicago Press, 1990.

Dainville, Francois de. *L'education des Jesuites: XVI–XVIII siecles*. Textes reunis et presentes par Marie-Madeleine Compere. Paris: Les Editions de Minuit, 1978.

Donohue, John W. *Jesuit Education*. New York: Fordham University Press, 1963.

Farrell, Allan P. *The Jesuit Code of Liberal Education: Development and Scope of the Ratio Studiorum*. Milwaukee: Bruce, 1938.

Good, Harry G., and James D. Teller. *A History of Western Education*. 3rd ed. London: Macmillan, 1969.

Grendler, Paul E. *Schooling in Renaissance Italy: Literacy and Learning, 1300–1600*. Baltimore: Johns Hopkins University Press, 1989.

Harney, Martin. *The Jesuits in History*. New York: America Press, 1941.

Highet, Gilbert. *The Art of Teaching*. London: Methuen, 1963.

Kennedy, George A. *Classical Rhetoric and its Christian and Secular Tradition from Ancient to Modern Times*. Chapel Hill: University of North Carolina Press, 1980.

Lynch, Edward Joseph, S.J. "The Origin and Development of Rhetoric in the Plan of Studies of 1599 of the Society of Jesus." PhD diss., Northwestern University, 1968.

Maryks, Robert Aleksander. *Saint Cicero and the Jesuits: The Influence of the Liberal Arts on the Adoption of Moral Probabilism*. Aldershot: Ashgate, 2008.

Monumenta Paedigogica Societatis Iesu Quae Primam Rationem Studiorum Anno 1586 Editam Praecessere. Madrid, 1501.

O'Malley, John. "How the First Jesuits Became Involved in Education," 43–62. In *A Jesuit Education Reader*, ed. Traub.

Padberg, John. *Colleges in Controversy: The Jesuit Schools in France from Revival to Suppression, 1815–1880.* Cambridge, Mass.: Harvard University Press, 1969.

Pavur, Claude, trans. *The Ratio Studiorum: The Official Plan for Jesuit Education.* St. Louis: Institute of Jesuit Sources, 2005.

Scaglione, Aldo. *The Liberal Arts and the Jesuit College System.* Amsterdam: John Benjamins, 1986.

Schneider, Herbert, and Carol Schneider, eds. *Samuel Johnson, President of King's College: His Career and Writings.* 4 vols. New York: Columbia University Press, 1929.

Traub, George, ed. *A Jesuit Education Reader.* Chicago: Loyola Press, 2008.

Vickers, Brian. *In Defence of Rhetoric.* New York: Oxford University Press, 1998.

Wise, John E. *The History of Education.* New York: Sheed and Ward, 1964.

PART II

POST-SUPPRESSION JESUIT
RHETORICAL EDUCATION
IN THE UNITED STATES:
LOSS AND RENEWAL IN THE
MODERN ERA

THE JESUITS AND RHETORICAL STUDIES IN NINETEENTH- AND TWENTIETH-CENTURY AMERICA

John C. Brereton and Cinthia Gannett

The twentieth century saw an enormous change in all of American higher education, and in Jesuit higher education in particular: The four-hundred-year legacy of rhetoric and the classical languages was gradually effaced as a required subject at Jesuit colleges, just as it had been in the late nineteenth century at colleges elsewhere. Rhetoric, once the center of the post-secondary curriculum, retreated to the periphery. Despite this enormous change, in mid-century Jesuit and Jesuit-trained scholars, alone or in concert with others, produced a remarkable outpouring of rhetorical thinking. As Jesuit colleges were turning away from their traditional reliance on rhetoric, Jesuit-educated scholars joined with others to help create a rich revival of classical rhetoric in American higher education. Today, thanks in part to the work of many scholars and teachers whose Jesuit connections have gone practically unnoticed, rhetoric plays a significant role for the thousands who teach college composition, the single largest course in the American academy. In Part II, five prominent contemporary rhetoricians—Frank D'Angelo, Michael Halloran, Paul Ranieri, Mike Rose, and Gerard Hauser—detail this change through accounts of their own Jesuit education and their studies of important Jesuit and Jesuit-trained figures.

INVISIBILITY OF JESUIT RHETORIC

For Americans in composition studies and communication, the four-hundred-year tradition of Jesuit rhetoric can practically seem invisible. Scholarly awareness of the Jesuits' strong historical connections with rhetoric has flickered on and off over the years, sometimes helped by the work of Jesuits themselves, equally often by secular scholars, mostly working in the fields of intellectual history or speech communications, not in rhetoric and composition. There is a rich bibliography of books and articles on Renaissance to eighteenth-century rhetoric, some of which mentions Jesuit contributions. But when it comes to general historical overviews, matters change. A nice example of wavering awareness occurs in James Murphy's *A Short History of Writing Instruction*, an excellent introduction to the field, containing chapters by eminent scholars treating many different eras. In the book's second edition (2008), the Jesuits are barely present in Don Paul Abbott's chapter on Renaissance rhetoric;

in the third edition (2012), the space devoted to them has increased markedly. Similarly, in Bizzell and Herzberg's widely adopted textbook *The Rhetorical Tradition*, the Jesuit connection to rhetoric was barely mentioned in the first edition (1990), but in the second edition (2001) it receives two full pages, still far from enough, but clearly an improvement.

Theoreticians of rhetoric have made highly variable use of mid-twentieth-century Jesuit and Jesuit-influenced thinkers whose work impinged on rhetoric. The important Jesuit-trained scholar Edward P. J. Corbett in at least two articles pointed out the need to examine the impact on rhetoric of the work of Jesuit-influenced Marshall McLuhan, but since the 1960s little has been done to follow up on that connection. The specifically rhetorical thinking of Walter Ong—who, under McLuhan's direction at Saint Louis University, wrote his master's thesis on the Jesuit poet Gerard Manley Hopkins—has also lacked sufficient interpreters, despite the books that have been written about his historical work. And Jesuit pedagogy, which had been the subject of significant scholarship from speech departments in the period from the 1930s through the 1960s, has since then been relatively unexplored.

Ironically, Daniel Fogarty, himself a Jesuit, completely omitted any mention of Jesuit historians or theoreticians of rhetoric in his 1959 study *Roots for a New Rhetoric* (see below), and though he included the important work of Francis Donnelly in his bibliography, he did so without including the affix S.J. to indicate that Donnelly was a Jesuit. (This trait of omitting the S.J.—connected with Jesuits' reputation for worldliness and their taste in clothing, away from the usual clerical habits—has helped many to overlook the religious connections of some prominent authors and thinkers. The editors of this volume met a renowned Jesuit scholar who was completely unaware that Albert Jonsen, the eminent scientist who collaborated with Stephen Toulmin on an important book on casuistry, had been a Jesuit.)

In truth, the role of Jesuit rhetoric has not always been promoted by the Jesuits themselves, particularly from the mid to the late twentieth century, as the traditional Jesuit educational enterprise was more and more being regarded as outdated. As Jesuits themselves started doing doctoral work (they started late: As late as 1938, Holy Cross had no Jesuits with PhDs [Kuzniewski, 283]), they quite naturally enrolled in programs in the disciplines where rhetoric was missing. Consequently, the past two generations of Jesuits have been heavily influenced by the norms and outlooks of the modern university's scholarly configurations. Traditionally, rhetoric had always transcended disciplines, as the work of Ong, Bernard Lonergan, and McLuhan demonstrates, and so in a disciplinary world it had, until very recently, tended to get overlooked or boxed into a narrow disciplinary framework.

RHETORIC AT THE CENTER OF THE INTERNATIONAL JESUIT CURRICULUM

Rhetoric at Jesuit colleges and universities formed the center of the curriculum that educated many of the main figures of the Enlightenment. But owing to infighting and internal jealousies, the Jesuits were suppressed by the pope in 1773 and permitted to resume their work only in 1814. This break in continuity meant that the Jesuits were forced to close down and then to reconstitute their educational establishments, laboratories, and libraries all over the world. Never again would they attain the influence they had in the seventeenth and eighteenth centuries, though in Europe they quickly assembled a collection of elite schools once again, all of which would face constant peril from secular-minded governments that ordered a series of suppressions throughout the nineteenth century. Partly as a result of these suppressions, and at the request of local bishops and congregations, many Jesuits moved to America, where they established a series of colleges and universities, beginning with Georgetown in 1789. Intended to train an educated group among the small but growing number of immigrant American Catholics, these American Jesuit colleges would follow the European model, offering up to seven consecutive years of education in the humanities, including the classical languages and rhetoric.

During the nineteenth century, Jesuit authorities in Rome viewed America as mission country. In America, unlike France, Portugal, Spain, Italy, and Belgium, Catholicism was decidedly a minority faith, tinged with a foreignness that signaled it out to nativists, and Jesuits were often regarded as foreign intriguers. Noah Webster's *American Dictionary of the English Language* (1850) fell back on age-old slanders, defining a Jesuit as a member of a "society remarkable for their cunning in propagating their principles. Hence . . . [a] crafty person, an intriguer"; and the definition for the word *Jesuitism* was "cunning deceit, hypocrisy, prevarication, deceptive practices to effect a purpose" (Mahoney, 53).

EARLY NINETEENTH-CENTURY AMERICAN ATTITUDES TO JESUITS

Clearly the Jesuits, like the eighteenth-century Illuminati, held a special place in the minds of some people. Witness the following exchange between John Adams and Thomas Jefferson, who both depict the Jesuits as evil schemers, always plotting to achieve mastery. On May 6, 1816, Adams wrote his friend Jefferson about the pope's reinstatement of the Jesuits after the suppression:

> I do not like the late Resurrection of the Jesuits. [The suppression had just ended.] They have a General, now in Russia, in correspondence with the Jesuits in the U.S. who are more numerous than every body knows. Shall

we not have Swarms of them here? In as many shapes and disguises as ever the king of the Gypsies . . . assumed? In the shape of Printers, Editors, Writers, School masters, etc. I have lately read Pascalls Letters over again, and four Volumes of the History of the Jesuits. If ever any Congregation of Men could merit eternal Perdition on Earth and in Hell. According to these Historians though like Pascal true Catholicks, it is this Company of Loiola. Our System however of Religious Liberty must afford them an Asylum. But if they do not put the Purity of our Elections to a severe Tryal, it will be a Wonder.

Jefferson replied on August 1, 1816:

I dislike, with you, their restoration; because it makes a retrograde step from light to darkness. We shall have our follies without doubt. Some one or more of them will always be afloat. But ours will be the follies of enthusiasm, not of bigotry, not of Jesuitism. Bigotry is a disease of ignorance, of morbid minds; enthusiasm of the free and buoyant. Education and free discussion are the antidotes of both. We are destined to be a barrier against the returns of ignorance and barbarism. Old Europe will have to lean on our shoulders, and to hobble along at our side, under the monkish trammels of priests and kings, as she can.

—Cited in Schroth, 57

This Adams–Jefferson exchange had its parallel in Europe, though with much more virulent attacks from anti-Catholic, anti-monarchist republicans who tried to purge the Jesuits (and all other Catholic orders) from the schools, finally succeeding by the turn of the twentieth century, in most countries, with harsh anticlerical laws. The slow, powerful growth of European anti-Jesuit feeling reminds us that the campaign to rid European education of Jesuit dominance took a very long time, while in America the secularist, anti-monarchist republicans were in charge from the beginning—they were the people Americans call the Founding Fathers.

GROWTH OF JESUIT COLLEGES

Jesuit colleges drew many different students from specific areas: Germans in the Midwest, Irish in the East, and Italians in the far West. And thanks to European expulsions, émigré Jesuit faculty too would be drawn from different countries, as Gerald McKevitt writes:

St. Louis University was run by Belgians; French expatriates launched institutions in Alabama, Kentucky, and New York; and Woodstock College, the Order's national seminary in Maryland was the creation of exiled Neapolitans. German Jesuits, deported by Bismarck's *Kulturkampf*, founded five schools across the Northeast from New York to the Mississippi River.

In the Far West, Italians and other immigrant priests operated colleges in Santa Clara, San Francisco, Denver, Spokane, and Seattle.

—McKevitt, "Jesuit Schools in the U.S.A., 1814–c.1970," 278

In fact, it was uncommon to find many American-born Jesuits in most nineteenth-century Jesuit colleges. Then the majority of American Jesuits could be characterized as English-language learners, capable of coping in their native tongue, as well as in Greek and Latin, but speaking English with an accent. For example, among the Jesuit missions to the Indian tribes in the nineteenth century, federal inspectors criticized the French and Italian Jesuit instructors for their broken English. At one Indian school, Father Giuseppe Cataldo noted, "We old timers make even Indian kids laugh when we misuse English" (McKevitt, "Habits of Industry," 386).

In the late nineteenth century, the growing number of Jesuit colleges (there were twenty-two by 1900) were operating within an American higher-education establishment that was the scene of enormous change, spurred by a modernization of the curriculum following the German model. Newly formed departments proliferated, graduate-degree programs in the disciplines were begun, and professional and vocational programs flourished. Many prominent American colleges that had been founded on religious principles gradually moved away from their Protestant origins, dropping required chapel and breaking longstanding denominational ties, even if some retained links to their associated seminaries. Catholic colleges, and particularly Jesuit ones, did not follow this pattern, remaining true to their founding principles.[1] Small, poorly endowed, and often struggling to attract students, the colleges clung to their classical curriculum in an increasingly professionalized world. As Eric Platt recounts in his history of Southern Jesuit colleges, many were opened but did not long survive (Platt, 130–62).

Rome took the lead in resisting change in higher education. In 1907, troubled by signs of worldwide secularization, Pope Pius X issued the encyclical *Pascendi Dominici Gregis*, attacking what he called "modernism," as part of his effort to help the Catholic Church counter new ideas in religion and education.[2] In the early twentieth century, the Jesuits, forced to follow this papal ruling, strongly resisted educational change, stuck to their traditional classical curriculum with rhetoric at its center, refused to break up their colleges into departments offering majors (as other colleges had done), and retained the traditional Jesuit seven-year curriculum closely binding high school and college.[3] This attitude is what has led some to call the era from the end of the suppression (1814) to the Second Vatican Council (1962–65) "the long nineteenth century," a time when Jesuits and the Roman Catholic Church as a whole, traumatized by the French Revolution, turned their backs on all kinds of up-to-date thinking, countering it with Thomistic philosophy, a love for things medieval (Gleason, 128–29), and a host of prohibitions affecting almost every area of modern life.

PRESSURES TO CHANGE

But despite the Jesuits' efforts to retain their traditional structures and curricula, their efforts at maintaining rhetoric at the center of the curriculum were not to last. At the turn of the twentieth century, the four-hundred-year tradition of intensive instruction in rhetoric and the classical languages still dominated American Jesuit colleges, but that tradition was increasingly coming under attack. In an enormous updating, secular colleges abandoned their commitment to a classics-dominated curriculum beginning in the 1870s, a trend that accelerated in the late nineteenth century (Brereton, 21–25). By 1900, secular accrediting agencies, founded in the 1880s, began pushing hard, asking Jesuit colleges to justify their allegiance to the classical curriculum. Ironically, the first half of the twentieth century, when immense forces conspired to do away with the Jesuits' devotion to classical letters, was witness to a great revival of classicism in European and American high culture, from the music of Prokofiev, Stravinsky, Hindemith, and many others to Picasso, de Chirico, and Leger in painting and to Balanchine and Ashton in ballet. Real classicism was being extirpated from Jesuit schools at the same time that an almost universal homage to classicism was being enacted and praised as a true form of modernism.

In the 1890s, Harvard caused controversy by publicly refusing to admit graduates of most Jesuit colleges to its law school; President Charles Eliot (a chemist who was himself the product of a classical education) called the uniform Jesuit classics curriculum "absurd," comparing it to the educational programs of madrasas (Mahoney, 88–89; see Halloran, Part II). And among Jesuit colleges, the liberal-arts ideal was slowly but steadily being displaced by career preparation, more prominently in the West, to a somewhat lesser extent in the Northeast, where the more traditional liberal-arts view persisted. Though with very small enrollments by today's standards (Gleason [84] presents a chart showing only eighteen Catholic colleges with more than three hundred undergraduates in 1926), Jesuit colleges were expanding, like all other colleges, even if not as quickly as their presidents wished. Many students (and their parents) wanted preparation for careers in business and the professions, which more and more were requiring college degrees for entry, so colleges were pressed to provide practical coursework and increasingly specialized majors.

The Jesuit educational response to this change in student attitudes was mixed. Some colleges aggressively pursued new professional opportunities as the century progressed. By 1909, Marquette began offering graduate degrees in law and medicine, admitted women undergraduates, and opened a journalism-based College of Communication in 1910; Saint Louis University would be offered and would accept a complete engineering college in the 1940s. As Katherine Adams recounts in her chapter, Jesuit colleges evolved a distinctive approach to professional communication. But other Jesuits clung to tradition, seeing themselves more as stewards, looking after their students' faith and refusing to run risks associated with modernism. These traditionalists, according to Leahy, "maintained that Catholic colleges and universities should continue their long-standing emphasis on humanistic, collegiate education and resist trends toward research, graduate schools, and professional programs" (34). The struggle between traditionalists and modernists can be understood as a conflict between what the Jesuits called "class men" and "branch men." Class men concerned themselves with every item on the highly restricted list of subjects a student would take each year, no doubt because Jesuits were trained in almost all the subjects across the curriculum. The class men abhorred electives. Opposed to them were those who preferred to specialize in a particular branch of learning, be it mathematics, history, or one of the new social sciences, such as sociology or anthropology, and welcomed electives (Gleason, 55–61). Over the first half of the twentieth century, Jesuit higher education, as secular higher education had a generation earlier, slowly but steadily moved away from class men and toward the different branches of knowledge. The stress on the class, most prominent in the East, meant that some Jesuit colleges had a curriculum that was coherent but ran the danger of seeming too parochial, too closed in, and losing a chance to educate some of the brightest American Catholic students.[4] Already, by 1900, Harvard, with a curriculum that was almost entirely elective, enrolled more Catholics than any other American college (Mahoney, 103). Still, the traditionalists saw themselves primarily as teachers, and their scholarship as applied. In the first half of the twentieth century, American Jesuits were all required to undergo up to twelve years of educational studies, but few earned PhDs, and fewer still published. (Leahy [42] reports that New England Jesuits held twelve PhDs in 1932 and that New York Jesuits held fifteen.) Rhetorical studies, long a teaching field that transcended disciplinary boundaries, rather than a field that encouraged original scholarly research, produced little published work. (It is hard to see where a Jesuit who wanted to conduct research or to earn a PhD in rhetoric could go. There was only one doctoral program in America specializing in rhetoric, Fred Newton Scott's at the University of Michigan, and that program—never very hospitable to classical rhetoric—was closed in the early 1920s.)

AMERICAN JESUIT RHETORICS

The venerable textbook by Charles Coppens, S.J., *A Practical Introduction to English Rhetoric* (1880), which Steven Mailloux discusses in the next chapter, was a breakthrough when first published, since it addressed rhetorical issues in the vernacular, not Latin; it still dominated teaching at Jesuit colleges, having replaced Kleutgen's Latin *Ars Dicendi* (Kitzhaber termed Coppens's book "anachronistic," 88; Wozniak traces its use at Fordham and Georgetown, 270). Bizzell's account of *Principles of Jesuit Education in Practice* (1934), another book by a Jesuit rhetorician, Francis P. Donnelly S.J., encapsulates his profoundly conservative outlook (Part I). Donnelly, a professor at a number of Jesuit colleges, wrote a series of books on rhetoric that were quite popular among Jesuits but do not seem to have been widely adopted elsewhere. His *Model English* (1919), *The Art of Interesting: Its Theory and Practice* (1920), and *Persuasive Speech: An Art of Rhetoric for College* (1931) are still listed in the catalogues of many Jesuit college libraries but are not found in such numbers in the libraries of other colleges. Edward P. J. Corbett was alone in noting that Donnelly was the only textbook writer to make use of the *topoi* of classical rhetoric in the first half of the twentieth century (1965, 380). Donnelly did participate in the larger educational world; he issued a ringing call for a traditional attitude toward composition (comparing it to science) at the 1934 conference of the National Council of Teachers of English in Washington, D.C. (*English Journal*, 315–16), and his rhetoric textbook *Persuasive Speech* was reviewed favorably, if somewhat condescendingly, in 1932 by the eminent University of Chicago classicist Paul Shorey in *Classical Philology*, but the book does not seem to have traveled outside of the relatively small orbit of Jesuit colleges.[5]

From 1900 to 1960, the classics- and rhetoric-centered curriculum died a slow death at Jesuit colleges, even in the Northeast. Holy Cross (see Halloran, Part II), the last holdout, dropped Greek as a graduation requirement in 1936 and Latin in 1959 (Bizzell, Part I). Latin and Greek persisted as majors with declining enrollments, but their days as universal requirements were over.

RHETORIC REPLACED BY PHILOSOPHY AND RELIGION

An examination of Loyola College of Maryland's undergraduate course requirements in classical languages clearly illustrates their dominance in 1855 and their dramatic decline over the generation 1895–1928. (See accompanying table.) It is easy to see that as classical languages and rhetoric receded, religion and religious-influenced philosophy (i.e., Thomism) began to take their place, with the largest percentage increase being in religion, a relative newcomer to the curriculum. Traditional Jesuit educational principles had always fostered religious practices in the extracurriculum, and relied on classical literature to address philosophical and moral issues in colleges; part of the attraction of great literature was that it foregrounded ethical questions and demonstrated the overwhelming importance of morality. As Gleason put it, "surprising as it may seem— . . . theology, or religion as such, had not attained the status of a full-fledged academic subject in Catholic colleges in the United States" (142). But once the classical curriculum was downgraded, religion (and, to a lesser extent, philosophy, which had often had a modest presence) rushed to fill the vacuum with their own newly minted required courses (Tetlow, 105–23). Loyola thus began to offer additional coursework and to appoint faculty in philosophy; it also began to require that undergraduates take theology, which had always been seen as a highly specialized professional subject offered only to graduate students preparing for the priesthood. As Gleason recounts it, religious studies (including the Bible and extending to the practical ways of living a moral life) and theology (the scientific study of religion, based on strict philosophical principles) represented widely divergent ways of coming at the subject, each with its own fervent adherents. It was a struggle that would mark Catholic higher education for the rest of the twentieth century, and it has still not been resolved (143–45). It is unknown how many Jesuits simply moved over from teaching classics and rhetoric to teaching theology, philosophy, or religion; they were, of course, trained in all three.

LOYOLA MARYLAND A.B. CURRICULUM, 1855–1928
1855: "PRECEPTS OF RHETORIC" TAUGHT WITH COMPOSITION THROUGHOUT
ALL FOUR YEARS.

Subject as a Percentage of A.B. Curriculum, 1895–1928

	1895	1912	1928
Latin	22	16	12 (Optional for some courses)
Mathematics	21	4	
Greek	15	10	(10) (Could be substituted for Mathematics)
English	13	7	9
History	0	7	4
Philosophy	12	23	23
Science	10	14	10
Languages	3	2	5
Religion	2	9	10 (No credit. Required only for Catholics)
Elocution	2	2	1 (No credit. Required only for Catholics)
Electives	0	6	15

Source: Varga, 225

TO REINTEGRATE THE COLLEGE CURRICULUM

In the first half of the twentieth century at most Jesuit colleges, rhetoric as an advanced course often disappeared, tied as it was to the classics curriculum. In its place, first-year composition was often left to bear much of the burden of teaching students to write effectively, the only required college course left that concentrated on producing excellent prose. What was lost was not only a thorough training in written and spoken communication. Rhetorical training had provided a center for the Jesuit curriculum, a means of integrating all instruction. As disciplines developed and rhetoric disappeared in the early twentieth century, faculty at all colleges—secular and religious alike—increasingly felt the absence of a common center to the curriculum. At Columbia and the University of Chicago, to name two prominent examples, concerned professors worked hard to create a trans-disciplinary framework, a common core, or what came to be called "general education," a means of tying together what had become dispersed as disparate subjects each in its own silo. Jesuit colleges felt this lack of integration keenly, having just given up the integrating force of rhetoric. Some Jesuits tried to fill the gap with coursework in philosophy and theology, requiring undergraduates for the first time to take courses in both. In the 1930s one Jesuit, William McGucken of Saint Louis University, chaired a National Catholic Educational Association committee charged with creating a consensus about what the curriculum of a Catholic liberal-arts education should contain. This turned out to be what Gleason calls a "long but ultimately fruitless endeavor" (189), in some ways similar to the failed series of attempts to determine the content of the religious- studies curriculum as opposed to the theology curriculum. Jesuits themselves could not agree on a common Core curriculum. It is clear that rhetoric's integrative force was missed.

RHETORIC'S SURVIVAL IN SPEECH

Rhetoric instruction survived nationally in speech departments, where it formed a small part of the public-speaking curriculum after 1914, when the discipline now known as communications (then called "speech") split off from English studies. The newly formed discipline of Speech emphasized the spoken language and favored social-scientific research into how oral language was used, a curriculum that emphasized "all the subjects that rely primarily on spoken language—public speaking, speech science, speech correction, oral interpretation, and dramatics" (Corbett, "Cornell School," 293). By 1922, Marquette University had hired a specialist to teach in the speech department. It founded a separate drama-and-oral interpretation-based School of Speech in 1926, now part of the Diederich School of Communication (Jung, 79).[6] At the same time, a traditionalist group of rhetoricians based at Cornell, all classically trained but not Jesuit-affiliated, emphasized a high level of humanistic—not social-scientific—scholarship in the rhetoric research and pedagogy they practiced throughout the first half of the twentieth century (Corbett, "Cornell School," 290–91).

In the mid-twentieth century, a few graduate speech departments, particularly in the Midwest, conducted and sponsored excellent research into rhetorical history, specifically among the Jesuits—notably at Minnesota, Northwestern, Iowa, and Illinois. For instance, Edward Joseph Lynch, S.J., wrote an important dissertation (1960), under Leland Griffin at Northwestern University, on the *Ratio Studiorum*. Thomas Flynn, S.J., for his doctoral dissertation (1955) at the University of Florida wrote a translation of Cypriano

Soarez's *De Arte Rhetorica*. Sister Mary Charlotte Jung at the University of Wisconsin wrote a master's thesis (1956) on the Jesuits' efforts to teach speech in schools and colleges. And Douglas Ehninger, Robert Lang, Warren Guthrie, K. V. Hance, Karl Wallace, and Marie Hochmuth Nichols, among others, published important historical studies of rhetoric, including the rhetoric of the Jesuits, from their posts in speech-communications departments at Midwestern universities in the 1930s, '40s, and '50s. This attention to American Jesuit education from secular scholars helps bring home the point that interest in Jesuit rhetoric was by no means confined to Catholic scholars or professors at religious-sponsored universities.

Another example: The Jesuit-trained rhetoricians who recount their educational experiences below all spent their careers at secular universities, where they found welcome outlets for the rhetorical approaches they first learned at Jesuit schools. As far as communications departments were concerned, though, no Jesuit university in the first half of the twentieth century had a doctoral program in speech, and relatively few had undergraduate departments. (Speech and communications, then as now, had difficulty gaining a foothold in many traditional Eastern universities, including Harvard, Yale, Princeton, Dartmouth, Williams, and Amherst, which to this day do not offer speech or communications as majors.) And still at present, no Jesuit university offers a doctorate in speech communications, though many offer a major and some a master's degree. To a Jesuit early in the twentieth century, the newly formed discipline of speech, with its emphasis on social-scientific research, must have seemed puzzling; on one hand it rightly emphasized the spoken word, but by breaking off into a separate department it shattered the unified humanistic tradition outlined in the *Ratio Studiorum*.[7]

RHETORIC FLOURISHES IN THE EXTRACURRICULUM

Yet just at the time that rhetoric was coming under assault in American Jesuit higher education, a remarkable efflorescence occurred in the extracurriculum. College debates had long been a staple of American and European higher education, of course, but the intercollegiate debates in the early twentieth century became a phenomenon of their own. For instance, Boston College's debating team competed with Harvard and Oxford in the 1920s in front of huge audiences, once filling Boston's Symphony Hall. Boston College in 1913 erected a purpose-built hall just for its Fulton Debating Society, its ceiling covered with extended passages from six rhetoricians: Demonsthenes, Cicero, St. Paul, Paolo Segneri, Louis Bourdaloue (the latter two were renowned Jesuit orators from the seventeenth century), and Daniel Webster—three religious and three secular figures, only one an American.[8] Head-to-head competitions between colleges attracted large, enthusiastic audiences, and that Jesuit students excelled in such a venue was a remarkable justification of the language- and rhetoric-infused traditional curriculum, even as that formal curriculum was on its way out (Donovan). Sister Mary Jung also details the prominence of debate at Fordham and Marquette in the mid-twentieth century (65, 80). As the century progressed, head-to-head debate competitions were also disappearing, being replaced by debate tournaments among participants from many colleges. During the first half of the twentieth century, Edgar Ray Nichols edited an annual series of volumes containing the winning arguments from these tournaments, testimony that intercollegiate debating was alive and well. But the success of debate shows that a subject can become lost in the extracurriculum, becoming confined to the most adept students and ultimately failing to reach the full network of possible sites of eloquence.

RHETORIC'S REVIVAL BY JESUITS: ONG, LONERGAN, FOGARTY, JONSEN

Despite the decline of rhetoric instruction in the early twentieth century, a remarkably rich, specifically Jesuit attitude toward rhetoric was to resurface in the 1950s and '60s. Perhaps most prominent was the work of Walter Ong, S.J., first with his 1958 study of the virulently anti-Jesuit seventeenth-century French rhetorician Peter Ramus, followed by his wide-ranging series of articles and books so ably analyzed by his student Janice Lauer Rice (Part II). Even though much of his historical work does not invoke the Jesuits formally, Ong represents a very Jesuit "take" on rhetoric. It's hard to imagine someone not trained by the Jesuits being capable of undertaking the enormous effort involved in understanding Ramus and his context in sixteenth-century France. In 1939, Harvard's Perry Miller wrote that "there is a crying need for a full study of Ramus and his influence" (*New England Mind*, 493). Ong—Miller's doctoral student—took up the challenge, mixing his fluency in Latin, French, philosophy, and literature with his training in the emerging field of media studies. After publishing his book on Ramus, Ong would erect a new approach to rhetorical studies from a distinctively Christian perspective, merging his profound historical scholarship with his explicitly Jesuit outlook. Ong would retain his close friendship with Marshall McLuhan, who shared his interest in the impact of new media. In the Ong–Mcluhan connection we already see the beginning of a Jesuit-and-non-Jesuit collaboration in rhetoric. We also see something of the traditional Jesuit approach to rhetoric reappearing: a broad interdisciplinary set of inquiries that transcends the modern breakup into disciplines and departments, a wide-ranging intellectual approach that calls on linguistics, history, philosophy, anthropology, religious studies, English, and a host of other areas of study. Ong himself, a prominent professor of English, and president of the Modern Language Association in 1978, never felt limited by his chosen field of literature and so ranged with a broad and capacious approach to all areas of humanistic inquiry. And the McLuhan–Ong trend of

Jesuit–lay collaboration would grow, as Jesuits diminished in numbers in the 1960s and lay faculty came to play a larger and larger role in Jesuit higher education. Ong's career path as well as his forward-thinking books and articles on communication and rhetoric form a key part of his legacy.

Bernard Lonergan also represents a notable exception to rhetoric's twentieth-century decline. As Paula Mathieu's chapter (Part II) so ably demonstrates, Lonergan's work remains fertile ground for new thinking about the connections between rhetoric and philosophy. Thomas Farrell (a student of Ong's) and Paul Soukup (a Jesuit teaching at Santa Clara University) edited a collection of essays, *Communication and Lonergan: Common Ground for Forging the New Age* (dedicated to Walter Ong), that is an important step in making Lonergan's work available to rhetoricians. Like Ong, Lonergan refused to be pigeonholed into a single narrow discipline; though he taught mostly philosophy, Lonergan's insights have had an impact on communications, rhetoric, and cultural studies. Stephen Toulmin, who knew a great deal about the subject, wrote about the ways in which Lonergan transcended narrow categories and disciplinary boundaries.[9] Interestingly, Toulmin entitled one of his last books *Cosmopolis* (1990), an echo of a key term for Lonergan (Mathieu, Part II).

Another mid-century Jesuit rhetorical scholar sought explicitly to replace classical rhetoric with more up-to-date rhetorics. Daniel Fogarty, dean of education at St. Mary's University in Halifax, published *Roots for a New Rhetoric* in 1959, a year after Ong's masterwork appeared. Fogarty, classically trained as all Jesuits were in the 1950s, wanted to bring to his readers' attention three modern alternatives to traditional Aristotelian rhetoric: what he called "philosophical rhetorics" as expounded by I. A. Richards, Kenneth Burke, and S. I. Hayakawa.

Today Fogarty's book's main claim to fame is as the source of the term "current traditional," which has since been used (by Richard Young and others, who have often omitted Fogarty's S.J. affix while adding a hyphen to Fogarty's original term [Young, 30]) to characterize the traditional rhetorics that were taught up to the 1950s and beyond. But for our purposes, Fogarty represents something quite different: one Jesuit's take on the possibility of updating the rhetoric taught in the first-year college course. He opens his book with a one-chapter overview of rhetoric's development, from the Greeks to the present age, claiming that the only true philosophical rhetorician had been Aristotle. (In this sense Fogarty's work can seem like a significant departure from Cicero and Quintilian, the traditional touchstones of Jesuit rhetoric.) It is only in the twentieth century, Fogarty claims, that true alternatives to Aristotelian rhetoric emerged. Fogarty makes no explicit connection to Jesuit rhetorics or to the long Jesuit traditions of teaching.[10] His book's three main chapters were based on extensive correspondence with Richards, Burke, and Hayakawa.

Fogarty's book—like the work of his Jesuit-trained contemporaries—represents a strong affirmation of rhetoric's centrality to modern thought and contemporary education, particularly to the first-year writing course, which he mentions explicitly. For a renewal of rhetoric, Fogarty looks not back to Aristotle but forward to Richards, Burke, and Hayakawa, whom he regards as full of promise for the future. (Note that Richards, Burke, and Hayakawa were all notable for sharing Ong's and Lonergan's wide-ranging interests, refusing to be limited to a narrow departmental silo, and taking all fields of humanistic inquiry for their subjects.) But even if he looks toward those three rather than back to Aristotle and the classical period, Fogarty's work reveals his Jesuit roots and his deep commitment to the rhetorical arts.

Another twentieth-century Jesuit connection to rhetorical studies is through Albert R. Jonsen, a Jesuit from 1949 to 1976, who collaborated with Stephen Toulmin on *The Abuse of Causistry* (1988), their groundbreaking study of moral reasoning. Jonsen, a bioethicist, served with Toulmin on the President's Commission on the Study of Ethical Problems in Medicine (1979–82). In describing the origins of their book, Jonsen stated that on the commission

> it occurred to many of us early on that the interesting features of bioethics were its cases; that when we talked about discontinuing life support it really came down largely, to use the title of that famous play and film, "Whose Life Is It Anyway?" or what kind of life is it? All of those are questions that are casuistic. Who is this person? What is their life at this point in time? What is it that the medical intervention can actually do for them? And a whole range of other questions like what costs are involved and so on. At that point the perception is that any theory as such is much too general in scope, much too general to deal with the kinds of questions that are of interest.
>
> —Jonsen, Acadia Institute, 91

This concern on the part of Jonsen and Toulmin led to their rich, detailed study of the "rhetorical character of causistical reasoning" (*Abuse*, 258), which was the traditional Jesuit way of arguing about the morality of specific cases, the very casuistry famously attacked by Pascal in the *Provincial Letters*. Jonsen and Toulmin attempted to rehabilitate casuistry from Pascal's attacks, urging that it be revived as a method of determining the moral and ethical response to a particular situation. Jonsen and Toulmin relied on an understanding of the rhetorical situation underlying such reasoning, writing that the Jesuits "were particularly insistent on the mastery of rhetoric, an art that . . . provides a structure of argument suitable for casuistry" (*Abuse*, 151).

The cases of Ong, Fogarty, Lonergan, and Jonsen demonstrate how closely the Jesuits remained associated with rhetoric, even at a time when actual teaching of it was declining in Jesuit higher education. They also demonstrate that early twentieth-century Jesuit rhetorical instruction was still capable of producing superb rhetorical thinking. Think also of the mid-twentieth-century French Jesuits Michel de Certeau, Henri de Lubac, and Teilhard de Chardin, the latter a great influence on Ong, who lived in the same Parisian Jesuit residence while researching his dissertation on Ramus (Farrell and Soukup, 4).

NON-JESUITS REVIVE RHETORIC

But as the chapters in Part II demonstrate, the Jesuit encounter with mid-twentieth-century rhetoric was also extended by a series of American Jesuit-trained secular scholars who brought their Jesuit backgrounds to bear on the actual teaching of writing, then and now the single largest enterprise in American higher education. Bizzell writes in Part I of "the bombshell effect of the 1965 publication of Edward P. J. Corbett's *Classical Rhetoric for the Modern Student*, which induced many people to incorporate elements of classical pedagogy in contemporary classrooms." Gerald Nelms (Part II) addresses Corbett's contribution, tracing his educational formation at Jesuit schools, including Marquette University High School (in Milwaukee) and at Creighton University (in Omaha), where much of *Classical Rhetoric* was written.

Corbett had an important predecessor as a mid-twentieth-century Jesuit-trained reviver of classical rhetoric for composition courses, P. Albert Duhamel, who collaborated with his Boston College colleague Richard E. Hughes on the writing textbook *Rhetoric: Principles and Usage* (1962), published by Prentice Hall. As Connors, Ede, and Lunsford rightly state, "The rediscovery of classical rhetoric in its application to writing pedagogy began in 1962, when P. Albert Duhamel and his colleague Richard E. Hughes published *Rhetoric: Principles and Usage*" (11; see Nelms, Part II).[11] Since little of his influence is known, despite scattered references to him, Duhamel's career bears a closer look. Trained by Henry Bean, S.J., at Holy Cross in the 1930s, the same teacher Michael Halloran reports that he wished he had had for rhetoric (Part II), Duhamel received his PhD from the University of Wisconsin, where he did his dissertation on Elizabethan rhetoric, under the direction of the Swift scholar Ricardo Quintana, and taught in the famous first-year writing program run by Robert Pooley and then Edgar Lacy.[12] Then he went on to teach at the University of Chicago, where he was part of the English 3 staff that included Wayne Booth, Richard Weaver (who shared an office with Duhamel), Wilma Ebbitt, Manuel Bilsky, McCrea Hazlitt, Robert E. Streeter, and Howard Sams (the director of composition). Kenneth Burke was a visiting professor at Chicago in 1949, when the sixteen-year-old Susan Sontag was his student.

Among the master's students at Chicago during Duhamel's time was Edward P. J. Corbett, and though there is no direct evidence that the two crossed paths, Corbett did cite Duhamel two separate times (Corbett, 1969) and included "Looking for an Argument," a *College English* article (1953) by Duhamel's Chicago colleagues Bilsky, Hazlett, Streeter, and Weaver, in the second, third, and fourth editions of his *Classical Rhetoric for the Modern Student*. Chicago at that time was heavily involved in reviving Aristotelian philosophy, including rhetoric, through the work of Richard McKeon and R. S. Crane. Duhamel himself contributed to this revival in essays he wrote while at Chicago, including "The Function of Rhetoric as Effective Expression" in the *Journal of the History of Ideas* (1949), which Gerald Hauser and Richard Weaver (as well as Corbett) have cited.[13] In 1949 Duhamel moved to Boston College, where he began to collaborate with Hughes on their textbook, which went through two editions in the 1960s. Hughes, a graduate of the Franciscan Siena College, received his master's degree at the Jesuit Boston College, taught writing with Duhamel at Wisconsin–Madison while earning his PhD, and moved to Ohio State, leaving before Corbett arrived there. He returned to Boston College as chair of the English Department in 1955. In 1968, Hughes and Corbett were among the founding board members of the Rhetoric Society of America. Hughes and Duhamel also collaborated on a rhetorically based collection of essays for college composition, *Persuasive Prose: A Reader* (1964), which partly anticipated the format and approach of *The Norton Reader*, which first appeared a year later, in 1965.[14]

Interestingly, that so many mid-twentieth-century rhetoric scholars had Jesuit connections was almost entirely unmentioned at the time, and ever since then as well. Corbett does refer to "Father Daniel Fogarty" in a *QJS* article (1965) that does not appear in the collection of his essays edited by Robert Connors. In that *QJS* article he also points out that "the inclusion of a section on the topics in Richard Weaver's freshman text *Composition* (1957) represented the first instance of the use of topics in a freshman rhetoric text since the appearance of Francis P. Donnelly's books in the 1930's," but Corbett does not note that Donnelly, too, was a Jesuit. It seems that often the Jesuit connection is simply tacit, often totally missing from the discourse of the era, and in fact in the discourse since that time as well.[15]

Hughes and Duhamel, along with Corbett, helped to bring the teaching of classical rhetoric into first-year writing courses exactly at the time when Jesuit colleges were dropping the subject. The subsequent flowering of interest in classical rhetoric has had to proceed without the direct help of Jesuits themselves. Very few Jesuits taught first-year composition from the 1970s on, since the dramatic thinning of the Jesuit ranks meant that many of the best concentrated their studies within the confines of individual academic disciplines or were recruited into administration. But the cause of classical rhetoric was greatly aided by Jesuit-trained or affiliated scholars, including Frank D'Angelo, Mike Rose, Gerald Hauser, Michael Halloran, and Paul Ranieri, all of whom contribute personal accounts to this volume.

In addition, Thomas Pace and Gina Merys examine the significant impact that another pivotal scholar with Jesuit connections, Paulo Freire, had on rhetoric and composition studies. Freire did not focus on classical rhetoric but nonetheless greatly affected the field of rhetoric and composition, reminding us that international connections are always present when studying the Jesuits.

Why isn't Freire better known as a religious educator? After all, his escape from Brazil's dictators and his arrival in America was facilitated in part by faculty at Union Theological Seminary, who early on recognized his deep spiritual roots, and he spent ten years working for the World Council of Churches. Perhaps the best explanation is that many of the progressive American scholars who have helped publicize Freire's insights—Henry Giroux, Donaldo Macedo, James Berlin, Stanley Aronowitz, Ira Shor—might be less than fully comfortable with his deeply religious connections. Tom Pace and Gina Merys in their chapter attempt to make up for that oversight and to right the balance in Friere's reputation.

The mid-twentieth-century Jesuit revival of the order's traditional interest in rhetoric is one of the untold stories of American higher education. Rhetoric, composition, and communications scholars are the beneficiaries of this revival, as will be demonstrated in Part III, where individual scholars recount the ways they are incorporating Jesuit rhetorical principles into their teaching and curriculum planning at a wide variety of colleges, religious as well as secular.

NOTES

1. Many Protestant colleges also refused to break denominational ties, of course. Baptist and Lutheran colleges, which throughout the twentieth century greatly outnumbered Jesuit colleges, tended to retain their denominational ties, though, because of their church polity, they were bound much less strictly to a central organizational principle than were the Jesuits.

2. The encyclical was preceded two months earlier by the *Syllabus of Errors*, a list of 65 doctrinal errors that the pope claimed were characteristic of the modern world. See http://www.catholicculture.org/culture/library/ view.cfm?id=3145.

3. To this day many Jesuit colleges are allied with high schools that were once closely connected to them. Thus Boston College has Boston College High School, Fairfield University has Fairfield Prep (on the same campus), Loyola New Orleans has Jesuit High School. There are many other examples.

4. Two twentieth-century American Jesuits, Thurston Davis and, to a lesser extent, Robert Harvanek, presented a vision af smaller, *collège*-like institution that would train a Catholic elite. See McDonough, 205–8, 403–9.

5. Shorey begins his review: "There is a certain rationality in the work of Catholic scholars which is very attractive to a critic who believes that the introduction into education of all the confusions of modern thought is one of our most disastrous mistakes. It would be inquiring too curiously to ask whether this 'sweet reasonableness' of our Catholic colleagues is due to the retention in their schools of the fundamentals of a 'classical education,' or to the fact that many major questions are settled for them and they do not have to unsettle all things at once. I merely note the fact and its exemplification in the book before us." *Classical Philology* 27, no. 1 (January 1932): 106.

6. See Sister Mary Charlotte Jung, S.S.N.D., "The Jesuit Philosophy of Speech Education and How It Functions in the Training of the Jesuit and in Two Jesuit High Schools and Two Jesuit Universities," master's thesis, University of Wisconsin (1956), 79.

7. To be sure, many of today's Jesuit communications scholars rightly claim descent from the Society's four-hundred-year-old tradition of rhetoric. See Robbin D. Crabtree, "Agents of Consumption and Objects of Desire: The Problematics of Communication Education for Jesuit Universities."

8. The ceiling forms a nice parallel with the reading selections, as listed by Steven Mailloux (Part II), in Coppens's textbook: Most are taken from classical and European Jesuit sources, but both reserve a prominent place for an American Protestant source as well: In Coppens, it is John Quincy Adams; in Fulton Hall, it is Daniel Webster.

9. See Francisco Sierra-Gutiérrez, "Education for Cosmopolis," note 10.

10. Fogarty does list three books by Donnelly in his bibliography: *Art Principles in Literature* (1923), *Literary Art and Modern Education* (1927), and *Persuasive Speech* (1931), without indicating that Donnelly was a Jesuit.

11. The Boston College student newspaper interviewed Hughes when the book was published: "We asked Dr. Hughes if he and Dr. Duhamel had formulated any new principles which would account for the good sale of the book. He said, 'The book actually makes use of some of the world's oldest principles. It is the first modern rhetoric text that follows the principles of Aristotle. Most other texts were watered-down affairs that insulted the student's intelligence.' Because of the success of the rhetoric text, the two professors are now working on a Freshman literary anthology designed as a companion volume. Dr. Hughes revealed, 'The new book is nearly one-quarter finished. Actually, it takes about three and one-half years to complete a text such as this one. In this Freshman anthology, we are attempting to get a fresh collection, embodying a combination of literary texts and suggestions for rhetorical analysis.'" The book, *Persuasive Prose: A Reader,* appeared in 1964. Mike Keady, "Drs. Hughes and Duhamel Publish Rhetoric Textbooks." *The Heights* 44, no. 10 (November 16, 1962). Richard Young in his 1978 essay cites Hughes and Duhamel's book, 36.

12. The linguist Robert Pooley led the Wisconsin writing program from 1945 to 1949, when Lacy took over. Hughes and Duhamel thank Lacy (misspelled "Lacey") and Ricardo Quintana in the acknowledgments to the first edition of *Rhetoric.*

13. Hauser, "Between Philosophy and Rhetoric: Interpositions within Traditions," *Philosophy and Rhetoric* 28, no. 3 (1995), iii–xvii; Weaver, *The Ethics of Rhetoric*, 3; Stanley Fish cites another of Duhamel's articles, "Milton's Alleged Ramism," in *Surprised by Sin: The Reader in Paradise Lost*, 127. See Duhamel's widely cited article "Milton's Allged Ramism," *PMLA* 67 (December1952): 1035–53.

14. Hughes and Duhamel thank their editor, Paul O'Connell, who would later go on to edit Susan Miller's early textbook, *Writing: Process and Product* (1974), along with other significant rhetoric textbooks. Duhamel's career at Boston College moved away from publishing scholarly works. He ran the BC honors program, began a book review column in 1966 for the *Boston Herald* (where ten years earlier Donald Murray had won his Pulitzer Prize), and hosted a book-discussion program on Boston's public television station, WGBH. Julia Child did her first TV cooking in 1962 on Duhamel's show, *People Are Reading.*

15. A nice instance of this erasure occurs in another piece of Corbett's, his *CCC* article "What Is Being Revived?" (1967), which does not appear in Connors's collection. There he writes that "some people see the roots of a new rhetoric in I. A. Richards' work on semantics and in the works stemming from that study" (57), which seems a pretty

explicit echo of Fogarty's title, *Roots for a New Rhetoric*, which had devoted a chapter to Richards but goes unmentioned in the article, including the notes.

WORKS CITED

Bizzell, Patricia. "Editing the Rhetorical Tradition." *Philosophy and Rhetoric* 36, no. 2 (2003): 110.f

Bilsky, Manuel, McCrea Hazlett, Robert E. Streeter, and Richard M. Weaver. "Looking for an Argument." *College English* 14 (January 1953): 210–16.

Bonachea, Rolando, ed. *Jesuit Higher Education: Essays on an American Tradition of Excellence.* Pittsburgh, Pa.: Duquesne University Press, 1989.

Brereton, John C. *The Origins of Composition Study in the American College, 1875–1925.* Pittsburgh, University of Pittsburgh Press, 1995.

Connors, Robert J., Lisa Ede, and Andrea Lunsford. "The Revival of Rhetoric in America" In *Essays on Classical Rhetoric and Modern Discourse*, ed. Robert J. Connors, Lisa Ede, and Andrea Lunsford. Carbondale: Southern Illinois University Press.

Cooper, Charles, and Lee Odell, eds. *Research on Composing: Points of Departure,* ed. Urbana, Ill.: NCTE, 1978.

Corbett, Edward P. J. *Classical Rhetoric for the Modern Student.* New York: Oxford University Press, 1965.

———. "The Cornell School of Rhetoric," 290–304. In *Selected Essays of Edward P. J. Corbett*, ed. Robert J Connors. Dallas: Southern Methodist University Press, 1989.

———. "Rhetoric and Teachers of English." *Quarterly Journal of Speech* 51, no. 4 (December 1965): 375–81.

———. *Rhetorical Analysis of Literary Works.* New York: Oxford University Press, 1969.

———. "What Is Being Revived?" *College Composition and Communication* 18, no. 3 (October 1967): 167–72.

Crabtree, Robbin D. "Agents of Consumption and Objects of Desire: The Problematics of Communication Education for Jesuit Universities." http://www.learningace .com/doc/2267593/c391216d345a874df85a1c2055580842/panel13_crabtree. Accessed January 21, 2013.

Donnelly, Francis P. *The Art of Interesting; Its Theory and Practice for Speakers and Writers.* New York: P. J. Kenedy and Sons, 1920.

———. *Art Principles in Literature.* New York: Macmillan, 1923.

———. *Literary Art and Modern Education.* New York: P. J. Kenedy and Sons, 1927.

———. *Model English.* Boston: Allyn and Bacon: 1919.

———"The Old Incentives to Composition in the New Era." *English Journal* 24, no. 4 (1935): 315–16.

———. *Persuasive Speech.* New York: P. J. Kenedy and Sons, 1931.

Donovan, Charles F. "Debate at Boston College: People, Places, and Traditions." Chestnut Hill, Mass.: Boston College, 1991. http://www.bc.edu/content/dam/files /schools/cas_sites/communication/pdf/Donovan-Debate-history.pdf. Accessed January 24, 2013.

Doherty, Paul. "Straight Arrow." *Boston College Magazine*, Winter 2007. http://bcm
.bc.edu/issues/winter_2007/linden_lane/straight-arrow.html Accessed January 20, 2011.

Duhamel, P. Albert. "The Function of Rhetoric as Effective Expression." *Journal of the History of Ideas* 10, no. 3 (June 1949): 344–56.

———. "Milton's Alleged Ramism." *PMLA* 67 (December 1952): 1035–53.

Farrell, Thomas J., and Paul A. Soukup, eds. *Communication and Lonergan: Common Ground for Forging the New Age*. Kansas City, Mo.: Sheed and Ward.

Fish, Stanley. *Surprised by Sin: The Reader in Paradise Lost*. Berkeley: University of California Press, 1970.

Fogarty, Daniel. *Roots for a New Rhetoric*. New York: Teachers College Press, 1959.

Flynn. Lawrence J. "The *De Arte Rhetorica* of Cipriano Suárez." PhD diss., University of Florida, 1955.

Gleason, Philip. *Contending with Modernity: Catholic Higher Education in the Twentieth Century*. New York: Oxford University Press, 1995.

Hauser, Gerard A. "Between Philosophy and Rhetoric: Interpositions within Traditions." *Philosophy and Rhetoric* 28, no. 3 (1995): iii–xvii.

Hughes, Richard E., and P. Albert Duhamel. *Rhetoric: Principles and Usage*. Englewood Cliffs, N.J.: Prentice-Hall, 1962.

Hughes, Richard E., and P. Albert Duhamel, eds., *Persuasive Prose: A Reader*. Englewood Cliffs, NJ: Prentice-Hall. 1964.

Albert R. Jonsen. Interview. Acadia Institute Projection of Bioethics in American Society. Interview with Albert Jonsen. https://www.google.com/search?q=Acadia +Institute+Projection+of+Bioethics+in+American+Society+A+l+Jonsen&ie=utf -8&oe=utf-8. Accessed December 11, 2013.

———. Interview. https://repository.library.georgetown.edu/bitstream/handle/10822 /557035/JonsenA.pdf?sequence=4. Accessed December 9, 2014.

———, and Stephen Toulmin. *The Abuse of Casuistry: A History of Moral Reasoning*. Berkeley: University of California Press. 1990.

Jung, Sister Mary Charlotte, S.S.N.D. "The Jesuit Philosophy of Speech Education and How It Functions in the Training of the Jesuit and in Two Jesuit High Schools and Two Jesuit universities." Master's thesis, University of Wisconsin–Madison, 1956.

Keady, Mike. "Drs. Hughes and Duhamel Publish Rhetoric Textbooks." *The Heights* 44, no. 10 (November 1962): 16. http://newspapers.bc.edu/cgibin/bostonsh?a=d&d =bcheights19621116.2.45. Accessed January 12, 2012.

Kitzhaber, Albert. *Rhetoric in American Colleges, 1850–1900*. Dallas: Southern Methodist University Press, 1990.

Kleutgen, Joseph. *Ars Dicendi Priscorum: Potissimum Praeceptis et Exemplis*. 2nd ed. Sylvae-Ducis: Verhoeveh fratres, 1855.

Kuzniewski, Anthony J. *Thy Honored Name*. Washington, D.C.: The Catholic University of America Press, 1999.

Hughes, Richard, and P. Albert Duhamel. *Rhetoric: Principles and Usage*. Englewood Cliffs, N.J.: Prentice Hall, 1962.

Leahy, William P. *Adapting to America: Catholics, Jesuits, and Higher Education in the Twentieth Century*. Washington, D.C.: Georgetown University Press, 1991.

Lucas, Thomas, ed. *Spirit, Style, and Story: Essays in Honor of John W. Padberg, S.J.*, Chicago: Loyola Press, 2003.

Lynch, Edward Joseph. "The Origin and Development of Rhetoric in the Plan of Studies of 1599 of the Society of Jesus." PhD diss., Northwestern University, 1968.

Mahoney, Kathleen. *Catholic Education in Protestant America: The Jesuits and Harvard in the Age of the University.* Baltimore: Johns Hopkins University Press, 2003.

McDonough, Peter. *Men Astutely Trained: A History of the Jesuits in the American Century.* New York: Free Press, 1992.

McGucken, William J. *The Jesuits and Education.* Milwaukee: Bruce, 1932.

McKevitt, Gerald. "Jesuit Schools in the U.S.A., 1814–c.1970." In *The Cambridge Companion to the Jesuits*, ed. Thomas Worcester. Cambridge: Cambridge University Press, 2008.

———. "'Habits of Industry': Jesuits and Nineteenth-Century Native American Education." In *Spirit, Style, and Story: Essays in Honor of John W. Padberg, S.J.*, ed. Thomas Lucas. Chicago: Loyola Press, 2003.

Miller, Perry. *The New England Mind: The Seventeenth Century.* Cambridge, Mass.: Harvard University Press, 1939.

Platt, R. Eric. *Sacrifice and Survival: Identity, Mission, and Jesuit Higher Education in the American South.* Tuscaloosa: University of Alabama Press, 2014.

Sierra-Gutiérrez, Francisco, "Education for Cosmopolis," note 10. *Paideia.* http://www.bu.edu/wcp/Papers/Educ/EducSier.htm. Accessed November 9, 2012.

Shorey, Paul. Review of *Persuasive Speech: An Art of Rhetoric for College*, by Francis P. Donnelly. *Classical Philology* 24, no. 4 (January 1932): 106–7.

Tetlow, Joseph A. "*In Oratione Directa*: Philosophy in the Jesuit Liberal Arts Curriculum in the United States." In *Jesuit Higher Education: Essays on an American Tradition of Excellence*, ed. Rolando E. Bonachea.

Varga, Nicholas. *Baltimore's Loyola, Loyola's Baltimore: 1851–1986.* Baltimore: Maryland Historical Society, 1990.

Weaver, Richard. *The Ethics of Rhetoric.* Davis, Calif.: Hermagoras Press, 1985.

Wozniak, John Michael. *English Composition in Eastern Colleges, 1850–1940.* Lanham, Md.: Rowman and Littlefield, 1978.

Young, Richard. "Paradigms and Problems: Needed Research in Rhetorical Invention." In *Research on Composing: Points of Departure*, ed. Charles Cooper and Lee Odell. Urbana, Ill.: NCTE, 1978.

RHETORICAL WAYS OF PROCEEDING: *ELOQUENTIA PERFECTA* IN AMERICAN JESUIT COLLEGES

Steven Mailloux

The Jesuit priest Francis Finn wrote a popular series of Catholic boy books at the end of the nineteenth century. Unlike his fictional namesake Huck, Father Finn is almost forgotten today, but his spirited stories about students at a Jesuit boarding school offer a useful introduction to my topic. In the novel bearing his name, the young hero, Tom Playfair, is described as having "a boyish eloquence which persuaded where it did not prove" (75). After hearing a sermon about Christ casting out devils, Tom convinces his compatriots to help him "exercise" (his word for *exorcise*) a fellow student "who curses and talks vile" (74). Failing in his first attempt, Tom finds other ways to reform the student, and his friend Alec ends up complimenting Tom's method: "You know how to talk"; and Tom replies, "That's what I've got a tongue for" (110).

The models for such eloquence become clear in later books in the Tom Playfair series. In *Harry Dee*, referring to their teacher, a Jesuit scholastic, "the boys of Rhetoric class . . . say that he's the most wonderful man they ever met. They say that when he gets started in class he talks like a book, and when he warms up to a subject he becomes really eloquent. His timidity all goes, his eyes flash, and he talks like an orator. He's a poet, too; and the leader of the class said that Mr. Auber was the nearest thing to a genius that he ever met" (180). Later these students, who had been giving their rhetoric professor quite a hard time, ask this same teacher to tell them a story. Reluctantly, hesitantly, he began and then was slowly "transformed. His eyes flashed and his hands moved in easy, striking gestures; and in a flow of English, strong, pure, simple, the like of which we had never heard, he poured forth a tale of heroism and adventure that set our eyes blazing, riveted us to our seats, brought the tears to our eyes, and convinced us that we were listening to the most eloquent story-teller we could hope to meet with" (197). After publishing several of his schoolboy books, Father Finn commented on contemporary juvenile literature: "We, who are Catholics, expect something more than outward respectability, or, as in the case of [Horatio] Alger's stories, rough honesty or courage from our young heroes. We have a right to demand that the supernatural element should pervade the character of the boy or the girl whom we delight to honor, and in proposing such heroes we need not depart from real life."[1]

Finn's narrative intention, in its theory and execution, illustrates nicely (what might be called) the Jesuits' rhetorical way of proceeding, a practical concern in their ministries of the Word for the virtuous shaping of character through *eloquentia perfecta*. To support this claim I track some rhetorical paths of thought running from Finn's fiction through his Jesuit formation and college teaching to his association with an influential Jesuit textbook author, Charles Coppens. In weaving together the stories of these two Jesuit writers, I attempt to trace a particular strand of Jesuit rhetorical education that emphasizes the connections among eloquence, learning, and virtue.[2]

The Society of Jesus became deeply involved in higher education soon after its establishment in 1540. The centrality of rhetoric within the Jesuit curriculum can be seen in the *Ratio Studiorum* of 1599, a plan for Jesuit education written collaboratively over three decades and structured as a hierarchy of student class levels and faculty professorships in grammar, humanities, rhetoric, philosophy, and theology.[3] Under "Rules for Professors of Rhetoric," the goal given for the rhetoric class is *eloquentia perfecta*: instructing students to attain perfect eloquence. This goal should be accomplished through teaching the arts of oratory and poetry, with oratory being given preference. The class should aim at both practical utility and cultural enrichment, meaning that perfect eloquence includes erudition as well as skill in the language arts. Erudition should derive from studying the history and customs of nations, scriptural authority, and Church doctrine (*Ratio atque Institutio Studiorum*, 424–25; "Ratio," 208–9). Such teaching must be adjusted to the capacities of the students. This pedagogical flexibility is part of a more general rhetorical accommodationism that Jesuits practiced in all their ministries, adjusting their teaching to their audiences' physical, emotional, and spiritual development, whether in the confessional, the lecture hall, or the foreign mission.[4]

The rules of the *Ratio* are quite specific regarding the preferred rhetorical theory and practice: Precepts should come primarily from Cicero, Quintilian, and Aristotle, and style should "be learned only from Cicero" ("Ratio," 208). For a rhetorical textbook, the *Ratio* recommends that of the Jesuit Cyprian Soarez, his *De Arte Rhetorica*, revised by the noted Jesuit orator and rhetoric professor of the Collegio Romano, Peter John Perpiñan, and reprinted 207 times in various forms from its first publication in 1562 through the late eighteenth century, when the Society was temporarily suppressed (Flynn, 44). In his opening address to the Christian reader, Soarez justifies imitating classical Greco-Roman examples and notes that his fellow Jesuits embrace this pedagogy as "they start training youth in virtue and learning" (105). Later returning to this educational principle of combining morals with erudition, Soarez declares his intention to assist beginners with reading "the learned books of Aristotle, Cicero, and Quintilian wherein lie the well-springs of eloquence" and concludes his initial address to readers by asserting his strong desire that they "possess every grace and scholarship and thus be pleasing and acceptable to the source and salvation of our life, Christ Jesus" (108–9).

In the introduction that follows, Soarez opens with an observation that the Greeks thought reason and speech so similar that they used the same term (*logos*) for both. He then elaborates: "Reason is a kind of light, so to speak, and illumination of life; speech is the glory and ornament of reason. Reason guides and keeps our own minds under control; speech changes the minds even of others." The "power and nature" of reason and speech "compel us to acknowledge that [God's] goodness, wisdom, power, and dominion" deserve admiration and wonder from all. Soarez rhetorically asks, "What can be more wondrous than for thoughts that are so numerous, so lofty, so varied and manifold to be entrusted to speech?" And what of speech's effects produced through our particular human embodiment? "What can be more wondrous than . . . for speech to pass into the minds of other people through very delicate passages of our ears, designed in such a unique and skillful manner, and to imprint its mark so perfectly and so fixedly on them that it comforts the sorrowful, arouses the languid, reanimates the discouraged, restrains those who have been carried away by empty pleasure, and, at length, moves the hearer to any mood whatever" (110–11).

Soarez argues that if speech has such "preeminence," then rhetoric must be "supreme," since it contains the theory for equipping speech. "Indeed, this same human reason that has invented the other arts has also illuminated the . . . art of speaking" (111). This "close union" of speaking with reason is the origin and dignity of eloquence. Soarez adds that those who learn the rules of rhetoric and dialectic should "hasten towards perfection in the other arts" as well (112). This combination of learning with eloquence must also be purified by Christian teaching. "Just as a conscientious farmer makes a vine more fruitful and better to behold by trimming it with his pruning knife when it runs wild and spreads out rather freely in all directions, in the same way eloquence will recover its marvelous beauty, if there is a pruning of the vanity of errors into which it has fallen through the fault of men ignorant of God's laws" (113). In his conclusion, Soarez describes eloquence as "nothing else but wisdom speaking fully" (428–29), and in an earlier chapter he follows Cicero in praising the "restraint and wisdom of the perfect orator," on which "depend not only the speaker's authority but the welfare of many individuals and especially that of the state as a whole." Continuing to echo Cicero's *De oratore*, he then declares that eloquence must be joined "with integrity and utter discretion. If we were to teach the ability to speak to people who lack these virtues, we would certainly not be training orators but would be providing mad men with weapons" (119–20).

For Soarez, Perpiñan, and others later in the Jesuit rhetorical tradition, the ideal rhetor unites eloquence with wisdom and virtue. Jesuit *eloquentia perfecta* might thus be characterized as a particular form of Christian rhetoric, a pedagogical elaboration of the classical ideal of the good person writing and speaking skillfully for the public good.[5] This strand of Jesuit rhetoric asserts that the teaching of eloquence should always be combined with critical thinking, moral discernment, and civic responsibility. Often quoting Quintilian's definition of the perfect orator as the good person speaking well, many Jesuit rhetoricians repeated his claim that virtuous character was required for true eloquence.[6] Such affirmations continued in the textbooks adopted in U.S. Jesuit colleges late in the nineteenth century and into the twentieth. I turn now to the rhetorical genealogy of these required texts of the 1880s and 1890s.

Eloquentia perfecta, as term and concept, remained a part of the Jesuit rhetorical tradition after the official restoration of the Society in 1814. The term still appears in the *Ratio Studiorum* of 1832, a revised version that was, however, never officially approved by the Society as a whole.[7] In fact, by midcentury in the United States, the explicit rhetorical theory promoted in Jesuit colleges differed little from that in non-Jesuit schools. In both, the classical theory of the Greco-Roman tradition (Aristotle, Cicero, and Quintilian) was often combined with the belletristic eighteenth-century British (more specifically, Scottish) tradition (especially Hugh Blair's *Lectures on Rhetoric and Belles Lettres*).[8] After the American Civil War, the curriculum in U.S. Jesuit colleges remained a classical course of study centered on Greek and Latin much longer than in most non-Jesuit schools, which were transformed by the elective system and the importation of the modern German research model.[9] However, English rhetoric textbook adoptions remained similar in Jesuit and non-Jesuit schools into the last quarter of the century.

The textbook situation changed as Jesuit colleges adopted at least three new rhetorics written by Jesuits. The first was *Ars Dicendi*, a Latin textbook by the German Jesuit Joseph Kleutgen, which appeared in the course lists of several Jesuit colleges as required for the Rhetoric Class's Latin instruction or as a reference work for the class's English rhetorical precepts.[10] The other two popular Jesuit rhetorics were *A Practical Introduction to English Rhetoric* and *The Art of Oratorical Composition*, English texts written by a Belgian-born Jesuit, Charles Coppens, and published in 1880 and 1885, respectively. Fr. Coppens taught at the Jesuit seminary, St. Stanislaus in Florissant, Missouri, and at several American Jesuit colleges, including Detroit, Xavier, and Creighton. At Saint Louis University in the late 1870s, as confessor and mentor, Coppens helped save the vocation of a future Jesuit novice, Francis Finn, by interesting himself in the student's "spiritual welfare" and leading him "to read some very good Catholic books" (Finn, *Father Finn*, 32). In the early 1880s, Coppens served as rector of St. Mary's College in Kansas when Finn taught there as a Jesuit scholastic. St. Mary's later became the basis of the fictional setting, St. Maure's, for Finn's Tom Playfair series, the early books of which he wrote while teaching at St. Mary's and Xavier in the 1880s and 1890s.[11] Throughout this same period Coppens's rhetoric textbooks were required at many Jesuit colleges across the country, a fact facilitated by the effort of the Missouri Province to standardize the curriculum and textbook adoptions of its Jesuit colleges. In the mid-1880s, one of Finn's benefactors Rudolph Meyer, S.J., , the Missouri provincial, called for the evaluation and standardization of the curricula in his province, and the resulting report recommended the adoption of Coppens's textbooks.[12]

In a 1920 autobiographical sketch, Coppens commented on the origins of his textbook writing:

> I was ordained, in 1865, and then employed for ten successive years in teaching, all alone, the juniorate at Florissant. Everything was very elementary in those early years of our province, and we were mostly well satisfied to do the best we could without any personal ambition. But meanwhile I felt my own unfitness for the work confided to me. The good Lord, however, assisted me, and during my professorship of the juniors I accumulated abundant notes on the science of rhetoric, which a few years later I ventured to publish as a text-book on the subject, chiefly because there was then no such work in English for the use of Catholic pupils. A few years later I published a companion volume to it on oratory. Both books were well received in Catholic colleges and academies, because they were the first text-books of the kind printed in America. They still have a fair circulation.
>
> —"Obituary," 200

The earliest textbook referred to here, the first Coppens published, is *A Practical Introduction to English Rhetoric: Precepts and Exercises*.[13] Adopted widely by Jesuit colleges, *A Practical Introduction* was required for the Classes of Humanities and Poetry at Xavier College, where Finn taught the Third Academic Class in 1885–86, and also for the same classes at St. Mary's College during his term there as rhetoric professor in 1894–95.[14] Finn used the textbook for his own courses at Marquette College in 1888–89 when he taught the Poetry Class and again at Xavier in 1897–98, when he returned to teach the Humanities Class and to lecture on "contemporaneous literature" in a postgraduate course.[15]

Book 1 of *A Practical Introduction* moves from "object-lessons" (names, parts, and qualities of objects, actions by or to objects, uses of objects) through chapters on words, sentences, paragraphs, and punctuation. Book 2, "The Ornaments of Composition," contains chapters on tropes, figures of words, and figures of thought; and book 3, "Style in Literary Composition," includes material on beauty, sublimity, wit, humor, and taste as well as the varieties and improvement of style. The final three sections focus on genres of prose composition and poetry: Book 4 covers imitation, letter-writing, narration, description, essays, dialogues, novels, and history, while book 5 explains versification and book 6 concludes the volume with the "Nature and Varieties of Poetry."

In the "Narration" chapter of *A Practical Introduction*, Coppens presents some "general rules for all good narration," one of which emphasizes choosing the proper subject for the "end intended by the writer." The options for narrative intentions are defined in Ciceronian rhetorical terms—to please, to move, and to instruct (152–53)—and Cicero is also the source for one of the examples Coppens provides of "simple narration": "Dionysius and Damocles" with its "every detail" adding to "the happy effect of the whole" (156). Other examples to be imitated include narratives with moral lessons such as "the humble are exalted" and "though a taste of pleasure might quicken the relish of life, an unrestrained indulgence is inevitable destruction" (154–55). In the chapter "Novels," Coppens defines the genre as "a fictitious narrative in prose, embracing a complete series of events, and exhibiting some phase of human life" (209) and lists examples of such phases: societal conditions, period manners, passions, institutional tendencies, and peculiar worldviews.

His informal taxonomy includes philosophical novels, society novels, and sensational novels. The latter two come in for some criticism. Society novels usually "ridicule the extravagances of prevalent tastes and practices" and are "chiefly taken up with the exhibition of character." Such novels "may be useful in their way," Coppens continues, "but unfortunately not many can be recommended for the perusal of those who care to keep their hearts undefiled by the contamination of vice." Coppens finds that "sensational novels are still more objectionable" because they "stir up the passions by frequent vivid sketches of exaggerated and unreal scenes" and in so doing "they create a morbid craving for exciting stories, and impair that calm of mind which is an essential element of a prudent and considerate character" (210).[16]

Instead of these negative effects of reading, Coppens suggests by contrast the positive benefits of reading philosophical novels, which include religious novels, though he still cautions that "the doctrines inculcated be sound" and emphasizes that "the composition possess literary beauty and proper interest" and that "the moral tone of the characters be favorable to virtue" (209–10). Of the last quality, Coppens notes that there is "no more excellent model" than Cardinal Nicolas Wiseman's *Fabiola; or, The Church of the Catacombs* (1854). It was this same novel that began "a new period" in the life of the young boy Francis Finn. Years later Finn recorded that "the beautiful story of those early Christian martyrs had a profound influence upon my life. Religion began to mean something to me. Since the day of reading 'Fabiola,' I have carried the conviction that one of the greatest things in the world is to get the right book into the hands of the right boy or girl" (*Father Finn*, 11).[17] On this point, the fiction writer Finn and the rhetorician Coppens appear to agree completely, and that agreement further illustrates the consistent preoccupation of the Jesuit tradition with connecting the language arts and Christian virtue.

The second textbook Coppens wrote was *The Art of Oratorical Composition, Based upon the Precepts and Models of the Old Masters*, which became a required text for the Rhetoric Class in Jesuit colleges both in and beyond the Missouri Province.[18] Father Finn used the text when he was professor of rhetoric at Marquette in 1889–90, at St. Mary's in 1894–95, and still again at Xavier in 1898–99.[19] Continuing the earlier nineteenth-century mixture of classical and belletristic rhetorics, *Oratorical Composition* added a more recognizably Jesuit character and an American flavor to the combination. Coppens often quotes Aristotle, Cicero, and Quintilian along with Blair but also cites the Jesuit Kleutgen's *Ars Dicendi* and refers to Jesuit orators as examples. Americans are represented by the speeches of Daniel Webster and the *Lectures on Rhetoric and Oratory* of John Quincy Adams, Harvard's first Boylston Professor of Rhetoric and Oratory. That Coppens uses Adams's lectures is somewhat unusual and perhaps even surprising given how the Boylston Professor explicitly rejects Quintilian's definition of the perfect orator: Adams declares that the Roman's arguments "in support of his favorite position, are not all worthy of his cause. They do not glow with that open, honest eloquence, which they seem to recommend; but sometimes resemble the quibbling of a pettifogger, and sometimes the fraudulent morality of a Jesuit" (Adams, 1:157).[20] Nevertheless, Coppens clearly found Adams's neo-classicism helpful in developing his own particular version of Jesuit rhetoric.

In his introduction, Coppens distinguishes among the terms *rhetoric, oratory,* and *eloquence*. Rhetoric is defined as "the art of inventing, arranging, and expressing thought in a manner adapted to influence or control the minds and wills of others," whereas oratory is "that branch of rhetoric which expresses thought orally." To define *eloquence*, Coppens prefers to use *Webster's Dictionary*: Eloquence is "the expression or utterance of strong emotion in a manner adapted to excite correspondent emotions in others" (*Oratorial Composition*, 12). This emphasis on strong emotion follows in a long Jesuit tradition, beginning at least with the rhetoric of the Ignatian *Spiritual Exercises*, and it is characteristic of other religious rhetorical traditions emerging out of the Renaissance.[21] Also typical of the Jesuit rhetorical way, Coppens asserts that eloquence is "not confined to oral discourse" but "applies also to written language" (*Oratorical Composition*, 12). He then describes oratory as "a noble art" and, like many Jesuit and non-Jesuit rhetoricians before him, quotes from the first book of Cicero's *De oratore*: "On the influence and the wisdom of a perfect orator depends not only his own dignity, but also, to a very great extent, the safety of multitudes and the welfare of the whole republic."[22] Coppens discusses "national variations," claiming that "American eloquence aims at the perfection of the Latin," which emphasizes "the beauty of eloquence, without, however, ignoring its usefulness" (14–15). The introduction concludes with a listing of the book's divisions, which, Coppens notes, agree with those in Quintilian's *Institutes*, "the most thorough and systematic work ever written on this subject" of training orators (16).

Oratorical Composition includes major sections on the invention, arrangement, and development of thought as well as "Memory and Elocution" and "The Different Species of Oratory." Consistent with the Jesuit emphasis I have been tracking, Coppens precedes all of these divisions with a section, "Sources of Success in Oratory," that highlights moral virtue along with natural talent and trained skills. "But far more important than any physical power in the orator," he writes, "are the moral virtues with which nature and his own efforts, with the help of God's grace, have adorned his soul." He then cites Blair: "In order to be a truly eloquent or persuasive speaker, nothing is more necessary than to be a virtuous man. This was a favorable position among the ancient rhetoricians: *Non posse oratorem esse nisi virum bonum*—'That no one could be an orator except a good man.'"[23] Among the virtues "most necessary for an orator," Coppens lists: probity, temperance, public spirit, compassion for the unfortunate, benevolence, modesty, confidence, self-command, and a habit of application and industry (26–31). He then makes the same association between a speaker's virtues and successful eloquence in the rhetorical genres of deliberative, forensic, and especially sacred oratory (230–32, 248–50, 271–72).

Of course, the close connection maintained between eloquence and virtue throughout the Jesuit rhetorical tradition is to be expected, given the long-standing educational goals of the Society. The founding *Constitutions* of 1558 declare that "very special care should be taken that those who come to the universities of the Society to obtain knowledge should acquire along with it good and Christian moral habits" (185), while the *Ratio Studiorum* of 1599 makes clear that students should be instructed so that "they may acquire not only learning but also habits of conduct worthy of a Christian." Under "Common Rules for the Teachers of the Lower Classes" (including rhetoric), the *Ratio* urges that "impressionable minds" be trained "in the classroom and outside . . . in the loving service of God and in all the virtues required for this service" (*Ratio* 62). These pedagogical goals continued to be stressed in course catalogues for U.S. Jesuit colleges and universities throughout the nineteenth century. A typical formulation emphasizes the value of a "liberal education" in the tradition of the *Ratio*, "which has met with success for centuries in the schools of the Society, both in Europe and in America." It aims "to develop the moral and mental faculties of the students, to make good Christians, good citizens, good scholars—men who shall be an ornament to religion and the upholders of Christian society."[24] Coppens's *Oratorical Composition* underlines the same point: "It is the chief duty of education to make men virtuous; any system of training which does not put virtue in the first place is a false system" (26).

The Jesuit tradition of *eloquentia perfecta* and its preoccupation with rhetoric and virtue thus fits well within the Society's general educational program. These Jesuit ways of proceeding, rhetorical and otherwise, emerge from another of the Society's founding documents, the *Spiritual Exercises* of Ignatius Loyola, a book that Coppens calls "one of the most remarkable and useful books in the world."[25] Ignatius's text has long been at the center of Jesuit formation, as testified by many members of the Society, including Francis Finn, who comments on his experience during his first novitiate year in 1877: "I can imagine nothing better calculated to make men close followers of Christ and by consequence true heroes of the cross, saintly missionaries, heroic martyrs, than the performance of the thirty days' exercises as laid down by St. Ignatius" (*Father Finn*, 42–43). Similar effects are recorded in the spiritual diary of Finn's provincial supporter, Rudoph Meyer, who responds to the call of the "Two Standards" meditation during several retreats over many years. The assumed narrative of that exercise pits those under Christ's banner against the followers of Lucifer, "the mortal enemy of our human nature," a conflict on which Meyer reflects, applying it to his own life and hearing it applied by his director to the history of the Jesuits.[26]

As Finn and Meyer suggest, the *Spiritual Exercises* are not simply to be read, they are to be performed. That performance includes a retreatant's working with a director in conjunction with Ignatius's text, which specifies a series of meditative and contemplative practices ordering the retreatant's life in preparation for a vocational election. The rhetoric of the exercises appeals to the intellect and emotions of the practitioners as it targets their narrative imaginations. In the contemplative practice called "composition of place," retreatants are instructed to use their imaginations to envision, sometimes through appeal to all five senses, a biblical narrative into which they will place their embodied selves as participants. Called to remember the story of Mary and Joseph's journey, retreatants are told to "see in imagination the road from Nazareth to Bethlehem. Consider its length and breadth, whether it is level or winds through valleys and hills." At the place of the Nativity, retreatants are supposed to imagine themselves as actors in the narrative scene: "I will make myself a poor, little, and unworthy slave, gazing at [the Holy Family], contemplating them, and serving them in their needs, just as if I were there, with all possible respect and reverence. Then I will reflect upon myself to draw some profit" (58–59). This explicit appeal to narrative imagination is thus combined with moral discernment and character formation. Such a rhetorical path of thought connects the exercises with both the intended effects of virtuous book-reading and the pedagogical tradition of *eloquentia perfecta* that I have been tracking throughout this essay.

NOTES

1. Finn, "Need of Juvenile Catholic Literature," 578. For more on Finn as Jesuit author, see Molson.

2. For more on tracking rhetorical paths of thought, see Mailloux, *Reception Histories* and *Disciplinary Identities*.

3. See Farrell.

4. See O'Malley, 255–56; Maryks, 79–82.

5. Cf. Quintilian, *Institutio Oratoria*, 12.1.1; see Meador.

6. See, for example, Reggio, 73: "*Christianus orator debet esse vir bonus*"; and note 10 below. However, not all Jesuits agreed that moral virtue was part of the formal defi-

nition of either rhetoric or eloquence. For example, in the mid-nineteenth century, the French Jesuit Frédéric-Marie Guérin approvingly quoted the earlier views of Perpiñan: "As to the contention of several very noble rhetoricians that eloquence is a virtue, and cannot be found except in a good man, that is a thing very much to be wished for, but there is little truth to it. . . . Nothing stands in the way of wicked men both possessing eloquence and abusing its power in order to weaken and overturn everything excellent" (Guérin ix–x, quoting Perpiñan's "De arte rhetorica discenda" [1561; English trans. J. Mark Sugars]). Still, the relation of eloquence to virtue was and remains an ongoing concern within Jesuit rhetoric, whatever disagreement there might be over the actual definition of eloquence itself.

7. Ratio Studiorum et Institutiones Scholasticae Societatis Jesu, 398; Farrell, 394.

8. See Johnson, and Carr, Carr, and Schultz.

9. On late nineteenth-century curricular debates and the Ratio, see Mahoney and McKevitt.

10. In line with the rhetorical tradition I am tracking, see Kleutgen, 136, for his use of Quintilian 12.1.1 ("vir bonus dicendi peritus") in a sample essay on the thesis "Nemo orator nisi vir bonus."

11. For biographical details, I have depended on Finn's memoir, Father Finn, confirming dates for both Coppens's and Finn's assignments by consulting the listings of faculty in the relevant college catalogues.

12. Course of Studies for the Colleges of the Missouri Province, 19–30. On Meyer's support for Finn, see Finn, Father Finn, 128, 148, 182; and on Meyer more generally, see Miros.

13. Stephen Carr places Coppens's textbook among what he calls the "composition-rhetorics" of the late nineteenth century, which combine rhetorical principles and rules with writing exercises (Carr, Carr, and Schultz, 66–68).

14. Catalogue of St. Xavier College, 1885–86 4, 12, 13; Catalogue of St. Mary's College, 1894–95, 18, 20.

15. Eighth Annual Catalogue of Marquette College, 1888–89, 4,17; Catalogue of St. Xavier College, 1897–98 3, 4, 15. Coppens's text was not without its critics among Jesuit instructors. During the 1886–87 consultation process leading up to the publication of a standard curriculum for the Missouri Province (see note 12 above), the Central Committee on Studies commented in a first draft of its report: "It is the sense of the committee, as of the colleges, that Coppens' Introduction, though the best textbook on the subject, stands in need of much improvement. The matter for Poetry is deficient; the treatise on Dramatic Poetry is wanting in development; that on Epic Poetry is too meager" (Jesuit Archive: Central United States, Missouri Province Collection, History of the Society of Jesus in Education, Course of Studies 1887).

16. On similar cultural anxieties over novel reading and the "Bad Boy Boom" of the 1880s, see Mailloux, Rhetorical Power, 99–129.

17. Also, in one of his schoolboy novels, Finn records the Jesuit prefect's thought that a student's admiration for Fabiola's characters was clear evidence of that student's "beautiful soul"; see Finn, Percy Wynn, 24.

18. After 1887, the standard catalogue description for the Rhetoric Class in many Jesuit schools was based on that in the Course of Studies for the Colleges of the Missouri Province, which included "English—Precepts: Coppens' Oratorical Composition; Dramatic Poetry; History. For reference: Quintilian, Kleutgen, Blair" (19).

19. *Ninth Annual Catalogue of Marquette College, 1889–90* 4, 16; *Catalogue of St. Mary's College, 1894–95*, 17; *Catalogue of St. Xavier College, 1898–99*, 4, 12.

20. After publication, Adams's lectures were only "very occasionally cited" in subsequent rhetorics (Carr, Carr, and Schultz 45).

21. See Shuger.

22. Coppens, *Oratorical Composition*, 12–13, quoting Cicero, *De oratore*, 1.8.

23. Coppens, *Oratorical Composition* 26; see Lecture 34 of Blair's *Lectures on Rhetoric and Belles Lettres* (Blair 381).

24. *Catalogue of Saint Joseph's College, 1893–94*, 3–4.

25. Coppens, *Who Are the Jesuits?* 7. Coppens writes further: "It is by going through the . . . exercises under the direction of a Jesuit that all the Jesuits of the world, in every succeeding generation, have been formed to their peculiar spirit. . . . From that book therefore we can most readily learn the spirit and the purpose of the Jesuits" (8).

26. *Spiritual Exercises* 65. For Meyer's comments on "The Two Standards," see Jesuit Archive: Central United States, Missouri Province Collection, Rudolph J. Meyer, Spiritual Diary; also see the later discussion in Meyer, *Science of the Saints*, 395–407.

WORKS CITED

Adams, John Quincy. *Lectures on Rhetoric and Oratory, Delivered to the Classes of Senior and Junior Sophisters in Harvard University.* 2 vols. Cambridge, Mass.: Hilliard and Metcalf, 1810.

Blair, Hugh. *Lectures on Rhetoric and Belles Lettres.* 2nd ed., 1785. Edited by Linda Ferreira-Buckley and S. Michael Halloran. Carbondale: Southern Illinois University Press, 2005.

Carr, Jean Ferguson, Stephen L. Carr, and Lucille M. Schultz. *Archives of Instruction: Nineteenth-Century Rhetorics, Readers, and Composition Books in the United States.* Carbondale: Southern Illinois University Press, 2005.

Catalogue of the Officers and Students of Saint Joseph's College, Philadelphia, Pa., 1893–94. Philadelphia: D. J. Gallagher, 1894.

Catalogue of St. Mary's College, St. Mary's, Kansas, 1894–95. Topeka: C. W. Douglass, 1895.

Catalogue of St. Xavier College, Cincinnati, Ohio, 1885–86. Cincinnati: P. T. Schultz, 1886.

Catalogue of St. Xavier College, Cincinnati, Ohio, 1897–98. Cincinnati: Edward Mountel, 1898.

Catalogue of St. Xavier College, Cincinnati, Ohio, 1898–99. Cincinnati: Keating, 1899.

The Constitutions of the Society of Jesus and Their Complementary Norms. St. Louis: Institute of Jesuit Sources, 1996.

Coppens, Charles. *The Art of Oratorical Composition, Based upon the Precepts and Models of the Old Masters.* New York: Schwartz, Kirwin and Fauss, 1885.

———. *A Practical Introduction to English Rhetoric: Precepts and Exercises.* New York: Schwartz, Kirwin and Fauss, 1880.

———. *Who Are the Jesuits?* St. Louis: B. Herder, 1911.

Course of Studies for the Colleges of the Missouri Province of the Society of Jesus. St. Louis: Nixon-Jones Printing, 1887.

Eighth Annual Catalogue of the Officers and Students of Marquette College, Milwaukeee, Wis., 1888–89. [Milwaukee]: Riverside Printing, [1889].

Farrell, Allan P. *The Jesuit Code of Liberal Education: Development and Scope of the Ratio Studiorum.* Milwaukee: Bruce, 1938.

Finn, Francis J. *Father Finn, S.J.: The Story of His Life Told by Himself for His Friends Young and Old.* Edited by Daniel A. Lord. New York: Benziger Brothers, 1929.

———. *Harry Dee; or, Making It Out.* New York: Benziger Brothers, 1892.

———. "The Need of Juvenile Catholic Literature," *American Ecclesiastical Review,* n.s. 5 (December 1896): 575–80.

———. *Percy Wynn; or, Making a Boy of Him.* New York: Benziger Brothers, 1891.

———. *Tom Playfair; or, Making a Start.* New York: Benziger Brothers, 1891.

Flynn, Lawrence J. "The *De arte rhetorica* (1568) by Cyprian Soarez, S.J.: A Translation with Introduction and Notes." PhD diss., University of Florida, 1955.

Guérin, Frédéric-Marie. *De la composition oratoire: Principes et applications.* Paris: Charles Douniol, 1861.

The Jesuit Ratio Studiorum *of 1599.* Translated by Allan P. Farrell. Washington, D.C.: Conference of Major Superiors of Jesuits, 1970. http://www.bc.edu/sites/libraries/ratio/ratio1599.pdf. Accessed February 2, 2015.

Johnson, Nan. *Nineteenth-Century Rhetoric in North America.* Carbondale: Southern Illinois University Press, 1991.

Kleutgen, Joseph. *Ars Dicendi Priscorum Potissimum Praeceptis et Exemplis.* Rome: Josephi et Francisci Salviucci, 1847.

Mahoney, Kathleen A. *Catholic Higher Education in Protestant America: The Jesuits and Harvard in the Age of the University.* Baltimore: Johns Hopkins University Press, 2003.

Mailloux, Steven. *Disciplinary Identities: Rhetorical Paths of English, Speech, and Composition.* New York: MLA, 2006.

———. *Reception Histories: Rhetoric, Pragmatism, and American Cultural Politics.* Ithaca, N.Y.: Cornell University Press, 1998.

———. *Rhetorical Power.* Ithaca, N.Y.: Cornell University Press, 1989.

Maryks, Robert Aleksander. *Saint Cicero and the Jesuits: The Influence of the Liberal Arts on the Adoption of Moral Probabilism.* Hampshire: Ashgate, 2008.

McKevitt, Gerald. *Brokers of Culture: Italian Jesuits in the American West, 1848–1919.* Stanford: Stanford University Press, 2007.

Meador, Jr., Prentice A. "Quintilian's 'Vir Bonus.'" *Western Speech* 34 (Summer 1970): 162–69.

Meyer, R. J. *The Science of the Saints.* Vol. 2, *The World in Which We Live.* St. Louis: B. Herder, 1919.

Miros, David P. "Rudolph J. Meyer and Saint Louis University: A Study of the Society of Jesus' Theological and Educational Enterprise at the Turn of the Century, 1885–1915." PhD diss., Saint Louis University, 2005.

Molson, Francis. "Francis J. Finn, S.J.: Pioneering Author of Juveniles for Catholic Americans." *Journal of Popular Culture* 11 (1977): 28–41.

The Ninth Annual Catalogue of the Officers and Students of Marquette College, Milwaukeee, Wis., 1889–90. Milwaukee: Riverside Printing, [1890].

"Obituary: Father Charles Coppens." *Woodstock Letters,* 50 (1921): 198–202.

O'Malley, John W. *The First Jesuits*. Cambridge, Mass.: Harvard University Press, 1993.

Ratio atque Institutio Studiorum Societatis Iesu. Monumenta Paedagogica Societatis Iesu, V. Ladislaus Lukács, S.J., ed. Rome: Institutum Historicum Societatis Iesu, 1986.

Ratio Studiorum et Institutiones Scholasticae Societatis Jesu, II. Edited by G. M. Pachtler. Berlin: A Hofman, 1887.

"The *Ratio Studiorum* of 1599." Translated by A. R. Ball, 119–254. In *St. Ignatius and the Ratio Studiorum*, ed. Edward A. Fitzpatrick. New York: McGraw-Hill, 1933.

Reggio, Carlo. *Orator Christianos*. Rome: Bartolomeo Zanetti, 1612.

Shuger, Debora K. *Sacred Rhetoric: The Christian Grand Style in the English Renaissance*. Princeton, N.J.: Princeton University Press, 1988.

The Spiritual Exercises of Saint Ignatius. Translated by George E. Ganss. Chicago: Loyola P, 1992.

JESUIT RHETORIC AND THE TEACHING OF PROFESSIONAL DISCOURSE IN AMERICA

Katherine H. Adams

Writing as taught within professional programs at American Jesuit universities involves a story that has not been told before. The Jesuits, who came to professional education both later and with more reticence than many other college administrators, engaged in a highly public denigration of these programs even as they embarked upon them. To many Jesuit educators, these programs seemed antithetical to the *Ratio Studiorum* and its emphasis on humanistic education—antithetical to their vision of what an educated man should be.

In the late nineteenth century, both state and private schools responded to a call for professional education, to better prepare the engineers, farmers, and businesspeople needed in a rapidly expanding nation. The Morrill Acts funded educational institutions by granting federally controlled land to endow "land-grant" colleges. As set forth in the initial 1862 Act, such schools would focus on the teaching of practical agriculture, science, and engineering as well as more traditional subject matters (Adams, 8–9).

Though the Jesuits embarked on professional education with many misgivings and though they often questioned whether they were making the right choice, they possessed a greater certainty about how to teach writing and speaking to students entering the professional programs that they began to develop in business, engineering, and other fields. The Jesuit tradition of *eloquentia perfecta*, defined by Robert Harvanek succinctly as "rhetorical gifts, combined with political insight, integrity, and wisdom," helped shape their approach, which would be different from that at state and other private schools and true to their educational goals (10). This curriculum involved students, throughout their degree programs, as makers of influential texts as well as readers, participating in Kenneth Burke's vision of an informed and engaged "unending conversation" (110–11). At a time when elective systems meant that many state and private-school students were taking only freshman composition before launching into other general education requirements and their majors, the Jesuits' tradition of rhetorical education led to another model for their professional as well as their classical programs.

From the beginnings at Georgetown, opening in 1789 with what would now be considered high school training and then gradually moving to higher-level instruction, the Jesuits established universities primarily in urban areas, to meet the needs of a Catholic population. Though 80 percent of Protestants lived in rural America at the beginning of the twentieth century, only 20 percent of Catholics did, and sons of these families certainly provided the primary audience for both secondary and university education administered by the Society of Jesus (Burtchaell, 564). Within cities, for a population interested in moving into the professionally employed middle class, the Jesuits maintained the *Ratio Studiorum*'s humanist education. As Father Joseph A. O'Hare, S.J., has written, the Jesuits always sought to provide "an integrated liberal education that develops habits of mind and powers of expression, both oral and written. . . . Moral education is as important as intellectual education; our graduates should not be simply successful careerists, but also responsible citizens" (145). His formulation recapitulates statements from many Jesuit university catalogs, such as Boston College's from 1894: "The end is culture, and mental and moral development" (quoted in Burtchaell, 568).

At a closer remove, especially for the Jesuits across town at Boston College, a more frightening experiment was also occurring at Harvard. Charles Eliot, president from 1869 to 1909, developed "spontaneous diversity of choice," an elective system through which, by the early 1880s, undergraduates selected most of their own courses, with the emphasis still on the liberal arts (Brubacher and Rudy, 114). This Harvard experiment soon spread to many other universities developing an array of new majors and classes. By 1894, Eliot concluded that the new system was "the most generally useful piece of work which this university has ever executed." In quoting Eliot in his history of the university, Samuel Eliot Morison wrote that "no principle in American higher education has ever spread so rapidly or gone so deep" (341). Eliot also transformed Harvard into a center of professional education, especially at the graduate level, in his new hires for the law faculty, expansion of the medical school from two years to three, and creation of a school of landscape architecture and a school of business administration.

With the American undergraduate curriculum changing fundamentally and with an array of professional programs also developing at the graduate level, the newly chosen superior general of the Society of Jesus, Father Luis Martin, S.J., in 1892 felt the need to stem this tide of change by contrasting the dominant system with what the Jesuits had to offer: "The training given by the Ratio was not to be specialized or professional, but general, and was to lay the foundation for professional studies. In this regard the Ratio stands in opposition to various modern systems which aim at the immediately useful and practical or, at best, allot a very short time to general education; it stands in sharp contrast with those systems which advocate the earliest possible beginning of specialization" (quoted in Herbermann, 655).

By the end of the century, the possible principles guiding higher education came into sharper contrast. In describing his elective system in the *Atlantic Monthly* in 1899, Eliot wrote that his most virulent opposition came from Muslim educators who insisted on education only in the Qur'an—as well as the overly dictatorial Jesuits, who strongly resembled them in brooking no opposition to their one form of instruction: "That these examples are both ecclesiastical is not without significance. Nothing but an unhesitating belief in the divine Wisdom of such prescriptions can justify them" (443). After the *Atlantic Monthly* refused to publish his response, Father Timothy Brosnahan, S.J., of Boston College, placed it in a Catholic magazine, *Sacred Heart Review*. There he argued at length for the superiority of the moral purpose and tradition of Jesuit education, which honored and valued students without abandoning them to the whims of temporary and inferior choices.

Into the twentieth century, Jesuits continued to contrast their educational goals with lesser, scattered approaches. In 1918, Fr. Francis P. Donnelly, S.J., of the College of the Holy Cross, wrote that "the evils of excessive specialization, of mere information instead of educated faculties, of neglected essentials and half-learned fads, of students who have a smattering in a thousand isms and a conceit fattened with some highly technical terms, and who at the same time cannot write or speak their own language;—these are evils which may be traced to the multiple and unrelated education of our time. . . . Modern schools have their highly specialized teachers for a hundred and one branches, each one striving to fill the memory with the technical terms and systematized information of some science. The old system held to the supremacy of language, mastered as an art." He then indicted the man who had spurred these evils: "Ex-President Eliot advocated all sciences as a means of education. Culture or educated faculties, he claimed, could be gained from 'chipping and filing and sawing' and, apparently, from anything else. . . . As a result, these multiplied sciences, these many trades, and these false theories, with the help of patient tax-payers, have turned our schools into laboratories, into foundries, into machine-shops, offices, farms, newspaper rows, art galleries, flower gardens, zoological parks, dairies, gents furnishing, ladies-tailoring, kitchens, dance-halls and what not" ("Discussion," 214).

But even though Jesuit leaders spoke against these professional programs, especially at the undergraduate level, their urban constituency sought this training. In *Conversations*, in fact, Jeffrey von Arx, S.J., argued that professional additions to the Jesuit curriculum—business, education, journalism, engineering, and other fields—occurred primarily in a "flurry" during the first decades of the twentieth century, stemming from "the desire for professional education from the rising Catholic middle class." In various cities, met with the need for a type of education that they had often decried, the Jesuits "backed into graduate and professional education without much of a plan" (7). Marquette's undergraduate school of engineering opened in 1908, and of business administration in 1909; Loyola Chicago began a law school in 1908 and an undergraduate education program in 1914; Georgetown's school of foreign service opened in 1919 with undergraduate and graduate programs; Boston College announced an undergraduate school of education that same year. As a result of this trend away from their traditional curriculum, as Charles L. Currie, S.J., reported in *Conversations*, Jesuit universities in 2009 were sponsoring four medical schools, three dental schools, fourteen law schools, twenty nursing and health-education programs, twenty-seven business schools, fourteen education schools or departments, eight engineering schools, five schools of social service, and one school of foreign service—this development, at both the graduate and undergraduate levels, similarly stated as occurring with "no master plan" (4). The Jesuits' commitment to this professional education, von Arx pointed out, has led to higher rankings for these programs than for their graduate schools in the humanities, even in fields such as philosophy, in which they might be expected to demonstrate superiority. For both Currie and von Arx, the well-ranked professional programs, a response to needs of particular students in particular cities, have often lacked a connection to the essentials of the universities' mission.

Because at all universities these new majors emphasized a set of professional skills, "there is little that is unique in form" about these programs as sponsored by the Jesuits, von Arx claims. However, the tradition of *eloquentia perfecta,* what Donnelly called "the supremacy of language, mastered as an art," led to a distinctive approach to oral and written rhetoric instruction if not to the overall curriculum.

At the beginning of the twentieth century, industry professionals and educators at non-Jesuit schools worked to shape the writing instruction that their professional students would receive. In his presidential address to the American Institute of Electrical Engineers in 1902, Charles P. Steinmetz spoke against the common tendency of philologists from the English department to insist on a "florid" literary style, from which "no useful results can be expected" (1148). In 1903, another industry leader, J. G. White, had a practical and non-florid content in mind for a course that would enroll engineering students: "It may be necessary to have a considerable part of the training incorporated into the writing of laboratory reports, examination papers, and other similar documents" (576). Similarly, in advocating new courses for agriculture majors, Harry R. O'Brien at the Oklahoma Agricultural and Mechanical College in 1914 disparaged the older curriculum as he spoke for the new: "We have been going on in the same old rut, teaching farmers how to get culture, how to write glowing descriptions, how to get local color into narratives; when instead we should be setting these farmers to putting practical knowledge into clear, concise English. We should be teaching them how to describe the workings of a fusilage cutter or a milking machine, how to relate the life history of a grasshopper or a liverfluke" (471). Business professors, such as David Kinley at the University of Illinois, also advocated practical training in writing various types of business documents (Adams, 128–29). These specialized courses could replace traditional freshman composition or appear at the sophomore level to engage students in real-world writing.

Thus at state schools particularly, the advanced writing instruction offered in professional programs became a more advanced and practical version of the expository forms, such as comparison and causal analysis, that reigned in the first-year course. In business-writing classes, students commonly considered the formats for various types of letters and reports; engineering students covered report forms and manuals in the civil and chemical fields; agriculture students wrote the county crop report and extension essay. At many schools, such forms appeared divorced from their real-world applications and may have seemed like little more than intricate exercises, the advanced version of the five-paragraph theme.

As the Jesuit universities embarked on professional education, they did so with other priorities: within their own appreciation for language and their own aversion to what Francis P. Donnelly referred to as a conglomeration of "what not," which in writing instruction could stem from an array of rules created for lectures on an array of formats. Instead of setting up special classes in writing for engineering or business, they relied on multiyear courses guided by Donnelly's textbooks, including two volumes of *Model English* (1920), *The Art of Interesting: Its Theory and Practice for Speakers and Writers* (1920), *Persuasive Speech: The Art of Rhetoric for College* (1931), and *Literature, the Leading Educator* (1938). His work continued that of Fr. Charles Coppens, S.J., author of *A Practical Introduction to English Rhetoric* (1880) and *Art of Oratorical Composition* (1885). Coppens taught Latin, Greek, and rhetoric at a number of universities, including St. Louis University, Creighton University, and Loyola University Chicago as well as St. Mary's College of Kansas, where he served as president from 1881 to 1884.

The influence of Coppens and Donnelly spanned years of instruction, in the professional as well as classical curricula of Jesuit universities. From Coppens's *A Practical Introduction to English Rhetoric,* students learned grammar, sentence formats, and figures of words and thought as they took on "species of prose composition," including school essays as well as business letters; magazine articles; scientific, historical, and political essays; histories and biographies; and dialogues, novel writing, and many forms of poetry. For Coppens, study of classical and modern literature in Latin and English, in college and the preparatory years, enabled students to write prose and poetry as well as write about it. Similarly, his textbook on oratory taught students to declaim as well as to write about famous orations. Francis P. Donnelly, who extended the influence of his textbooks through frequent addresses at meetings of classics and English teachers, similarly advocated an education in oratory and literature that provided models to imitate: orations, essays, and poems. "The drill was centered upon expression," he wrote in *Literature: The Leading Educator* (1938), "not upon history, archaeology or antiquities" (127). "Art is doing and you learn to do by doing," he asserted further. "Original composition from the first day of kindergarten to the day of college graduation will ensure that literature is taught as an art" (178). This approach acquainted students with prose and poetry understood as arts to appreciate and to imitate, as students became immersed in various forms of rhetoric.

This active form of education in written and oral discourse, in the "unending conversation," continued in co-curricular events that provided a major part of college life. Georgetown's first non-religious organization was the Philodemic Society, formed by seniors in 1830, to further both eloquence and liberty. Its activities included banquets and regular meetings at which students recited famous orations such as Washington's Farewell Address; students and alumni served as guest orators, reciting their own original speeches, dialogues, and poetry; and debaters took on topics drawn from contemporary politics, such as the reasons for and effects of tariffs. Students also read papers concerning famous rhetors, comparing Cicero and Patrick Henry as political speakers, for example. This club, and additional ones for students in the sophomore and junior years, furthered a tradition begun at regular exhibitions and at commencements that might go on from 9:00 AM to 2:30 PM and involve twenty-five to thirty speakers (Daley, 233–38). On its current website, the Philodemic Society claims that "it is the dedication of our members—both past and present—which has given our society the distinction of being not only the oldest student organization on campus, but also one of the long-running collegiate debating societies in the country. While other organizations occasionally engage in debate on-campus, the Philodemic Society strives to consistently be the premier forum for debate at Georgetown University" ("History").

Even before the publication of texts by Coppens and Donnelly, Jesuit schools provided complete programs in imitation and rhetorical skill. One of the earliest forays into professional education at Jesuit universities occurred in separate "commercial courses," in which students learned bookkeeping and other technical skills, in curricula varying from two years to four, perhaps with less Latin instruction than in the "classical course" but still very much with the Jesuit emphasis on rhetoric. As the catalog indicated, Marquette University's commercial course in 1879, involving bookkeeping, math, and physics, included two years of basic study of words and sentences guided by Lindley Murray's ubiquitous *English Grammar*, along with a third year in which John Seeley Hart's *A Manual of Composition and Rhetoric* spurred additional grammar review and study of the sentence types and figures of speech that would enable students to succeed at an array of genres: versification, letter writing, diaries, news writing, history, and fictional narrations. The fourth year provided the opportunity to "perfect the student in rhetoric and the higher styles of composition," with Abraham Mill's edition of Hugh Blair's *Lectures on Rhetoric and Belles Lettres* as the text (10). These students, clearly viewed as active rhetors, not just writers of business reports, also took required elocution lessons through the years.

After Fr. Coppens published his *A Practical Introduction to English Rhetoric* (1880) and *Art of Oratorical Composition* (1885), these books frequently guided the extended rhetoric curriculum within professional programs. Gonzaga University, founded in 1887, had a commercial course whose curriculum, as the 1893–94 *Catalogue* maintained in good Jesuit fashion, enabled the student to have "all his powers developed by a liberal education" so that he could "bring a ten-fold effort to mercantile pursuits" (4–5). This program included bookkeeping, stenography, and typing; Latin, French, German, and philosophy; and poetry and orations in English. To form the most successful businessman, as the *Catalogue* stated, "an English narration, description, or other composition, in prose or verse, is written by every student once a week" (5). The commercial course in 1901–2 provided more specifics about the English study. Guided by Coppens's *A Practical Introduction,* students mastered grammar and style as they read and imitated letter writing, short stories, and various verse forms. First-year students also took elocution once a week along with chemistry, commercial law, bookkeeping, and other subjects. In the second year, reading models and doing imitations continued, as did letter writing, both receiving further emphasis in the third year, along with etymology (*Catalogue, 1901–1902,* 24–26).

As professional programs developed, this set of classes and assignments permeated more than the first commercial courses. In 1912–13, as the Loyola University New Orleans bulletin indicated, for the second year that this college was on St. Charles Avenue, the emphasis on reading, writing, and rhetorical study reiterated the stated goal of providing "general, vigorous and rounded development" that would ensure "mental growth" (8). Students in the premedical program studied fiction, poetry, and essays, using Coppens's *Practical Introduction* as the text. The prose readings included essays by Newman, Macaulay, Arnold, and De Quincey; the poetry, Coleridge, Tennyson, Milton, and Shelley; the plays, *The Tempest* and *Julius Caesar.* This study resulted in weekly exercises in writing essays, poems, and dialogues, as Coppens directed. In the two-year pharmacy program, instruction included Latin language and literature along with fiction and poetry in English, with the home reading including the novels of James Fenimore Cooper and the composition assignments including letter writing and narratives. In the four-year scientific course, along with the science, bookkeeping, commercial law, and a modern language instead of Latin, students did declamations once a week while studying the same literature as the did pharmacy students and doing the same writing exercises. The scientific curriculum also included the study and imitation of orations such Edmund Burke's speech to the electors of Bristol, concerning the independence that an elected representative ought to be granted, along with precepts of oral argumentation. Seniors received special "practice in the writing of essays, magazine articles, and short stories" (80).

By the 1920s, Jesuits schools were availing themselves of the many textbooks by Francis P. Donnelly, such as the two volumes of *Model English* (1920), which drew students further into imitation of models. Rockhurst University, as its curricular prospectus from 1915 stated, sought to embody Jesuit theories of education throughout the curriculum: "A young man well trained in general and classical studies succeeds better afterwards in professional preparation than one whose early training was distracted by an assorted smattering of quasi-professional studies" (quoted in Owens, 39). To construct this education that would not be a "smattering," in the pre-legal and premedical certificate programs in 1925–26, the Jesuits included regularly meeting classes in English and public speaking. Using Donnelly's texts, teachers turned to literature and to orations to provide models for writers that would engage them in effective responses to various rhetorical situations (Owens, 62).

In using Donnelly's *The Art of Interesting: Its Theory and Practice for Speakers and Writers* as well as his *Model English*, the Jesuits further connected speaking, writing, and reading to the active role in society that they intended for all their graduates. At Canisius College in the 1920s, as its historian Charles A. Brady has asserted, the Jesuits judged that, because of the "accelerated tempo of business development," they had a responsibility to move into business education, establishing a more advanced and developed curriculum than had been offered in the earlier commercial course. With the initiation of this program in 1926, Canisius "formally acknowledged its responsibility in the matter of helping establish an ethos for business within the American culture that, more than any other in history, was now attempting to ground a large part of its civilized values upon the primacy of commerce and manufacturing," the Canisius Jesuits thus committing themselves to instilling ethical values, not just preparing men for work (Brady, 159). As Father J.A. Panuska, S.J., commented in his study of Jesuit education for the professions, such a program reflected the "very definite and dynamic reform thrust" that underlies Jesuit training (127). To fulfill their goal of "installing systematic business curricula within a balanced educational process," Canisius's teachers established an accounting major that involved English study each year: poetry and drama as well as orations and debates, the textbooks by Francis P. Donnelly providing an emphasis on models (Brady, 157). *The Art of Interesting* especially provided a focus on oral persuasion, on how to avoid being a "tiresome speaker" lacking eloquence and directness (3). For training priests as well as businessmen, Donnelly provided advice and exercises that could bring imagination and interest to any discourse, with imitation of famous orations a key part of the process.

Other professional programs also adopted this combination of the written and the spoken through models. A Gonzaga program in engineering, discussed by the college administration as early as 1912, actually began in 1934, providing courses in chemical, civil, and electrical engineering, thirty-one students in the first class, with religion and English in the first two years of a three-year curriculum, the third still being worked out when classes began (Schoenberg 368). First-year students did public speaking, through imitation of models, along with reading and writing both prose and poetry. While the Jesuits did not require Latin in this curriculum, they did maintain their commitment to training in English.

Another addition to professional education, which led to the enrollment of women in Jesuit schools, was summer-school education and then full-time programs for teacher education, at first for Catholic sisters and then for other women as well as men. It was another department or college influenced by the Donnelly approach to reading and writing, one through which Jesuit professors could extend their influence on rhetorical instruction in the lower schools. Fordham began teacher-education classes in 1916, leading ten years later to 720 women enrolled in its teaching college, 80 percent of the students (Leahy, 75). At Gonzaga, a new summer department for education training in 1923–24 enrolled women when the rest of the university did not, the first enrollees including fifty-eight sisters, five laypeople, six scholastics, and one priest (Schoenberg, 305). Fr. Timothy Driscoll, S.J., offered instruction in English, involving analysis of various forms of literature as well as imitation of models, and Lilly Snow taught expression in the summer course for an additional hundred dollars (Schoenberg, 305–6). As Driscoll made assignments based on regular analysis and imitation of models, he discussed his purposes and methods and their applicability to various age groups. When he switched to Seattle University in 1925, he continued his use of complex reading and writing assignments, which some students found shocking. In *Reminiscing*, Archie J. Richardson recalls the workload of one of Driscoll's classes: "About two weeks into the course, he announced our written assignment for two semesters of in-depth Shakespeare—a 6,000 word paper consisting of personality analyses of 12 major and 12 minor characters from any plays of our choice. With that announcement came five drop-outs" (31). Along with this extended assignment, students created monologues, dialogues, and orations and discussed the purposes of this intense combination.

Along with other professional programs, Jesuit schools established professional education in journalism, certainly another opportunity to engage students in the purposes and methods of rhetoric. Within its business school beginning in 1910, Marquette launched this instruction with leadership from Fr. John E. Copus, S.J., who had worked as a journalist. From England, he had immigrated to Canada, where he worked for a rural paper, the *Kingsville Weekly Reporter*, published by his brother, and then edited two other small-town Canadian papers before becoming a reporter for the *Detroit Morning Times*. He was writing novels, primarily juvenile fiction about key stories of the Bible and the choice of faith, himself a convert to Catholicism in his youth, when he came to Marquette to teach English literature in 1907. In 1910, when only two other American universities had such programs, he established the first Catholic journalism school. He felt that state universities oriented their instruction to skills and to the big-city dailies but a Jesuit school could foster another emphasis for young journalists: on "the ideals of their vocation," a type of study that would enable Marquette graduates to "displace the prevalent journalistic sensationalism and sordid materialism" (Hamilton, 99). At the beginning, Copus was the only teacher. Two years led to a diploma, three to a bachelor's degree in journalism. The first four young men met in Copus's room in 1910 as they began the two-year program. In 1914 students completed the first bachelor's degrees. As Copus's obituary in the *Milwaukee Sentinel* in June 1915 described them, "his classes were without doubt the most informal of any in the school," and he concentrated not on the format of the news article but on the ethics of reporting, on the role of the press in a democracy, and on the newspaper's duty to its city and state ("Illness Is Fatal").

Fr. John Danihy, S.J., replaced Copus as director in 1915, separating journalism from its first home in the college of business. He sought a regular student newspaper, first called *The Blue and Gold* and then in 1916 *The Marquette Tribune,* created with used press and composing-room equipment, turning out five hundred copies by the third issue. Danihy also established the college yearbook, the *Hilltop,* and formed Phi Epsilon, Marquette's journalism honor society. Other Jesuit colleges followed in offering journalism courses and colleges, including Fordham, whose first courses were given in 1917 and 1918, along with the publication of the *Ram* (Schroth, 136–37).

While the Jesuits developed a significant curriculum in rhetoric in their undergraduate professional programs, they did so also in their law schools, in which their commitment to rhetorical training long predated the twentieth century's legal-writing courses. One of the earliest legal-writing courses began at the University of Chicago in 1938, a yearlong curriculum involving legal memoranda, editorials, contracts, and other assignments (Sheppard, 833). Jesuit schools did not begin this trend toward a separate course, but they had always incorporated oral and written argumentation in what they required of law students. In the 1890s, Georgetown Law School, with the classics department of the college providing instruction in Latin "to relieve the embarrassment of those who find a knowledge of the Latin language essential to the study of law" and presumably came from non-Jesuit colleges that didn't have it, created one of the first moot-court programs, for second and third-year students who participated three times a week, making arguments before a circuit court and a court of appeals (Sheppard, 546). The St. Louis University Law School in 1891 required weekly exercises in the pleading of cases. At Gonzaga Law School, as the 1920 catalog indicated, students studied debating each week and participated in the Philhistorian Debating Senate, concerned with issues of politics, ethics, and law. They took Oratory of Pleading in the second year: "a study of the principles of argumentation, with regular practice in outlining and briefing arguments and in debates" (22).

Though state schools seemed to be the leaders in establishing writing courses as part of professional education, Jesuit universities involved all of their students in several years of writing and speaking. In the Jesuits' professional programs, Latin might be eliminated but certainly not English. Student studied grammar, sentence style, and a variety of types of poetry and prose, including essays, short stories, magazine articles, histories, and letters. They read widely not just to appreciate literature but to create their own. Oration and debate exercises engaged students in oral disputation, often about current economic or political issues. Opportunities for oral practice continued in clubs and at special events. The Jesuits perhaps did not lead in the creation of courses on business reports or law briefs, but they did lead in a commitment to rhetoric, for every semester and year, with some of the style certainly "florid," as engineer Charles P. Steinmetz maintained, but with a great deal of variety in the reading and writing assignments. In these beginnings, the Jesuits created a curriculum by which they engaged professional rhetors in larger questions, in addressing various audiences through an array of genres—in the "unending conversation" of well-schooled citizens, business leaders, and scholars. As major curricula grew in credit hours in the twentieth century, not all Jesuit universities maintained this commitment, but they did provide a model for what the rhetoric component of a professional program can be.

WORKS CITED

Adams, Katherine H. *A History of Professional Writing Instruction in American Colleges: Years of Acceptance, Growth, and Doubt.* Dallas: Southern Methodist University Press, 1993.

Brady, Charles A. *The First Hundred Years, Canisius College, 1870–1970.* Buffalo: Canisius College, 1969.

Brosnahan, Timothy. "President Eliot and Jesuit Colleges." *Sacred Heart Review* 13 (January 1900). Reprinted by Woodstock College. California Digital Library, Ebook and Texts Archive. Accessed February 27, 2012.

Brubacher, John Seiler, and Willis Rudy. *Higher Education in Transition: A History of American Colleges and Universities.* Piscataway, N.J.: Transaction, 1997.

Burke, Kenneth. *The Philosophy of Literary Form.* Berkeley: University of California Press, 1941.

Burtchaell, James Tunstead. *The Dying of the Light: The Disengagement of Colleges and Universities from Their Christian Churches.* Grand Rapids, Mich.: Eerdmans, 1998.

Catalogue of Gonzaga College, 1893–1894. Spokane: Quick Print, 1894.

Catalogue of Gonzaga College, 1901–1902. Spokane: Inland Printing, 1902.

Catalogue and Bulletin of Gonzaga University. Spokane: Gonzaga University, 1920.

Coppens, Charles. *Art of Oratorical Composition.* New York: Schwartz, Kirwin, and Fauss, 1885.

———. *A Practical Introduction to English Rhetoric, Precepts and Exercises.* New York: Catholic Publication Society, 1886.

Currie, Charles L. "Jesuit Graduate Professional Schools: Anything Distinctive?" *Conversations on Jesuit Higher Education* 35, no. 1 (Spring 2009): 2–6.

Daley, John M. *Georgetown: Origin and Early Years*. Washington, D.C.: Georgetown University Press,1957.

Donnelly, Francis P. *The Art of Interesting: Its Theory and Practice for Speakers and Writers*. New York: P. J. Kenedy and Sons, 1920.

———. "Discussion of 'The Coordination of Language Study.'" *NCEA* 15, no. 1 (November 1918): 212–17.

———. *Literature: The Leading Educator*. New York: Longmans, Green, 1938.

———. *Model English, Book I: The Development of Thought*. 1902. Boston: Allyn and Bacon; 2nd ed., 1920.

———. *Persuasive Speech: The Art of Rhetoric for College*. New York: P. J. Kenedy and Sons, 1931.

Eliot, Charles W. "Recent Changes in Secondary Education." *Atlantic Monthly* 84 (October 1899): 433–45.

Hart, John Seeley. *A Manual of Composition and Rhetoric*. New York: Hammett, 1871.

Hamilton, Raphael N. *The Story of Marquette University: An Object Lesson in the Development of Catholic Higher Education*. Milwaukee: Marquette University Press,1953.

Harvanek, Robert F. *The Jesuit Vision of a University*. Chicago: Loyola University Press, 1989.

Herbermann, Charles George. *The Catholic Encyclopedia: An International Work of Reference on the Constitution, Doctrine, Discipline, and History of the Catholic Church*. Vol. 12. New York: Universal Knowledge Foundation, 1913.

"Illness Is Fatal to Father Copus." *Milwaukee Sentinel* June 13, 1915, 1:4.

Leahy, William P. *Adapting to America: Catholics, Jesuits, and Higher Education in the Twentieth Century*. Washington, D.C.: Georgetown University Press, 1991.

Loyola University, New Orleans, La., 1912–1913. New Orleans: Loyola University, 1912.

Marquette College Catalogue, 1879–1880. Milwaukee: Marquette College, 1879.

Mill, Abraham, and Hugh Blair. *Lectures on Rhetoric and Belles Lettres*. London: Carvill, 1829.

Morison, Samuel Eliot. *Three Centuries of Harvard, 1636–1936*. Cambridge, Mass.: Harvard University Press, 1986.

Murray, Lindley. *English Grammar: Adapted to the Different Classes of Learners*. London: Wilson, Spence, and Mawman, 1795.

O'Brien, Harry R. "Agricultural English." *English Journal* 3 (1914): 470–79.

O'Hare, Joseph A. "Jesuit Education in America." In *The Jesuit Tradition in Education and Missions: A 450-Year Perspective*, ed. Christopher Chapple, 143–54. Scranton, Pa.: University of Scranton Press, 1993.

Owens, Hugh M. *History of Rockhurst College: The First Quarter Century (1914–1939)*. Kansas City, Mo.: Rockhurst College, 1953.

Panuska, J. A. "The Jesuit Experience with Graduate Education and Education for the Professions." In *Jesuit Higher Education: Essays on an American Tradition of Excellence*, ed. R. E. Bonachea, 124–33. Pittsburgh: Dusquesne University Press, 1989.

The Philodemic Society of Georgetown University. http://philodemicsociety.org. Accessed February 22, 2012.

Richardson, Archie J. *Reminiscing: A Seventy Year Collection of Memoirs and Stories about the Jesuits Who Built Seattle University.* Seattle: Seattle University Alumni Association, 1980.

Schoenberg, Wilfred P. *Gonzaga University: Seventy-Five Years, 1887–1962.* Spokane: Lawton, 1963.

Schroth, Raymond A. *Fordham: A History and a Memoir.* New York: Fordham University Press, 2008.

Sheppard, Steve. *The History of Legal Education in the United States: Commentaries and Primary Sources.* Vol. 1. Clark, N.J.: Lawbook Exchange, 2007.

Steinmetz, Charles P. "Presidential Address." *Transactions of the AIEE* 19 (1902): 1145–50.

Von Arx, Jeffrey. "Professional Education." *Conversations on Jesuit Higher Education* 35, no. 1 (Spring 2009): 7–8.

White, J. G. "The Problems That Are Facing the Electrical Engineer of To-day and the Qualities of Mind and Character Which Are Needed to Meet Them." *Transactions of the AIEE* 20 (1903): 569–78.

WALTER ONG: A JESUIT RHETORICAL AND INTERDISCIPLINARY SCHOLAR AND EDUCATOR

Janice Lauer Rice

Over the years since I studied with Fr. Walter Ong from 1959 through 1961, I have realized how many of his concepts have impacted literacy education and forecast major rhetorical ideas in the field of rhetoric and composition. His rhetorical works have, in fact, helped to awaken the entire field of English studies to an understanding of the disciplinary nature of the study and teaching of written discourse.

Fr. Ong was an exceptional scholar and Jesuit priest. His significant contributions to modern culture place him high in the ranks of the most prominent Jesuit educators of the twentieth century. His 457 publications include highly influential books, many of them translated into other languages, and numerous essays, reprinted extensively. His rhetorical work must therefore be contextualized in a complex interdisciplinary matrix of studies. This essay can offer only a thin layer of his insightful ideas that penetrate some of the major dialogues in the academy, religion, and culture at large. Below is a sample of the areas to which he has contributed books and essays:

Literary studies: Hopkins, Yeats, Kafka, Joyce, medieval hymnody, the Green Knights, Tudor prose style, Swift, New Criticism, Chesterton, T. S. Eliot, and Conrad.

Rhetoric: "The Province of Rhetoric and Poetic"; Hobbes; *Ramus and the Talon Inventory*; *Ramus, Method, and the Decay of Dialogue*; "The Writer's Audience Is Always a Fiction"; Interfaces of the Word: Studies in the Evolution of Consciousness and Culture, and *Orality and Literacy*.

Contemporary culture: Comics, Hollywood, "Evolution and Cyclicism in Our Time," *The Barbarian Within, Technology and Culture, Frontiers in American Catholicism, In the Human Grain, Fighting for Life*, and "American Culture and Morality."

Religion and the Jesuit ethos: *The Presence of the Word*, "St. Ignatius' Prison-Cage and the Existentialist Situation," "Scholarly Research and Publication in the Jesuit College and University," "Voice as Summons for Belief: Literature, Faith, and the Divided Self," "Teilhard de Chardin," and "Realizing Catholicism: Faith, Learning, and the Future.

Interdisciplinary studies: "Philosophical Sociology," "The Agonistic Base of Scientifically Abstract Thought," "An Exchange on American Sign Language and Deaf Culture," "Government and Human Values," "Communications as a Field of Study."

Ong's entire list of publications can be found in "The Walter J. Ong Bibliography" complied by Thomas Walsh in *Language, Culture, and Identity: The Legacy of Walter J. Ong, S.J.,* edited by Sara van den Berg and Thomas M. Walsh (Cresskill, New Jersey: Hampton Press), 2011, or online at http://bibs.slu.edu /ong/searchForm.php. All of the above works show evidence of the importance of discourse, particularly written discourse or rhetoric. Thomas Farrell in "An Introduction to Walter Ong's Work," in a three-volume collection of Fr. Ong's essays and studies, *Faith and Contexts* (xix–lv), lists his many national roles, including as a member of a White House Task Force in Education; president of the Modern Language Association; regional associate for the American Council of Learned Societies; cochairman of the National Endowment for the Humanities' Committee on Science, Technology, and Human Values; and advisory-board member of the John Simon Guggenheim Memorial Foundation. He also served on the National Commission on the Humanities sponsored by the Rockefeller Foundation and as president of the Milton Society of America and of the Central Renaissance Conference. He was a member of the National Endowment for the Humanities. His honors included France's Chevalier dans l'Ordre des Palmes Académiques; the Jesuits' Sword of Ignatius Loyola; the Lifetime Achievement Award of the Conference on Christianity and Literature; and various honorary degrees. He lectured extensively throughout the United States, Canada, Europe, the Middle East, Central and West Africa, Northern Africa, East Asia, and Latin America and offered visiting-lecture series at major universities in the United States and Canada. Despite these accolades and international renown, he was a humble person, a faithful friend, and a dedicated priest. During his thirty-six years as a faculty member at Saint Louis University he could be found saying the early daily Mass at the university church.

In 1960, I first encountered his rhetorical work when I studied for my master's degree at Saint Louis University. I took two classes from him. Our sessions were permeated by his subtle humor, including an occasional reference to his hobby, fly-fishing. Paramount was his great respect for each student. The first course was the required boring bibliographic course, which he occasionally enlivened by accounts of the history of printing and bookmaking. The high points of the course, however, were the times we got him off subject to talk about his rhetorical writings. (Both of his books on Ramus were published the year before I took his course.) Those moments prompted me to find and begin reading his work on rhetoric.

The second course was entitled "Prose Criticism." In this course he shared his broad reading background with us. This course opened my mind to a diverse set of readings and ideas. Among the twenty-two books and numerous journal essays we consumed, including several of his own, were Marshall McLuhan's *The Mechanical Bride,* Margaret Mead's *And Keep Your Powder Dry,* Aristotle's *Art of Rhetoric,* Bernard Rosenberg and David White's *Mass Culture,* Herbert Read's *English Prose Style,* William Lynch's *Image Industries,* and M. H. Abrams's *The Mirror and the Lamp.* In the forty-four pages of notes that I took from his lectures and still have, he introduced notions such as orality and literacy, emerging electronic communications, popular culture and media, and new movements in philosophy. The course not only introduced me to current interdisciplinary studies of a wide range of print media, it also awakened me to rhetoric as a whole and especially to Aristotle's rhetoric and its discussion of invention and probability as the province of rhetoric.

What an eye-opener! Especially central to me was his work on Ramus, which catapulted me into trying to restore rhetorical invention to teaching written discourse both in theory and in pedagogy. I had been teaching the categorical syllogism to my composition students as a way to generate arguments. After that I began to rethink my inventional pedagogy. Only through the years that followed did I realize how much Ong's courses penetrated my teaching, writing, and efforts to educate others to connect composition and rhetoric. During this course he invited Perry Miller, his professor at Harvard, to visit our course and meet with the class, requesting us to read some of Miller's books so we would be able to carry on a dialogue with him. Each of us read one book and shared our notes beforehand. As we sat around a large table with Perry Miller, there was an awkward silence. I asked a question that stimulated Miller's response. Silence followed. I asked another question, and so it went. For this effort, I think I earned Ong's eternal gratitude!

A year later, in 1962, when I started my doctoral work at the University of Michigan, I told Warner Rice, the English-department chair, that I wanted to study rhetoric. Surprised but interested because he remembered that the department had once been a department of rhetoric, he informed me that, although the department currently had no graduate rhetoric program, he would advise me through a somewhat unorthodox program that enabled me eventually to write my dissertation, "Invention in Contemporary Rhetoric." Later, in 1976, joined by Ross Winterowd, I initiated a summer two-week seminar, entitled "Rhetoric Seminar on Current Theories of Teaching Composition," as a venue for composition instructors to become acquainted with the accumulating body of rhetorical theory and research on written discourse and the emerging field of study. It was held for thirteen summers from 1976 to 1988, first at the University of Detroit and then at Purdue University. The seminar annually enrolled around fifty new and seasoned college, university, and community-college English professors, some high-school teachers, and a few administrators and scholars from other disciplines, most funding themselves, from all around the United States and Canada and from England. It featured as faculty eight or nine prominent "rhetoric and composition" scholars and was one of the earliest English courses to offer graduate credit for rhetorical studies. Not surprisingly, the first seminars were offered at the University of Detroit, a Jesuit university. Ong graciously came to five of the thirteen seminars, offering lectures and discussions on such topics as "Audience as Silent Reader," "Writing Is a Technology That Changes Thought," and "Plato, Writing, Print, and Computers." During his last seminar visit, in 1986, after giving his lecture he excused himself from the usual discussion and came to my home to rest. How dedicated and typical of him to come to the seminar in ill health!

RHETORICAL SCHOLAR

Let me turn now from the above personal memories to Ong's rhetorical scholarship. Three of Ong's intellectual influences were Marshall McLuhan, who directed his master's thesis at Saint Louis University in 1944; Perry Miller, who supervised his dissertation at Harvard in 1955; and the Jesuit rhetorical tradition. One of the ways that Ong typically treated a scholarly subject was to historicize it, a practice he credited to Marshall McLuhan. Then as a student of the Renaissance at Harvard, he began to investigate the role of Peter Ramus in the study and teaching of rhetoric. As a Jesuit he would also have been familiar with the Jesuit *Ratio Studiorum*, published in its final form in 1599. This curricular document recommended that students be taught rhetoric from *De Arte Rhetorica*, a classical rhetorical-theory text by Cypriano de Soarez. In a recent essay on Jesuit rhetoric, Kristine Johnson and Paul Lynch claimed that the Jesuits in their *Ratio* "founded the first global rhetorical curriculum" (99). Thus, at the time when Ramus was reducing rhetoric, the Jesuits were teaching a full art of rhetoric, including invention, as Johnson and Lynch argued, "through a medieval curriculum with humanistic and religious aims, ultimately producing a distinctive rhetorical tradition" (101). The *Ratio* devoted "significant attention to invention," as these authors pointed out, concluding "that invention remained within the province of rhetoric is perhaps a pedagogical reflection of Jesuit resistance to Ramus" (104).

In 1958, Ong helped to initiate this rescue of invention in his dissertation at Harvard and in subsequent book, *Ramus, Method, and the Decay of Dialogue*. He saw connections between Ramus's reorganization of logic and rhetoric in the sixteenth century and the literacy problems of the twentieth century. In that text and others he investigated Ramus's role in excluding invention from the study of rhetoric and relegating it to logic, thereby ignoring the distinction that Aristotle made between rhetorical and philosophical reasoning: Rhetoric starts from premises accepted by the audience in a particular culture and reaching probable conclusions, whereas logic (philosophy) stems from self-evident principles and reasoning to absolute conclusions. He traced how Ramus combined invention and disposition into one "method" under dialectic (logic).

Attempting to explain how this happened, Ong and others, including Albert Duhamel, pursued extensive and complex studies of Ramus's "method," linking it to many cultural and intellectual propensities of the time. One was a contemporary drive toward the reduction of complexity. Ong contended that Ramus's logics "manifest an express concern for simplification for pedagogical purposes, based on simple spatial models" (*Ramus, Method* 169). He referred to Ramus's method as a "kind of intellectual commercialism" ("Ramist Method," 172) and "corpuscular epistemology" ("Ramist Method," 203), labeling this "method" a "cold-blooded, analytical, diagrammatic, even mechanistic view of communication" ("Ramist Method," 173). He also noted that "this concept of method was transferred to logic, being rigidified in a sort of mechanical way in the process" ("Ramist Method," 178).

RHETORIC AND COMPOSITION

The above work had an important impact on the development of the field that came to be called "rhetoric and composition." The above reduction of rhetoric over the centuries ultimately led composition instructors and textbooks to narrow writing instruction to a focus on the five-paragraph theme and expository style and resulted in the popular view, still prevalent, of rhetoric as decoration, empty bombast, or even misleading verbiage. In the 1960s and seventies, students were entering (and sometimes leaving) colleges and universities with literacy problems. Many causes have been advanced for this situation in numerous books and essays over the last five decades. One of these culprits was the narrow emphasis, in composition courses, on teaching expository style and traditional grammar, a residue of Ramus's pedagogy. In such classes, students scrutinized examples of good expository prose to imitate but were largely left on their own to get ideas and arguments. Some classes at the time used casebooks to provide content or taught symbolic logic (categorical syllogisms, etc.) to improve students' arguments and stimulate ideas. For a period of time, I taught using these pedagogies and shared in the frustration about their ineffectiveness. So how did things begin to change?

Although many readers may be familiar with the story below, I wish to offer my narrative here especially for those outside the field of rhetoric and composition or for newcomers to it. In the sixties, a few English professors who were involved in teaching writing began to go more deeply into the above problems, engaging in historical investigations that prominently included Fr. Ong's seminal studies. Edward Corbett, Frank D'Angelo, Janet Emig, Janice Lauer, Gordon Rohman, Ross Winterowd, Richard Young, and other English professors began offering ways to return invention and disposition to the teaching of writing, bringing with it an inevitable attention to the writing process. Such efforts were a strong part both of the development of the field of rhetoric and composition and of the revival of the study of written discourse as a scholarly discipline in the academy. At the present time, these moves continue to generate extensive multimodal research, fruitful subfields, theoretically educated and devoted instructors of writing, interdisciplinary collaboration, vigorous dialogues and rhetoric and composition programs at undergraduate and graduate levels. While the paths and trajectories of such developments since the sixties have been only minimally delineated here (in contrast to available rich theoretical and historical accounts), Ong must be credited as one of the seminal movers.

Another of Ong's contributions to rhetoric and composition studies, his popular *Orality and Literacy*, which was translated into at least ten languages, illustrates a key trait of a Jesuit educator: one who not only publishes in-depth scholarship but also offers books for the public that incorporate a copious range of theoretical and interdisciplinary theory and research. Jesuits have been the educators of educators, exemplifying Jesuit education at its best. *Orality and Literacy* has played that role: It is prescient, penetrated by salient scholarship, and replete with current implications. This text helped to heighten the importance of writing instruction and to foreground the crucial nature of writing. Ong boldly asserted there: "Writing, in this ordinary sense, was and is the most momentous of all human technological inventions. It is not a mere appendage to speech" (*Orality and Literacy*, 85). He went on to explain one of the relationships between orality and literacy: "Persons who have interiorized writing not only write but also speak literally, which is to say that they organize, to varying degrees, even their oral expression in thought patterns and verbal patterns that they would not know of unless they could write" (*Orality and Literacy*, 56–57). In this book he also reviewed interdisciplinary studies of literacy and orality, ending with pedagogical implications like the following: "At a more practical level, our deeper understanding of the psychodynamics of orality in relation to the psychodynamics of writing is improving the teaching of writing skills, particularly ... in residually oral subcultures in dominantly high-literacy societies ... such as urban black subcultures or Chicano subcultures in the United States" (*Orality and Literacy*, 160). He enacted this point when he taught inner-city youths in St. Louis and religion classes for boys at a correctional center. Many of us did not know of these commitments until after his death, and learning of them has strengthened our understanding of one of the best traits of Jesuit scholars, a compassion for and dedication to meeting the needs of those at all levels of education. Having studied and taught in Jesuit universities, I can attest to the importance placed on the ability to communicate. It is a central focus in their university education, influencing every discipline.

INTERDISCIPLINARY CONTRIBUTIONS

In Ong's extensive interdisciplinary contributions, which contextualize his rhetorical work, his voice can clearly be heard to resonate. In 1970, Saint Louis

University named Fr. Ong University Professor of Humanities in Psychiatry because his scholarship was too interdisciplinary to fit in any department. In an interview with Ong in 1996, Michael Kline and Fredric Gale asked him, "Well, first of all, are you a rhetorical theorist?" He responded: "I don't think of myself as a rhetorical theorist nor do I desire to be precisely a rhetorical theorist. . . . I am basically a cultural historian focusing in great part, but not exclusively, on relations between technology and the evolution of consciousness." He went on to say that a great deal of his thought "springs ultimately from what I first worked through historically in Ramus, *Method and the Decay of Dialogue*" (66–67).

The following sections offer a glimpse of Ong's thinking across disciplines, much of it colored by his rhetorical bent. In these writings he not only offered significant insights into their reigning doctrines but also connected them to global conditions, writing, and religion. Unlike those who held that contemporary ideologies and theories were incompatible with religion, he demonstrated their enriching relationships.

In his essays on the humanities, Ong explained that "over the centuries, the shift from orality through writing and print to electronic processing has profoundly affected and, indeed, basically determined the evolution of verbal art genres and of course simultaneously the successive modes of characterization and of plot" (*Orality and Literacy*, 158). The implications of this rhetorical influence on literature were new for critical interpretation but gradually took hold among some critics. Placing psychology and literary studies under the influence of writing and print, he pointed out that "in so far as modern psychology and the 'round' character of fiction represent to present-day consciousness what human existence is like, the feeling for human existence has been processed through writing and print" (*Orality and Literacy*, 155). Adding to this cogent observation, he offered a broader view: "In the shift from a world in which man finds himself embedded in nature to one in which he finds himself more and more externally managing nature lies the core of the problem concerning the relation of religion and the humanities today, if by the humanities we mean those disciplines which are of special concern to man as man and to his place in the scheme of things. For this place is undergoing a profound change" ("Religion, Scholarship," 96). The shifting relationship of humanities with nature remained an abiding interest in Ong's thought.

Theorizing about interiority, one of his other main themes, Ong pointed out that the printed word held some responsibility for the state of current and religious interior life: "Heretofore the religious matrix was I-and-my-universe (including other men) open to God. Now, with the physical world more and more at our command, the religious matrix is becoming more I-alone or we-alone open to God" ("Religion, Scholarship," 95). But he continued: "The knowledge of man's physical place in the cosmos has been very little assimilated to his knowledge of his own interior" ("Religion, Scholarship," 96).

His interest in interiority can be seen in many of his writings on literary authors. He probed their characters' interior lives and the influence of print, explaining the source of the emphasis on interiority: "Print was also a major factor in the development of the sense of personal privacy that marks modern society" (*Orality and Literacy*, 130). This view of interiority may have been partially responsible for the underdeveloped sense of audience in teaching composition and theorizing written discourse at that time of the writer's ideal of the well-wrought urn. His widely reprinted essay "The Writer's Audience Is Always a Fiction" helped to trigger an interest in audience both in composition theory and pedagogy.

In response to the prevalence of interiority, he posed a challenge for the humanities. "What is needed in this situation is to unite the interior and the exterior, to restore man to his home in the cosmos; . . . in this mortal life man will not find his permanent home here. And yet the material universe is in some sense his permanent home here [because] his material body is part of his person, and in Christian teaching it becomes again a living part of each individual in the resurrection" ("Religion, Scholarship," 99). He announced that "what religion would most welcome from humanistic scholarship, I believe, is the resituation of man within the natural universe, from which his . . . development of technology has removed him" ("Religion, Scholarship," 97). In his religious community he was known for noticing natural details and caring for every houseplant in Jesuit Hall. He maintained that "religious man needs a knowledge of the whole background, as far as this can be ascertained, against which his personal salvation is being worked out" ("Religion, Scholarship," 104). This statement echoes one of his frequent themes: the need for a global interdependent culture.

Ong also had a considerable amount to say about the development of communications and technology, contending that the deepest effect of secularization and technology had been on the arts of communication. Offering a historical perspective, he explained that, during the period of the early pretechnical arts (rhetoric, logic, and grammar), persons achieved a high degree of self-consciousness and self possession ("American Culture," 120) but that very gradually, especially in the nineteenth century, attention was weaned from the oral to written discourse and then later to mass communications ("American Culture," 121). He critiqued this current model of communication as transportation of a message from a sender to a receiver, saying that it doesn't work, especially for the Christian message itself and specifically for Christian theology, because "the Word of God is not a message separate from a person . . . but indeed is a person . . . Jesus Christ" ("Communications Media," 156–57). Later he offered a striking insight about rhetorical contexts: "Fully formed studies of communication show an intimate awareness that communication and human knowledge, which is inevitably communication, cannot exist except in a context of love. At this point, scholarly interest abuts on what is specially and centrally religious" ("Religion, Scholarship," 103). Extending these observations to the cyber world, he claimed that "technology has made possible an enlargement of the range of love" ("Religion, Scholarship," 93).

Exploring these relationships further, he asked: "In today's technological society, what does religion expect from scholarship, in particular from humanistic scholarship?" ("Religion, Scholarship," 88). In his response, he analyzed the impact of technology on theology historically, explaining that present-day Catholic theology has increasingly shifted from basic orality (entailing Latin, disputation, and sexual polarization) to a multimedia theology that is non-Latin, non-mnemonic, noncombative, and text-oriented, and thus historically oriented (as against mythology) and dependent on writing ("Communications Media," 170). Counter to historical theology present-day Catholic theology as he described it is print-oriented, computer-oriented, nonformulaic, original, spontaneous, casual, rapidly expanding and exploding, and interlocking with other disciplines such as anthropology, psychology, biology, sociology, and history ("Communications Media," 170–73). This emphasis on interdisciplinarity has remained important to me and found a voice in my essay "Dappled Discipline" and in my efforts to instantiate multimodality (the use of different modes of inquiry) in the graduate program in rhetoric and composition at Purdue.

Pointing out the impact of technology on global human unity, Ong contrasted oral and literate cultures: "These technologies of the word do not merely store what we know. They style what we know in ways which made it quite inaccessible and indeed unthinkable in an oral culture" (*Orality and Literacy*, 155). Further, he explained, "technologies are not mere exterior aids but also interior transformations of consciousness, and never more when they affect the word. Such transformations can be uplifting. Writing heightens consciousness" (*Orality and Literacy*, 82). This impact of writing on thinking was a repeated theme in his work. In "God's Known Universe and Christian Faith," he concluded: "Thanks to the remodeling of time and space through the technologizing of the word by writing, print, and electronics and other vast developments in circulating knowledge, the human race is one people as never before" (228). Elaborating, he noted: "Technology has made possible the total exploration of the earth's surface. . . . . The resulting sense of the solidarity of the human race is new, it has immediate religious relevance" ("Religion, Scholarship," 93).

Over the years, Ong also had an increasing interest in the sciences. With Charles Hofling, MD, he founded and codirected a joint program at Saint Louis University for residents in psychiatry and PhD students in English. In this area, Thomas Farrell notes that Ong found compatibility between his and Bernard Lonergan's levels of consciousness, the overvalorization of propositional truth, and Second Realities ("An Introduction to Walter Ong's Work," liii–liv).

Another interest of his was the biological setting for human intelligence and culture. He also critiqued in a number of places the prevalent view of an incompatibility between religion and science. In 1968 he noted that "by removing a great deal of this ignorance [of the physical universe], scientific advance has improved the religious prospect. God's cause is not served by ignorance as such" ("American Culture," 119). But he insisted that "despite the great advance in knowledge, . . . there will always remain room for . . . faith, [because] knowledge is clearly not moving at all in any direction that would engage the problems of existence that faith meets head-on" ("Knowledge in Time," 149). He continued: The "commitment to something beyond does not in the least exonerate the Christian from the common obligation . . . to do something about the here and now and the future of man on earth . . . —the alleviation of suffering, the improvement of living conditions, the promotion of world peace, the general improvement of mankind, and the advance of knowledge" ("Knowledge in Time," 151).

For Fr. Ong, such advancement also entailed rhetorical activity through writing, multimedia, printing, and computing. In tune with such efforts, the field of rhetoric and composition has promoted such advancements through its programs of writing across the curriculum (WAC) and its research on writing in the disciplines (WID). This interest in science continued throughout his life. On my last visit with him in the Jesuit retirement house in St. Louis, he enthusiastically shared some of his latest ideas on religion and science, and as I left he hurried off to a science conference being held at the university. What a great example for retirement.

SCHOLARSHIP AND CATHOLICISM

In this volume on Jesuit education, this last section offers some of Ong's discussions of the importance of scholarship, highly valued by the Jesuits and a crucial endeavor in Catholicism. In essays such as "Scholarly Research and Publication in the Jesuit College and University," he addressed this topic specifically. Other essays treat this subject more broadly. In "Realizing Catholicism," Ong defined "Catholic" as meaning 'throughout the whole, without boundaries—expansive, growing, open, representing all races and regions of the earth" ("Realizing Catholicism," 2). He stated that "Christianity is an incurably future-oriented religion" ("Realizing Catholicism," 6), looking toward a future that "cannot be independent of this real created world" ("Realizing Catholicism," 7). In several essays he directly discussed this character. In 1989, he wrote: "What the task of Catholic scholarship is, if truly catholic, is to seek to understand the whole of actuality. . . . We have a faith that seeks understanding" ("Realizing Catholicism," 8). But he added, "The scholarship–faith question is affected today by the incommensurability of the universe as we know it today" ("Realizing Catholicism," 6). He went on to share: "In my own life, the biblical and Catholic conviction that, however vast the universe in time and space, God made it all, has, I trust, been the sustaining force uniting faith and science and scholarship of all the kinds with which I have been in contact"("Realizing Catholicism," 8–9). He reassured scholars of faith: "Faith does not confront the universe. . . . Faith penetrates the universe . . . in which the humanity of Jesus Christ is rooted, the universe in which the Son of God became a human being who died for us and rose to bring us to a new life" ("Realizing Catholicism," 8). He went on: "There are obvious connections between the dynamic aspects of American life and the theology of mission of the Incarnation lying at the center of Catholic teaching" ("The American Catholic Complex," 35). These words could surely be the mantra of the Catholic scholar.

All of these inspiring thoughts as well as Ong's life as a Jesuit have encouraged me as a Catholic, a rhetorical scholar, a writing teacher, and a community member. His annual Christmas card with an included bibliography of his writing and notations kept me theoretically expanded and apprised of his wide-ranging scholarship. Remaining a friend until his death, he embodied for me a scholar and teacher in a complex universe motivated by faith and concern for others. Walter Ong has left us a vast and valuable corpus of ideas that we will be mining for years to come.

WORKS CITED

Duhamel, Pierre A. "The Logic and Rhetoric of Peter Ramus." *Modern Philology* (1949): 163–71.

Farrell, Thomas J. "An Introduction to Walter Ong's Work." Farrell and Soukup xix–lv.

Farrell, Thomas J., and Paul Soukup, eds. *Faith and Contexts.* Vol. 1., *Selected Essays and Studies, 1952–1991.* Atlanta, Georgia: Scholars Press, 1992.

Johnson, Kristine and Paul Lynch. "Ad perfectum eloquentium: 'The Spoils of Egypt' in Jesuit Renaissance Education." *Rhetoric Review* 31 (2012): 99–116.

Klein, Michael and Fredric Gale. "The Elusive Presence of the Word: An Interview with Walter Ong." *Forum* 7 (1996): 63–86.

Ong, Walter, S.J. "The American Catholic Complex." In *Faith and Contexts*, ed. Farrell and Soukup 19–37.

———. "American Culture and Morality." In *Faith and Contexts*, ed. Farrell and Soukup 16–126.

———. "Communications Media and the State of Theology." In *Faith and Contexts*, ed. Farrell and Soukup 154–74.

———. "God's Known Universe and Christian Faith: Pastoral, Homiletic, and Devotional Reflections." In *Faith and Contexts*, ed. Farrell and Soukup 219–38.

———. "Knowledge in Time." In *Faith and Contexts*, ed. Farrell and Soukup 127–53.

———. *Orality and Literacy: The Technologizing of the Word.* London and New York: Methuen, 1982.

————. "Ramist Method and the Commercial Mind." *Rhetoric, Romance, and Technology*. Ithaca and London: Cornell University Press, 1971. 165–89.

————."Realizing Catholicism: Faith, Learning, and the Future." In *Faith and Contexts*, ed. Farrell and Soukup 1–18.

————. "Religion, Scholarship, and the Resituation of Man." In *Faith and Contexts*, ed. Farrell and Soukup, 88–105.

————. *Ramus, Method, and the Decay of Dialogue*. Cambridge, Mass.: Harvard University Press, 1958.

————. "The Writer's Audience Is Always a Fiction." *PLMA* 90 (1975): 9–21.

EDWARD P. J. CORBETT, THE REVIVAL
OF CLASSICAL RHETORIC, AND
THE JESUIT TRADITION

Gerald Nelms

In 1989, for my dissertation "A Case History Approach to Composition Studies," I conducted thirteen hours of interviews with Edward P. J. Corbett, one of the most prominent figures in the early post–World War II development of composition studies and, in particular, the adaptation of classical rhetoric for our understanding and teaching of written composition. During those interviews, Corbett retold his account of how he discovered classical rhetoric for himself, leading him to apply classical principles and pedagogy to his teaching of composition. It's an account he had told many times before.

It was Corbett's first year of teaching at Creighton University, and he "was saddled with four sections of freshman English and a section of English Survey." Corbett had come out of the tradition of New Criticism, and he had no trouble talking about poetry, fiction, and drama, but he didn't know how to teach nonfiction prose, the next unit of the English survey that he was to teach. In "desperation," he admitted, he went to the library. (This was 1948, back when people actually physically went to libraries.) He happened into a section where there were books on rhetoric, one of which was Hugh Blair's *Lectures in Rhetoric and Belle Lettres*. Corbett said it was the "belles lettres" part of the title that intrigued him. He said he didn't know what "rhetoric" was referring to. (His teaching of composition followed the current-traditional pedagogical model common at the time.) He happened to open the book onto Blair's analysis of one of Addison's *Spectator* papers and was stunned. "For the first time in my life, I saw someone talking sentence-by-sentence about the style of an essay." Corbett had found a way to talk about nonfiction prose but, more importantly, in volume 2 of these *Lectures*, Corbett would find Blair turning away from his discussion of stylistic devices and taking up the history and theory of classical rhetoric, leading his reader back to the three classical rhetoricians who would become the major influences on this young man's scholarship: Aristotle, Cicero, and Quintilian.

In this story, we find all the clues we need to understand the immense but tacit influence of Jesuit thinking on Edward P. J. Corbett. We find the Jesuit commitment to education. How many of his English Department colleagues would have taken the time to seek out ways to teach literature? We find the Jesuit affinity for what Hellwig calls "the cumulative wisdom of the past" (249), which privileged pagan classical traditions as much as the Christian tradition—and, as Maryks shows, especially Ciceronian thought. We find not only the Jesuit interest in scholarship but in scholarship put to instrumental service (in this case, teaching). The first fundamental principle of Jesuit education that Newton lays out in his *Reflection on the Educational Principles of the Spiritual Exercises* is that Jesuit education is instrumental, not an end in itself but a means of service to God and others (275; see also Hellwig, 249–50; and O'Hare, 145–46). We find the centrality of libraries to the Jesuit mission, a feature of Jesuit education from its earliest days in sixteenth-century Europe (Hellwig, 252). We find, too, more subtle features of Jesuit thought in Corbett's story, especially an integration of the analytical and the generative, or, more specifically, of textual analysis and rhetorical composition. When telling his story, Corbett emphasized his good fortune, the happenstance of finding Blair. In fact, I suggest here, chance played only a very small role. It was not chance at all that led Corbett to the library, that attracted him to a book with "belle lettres" in its title, that he would find himself immersed in the rhetoric of Aristotle, Cicero, Quintilian, and Blair—and, most important, that he would, then, recognize the applicability of classical rhetoric to the teaching of composition—or that he would pursue a life's career of advocating for that application. I suggest that Corbett's Jesuit education helped to shape his values in such a way as to prepare him for his career adapting classical rhetoric to modern composition studies and influenced how classical rhetoric would be adapted.

LIFE, EDUCATION, AND EARLY CAREER

Edward P. J. Corbett was born in North Dakota in 1919. His father was the son of Irish immigrants. When he was nine or ten, his parents separated, and his father moved his brother, two sisters, and him to Milwaukee to live with their paternal grandmother. During the Depression, his father was often without a job, and the family was very poor. Neither of his parents had more than a grade-school education. The children went to Catholic grade school, and Corbett received a scholarship to Marquette University High School. He spoke of this "break" with great emotion, but it certainly was not happenstance. As Hellwig notes, one of the "characteristic emphases and understandings" of the Jesuits is "an anti-elitist bent" (249). While it is true that the Jesuits have often served the most elite members of society, it also true that the Society of Jesus has long sought to educate the lay underprivileged, and high-school and college scholarships have long been one means of fulfilling that mission. It was this mission of the Jesuits that gave Corbett his educational break, and it was this characteristic of the Jesuits that Corbett often spoke of and that may well have influenced his ultimate move into the profession of teaching. Corbett's natural humility, epitomized in his preference for his students to call him "Mister" rather than "Professor" Corbett and in his insistence that he was never an "innovator," probably had its origins not only in his family life but in his exposure in school to the anti-elitism of the Jesuit mission.

It is clear from Corbett's description of his high-school education that Marquette was highly influential in shaping his values. Corbett distinctly recalled his courses in Latin and Greek. Latin had been part of the curriculum since well before Corbett arrived, but Greek was not offered until the school hired a PhD in Greek who had been teaching at Saint Louis University but preferred teaching at the secondary-school level. Corbett spoke to me of this opportunity to learn Greek as a blessing and turns it, with his characteristic compassion, to fellow human beings:

> Four years of Latin and Greek just turned my life around—and why me, Lord? Why me, Lord?—that I got those kinds of breaks despite the fact that I was dirt poor. And my life could have been the very opposite. Why does it happen to certain people?
>
> —October 2, 1989

Later, in his essay "Teaching Style" (1986), Corbett would speak of the Renaissance schoolboy's immersion in "words—English words, Latin words, sometimes even Greek words," reciting grammatical rules, parsing sentences, translating Latin into English and English into Latin, paraphrasing, imitating, and creating sentences (308). Corbett's own education at Marquette appears to have been similarly immersive in language, both modern and classical.

Certainly Corbett's affinity for classical philosophy and literature was deeply influenced by his high-school education in Latin and Greek. After graduating from high school in 1938, Corbett studied for the priesthood at Venard College (later known as Maryknoll Apostolic College) in Pennsylvania, where he continued his study of Latin and Greek. Corbett spent an additional year taking classes in the seminary at Maryknoll, New York. The Maryknoll archives indicate that Corbett took coursework at the Venard in Latin, English, French, Scripture, speech, music, history, science, astronomy, geology, botany, agronomy, and economics and, at the Maryknoll seminary, coursework in philosophy, missionology, Chinese, Japanese, political science, and physiology (Walsh, email). In addition, Corbett told me that while the Venard did not offer courses in Greek, he continued his study of Greek on his own, reading a New Testament edition in Latin and Greek on facing pages. He kept that book in his office during his entire career. Corbett insisted to me that he never encountered classical rhetoric per se during his early schooling or undergraduate education, but he certainly encountered practical applications of it, reading Cicero and other classical authors, both in translation and in the original Greek and Latin.

In July 1943, Corbett left his missionary training. He spent the remainder of that summer working in the Schlitz Brewing Company icehouse in Milwaukee. In November, he was inducted into the Marines. His brother had been a Marine and was wounded at Saipan. The inspiration of his brother motivated Corbett's enlistment. Corbett was trained as a radar technician and was shipped to Majuro Island in 1945 and eventually reassigned to Tsingtao, China, where he was appointed NCO in charge of the Communications unit there. He never saw combat, and while serving in the south Pacific he got hold of a military edition of Mortimer Adler's *How to Read a Book.* In this work, Adler first makes his arguments that would become the foundation for the "Great Books" movement. He sets forth three levels of analytical reading that mirror New Critical close reading with its focus on textual analysis and exclusion of authorial, historical, cultural, and reader contexts. This may not have been Corbett's initial introduction to close reading and New Criticism, but it certainly was the most formative such influence on him.

Corbett used the GI Bill to acquire a master's degree in English at the University of Chicago. The program, he told me, consisted entirely of literary study. The University of Chicago at this time was, interestingly, both a hothouse for the Great Books movement with its emphasis on reading primary texts and on general education and also a hothouse for developing applications of classical rhetoric, and sometimes these two movements did not coexist amicably.

In 1937, under the leadership of the president, Robert Maynard Hutchins, who was influenced by the philosopher Mortimer Adler, the University of Chicago implemented a new undergraduate curriculum that did away with majors and consisted entirely of the study of what were considered seminal primary texts in the sciences, philosophy, history, the arts, and the humanities. All Chicago undergraduates were required to take the same courses, and that curriculum included a required composition course every year except the last. The undergraduate composition program was chaired by Henry Sams, but in interviews I conducted in the 1990s with several former faculty members of Chicago's undergraduate composition program in the 1940s and early '50s, they indicated that the composition curriculum was primarily under the influence of Richard Weaver. While Weaver is typically considered a Platonist, he insisted that Chicago's undergraduate composition curriculum be based on Aristotelian and Ciceronian rhetoric. In fact, four of the composition faculty at Chicago at the time, including Weaver and Robert E. Streeter, published an article, in a 1953 issue of *College English,* that set forth an argument for teaching the classical *topoi,* or "topics," in freshman English composition courses (Bilsky et al.). In 1954, Chicago's composition-program chair Henry Sams published an explicit call in *College Composition and Communication* for the recovery of the rhetorics of Aristotle, Cicero, and St. Augustine to inform our teaching of writing.

That said, because the separation between the undergraduate college and the Chicago graduate programs was fairly strict with respect to faculty and curricula, Corbett apparently had no contact with the composition faculty there. At least, he has mentioned no such contact in my and others' interviews with him. On the other hand, Chicago's graduate English department, beginning in the 1940s, became known for its so-called neo-Aristotelian approach to literary criticism. The Chicago School, as it came to be called, is most associated with Ronald Crane, English department chair from 1935 to 1947, and Richard McKeon, of Chicago's Philosophy department. McKeon distanced himself from Crane and his English department colleagues over their almost exclusive emphasis on Aristotle's *Poetics*. McKeon advocated for what he saw as Aristotle's "pluralism": the notion that no one critical approach alone is sufficient for understanding any text. McKeon also advocated for the study of rhetoric and the use of Aristotelian rhetoric in critical analysis.

This distinction between the neo-Aristotelianism of Crane and that of McKeon is important for understanding why Corbett was not introduced to Aristotelian rhetoric while a master's student at Chicago. In a 1993 retrospective CCCC talk, Corbett echoes McKeon, noting that "the so-called Chicago School of Criticism was rooted in Aristotle's *Poetics*, not in his *Rhetoric*" ("From Literary Critic to Rhetorician"). In my interviews with Corbett, too, he never mentioned any introduction to rhetoric while working on his master's. He never mentioned any instance of rhetoric being discussed in any classes. Most of his exposure to the Chicago School seems to have come through reading their publications, and it is not clear that Corbett read any of McKeon's works on rhetoric during his two years at Chicago. However, in his introduction to his book *Rhetorical Analyses of Literary Works*, Corbett notes that the Chicago School was not a unified group, sides with McKeon in viewing Aristotle's *Rhetoric* as more formative to modern criticism than is the *Poetics*, and is clear that he views the Chicago School's approach as related to that of the New Critics. At any rate, Corbett spent only two years at the University of Chicago.

With MA in hand, he was hired as an English instructor at Creighton University in Omaha, Nebraska, in 1948. And it was during his two years there that Corbett discovered Blair's *Lectures in Rhetoric and Belle Lettres*. And after teaching for several years at Creighton—and discovering classical rhetoric—he entered the PhD program at Loyola in Chicago in 1950. He returned to Creighton in 1954, completed his dissertation on Hugh Blair's rhetorical theory in 1956, and was promoted at Creighton to the rank of associate professor in 1957. During the mid-'50s, Corbett began his scholarly publishing. He published a small piece in *Notes and Queries* in 1954, but his first important publication was "Hugh Blair as an Analyzer of English Prose Style" (1958). He followed with numerous articles on rhetoric throughout the 1960s, '70s, and '80s.

We should note that Corbett's scholarly connections to the Jesuit tradition were not altogether indirect. He also published in religious magazines, including *America*, *Commonweal*, *Benedictine Review*, and *Pastoral Life*, as well as in the *Nation* early in his career. One of his most widely reprinted essays was his 1961 defense, in the Catholic weekly magazine *America* (published by the Jesuits), against school censorship of J. D. Salinger's *The Catcher in the Rye*. This desire to speak to a broader audience beyond his discipline and the academy generally echoes the apostolic mission of the Jesuits. As Traub points out, Ignatian spirituality is summed up in the phrase "finding God in all things. It invites a person to search for and find God in every circumstance of life." (393). And that mission provides the eminent rationale for the Jesuit emphasis on education: "Its goal is to produce an independent learner who internalizes the skills of learning and eventually is able to act without the support of the formal educational environment" and able, therefore, to find God in all things (Newton, 275). Translating this religious principle into a more secular, postmodern articulation, we might say, instead of "finding God in all things," that rhetoric provides a means for *discerning meaning* in all things. And in fact, Jesuit scholars (Traub, 391; Kolvenbach, 2) identify *discernment* as the operational tool for finding God in all things.

Whether Corbett absorbed this Jesuit value in his early education or not, it certainly became a defining feature of his attitude toward publication, even his scholarly publication. His scholarly writing is always done in service to others: students, teachers, the public. While often treated as a scholarly treatise on classical rhetoric and even, at times, as a reference work, Corbett's most influential book, *Classical Rhetoric for the Modern Student*, is in fact a composition textbook addressed to students learning to write rhetorically. It is easy to see how the popularity of CRMS as both textbook *and* scholarly treatise of sorts continued the powerful Jesuit tradition of composition/rhetoric textbooks with scholarly influence, a tradition that began as far back as Cypriano Soarez's textbook of 1590—a tradition that itself may well have been influenced by the earliest rhetorics of classical Greece and Rome, which functioned both as textbooks and treatises.

THE JESUIT RHETORIC OF EDWARD P. J. CORBETT

Rhetorical Norms

As noted above, while the foundational principle of Jesuit belief is the idea that God's work is evident in all things, that doesn't guarantee that we humans *will* perceive God's work in the world—or any meaning whatever, for that matter; *discernment* is required. Rather than shying away from teaching independent, critical thinking, the Jesuit tradition embraces that teaching as a way of ultimately enhancing a learner's ability to *discern* God's work and thereby enhance her or his faith. But discernment is complicated by the fact that we live in a world of contextual contingencies. The world does not consist of simple good–bad, black–white dichotomies but rather of gradations, probabilities, and limiting contexts. Thus, Traub identifies *discernment* as a "process for making choices . . . when the option is not between good and evil, but between several possible courses of action, all of which are potentially good"

(391). If the connections between Jesuit belief and rhetoric were not obvious, Maryks has shown how Ciceronian rhetoric, "built on epistemic premises of probability" (4)—that is, on a recognition of the inherent probabilism of our existence—shaped Jesuit theology and education almost from its beginnings. Following Cicero, Jesuit education teaches that decisions always occur in context. That said, however, Maryks makes clear that Jesuit relativism is never absolute, quoting from Cicero's *De Partitione Oratoria*: "We are men who wish to discover the truth and our discussion has no other purpose than to force to the surface the truth or what *most nearly* approaches it" (7, Maryks's emphasis). In sum, following Cicero, the Jesuits recognize that while God's truth is absolute, we do not have direct access to it. Discernment requires rhetoric, and rhetoric "is situationally conditioned" (Maryks, 99).

Edward P. J. Corbett in his writings expressed that same Ciceronian probabilistic view of reality as the foundational rationale for rhetoric. Corbett believed in an objective, absolute truth but did not believe that the average human being could have direct, objectively obtained access to it. As Corbett said to me in our interviews, "There is more than one avenue to arrive at the truth" (October 11, 1989). And then he went on to give the example of witnessing a car accident. The accident clearly happened, but different perspectives on it yield different interpretations of exactly what happened and who was at fault, all based on limited perspectives that never yield an omniscient understanding, only probable truth.

It is true that we can see Corbett's probabilism evolving over the years. For example, in the 1965 (34) and 1971 (45) editions of *Classical Rhetoric for the Modern Student* he wrote that "the beginning of all discourse is a subject," but in the 1990 edition that statement had evolved to "the beginning of all discourse is a topic, a question, a problem, an issue" (32). As we can see, Corbett moved from a more discourse-bound view to one more thoroughly based on a view of contingency and context. Of course, this tension was evident in rhetorical discussions throughout the history of rhetorical studies, beginning with Aristotle's tying particular rhetorical processes to different rhetorical genres with different formal structures: deliberative, forensic, and epideictic.

That said, Corbett is very clear that he believes rhetoric to be fundamentally based on a basic, universal human contingency. Corbett's probabilism is clearly evident in what I see as his most important contribution to the teaching of composition, his discussion of what he identified as "rhetorical reference points" in which "rhetorical norms" are found. In "Rhetoric in the Senior High School," Corbett defines rhetorical norms as "a set of norms or criteria" that allow us to make "the best choices from available matter and form" (26). He identified the rhetorical reference points as categories of decisions that speakers and writers must make: decisions on the *purpose* of the text, the *audience* for the text, its *subject matter*, and "the competencies and personality of the speaker or writer," the textual *ethos* (27). Corbett's description of rhetorical decision-making mirrors that of Jesuit discernment: "When an author was faced with making a selection among two or more available means [of persuasion], he [or she] made [that] decision by relating the available means to one or more of these reference points" ("The Relevance of Rhetoric to Composition," 6–7).

By aligning rhetoric with discernment, we resolve a discrepancy between the characterization (notably by Berlin) of Corbett as a traditionalist and the fact that, for someone devoted to the classical tradition, Corbett expanded the scope of rhetoric to a remarkable breadth, including not only formal oral and written communication but also television, film, symposia, panel discussions, and interviews ("What Is Being Revived?" 59), advertising (*Classical Rhetoric for the Modern Student*, 1990, 4–9), and cartoons, comic strips, and music ("Rhetoric, Whether Goest Thou?" 27; "Rhetoric in Search of a Past, Present, and Future," 173).

The problem for the critics has been twofold. They have assumed that Corbett uncritically adopted classical rhetoric and that classical rhetoric itself was objectivist and narrowly product-oriented. In fact, however, as Kennedy, Conley, Jarratt, and other historians have shown, the history of rhetoric has never been a smooth, gradual transition from objectivism to relativism, and the epistemologies of even those major classical rhetoricians thought to be the most traditional, including Aristotle and Cicero, are much more complicated than even a superficial study reveals. As early as 1967, in "A New Look at Old Rhetoric," Corbett accepted Cicero's efforts "to extend the province of rhetoric" (105), and he found this same tendency in Aristotle's definition of rhetoric as "the faculty of observing *in any given case* the available means of persuasion" (my emphasis). Corbett makes much of Aristotle's lack of specificity. "In any given case" suggests a role for rhetoric beyond oratory and written communication. And in fact, Corbett himself finds rhetoric everywhere, much as the Jesuits find God in all things. Rhetoric, for Corbett, as it was and is for the Jesuits, provides humans with an innate, intrinsic, instinctive tool for discerning meaning.

Rhetoric as Analysis and Composition

Corbett's reading of Mortimer Adler's *How to Read a Book* while in the South Pacific during World War II had a profound effect on him. The way that Corbett described that effect is revealing. "Rhetoric," he said, "is in a sense a synthetic art, putting something together, composing it, but this was rhetoric in reverse. . . . Adler was really giving me the key, the secret to studying discourse . . . , and then, of course, I discovered rhetoric, which is the art of putting it together, but I was being prepared for that by Adler's book" (interview, October 2, 1989). Throughout his career, Corbett embraced this paradoxical view of rhetoric as both different in function from poetics and other kinds of analysis yet also inherently, perhaps systematically, connected—analysis being necessary for the rhetorical process of generating text, and that generation being a natural result of analysis. On many occasions, Corbett made no effort to divide analysis from rhetorical composition, the analytical from the productive and creative. His analysis of advertising, at the beginning of the 1990 edition of *Classical Rhetoric for the Modern Student*, epitomizes this synthesis. So do his discussions of two different kinds of protest rhetoric in "The Rhetoric of the Open Hand and the Rhetoric of the Closed Fist" and "The Rhetoric of Protest." In both cases, the reader is asked to use analysis to better learn to produce rhetorical texts.

While Corbett attributes his unified view of rhetoric to his reading of Adler, I suspect that his Jesuit education prepared the ground for that seed. In their earliest educational documents, the *Spiritual Exercises* of St. Ignatius (O'Hare, 147) and the *Ratio Studiorum*, or Jesuit "Plan of Studies" (part H27, section 396), assignments in both analysis and rhetorical composition were recommended. The Jesuit purpose of learning to think critically remains the enhancing of spiritual *receptivity*, an individual's willingness to use *discernment*/rhetoric to perceive God in all things (Muldoon, 291–94). It is likely that the Jesuit curriculum provided Corbett with models that blended analysis and composition, without being fully conscious of it. And we certainly see his integration of analysis and composition in his discussion of rhetorical invention, one of rhetorical "canons."

Rhetorical Canons
The revival of classical rhetoric in the 1950s and early 1960s tended to focus on reviving the Aristotelian canons of rhetoric of *invention, arrangement*, and *style* (Nelms, "Rise of Classical Rhetoric," 11–17), and in discussing invention, the focus has been on the three modes of persuasive appeal (*logos, pathos*, and *ethos*) and on the methods for developing material to use in those appeals (most notably the Aristotelian "topics"). Following Aristotle and Cicero, Corbett views these decisions involved in invention as directed by rhetorical norms.

Critics such as Berlin have argued that the revival of classical rhetoric was *logos*-centric, privileging logical argument, and in interviews Corbett admitted his bias for *logos*. That said, however, Corbett always recognized the power of ethical and emotional appeals, both in his interviews and in his published scholarship. In fact, Corbett frequently identified *ethos* as probably the most powerful of the three persuasive appeals ("Rhetoric, the Enabling Discipline," 204; introduction to *The Rhetoric and Poetics of Aristotle*, xvii; "The Ethical Dimensions of Rhetoric," 256ff.). In "The Ethical Dimensions of Rhetoric," Corbett writes, "When we understand all that is implicit in Aristotle's notion of the ethical appeal, we can see why *ethos* could be the most potent means of persuasion" (259). And indeed, Corbett's own teaching was indicative of his high regard for *ethos*. He relied on analyses of model ethical appeals, aligning *ethos* with "voice," "posture," and "persona." He believed that raising student awareness of *ethos* in other texts would assist students in developing their own ethical appeals (interview, October 16, 1989).

Corbett's views on *pathos* were more complicated. Rhetorical analyses all too often reveal attempts to manipulate emotions that seem deceptive and insidious, and Corbett never privileged *pathos* as he did *ethos*. Still, he does recognize that a suspicion of *pathos* as always deceptive has no historical basis (*Classical Rhetoric for the Modern Student*, 1990, 86; "Rhetoric, the Enabling Discipline," 202–3; "Ethical Dimensions," 265–66):

> Part of the enabling process [of rhetoric] is making people aware that there are occasions when appeals to emotion are not only inappropriate but reprehensible. . . . [Still], we need to be made aware of the role that emotion plays in human relations generally and in the communication process particularly, to be made aware that the stirring of the appropriate emotion at the appropriate time can be a legitimate and effective tactic.
> —"Rhetoric, the Enabling Discipline," 203–4

Corbett recognized that any narrowing of rhetorical appeals would only weaken rhetoric's ability to effect *discernment*, or meaning-making, and this recognition mirrors the Jesuit understanding that, as Korth states, learning "involves the whole person—mind, heart, and will—because without internal feeling joined to intellectual grasp, learning will not move a person to action" (282). As Traub notes, a major characteristic of Jesuit understanding is its respect for the use of imagination and emotion as well as intellect (395). This emphasis on emotion is most obvious in the numerous Jesuit rhetoric textbooks that followed the distribution of the *Ratio Studiorum*. As Conley points out, "The *Ratio studiorum* directed that all students were to be trained in eloquence," and when the *Ratio* came out in 1599, rhetoric "was a central element in the curriculum of Jesuit schools" (152–53). Cypriano Soares's *De arte rhetorica* is representative of these textbooks and one of the most widely used (Conley, 153). And as Conley writes, "Soares . . . seems to place an unusually high premium on emotion as a component of persuasion, for it is evidently emotion that mainly *moves* the souls of men—that is, persuades them, in addition to teaching them" (154).

A reading of composition textbooks that have centered around rhetoric further reveals how classical rhetoric has been *adapted* more than *adopted* by composition scholars. Indeed, what distinguished *Classical Rhetoric for the Modern Student* at that time was Corbett's purposeful confinement of it to content that had its origins with classical rhetoricians. Other textbooks were not so confined. Richard Weaver's *Composition: A Course in Writing and Rhetoric* (1957) gives considerably less space to invention than does *Classical Rhetoric for the Modern Student*. In fact, Weaver collapses invention and arrangement into sixteen pages, while allotting seventy-six to "The Sentence," "The Paragraph," and "Diction" and sixty-six pages to grammar and usage. Weaver's approach in *Composition* seems ironic, given his leadership in developing the strikingly classical undergraduate composition curriculum at the University of Chicago (see above).

Richard Hughes and Albert Duhamel's *Rhetoric: Principles and Usage* (1962), probably the most important rival to *Classical Rhetoric for the Modern Student*, is considerably more "classical" by comparison, but still not so confined as Corbett's textbook. Both Hughes and Duhamel had connections to the Jesuits. Duhamel attended St. Thomas Eminday School in Bloomfield, Connecticut, and first became interested in classical rhetoric in 1936, as a "student of Jesuit tradition at Holy Cross," and later taught, along with Hughes, at Boston College, another Jesuit institution of higher education (Nelms and Goggin, 16). In *Rhetoric: Principles and Usage*, these authors rearrange the traditional presentation of the canons, devoting their first four chapters to "Organization" (arrangement), the second five to "Invention," and the final three to "Style." Moreover, like Weaver, Hughes and Duhamel include discussions of modes of discourse (description, narration, exposition, etc.), something that neither classical rhetoricians nor Corbett did.

That said, it is wrong to view Corbett as simply an *adopter* of classical rhetoric. He does a good bit of *adapting* in *Classical Rhetoric for the Modern Student*, and in later textbooks, notably *The Little Rhetoric*, first published in 1977, he blends Aristotelian-Ciceronian rhetoric and modern composition strategies and views of composing processes. For example, in *The Little Rhetoric*, Corbett overlays the composing process onto the classical rhetorical canons and organizes the text to take the student chronologically through that process: "Finding a Subject," "Finding Something to Say" (invention), "Selecting and Organizing Material" (arrangement), and "Expressing What Has Been Discovered, Selected, and Arranged" (style). Moreover, invention here is not limited to the classical topics. Corbett also includes modern heuristics: brainstorming, meditation, observation, interviewing, surveying, experimenting, and reading as well as Kenneth Burke's dramatistic pentad.

It's surprising, too, that Corbett excludes Aristotle, Cicero, and other classical rhetoricians—and Hugh Blair also, for that matter—from his short list of the "master rhetoricians" he idolizes. Instead, in the headnote to his article "Some Rhetorical Lessons from John Henry Newman" in *Selected Essays of Edward P. J. Corbett*, he states that "my three gods are Tom More (Thomas More of *A Man for All Seasons*), Dr. Samuel Johnson, and John Henry Newman" (209). He notes that in addition to being "master rhetoricians," they "were all religious men" (209). Newman, of course, left the Church of England for the Roman Catholic Church in 1845 and rose to rank of cardinal. Newman also claimed to have translated Cicero daily. Bottone states, "Cicero was a central figure for the development of John Henry Newman's thought. After Aristotle, he is the main source of inspiration for Newman's idea of liberal education"

(1). Corbett calls Newman "the nineteenth-century epitome of Cicero" (209). Corbett was introduced to Newman in a Victorian-prose course he took with Martin Svaglic while working on his PhD at Loyola. In his essay on Newman, Corbett is able to locate him within the Aristotelian-Ciceronian line of rhetoric, focusing particularly on Newman's own probabilism, his recognition that "many of our most obstinate and most reasonable certitudes depend on proofs which are informal and personal, which baffle our powers of analysis and cannot be brought under logical rule, because they cannot be submitted to logical statistics" (*Grammar of Assent*, chap. 8, 230, quoted by Corbett, 222). But in typical Corbett style, toward the end of this essay he addresses the question of what relevance Newman's rhetoric might have for teaching, concluding that the *Grammar of Assent* "is a book for us teachers of rhetoric and composition to read and absorb and then make use of in our own way in the classroom" (221).

The Topics

The revival of classical rhetoric for modern composition, beginning in the early 1950s, tended to focus on reviving the Aristotelian appeals (*logos, pathos,* and *ethos*) and then those strategies (or *topoi,* "topics") from classical rhetoric used to develop actual arguments within each of those appeals. Corbett defines the topics as "the method that classical rhetoricians devised to aid the speaker in discovering matter for the three modes of appeal. . . . To put it another way, the topics constituted a method of probing one's subject to discover possible ways of developing that subject" (*Classical Rhetoric for the Modern Student*, 1990, 24). Many discussions of these invention strategies have presented them as an artificial heuristic. Corbett, however, viewed them as the result of "the characteristic ways in which the human mind reasons or thinks" ("The *Topoi* Revisited," 47), "a form of epistemology [that] . . . accurately catergorize[s] the mental processes involved in any kind of inquiry" (66). As such, the topics represent a natural way of making decisions about which mental operations are the most appropriate for a writer to use, given her or his purpose, audience, subject matter, and *ethos:* The human mind's "constant tendency is to rise above the particulars and to abstract, to generalize, to classify, to analyze, and to synthesize. The topics represented the system that the classical rhetoricians built upon this tendency of the human mind" (*Classical Rhetoric for the Modern Student*, 1990, 300). Thus, the topics provide a method for making conscious our *discernment* of what's meaningful in the subject matter before us.

Style

As indicated above, Corbett first became aware of classical rhetoric through Hugh Blair's stylistic analyses, no doubt drawn to Blair's analyses by his intensive language study, his Renaissance schoolboy-like immersion in Greek and

Latin during his education at Marquette High School and the Venard Mary-knoll College, and on his own. In "Teaching Style," he defines style as "the choices that an author made from the lexical and syntactical resources of the language" (24), but for Corbett, as for Blair and the classical rhetoricians who influenced him, these choices involve more than simply providing verbal ornamentation to prior thoughts. In *Classical Rhetoric for the Modern Student*, Corbett quotes Newman: "Style is a thinking out into language" (1990, 380).

Pedagogically, Corbett focused almost exclusively on imitation. In classical education, however, imitation was more than simply a set of pedagogical exercises, and Corbett traced its long history in rhetorical instruction in "The Theory and Practice of Imitation in Classical Rhetoric." For the classical Greek and Roman student, a major part of instruction through imitation involved translation (Latin to Greek, Greek to Latin), paraphrasing, and exploring different ways of saying the same thing, and he often cited writers who had used imitation copying, such as Benjamin Franklin, Somerset Maugham, and Malcolm X. In adapting imitation for modern composition pedagogy, Corbett emphasized the practice of copying passages of texts verbatim ("The Usefulness of Classical Rhetoric," 18–19; "The Theory and Practice of Imitation," 185–86; "Teaching Style," 31; *Classical Rhetoric for the Modern Student*, 1965, 465; 1971, 510; 1990, 475; *Style and Statement*, 75–111). Corbett himself copied a page of text every morning. He believed that imitation copying helped him see the stylistic choices the writer had made, giving him experience with composition at the sentence level and helping him expand his stylistic repertoire (interview, October 4, 1989). He also assigned imitation copying in virtually every course that he taught, even graduate courses. Sometimes, he would assign ten minutes of copying, but in writing courses he required students to submit a page of copied text at the beginning of every class meeting. He would read a few of these out loud and ask students what they noticed about them—thereby extending classical practice to include modern reflection (interview, October 4, 1989).

Significantly, it was this aspect of rhetorical education that Corbett admitted to learning at Marquette High School. He was assigned the practice by an English teacher and continued on with it. As Maryks notes, "Ciceronian imitation became an important part of the new Jesuit identity after 1548 and perhaps had an influence on non-Western thought as well" (4). Maryks shows how the *Ratio Studiorum* assigns Cicero as the primary stylistic role model. In the section "Rules of the Teacher of Rhetoric," the *Ratio* gives this precept: "Cicero is to be the one model of style. . . . All Cicero's works are appropriate models of style" (88). And the *Ratio* recommends to humanities teachers that they assign their students "exercises choosing phrases from previously read passages and expressing them in different ways, reconstructing a passage from Cicero that had been disarranged for this purpose" (Maryks, 89). Corbett's understanding of style, then, seems clearly to have had its origins in his Jesuit education.

CONCLUSION

Of all those involved in the revival of classical rhetoric for modern composition studies, Edward P. J. Corbett may have exerted the widest influence. In his twenty-four years at the Ohio State University, he taught numerous undergraduate and graduate students, some of whom entered into rhetoric and composition—including Andrea Lunsford, Lisa Ede, Robert Connors, Gail Hawisher, Cheryl Glenn, Krista Radcliffe, and Sheryl Finkle, among many others too numerous to name here—and thereby indirectly influenced the many students of his students. And there were the many scholars and teachers whom Corbett inspired through his involvement in NEH seminars and the Summer Rhetoric Seminars and through his many conference presentations and invited talks at universities and colleges nationwide. In addition, Corbett edited *College Composition and Communication* from 1974 to 1979, chaired the CCCC's program in Seattle in 1970 and the entire CCCC in 1971, was a member of a number of editorial boards of professional journals and of committees and commissions of the National Council of Teachers of English and of the Modern Language Association; he chaired the Rhetoric Society of American from 1973 through 1977. Finally, Corbett's articles, scholarly books, and especially textbooks continue to find readers, and not only rhetoric and composition scholars but also their students.

What distinguished Corbett's adaptations of the principles and strategies of classical rhetoric was their comprehensiveness—and perhaps equally important, the influence of Jesuit thought on those adaptations. In this, Corbett was not alone. We've noted above the adaptation of Aristotelian-Ciceronian rhetoric in the University of Chicago undergraduate program in the 1940s and '50s as well as the textbooks by Weaver and Hughes and Duhamel, published in the 1950s and early 1960s. In addition, Nelms has charted the rise of classical rhetoric through the 1950s and '60s, noting also tacit emphases on the rhetorical reference points and rhetorical norms in Brooks and Warren's *Modern Rhetoric with Readings* (1949) and McCrimmon's *Writing with a Purpose* (1950) ("The Rise of Classical Rhetoric in Modern Composition Studies," 8–11), though without reference to Jesuit or Catholic connections. And Nelms and Goggin found other major figures involved in this revival who had Jesuit or at least Catholic educations or taught in Jesuit institutions, including not only Duhamel (Holy Cross and Boston College) and Hughes (Boston College), already mentioned, but also Michael Halloran (Holy Cross) and James Kinneavy (St. Mary's in San Antonio and Catholic University). I don't want to overstate the possible influence that Jesuit pedagogy, educational theory, and theology had on the development of modern composition instruction, but the Jesuit influence on the adaptation of classical rhetoric for composition teaching is clear and well supported, and classical rhetoric was a major force in the early post–World War II development of composition studies, providing this emerging discipline with a theoretical and pedagogical structure and language that continues to this day.

WORKS CITED

Adler, Mortimer. *How to Read a Book: The Art of Getting a Liberal Education.* New York: Simon and Schuster, 1940.

Berlin, James A. *Rhetoric and Reality: Writing Instruction in American Colleges, 1900–1985.* Carbondale: Southern Illinois University Press, 1987.

Bilsky, Manuel, McCea Hazlett, Robert E. Streeter, and Richard M. Weaver. "Looking for an Argument." *College English* 14 (January 1953): 210–16.

Blair, Hugh. *Lectures on Rhetoric and Belles Lettres.* Edited by Linda Ferreira-Buckley and S. Michael Halloran. Carbondale: Southern Illinois University Press, 2005.

Bottone, Angelo. "The Influence of Cicero on Newman's Idea of a Liberal Education." In *Yearbook of the Irish Philosophical Society* (2009), ed. Cyril McDonnell, 1–14. Dublin: Irish Philosophical Society, 2010.

Brooks, Cleanth, and Robert Penn Warren. *Modern Rhetoric with Readings.* New York: Harcourt, 1949.

Conley, Thomas M. *Rhetoric in the European Tradition.* Chicago: University of Chicago Press, 1990.

Corbett, Edward P. J. "America's Sainte-Beuve." *Commonweal,* May 13, 1960: 173–75.

———. *Classical Rhetoric for the Modern Student.* New York: Oxford University Press, 1965. 2nd ed., 1971. 3rd ed. 1990. 4th ed., with Robert J. Connors, 1998.

———. "The Collegiate Muse: Gone Feminine." *America,* December 1, 1956.

———. "Education at the Crossroads." *Benedictine Review* 12 (Summer 1957): 5–10.

———. "The Ethical Dimensions of Rhetoric." DeKalb: Northern Illinois University, 1984. Reprinted in *Selected Essays,* 255–67.

———. "From Literary Critic to Rhetorician: A Professional Journey." Conference on College Composition and Communication. Cincinnati, 1992. www.eric.ed.gov/ERICWebPortal/recordDetail?accno=ED358482. Accessed July 12, 2012.

———. "*Gone with the Wind* Revisited." *America,* August 14, 1957: 524–26.

———. "Hugh Blair as an Analyzer of English Prose Style." *College Composition and Communication* 9 (May 1958): 98–103. Reprinted in *Selected Essays,* 4–13.

———. "Hugh Blair's Three (?) Critical Dissertations." *Notes and Queries,* n.s. 1 (November 1954): 478–80.

———. "Letter on 'The Lay Professor.'" *Commonweal,* May 9, 1958.

———. *The Little Rhetoric.* New York: Wiley, 1977.

———. "A New Look at Old Rhetoric." In *Rhetoric: Theories for Application,* ed. Robert M. Gorrell, 16–22. Papers Presented at the 1965 Convention of the National Council of Teachers of English. Champaign, Ill.: NCTE, 1967. Reprinted in *Selected Essays,* 63–72.

———. Personal interviews. October 2, 4, 9–12, 16–17, 1989.

———. "Professors, Old and New." *America*, September 16, 1961: 734–36.

———. "Raise High the Barriers, Censors." *America*, January 7, 1961. Reprinted in *If You Really Want to Know: A "Catcher" Casebook*, ed. Malcolm M. Marsden, 68–73. Chicago: Scott Foresman, 1963:

———. "The Relevance of Rhetoric to Composition." *Kentucky English Bulletin* 17 (Winter 1967–68): 3–12.

———. "Rhetoric in Search of a Past, Present, and Future." In *The Prospect of Rhetoric*. ed. Lloyd F. Bitzer and Edwin Black, 167–78. Englewood Cliffs, N.J.: Prentice-Hall, 1971.

———. "The Rhetoric of the Open Hand and the Rhetoric of the Closed Fist." *College Composition and Communication* 20 (December 1969): 288–96. Reprinted in *Selected Essays*, 99–113.

———. "The Rhetoric of Protest." *Rhetoric Society Quarterly* 4, no. 2 (1974): 4.

———. "Rhetoric, the Enabling Discipline." *Ohio English Bulletin* 13 (May 1972): 2–10. Reprinted in *Selected Essays, 194–208.*

———. "Rhetoric, Whether Goest Thou?" In *A Symposium in Rhetoric*, ed. J. Dean Bishop, Turner K. Kobler, and William E. Tanner, ed. 44–57. Denton: Texas Women's University, 1975. Reprinted in *Rhetoric and Change*, ed. William E. Tanner and J. Dean Bishop, 15–30. Mesquite, Texas: Ide House, 1982.

———. *Rhetorical Analyses of Literary Works*. New York: Oxford University Press, 1969.

———. "A Romp with Pop." *Nation,* January 17, 1959: 51–53.

———. "The Sagging Pulpit." *Homiletic and Pastoral Review* 59 (June 1959): 821–26.

———. *Selected Essays of Edward P. J. Corbett*. Edited by Robert J. Connors. Dallas: Southern Methodist University Press, 1989.

———. "Some Rhetorical Lessons from John Henry Newman." *College Composition and Communication* 31 (December 1980): 402–12. Reprinted in *Selected Essays*, 209–24.

———. "Teaching Style." In *The Territory of Language: Linguistics, Stylistics, and the Teaching of Composition*, ed. Donald A. McQuade, 23–33. Carbondale: Southern Illinois University Press, 1986.

———. "The Theory and Practice of Imitation in Classical Rhetoric." *College Composition and Communication* 22 (October 1971): 243–50. Reprinted in *Selected Essays, 179–91.*

———. "The *Topoi* Revisited." In *Rhetoric and Praxis: The Contribution of Classical Rhetoric to Practical Reasoning*, ed. Jean Dietz Moss, 43–57. Washington, D.C.: Catholic University of America Press, 1986.

———. "The Usefulness of Classical Rhetoric." *College Composition and Communication* 14 (October 1963): 162–64. Reprinted in *Selected Essays*, 16–21.

———. "A View from the Pews." *Pastoral Life* 9 (July–August 1961): 3–7.

———. "What Hath Webster Wrought." *America*, October 20, 1962: 929–31.

———. "What Is Being Revived?" *College Composition and Communication* 18 (October 1967): 1 166–172. Reprinted in *Selected Essays, 49–60.*

Corbett, Edward P. J., and Ruth Anderson. "Rhetoric in the Senior High School." *Breakthrough* 1 (May 1966): 25–28.

Corbett, Edward P. J., and Robert J. Connors. *Style and Statement*. New York: Oxford University Press, 1998.

Hellwig, Monika K. "The Catholic Intellectual Tradition in the Catholic University." In *Examining the Catholic Intellectual Tradition*, ed. Anthony J. Cernera and Oliver J. Morgan, 1–18. Fairfield, Conn.: Sacred Heart University Press, 2000. Reprinted in *A Jesuit Education Reader*, ed. George W. Traub, 242–59. Chicago: Loyola Press, 2008.

Hughes, Richard, and P. Albert Duhamel. *Rhetoric: Principles and Usage*. Englewood Cliffs, N.J.: Prentice Hall, 1962.

Jarratt, Susan. *Rereading the Sophists: Classical Rhetoric Refigured*. Carbondale: Southern Illinois University Press, 1991.

Kennedy, George A. *Classical Rhetoric and Its Christian and Secular Tradition from Ancient to Modern Times*. 2nd ed. University of North Carolina Press, 1999.

Kolvenbach, Peter-Hans, S. J. "Themes of Jesuit Higher Education." Based on two addresses at Georgetown University, June 7, 1989, summarized and edited by John J. Callahan, S. J. http://onlineministries.creighton.edu/Heartland3/r-themes .html. Reprinted in *Foundations: The Jesuit Tradition at Regis University*, by John J. Callahan, 22–26. Regis University, 1997. www.regis.edu/content/ars/pdf/ ars.asn.FoundationsJackCal.pdf. Accessed 14, February 2012.

Korth, Sharon J. "Precis of Ignatian Pedagogy: A Practical Approach." *A Jesuit Education Reader*, ed. George W. Traub, 280–84. Chicago: Loyola Press, 2008.

Maryks, Robert Aleksander. *Saint Cicero and the Jesuits: The Influence of the Liberal Arts on the Adoption of Moral Probabilism*. Aldershot, Hampshire, England: Ashgate, 2008.

McCrimmon, James M. *Writing with a Purpose: A First Course in College Composition*. Boston: Houghton Mifflin, 1950.

Muldoon, Tim. "Postmodern Spirituality and the Ignatian *Fundamentum*." In *A Jesuit Education Reader*, ed. George W. Traub, 285–98. Chicago: Loyola Press, 2008.

Nelms, Gerald. *A Case History Approach to Composition Studies: Edward P. J. Corbett and Janet Emig*. PhD diss., Ohio State University, 1990. Ann Arbor: UMI, 1991.

———. "The Rise of Classical Rhetoric in Modern Composition Studies." *Focuses* 8, no. 1 (Summer 1995): 3–30.

Nelms, Gerald, and Maureen Daly Goggin. "The Revival of Classical Rhetoric for Modern Composition Studies: A Survey." *Rhetoric Society Quarterly* 23, nos. 3–4 (Summer–Autumn 1994): 11–26.

Newton, Robert R. "Summary Conclusion." In *Reflections on the Educational Principles of the Spiritual Exercises and Questions for Teachers*. Washington, D. C.: Jesuit Secondary Education Association, 1977. 26–33. Reprinted as "Reflections on the Educational Principles of the *Spiritual Exercises:* Summary Conclusions and Questions for Teachers." In *A Jesuit Education Reader*, ed. George W. Traub, 274–79. Chicago: Loyola Press, 2008.

O'Hare, Joseph A. "Jesuit Education in America." *The Jesuit Tradition in Education and Missions: A 450-Year Perspective*, ed. Christopher Chapple, 143–54. Scranton, Pa: University of Scranton Press, 1993.

Ratio Studiorum: The Official Plan for Jesuit Education (Ratio atque Institutio Studiorum Societatis Iesu). Translated by Claude Pavur. St. Louis: Institute of Jesuit Sources, 2005. http://www.slu.edu/colleges/AS/languages/classical/latin/ tchmat/pedagogy/rs/rs1.html#rs-data. Accessed February 14, 2012.

Sams, Henry W. "Fields of Research in Rhetoric." *College Composition and Communication* 5 (1954): 60–65.

Traub, George W. "Do You Speak Ignatian? A Glossary of Terms Used in Ignatian and Jesuit Circles." Jesuitresource.org, Xavier University, 2008. http://www.jesuitresource.org/ignatian-resources/do-you-speak-ignatian.cfm. Reprinted in *A Jesuit Education Reader*, ed. George W. Traub, 390–409. Chicago: Loyola Press, 2008.

Walsh, Mike, MM Maryknoll Mission Archives. "Re: Research Assistance." Email to the author. June 19, 2012.

Weaver, Richard M. *Composition: A Course in Writing and Rhetoric*. New York: Holt, 1957.

BERNARD LONERGAN'S RHETORICAL RESONANCES: A PRELIMINARY INQUIRY

Paula Mathieu

> An insight is not just a slogan, and an ongoing accumulation of insights is not just an advertising campaign. A creative process is a learning process. It is learning what hitherto was not known.
> —Bernard Lonergan, "Healing," 101

BECOMING A STUDENT OF LONERGAN

I discovered Bernard Lonergan's work as a doctoral student in rhetoric, much in the same way I suspect many other Lonergan students do: at the suggestion of a Jesuit or, in my case, an almost-Jesuit. Thirty years before we met, my graduate-school mentor, Jim Sosnsoski, had completed a PhL from West Baden College on his way to becoming a Jesuit priest but then chose a different path in life, which included nearly forty years of academic teaching and mentoring. Jim arrived at the University of Illinois at Chicago just as I was working to revise my master's thesis—a discourse analysis of the Starbucks coffee company—into what would become my first published article. During this revision process, I puzzled over how to talk in new ways about cultural studies and rhetoric. While I was firmly grounded in materialist ideas, the Marxist concept of ideological mystification seemed an incomplete way to explain how and why we as individuals accept certain ideas as true while entertaining huge inconsistencies and blind spots in our thinking. Jim's response at the time was simple. He said, "Take a look at Bernard Lonergan's *Insight*. Read especially what he has to say about scotosis."

While the suggestion was simple, the task was not. At the time I had no idea of the scope and depth of Lonergan's work, how dense and ranging a work *Insight* would be, how vast a body of scholarship Lonergan had written in addition to *Insight*, or how complex, confounding, and visionary were Lonergan's ideas, even for those deeply schooled in the philosophical and theological traditions to which he wrote and responded.

Now, more than a decade after I first encountered Lonergan's scholarship, I still categorize myself, even after writing this essay, as a beginning student of Lonergan's work. And if that claim sounds overly apologetic, consider that Frederick Crowe, the general editor of Lonergan's collected works, biographer and author of numerous works about Lonergan—clearly a scholar who spent much of his career wrestling with "the several million words of Lonergan's lifetime production"—wrote in 1984 that "I do not understand him after thirty-seven years of study" (4). Rather than stating this to deter others from exploring the relevance of Lonergan's ideas to contemporary issues and problems, however, Crowe intends his words as a call for more communal discussions of this scholarship:

> It is the nature of seminal thinking to become clarified only in the harvest, and the harvest will raise as many questions as it solves. The process, then, is a to and fro movement in which we bring our limited understanding to bear on a problem area, discover in that effort our need for deeper understanding, return with more specific questions to our seminal source, and so advance through lesser and lesser measures of failure to greater and greater measures of success.
>
> —Crowe, 4

Crowe argues that only in the act of applying Lonergan's ideas to contemporary problems will greater clarity of his works' meaning and relevance become manifest. Thus, in this essay, I attempt no comprehensive understanding of Lonergan's scholarship and offer no specific argument about its relevance to the rhetorical tradition. Instead, in the spirit of Crowe's recommendation, I merely suggest some of the deep and often implicit rhetorical resonances of Lonergan's work, in order to begin exploring what I see as some of its potentially fruitful applications to important issues of the day surrounding language, public debate, and public meaning—issues relevant to rhetorical studies. To do that, I first give a brief overview of who Bernard Lonergan was, outline what previous scholars have said about connections between Lonergan and rhetoric, and then select a few concepts of Lonergan's that speak most strongly to me. I then tease through some of their potential implications. My selections are but a handful of other equally relevant of Lonergan's ideas, concepts, and arguments. And since the very concept of inquiry is so central to Lonergan's thought, this chapter is intended as an introductory inquiry that will serve, I hope, as an invitation to other rhetoricians who might become interested in the process of asking questions about Lonergan's thought and its connections to the field of rhetoric and writing studies.

BERNARD LONERGAN, S.J.

Twentieth-century Jesuit priest, philosopher, theologian, and economist, Bernard Joseph Francis Lonergan was born in Buckingham, Quebec, an English-speaking enclave of francophone Canada, in 1904. Some scholars suggest that his growing up as a "minority within a minority" shaped some of his later unconventional ideas (Byrne, "Insight 1"). In 1918, at the age of thirteen, Lonergan went as a boarder to Loyola College, a Jesuit school in Montreal, and joined the Jesuit order at age eighteen. While he followed a fairly traditional course of Jesuit formation, including classical languages, mathematics, and rhetoric, he also held "a lifelong dissatisfaction with the intellectual standards of Jesuit schools in particular, and the state of Catholic education more generally" (Boston Collaborative). He pursued doctoral studies in Italy until 1940, when he was forced to return to Canada owing to the war in Europe. That year he began teaching at the Collège de l'Immaculée Conception in Montreal, and then at the Jesuit seminary in Toronto from 1947 to 1953, and at Gregorian University from 1953 to 1965. From 1965 to 1975 he was professor of theology at Regis College, Toronto, while serving as the Stillman Professor at Harvard University from 1971 to 1972. An article in *Time* magazine (1970) asserted that many intellectuals believed Lonergan to be the finest philosophical thinker of the twentieth century. In 1975, Lonergan became a Distinguished Visiting Professor of Theology at Boston College and taught there until his retirement. In 1983 he returned to Canada, where he died in 1984.

After Lonergan's death, Fr. Crowe and others discovered a wealth of Lonergan's unpublished writing from the 1930s that offers insights into Lonergan's most significant early influences, which included Plato, John Henry Newman, the Catholic social encyclicals of the 1930s (especially those calling attention to the plight of workers), Hegel and Marx (Byrne, "Insight, Lecture 1"). While this may seem surprising of someone most widely considered a Thomist, a student of St. Thomas Aquinas, it underscores Lonergan's abiding interest in the problem of human history (Byrne, "Insight, Lecture 1").

Lonergan's collected works, which are in the process of being published by the University of Toronto Press, number twenty-five volumes. His major works are the later *Method in Theology* (1972) and, his best-known, *Insight: A Study of Human Understanding* (1957). *Insight* takes on the question "What am I doing when I am knowing?" and traces a common process or method of inquiry through various kinds of knowing—scientific, common sense, aesthetic. Lonergan's writing style, especially in *Insight*, is dense and not easily accessible by many accounts. One reviewer of *Insight* commented as follows: "Many readers who begin *Insight* in hope of realizing its wealth will soon feel like the pioneers confronting the Great Plains or the Rockies" (Campbell, 476). The scope of Lonergan's philosophy ambitiously takes on topics of human understanding both within academic disciplines and through everyday reasoning, theological method, and, later in his career, economics. Some scholars suggest that Lonergan's greatest interest was not topics of his inquiry but the method of inquiry itself:

> Lonergan's primary intention was neither philosophical nor theological nor, more recently, economic, but methodological; . . . his contribution lay less in particular areas of those disciplines than in radical methodological proposals cutting across and expanding the boundaries of many disciplines. The implementation of this method requires not only the self-appropriation essayed in Lonergan's work but also familiarity with the questions, tech-

niques, and data of many specialized fields. The implementation requires, furthermore, not a solitary individual working in a single area on one project, but the ongoing and dialectical cooperation of many individuals involved in different fields, diverse projects, and various types and stages of works.

—Riley and Fallon, foreword, viii

Similar to Crowe's call for the to and fro of scholars working together to understand and tease out the relevance of Lonergan's ideas, Riley and Fallon argue that they can be relevant to all academic disciplines and even more usefully in interdisciplinary or post-disciplinary investigations. Like rhetoric itself, Lonergan's work can be viewed as a method for seeking truth or forging greater understanding in a given situation.

LONERGAN AND RHETORIC

Despite abiding interests in inquiry, human understanding, and how beliefs change, Lonergan himself makes scarce direct mention of rhetoric in most of his scholarship. The reasons for this could only be speculations, but they might include his abiding interest in Plato, which drew stark distinctions between the realms of philosophy and rhetoric, according the former with the weighty issues of discovering truth and relegating rhetoric to facility with language. In fact, Enlightenment understandings of rhetoric as a practice not centrally occupied with discovering truth but only with adorning language still endure today, though they were more persistent at the time of Lonergan's education. Influential books reshaping rhetorical theory, such as Perelman and Olbrechts-Tyteca's *The New Rhetoric* or Kenneth Burke's *A Rhetoric of Motive*, weren't published in English until 1968, after much of Lonergan's opus was written.[1] And although Lonergan does not discuss the concept of rhetoric per se, his works help clarify, define, and refine rhetorical processes and methods in a tradition similar to these groundbreaking works.

Despite the rhetorical richness of Lonergan's work, only a handful of scholarly articles seek to apply Lonergan's thought to issues related to rhetoric and writing studies. Likely the first and most direct article to connect Lonergan and rhetoric is "Insight and Understanding: The 'Common Sense' Rhetoric of Bernard Lonergan," John Angus Campbell's 1985 book review of *Insight* for the *Quarterly Journal of Speech*.[2] Campbell attempts to tease out "Lonergan's implicit perspective on the role of rhetoric in human self-understanding" (476). Campbell focuses on three (of many) themes that Lonergan explores in *Insight*: the science of human action, the connection of cognition to practical living, and the understanding of how common sense and language help constitute the lives of individuals and communities (477). From these ideas, Campbell argues that Lonergan would place rhetoric within a larger human quest for knowledge and order, not as a theory of persuasion but "a specialization of human intelligence" and that it should be described as "a rhetoric of common sense" (477). Campbell sees in Lonergan the promise of rhetorical theory that helps individuals ethically wrestle with the challenges of their day:

> A Lonergian rhetoric would generate strategies for commending intelligence and reasonableness as normative guides for men and women as they struggle in uncertainty to make sense of themselves and their worlds. In brief, according to Lonergan, what one intends in asking a question and what one knows in reaching a correct judgment—a judgment that satisfies the relevant questions—is "being," apart from which there is nothing.
>
> —Campbell, 486

Two other rhetorical scholars—Janice Lauer and Thomas J. Farrell—focus on the significance of Lonergan's work for the teaching of writing. Lauer's article "Writing as Inquiry: Some Questions for Teachers" (1982) was written at a time when some universities were beginning to explore the possibility of replacing core-distribution requirements with a focus on developing skills, including the skill of inquiry. Lauer argues that "if we want to engage students in writing as inquiry, we must understand the nature of inquiry," and she goes on to use Lonergan's deep understanding of inquiry to tease out relevant questions related to a writing pedagogy of inquiry. Working from Lonergan's idea that insights come as a result of the "tension of inquiry," she wonders what inner conditions compel some writers but not others to ask deep and insight-provoking questions (90). Beyond the inner motivations of writers, Lauer turns to broader societal concerns that trivialize or delegitimize inquiry. She asks how students who are raised in a culture that "extols certainty" and are taught by "an educational system that rewards right answers" can awaken their minds to the enigmas that they experience: "What kinds of writing assignments can we set to avoid trapping students in contexts so narrow or artificial that they preclude genuine puzzlement or curiosity? What strategies can we offer to guide students to state the unknowns well?" (910). These questions are as—or more—salient and challenging to writing teachers today as when they were written thirty years ago.

Part of the broader societal issues that trivialize inquiry are obstacles to inquiry and insight that are psychological and cultural, what Lonergan describes as "flights from understanding" (*Insight*, 5). They include a tendency to dismiss inquiries that do not seem immediately practical and the fear of discovery that can disrupt one's complacency or force unwanted change. Lauer trenchantly writes:

> These powerful psychological and cultural obstacles pose more serious threats to developing writers than lack of syntactic maturity or poor control of conventions. . . . Could not these very problems become catalysts to our

own inquiry, creating the tension necessary to spark our explorations for insights about the teaching of composition itself—as inquiry?

—Lauer, 92

In Lauer's article and the questions she generates, one can easily see important ways that Lonergan's ideas about inquiry can be useful in training teachers and perhaps also in sharing with students. As writing classes increasingly take on questions of inquiry and questions about the nature of writing itself, Lonergan's thoughts might make useful additions.

Thomas Farrell in "Writing, the Writer, and Lonergan" explores the value of Lonergan's thought on developing a greater awareness of one's process as a writer. Farrell underscores the importance of Lonergan's idea that human subjectivity is actually intersubjective—in that it is formed both by the communities in which one lives and by the process of inquiry one undertakes—as a possible way to disrupt the romantic notion of a solitary writer who exists outside community or history. Farrell believes that Lonergan's ideas can directly help students compose more authentic academic prose and more organically incorporate external sources into their arguments. He argues that when students engage in the process of inquiry, something akin to a parliamentary debate takes place within one's subjectivity students, which he believes is helpful in preparation for entering academic disciplines and incorporating external sources. Adopting Lonergan's idea that one's subjectivity is always in process, Farrell argues that the goal of education should be to help students "expand their intersubjectivities by learning the meanings and values of different academic disciplines" (46).

Farrell's essay appears in the collection *Communication and Lonergan: Common Ground for Forging the New Age* (1993), edited by Farrell and Paul Soukup. The collection combines essays by traditional Lonergan scholars with essays by Farrell, Campbell, and other rhetoricians, the goal being to make Lonergan's thought relevant not only to rhetorical study but to our common situation. Farrell and Soukup explore these connections in the preface to the collection:

> The very world we live in lies under threat of war, of environmental collapse, of the interpersonal and structural violence that leads to abominations such as the Holocaust or "ethnic cleansing." How can we transform the wasteland of limited vision and distorted communication?
>
> Lonergan's philosophical and methodological work invites us to see with different eyes and to reflect with transformed understanding on what we do. He urges all human beings to "authenticity"—a word that in his writings summarizes honesty, integrity, attentiveness to experience and overcoming distorted communication through faithfulness to his five "transcendental" or "self-affirming" precepts: Be Attentive, Be Intelligent, Be Reasonable, Be Responsible, and Be in Love.
>
> —Farrell and Soukup, xvii

Later in the preface and throughout the collection, contributors further explicate the meaning of Lonergan's precepts and the implications they have for questions of communication.

Another collection honoring Bernard Lonergan, published in the year of his death (1984), contains several essays that make explicit connection between Lonergan's work and rhetorical methods. In the preface, editors Timothy Fallon and Philip Boo Riley describe Lonergan's scholarship as a meta-method of interpreting religion and culture, which requires collaborative study.

Contributor Stephen Toulmin argues that Lonergan's work intervenes importantly and productively in the split between absolutism and relativism, especially within the discipline of theological studies—to determine what the historical meaning and relevance of religious dogma is, for example. Lonergan's relevance, according to Toulmin, extends far beyond the discipline of theology in its suggesting an epistemological method for making good decisions across many domains, including science, law, and Judaic studies. Toulmin sees Lonergan as fruitfully helping intellectuals consider how to identify whether disciplinary changes point in fruitful directions, or which colleagues should be accorded more respect as carrying rational authority (22). And again, while Toulmin does not describe such terms as rhetorical, they do outline a method for understanding and making decisions in a historical changing world. Lonergan's work, as Toulmin describes it, serves an important rhetorical function, that of keeping open debate and discussion: "It is one of Lonergan's most striking virtues that he has always been committed to finding a language in which to keep constructive discussions going, across all the boundaries between different historical epochs and different contemporary cultures" (17).

Stephen Happel goes further, asserting that Lonergan's methods themselves can be considered a rhetoric. In "Religious Rhetoric and the Language of Theological Foundations," Happel asserts that Lonergan's *Method in Theology* provides a valuable analysis of the persuasive arguments claiming truth value within theological study: "By revitalizing theology as a 'generalized empirical method,' Lonergan has rethought rhetoric as a contemporary public language which integrates both head and heart, truth about reality and the affective desire for that reality" (Happel 191). What Happel so usefully points out is that rhetoric, as envisioned by Lonergan (though without using the term), unites intellectual and affective aspects of persuasion and understanding as well as making a place for religious practice, symbols, images, and faith within the realm of decision-making. I most appreciate Happel's following claim, which creates a full sense of rhetoric that revels in the everyday and in the sacred, linking common sense and intersubjective awareness as a metaphor for the divine:

When Lonergan maintains [in *Method in Theology*, 292] that "genuine objectivity is the fruit of authentic subjectivity," he goes on to say that ascertaining the real requires the converting affect, intellect, decision and religious sense. Lonergan develops an ontological rhetoric which, through its differentiation of interiority and its proper appropriation transforms common sense and theory. Common sense and theory grounded in an ontological interiority become the dominant entry into a disclosure of differentiated transcendence itself. Intersubjective interiority in our religious common sense has become the primary metaphor for the presence of God.

—Happel, 196–97

It is in this interior subjectivity that most explicitly shows the connections between Lonergan's notion of rhetoric and Jesuit theology. Here Lonergan certainly enacts the Jesuit notion of finding God in all things. Beyond that, he shows that a process of intersubjective interiority, or what he calls elsewhere "an orientation to transcendent mystery," is, as he goes on to say, "the primary and fundamental meaning of the name, God" (*Method*, 341). His process of questioning and discovery, in search of self-appropriation, with a sense of faith, is, to Lonergan, God.

LONERGAN AND RHETORICAL CONCEPTS

Most of the existing scholarship on Lonergan and rhetoric focuses on his scholarship as method or process, but I would like to extend his discussion of process to pinpoint some heuristic concepts he uses to aid in that process, which I see as fruitful and relevant to the study of language, persuasion, and the shaping of truth claims. Certainly Lonergan's highest authority is the process of seeking knowledge itself, the individual but communal act of asking questions and seeking answers, what becomes a self-correcting cycle of inquiry, reflection, judgment, and further inquiry. A key idea for Lonergan is process—gaining knowledge is a process, self-appropriation is a process, history (of progress or decline) is also a long process. But for such processes to be meaningful, authentic, objective, and intelligent, they have to be taken on deliberately, bravely, carefully, continually, and lovingly. And any meaningful process as envisaged by Lonergan never reaches an ending point. It merely opens up new questions, new challenges, or new languages to be articulated, as is clear from the following quote:

> To learn, to be persuaded, to become adapted, occur within living and through living. The living is ever now, but the knowledge to guide living, the willingness to follow knowledge, the sensitive adaptation that vigorously and joyously executes will's decisions, these belong to the future, and when the future is present, there will be beyond it a further future with steeper demands.
>
> —Lonergan, *Insight*, 711

The process of human knowing begins with but is not limited to human experience. We experience the world, but only by paying attention and asking questions can we gain the insights that lead to further questions of fact and judgment. Lonergan focuses centrally on the individual, in that his work is an "invitation to a personal, decisive act to know oneself" (Byrne, "Insight 1"), yet at heart this is an individual who is rhetorical in two ways. Internally, we persuade ourselves to pay attention or not, to reflect or not, to act based on or insights or not. Secondly, the individual in Lonergan's work is a historical one, raised in specific communities, with historically and culturally shaped ideas and beliefs.

Lonergan spends two full chapters of *Insight* on common sense, which he describes as an important form of knowledge that is both intelligent and rational—but incomplete, as are all branches of knowing, including scholarly knowledge, artistic knowledge, etc. Common sense is intellectual because it is a communally tested fund of insights and because of its methods, a self-correcting process: Inquiries lead to insights lead to actions lead to patterns of experience, which lead to further insights. Ultimately, common sense is shared, as an inventory of insights that can be passed on generation to generation.

While Lonergan's preoccupation in *Insight* is the uncovering of a process or method for gaining insights via inquiry, he deploys along the way various concepts as heuristics for understanding or interrogating our processes of understanding. He importantly acknowledges that humans regularly engage in various "flights from understanding" (5) that are rooted in problems of psychology, culture, and emotion:

> For insights can be implemented only if people have open minds. Problems can be manifest. Insights that solve them may be available. But the insights will not be grasped by biased minds. There is the bias of the neurotic fertile in evasions of the insight his analyst sees he needs. There is the bias of the individual egoist, whose interest is confined to the insights that would enable him to exploit each new situation to his own personal advantage. There is the bias of group egoism blind to the fact that the group no longer fulfills its once useful function and that it is merely clinging to power by all the maneuvers that in one way or another block development and impede progress. There is finally the general bias of all 'good' men of common sense, cherishing the illusion that their single talent, common sense, is omnicompetent, insisting on procedures that no longer work, convinced that the only way to do this is to muddle through, and spurning as idle theorizing and empty verbiage any rational account of what has to be done.
> —Lonergan, "Healing," 102

Lonergan's discussions of such flights from understanding—like scotosis, general bias, group bias—first interested me in his work, and concepts such as these helped me see potential richness for rhetorical studies.

Scotosis: Lonergan describes scotosis as an unconscious process of censorship of information or insights, a process occurring in one's psyche. Yet, he says, "the whole process is not hidden from us," because contrary insights do arise and must be rationalized or brushed aside "in an emotional reaction of distaste, pride, dread, horror, revulsion" (*Insight*, 215). So while we do not choose or knowingly create a scotosis, by refusing to engage in a process of self-appropriation, we unconsciously allow certain blind spots to persist and remain unexamined.

Many of Lonergan's concepts, like scotosis, are made all the richer by the etymological reverberations of the terms he chooses to describe them. According to the *Oxford English Dictionary*, the etymology of the word *scotoma* suggests dizziness and "to darken, to make dimsighted." A scotoma is a blind spot, either in one's eye or on the sun. The metaphor of blind spot is a useful one for Lonergan and rhetorical theory, in that whatever blind spots an audience holds can forestall what Aristotle called the "available means of persuasion." A scotosis is not rational, but it's real, and we as individuals can't often see our own blind spots, so it requires dialogue and shared community processes to allow one to see and address what we cannot. Lonergan details other forms of bias, which include egoism, group bias, and general bias.

Egoism, or individual bias: Lonergan ascribes egoism to an "incomplete development of intelligence" and is a more deliberate case of oversight than scotosis, which can often be preconscious or rooted deeply in one's psyche. One suffering from individual bias has a tendency to act only in one's own best interests, disregarding the knowledge of common wisdom and personal intelligence. An egoist, in Lonergan's view, acts and is aware of his actions and as a result might suffer from "an uneasy conscience, for it is not by sheer inadvertence but also by a conscious self-orientation that he devotes his energies to sizing up the social order, ferreting out its weak points and its loopholes, and discovering devices that give access to its rewards while evading its demands for proportionate contributions" (*Insight*, 246). This uneasy conscience is a result of the egoist who uses intelligences to further his own interests but who "will not grant serious consideration to its further relevant questions" (247).

Group bias: Lonergan shows that groups of people tend to resist insights that would reveal their "well-being to be excessive" or that point to the limits or ends of their usefulness (248). In other words, groups in power seldom choose to relinquish that power, which leads to class tensions and resentments: "The advantage of one group is commonly disadvantageous to another, and so some part of the energies of all groups is diverted to the supererogatory activity of devising and implementing offensive and defensive mechanisms" (249). Central to group bias, and all bias, are emotions (what he calls "feelings"), a topic that Lonergan further explores in his *Method in Theology*. While bias generates winners and losers in terms of social class, sentiments run high and can turn to militant force or violence (*Insight*, 250).

General bias: It exists within all humans and within the realm of common sense—a tendency to focus on the concrete and particular and to rule out less immediately practical forms of human knowledge as useless or invalid. Again, general bias is a form of rationalization that occurs because common sense cannot analyze itself, cannot realize its own limitations. Thus a focus on the concrete and immediate tends to supersede the importance of larger issues or long-term results (250–51). One can see such shortsightedness in resistance to government funding of long-term infrastructure projects or in the stock market, which prizes immediate gains beyond all else.

In my earlier work on rhetoric and cultural studies, which led me to Lonergan,[3] I found his notions of scotosis and bias to be useful heuristics, for thinking through not only how individuals have unexamined places in their psyches but also how our consumer culture encourages blind spots and biases in individuals and groups by circulating and selling fragmented but comforting narratives that allow us to entertain myopic visions that disconnect our choices, our consuming, and our ethics from each other, from their long-term consequences, and from the material conditions of our planet. Such blind spots can easily persist because they allow us to remain within a comforting narrative frame and not ask questions and engage in the process of inquiry that might shed light on that darkness. If scotosis or bias allows one to accept the rhetorical presence of a given narrative frame and to act in the directions that frame suggests, one question for rhetorical studies to consider is how rhetoricians and teachers of writing can help to raise questions about the blind spots in each of us. How can we learn to ask questions that shine light on our unexamined spaces within? How can the realm of the polis or public debates more productively focus on genuine inquiry and less on spinning narrow, biased stories with predetermined aims?

Although the focus of much of Lonergan's work is on the internal workings of human intelligence and emotions, his interests clearly relate to problems of history, civilizations, and inequality. He does not, however, offer direct ways to address or mitigate bias as it shapes "the longer cycle" of history (*Insight*, 251–63). The goal of his philosophy of self-appropriation is to help people heal individually as well shape the unfolding of human history. Since the search for insight, knowledge, and understanding always takes place in a busy, practical world, the connections between theoretical intelligence and messy reality is always filled with gaps and unintelligibilities. Because of this, Lonergan argues, aims of progress and higher integration never match up perfectly with the realm of the practical, resulting in a "residue" that he calls "the social surd" (255). Once again, Lonergan chooses a rich term that reverberates deeply through its etymology. *Surd* comes from mathematics, as a term to describe an irrational number, and so the expression "social surd" implies that society lacks in rationality in various ways. But *surd* is also a term from phonetics, to denote speech that is uttered with the breath and not sound—in some ways speechless but speech at the same time. The Greek and Latin roots (*alogos* and *surdis*) reverberate with the ideas both of irrationality and of speechlessness, echoing the close connection Lonergan makes between knowledge and language, or "expression," as he calls it. Campbell claims that a social surd results when societies lack a public forum for reflection, which is indeed true, but Lonergan seems to suggest that the social surd is a more general malady facing all human societies because progress is perpetually hampered by the various biases and the preoccupation with practicality that he catalogs. Despite this critique of history as a long cycle of decline, Lonergan holds out hope for a better kind of world, which he describes via the concept *cosmopolis* (*Insight*, 263–269).

Cosmopolis: Interestingly, rather than describing what a cosmopolis is or could be, Lonergan primarily defines it in terms of what it is not:

> It is not a group denouncing other groups; it is not a superstate ruling states; it is not an organization that enrolls members nor an academy that endorses opinions, nor a court that administers a legal code. It is a withdrawal from practicality to save practicality. It is a dimension of consciousness, a heightened grasp of historical origins, a discovery of historical responsibilities.
>
> —Lonergan, *Insight*, 266

Lonergan describes the idea of cosmopolis as a heuristic, something that can be learned only in the process, and so the idea itself is just a placeholder, "an X, what is to be known when one understands" (263). Its goal is to help guide people to make insights—and take actions—that are not just practical or beneficial in the short term but can focus on long-term benefits. Cosmopolis is a helpful challenge, an invitation to engage the process of inquiry with an eye toward a more humane world.[4] And the values of such a world, according to Lonergan, would be "founded on the native detachment and disinterestedness of every intelligence, that commands man's first allegiance, that implements itself primarily through its allegiance, that is too universal to be bribed, too impalpable to be forced, too effective to be ignored" (263). Thus even solutions of historical and social problems, for Lonergan, begin in the concerted efforts of individuals to know themselves and to increase their understanding. Ultimately the process of inquiry should lead to self-appropriation, guided by his precepts of Be Attentive, Be Intelligent, Be Reasonable, Be Responsible, and Be In Love. Love in the broadest sense—which includes the familial, the romantic, the intellectual, the religious, the altruistic, etc.—becomes the basis for guiding the process of self-appropriation:

> Where hatred reinforces bias, love dissolves it, whether it be bias, unconscious motivation, the bias of individual or group egoism or the bias of

omnicompetent, shortsighted common sense. Where hatred plods around in ever narrower vicious circles, love breaks the bonds of psychological and social determinisms with the conviction of faith and the power of hope.

—Lonergan, "Healing," 103

A key necessity for overcoming blind spots and being guided by love, according to Lonergan, is a focus on the connection between knowledge and expression—in other words, language. In fact, late in his teaching career at Boston College, Lonergan taught courses focused on analogies and the meaning of symbols (Byrne, interview). But even early in his scholarship, Lonergan is quite explicit that "the interpenetration of knowledge and expression implies a solidarity, almost a fusion, of the development of knowledge and the development of language" (*Insight*, 577).[5] For Lonergan, beyond simple expression is interpretation, which becomes problematic because it is relative to the viewpoint of the interpreter. He offers another heuristic concept, that of a "universal viewpoint," which is unreachable in practice but would contain all possible interpretations of all possible interpreters (587–95). It's an idea that all views and voices must be heard in order to interpret fully. And not surprisingly, the totality of viewpoints would be concerned with acts of critical reflection and the gathering of the insights of the interpreters (588).

Something that might aid in the process of critical reflection, according to Lonergan, is satire and humor (647–48). While his discussion of humor is brief, he stresses its important rhetorical potential to break through a person's biases and preoccupation with practicalities: "If men are afraid to think, they might not be afraid to laugh. Yet proofless, purposeless laughter can dissolve honored pretense; it can disrupt conventional humbug; it can disillusion man of his most cherished illusions, for it is in league with the detached, disinterested, unrestricted desire to know" (649). Thus, while Lonergan's focus is on inquiry, reflection, and self-appropriation, such processes should be not somber, humorless endeavors but rather creative processes engaged with the rich complexity of life itself. For Lonergan, the dialectic between creativity and healing are central: "For just as the creative process, when unaccompanied by healing, is distorted and corrupted by bias, so too the healing process, when unaccompanied by creating, is a soul without a body" ("Healing." 105).

FURTHER DIRECTIONS AND AN INVITATION TO COLLABORATION

Since Lonergan's opus is so extensive, there is vastly more to say about connections between rhetorical scholarship and his ideas found in, for example, his work on feelings, religious conversion, judgment, etc. I hope others will take up these themes. My hope is that this essay suggests that the scholarship of Fr.

Bernard Lonergan is a rich and largely untapped source for methods of studying and theorizing rhetorical practices.

I now teach at Boston College, beginning my academic teaching career on the campus where Lonergan completed his. During the writing of this article, I have had the occasion to read, sit with, and puzzle over many of Fr. Bernard Lonergan's words and ideas and have come to appreciate their relevance not only to rhetorical study but to the more demanding process of everyday living.[6] Fortunately, I did not have to endeavor this inquiry alone. I have been fortunate to have had the opportunity to call on a colleague of mine, Patrick Byrne, who is a former student of Lonergan's, was later his junior colleague, and is now professor of philosophy and director of the Lonergan Institute at Boston College. In 2010, Byrne taught a two-semester course on Lonergan's *Insight*, and the video of the lectures and the notes of both semesters are available for watching and downloading at the Lonergan Institute's website. I am so grateful for this invaluable resource and for Pat's willingness to have several lunches with me. While I puzzled over Lonergan's ideas or asked basic questions of interpretation, Pat generously offered patient advice and suggestions for further reading, which were beyond useful. What I appreciated most about this interaction, however, was a chance to sit down with a colleague, to discuss deep and important issues, and to puzzle over big questions of how better to analyze, teach, or learn more just and humane ways of being in the world.

This process of becoming Lonergan's student has helped remind me of the value of community and collaboration, exactly what so many Lonergan scholars argue is necessary for learning, understanding, and applying these ideas. Lonergan's ideas demand conversation, collaboration, and shared inquiry. They invite people to think and talk through ideas to form new questions about self-appropriation and creating a better world. If Lonergan's work is to remain relevant in the twenty-first century, it is through collaboration that it will happen. Various resources exist to help foster that collaboration. In addition to the Lonergan Institute at Boston College, several other centers for Lonergan studies host symposia and conferences where interested people can gather to inquire together: at Regis University, Marquette University, Seton Hall University, Loyola Marymount College, Concordia University, and others. My hope is that at these gatherings and at disciplinary conferences of rhetoric and writing studies, other scholars might join together to together in seeking new ways to bring some of Lonergan's concepts to light—and to life.

NOTES

1. Perelman and Olbrechts-Tyteca's *The New Rhetoric* was originally published in French in 1955.

2. Campbell later revised this essay for inclusion in the collection *Communication and Lonergan*, edited by Thomas Farrell.

3. See Mathieu, "Economic Citizenship and the Rhetoric of Gourmet Coffee."

4. For an essay more fully explicating the concept, see Martin Lopez Calva, "Cosmopolis: From Common Sense to a Sense in Common: Educational Challenges in a Change of Epoch."

5. For more on Lonergan and expression, see especially *Insight*, 586–87.

6. I don't think it would be possible for me to overstate how indebted I am to Professor Patrick Byrne, director of the Lonergan Institute at Boston College, for his help and support in my writing of this article. Thank you, Pat, for your patience, insight, and support.

WORKS CITED

"Bernard J. F. Lonergan (1904–1984)." In *Boston Collaborative Encyclopedia of Western Theology*. http://people.bu.edu/wwildman/bce/lonergan.htm. Accessed September 10, 2012.

Byrne, Patrick. A Course on Insight. The Lonergan Institute at Boston College. Fall and Spring 2010. http://bclonergan.org/2011/04/insight-course/.

———. Interview. June 26, 2012.

Campbell, John Angus. "Insight and Understanding: The 'Common Sense' Rhetoric of Bernard Lonergan." *Quarterly Journal of Speech* 71 (1965): 476–506.

Crowe, Frederick E. "The Task of Interpreting Lonergan: A Preliminary to the Symposia." In *Religion and Culture: Essays in Honor of Bernard Lonergan, S.J.*, ed. Timothy Fallon and Philip Boo Riley, 3–16. Albany: SUNY Press, 1987.

Fallon, Timothy, and Philip Boo Riley. Foreword to *Religion and Culture: Essays in Honor of Bernard Lonergan, S.J.*, ed. Timothy Fallon and Philip Boo Riley. Albany, N.Y.: SUNY Press, 1987.

Farrell, Thomas J. "Writing, the Writer ,and Lonergan: Authenticity and Intersubjectivity." In *Communication and Lonergan: Common Ground for Forging the New Age*, by Farrell and Soukup, 23–47.

Farrell, Thomas J., and Paul A Soukup. *Communication and Lonergan: Common Ground for Forging the New Age*. Kansas City, Mo.: Sheed and Ward, 1993.

Happel, Stephen. "Religious Rhetoric and the Language of Theological Foundations." *Religion And Culture: Essays in Honor of Bernard Lonergan, S.J.*, ed. Timothy Fallon and Philip Boo Riley, 191–203. New York: State University of New York Press, 1987.

Lauer, Janice M. "Writing as Inquiry: Some Questions for Teachers." *College Composition and Communication* 33, no. 1 (February 1982): 89–93.

Lonergan, Bernard. "Healing and Creating in History." In *Macroeconomic Dynamics: An Essay in Circulation Analysis. Collected Works of Bernard Lonergan*, ed. Frederick G. Lawrence, Patrick H. Byrne, and Charles C. Helfling,Jr., 97–106. Toronto: University of Toronto Press, 1999.

———. *Insight: A Study of Human Understanding*. 1957. Toronto: University of Toronto Press, 1992.

———. *Method in Theology*. Toronto: University of Toronto Press, 1971.

Calva, Martin Lopez. "Cosmopolis: From Common Sense to a Sense in Common: Educational Challenges in a Change of Ppoch." Lonergan en Latinoamérica.

http://lonerganlat.com.mx/wp-content/uploads/2011/01/cosmopolis-english.pdf. Accessed July 15, 2012.

Mathieu, Paula. "Economic Citizenship and the Rhetoric of Gourmet Coffee." *Rhetoric Review* 18, no. 1 (Autumn 1999): 112–27.

Matthews, William A. *Lonergan's Quest: A Study of Desire in the Authoring of Insight.* Toronto: University of Toronto Press, 2006.

"Religion: The Answer Is the Question." *Time*, April 20, 1970. http://www.time.com/ time/magazine/article/0,9171,944048,00.html#ixzz2owC3faNK

Toulmin, Stephen. "Pluralism and Authority." In *Religion and Culture: Essays in Honor of Bernard Lonergan, S.J.*, ed. Timothy Fallon and Philip Boo Riley, 17–29. New York: State University of New York Press, 1987.

PAULO FREIRE AND THE JESUIT TRADITION: JESUIT RHETORIC AND FREIREAN PEDAGOGY

Thomas Pace and Gina M. Merys

For most scholars in rhetoric and composition studies, Paulo Freire's insistence on problem-posing education has been critical in the teaching of reading and writing since his *Pedagogy of the Oppressed* first appeared in 1968. Freire's book has become a type of "ur text" for what is now known as critical pedagogy, a theory and practice of teaching that, as Ann George states, "envisions a society not simply pledged to but successfully enacting the principles of equality, of liberty and justice for all" ("Critical Pedagogy," 92). James Berlin in his essay "Freirean Pedagogy in the U.S." (1991) argues that Freire's work is of particular interest to compositionists, in part because of Freire's assertions that thought and knowledge are socially constructed: "Language—in its mediation between the world and the individual, the object and the subject—contains within its shaping force the power of creating humans as agents of action" (170). Advocates of critical pedagogy strive to enact a kind of writing instruction that leads students to use language sensitively and thoughtfully within a number of rhetorical situations—in other words, a writing pedagogy that teaches students to use language within a variety of contexts.

It is hard to overstate the influence Freire's work has had on the field of rhetoric and composition and beyond, since his influence extends to various religious, including Jesuit, contexts as well. For example, both Freire and the Jesuits share the common belief in the powerful role that language plays as the principal means of coming to know the world, in organizing daily reality, and in transforming the self and the world. Language, for Freire and the Jesuits, is both a reflective and an active practice. In *Pedagogy of the Oppressed*, he recognizes that knowledge of the world begins with knowledge and understanding of the word and that knowledge of language should lead to action within the world. He insists that literacy and language make students "discover the world is also theirs . . . and [is a matter] of helping the world be a better place" (68). Similarly, the Jesuits enact what John O'Malley calls "the ministry of the Word," in which Jesuit educators, particularly during the early modern period following their foundation in 1540, fostered the development of students who used language and rhetoric to be informed, ethical, sympathetic, and articulate writers and speakers, willing and committed to engage with their larger communities through the careful use of words (O'Malley 89). This concept, known to the Jesuits as *eloquentia perfecta*, aimed to produce a Christian version of the classical ideal orator, a good person writing and speaking well for the common good. For both Freire as well as for the Jesuits, this interaction with language should lead to reflective practice and action through persuasion.

Freire's work also wielded a significant influence on what became known as liberation theology, a political movement in Christian theology that interprets the teachings of Jesus Christ in terms of a liberation from unjust economic, political, or social conditions. Liberation theology, which grew as a movement in the Roman Catholic Church in Latin America in the 1950s–'60s, was forged as a moral response, primarily, to the harsh economic conditions caused by various social injustices in Latin America. Many of the Catholic workers in Latin America who were part of the movement were Jesuit and were influenced heavily by Freire's writings about education and social justice. Specifically, his theories of what he termed *conscientization* and *praxis* influenced heavily the work of Jesuit Catholic liberation theologians. This chapter argues that the Jesuit influence in Brazil, and elsewhere, helped shape Freire's educational theories and practices, while Freire's theories subsequently impacted the Jesuits. Specifically, we trace the dialectic route between Jesuit traditions of rhetoric and education and Freire's ideas about education on Jesuit notions of liberation theology, particularly examining the impact that the French Jesuit priest Pierre Teilhard de Chardin wielded on Freire's early educational thinking. In the process, we also examine Jesuit concepts of pedagogy and their Freirean parallel. By looking at Freirean pedagogy through the lens of his interactions with the Jesuit tradition, this chapter unveils a relationship previously unexplored by compositionists and those interested in Jesuit education more broadly.

Before exploring the connection between Freirean pedagogy and the Jesuits, it is important to offer a definition of liberation theology. Peruvian theologian Gustavo Gutiérrez, considered the father of liberation theology, developed the movement in response to the large amount of poverty and injustice he witnessed in Latin America, arguing in his *A Theology of Liberation* that the world should be looked at through the perspective of the poor. In *Gustavo Gutiérrez: An Introduction to Liberation Theology*, Robert McAfee Brown, arguing that Gutiérrez stressed that the work of liberation theology should cure what Gutiérrez calls "historical amnesia," suggests that God is "revealed only in the concrete historical context of liberation of the poor and oppressed" (13). In short, liberation theology examines the material conditions and historical contexts that contribute to poverty and argues that the work of the Catholic Church should be conducted through the prism of the poor.

One of the leading scholars and historians of liberation theology, Philip Berryman, defines it as an "interpretation of Christian faith out of the experience of the poor. It is an attempt to read the Bible and key Christian doctrines with the eyes of the poor" (*Liberation Theology*, 5). Berryman goes on to list three features of liberation theology:

1. An interpretation of Christian faith out of the suffering, struggle, and hope of the poor.
2. A critique of society and the ideologies sustaining it.
3. A critique of the activity of the church and of Christians from the angle of the poor.

—Berryman, 6

One of the main features of liberation theology is its insistence on action in relation to religion. In other words, liberation theology is very much concerned about the enacting of Christian faith in the world. In *The Cambridge Companion to Liberation Theology*, Christopher Rowland suggests connections between liberation theology and the Ignatian tradition of putting into practice one's faith:

> Liberation theology is a way, a discipline, an exercise which has to be lived rather than acquired as a body of information. It has parallels in the classic texts of Western Christian spirituality. The Spiritual Exercises of Ignatius Loyola, the founder of the Jesuits, for example, seems at first sight to be a rag-bag of Christian platitudes. To read them without putting the advice into practice for oneself, however, fails to do justice to the fact that it is only when one actually *uses* them that the significance and function of the Exercises becomes apparent.
>
> —Rowland, 4

Rowland compares the *Spiritual Exercises* to tenets of liberation theology, stressing that "engagement with the texts of liberation theology offers an understanding of God from within a commitment to the poor and marginalised and a means of thinking afresh about reality" (4). In other words, liberation theology stresses the importance of a dialectic relationship between theory and practice, between thought and action, ideas that grew out, in large part, from these theologians' reading of Freire. Denis E. Collins, S.J., former professor of education at the University of San Francisco and a biographer of Freire, insists that Freire and Gutiérrez were not only good friends but also "fellow travelers" in their work with the poor and that Freire's "thinking was in consonance with liberation theology" (Collins, interview).

Since its inception, though, liberation theology has been criticized by the Vatican, particularly in recent years, notably by John Paul II and by Benedict XVI (Joseph Ratzinger). Even the current pope, the more moderate Jesuit Francis, appears to take a middle ground on questions of liberation theology. In a 2013 piece in the *Nation*, Harvey Cox points out Francis's conflicted stance:

> As head of the Jesuits in Argentina and then as a bishop, Francis never joined in the attack on liberation theology—but he was never a forceful defender of it either. As a bishop, he claimed that he favored it, but not in an ideological way. When debates about the movement split both the church and the Jesuits, Francis tried to patch up the divisions. He has subsequently conceded that he often did it with a heavy hand, which he now regrets.

His two predecessors, however, were less conflicted. During John Paul II's tenure as pope, for example, Ratzinger served as the prefect for the Congregation for the Doctrine of the Faith (CDF), the Vatican's office for Church orthodoxy. During his tenure, Ratzinger was highly critical of liberation theology, publishing the official criticism of it in 1984, a critique that primarily stresses liberation theology's Marxist leanings:

> The present Instruction has a much more limited and precise purpose: to draw the attention of pastors, theologians, and all the faithful to the deviations, and risks of deviation, damaging to the faith and to Christian living, that are brought about by certain forms of liberation theology which use, in an insufficiently critical manner, concepts borrowed from various currents of Marxist thought.

Here Ratzinger, speaking as head of the CDF, suggests that liberation theology's association with Marxism makes it incompatible with what the CDF views as appropriate "Christian living." A year later, Ratzinger published what he called his own private criticism of liberation theology, again noting that traditional Christianity is discussed through a Marxist lens in liberation theology. He stresses that "an analysis of the phenomenon of liberation theology reveals that it constitutes a fundamental threat to the faith of the Church" (Ratzinger). Ratzinger's critique extended into his tenure as pope and included strong warnings to Jesuits who are part of the movement. In a BBC News report in 2007, Benedict criticized one of the leading proponents of liberation theology, Father Jon Sobrino, S.J. BBC News reported that the pope said that Sobrino's "writings give too much emphasis to Jesus Christ as a mortal man." It later quoted Ratzinger as saying that "these works contain propositions which are either erroneous or dangerous and may cause harm to the faithful" ("Pope Warns").

An open issue that emerges from these debates about liberation theology and their connection to Freire is whether Freire himself was a Marxist. He certainly cites Marx as a significant influence in his work, but he never assumes that one can't learn from Marx and still be Christian. Indeed, in his brief biography of Freire, Peter Lownd stresses that "Freire vehemently maintains that his familiarity with Marxism never distanced him from Christ" (Lownd). Here, Lownd quotes Freire explaining how he synthesizes Marx with Christ:

> I never understood how to reconcile fellowship with Christ with the exploitation of other human beings, or to reconcile a love for Christ with racial, gender and class discrimination. By the same token, I could never reconcile the Left's liberating discourse with the Left's discriminatory practice along the lines of race, gender, and class.

Indeed, throughout much of his work—not unlike much Jesuit thinking—Freire does not assume dichotomies or opposites. As in his breakdown of the teacher–student dichotomy in *Pedagogy of the Oppressed* and other major works, he also refuses to work from the premise that drawing from the works of Marx and drawing from the teaching of Christ are somehow mutually exclusive.

One question this quote might raise is why many U.S. Freireans do not speak of Freire's strong Catholicism. Indeed, a kind of veil of silence about the fact that Freire was a Christian educator pervades U.S. critical pedagogy studies, an indication that perhaps many of these educators are Marxist sympathizers who have shied away from or ignored Freire's strong Catholic roots. Another reason, though, may be, as Shari Stenberg argues in her essay "Liberation Theology and Liberatory Pedagogies: Renewing the Dialogue," that many Freireans and critical pedagogues, such as Henry Giroux and Peter McLaren, were also influenced by the Frankfurt School and neo-Marxism, thinking that "challenges foundational knowledge and universal truths" such as Christianity and other forms of religion (275). Specifically, she argues that the multiple discourses of critical pedagogy have had the effect of separating religion from such types of pedagogy: "Indeed, because of the deep chasm between intellectualism and spirituality, many of the values from which Freire wrote have been severed from critical pedagogy discourse in the United States—a split that I contend limits the potential effectiveness of critical pedagogy's work" (275).

Many U.S. Freireans have shied away from Freire's Catholicism largely because of their own rejection of theologies such as Christianity that, as Stenberg stresses, "are designed to provide final answers," and as a result those theologies have been viewed as incompatible with the contemporary university's move toward critical theory and its "tolerance for many ideological perspectives" (276). Stenberg writes:

> So even as critical thought is the reigning religion in our contemporary universities, an ethos that theoretically encompasses a respect for diverse ideologies, faith-based perspectives—particularly Christian—remain distinct from the privileged category of rationalism. As such, faith is often regarded as a false consciousness through which critical thought should cut, not something it should work alongside.
>
> —Stenberg, 277

While Stenberg's argument about the disconnect between critical pedagogy and Christianity sheds light on why U.S. Freireans have turned from Freire's Catholic tradition, a closer look at this background reveals the crucial importance that Catholicism, liberation theology, and subsequently Jesuit thinkers actually play in his work.

Born in Recife, Brazil, in 1921, Freire grew up in a family influenced heavily by his mother's Catholicism (Gadotti, 4; Kirylo, 3–7). Recife, like many Brazilian cities, was saturated with Jesuit thinking between social action and educational formation. Many times over the course of his career, Freire noted the influence of Catholicism, specifically through the figure of his mother, on his life and work. In his biography of Freire, Moacir Gadotti notes how much

Catholicism influenced his life, and how his mother raised him to be a strong Catholic:

> His mother brought him up in the Catholic religion, and this would also be an important influence both on his pedagogical theories and on his practice. . . . Freire never denied his Christian upbringing; in fact, he has always considered Christianity progressive. But he would criticize what he called the church of the oppressors, opposing it to the prophetic church, the church of the oppressed: "The prophetic church is the church of hope, hope which only exists in the future, a future which only the oppressed classes have, as the future of the dominant classes is a pure repetition of their present state of being the oppressors."
>
> —Gadotti, 4

In a more recent biography, *Paulo Freire: The Man from Recife*, James D. Kirylo also stresses the importance that young Paulo attached to Catholicism, noting that "very early on he learned from his parents that in order for religious beliefs to be authentic, faith and action must be consistent" (6). Collins has noted that Freire's mother had no direct connections with the Jesuits (Collins, interview), although Freire does specify in *Letters to Cristina* that his mother's Catholicism, as well as his father's own spiritualism, influenced his understanding of tolerance and, especially, dialogue: "Although my mother was Catholic and my father was a spiritualist, they always respected each other's religious opinions," Freire writes. "From them, I learned early on the value of dialogue. I never was afraid to ask questions, and I do not recall ever being punished for disagreeing with them" (28). Kirylo notes the strong influence that Catholicism as a whole exerted on him, writing that Freire's Christianity was one "dedicated to his understanding of Catholicism, one of a radical love that blended a spiritual and social commitment as a way of life" (125). A dialectic relationship arose between Freire and many Catholics and Jesuits; his theories of education were influenced heavily by his Catholic roots and, in turn, his theories of education would strongly influence both Jesuit and non-Jesuit theologians who helped spread liberation theology. In his foreword to the first edition of *Pedagogy of the Oppressed* in 1968, Richard Shaull writes that "the methodology he developed was widely used by Catholics and others in literacy campaigns throughout the North East of Brazil" (Freire, *Pedagogy*, 13).

This influence stems in large part from the Jesuit influence in Freire's native Brazil. The history of Brazil, from the sixteenth century onward, can at times be seen as a history of colonization on the part of the Jesuits. Indeed, many of the educational institutions in Brazil were heavily influenced by the Jesuit missionaries of the sixteenth century who laid a foundation of Jesuit-oriented teaching that has since pervaded much of the country's culture. São Paulo, where Freire made his name, was founded by the Jesuits in 1554. In the sixteenth century, the Jesuits founded a network of colleges for humanistic learning. And even though the Jesuits were expelled from Brazil in the late eighteenth century during their general suppression worldwide, their history in the region pervaded much of the area's religious leanings. For example, Thomas Bruneau in his book *The Political Transformation of the Brazilian Catholic Church* points out that the Jesuits wielded a greater influence on Brazilian culture, education, and society than did other Catholic groups. He argues that "what made the Jesuits more effective was their greater degree of organization, independence, and discipline" (19). This organizational strength reared itself especially in education, where, as Bruneau points out, Jesuits "founded schools . . . developed new methods of teaching . . . [and] made the Church somehow important in the early [Brazilian] society" (18–19). In *Catholic Radicals in Brazil,* his history of the political and economic work of Catholics in Brazil during the 1950s and '60s, Emanuel de Kadt notes the influence of Jesuits on education in Brazil in general. "The Jesuits also played an important educational role," de Kadt argues. "Their schools represented all that existed in the way of a structured educational system during the first two centuries of the colonial period" (52). In short, by developing schools and bringing in new methods of teaching and learning, the Jesuits wielded enormous influence on Brazilian Catholic culture for generations.

Two areas where the Jesuits wielded their influence occurred through the Catholic Action movement and the subsequent spreading of liberation theology, in which Freire was very much involved. Gadotti's biography, reporting that as a young man Freire was heavily involved in Brazilian Catholic Action, calls him "a militant" in the movement (4). Catholic Action was a worldwide organization that throughout much of the twentieth century, especially during the 1950s and later during the post–Vatican II era, played "an important role in the formation and organization of the struggle for grassroots reforms" (Gadotti, 162). Catholic Action encompassed several communities of laypeople who encouraged a Catholic influence on society. Brazilian Catholic Action helped spread liberation theology, with the Jesuits heavily involved in the movement; much of liberation theology took root in Brazil through Catholic Action's role. Freire and his wife Elza found Catholic Action appealing and began participating shortly after World War II (Kirylo, 40). In Recife they began meeting with other couples interested in Catholic Action and "aiming to bring to light the contradiction between living a life of privilege and the radical teachings of the Gospel" (Kirylo, 40).

Early leaders of the movement in Brazil included two Jesuits: Leopoldo Brentano and Pedro Belisario Velloso. In his history of the Jesuits in Latin America, Jeffrey Klaiber, S.J., claims that both Brentano and Velloso played key roles in the development of these circles. Their focus was on social activism: "The circles aimed at forming socially conscious Christian leaders among workers," Klaiber writes. "By 1951 the circles had almost 233,170 members. Brentano served as national director of the circles until 1955. His successor as moderator of the circles was Pedro Belisario Velloso" (232). Since the 1960s, many of the leading proponents of liberation theology have been Jesuit, and the Jesuit focus on education in rhetoric and argumentation helped propel many of these socially progressive ideas. Specifically, according to de Kadt, two Jesuits whose work influenced these Catholic activists during the 1960s included Pe Henrique de Lima Vaz and Pierre Teilhard de Chardin. Pe Vaz influenced Catholic Action overall with his work on what de Kadt calls "historical consciousness" and the idea that "transformation of the world" can take place based on "real understanding of the real conditions fond in the here and now . . . , a transformation which *humanizes* the world" (87–90). But it was ultimately Teilhard's work where we see the most significant influence of a Jesuit on Freire's thinking.

Freire, of course, was well aware of these Jesuit scholars, and their work, especially Teilhard's, influenced his significantly. Another Jesuit who notes the influence of Freire on liberation theology is Jose L. Gonzalez Faus. According to Emilio A. Nunez, whose work explores the history of liberation theology and the connections among Freire's work, liberation theology, and Jesuit culture, in the 1960s Freire's work was well known by many pioneers of liberation theology, notably the ISAL (Church and Society in Latin America) (Nunez 58). One notable liberation theologian Nunez identifies, the Jesuit Jose L. Gonzalez Faus, "sees that the ethical, anthropological principles upon which Freire's pedagogy rests 'have a very close relationship with theology'" (58). To expand this idea, Nunez cites a 1972 interview with Freire in which Freire stresses that "as I see it, the role of the church is that of the liberator, the humanizer, of man. . . . For that reason I believe that theology should be actively involved with liberating education and liberating education with theology" (Nunez, 58–59).

Most significant, however, is the influence on Freire from Teilhard, a philosopher trained as a paleontologist and biologist. Teilhard abandoned the strict interpretations of creation depicted in the Book of Genesis and attempted to synthesize theology and science. His writings on theology, though, would influence liberation theology, especially through the work of Gutiérrez. In his *Theology for a Liberating Church*, Alfred Hennelly, S.J., quotes from Gutiérrez's *A Theology of Liberation: History, Politics and Salvation* where Gutiérrez notes the similarities between his work and Teilhard's:

> Teilhard de Chardin has remarked that man has taken hold of the reins of evolution. History, contrary to essentialist and static thinking, is not the development of potentialities preexistent in man; it is rather the conquest of new, qualitatively different ways of being a man in order to achieve an ever more total and complete fulfillment of the individual in solidarity with all mankind.
>
> —Gutiérrez, 189–90

Here Gutiérrez notes that Teilhard's insistence on the human construction of reality and knowledge corresponds to liberation theology's focus on the material conditions of the poor and their connection to all of humankind. As a result, Teilhard wielded influence on Catholic Action as well as on Freire. In his history of Catholic radicals in Brazil, de Kadt stresses that Teilhard "had a substantial following at the apex of the Movement [Catholic Action]: 80 percent mentioned him. Of the intermediate group, 29 per cent were in some way familiar with his work" (142). Indeed, Teilhard's focus on the solidarity of humanity would influence Freire as well. In his book *Paulo Freire: Pedagogue of Liberation*, John Elias notes how comfortable Freire was with the language of religion, citing numerous religious influences on Freire's thinking, especially Teilhard (Elias 38–42). So, although Freire did not attend a Jesuit school, strong traces of Jesuit influence on his thinking about education and, conversely, his influence on Jesuit thinking are evident.

While it is difficult to trace a direct line from Jesuit teaching to Freire's work, it is reasonable to suggest that the tradition of the Jesuits, through their role as colonizers in Brazil, through the filter of Catholic Action, through the work of Jesuit priests such as Teilhard and others, and through the influence of liberation theology, ultimately played a significant role in the development of Freire's ideas. And conversely, Freire is a key example of the influence that liberation pedagogy had on Jesuits. Since the 1960s he has been an extremely fruitful source of ideas and inspiration for Jesuits worldwide.

For instance, Maltese Jesuits established the Paulo Freire Institute in Zejtun to promote literacy and community development ("The Paulo Freire Institute"). In Colombia in 1972, a group of Jesuits founded a center that, as Jeffrey Klaiber, S.J., describes it, "would combine research, reflection, and social action especially oriented toward the lower classes" (289). Called the Center for Research and Popular Education (CINEP), this institution still exists and was "powerfully influenced by the ideas of Paulo Freire" (Klaiber 289). Also in 1972, on one of his earliest visits to the United States, Freire spoke at Fordham University. John W. Donohue, S.J., covered the visit for the Catholic magazine *America*, where he was associate editor for thirty-five years. Speaking to a packed house of Jesuit and non-Jesuit listeners, laypeople and clergy, students and faculty, Freire insisted on the dialogic nature of education (Donohue 178). " 'We *exist* explains *I exist*,' he told the young people at Fordham. 'I cannot be if you are not. I cannot know alone. For me to know, it is necessary for you to know'" (178).

Significant, too, is the work of Denis Collins, S.J., author of *Paulo Freire: His Life, Works, and Thought* (1977), one of the first biographies of Freire. Collins tells a story about interviewing him at a Jesuit conference in Seattle in 1973. "He was interested in us," Collins notes, "and had come to talk with the Society of Jesus" (Collins, interview). Collins says that, although no minutes of the meeting remain, Freire did speak at the meeting to representatives from the ten Jesuit provinces in the United States who were responsible for international ministry. Freire's topic that day, Collins remembers, was the Church's international ministry in light of current socioeconomic and political realities. Collins says that Freire stressed to the audience that they should go to the people of these countries and through a dialectic engagement learn from the poor about what their needs are.

It was fortuitous, Collins says, that Freire even spoke at the meeting. Freire just happened to be in Seattle to work with groups of student activists on a separate issue, and he was invited to attend the Jesuit meeting by one of the directors of the Jesuit conference from Washington, D.C. (Collins, interview). Freire was still living in exile, in Geneva, and asked that all recording devices be turned off. "I later arranged to meet with him, had lunch with him and his wife, and took him back to his dorm," Collins recollects. "He offered more of an approval to what the Jesuits were trying to accomplish in Latin America at the time. I would say that Freire's work is in consonance with Jesuit spirituality" (Collins, interview). Later, Collins wrote a reflection of his experience with Freire in Seattle, where he told of Freire's response to his question about implementing Freirean pedagogy at Jesuit schools: "When I told him I was probably going to work with Jesuit educators in the U.S. and I asked him (not so naively as the reader might suspect) whether he thought we could ever implement his educational philosophy in Jesuit schools in this country, he reached over, put a hand on my knee, and smilingly replied, 'Not until you succeed in overthrowing your government'" (Collins "Seattle, January 1973," 28). The experience helped reinforce for Collins the connections between the Jesuits and Freire's work. Perhaps most important is the influence that Freire's concepts and theories—many of which have Jesuit parallels—have had on Jesuit pedagogy.

Concepts such as *cura personalis* and *eloquentia perfecta* have been embraced as the ideals of Jesuit education; these ideas held within the rhetorical tradition of Jesuit education can be found and enacted through contemporary liberation pedagogy and particularly through concepts such as Freire's *word* and *problem-posing method*. For instance, *cura personalis,* care for the (individual, whole) person, is a concept that, in teaching, focuses on the personal relationship between teacher as guide and student as journeyer, a relationship in which the teacher listens to the student during teaching and draws students toward personal initiative and responsibility for learning, especially learning that leads a student into the world. It also focuses on being present to the student at every point in the learning process. Being present, in the Ignatian spirit, is more than a simple availability during office hours. It centers on an effort to understand the student as a person and a learner at every point in that student's journey in education. When a student truly experiences *cura personalis,* he or she is then called to enact this charism or rhetorical action in relation to others he or she encounters; we see this mindful presence not only in Ignatian pedagogical principles for the classroom but also in the Catholic Action movement on the streets and in the world.

The ideas behind *cura personalis* are paralleled by Freire's *Problem Posing Method*, the posing of issues that distinctly stem from the realities faced by human beings in their relationship with the world: a process by which the teacher is present with the student through the learning process in such a way as to make both teacher and student jointly responsible for discernment, growth, and development. In this process, students are co-investigators with the teacher. The role of the problem-posing educator is to create the conditions under which knowledge, in the sense of surface facts or popular opinion, is superseded by true knowledge at the level of logic or reasoning. Thus *cura personalis*, as a "humanist, liberating praxis," as Freire would say,

> posits as fundamental that the people subjected to domination must fight
> for their emancipation. To that end, it allows teachers and students to be-
> come Subjects of the educational process by overcoming authoritarianism
> and an alienating intellectualism; it also enables people to overcome their
> false perception of reality. The world—no longer something to be described
> by deceptive words—becomes the object of that transforming action by men
> and women which results in their humanization.
>
> —Freire, *Pedagogy of the Oppressed*, 86

Much like the Ignatian pedagogical paradigm (see, in this volume, Mailloux, Fitzsimmons, and Deans), the *problem-posing method* and all of Freirean pedagogy moves through a learning cycle that sets as an ideal the process of moving through that cycle: *context, experience, reflection, action,* and *evaluation.* These terms are used with specific intention by Ignatian pedagogues, as each term encompasses many layers of meaning. *Context* includes the whole of the student's and the teacher's existing knowledge, skills, and experiences as well as the positioning of a course within a whole curriculum that is then individualized by students. *Experience* looks to each learning situation within a class as a way for students to be involved in knowledge-making. *Reflection* acts as an important step for students to integrate, synthesize, and analyze the knowledge they have created through the experiences of the class. *Action* moves the student to apply the knowledge she has created and integrated, ideally, for the "greater glory of God" through the betterment of the world beyond the classroom. Working not only as a means for judgment of the type, quantity, and quality of student learning by the teacher, *evaluation* also, perhaps more importantly, is a time for self-assessment by both student and teacher about the learning of the class in order to reenter the cycle at a deeper level of awareness. All of these specific terms, with their multifaceted meanings, must work in concert with each other within the complex web of the paradigm. When analyzed carefully, it can be seen that the learning cycle Freire sets up in his theories includes similar complex elements, beginning with a sharp and intentional awareness of context and moving to the core of his theories, *praxis* (action + reflection), and ending with a transformational experience that interpellates us to continue the cycle, going ever deeper into knowledge and naming (*word*) of the world.

We can continue noting the additional parallels in these two pedagogical approaches by reaching deeper into the rhetorical tradition of *eloquentia perfecta* and comparing it with Freire's pedagogy of the *word*. *Eloquentia perfecta* goes beyond just perfect eloquence in words. It calls us to use speech or communication that focuses on truth, accuracy, and comprehensiveness as a path into the world, especially used in order to stand for the silenced, excluded, or impoverished. We cannot forget Ignatius's and the Jesuits' preferential option for the poor. At the same time, as mentioned above, Freire's concept of the *word* is action + reflection, or *praxis*. He states that to speak a *true* word is to transform the world (Freire, *Pedagogy of the Oppressed*, 88). The idea that speaking (not to be confused with chatter) is the right of all, and that speaking evokes dialogue that has the capacity to change the world, which is to be transformed and humanized, especially for and from those whom have been silenced, excluded, or impoverished, parallels what the Jesuit rhetorical tradition has been advocating for centuries.

Thus, the Jesuit rhetorical tradition of *eloquentia perfecta* is "education as the practice of freedom." It works together with *cura personalis* "as [opposition] to education as an act of domination—denies that a person is abstract, isolated, independent, and unattached to the world; it also denies that the world exists as a reality apart from people" (Freire, *Pedagogy of the Oppressed*, 81). *Cura personalis*, the Ignatian pedagogical paradigm, and *eloquentia perfecta* now carry the Jesuit rhetorical tradition, and with them the Ignatian educator, toward collaboration, in this case as teachers and students, in order to address the world through real education and real understanding of all of the world, including and especially those parts beyond the ivory tower. As educators who see the parallel approaches of the Ignatian and Freirean models, we are called to be and to teach our students to be what Superior General Hans Peter Kolvenbach has called "whole persons in solidarity for the real world," beginning with how and what we teach in our classrooms and programs. With Kolvenbach's statement, we must acknowledge that what we see as parallel pedagogical theories are actually intertwined theories in our contemporary educational reality.

WORKS CITED

Berlin, James. "Freirean Pedagogy in the U.S.: A Response." In *(Inter)views: Cross-Disciplinary Perspectives on Rhetoric and Literacy*, ed. Gary A. Olson and Irene Gales, 169–76. Carbondale: Southern Illinois University Press, 1991.

Berryman, Phillip. *Liberation Theology: Essential Facts about the Revolutionary Movement in Latin America—and Beyond*. Philadelphia: Temple University Press, 1987.

Brown, Robert McAfee. *Gustavo Gutiérrez: An Introduction to Liberation Theology.* Maryknoll, N.Y.: Orbis, 1990.

Bruneau, Thomas C. *The Political Transformation of the Brazilian Catholic Church.* Cambridge: Cambridge University Press, 1974.

Collins, Denis. *Paulo Freire: His Life, Works, and Thought.* Mahwah, N.J.: Paulist Press, 1977.

———. "Seattle, January 1973." In *Memories of Paulo*, ed. Tom Wilson, Peter Park, and Anaida Colon-Muniz, 27–29. Rotterdam and Taipei: Sense, 2010.

———. Personal interview. May 19, 2014.

Congregation for the Doctrine of the Faith. "Instruction on Certain Aspects of 'Liberation Theology.'" August 6, 1984. http://www.vatican.va/roman_curia/congregations/cfaith/documents/rc_con_cfaith_doc_19840806_theology-liberation_en.html. Accessed August 14, 2012.

Cox, Harvey. "Is Pope Francis the New Champion of Liberation Theology?" *Nation*, December 18, 2013. http://www.thenation.com/article/177651/pope-francis-new-champion-liberation-theology Accessed May 12, 2014.

de Kadt, Emanuel. *Catholic Radicals in Brazil.* Oxford: Oxford University Press, 1970.

Donohue, John W. "Paulo Freire—Philosopher of Adult Education." In *Molding the Hearts and Minds*, ed. John A. Britton, 177–85. Wilmington, Del.: Scholarly Resources, 1994.

Elias, John. *Paulo Freire: Pedagogue of Liberation.* Malabar, Fla.: Krieger, 1994.

Freire, Paulo. *Pedagogy of the Oppressed.* New York: Continuum, 1997.

———. *Letters to Cristina.* New York: Routledge, 1996.

Gadotti, Moacir. *Reading Paulo Freire.* Trans. John Milton. Albany: State University of New York Press, 1994.

George, Ann. "Critical Pedagogy" Dreaming of Democracy." In *A Guide to Composition Pedagogies*, ed. Gary Tate, Amy Ruppier, and Kurt Schick, 92–112. New York: Oxford University Press, 2001.

Gutiérrez, Gusatvo. *A Theology of Liberation: History, Politics, and Salvation.* 1973. Translated by Caridad Inda and John Eagleson. Maryknoll, N.Y.: Orbis, 1988.

Hennelly, Alfred. *Theology for a Liberating Church.* Washington, D.C.: Georgetown University Press, 1989.

Kirylo, James D. *Paulo Freire: The Man from Recife.* New York: Lang, 2011.

Klaiber, Jeffrey L. *The Jesuits in Latin America, 1549–2000.* St. Louis: Institute of Jesuit Sources, 2009.

Kolvenbach, Hans Peter. "The Service of Faith and the Promotion of Justice in American Jesuit Higher Education." www.marquette.edu/mission/documents/TheServiceofFaithandthePromotion ofJusticeinAmericanJesuitHigher Education—Kolvenbach.pdf. Accessed July 1, 2014.

Lownd, Peter. "Freire's Life and Work: A Brief Biography of Paulo Freire." http://dmnier weber.iweb.bsu.edu/teachingguide/Freire%20bio.html. Accessed August 14, 2012.

Nunez C, Emilio A. *Liberation Theology.* Chicago: Moody, 1985.

O'Malley, John. *The First Jesuits.* Cambridge Mass.: Harvard University Press, 1995.

"The Paulo Freire Institute." *Jesuits in Malta.* Jesuit.org.mt. Accessed May 12, 2014.

"Pope Warns Liberation Theologian." BBC News Europe. March 14, 2007. Accessed August 14, 2012.

Ratzinger, Joseph. "Liberation Theology: Preliminary Notes." *Joseph Cardinal Ratzinger Homepage.* December 9, 2004. Accessed August 14, 2012.

Rowland, Christopher, ed. *Cambridge Companion to Liberation Theology.* 2nd ed. Cambridge: Cambridge University Press, 2007.

Stenberg, Shari J. "Liberation Theology and Liberatory Pedagogies: Renewing the Dialogue." *College English* 68, no. 3 (2006): 271–90.

RHETORICIANS REFLECT ON THEIR JESUIT EDUCATION

BEING EDUCATED BY THE JESUITS

Frank D'Angelo

I entered Jesuit High School in New Orleans when I was twelve, going on thirteen. Jesuit at that time was a college preparatory school. Luckily, most of my teachers were either Jesuit scholastics (young men studying to be priests) or Jesuit priests. This is not to denigrate the fine lay teachers who were to follow, but the value of being taught by the Jesuits is that they shared the same educational philosophy, a curriculum and methodology based loosely on the *Ratio Studiorum* of Ignatius Loyola, but ultimately on the earlier Greek and Roman *paideia*. As a result of this kind of education, most of my classmates later became successful public servants and outstanding citizens—judges, doctors, lawyers, educators, and businessmen. (In those days, Jesuit was an all-male school.)

Although science and math classes were taught (chemistry, biology, physics, algebra, geometry, and trigonometry), all were in the service of a liberal education. In all of our classes we were taught to speak and write proficiently enough to become outstanding public servants. In all of our classes, we had to speak, write, outline, take copious notes, imitate, memorize, and analyze texts. The curriculum consisted of four years of English, Latin, elocutio (spoken rhetoric), math, and theology; two years of Greek (for some students), a modern foreign language (French or Spanish), history, and science. No electives!

In retrospect, I realize that my early education was agonistic (a competition for superiority and victory, a dramatic conflict, verbal disputation, reasoning aimed at demonstrating truth or falsehood). There was competition within each class, between classes, and on various levels, in academic subjects and intramurals. To foster competition, the Jesuits would give out gold-colored cards for first place in any subject, silver-colored cards for second place, and bronze-colored cards for third place. I received my share of gold and silver cards when I attended Jesuit High School. I was a good student. I excelled in English, elocution, Latin, and religion. I even got a first card in algebra. (Math was not my favorite subject, but I did like plane geometry, perhaps because of the logical thinking involved in the axioms and postulates.)

We had our moments of laughter and playfulness at Jesuit. As a freshman, I was taught Latin by a scholastic. (He also taught me English, a common practice then.) One day he asked the class to conjugate the verb *scio* in the present tense. So we responded loudly:

scio

scis

SHIT! [scit]

We spoke Latin with an Italian accent. Naturally, the class laughed aloud. We thought we were putting one over on this young scholastic, but he sent the entire class to Penance Hall.

Penance Hall (great shades of James Joyce) was simply the name given to the classroom where students who disrupted the class were sent to spend two hours after school. (The Jesuits even made Penance Hall educational.) In Penance Hall we had to memorize short poems, passages from speeches, prose passages, and passages from plays. If you could memorize the selected passage in a short time, you could go home early rather than stay the entire two hours. Needless to say, I learned how to memorize quickly, efficiently, and effortlessly, a resource I later drew on as a professor of English. Because I was fond of making puns in class (the Jesuits encouraged wordplay), thereby causing a disruption of the school lesson, I was sent to Penance Hall from time to time. "D'Angelo, get thee to Penance Hall!" my Jesuit teacher would intone. "You're disrupting the class!"

I can't understand the neglect of memory in today's educational system. To Aristotle, memory was one of the five canons of rhetoric. To Vico, memory, in one of its forms, was related to invention. In antiquity, memory is the mother of the Muses, who is associated with the arts of civilization. It won't do to say that computers have memories. Computers do store information. But information has to be put into a conceptual framework in order to become knowledge. That is where education comes in. The various disciplines provide conceptual frameworks within which thinking, reasoning, and imagining might take place. My Jesuit teachers would have scoffed at anyone who was not trained to memorize. Imagine an educator or a politician being able to survive today without the art of memory. Before a public servant or anyone can speak or write, he or she should have memorized certain basic facts worth remembering. Most of us have seen Jay Leno's "man in the street." These adults on that segment of the program seem to remember almost nothing. Wait a minute (one might say), I'll look it up on the computer. Of course, in any field, we have to consult references. But "our whole discipline," said Quintilian, "relies on memory."

At Jesuit, in elocution classes I first had to memorize and imitate the poems (Edgar Allan Poe) and speeches (Tom Paine, Patrick Henry, Abraham Lincoln) of others. In the next two years I prepared and delivered my own speeches (on public issues that are by now probably out of date). Finally, in my senior year, I had to deliver extemporaneous speeches on any subject.

My biggest influence at Jesuit High School was Fr. Lynette. I was lucky enough to have him as a teacher for two years. He taught me elocution, English,

Latin, and religion. In elocution classes, Father Lynette was a tough taskmaster. If you gave a speech in his class, you had to speak clearly, intelligently, effectively, and forcefully, and articulate each word. I had a bad habit of interspersing my speeches with the words "well," "well." To rid me of the habit, Fr. Lynette would comment: "Well! Well. Two holes in the ground." It didn't take me long to get rid of this habit.

Because he taught me English and Latin in the same years, in the classes dealing with grammar and vocabulary Fr. Lynette would make cross-references from one language to another. For example, in English class he would put the word *lucid* on the blackboard. (The board was black in those days.) Then he would explain: "The word *lucid* comes from the Latin *lux, lucis*. Notice the similarity in the English and Latin forms. The word *lux* means *light*. If you shed light on something, you make it clear. Therefore, the word *lucid* means *clear.*"

In composition classes (in both English and Latin), we moved from grammar to sentences to paragraphs to essay writing. Before Piaget, the movement in all our classes was developmental—from parts to the whole, from the simple to the complex. In writing classes, we moved from expository writing to persuasive writing. In most of our classes, the emphasis was on analysis, logic, and reasoning.

Except in religion classes and literature classes! There, the emphasis seemed to be more on ethics, moral reasoning, and thematic analysis. In religion classes, the emphasis was more on everyday moral problems of adolescents than on cosmology and apologetics. (That was to come in college.) On every paper we turned in, we had to put the letters A.M.D.G. (Ad Majorem Dei Gloriam) in the upper left-hand heading—all for the greater honor and glory of God. In literature classes, as best I can remember, the emphasis was on the thematic and moral aspects of the poetry and prose we studied. We studied writers such as O. Henry, Longfellow, and John Greenleaf Whittier, writers no longer anthologized.

Even in intramurals there was competition, one class pitted against another, with prizes awarded. (A sound mind in a sound body!) Those of us who did not play on a varsity team had to compete with the other classes in intramurals (touch football, basketball, handball, and horseshoes) in season. And compete we did! Fiercely and playfully, competitively, as we did in the classroom.

The Spanish influence was everywhere. After all, Ignatius was a Spanish soldier and educator. We called our Spanish Jesuit teacher "Mr. Muy Bien," because whenever we would answer a question in Spanish, he would say, "Muy bien, muy bien." I never learned to speak Spanish properly, although I could read it fairly well. But the Spanish influence in New Orleans was strong when I grew up. I attended Jesuit High School (taught by the Jesuits, an order with roots in Spain), later went to Loyola University, and attended a Jesuit Spanish church (Gothic, Spanish, and Moorish architecture) once a month on Baronne Street, went to the Cortez movie house, lived on Palmyra and Gayosa (near

Galvez Street), and visited the French Quarter frequently (constructed mainly of Spanish Creole colonial buildings and courtyards).

I came to higher education late. My father died when I was a junior in high school, so after graduation I went to work to support my mother and brother. Then I got drafted. I spent eighteen months in Korea, and after I returned home I got married and enrolled at Loyola in New Orleans. Because I got such an excellent education at Jesuit High School, I found my undergraduate classes relatively easy. Despite working at a full-time job, I graduated with honors, switching from business to English education. I then taught English at De La Salle High School (a rival of Jesuit) until I entered graduate school.

Unlike the Jesuits at my high school, Loyola's Jesuits taught me scholastic philosophy (logic, ethics, metaphysics, epistemology, rational psychology) and theology. The courses in philosophy emphasized Aristotle, Thomas Aquinas, and Duns Scotus. In all of these classes, we analyzed, reasoned, argued, disputed, and tried to reconcile scholastic philosophy with classical philosophy and modern science. We paid little attention to the history of philosophy but focused more on logic, ethics, and reasoning and being able to refute the ideas of other philosophers. I had little awareness at that time of the quarrel between philosophy and rhetoric, or of the battle of the seven arts, or of the quarrel between the ancients and moderns.

However, after I became a college teacher and taught courses in the history of rhetoric, literary theory, cultural studies, poetry, fiction, and drama, I called on all of the resources and the mental training I received from the Jesuits. I could quote (from memory) lines and passages from speeches, poetry and prose. I could analyze almost any kind of text. (In high school, I had to keep a notebook for every class I took and outline every chapter.) The canons of rhetoric (invention, arrangement, style, memory, and delivery) were already familiar to me from my classes in philosophy, as was inductive and deductive thinking. I could argue, debate, and refute with the best students.

In theology class, we took reason as far as we could take it, and then took a leap of faith. I was surprised at some of the comments of my Jesuit philosophy mentors, which I'll not exemplify here. But I was impressed by their vigorous reasoning and skeptical attitude. I guess that's why my favorite Jesuit-trained thinkers were Gracián, Vico, and later Teilhard de Chardin, himself a Jesuit. In sum, what I received from my Jesuit education was the literary-humanistic ideal of antiquity combined with the theological ideal of the Middle Ages. Jesuit education today is still excellent, but judging from the course work of my nephews, who are currently attending Jesuit institutions, there seems to be more emphasis on science than on liberal education.

JESUIT RHETORIC AT HOLY CROSS COLLEGE, CIRCA 1957–1958

S. Michael Halloran

In *Thy Honored Name*, his history of Holy Cross College, Anthony Kuznewski, S.J., identifies 1960 as the year when the school bottomed out in an organizational and curricular rut. Coincidentally, 1960 was the year in which I graduated from Holy Cross.

Organizationally, Holy Cross was slow in coming to terms with the changes effected by the return of the World War II veterans. With a student body approaching two thousand, the college was administered in much the same way as it was in the 1930s, when it had fewer than 800 students. Educationally, its curriculum had become an inconsistent mishmash of timid electivism grafted onto the compromised remains of a fully prescribed classical curriculum based in the *Ratio Studiorum* (1599). Juniors and seniors took six credit hours per semester of prescribed philosophy courses regardless of their majors, and they were required to participate in end-of-year oral disputations similar to those that had been abandoned by most secular liberal-arts colleges before the turn of the twentieth century. There were some on the faculty who believed that Holy Cross had started down the slippery slope to decadence when Latin gave way to English as the language of the disputations. Perhaps they were right.

Or perhaps not. My own experience with the philosophy curriculum proved edifying, though probably not in the way intended by the Jesuit faculty. In one course—I forget which one—I chose to write a term paper on Jean-Paul Sartre. I had to get special permission to read his *Being and Nothingness*, which was on the Vatican's Index of forbidden books. And while no one told me in so many words, I understood that if I hoped for a grade other than F on my term paper, it would have to include an eloquent refutation of M. Sartre. Postscholastic philosophers (inconsequential figures such as Immanuel Kant, John Locke, and of course Jean-Paul Sartre), if they were mentioned at all in the textbooks we used, were classified as "adversaries" whose doctrines were to be dismissed in terse and tidy syllogistic paragraphs. I dutifully included in my term paper the expected refutation of M. Sartre and got a grade of B, as I recall. But in graduate school I followed up on my interest in existentialism, and my dissertation drew heavily on that interest.

One curricular remnant that some of us regarded as particularly burdensome was a yearlong course in rhetoric that was required of all sophomores. Rhetoric was among the less popular courses, and it was surely the least fashionable one, offered by an English department that, under the chairmanship of Fr. Thomas Grace, was struggling to forge an academic community and a program of study current with the national standards of its discipline. In the upper-division electives for English majors, we studied current scholarly approaches to Shakespeare, T. S. Eliot, and—the special field of Fr. Grace and a particular favorite of mine—Middle English literature.

In rhetoric, we studied a dispute—conducted around the turn of the twentieth century by President Charles Eliot of Harvard and the Reverend Timothy Brosnahan, S.J., of Boston College—over the relative merits of the elective system as practiced at Harvard and the classical curriculum as prescribed in Jesuit colleges. Brosnahan took issue with Eliot's refusal to recognize the diplomas of Holy Cross and Boston College as adequate preparation for Harvard Law School. Eliot made his case against the Jesuit curriculum in the pages of the *Atlantic Monthly*. Brosnahan's detailed rebuttal was turned down for publication by the *Atlantic*, so he had it printed in the form of a pamphlet that sold originally for ten cents and remained in print (mostly for the use of rhetoric students at Holy Cross, Boston College, and perhaps a few other Jesuit schools) well into the 1950s. To no one's surprise, Fr. Brosnahan and the prescribed classical curriculum carried the day when we studied his pamphlet in rhetoric; so resounding was his victory that it was deemed unnecessary—and perhaps unwise—for us to read the article by President Eliot to which Brosnahan's brilliant performance was a response. The winter 2012 issue of *Boston College Magazine* has a full account of the dispute and Brosnahan's role in it.

What I learned (as opposed to what I was taught) in the philosophy and rhetoric courses, in addition to my surreptitious and probably sinful interest in forbidden writers such as Sartre and Camus, was a degree of skepticism about the fixed and final principles we were supposed to be able to defend through syllogistic logic adorned with classical eloquence. An unsigned and undated memorandum in one of the boxes labeled "English Department, Early Records" in the Holy Cross archives says, in specific connection with the rhetoric course, that "the post war approach of our Society [i.e., the Jesuit order] to the problem of education will not be one of further capitulation to the scientific and commercial and pragmatic and utilitarian trend of so many educators outside our ranks, but rather a courageous approach unto the devising of ways and means for the production of the Christian cultured gentleman." Clearly, this species of "gentleman" was assumed to be at odds with the modern world, beset by an ever-growing army of "adversaries" including science, commerce, pragmatism, and utilitarianism—not to mention Sartre and films condemned by the Catholic Legion of Decency. What the Christian cultured gentleman needed, and what the philosophy and rhetoric courses were supposed to provide, were intellectual tools to defend against these multiple adversaries.

After graduating in 1960, I spent three years in the navy and four teaching high-school English. Then I was accepted to the doctoral program at Rensselaer Polytechnic Institute, a school that gloried in the scientific and commercial and pragmatic and utilitarian trend so scorned by the author of that anonymous memorandum on the Holy Cross rhetoric course. At RPI, I discovered

that "rhetoric," that fossil remnant of what in the late 1950s had been an obsolete curriculum, was enjoying a national renaissance. As a first-year teaching assistant, I had as my assignment to teach a section of a freshman course
called "Rhetoric and Writing" from a textbook that epitomized the new current of thought and yet brought back strong memories of my sophomore
English course at Holy Cross: Edward P. J. Corbett's *Classical Rhetoric for the
Modern Student.* In graduate seminars I pored over Aristotle, Cicero, and Quintilian, and I argued with teachers and fellow students over the relevance of
these and other ancient authors to the conflicts that raged on the campuses and
in the streets of that tumultuous time. In the years that followed I wrote articles and participated in scholarly conferences on rhetoric. I taught undergraduate and graduate courses on rhetoric. I became a specialist in the very subject
I had most scorned as an English major at Holy Cross.

In his preface to *Classical Rhetoric for the Modern Student,* Corbett characterizes the book as an adaptation of the system of classical rhetoric to the
modern task of teaching and learning composition. He claims that, while developed long ago by Aristotle, Cicero, and Quintilian, the system is nonetheless
new in that "the kind of rhetoric set forth in this book has been absent from
American classrooms for about a century, and has been replaced by other systems of teaching whatever is teachable about composition." And yet classical
rhetoric as synthesized and adapted in Corbett's widely influential text has
unmistakable affinities to the rhetoric taught at Holy Cross during the post–
World War II years.

In an earlier draft of this paper I rehearsed in tedious detail the many similarities and the mostly inconsequential differences between Corbett's version
of classical rhetoric and the rhetoric codified in two sources—*Precepts of
Rhetoric,* by Sidney J. Smith, S.J., a locally printed textbook used in most sections of the Holy Cross rhetoric course, and the standard syllabus for that
course developed in 1949 by Harry Bean, S.J., who chaired the meetings of the
sophomore English faculty that were held almost monthly throughout the 1950s.
Here I will summarize.

Both Corbett and the Holy Cross Jesuits gave heaviest emphasis to the invention of arguments in the mode of appeal called *logos,* though neither Smith's
text nor Bean's syllabus used that term, and unlike Corbett they did not position their preferred mode of appeal in the traditional triad of *logos, pathos,* and
ethos. Like Corbett's rhetoric, the Jesuit rhetoric of Smith's text and Bean's
syllabus excluded consideration of memory and delivery. On both counts the
adaptation was to a print culture and focused on the art of writing and on reading persuasive "speeches" rather than on oral discourse per se. Bean in a post-
script to his syllabus noted that, while the course as outlined did not include
practice in public speaking, it would be a good idea to include such practice if
time permitted. Whether public speaking should be included in the course was

a recurrent and unresolved topic in the minutes of the meetings of the sophomore English faculty.

The one truly important contrast between the Jesuit rhetoric and that of Corbett's *Classical Rhetoric for the Modern Student* is that Corbett's text offers a sense of historical perspective that is difficult to find in the Jesuit rhetoric, at least as it is codified in Smith's *Precepts* and the Bean syllabus. For Corbett, rhetoric is an art that originated in ancient Greece, developed over the centuries, and continues to develop in the present time as it is applied to new public controversies. Corbett's text includes a brief historical survey of rhetoric, and it captures something of the excitement that was in the air at conference discussions of rhetoric and in public forums during the 1960s and '70s. But Smith's *Precepts* seems to codify a fixed and timeless system applicable to issues that are well settled for everyone but misguided adversaries, and for the most part Bean's syllabus conveys the same sense that what students need to learn is not so much a living art as a set of timeless formulas. There appears to be nothing new under the sun of the Jesuit rhetoric, no need to probe and question, no room for reconsideration or innovation.

In justice to Harry Bean, I must add that in practice he was less constrained by the authoritarian tone of the syllabus he wrote than were most of his colleagues. In a meeting of the rhetoric faculty held on November 9, 1954, it was reported, Smith's *Precepts of Rhetoric* was used "by all attending except Fr. Bean." While other members of the rhetoric faculty pondered at length whether it would be acceptable to use a text by a non-Jesuit author and, by consulting the authority of "the Jesuit fathers," sought to resolve the nagging question of whether to include public speaking in the rhetoric course, Bean adopted Mortimer Adler's *How to Read a Book* as the text for his section of rhetoric and had his students writing papers on Dorothy Thompson and Fielding's *Tom Jones*. Those of us who did not make it into Bean's section (which was reserved for "section A," the most elite group of undergraduates) listened enviously to stories of the interesting things that went on in his "rhetoric" class, which I assumed to be "rhetoric" in name only. A classmate who did make it into section A recalls Bean as "the best teacher I had at Holy Cross." And John Brereton and Cinthia Gannett have informed me that Pierre Albert Duhamel, who together with Richard E. Hughes published a composition textbook grounded in classical rhetoric three years before Corbett's came out, studied under Bean at Holy Cross.

Ed Corbett attended a Jesuit high school and taught for several years (including the time during which he would have been working on *Classical Rhetoric for the Modern Student*) at Creighton University, a Jesuit school in Omaha, Nebraska. So his assertion that the version of rhetoric offered by his textbook "has been absent from American classrooms for about a century" is a bit puzzling. How could he have been unaware that a lineal descendent of the rhetoric prescribed in the *Ratio Studiorum,* a rhetoric in most of its technical details so close to the rhetoric purveyed by his own text as to be barely distinguishable from it, was being taught at Jesuit colleges in the United States beyond the midpoint of the twentieth century?

The answer, I suspect, is that what I have termed "the Jesuit rhetoric" was never quite the fixed and final system I took it to be and that, at the time when I first experienced it, was being replaced, at differing rates of speed, by something more up to date at Jesuit colleges across the United States. Many of the Jesuit colleges were adapting quite easily "to the scientific and commercial and pragmatic and utilitarian trend of so many educators outside [the] ranks" of the Jesuit order, and the anonymous author of that memorandum approving the Holy Cross rhetoric syllabus in the late 1940s was probably whistling against the wind of his own order. As early as 1951, Creighton University offered, in addition to the traditional programs leading to bachelor-of-arts and bachelor-of-science degrees, programs leading to the bachelor of science in chemistry and to the bachelor of science in medical technology. With the development of the medical-technology program, Creighton had gone coeducational, a step Holy Cross would not take for another twenty years. The catalog description of the two-semester Rhetoric and Composition course in Creighton's 1951–52 bulletin (which lists Edward P. J. Corbett as an instructor) sounds like an utterly conventional and resolutely non-classical course of the sort Richard Young would one day dub "current-traditional." It's quite possible that Ed Corbett, despite his abundant contact with the Jesuits, never saw in action the rhetorical remnant of the *Ratio Studiorum* that was part of my experience in a conservative corner of New England.

Holy Cross was one of the slowest, quite possibly *the* slowest of the Jesuit colleges to move into the twentieth century. Its philosophy program seemed fully ossified, and in its official version (the one that I endured in academic year 1957–58) the rhetoric course was equally rigid and retrograde. But even at traditionalist Holy Cross, variety and change were in the air, as the example of Harry Bean's rhetoric section illustrates.

In addition to being the year of my graduation and the year of my *alma mater's* deepest slump, 1960 was the year in which the United States elected its first Roman Catholic president, and it was a year in which Pope John XXIII was preparing to throw open the windows of a church that had grown as doctrinally ossified as those dreary philosophy courses with their snide dismissal of all adversaries. The Second Vatican Council, formally convened in 1962, would foster a climate in which "the Christian cultured gentleman" and gentlewoman began to believe that they could reason and argue about matters of conscience for themselves, and even conclude against the ex cathedra word from Rome. In this new climate, rhetoric could forgo the task of defending fixed and final principles and begin to take on the job of testing ideas, of finding in each particular case what are the available means of persuasion on both sides of an issue. I have a suspicion that Harry Bean, S.J., sly Jesuit that he was, had something like this in mind as an agenda to hide beneath the surface of the authoritarian syllabus he wrote back in 1948, an agenda that would not have passed muster with whoever wrote the memorandum approving it.

THE CUTTING EDGE OF ENGAGEMENT

Gerard A. Hauser

For many years, social scientists believed that political events were best explained by economic or political models. For example, an economic down-turn and loss of jobs would prompt citizens to discern that acting on self-interest was the most rational course of action. However, the weird politics of the past decade at least, and surely during the Obama administration, gives reason to wonder about the efficacy of rational choice as a model for explaining po-litical behavior. Citizen choice seems not to be based exclusively on self-interest. Such alternative criteria as the value structure of religious beliefs (which can work against economic self-interest), or dislike of one political persona more than another (which also can lead to choices that work against economic and social self-interest), or blind prejudice absent factual foundation (another for-mula for producing a bad result in terms of self-interest) seem to defy the mod-els of economics and political science.

On the other hand, they fit quite comfortably with rhetorical models for interpreting and understanding public choice, which have always been fasci-nated with the struggle between reason and passion. I should add, however, that the current weirdness of domestic politics in the United States is a permuta-tion that exceeds deliberation as the ancients conceived it. Present-day dustups highlight control (invention) of information and information flow, framing (disposition) and depiction (style) of problems, circulating (delivery) content through riveting images that influence message and choice. It is a new way of deliberation and debate, less concerned with factual fidelity to the realities it inscribes (memory) and more with visions of a world as one wishes it were, the facts be damned. It highlights how deeply the choices of publics are in-fluenced by more basic emotional states of attraction and avoidance and how these intersect with beliefs and perceptions of reality rather than informed rea-son. Some might call it propaganda, but that valorizes rhetoric more than it deserves by reserving it for discourse that instigates social imaginaries we pre-fer and that connects them to material conditions we choose to emphasize as defining reality. Absent a "magic circle" argument that admits only the (pre-ferred) "good" to a legitimate claim on rhetoric, rhetoric must be considered as open to all, issuing calls that may be just and unjust alike and asking (even demanding) choice. I learned this as a college student studying at a Jesuit institution, Canisius College, in my hometown of Buffalo, New York, where I was first introduced to rhetoric as a discipline and as a lens onto the human world.

I invite you to imagine how confusing it was for the grandson of a Greek gun runner to be a first-generation college student at a private Jesuit college, how this quintessential American experience colored what it meant to attend college in terms of family pride and expectations absent an understanding of what attending college meant other than a public claim to be among the educated class and the expectation that this would lead to a profession. The sustaining expressions of pride and support by my parents, grandparents, aunts, and uncles gave me status in the family, although its gravitas was not always appreciated by cousins who thought my celebrity was casting a cloud of pressure on their devil-may-care high school days. As for me, my family's attitude, which might best be described as a matter of *omne ignotum pro magnifico*, occasionally gave my matriculation the disconcerting aura of a novelty act. There is more. I am also the only member of my family to have received a Jesuit education. I was able to attend Canisius only because I had qualified for the Regents Scholarship, awarded on the basis of a competitive exam to high-school graduates in New York State. For my siblings, the economic realities of a blue-collar family made such an opportunity beyond their means, if not beyond their dreams.

Still, in the absence of a relevant reference point, the dream of attending Canisius was largely in the realm of the mysterious. I was embarked on a journey to a new country with images from the good friars of St. Francis, who had tended to my high-school education, and with the barest help from conventional wisdom learned in the street about what to expect from the Jesuits, whose reputation for intellectual acumen and, shall we say, ingenuity in crafting arguments had preceded them.

I should acknowledge that not all was mysterious, or at least not for long. I was aware that the Jesuits' reputation for fostering intellectual rigor, which had entered the realm of mythos in my hometown of Buffalo, gave my attending Canisius considerable cachet in local spas that seemed really important to a freshman—especially the college bar scene. I soon became aware as well of certain mental habits that were expected of us if we actually were to think on the cutting edge. How to read and critically analyze a text, the importance of making distinctions and establishing logical relations, how to make an academic argument, how to write an academic paper, how to use the English language with precision, and, most important, the centrality of intellectual integrity to all of the above were stressed across the curriculum. These are enduring habits that seem more difficult to inculcate across the curriculum in the large public institutions where I have spent my career. There they are regarded as skills, such as critical thinking to be learned by taking a required critical-thinking course.

Perhaps it is a problem of scale, but curricular requirements treat intellectual virtues as if they were techniques to be mastered, much like multiplication and division in math, rather than the product of intellectual habits one acquires from the experience of living in a particular intellectual culture. The more elusive outcome of my education, which I had to discover and which is tremendously powerful and important in our society, didn't come clear to me until later.

I matriculated at Canisius in a pre-engineering program linked to the University of Detroit. The game plan was to transfer after my sophomore year, become an engineer, and enjoy the good things of life that children of working-class families read about but seldom experience. Professor Tidd began the first day of Calculus 101 by asking us to look to the students seated on our immediate right and left. He then imparted the sobering news that two of the three would not be here by the end of the semester. He certainly was prescient in my case, at least. Receiving a cutting-edge education started out with me on the dull side of whatever blade the college was using, which left me wondering "What next?" for most of my freshman year. As June arrived, I faced reality. I was not cut out to be an engineer. And while I was going great guns in Professor Starr's Chemistry 101, I realized my heart wasn't in it. My main accomplishment during my first year was making the college debate team and, through that, developing an interest in rhetoric. The closest major to that pursuit was English.

The English department was located on the fourth floor of Old Main, aka "the attic." I still remember trudging up four flights of stairs on a beastly hot June day to the office of Professor Lovering, department chairman, as they were called fifty years ago, to have him sign my declaration of major. Papers signed, Lovering welcomed me to the major with, and I quote: "Mr. Hauser, I hope you are not choosing the English major because you think it will lead to a career. Our purpose is not to prepare you for gainful employment but to cultivate your sense of taste." Oh, great! How will I explain this to my parents? Little did I realize that this was a signal encounter with the reputed cutting-edge thought Jesuit education was supposed to impart.

Fortunately, my involvement with debate drew me into the orbit of Donald Cushman, who, in addition to instructing me in the intricacies of constructing and attacking the first affirmative case, encouraged me to write papers analyzing the rhetorical character of the texts we were reading in my English and philosophy courses. Cushman had a pragmatist's sense for big ideas, with little tolerance for academic debates, which provided effective counterpoint to the ideals Professor Lovering espoused. Possessing a remarkable knack for sharing and instilling enthusiasm for ideas that were consequential in the world, he was a crafty interrogator of arguments. He spent a great deal of time with his debaters, engaging us on the underlying assumptions of whatever we happened to be studying. The cutting edge in my undergraduate education lay in this rhetorically constituted culture of continuous intellectual discussion and deliberation that challenged my colleagues and me to think critically and constructively.

Together, Lovering's benediction to taste and Cushman's remorseless interrogation of ideas were formative and consequential, as is illustrated by this representative anecdote. In the spring of 1965, a group of students from Canisius traveled by bus to Alabama to participate in the Selma freedom march. On their return, they met with the other students in a public convocation to share their experience. Men we had come to know and whose political register was no secret shared—publicized—what they had experienced and how it had transformed their lives. The searing experience of local white responses to nonviolent protest, juxtaposed with the hospitality of local blacks who opened their homes and their hearts to my classmates, had made the abstraction of segregation excruciatingly concrete as an evil that challenged everything we had studied and debated, the values we cherished most and the hopes we shared for the future—ours and our society's. It was another signal moment that merged the critical habits of mind basic to Jesuit education: the emphasis on informed dialogue to reach a considered and sound judgment; the relationship between those hallmarks of the Society of Jesus, knowing and doing; the integration of the commitment to social justice with the decidedly pragmatic turn of using the means at your disposal to accomplish a good end, and the living up to the responsibility to use one's gifts for the service of others. The cutting edge of Jesuit education, for me at least, turned out to be a mode of intellectual and moral formation more than marketable skills.

The intellectual habits of Jesuit education that are often celebrated are a product of open dialogue. This is an achievement of an educational culture that depends on professors being accessible, demanding, and demonstrably caring for the whole person of their students. Cushman was representative of the spirit of my alma mater, which taught through intellectual companionship and capacitated me to experience my courses as offering a perspective on the human condition and to see the human world as a product of human ingenuity—a rhetorical construction of the most essential sort. The point, as Lovering informed me, although I did not realize it at the time, is not to squander your education on techniques for getting ahead at the expense of cultivating exquisite sensitivity to the world as you find it, of knowing what you believe and why you believe it, of articulating and defending your own thoughts, of bringing an informed moral register to your life, and of using these as the enlightening platform from which to engage the community in which you live in order to help shape it into a better place. At those times when I have been at my best, it is because these were the central concerns of my professional life as a teacher and student of rhetoric and as a person. In that respect, as with most college graduates, I may have flown away from my alma mater to pursue my dreams, but my alma mater has flown with me.

REREADING *LIVES ON THE BOUNDARY*

Mike Rose

FATHER ALBERTSON, S.J.

When Father Albertson lectured, he would stand pretty much in one spot slightly to the left or right of center in front of us. He tended to hold his notes or a play or a critical study in both hands, releasing one to emphasize a point with a simple gesture. He was tall and thin, and his voice was soft and tended toward monotone. When he spoke, he looked very serious, but when one of us responded with any kind of intelligence, a little smile would come over his face. Jack McFarland had told me that it was Clint Albertson's Shakespeare course that would knock my socks off.

For each play we covered, Father Albertson distributed a five- to ten-page list of questions to ask ourselves as we read. These study questions were of three general types.

The first type was broad and speculative and was meant to spark reflection on major characters and key events. Here's a teaser on *Hamlet*:

> Would you look among the portrait-paintings by Raphael, or Rembrandt, or Van Gogh, of El Greco, or Rouault for an ideal representation of Hamlet? Which painting by which of these men do you think most closely resembles your idea of what Hamlet should look like?

The second type focused on the details of the play itself and was very specific. Here are two of the thirty-eight he wrote for *As You Like It*:

> ACT I, SCENE 2:
>
> How is Rosalind distinguished from Celia in this scene? How do you explain the discrepancy between the Folio version of lines 284–287 and Act I, scene 3, line 117?
>
> ACT II, Scenes 4–6:
>
> It has been said these scenes take us differently out of the world of reality into a world of dream. What would you say are the steps of the process by which Shakespeare brings about this illusion?

The third kind of question required us to work with some historical or critical study. This is an example from the worksheet on *Romeo and Juliet*:

> Read the first chapter of C. S. Lewis's *Allegory of Love*, "Courtly Love." What would you say about Shakespeare's concept of love in relation to what Lewis presents as the traditional contradictory concepts in medieval literature of "romantic love" vs. "marriage"?

Father Albertson had placed over one hundred fifty books on the reserve shelf in the library, and they ranged from intellectual history to literary criticism to handbooks on theater production. I had used a few such "secondary sources" to quote in my own writing since my days with Jack McFarland, but this was the first time a teacher had so thoroughly woven them into a course. Father Albertson would cite them during lectures as naturally as though he were recalling a discussion he had overheard. He would add his own opinions and, since he expected us to form opinions, would ask us for ours . . .

His questions forced me to think carefully about Shakespeare's choice of words, about the crafting of a scene, about the connections between language and performance. I had to read very, very closely, leaning over my thin Formica desk . . . , my head cupped in my hands with my two index fingers in my ears to blot out the noise from the alley behind me. There were times when no matter how hard I tried, I wouldn't get it. I'd close the book, feeling stupid to my bones. . . . The next day I would visit Father Albertson and tell him I was lost, ask him why this stuff was so damned hard. He'd listen and ask me to tell him why it made me so angry. I'd sputter some more, and then he'd draw me to the difficult passage, slowly opening the language up, helping me comprehend a distant, stylized literature, taking it apart, touching it. (56–57)

Rereading this passage and trying to put myself back into that period of my life, several things strike me:

First this is my introduction to doing literary and rhetorical scholarship. I was an average student for most of my K–12 career, and it was a high-school senior English teacher, Jack McFarland (mentioned above), who got me excited about schooling and turned my life around. There were about a half-dozen faculty at Loyola (now Loyola Marymount) who took the baton and further educated me, and it was Fr. Albertson who showed me how to use scholarship—historical, sociological, literary theoretical—to further understand a literary text, to consider its time, its connection to other art, to politics and science, to ideas in the air. It has been decades since I've done any literary analysis, but I use the tools and the approach to inquiry that Clint Albertson taught me every time I analyze a historical text or a political speech or one of the endless documents that issue like pollen from the world of social policy.

Second, Fr. Albertson guided me to new ways of thinking about how language is used, what it does, and how an effect is achieved—and how all this is contextual, how you have to know things about time and place to think well about language use. Something else, and I don't know how to express this in other than physical terms: The course he set up required that I think hard, that I push myself, not settling for the obvious or the easily executed. He provided the guided experience of staying with a problem, focusing on it, prying off the surface features of it, coming up short, but going back at it again. This sounds more aggressive than I want it to, for part of this process also involved reflection and noodling, and at times the process involved—when I was lucky—a gestalt shift, seeing the issue in a very different way. I use physical language, I guess, because to this day my recollection is that what I was trying to do involved exertion—which felt physical in its demands. It is this kind of intense focus, this going beneath the surface, that I try to engender in my students today—and that, when I'm lucky, I can achieve in my own writing.

STANDING THE TEST OF TIME: LIBERAL EDUCATION IN A JESUIT TRADITION

Paul Ranieri

In 1977, after seeing the movie *Oh, God!* with fellow students from Xavier University and a Jesuit friend, I remember someone saying, "Boy, George Burns is just how I want God to look." We all laughed at the absurdity of such a thought, though our young Jesuit brought us up short with his response, "You know, you only understand God through his reflection in those around you."

After sixteen years of Catholic education, of consciously conceiving a divine power beyond our physical world, this sense of meeting the divine only within the physical form of others suddenly seemed to focus my nonconscious, lived experience in a way my formal education had not. Xavier prepared me well, an English major specializing in secondary education from 1971 to 1975, in close analysis of literature and in a broad array of core subjects that have grounded my teaching to this day (i.e., philosophy, theology, calculus, Spanish, history, psychology, chemistry). Looking back, I realize that we addressed little in the way of rhetoric or even style, but clearly we came to value critical thinking, continual reflection, and an essential need to act on our values, to tie thought to speech to act (think → say → do).

In 1977 then, my undergraduate program at Xavier only just behind me, I knew instinctively that my Jesuit friend, Terry Charlton, S.J., was right. Understanding exactly why would focus my journey through the history and theory of rhetoric and composition.

The history of liberal education, whether seen from antiquity (e.g., H. I. Marrou's *A History of Education in Antiquity*) or the late twentieth century (e.g., Bruce Kimball's *Orators and Philosophers: A History of the Idea of Liberal Education*), is the story of two competing traditions: that of the philosopher and that of the scribe (Marrou) or orator (Kimball). As Kimball documents in *Orators and Philosophers*, the contemporary version of the philosopher tradition—rooted largely in Plato and Aristotle—has deep ties to the American individual as above all "autonomous" and "free," including:

An emphasis on freedom, "especially freedom from a priori strictures and standards,"

An emphasis on intellect and rationality, leading to an Enlightenment stress on reason, mathematics, and science at the expense of sensory experience and the emotions,

A skepticism that is often expressed as a value for "critical thinking,"

A tolerance for new experiences that follow from skepticism,

An egalitarianism rooted in the freedom and nature of all humans,

An emphasis on the "volition of the individual rather than upon the obligations of citizenship,"

A pursuit of these ideals as an end in themselves.

—Kimball, 119–23

In summary, the philosophical tradition (what we largely studied directly in my philosophy courses at Xavier) lies at the root of a Platonic and Aristotelian tradition of liberal education focused on the autonomous, free individual pursuing knowledge (even truth) through reason, skepticism, and critical thought. Any mention of civic purpose is assumed to follow from knowledge, though how exactly the conceptual (what we "know") becomes the practical (what we "live" or "do") is usually left up to the individual learner.

When I completed my degree at Xavier and earned certification to teach English at the secondary level, my head was filled with many potentially useful concepts from English essays and literature, philosophy, theology, history, psychology, and mathematics. Only later would I fully understand that the gap between the concepts that followed from the *curriculum* and how we would "act" in our lives was to be filled by our *non-curricular* experiences (e.g., social and religious) with the Jesuits outside the classroom. In those contexts—our retreats, our discussions of ethics, our lived experiences—we were encouraged to "act on our knowledge, "to do the right thing," to translate concepts and precepts into behavior. In our weekly service work, in our expected behavior on campus, and in the way the Jesuits modeled living and learning, we were taught how to integrate our thinking with our speaking and our doing (think → say → do).

In 1980, after four years of teaching high school, I moved to Austin, Texas, and enrolled in the University of Texas to pursue a doctorate in English education. There I took half my courses in the rhetoric area of the English department and a few others in philosophy and speech communications, seeking out the same multidisciplinary curricular experience I had enjoyed at Xavier. However, studying with Ed Farrell in English education and with James Kinneavy in English, I also began to identify the orator tradition as what linked my two experiences at Xavier (the curricular and the non-curricular), binding the conceptual to speaking and to action.

In Classical Rhetoric with James Kinneavy, we studied Plato's contemporary Isocrates, who clearly was the educational power of classical Athens. According to Marrou, the two rival streams, or "two pillars," of ancient education were exemplified by Plato and Isocrates (91), though "on the whole it was Isocrates, not Plato, who educated fourth-century Greece and subsequently the Hellenistic and Roman worlds" (79). "On the level of history," says Marrou, "Plato had been defeated: posterity had not accepted his educational ideals. The victor, generally speaking, was Isocrates, and Isocrates became the educator first of Greece and then of the whole ancient world" (194). Kimball also identifies Plato and Isocrates as the roots for "liberal education," but then adds that humanistic culture can be "traced . . . through the Roman educational theorists to Isocrates, rather than to Plato or Aristotle" (19). Werner Jaeger in *Paideia: The Ideals of Greek Culture* acknowledges Isocrates as the "father of 'humanistic culture,'" saying that "there is no doubt that since the Renaissance he has exercised a far greater influence on the educational methods of humanism than any other Greek or Roman teacher" (3:46). Finally, Cicero in his dialogue *De Oratore* writes, "Then behold! there arose Isocrates, the Master of all rhetoricians, from whose school, as from the Horse of Troy, none but leaders emerged" (269, sec. 2.22).

On the one hand I was perplexed by how I had missed in my studies at Xavier such an instrumental figure in ancient education. I could see most clearly in Plato and Aristotle the roots of the broad multidisciplinary, philosophy-centered curriculum at Xavier. On the other hand I became conscious that Isocrates provided the intellectual roots tying what I had learned in my *non-curricular* experiences at Xavier to what I had learned in the formal *curriculum*. By studying Isocrates, I began to connect more explicitly what my courses taught me to think with how my non-classroom experiences fostered a decision-making that translated those thoughts into speech and action.

In 1985, shortly after I began my university teaching career, Ed Corbett would bring to the forefront first how different the orator tradition of Cicero and Quintilian is from the philosophical tradition of Aristotle, but also how indebted Cicero and Quintilian were to the ideas of Isocrates:

> What I began to realize as time went on is that Aristotle is not responsible for the liberal-education aspects of rhetoric. It's Cicero and Quintilian. What you realize when you study them more is that their progenitor is Isocrates. . . . Isocrates is the great proponent and the great promoter of liberal education and the study of rhetoric as a liberal discipline.
>
> —Corbett, 267

Briefly wondering why Cicero and Quintilian have been viewed as playing a greater role in "promoting the humanistic brand of rhetoric throughout the Western world" (275), Corbett speculates that their texts were "more readily accessible" (275) than Isocrates'. Regardless, by 1985, Corbett could state both that "Isocrates was the true fountainhead of humanistic culture" (275) and that his intellectual roots, like Cicero's and Quintilian's, lie in the "Greek sophistic tradition" (269).[1]

Since those early watershed years, I have come to identify four key aspects of that "sophistic tradition," aspects that separate the orator and philosopher traditions of liberal education.

Isocrates' approach to liberal education and life begins with *logos*.[2] He returns to an older sophistic notion of *logos*, defined not as "reason" or "the rational" but as a dynamic combination of thought and word. As he explains in *Antidosis*,

> we ought, therefore, . . . [not] show ourselves intolerant toward that power which . . . is the source of most of our blessings. For in the other powers which we possess . . . , we are in no respect superior to other living creatures; nay, we are inferior to many in swiftness and in strength and in other resources; but, because there has been implanted in us the power to persuade each other and to make clear to each other whatever we desire, not only have we escaped the life of wild beasts, but we have come together and founded cities and made laws and invented arts; and, generally speaking, there is no institution devised by [humans] which the power of speech has not helped us to establish.
>
> —Isocrates, *Antidosis*, 327, sec. 253–54

As a Greek concept *logos* identifies a linking of thought and word (as "thought into word," or "thought → word"). As twenty-first-century humans we are jaded by those whose words do not reflect their thoughts. For Isocrates, however, we fulfill our humanness by expressing thoughts clearly, and then using *logos* to create the society that free humans are capable of building.

Notice that *logos* is by definition a social power. Collaboration and cooperation are not optional human activities. His last sentence from the passage cited earlier extends the power of *logos* to our actions: "Through [*logos*] we educate the ignorant and appraise the wise; for the power to speak well is taken as the surest index of a sound understanding, and discourse which is true and lawful and just is the outward image of a good and faithful soul" (327, sec. 255). For Isocrates, *ethos* was determined by how well our thoughts, words, and actions were consistent *and* to the advantage of those goals that society most valued.

Inherent to both a *logos*-based education and one tied to democracy is *nomos*, the necessary deliberation, collaboration, and cooperation required to "hit the mark," an archery term for making the right decision. Homer reflects this sense of decision-making in the *Iliad* as the warriors gather in a group to decide a course of action, recognizing each speaker in turn by passing around the staff, which temporarily grants one the authority to speak. Susan Jarrett identifies this rhetorical process as *nomos*, which would evolve to signify "habitual practice, usage, or custom" (89). The essential feature to be stressed here is "human agency" (89). "In epistemological terms," continues Jarrett, "*nomos* signifies the imposition of humanly determined patterns of explanation for natural phenomena . . . to construct knowledge across a range of fields and to codify norms of behavior in communally sanctioned forms" (90). *Nomos*, then, requires that as humans we identify the ideals and goals by which we want to live and that we accept responsibility for the day-to-day decisions exemplifying our commitment to them.

Logos (with *nomos* inferred) is thus, by definition, context-bound, or knowledge "embedded in the conditions of life" (Gilligan 148)—and here Terry Charlton's caution echoes clearly: Some knowledge is indeed "conceptual," but other knowledge comes to exist only as it comes to be "embodied" in our and others' lives. Simply knowing ideas and concepts is not enough; one must also master the ability to adapt that knowledge to particular situations. According to Takis Poulakos, in his essay "Isocrates' Use of *Doxa*," "Isocrates conceives of learning not so much in terms of possessing a specialized body of knowledge as in knowing how to apply principles to specific situations" (61). Isocrates calls this type of wisdom *phronesis*, or "practical wisdom." Poulakos continues: "By guiding students in how to apply rhetorical principles to practical situations, how to make choices about future courses of action with an eye to potential consequences, and how to adjust choices made to the demands of changing circumstances, [Isocrates] is in fact preparing students to participate in their city's deliberations as citizens" (62).

A critical aspect of this type of "context-bound" knowledge is to consider not whether speakers are "right" or "wrong" but whether they accurately perceive shared goals for a decision and whether a decision or action reaches that practical goal. Poulakos elaborates:

> Understood in these terms, deliberation calls for the pronouncement of a judgment in the uncertain world of politics [or business, or life], a conjecture that aims to hit the mark. . . . Like the skill of an archer who bends the bow in the direction of the target, a person skilled in deliberation knows how to aim and hit the right course of action. Hence, Isocrates' reference . . . to a wise person as someone "who possess[es] a judgment . . . which is accurate in meeting occasions as they arise and [who] rarely misses the expedient course of action."
>
> —Poulakos, 71

Up to this point one might be led to a detour down the Platonic path, to argue that knowledge based on the contextual, the contingent, cannot be based on truth. Isocrates might respond that as a society we define what values give us direction. His values were centered on those of a Panhellenic society, one that exemplified piety, moderation, justice, and virtue ("On the Peace," sec. 63). Such goals might be idealistic (not Ideal), but they give us direction as a society, and as rhetors,[3] we "are to be guided by [our] experience with and understanding of the community's shared beliefs, values, and traditions" (Poulakos, 72). Of course, we are not committed to the Isocratean goals of twenty-five centuries ago, but we do share goals tied to our sense of "democracy." We cannot define here what values make up the American *ethos*, but suffice it to say that a small list would include liberty, dignity, freedom of speech, dialogue, responsibility, respect, and justice.

With a *logos*-based culture stressing a continuum of thought-word-action, one in which decisions critical to one's context are made based on group norms and goals guiding actions that best address the needs of the moment, we find a catalyst for decision-making in the rhetorical principle of *kairos*. Richard Leo Enos notes that the Roman orator and educator Quintilian "saw *dunamis* [from which we have the word *dynamic*] as the power (*vim*) of persuasion and credited Isocrates with first recognizing this faculty in rhetoric" (3). The ancient sophist Gorgias referred to *kairos* as the ability to "say or keep silent, do or not do, the necessary thing at the necessary moment" (Freeman 130). *Kairos* is not "audience analysis," as it often appears in textbooks, but rather "an awareness" that the answer to *this* question at *this* point in the decision-making process has presented itself. It is a powerful rhetorical moment when *kairos* presents itself, and the rhetor, intricately aware of the moment, senses it and steers the decision-making process toward the best conclusion.

After all these years, then, I now more clearly recognize how the philosopher tradition of liberal education emphasized in Xavier's *curriculum* synthesizes with the rhetor tradition emphasized in Xavier's *co-curricular* experience. The reason Terry Charlton's comment in 1977 struck me as accurate was that concepts, knowledge, ideas make sense not only in isolation but in a distinctly human way, within rhetorical contexts as well. "Studying rhetoric" (or philosophy, or biology, or engineering, or educational theory) eventually must evolve to "doing rhetoric." Today my "philosopher side" pulls me to thought and reflection, while my "rhetoric side" prompts those thoughts to expression and action, in the process defining my ethos as a human being, to myself and to other people. We are rhetorical, *logos*-driven, contextually bound beings who draw our identities as much from our relationships with others as from our own autonomous selves. As rhetorical beings we seek to respond to the *kairos* in our lives, to the problems we face as humans, bringing to bear on those problems not only the wealth of our ideas but also the rhetorical skills we have to work in *nomos*-driven contexts with each other. The rhetoric tradition pulls us to action, meeting the philosopher tradition over *logos*.[4]

Unfortunately, the political, social, and epistemological environment of contemporary higher education makes it difficult to help students see the value of the rhetoric tradition in their lives, to "do rhetoric," to develop an "ear for *kairos*," to develop the ability to "hit the mark," to work with the dialectic that shifts rapidly between the philosophic and rhetorical. Our education system is developmentally impaired, our society prefers passive consumers and voters even as it bemoans the lack of civic participation, and the digital revolution compounds the challenge of students' developing these ways of knowing even as the need for them becomes clearer every day. These are the challenges many of us face working with young adults, especially in a large, state comprehensive university. However, I relish the challenge to education and democracy posed every day in my work. In my thirty-fve years as a teacher, and my fourteen years as an administrator, I have experienced the success of "studying rhetoric" but also, in a more everyday sense, I have known the success of "doing rhetoric," of bringing rhetoric to my administrative, teaching, and civic work.

Besides, in a kind of springtime, we now see signs that the orator-rhetoric tradition is emerging from the historical winter in which it has languished for at least the last three centuries:

> Each year Xavier University awards a small number of Community Engaged Fellowships, to students who have "demonstrated extraordinary leadership or initiative in the area of community engagement of service . . . and who have shown high academic achievement" ("Service Awards"). These students are expected to continue their service work at Xavier with "hands-on community opportunities."
>
> The Association of American Colleges and Universities (AAC&U), of which Xavier and my institution are members, argues for a liberal education that includes both knowledge and engagement, "a vision of excellence that includes a practical and engaged liberal education for all students" ("Liberal Education"). Recently AAC&U participated in a national meeting at the White House arguing for civic learning as a priority for all students.
>
> My own institution has invested in "immersive learning," "which pulls together interdisciplinary student teams guided by expert faculty to create unique, high-impact learning experiences that result in real world solutions" ("Immersive Learning").

Granted, such efforts do not affect most students, yet they highlight the tenacity and value of "doing rhetoric," even in a climate that limits much real innovation in higher education.

All that said, however, more is at stake for Jesuit education, marking a possible *kairos* moment in American higher education. As other essays in this collection make clear, the Jesuits did preserve the rhetorical tradition when many other intellectual traditions reduced it to the skills of freshman writing. However, mere preservation or mere conceptual curricular changes are not enough. Historically the Jesuits retained rhetoric within the *Ratio Studiorum* at the college-preparatory level, but it was clearly subordinate to philosophy, theology, and later the sciences at the university level (Donnelly). Recently, in "How to Build a Better Student," academics at Saint Louis University, Fordham University, and Loyola Marymount University (see essays by contributors from the latter two institutions in this collection) argue for revising a rhetoric-based education, aimed at *eloquentia perfecta* and rooted in the *Ratio Studiorum,* that emphasizes reason, digital sophistication, classroom discussion, collaboration, active learning, and the ability to put words (both written and oral) to thought, even as they hope to push such learning beyond improving only in-class performance (Clarke). Educators need to do more than "hope" that students can push beyond in-class performance. Only by fully reviving the rhetoric tradition of liberal education will students fully benefit from the dynamic power of *logos, nomos, phronesis,* and *kairos.*

In this volume, David Leigh goes right to the heart of the need to synthesize the philosopher tradition with a rhetoric-based liberal education in a distinctly Jesuit way:

> Three of these principles [that form the basis of Jesuit liberal education] call for an education that is *incarnational,* that is transforming, and that is socially and historically embedded. As incarnational, Jesuit spirituality believes in the entry of God into the human condition in Jesus Christ; such a belief leads to the study of 'all things human' as the place of finding God. . . . Jesuit liberal education has taught its students that to develop their human talents is to develop the very image and likeness of God within them. As *transformative,* Jesuit spirituality calls not for a quietistic or private religious or philosophical life, but for an education that prepares students for responsible service of others to transform a broken world . . . Finally, as *historically embedded,* Jesuit spirituality calls for its followers to adapt to and critique the time and place and culture into which they move. [Emphasis added]

Leigh's passage clearly echoes those aspects of the rhetoric tradition discussed earlier, a focus on *logos, kairos, nomos,* and on solving problems in a context-bound world (*phronesis*). Or, to paraphrase Terry Charlton, our human sense of the divine relies on how each of us embodies a *logos* that reflects the divine *Logos,* the perfect embodiment of an ethereal God in human form. Christians are called to model themselves on the *Logos,* aiming to "hit that mark" in a way others can know. That is the essence of life or of an education that is *incarnational.*

Rhetoric-based liberal education and Jesuit liberal education both center on *logos/Logos.* The *Logos* of Jesuit liberal education blends rhetorical *logos* with

Leigh's call for the incarnational. In John 1:1–18, we are told the Messiah is the Word made flesh, dwelling among us, who reveals God to us (as our words reveal our thoughts) and who models Christianity for us (as actions follow from thought/word in the rhetorical tradition). C. H. Dodd in *The Interpretation of the Fourth Gospel* notes how a tendency to "attribute to the spoken word an existence and activity of its own" (264) is deeply rooted even in Hebrew, and that in the Greek of the New Testament, the incarnate Logos, the Son of God, is "the ultimate reality revealed" (267). *The Dogmatic Constitution on Divine Revelation*, or *Dei Verbum*, captures a flavor of this rhetorical tradition inherent in the Word, saying "*for when the fullness of time arrived* (see Gal. 4:4), *the Word was made flesh* and dwelt among us in His fullness of graces and truth (see John 1:14). Christ established the kingdom of God on earth, *manifested His Father and Himself by deeds and words*" (section 17, emphasis added). Inherent in such passages is not only the sense of rhetorical *logos* and *kairos* but also the *ethos* of tying thought to word and to action. Benedict XVI recently noted as well that "in the Son, '*Logos made flesh*' (cf. *Jn* 1:14), who came to accomplish the will of the one who sent him (cf. *Jn* 4:34), *God, the source of revelation, reveals himself as Father* and brings to completion the divine pedagogy which had previously been *carried out through the words of the prophets and the wondrous deeds accomplished in creation and in the history* of his people and all mankind" (section 17, emphasis added). Here one again senses the rhetorical notions of *logos* and *kairos* as well as the tie of thoughts to words and to actions. In biblical terms: Only by their fruits will we know them (Matt. 7:16–20).

Space does not allow a more detailed analysis of the connection between the rhetoric tradition of liberal education and an incarnational view of Christianity, a connection that serves as a necessary, proper, and fitting reaction to the demands of contemporary life. However, just as a dialectic between the philosophy and rhetoric traditions of liberal education can yield a more human, embodied sense of action within modern democracy, one that heals the fragmented contemporary human by seeking an integration of thought and action through *logos*, so too would a dialectic between the philosophical and the incarnational traditions of Catholicism bring to today's Jesuit education a powerful dialectic of thought and action, mediated by the *Logos*.

Today, early in the twenty-first century, Jesuit universities are poised to do for Catholic liberal education what such institutions as Worcester Polytechnic University are already doing for secular liberal education: to bring the informed, reflective, committed mind to the modern agora.[5] Maybe the emerging "theology of the body" credited to John Paul II is another sign that we are beginning to refocus on the contextual, the embodied Logos/logos as the center of our physical, intellectual, and spiritual existence.

In the end, having left Xavier in 1975 wondering how the philosophy of my Jesuit education would "play out" in my career and life, I understand now that the philosopher tradition of liberal education (i.e., what I studied initially in the classroom at Xavier) informs the orator tradition (i.e., what I saw modeled outside the classroom in the Jesuit tradition)—and that we need once again to bind the two traditions more tightly together. Whether I encountered the use of rhetoric teaching high school, teaching at the university level, administering various university and professional programs, or encountering socially the various communities in which I live, I appreciate my evolving understanding of rhetoric in both its conceptual and its practical or lived senses—and I hope I have taken Terry Charlton's advice to heart, to reflect *Logos* in my own thoughts, words, and actions even as I seek that reflection in others.

Life inside the classroom and inside my office "studying rhetoric" deepens my appreciation for the rhetorical traditions that lead directly to us across twenty-five centuries. Life outside the classroom, "doing rhetoric," embodies Logos/logos, making relevant to the human context our deepest thoughts and ideals. The continuous struggle of life is to clearly reflect one's thoughts in one's words and actions. For the educated person living in the "real world," that means making the actual possible through human logos. For those of us trained by the Jesuits, however, that also means remembering that the image and likeness we reflect in our words and actions is not just of our own individual consciousness but of the divine Logos we are called to imitate as well.

NOTES

1. I might also note that, though Cicero does credit Isocrates with a major role in his own view of the education and duty of the orator, near the end of his life Cicero in *Orator* is already laying the foundation for the separation of thought from language, a division that would, by the sixteenth and seventeenth centuries, undercut the orator tradition of liberal education even though it still managed to serve in the Renaissance as the core of humanist education.

2. We would make a mistake to see Isocrates as either "idealistic" (see, for example, Norlin) or as one whose contribution to Western education is largely "literary" (see, for example, O'Malley and Covington). The former confuses Isocrates' commitment to Panhellenic values with being impractical, something he was not. The latter is a tag that follows from a nineteenth- and twentieth-century interpretation of liberal education, a topic both Marrou and Kimball discuss in detail. Unfortunately such scholarship is cited often, obscuring the "sophistic tradition" at the core of Isocrates' rhetoric.

3. *Rhetoric* is a broader term now than *orator* but built on the same tradition. It also more easily adapts to today's digital world, one that involves the speaker's interacting with the audience about a topic within a multimodal context.

4. As faculty members and as members of our civic communities, we bear the same responsibility to model the dialectic of these two traditions of liberal education as did the Jesuits I knew at Xavier. Richard Light makes this point clear in the report on his research with college seniors. His book *Making the Most of College: Students Speak Their Minds* revealed what I discovered Isocrates knew, that just as education could and often does mirror the less admirable traits of culture, we have the chance to be a microcosm of what society should be. Students surveyed by Light often commented

that, while classwork was important, more so was how they saw those ideas in practice in their residence halls, within student organizations, and as exemplified by the actions of faculty and administrators. If we want our graduates to be ethical, responsible, courageous agents in their adult endeavors, then we need to be sure that their university microcosm exhibits those same values, and that we give them the chance to participate in that environment—as agents, as apprentices, as reflective, intentional learners. They need to be guided through the process of decision-making until they too have developed a sense of, an "ear for," the *kairos*.

5. WPI's "Interactive Qualifying Project," an excellent example of an institution-wide effort to synthesize the conceptual (the "knowing") and the practical (the "doing"), challenges students to develop a "broad understanding of the cultural and social contexts of [engineering and science], and thus be more effective and socially responsible practitioners and citizens. . . . [S]mall teams of students work under the guidance of faculty members from all disciplines to conduct research . . . directed at a specific problem or need. Students deliver findings and recommendations . . . to advisors. . . . About half of all IPQs are completed off-campus through the Global Projects Program (GPP)."

WORKS CITED

Benedict XVI. *Verbum Domini*. September 30, 2010. http://w2.vatican.va/content/benedict-xvi/en/apostexhortations/documents/hfben-xviexh20100930verbum-domini.html. Accessed November 12, 2010.

Cicero, Marcus Tullius. *De Oratore*. 2 vols. Translated by E. W. Sutton and H. Rackham. Cambridge: Harvard University Press, 1959.

Clarke, Kevin. "How to Build a Better Student." *America* 204, no. 16 (May 16, 2011): 12–17.

Corbett, Edward P. J. "Isocrates' Legacy: The Humanistic Strand in Classical Rhetoric." In *Selected Essays of Edward P. J. Corbett*, ed. Robert J. Connors. Dallas: Southern Methodist University Press, 1989. 267–77.

Covington, Faries McRee. *Friedrich Blass: On the Rhetorical Theory of Isocrates*. Diss., Ball State University, 1994. An Arbor, UMI, 1995.

Dodd, C. H. *The Interpretation of the Fourth Gospel*. New York. Cambridge University Press, 1968.

Donnelly, Francis P., S.J. *Principles of Jesuit Education in Practice*. New York: P. J. Kenedy and Sons: 1934.

Enos, Richard Leo. *Roman Rhetoric: Revolution and the Greek Influence*. Prospect Heights, Ill.: Waveland, 1995.

Freeman, Kathleen. *Ancilla to the Pre-Socratic Philosophers: A Complete Translation of the Fragments in Diels*, Fragmente der Vorsokratiker. Cambridge: Harvard University Press, 1957.

Gilligan, Carol. *In a Different Voice: Psychological Theory and Women's Development*. Cambridge: Harvard University Press, 1993.

"Immersive Learning." Ball State University, 2015. http://cms.bsu.edu/academics/undergraduatestudy/beyondtheclassroom/immersivelearning. Accessed March 1, 2015.

"Interactive Qualifying Project." Worcester Polytechnic Institute, Interdisciplinary and Global Studies Division, June 15, 2014. http://www.wpi.edu/academics/igsd /iqp.html. Accessed March 1, 2015.

Isocrates. *Antidosis*. In *Isocrates*, vol. 1, trans. George Norlin. Cambridge: Harvard University Press, 1968. 181–65.

———. *On the Peace. Isocrates.* vol. 2, trans. George Norlin. Cambridge: Harvard University Press, 1968. 2–97.

Jaeger, Werner. *Paideia: The Ideals of Greek Culture*. Translated by Gilbert Highet. 3 vols. New York: Oxford University Press, 1944.

Jarrett, Susan. "The Role of the Sophists in Histories of Consciousness." *Philosophy and Rhetoric* 23, no. 2 (1990): 85–95.

Kimball, Bruce A. *Orators and Philosophers: A History of the Idea of Liberal Education*. Expanded edition. New York: College Board, 1995.

Leigh, David. "The Changing Practice of Liberal Education and Rhetoric in Jesuit Education: 1600–2000." In this volume, 125–37.

"Liberal Education." Association of American Colleges and Universities." 2012. http://www.aacu.org/resources/liberal-education. Accessed January 13, 2012.

Light, Richard. *Making the Most of College: Students Speak Their Minds*. Cambridge: Harvard University Press, 2001.

Marrou, H. I. *A History of Education in Antiquity."* Translated by George Lamb. Madison: University of Wisconsin Press, 1982.

Norlin, George. Introduction, ix–li. *Isocrates*, vol. 1. Cambridge, Mass.: Harvard University Press, 1968.

O'Malley, John W. "Eloquentia." *America* 204, no. 16 (May 16, 2011): 17–18.

Paul VI. *Dogmatic Constitution on Divine Revelation: Dei Verbum*. November 18, 1965. http://www.vatican.va/archive/histcouncils/iivaticancouncil/documents/ vat-iiconst19651118dei-verbumen.html. Accessed April 2, 2012.

Poulakos, Takis. "Isocrates' Use of *Doxa*." *Philosophy and Rhetoric* 34, no. 11 (2001) 61–78.

"Service Awards." Xavier University, 2012. http://www.xavier.edu/undergraduate-admission/scholarships/service.cfm. Accessed January 13, 2012.

PART III

JESUIT RHETORIC AND IGNATIAN PEDAGOGY: APPLICATIONS, INNOVATIONS, AND CHALLENGES

THE UNFINISHED BUSINESS OF *ELOQUENTIA PERFECTA* IN TWENTY-FIRST-CENTURY JESUIT HIGHER EDUCATION

Cinthia Gannett

Thus the past is the fiction of the present.
—Michel de Certeau, S.J.

It's a funny kind of history that only looks backwards.
—Lewis Carroll

There is no one like the Jesuits for doing pirouettes.
—M Despois, *Le Theatre Français sous Louis XIV*, cited by Judith Rock

CREATING A USABLE PAST

The president of Fairfield University, Jeffrey von Arx, S.J., often claims that "in the phrase 'Jesuit university,' *university* is the noun and *Jesuit* is the adjective." This statement asserts that Jesuit colleges are now in the full mainstream of American higher education and that the adjective *Jesuit* works in accord with the modern university in all its variety. As for the noun *university*, the state of American higher education is in a period of rapid transformation: New technologies are changing the ways in which we gather, create, and share cultures, information, and ideas. New media are transforming the teaching-learning exchange, reshaping the ways we communicate, present, and represent ourselves in local and global contexts. Proliferating forms of professional and scholarly disciplinarity have created countless life-enhancing innovations and advances in knowledge. But these sites of increased specialization can also displace holistic and integrative educational experiences, focusing more narrowly on preparation for specific expert roles or careers rather than on the broad flexible intellectual, civic, and social competences that graduates also need. Similarly, corporatized educational models, with their bureaucratic forms of increased public accountability and assessment regimes, often rely on reductive cost–benefit and outcomes analyses, which produce simplistic measures of college "productivity."

In addition, the dramatically increased costs of higher education create serious burdens for many families, adding pressure to concentrate on vocational and professional courses of study and reducing the traditional focus of an integrative foundational liberal arts curriculum. Jesuit institutions, along with other liberal arts colleges and universities, are asking what is the value and vitality of the humanities and how might they be sustained and nourished in a coherent way now and in the future (Biondi, Crabtree, Tripole).

How then might we construe *Jesuit* as a modifier, as a means of distinguishing the higher education experience in the twenty-first century? As with any strong mission-based educational project, it evokes its own complex and even conflicted history, as we (and many others) draw on what we find important and valuable about all its past incarnations, while bracketing or eliding aspects that may seem troubling, or simply as no longer "speaking" to the present. As Michel de Certeau, the late-twentieth-century Jesuit philosopher and cultural historian, so aptly reminds us: "History endlessly finds the present in its object, and the past in its practice. Inhabited by the uncanniness that it seeks, history imposes its law upon the faraway places that it conquers when it fosters the illusion that it is bringing them back to life" (36).

Responding to the current educational scene and creating the educational cultures of the future, many Jesuit-affiliated educators are bringing some version of the historical Jesuit educational and rhetorical project "back to life." As this volume relates, over its four-hundred-year history, the Society of Jesus has undergone dramatic changes in its ministries and missions, wielding great educational, cultural, and civic influence in some sites and periods, while at other times and places being actively suppressed (in many countries on multiple occasions even in the twentieth century), exiled, marginalized (Codina, 4–8). The Society has participated in moments of great forward thinking, innovation, and creativity, and experienced periods, such as the nineteenth and early twentieth centuries, characterized even by Jesuit historians as times of conservative, often backward-looking insularity. In the United States, Jesuit colleges have undergone major shifts in focus and curriculum. The traditional seven-year classical curriculum across the nineteenth and early twentieth centuries with its broad cross-disciplinary rhetorical underpinning was gradually reconfigured to admit a variety formalized courses of disciplinary study, with the newly-formed undergraduate departments of philosophy and theology providing the obvious "Jesuit" aspect of the curriculum (See Brereton and Gannett, Part II; McInnes, *Philosophy*; O'Hare).

Since the 1960s, American Jesuit education has taken its third turn, through recent congregation meetings and Vatican II reforms, recommitting to a focus on education for social justice (McKevitt, 291; see also Bonachea; Leahy; McInnes, *Jesuit Higher Education*; Schroth). Indeed, the Jesuits have undertaken a massive set of revisions across all their ministries, with substantive changes for their educational project in the United States and across the globe. As Jesuit philosopher Stephen Rowntree's "Ten Theses on Jesuit Higher Education" (1994) explains the transformation, in the postwar surge of U.S. higher education the Jesuits gave up control over hiring, curricula, and even relinquished control over boards of trustees: "In the late 1960s, Jesuit colleges 'went native' . . . accommodating [their mission] to the tribal customs and mores of the wider U.S. higher education culture" (6). Vatican II also opened the door for greater ecumenism, and colleges continued to open their communities to students of both sexes and to faculty from many religious and philosophic orientations, and sponsored the growth and development of Jesuit higher education as commensurate with other public higher-educational institutions (7). The success of these changes can be seen in the twenty-eight Jesuit colleges and forty-six secondary schools in the United States that have now educated well over a million living graduates.

All these changes, however, increase the challenge of retaining or forging some particular, if evolving, notion of Jesuit identity and mission (Rowntree, 7–8). The question of identity is crucial because Jesuit higher education is increasingly enacted by lay (and often non-Catholic) faculty, staff, and administrators for an increasingly diverse student body. As Jesuit schools and colleges have grown in the United States and worldwide, the number of Jesuits available to support them has decreased dramatically in the past fifty years, from 36,000 in the early 1960s to approximately 19,000 in 2013, with a good many of the 19,000 near retirement age. Many Jesuits are engaged in other Jesuit ministries and social-justice work worldwide; as of 2000, Jesuits constituted only 5.8 percent of Jesuit-school faculty and staff (Codina, 21). One way to understand the current incarnation of Jesuit higher education is that, as John Callahan, S.J., puts it, "no longer is Jesuit education the exclusive property of Jesuits. Rather, Jesuit education is the property of all the men and women who work in educational institutions which claim the Ignatian heritage" (Callahan, "Jesuits and Jesuit Education"; see also *Characteristics*, 1–2).

Clearly, our contributors believe that one promising means of claiming this heritage is to embrace a broad, capacious, reforged notion of rhetoric and its reimagined aim of *eloquentia perfecta*. The notion of rhetoric as an integrative force across the curriculum is true to the Jesuit heritage, and also bears on curricular and pedagogical conversations across higher education under the broad rubric of writing, speaking, and composing in, across, and beyond the curriculum. The aim of eloquence can also speak to the reform of general-education programs and to other transdisciplinary projects such as writing centers, civic literacies, writing as reflection, service learning, global rhetorics, and information literacies, all of which are themselves immersed in the new universe of digital and performative rhetorics.[1]

As the chapters in this volume demonstrate, however, until recently many lay scholar-teachers have had little access to the complex histories of Jesuit rhetorical scholarship and pedagogy, practices that might help them claim and reformulate this area of the Ignatian and Jesuit heritage. Indeed, scholars at Jesuit institutions and elsewhere are having to "back into" the larger inquiries about Jesuit educational and rhetorical traditions. Understandably, the substantial dispersal and effacement of explicit rhetorical practices and pedagogies in Jesuit education, and the rapid shift from Jesuit-staffed colleges to those primarily populated by faculty not connected to Jesuit traditions, has magnified the knowledge gap for those now working in rhetoric, composition, literature, theater, communication, and any of the arts of eloquence across disciplines at Jesuit schools.[2]

In this final part of the collection, then, those engaged in de Certeau's "network of human realities" (11) connected to Jesuit colleges and universities, and those interested in fuller histories of discursive education, are attempting to engage these recovered "usable pasts," even as they understand their partial and provisional natures. They want to relocate these traditions in dialogue with the current situation of American higher education in the liberal and literate arts. While the scope of the term *rhetoric* has waxed and waned across the centuries, both the sixteenth century and the period of the twentieth and twenty-first centuries share a capacious and multiform view of rhetoric.[3] The twentieth-century mini-renaissance of rhetoric in American arts and letters, the subject of Part II of this volume, focuses on the essential rhetorical nature of all human sciences, and on the concomitant "revival" or reemergence of rhetoric in all its variety as a deep, if contested, set of theoretical and pedagogical projects. Although channeled and constrained through various disciplinary and departmental filters, language, literature, communications, information literacies, and media studies all share in this rhetorical grounding (Conley; Mailloux, *Disciplinary*; Murphy; Nelms, Part II; Kennedy; Welch; Farrell and Soukup).[4] Indeed, noting that the Renaissance was a time when rhetoric was *reintegrated* after having been dispersed since the fall of Rome, Don Paul Abbot suggests that the time is right for *integration* again, as "the integrated rhetoric so valued by the Renaissance humanists gradually disintegrated into dualities of literature and composition, speaking and writing" (in Murphy, 170). We see this as a kairotic moment, a convergence of specific time, place, and situation that provides the opportunity for meaningful scholarly discourse on the potential for this kind of integration (see O'Malley, "Historiography," "Eloquentia"; Ranieri, Part II; Peters, Part III).[5]

Calling on Ong, Corbett, Freire, and other key figures discussed in Part II, the authors in this final part take up the current status of *eloquentia perfecta* and its associated humanistic rhetorical curricula, documenting current efforts to locate, name, redefine, and reanimate it in scholarly work, curricular initiatives, and broader educational cultures. The contributors address three main questions: What does it mean to "bring it [rhetoric] to life" in present places, times, and contexts? What might it mean to promote, in the twenty-first century, *eloquentia perfecta* as a transdisciplinary integrative anchor for the humanities and the liberal arts? What are the affordances and limitations to promoting these initiatives at Jesuit schools and beyond?

CURRENT EXPERIMENTS IN JESUIT EDUCATIONAL
AND RHETORICAL IDENTITY

Jesuit institutions in the United States and globally are engaged in a series of discussions and initiatives to create a twenty-first century identity that updates their historical missions and ministries. There have been large-scale Jesuit-sponsored efforts at defining identity, and a host of individual or small-group efforts as well. A copious array of pamphlets, brochures, essays, statements, and monographs describe versions of current Jesuit educational mission, offering lists of characteristics, traits, features, and principles. It is an age of rich, sometimes confusing, experimentation, with terms or constructs like "men and women for others" (or social justice), *cura personalis* (the care of the whole person), *magis* (the more), and "discernment" (processes of internal decision-making informed by or as metaphorically similar to the inner dialogic process of the *Spiritual Exercises*). These terms are often invoked, individually or collectively, and sometimes almost at random, to describe the special Jesuit and Ignatian spirit of education.

To date, the major official initiative has been the development of "Ignatian pedagogy," a broad set of learning processes or principles identified as the real through line of Jesuit education. International groups of Jesuits began to work on common criteria in 1960 (Codina, 18) at the direction of Superior General Janssens, and Superior General Arrupe established the Secretariat for Jesuit Education in 1967. The largest effort to remake Jesuit educational identity started in 1980, when Arrupe brought Jesuit and lay leaders together to reimagine Jesuit education. They decided not to undertake another revision of the official Jesuit plan of studies, the *Ratio Studiorum*. As one Jesuit scholar put it rather colorfully:

> Certainly Jesuit education cannot be defined in terms of the *Ratio*. That was only one of many Renaissance school plans, Protestant as well as Catholic; all of which looked alike on paper. They were all inspired by the ideal of perfect Latin eloquence that Cicero had exemplified and Quintilian, the first-century teacher of rhetoric whom some 16th-century Jesuits called "our Quintilian," had codified. In any case, the *Ratio* bears as much relationship to contemporary Jesuit education as Harvey on the circulation of blood bears to contemporary medical practice.
>
> —Donohue, 4

While the specific curriculum of the *Ratio* of 1599 itself is clearly obsolete, along with its attendant seven-year training in "latinitas" and other classical languages, grammar, humanities, and rhetoric for the continental *collège* (that combination of what we would now call high school and the first half of college), the rhetorical nature of all knowledge-making is readily reclaimable, as we have seen throughout this collection. Donohue himself argues elsewhere that "certain principles of sixteenth-century Jesuit education may be applied to our contemporary school actualities but they will usually require transposition into a new key" (in Duminuco, 148). "For instance, the rhetorical ideal of 'Ciceronian grace' has a wider aim that 'rests on the conviction that the truly human mind must possess both wisdom and eloquence, must know something and be able to say what he knows, must be able to think and communicate'" (cited in Duminuco, 148). Or as Claude Pavur, S.J., who has recently published a new translation and commentary on the *Ratio*, remarks: "Having recently rediscovered the *Spiritual Exercises* and the *Constitutions* of Ignatius, the Society of Jesus and its collaborators should be ready to discover the institutional educational genius expressed in this document" (2005, ix).

However, it was decided to use the "rediscovery of the Exercises of Ignatius as the inspiration for its educational renewal, rather than the formality of a predetermined pedagogical code" (Codina, 30).[6] The codification of this renewed educational project appeared in 1986 as "The Characteristics of Jesuit Education" (Duminuco, 161–230), along with companion guides, "Ignatian Pedagogy: A Practical Approach" (1993, Duminuco, 231–93) and "Précis of *Ignatian Pedagogy: A Practical Approach*" (Korth, 280–84). In the new "Characteristics," explicit mention of eloquence is relegated to a single item (number 29), out of the nearly two hundred separate numbered paragraphs. Of course, a few other paragraphs may speak to the more capacious notion of rhetoric and eloquence explored in this collection, but those connections are no longer visible, and the term *rhetoric* is omitted entirely. Indeed, *eloquentia perfecta* is not even mentioned in Traub's widely reprinted glossary, "Do You Speak Ignatian?" which is given out routinely at Jesuit colleges. And the entry under the *Ratio* simply dismisses it altogether: "Much of what the 1599 *Ratio* contained would not be relevant to Jesuit schools today" (12). Other new collections of essays applying Jesuit educational principles to the current scene make little or no reference to rhetoric or *eloquentia perfecta* (Traub, *Reader*, Tripole).

In essence, the broad legacy of the *Ratio*, informed by Ignatius's intimate spiritual *discursive* education, but also drawing on his and his confrères' other educational experiences and the larger dynamic project of Jesuit rhetorical education, has been, however inadvertently, stripped away from many new versions of Jesuit education. In the new view, the *Spiritual Exercises* are the metaphorical source of "renewable" Jesuit educational energy, while the *Ratio* and its related documents and enactments, still imbued with the "spirit" of the *Spiritual Exercises*, appear to have run out of steam.

Ignatian pedagogy is based on three broad principles or processes extracted from Loyola's own "spiritual growth" documented in the *Spiritual Exercises* and applied to the formal teaching and learning encounter: specifically, the sequence of experience, reflection, and action. These are important, accessible, useful, and productive constructs for the teaching and learning encounter, and faculty and students benefit from their mindful application daily. Noting that *all* the colleges and universities of the Society have taken up the "Characteristics," Codina explains their power this way:

> The impact of the Characteristics continues to be extraordinary, not only for the Jesuit colleges, both also for other educational centers of Ignatian spirituality. Some 2000 educational institutions all over the world lay claim to an inspiration that is Ignatian, if not necessarily Jesuit. This is not an idle distinction. The Characteristics have established a sense of identity and have certainly brought greater clarity to the work and being of Jesuit education than no other document since the Ratio. The Characteristics are absolutely not a new Ratio. And yet, they project a vision and a sense of purpose which far transcends the formality of the Ratio.
>
> —Codina, 31–32

Yet, for lay collaborators, it may seem difficult to find the balance between "Jesuit" and "university" here. Most Ignatian pedagogical paradigm materials invoke explicitly Christian, Catholic, and Ignatian spiritual references, and that language may have the unfortunate effect of excluding faculty and students outside this faith tradition, and the broader, flexible reflective practices it endorses as habits of mind. On the other hand, the short summary forms often provided as handouts in pedagogical workshops can easily be read simply as modern educational philosophy unmoored from any Jesuit context.[7] As a colleague who uses "Ignatian pedagogy" in her classes once put it in conversation, "It's just Dewey warmed over."

WHAT MIGHT JESUIT *ELOQUENTIA PERFECTA* MEAN IN THE TWENTY-FIRST CENTURY?

In the United States, one critical resource in this work of recovery and regeneration has developed over the past fifteen years, as faculty at Jesuit institutions have formed a network of scholar-teachers, along with other interested scholars, to explore and re-envision the complex traditions of Jesuit rhetorical education that they have inherited. The Jesuit Conference on Composition and Rhetoric (JCRC), established formally in 2007 as one of the AJCU (American Jesuit Colleges and Universities) conferences, meets regularly at academic conferences and has an active listserv. Indeed, this collection was prompted by discussions at early JCRC meetings. Members of the JCRC (e.g., Gillespie; Johnson and Lynch; Mailloux, *Enactment*) have begun publishing on Jesuit rhetorical traditions in multiple scholarly venues. Presentations on Jesuit rhetoric have been featured at panels at several recent scholarly meetings of national organizations: the Conference on College Composition and Communication, the Rhetoric Society of America, the International Society for the History of Rhetoric, the European Association of Teachers of Academic Writing, and Writing Research across Borders. Jesuit *eloquentia perfecta* has even been the theme of recent conferences and symposia at Loyola Marymount in 2012, Loyola University of New Orleans in 2013, and the College of the Holy Cross in 2014 among others.

Clearly, the enduring integrated and integrative legacy of *eloquentia perfecta* has much to offer in the remaking of Jesuit education. As Paul Lynch, professor of rhetoric and composition at Saint Louis University, argues, Ignatian pedagogy appears to reject any focus on academic competition (*aemulatio*) and the training for powerful argumentation that clearly marks the *Ratio* in important ways, replacing argumentation with irenic notions of "experience, reflection, and action" and positioning the teacher as a sort of spiritual director rather than someone who might model or require practice in negotiating public disagreements (*Conversations*, 8), rather than balancing them. Lynch agrees that competition for its own sake or for individual gain or control is not desirable, but he argues that the new paradigm of Jesuit education is not really coherent without educating students to engage important public issues and controversies and to develop the discursive skills and knowledge to be powerful advocates for social justice (8–9). For Lynch, rhetoric is something that students *experience* as well as *do* all the time and should be joined to Ignatian pedagogy:

> They [students] write papers, request extensions, discuss politics, sports and music (and occasionally the work we assign). They apply for scholarships and jobs and further schooling. They perform a great deal of community service around our campuses and around the world, and these projects demand constant communication. In other words, our students are already immersed in both the *experience* of receiving rhetoric and the *action* of producing it. As teachers of perfect eloquence—no matter our discipline—our job would be then be to lead students through the reflection that makes rhetoric intentional. Ignatian pedagogy thus provides the perfect vehicle for crafting an *eloquentia perfecta* appropriate to our moment, shaped by deep erudition, manifested in a range of communication media, and, most importantly, unwaveringly committed to justice.

With Lynch, we think that it is possible to integrate these overlapping discursive traditions: Ignatian pedagogy, with its roots in Loyola's personal dialogic spiritual education, contextualized with the symbolic devotional practices of the Renaissance, particularly the *devotio moderna* (Fumaroli, 92–95), as well as the multiple traditions that carry forth and continually remake *eloquentia perfecta* from its classical and, later, Renaissance and humanistic roots. Calling on the outward-looking discourses that explore, persuade, inspire, teach, and delight in the public world for the common good, and on the intimate discourses of conversation, care, devotion, prayer, witnessing, reconciliation, or simple reflection and mindfulness that align mastery of the word with ministries of the word, we find they can offer a powerful and distinctive means of

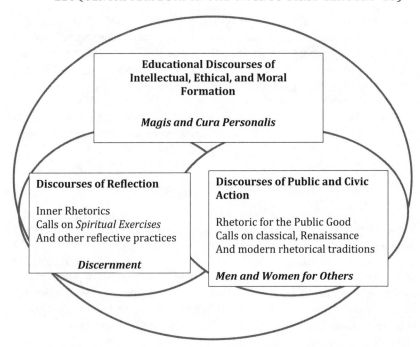

Figure 1. Jesuit education and Jesuit *eloquentia perfecta*: rhetorics of formation, reflection, and action.

renewing Jesuit educational identity. Together, they reconnect the active, imaginative, and contemplative aspects of human life. John O'Malley, in "Not for Ourselves Alone," sets them in relation this way: "The virtue the rhetorical tradition especially wants to inculcate is prudence, that is, good judgment, the wisdom that characterizes the ideal leaders and makes them sensitive in assessing the relative merits of competing possibilities in the conflict of human situations. It hopes to turn students into adults who make humane decisions for themselves . . . [and] tries to instill a secular version of what we in the tradition of the *Spiritual Exercises* of Saint Ignatius call discernment" (5; see also Gillespie; Hendrickson; O'Malley, *Eloquentia*; Parmach; Rowntree; and Worcester 2010).

Like Lynch and O'Malley, Steven Mailloux argues that *eloquentia perfecta* calls on "the classical ideal of the good person writing and speaking well for the public good and promotes the teaching of eloquence combined with erudition and moral discernment" ("A Good Person" 13). A working definition of this admittedly aspirational conception might be the following: Jesuit *eloquentia perfecta* combines the development of strong intellectual and integrative habits of mind, fosters ethical and moral formation through ongoing reflection, permits but does not force spiritual formation, and cultivates the uses of knowledge and eloquence for the public good (see Figure 1). This figure offers possible intersections and alignments between *eloquentia perfecta* and the Ignatian pedagogical paradigm. Jesuit rhetorical practice and pedagogy is influenced by Renaissance humanist rhetorics as well as by the intimate inter- and intrapersonal rhetorics of reflective devotional practices, of which the *Spiritual Exercises* is a paradigmatic instance. *Eloquentia perfecta* (EP) joins the discourses of all subject areas (erudition) with the cultivation of con- science and compassion (the inner rhetorics of reflection and discernment) to foster the development of people as informed, articulate, civil, compassionate, and willing to act in the service of the greater community good.

THE STATUS OF RHETORIC AND *ELOQUENTIA PERFECTA* AT JESUIT COLLEGES AND UNIVERSITIES

While by no means widely shared, these ideas and practices are circulating across Jesuit colleges and universities. Indeed, given all the ways in which the rhetorical legacy of modern Jesuit schools has been effaced and the ways in which Jesuit higher education has entered the "mainstream" of public higher education, it is not surprising that, from the outside, the writing and rhetori- cal curricula at Jesuit colleges often look pretty much like writing programs at other American colleges and universities. Naturally, programs vary consid- erably in size, shape, character, and structure according to their larger insti- tutional cultures: larger research universities and very small liberal-arts colleges, expensive elite schools and schools with particular missions to serve the urban poor.

In order that the current landscape of Jesuit education with regard to these initiatives might be better understood, Jesuit writing programs (JCRC Survey 2012–14) were recently asked to inventory their current curricular and admin- istrative structures and to comment on the ways in which they do or do not draw on Ignatian pedagogy or Jesuit educational elements in their work.[8] The generative and dynamic snapshots demonstrate the multiple ways and degrees to which current programs and curricula have decided to enact site-specific appropriations of Jesuit mission and identity.

The JCRC gathered data from twenty-six of the twenty-eight American col- leges and universities. Naturally all the institutions offer some kind of under- graduate degree (in writing, rhetoric, English, or writing studies); eight offer master's degrees in English, and five programs offer English PhDs. Of the PhD programs, only St. Louis University has a specialization in rhetoric; the rest are in English literature. Given that many of these are fairly small liberal-arts colleges and that some have no graduate programs, it is understandable that there would not be more graduate programs in rhetoric or writing studies as stand-alone disciplinary specializations.

As for first-year writing curricula, only Holy Cross has no required writing course at all, but its two required first-year seminars in its Montserrat program constitute an ambitious, "rhetoric-intensive" integrative multidisciplinary year-long sequence (Whall). All the other schools require at least one course, and ten of the reporting schools have a two-course sequence. Nineteen of the schools reported some kind of first-year seminar, and thirteen schools reported some level of "writing-intensive" course beyond first-year writing (Spinner). The relatively high number of schools reporting a full year-long course of study in writing and rhetoric, which is clearly not as common in American higher education any more, as well as the preponderance of institutions with multiple writing-intensive courses, does suggest—at least tacitly—that the Jesuit rhetorical legacy is still active in the curriculum.

We also asked whether schools drew on some aspect of Jesuit or Ignatian mission or identity in their writing programs. At some schools (Georgetown, Le Moyne, Rockhurst, Santa Clara, St. Louis, Xavier, and Wheeling, for example), respondents reported making (or finding) little explicit reference to Jesuit heritage or pedagogies, although they themselves were often interested in promoting these conversations. Well over half (eighteen) reported positively. Sixteen reported they engaged their Jesuit educational heritage (listing such specific attributes as eloquence or EP, *cura personalis,* and social justice). Thirteen institutions reported that they drew explicitly on the frame of Ignatian pedagogy. Interestingly, social justice was the only feature cited as belonging to both categories. Ten institutions answered that they drew on both "Jesuit" and "Ignatian" features. (See appendix, "Selected Data.") The findings of this JCRC survey parallel our discussion of the complex understandings circulating about Ignatian pedgogy and Jesuit *eloquentia perfecta.*

When in use, notions of *Jesuit* or *Ignatian* are employed in a variety of configurations, along with terms for particular Jesuit values, such as *cura personalis* or "women and men for others." Sometimes they are invoked separately, sometimes linked as partners, often with one or the other leading educational conversations taking place at the schools. We also asked about some specific features of Jesuit education that are often connected with both Ignatian pedagogy and Jesuit *eloquentia perfecta.* A full half of the reporting institutions, thirteen, join oral and written rhetoric in their courses, and eleven encourage or require ethical reflection as a programmatic aspect of their course aims and objectives, while thirteen treat civic engagement as a direct or encouraged part of rhetorical training. While there is no set of comparative national data, these indicators do speak to the liveliness and commitment to these acknowledged elements of eloquence across the array of Jesuit schools and colleges. As Paula Gillespie explains in "Writing in a Jesuit School," these practices may look very much like current practices and trends in composition (including WAC, WID, and writing as service learning, or civic engagement), but they are also imbued with their own distinctive sense of a Jesuit rhetorical legacy (146). And in fact many of these current practices may have been first developed or influenced by some of the Jesuit-trained scholar-practitioners identified in this collection.

Importantly, several Jesuit colleges and universities are currently undertaking Core revisions intended to highlight their historical mission and identity while incorporating the best of current educational practices and principles. The Core curriculum is still a distinctive feature of Jesuit schools, which tend to require more common courses than other schools, including multiple courses in English (writing and literature), philosophy, ethics, and theology, in the service of an integrated educational experience. A summary of Cores at Jesuit colleges and universities shows several schools with strong liberal-arts Cores constituting up to 50 percent of the entire curriculum (Davis, 16). At LeMoyne College in 2011, for example, Laura Davies and Erin Mullally (*Conversations*) piloted sections of the first-year writing course modeled on Ignatian pedagogy. The focus was on "teaching writing through a holistic pedagogical framework that emphasized 1) care of the individual person, 2) individual reflection and self-evaluation, and 3) a concern for the ethical ramifications of rhetorical acts" (21), and calling on Jesuit education, the liberal arts, and rhetoric as subject matter (22). Regis University has also revised its first-year writing course, using *eloquentia perfecta* as a heuristic from which to redesign engaged pedagogy that supports students entering into the dynamic world of the 21st century (Reitmeyer). Santa Clara University has added two new tenure-track faculty to support its rhetoric-intensive core curriculum and has used the recent *Conversations* volume on *eloquentia perfecta* (2013) as a prompt for sponsoring a series of faculty-development seminars on Jesuit ways of enacting writing across the curriculum, funded by its Ignatian Center (Billings, personal communication, March 2015).

Loyola University Maryland has an extended recent history with *eloquentia perfecta* projects. For example, Barbara Walvoord, one of the major figures in the development of writing scross the curriculum (WAC), was at Loyola Maryland for decades. Certainly, Walvoord's WAC work started before she arrived at Loyola and continued to develop at different institutions and in new directions after her time there. Yet there has been little consideration of how her extended immersion in a Jesuit institution connects her in substantive ways to Jesuit rhetorical traditions. Indeed, NEH grant proposals that she wrote with several Loyola faculty to fund the development of the "Empirical Rhetoric Project Phase II, 1982–88"[9] helped to create the famous BAC-WAC (Baltimore Area Consortium on Writing Across the Curriculum), as well as a curricular sequence and writing across the curriculum at Loyola (Walvoord et al., 1990), Walvoord [then Fassler]). The grant calls directly on the Jesuit rhetorical heritage: "Appropriate to an institution rooted in the Renaissance ideal where rhetoric was the synthesizing discipline, writing is a common component to all core courses" (*Empirical Rhetoric II Proposal*, 3).

Loyola Maryland continued its strong engagement with *eloquentia perfecta*, retaining it as an explicit aim of the full undergraduate curriculum, continuing to develop its WAC program and writing center, and organizing its own independent writing department.[10] Currently, Peggy O'Neill, Lisa Zimmerelli, and Allen Brizee have been developing *eloquentia perfecta* (one of the department and college aims) in several ways, emphasizing the central role that writing and rhetoric play in communication through Core writing courses and the incorporation of new media (what some are calling *Eloquentia Perfecta* 2.0; Brizee and Fishman, 2013). The writing center supports the whole university community and also sponsors literacy projects in the larger community, very much in the Jesuit rhetorical tradition of using language to serve others. It continues to offer writing-across-the-curriculum support and a writing minor and major (Gannett et al., 2011; Bean, 2013; Britt-Smith et al., 2013). Loyola Maryland (O'Neill and Gannett) and Marquette have also created their own institutional guides for writing across the curriculum and writing in the disciplines, in collaboration with other disciplinary faculty, to support both faculty and students in Core and major courses. Rockhurst, too, is directing significant efforts to curriculum reform through faculty and pedagogical development in Jesuit rhetoric and reflection (John Kerrigan, personal communication).

In terms of larger Core revisions, Holy Cross has developed the Montserrat Seminar sequence (Whall, 16). St. Joseph's University has revised its Core to require a writing-intensive course every year (Bean 2013). The University of Detroit Mercy has adopted new Core curriculum learning outcomes intended to develop students' sense of ethos and to foster enduring rhetorical competences (Britt-Smith et al., 2013; Britt-Smith, personal correspondence, June 2014). John Carroll University in Cleveland has also just completed a Core curriculum review, which will require writing and rhetoric-intensive courses across the whole vertical curriculum, infusing *eloquentia perfecta* at every level, and joining oral and written rhetoric courses in its foundational sequence (Report of the John Carroll Curriculum Working Group, June 2013). Scranton University, in the process of revising its Core curriculum, has taken *eloquentia perfecta* as one of its principal aims, which it is infusing into first-year writing and the first-year seminar, including digital literacies and oral communication in its foundational level. Scranton is now working on integrating *eloquentia perfecta* into its level-2 courses (Grettano, personal communication, March 13, 2015).

At St. Louis University, according to Vincent Casaregola (personal correspondence, June 26, 2014), students can take a preliminary first-year writing course in a "stretch" pattern across the full year, while others start with their "Advanced Strategies of Rhetoric and Research," in keeping with the developmental principles of early Jesuit education promoted by the *Ratio*. SLU is also experimenting with linking first-year writing and ethics courses for business students and has created a "rhetoric, writing, and technology" track, with many new-media courses to engage new forms of *eloquentia perfecta,* as well as a new required English-major course, Rhetoric and Argument. He explains the power of *eloquentia perfecta* as an animating principle this way: "I see EP not as a separate track, but as a multiplicity of paths, leading in part from our fundamental work in writing pedagogy, spreading, vine-like, into and through the whole of the curriculum in both formal and informal ways that enrich all the learning through an enhanced sense of the discourse arts and an intensified realization that learning must fulfill the self only so that the self can be of service to others. The perfection of eloquence is achieved not merely by the mastery of the discourse arts but by the recognition of their fundamental importance in and through all areas of learning, and their fundamental purpose of leading to public action" (personal correspondence, June 26, 2014).

Fairfield University is also revising its Core. Current recommendations from the Core Currriculum Task Force Report (December 2014) would reduce the writing and literature requirements from three courses to two, presumably cutting the full-year writing sequence to one course, but would infuse writing more deliberately in other Core courses. *Eloquentia perfecta* is not identified as a specific goal or aim of the new program, but the process is ongoing. The Core Pathways initiative, an earlier Core reform initiative that identifies common, integrative habits of mind that traverse the Core, includes a Rhetoric and Reflection Pathway, which explicitly calls on the Jesuit rhetorical heritage.

For now, Fairfield's current full-year, two-course sequence, the Core Writing Program, is working to create new "coalitions of the willing." The Fairfield Writing Center and the Connecticut Writing Project, related writing initiatives, are engaged in several literacy and WAC projects to serve various departments and the larger local community. Core Writing is investigating ways to work with the Center for Faith and Public Life on service-learning and JUHAN (Jesuit Universities Humanitarian Action Network) projects. It also collaborates with the Center for Academic Excellence to sponsor and support faculty writers through a series of writers' retreats and workshops.

Currently, Fairfield's Core Writing sequence has undertaken a novel curricular project, in which several sections of its Core writing courses have agreed to focus on *eloquentia perfecta* and integration *across* the whole Core curriculum (fall 2013–spring 2015). Students practice writing in an Ignatian reflective tradition and also create public arguments and inquiries intended to integrate their discursive work across the curriculum and co-curriculum, which they capture in a full print, electronic portfolio, or both. The program produces a Core writing anthology each year for use across all sections to celebrate and integrate student writing and learning across the Core, and hosts the National Day on Writing for the whole campus community in the spirit of *eloquentia perfecta*. The Core Writing Program has also worked to partner with university themes, theater, new media, service learning, and arts curricula in a much more robust way, exploring them as sites for the co-development of *eloquentia perfecta* in its full capacious sense.[11] While the days of Jesuit-sponsored grand ballet and theater productions at Louis-le-Grand are long gone, Fairfield is discovering once more that "there is no one like the Jesuits for doing pirouettes" (Rock, 39).

ELOQUENCE IN ACTION: FORDHAM UNIVERSITY, LOYOLA MARYMOUNT UNIVERSITY, SEATTLE UNIVERSITY

To offer a fuller profile of selected Jesuit colleges and universities that have undertaken major kinds of curricular reforms and initiatives, Part III features three distinct experiments with *eloquentia perfecta*. These essays describe the institutional contexts and processes for their curricular projects and Core revisions and discuss both the successes and serious challenges entailed in these initiatives. Anne Fernald and Kate Nash recount how a renewed focus on rhetoric and an explicit vertical sequence of four *eloquentia perfecta* courses was developed at Fordham through a formal revision of the Core curriculum begun in 2003 and implemented in 2008. The emphasis on EP, which Fordham described as the arts of reading, listening, observing, thinking, and thoroughly understanding a topic under consideration, was identified as an aspect of "intellectual excellence," a primary integrative thread across the Core. The final version included the current required Composition and Rhetoric course (EP 1) as part of a four-course *eloquentia perfecta* requirement, which dispersed reading and writing instruction across the full four years of college (EP2: Texts and Contexts; EP 3: Designated sections of Core, major, and electives; EP 4: Values seminar). The writing-intensive courses include training in rhetoric and argumentation, and opportunities to develop social responsibility and moral discernment. Initial program support came from the Center for Teaching Excellence, which offered a series of faculty-development workshops, a practicum course for graduate students, and a Jesuit pedagogy seminar.[12] Challenges for the future include programmatic support, faculty development, and staffing. Fernald and Nash do note that the preponderance of EP 1 and EP 2 courses are taught by doctoral students and adjuncts, but they insist that there is a "rich range of sections and diverse and dynamic community of scholars."

While Fernald and Nash offer a fairly straightforward account of Fordham's Core revision process, K. J. Peters, in his analysis of Loyola Marymount's revision of the Core efforts to restore rhetoric to a central place in the curriculum, addresses several challenges and obstacles that such major cross-disciplinary projects can entail. Considering how Core curriculum discussions are generally shaped in obvious and in indirect ways by "disciplinary thinking, departmental ambition, and individual disposition," Peters details some critical obstacles to this kind of serious consensus-building: first, the splintering of rhetoric and humanities into literature, rhetoric, communication, and philosophy, disperses advocacy for *eloquentia perfecta*; second, the reduced Jesuit presence attenuates the rich understanding of Jesuit educational history;

and third, "the great horde of contingent instructors, who often carry the burden of the core" have little or no voice in curricular conversations.

Even so, the new LMU Core has been thoughtfully structured as a three-tiered set of courses across the whole curriculum, based on broad developmental constructs: foundations, explorations, and integrations. Peters, then director of composition, and Steven Mailloux, newly hired as President's Professor in Rhetoric, worked to create a rigorous foundations course inspired by both *eloquentia perfecta* and the *Spiritual Exercises*. But the Core-revision process ran into some fairly serious, though not uncommon, roadblocks: strong pressure to reduce the Core to make room for electives and major courses, and departments contesting for the reduced curricular territory—while trying to retain a particularly Jesuit flavor. In the final version (fall 2013), philosophy and communication were represented, but literature was not, even though literary studies are clearly foundational, and the *eloquentia perfecta* course became reframed as Rhetorical Arts. Also, as at Fordham, non-tenure-track faculty teach a much greater share of the first-year courses in support of full-time faculty and will undertake most of the faculty development for this part of the curriculum—again, with very little voice in the process. In the new sequence, students take a first-year seminar in the first semester, and rhetorical arts in the second semester. Peters, though convinced that the new Core is innovative and will be taken up with seriousness of purpose, appreciates the striking divergence between "aspiration" and "articulation" and notes the difficulty of sustaining a substantive sense of mission when much of the historical context has been effaced (see also Mailloux, Part II).

At Seattle University, efforts to highlight rhetoric across the curriculum have been ongoing for over twenty-five years. In their program profile, Bean, Nichols, and Philpott chronicle the development of a "multilayered approach for teaching *eloquentia perfecta* within our undergraduate curriculum." Two major revisions of the Core—a major writing-across-the-curriculum initiative, the development of a very strong writing center, a serious effort to professionalize the contingent faculty, and the redesign of the first-year writing seminar to address rhetoric as civic action focused on social justice—have all been coordinated (both mindfully and through serendipity) to create a very robust and vital rhetorical educational culture. The authors acknowledge that "at every stage of its development, rhetoric across the curriculum has been influenced by our institution's Jesuit ethos." The 1986 Core set the stage, by requiring rhetoric-rich courses across all four years, crowned by a "senior synthesis course that linked the Core and the major."

Hired to support faculty development for this new Core, John C. Bean, an important national (and international) figure in writing across the curriculum, along with his colleagues Jeffrey S. Philpott and Larry C. Nichols, detail the writing of an in-house guide that calls explicitly on the Jesuit heritage of active rhetorical training as the center of intellectual work. Bean's work, revised and with its overt Jesuit context removed, would become *Engaging Ideas: The Professor's Guide to Integrating Writing, Critical Thinking, and Active Learning in the Classroom* (2011), probably the best-known writing-across-the-curriculum guide in print. This is another fascinating example of a hidden Jesuit connection and contribution to the larger field of composition-rhetoric and writing across the curriculum.

The Jesuit rhetorical connection was enhanced when Seattle, needing both to revisit its Core and to initiate a serious assessment conversation, asked Barbara Walvoord of Loyola Maryland to facilitate the dialogue. It is easy to see how their common sensibilities concerning the central and integrative power of rhetoric, informed by a Jesuit rhetorical culture, and balanced with a respect for disciplinary discourse fed into the new "organic" assessment based on "embedded assignments" in Core and disciplinary courses. This important institution-wide assessment project led to the development of Core revision based on four broad learning outcomes, including effective communication, based on clear rhetorical principles and the "key elements of *eloquentia perfecta*" (Bean). Importantly, by creating a committee infrastructure to support the Core and a permanent budget for ongoing faculty development, Seattle University clearly has developed a vital and viable means of joining the Jesuit transdisciplinary notion of *eloquentia perfecta* with current thinking on rhetorical and communication-arts education.

RELATING *ELOQUENTIA PERFECTA* WITH SPECIFIC JESUIT CONSTRUCTS IN PARTICULAR CLASSES: *CURA PERSONALIS* AND "MEN AND WOMEN FOR OTHERS"

The next pairing of chapters treats the engagement of *eloquentia perfecta* with various Ignatian pedagogical concepts in specific classes. Since Jesuit colleges and universities have been, for over a decade, systematically including Ignatian pedagogy in mission statements and introducing faculty to the Ignatian pedagogical paradigm and specific Jesuit "values," such as *cura personalis, magis*, discernment, and "men and women for others" (or solidarity), many faculty see these constructs as foundational. They are just beginning to explore how notions of Jesuit rhetoric and eloquence can be usefully deployed as a means of "seeing" and "making" classrooms work, or to consider how the Ignatian pedagogical paradigm is inherently infused with rhetorical thinking. Both Karen Paley's study of *cura personalis* in two disciplinary courses and Ann Green's analysis of discernment in her own service-learning course use the language of Ignatian pedagogy to highlight the aim of fostering moral, ethical, and intellectual formation (*eloquentia perfecta*) in an integrated way.

Paley, then director of the writing program at Loyola Marymount University, takes an ethnographic approach, combining classroom observation with student interviews to examine the classroom pedagogy and assignments that she calls a "pedagogy of *cura personalis*." In a philosophy class and a theology class, Paley analyzes the kinds of reflective assignments that foster individual discernment (articulating one's own philosophy of life), and coming to terms imaginatively with inequality and the suffering of others. Paley examines the sources of *cura personalis* and the newly formed Ignatian pedagogy in the 1970s, describing *cura personalis* as a modern incarnation of *eloquentia perfecta*.

Ann Green at St. Joseph's University reveals how an assignment built on the process of discernment from the *Spiritual Exercises* supports her service-learning writing course. She created a variety of specific genres of writing for this work, adapting the Jesuit language of the "desolation" and "consolation" associated with a retreatant's experiences during the *Spiritual Exercises*. This kind of experience–reflection–action sequence accords directly with the intimate, interpersonal rhetorics of Ignatian pedagogy. Green balances the discursive work of her course by also incorporating aspects of more public persuasive rhetoric in the class, such as using readings (of, e.g., bell hooks) that offer strong and critical arguments to be engaged (see also Green, 2001, 2003, 2004).

EP 2.0: *ELOQUENTIA PERFECTA* ENCOUNTERS NEW MEDIA AND NEW LITERACIES

Jenn Fishman and Rebecca Nowacek of Marquette University and Vincent Casaregola of St. Louis University address the possibilities and perils offered by the new communication environments to traditional notions of rhetoric based on voice (orality) and print (literacy), pedagogical issues that have become very important to faculty in most university settings (Turkle, 1997, 2013).

Fishman and Nowacek (Marquette University) locate their chapter "at the current juncture of education change and literacy evolution." Mindful of Ong's work on literacy in *Interfaces of the Word*, and aware that the specific rules-based tradition of the *Ratio Studiorum* is out of date, they want to call on the larger Jesuit principle of rhetorical accommodationism to think toward the future. Using Richard McKeon's notion of the epistemic and architectonic character of rhetoric, they argue that the open rhetorical system of virtual networks offers valuable new sources of "rhetorical praxis." Their overview of two campus and community-based initiatives at Marquette University, "Who Counts" and "Social Innovation," demonstrates how *eloquentia perfecta* is being productively reimagined as "global, multimodal writing for reflection and social action." They recommend ways to increase collaboration, visibility, and support for sustainable change for future "stewards of *eloquentia perfecta*."

Vincent Casaregola writes as someone accustomed to traditional orality and print literacies now engaging students whose approaches to learning and communication are increasingly shaped by technologies that seem to work against the cultivation of sustained attention to texts through reading, writing, and the development of "voice" through repeated practice with speaking and listening. He acknowledges that new media offer "wonderful opportunities to expand our teaching" but is concerned about the "unanticipated consequences" of moving too quickly to new media, reminding us that the move to print, another critical technology, also had important cultural consequences. He is concerned that, as Diana Owen in *"Eloquentia Perfecta* and the New Media Landscape," writes,

> the complexity and cultural underpinnings of the current media landscape present challenges for Jesuit colleges and universities seeking to adapt the tenets of *eloquentia perfecta* to the modern-day curriculum. Students are bombarded with information from a constantly evolving array of platforms that require increasingly specialized skill sets to navigate successfully. The questionable quality and vitriolic tone of much of the content disseminated via media run in direct opposition to the fundamental principles of *eloquentia perfecta*. A tradition of well-reasoned, carefully articulated arguments is more difficult to achieve in a media environment that encourages an abundance of information expressed in brief. In these times, rhetorical training that emphasizes substance, civility and responsibility is vital.
>
> —Owen, 14

Concerned that virtual connectivity and massively mediated communication may be acting as substitutes for physical presence, Casaregola wants students engaged in sufficient personal and "voiced" interactions to develop the kind of substance, civility, and responsibility crucial to effective rhetoric. His solution, calling on the spirit of the *Ratio Studiorum*, is to introduce students to what he calls "the oral performance environment" through the "voices" of NPR (National Public Radio) programming, including StoryCorps and *Morning Edition*. Paying close attention to "the richness of oral performance," Casaregola's students learn how to compose their own oral and written "performances," an updated echo of the early days of Jesuit pedagogy. Casaregola revives the rhetorical emphasis on voice and delivery, combining multiple forms of media to bridge students' new communicative modes with writing and speaking for real audiences.

SITES OF ELOQUENCE: DISPERSALS, COALITIONS, AND NEW CONSTELLATIONS

There are many challenges to these efforts to renew Jesuit education: balancing disciplinarity and professional preparation with a holistic education, balancing the adjective *Jesuit* with the noun *university* (i.e., balancing historical mission with the modern world, or the spiritual with the secular); finding ways to increase effective Jesuit-lay collaboration; negotiating the tensions between educating the elite for leadership and serving the aims of social justice for all;

and addressing the global and virtual realities that shape communication, re-lationships, knowledge, and action.

One of the most serious challenges to this effort, and to any serious *common integrative* Core curriculum, has been the dis-integration of unified knowl-edge communities into a growing number of discrete disciplines (majors and concentrations). Courses of study are organized vertically through college and departmental structures that control academic decisions and resources, and through modern university structures that separate the formal curricular elements of education from the larger educational cultures of the institution, the *paideia*. Increasing accrediting requirements for professional courses of study (health studies, business, engineering, etc.) also determine the size and shape of any Core curriculum, and tenured faculty in all departments often prefer to teach a wide variety of specialized upper-division electives rather than "common" courses.

These structures also encourage the invisibility of modern staffing structures through which our foundational ("non-" or "proto-disciplinary") courses are frequently taught by a marginalized underclass of graduate students and contingent labor. This fragmentation and de-professionalization of com-position and rhetoric faculty is a pressing educational issue everywhere in American higher education but has special salience in Jesuit education, where rhetorical education has been a central anchor for the whole curriculum. If the Jesuit eloquence initiative is to flourish and endure, we must all work together *at every level* to ensure that all our faculty are well supported, have permanent or long-term appointments, and the right to function as real members of our academic communities.[13]

The unified and unifying aim of *eloquentia perfecta,* fostered through every aspect of the curriculum and co-curriculum for centuries, has been dispersed into countless different sites, many of which have lost connection with each other. While the likelihood of rhetoric's returning as the organizing mechanism of all disciplines is remote at best, it can serve as a conscious integrative proj-ect, a means by which we mindfully seek the diverse sites where eloquence is fostered, gather the fragments, and bring them back into conversation, coali-tion, and collaboration (Hendrickson, Lakeland). Figure 2 identifies a wide array of sites where *eloquentia perfecta* may be found and fostered.

All of these initiatives have a common purpose: to infuse the Jesuit curric-ulum with a reimagined notion of rhetoric, aligned with both historical heri-tage and modern embodiments. This work can be integrated with current Ignatian pedagogical principles through deliberate reclaiming, reframing, and renaming of *eloquentia perfecta* and has the potential to contribute to the on-going reshaping of Jesuit education in the twenty-first century. In the final chapter of this part, Krista Ratcliffe, eminent rhetorician and author of *Rhe-torical Listening,* offers one way of thinking about how the twentieth-century Jesuit rhetorical heritage is being passed on, person to person, and remade

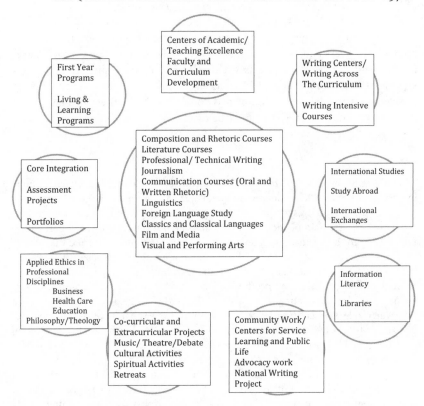

Figure 2. Jesuit *eloquentia perfecta*: finding and fostering sites of eloquence in the twenty-first century.

anew. A student of Edward P. J. Corbett, she notes that the "Jesuit resonances in rhetoric theories and praxes and even in his [Corbett's] pedagogy" were not "audible" to her when she was studying with him in graduate school, but after many years at Marquette, she is aware of those echoes, not only at her own Jesuit institution but more broadly across the whole field of rhetoric and composition. She offers several working principles for bringing eloquence and rhetoric into conversation with many other critical Jesuit values we have considered: modeling and *magis*, reflection and discernment, *cura personalis*, social justice and civic engagement, and education as personal and social transformation.

The book concludes with a deliberately provocative essay by Joseph Janangelo from Loyola University Chicago, a prominent composition scholar and former president of the Council of Writing Program Administrators. He takes a hard look at the possibilities of *mission*, an important word for secular and Jesuit education alike. It may be that all colleges that take their missions seriously will have some difficult questions to face as they try to live up to the lofty goals that they profess in their mission statements. Janangelo focuses on two, technology and diversity, where all higher education faces challenges. It's worth remembering, Janangelo reminds us, that missions are aspirational, always serving as guides and marks of excellence rather than simple, already achieved goals. He leaves us not with a finished conclusion but rather with a series of questions to contemplate as we face the future.

NOTES

1. The enduring Jesuit interest in an expanded view of rhetoric and eloquence finds important allies and intersections with several current movements in rhetoric and composition more generally. One important alignment is the renewed emphasis on language as civic action and social justice. Paulo Freire, the famous Brazilian whose relationship to the Jesuits, profiled by Pace and Merys in Part II, offered the famous critique of "the banking concept of education," and promoted "conscientizao," a coming to conscious awareness and agency for those without political or economic power through language education, specifically through the naming and reclaiming of language, through reconnecting "the word and the world." In the late 1960s and 1970s, a time when colleges in Latin America were becoming increasingly elite as repressive state governments took away public funding that would ensure open access to all classes of students, "the Latin American bishops addressed Catholic institutions and called for 'liberating education' inspired by Paolo Freire" (25).

Also, while higher education confronts the new challenges of the internationalization, indeed, globalization of education, and composition-rhetoric has taken its own international turn, we can recall that the Jesuits were, from the very beginning, a fully internationalized and global order, engaging cultures and languages in complex forms of exchange and creating a global educational project centuries ago. In "The Jesuits and Jesuit Education: A Primer," this feature is highlighted in terms of its relevance for today: While inherently multicultural and multilingual, "Jesuit education, in Rome and elsewhere, was a network that transcended boundaries of language, culture, and nationhood, one that was intercultural and global in perspective" (*Jesuit Reader*, 41).

Currently there are 3730 Jesuit-run schools and educational projects across the globe, with 2.5 million students, and there is increasing interest and effort to use this unique global network to undertake education for global citizenship. James W. Sauvé, S.J., in "Jesuit Higher Education Worldwide," notes that in 1989, nearly 200 Jesuit postsecondary institutions offered education for about 450,000 students in multiple institutional formats (161–62) in the United States and Canada (36), Europe (53), Latin America (24), India (41) East Asia (24), the Near East (1), and Africa (5). (162). Sauvé suggests that the time is right to recreate the kind of rich inter and transnational educational exchange and correspondence that led to the original *Ratio*. However, such interaction aims at more than simply coherence—it is the "vital concerns of the day: peace and justice, the world economy, the search for a society that will more effectively promote and defend human dignity." Evidence that this work has begun in earnest is readily available. *Education for a Globalized World: A Profile of the Internationalization of U.S Jesuit Campuses* (DiLeonardo, AJCU, 2007) describes an impressive array of projects that work with multicultural engagement, internationalized education for social justice, global partnerships, shared humanitarian action projects, and cross-border academic engagement.

It is critical to reconnect this work with *eloquentia perfecta* and the work of rhetoric. As Charles F. McCormack, former CEO of *Save the Children*, explained in his keynote luncheon address to a group of JUHAN (Jesuit Universities Humanitarian Action Network Meeting) at Fairfield University in August, 2013, the current worldwide network of Jesuit universities is uniquely positioned to create global citizens and global humanitarian leaders through transnational education and exchange. Equally important is the *kind* of educational skills, competences, and predispositions that Jesuit colleges and universities can offer. While technical skills are useful, McCormick stressed that the next generation of leaders need to have both a "strong cross-curricular liberal arts education," to foster the capacity to be lifelong learners, and a "whole range of communicative capacities" and education and experience with multicultural, specifically multilingual environments, as well as an enduring commitment to work for the greater public good. Sounds just like *eloquentia perfecta*, does it not?

2. As several of our Jesuit colleagues have remarked, even many Jesuits are no longer in touch with these traditions, for many reasons (Jim Bowler, S.J., personal communication).

3. The rhetorical revival of the late twentieth century included attention to rhetoric as an academic subject as well as the general term for communicating through speech, writing, and the visual arts. One such alignment is an interest in multimodal forms of rhetoric: From the beginning of the order, the Jesuits exploited the communicative possibilities offered by the new medium of the printing press, and by all the visual and performative rhetorical arts (emblematics, theater, dance, music, visual arts, and architecture), just as we are engaging proliferating forms of new public, social, and private modes of interaction and discourse and employing rhetorics intended to move all the senses.

4. As Stephen Toulmin (1990) and others (see Schlosser [2014], for example) have explained, we find ourselves in another era in which discourse is a central preoccupation and orientation for social and intellectual life. As Marc Fumaroli puts it, "Indeed, the Renaissance humanist critique of scholastic formal grammar and its own investigations into grammar, rhetoric, ethics, and religion, not only pursued highly original aims but has striking kinship with such twentieth-century schools of thought as those of Peirce, Wittgenstein and Austin, philosophers who scrutinize the links among performative language, ethical inquiry, and social practices" ("Fertility and Shortcomings," 291; see also Mailloux, in Part II).

5. First, recent Jesuit scholarship has improved in quantity and quality. Also, the number of non-Jesuit scholars of communication, rhetoric, and composition history interested in Jesuit rhetoric is also on the rise. Another related trend can be seen in the renewed interest in rhetorics of faith and spirituality (see Pernod). Scholarly work on the rhetoric of spiritual discourse (and the spirituality of rhetoric) has received increased attention by Jesuit-influenced scholars and non-Catholic scholars alike. Several colleges and universities now offer upper-division courses on "Spirituality and Writing" or "Rhetorics of Faith" (WPA listserv), and there is a new special-interest

group on rhetoric and spirituality at the Conference on College Composition and Communication (2013). Regina Foehr and Susan Schiller have edited a collection, *The Spiritual Side of Writing* (1997). Natalie Goldberg's *Writing Down the Bones* is a well-known Buddhist-inflected writing guide. And creative writers such as Paul Mariani of Boston College, Ron Hansen of Santa Clara University, and Patricia Hampl of the University of Minnesota have been actively exploring these relationships in fiction, essay, and memoir. The connected interest in rhetoric and language for healing and reconciliation is exemplified by works including Eric Doxtader's award-winning 2009 examination of the Peace and Reconciliation talks in South Africa, *With Faith in the Works of Words: The Beginning of Reconciliation in South Africa, 1985–1995*. Doxtader speaks to the irenic power of this special kind of intimate, and yet public, discourse: "Making engaged opponents out of sworn enemies, reconciliation's fragile words come to constitute the potential for politics and a politics of potential" (ix). He argues for the singular transformative power of words and of the actions of mindful listening and speaking not to persuade but rather to bring humans back together in community: "In the domain of art far more than science, reconciliation appears to begin with those words that hold the seemingly miraculous capacity to form and fashion human relationships" (x). Certainly, many modern rhetoric and composition scholars are engaged with this exciting set of scholarly and curricular projects, both by education and by inclination. And Jesuit higher education is one salient site for this kind of reintegrative work.

6. Interestingly, the *Spiritual Exercises* as a text is difficult to read and apply directly, and needs critical contextualization, just like the *Ratio*. O'Malley offers two reasons. First, it is a "set of materials, directives, and suggestions" for the person who guides the retreatant, not the retreatant him- or herself. Second, the book "consists of interspersed pieces from many different literary genres—directives, meditations, prayers, declarations, procedures, sage observations, and rules. . . . The book is not laid out in continuous discourse and lacks literary grace. Points critical for understanding it sometimes appear in what seem to be subordinate or supplementary sections. These qualities are surely due in part to limitations of the author, but are also due to the kind of book they are and what they hope to accomplish" (O'Malley, *First Jesuits*, 37).

7. See, for example, Sharon J. Korth, "Précis of Ignatian Pedagogy: A Practical Approach" in *A Jesuit Education Reader*, ed. George W. Traub.

8. The JCRC survey covers many aspects of institutional profile, curriculum, program structure and features, and types of faculty positions. Jenny Spinner at Saint Joseph's also collected JCRC data that are slightly different but very useful. The data, of course, represent single snapshots of programs that are constantly changing. A copy of the survey is available at http://fordham.bepress.com/relig/12/ or from cinthiagannett@gmail.com.

9. NEH grant proposal (unpublished, undated), Loyola Maryland Writing Department Archives.

10. The author helped establish the writing center and current version of writing across the curriculum at Loyola Maryland from 2002 to 2008, worked on a Core review that resituated *eloquentia perfecta*, and helped in development of the faculty guides to writing. The faculty were generally quite interested in reclaiming these aspects of the Jesuit heritage. She was fortunate to be able to do the Ignatian pilgrimage trip, which immersed her directly in the history of the Jesuits and she followed the life of Loyola

from his birth near Bilbao to his time as the head of the Society of Jesus in Rome. Along with Peggy O'Neill, she helped organize an RSA Summer Institute (2006) on the history of Jesuit rhetoric and current possibilities for reclaiming EP for today's classroom. Discussions at the RSA Institute provided an important prompt for this collection.

11. The Fairfield Core Writing sequence, a year-long sequence of linked courses, *EN 11: Texts and Contexts I: Writing as Craft and Inquiry,* and *EN 12: Texts and Contexts II: Writing about Literature,* promotes the development of *eloquentia perfecta* along with other curricular and extracurricular programs across the University. The aims of English 11 include the following:

- Gain facility with writing/reading/speaking processes as intellectual inquiry by practicing careful reading, invention, drafting, revising, giving feedback, and presenting/performing texts.
- Gain familiarity and facility with different modes, genres, and audiences by practicing informal (composing to learn/reflective) writing to sponsor your learning and formal (composing to communicate) assignments to demonstrate and apply your learning.
- Increase your inquiry skills and researching skills by practicing ways to prompt your curiosities and ask important questions. Generate increasingly complex claims based on multiple sources of evidence and learn effective college researching practices.
- Develop as readers, writers, speakers, and critical/reflective thinkers and citizens by integrating EN 11/12 with all Core courses and larger notions of reading and writing as intellectual and social action.

12. Recent correspondence with Dr. Fernald suggests that the program is in some flux, and ongoing support through the Center for Teaching Excellence is uncertain.

13. See "Seven Characteristics." Under the principle of Integrity, it states: "In its management practices the university should offer compensation and benefits which demonstrate a commitment to fairness, equity and the well-being of employees" (2012, 39). The JCRC is gathering data on the labor categories and positions for those primarily charged with teaching rhetoric and composition in Jesuit colleges and universities, and will develop an analysis and white paper on this critical topic.

WORKS CITED

Abbot, Don Paul. "Reading, Writing, and Rhetoric in the Renaissance." In *A Short History of Writing Instruction from Ancient Greece to Contemporary America,* ed. Murphy. New York: Routledge, 2012.

Bean, John C. *Engaging Ideas: The Professor's Guide to Integrating Writing, Critical Thinking, and Active Learning in the Classroom.* 2nd ed. San Francisco: Jossey-Bass, 2011.

——. "Round-Up." *Conversations on Jesuit Higher Education* 43 (2015): 22.

Biondi, Lawrence, S.J., "Educational Aims of the Liberal Arts Curriculum: Contextual Education," 94–104. In *Jesuit Higher Education,* ed. Bonachea.

Bonachea, Rolando, ed. *Jesuit Higher Education: Essays on an American Tradition of Excellence.* Pittsburgh: Duquesne University Press, 1989.

Boryczka, Jocelyn M., and Elizabeth Petrino. *Jesuit and Feminist Education: Intersections in Teaching and Learning for the Twenty-First Century.* New York: Fordham University Press, 2012.

Britt-Smith, Laurie A., Lisa Zimmerelli, Cinthia Gannett, and John Kerrigan. "Spread Out, but Close." *Conversations on Jesuit Higher Education* 43 (2013): 20.

Brizee, Allen, and Jenn Fishman, "From Class to Community: EP 2.0 and the New Media Legacy of Jesuit Education. *Conversations on Jesuit Higher Education* 43 (2013): 31.

Callahan, John J. "Jesuits and Jesuit Education." Academic.regis.edu/tleining/pdfs/ Jesuit_Education.pdf. Accessed September 7, 2014.

Certeau, Michel de. *The Writing of History.* Translated by Tom Conley. New York: Columbia University Press, 1988.

Codina, Gabriel. "A Century of Jesuit Education, 1900–2000." In *Jesuits: Yearbook of the Society of Jesus,* 2000. Translated by John F. Dullea. www.bc.edu/content/dam/ files/offices/mission/pdf1/ju3.pdf. Accessed November 9, 2013.

Conley, Thomas. *Rhetoric in the European Tradition.* Chicago: University of Chicago Press, 1990.

Cosgrove, Cornelius, and Nancy Barta-Smith, *In Search of Eloquence: Cross-Disciplinary Conversations on the Role of Writing in Undergraduate Education.* New York: Hampton Press, 2004.

Crabtree, Robbin D. "Agents of Consumption and Objects of Desire: The Problematics of Communication Education for Jesuit Universities." http://.learningace .com/doc/2267593/c391216d345a874df85a1c2055580842/panel13_crabtree. Accessed January 21, 2013.

Cueva, Edmund P., Shannon N. Byrne, and Frederick Benda, eds. *Jesuit Education and the Classics.* Newcastle upon Tyne: Cambridge Scholars, 2009.

Davies, Laura, and Erin Mullally. "A Course to Blog About." *Conversations on Jesuit Higher Education:* 21–22.

Davis, Margaret. "Summary of Jesuit College and University Graduation and Core Hours." *Conversations on Jesuit Higher Education* 38 (2010): 16.

Deans, Thomas. *Writing Partnerships: Service-Learning in Composition.* Portsmouth, N.H.: Boynton/Cook: 2005.

Donohue, John W. "Notes on Jesuit Education." *America* (October 26, 1985). americamagazine.org/issue/100/notes-jesuit-education. Accessed January 24, 2015.

Doxtader, Eric, *With Faith in the Works of Words: The Beginning of Reconciliation in South Africa, 1985–1995.* Lansing: Michigan State University Press, 2009.

Duminuco, Vincent J., ed. *The Jesuit Ratio Studiorum: 400th Anniversary Perspectives.* New York: Fordham University Press, 2000.

Farrell, Thomas J., and Paul A. Soukup. *Of Ong and Media Ecology: Essays in Communication, Composition, and Literary Studies.* New York: Hampton Press, 2012.

Foher, Regina, and Susan Schiller. *The Spiritual Side of Writing.* Portsmouth, N.H.: Heinemann, 1997.

Fumaroli, Marc. "The Fertility and Shortcomings of Renaissance Rhetoric: The Jesuit Case." In *The Jesuits II: Culture, Sciences, and the Arts, 1540–1773,* ed. O'Malley et al. Toronto: University of Toronto Press, 1999.

Gannett, Cinthia, Lisa Zimmerelli, Beth Boquet, Laurie Britt-Smith, John Kerrigan. "The Spiritual Life of Writing." Conference of European Association of Teachers of Academic Writing. University of Limerick, June 2011.

Gillespie, Paula. "Writing in a Jesuit School." In *Composition(s) in the New Liberal Arts*, ed. Joanna Caster Post and James A. Inman. New York: Hampton Press, 2009.

Goldberg, Natalie. *Writing Down the Bones*. 2nd ed. Boston: Shambhala, 2005.

Green, Ann. "But You Aren't White: Racial Perceptions and Service-Learning." *Michigan Journal of Community Service-Learning* 8, no. 1 (2001): 18–26.

———. "Difficult Stories: Service Learning, Race, Class, and Whiteness." *College Composition and Communication* 56, no. 2 (2003): 276–301.

———. "The Writing Center and the Parallel Curriculum: Creative Writing and Service-Learning in the Writing Center." *Praxis: A Writing Center Journal* 2, no. 2 (2004).

Greenbaum, Andrea, and Deborah Holdstein, eds. *Judaic Perspectives in Rhetoric and Composition*. Cresskill, N.J.: Hampton Press, 2000.

Hampl, Patricia. *Virgin Time: In Search of the Contemplative Life*. New York: Ballantine, 1993.

Hansen, Ron. *A Stay Against Confusion: Essays on Faith and Fiction*. New York: Harper Perennial, 2002.

Hendrickson, Daniel Scott. "The Jesuit Imaginary: Higher Education in a Secular Age." PhD diss., Columbia University, 2012.

Kennedy, George A. *Classical Rhetoric and Its Christian and Secular Tradition from Ancient to Modern Times*. 2nd ed. Chapel Hill: University of North Carolina Press, 1999.

Korth, Sharon J. "Précis of Ignatian Pedagogy: A Practical Approach" in *A Jesuit Education Reader*, ed. Traub.

Johnson, Kristine, and Paul Lynch. "*Ad perfectum eloquentiam*: The 'Spoils of Egypt' in Jesuit Renaissance Rhetoric." *Rhetoric Review* 31, no. 2 (2012): 99–116.

Lakeland, Paul. "Ignatian *Paideia* and the Mission of Fairfield University." In *Jesuit Education: A Vision of Human Flourishing*. Fairfield University, 2007.

Lay–Jesuit Collaboration in Higher Education: A Forum with Theodore Cardinal McCarrick, Howard J. Gray, S.J., and John J. DeGoia. St. Louis: Institute of Jesuit Sources, 2002.

Leahy, William, P. *Adapting to America: Catholics, Jesuits, and Higher Education in the Twentieth Century*. Washington, D.C.: Georgetown University Press, 1991.

Lynch, Paul. "The Best Training for Public Life: Reconciling Traditions: Jesuit Rhetoric and Ignatian Pedagogy." *Conversations on Jesuit Higher Education* 43 (2013): 6–9.

MacCormack, Charles F. "Reflections from the Field." Presentation at Teagle Project Meeting, Fairfield University, August 19, 2013.

Mailloux, Steven. "Disciplinary Identities: On the Rhetorical Paths between English and Communication Studies." *Rhetoric Society Qurarterly* 30, no. 2 (2000): 5–29.

———. "Enactment History, Jesuit Practices, and Rhetorical Hermaneutics." In *Theorizing Histories of Rhetoric*, ed. Michelle Bailiff. Carbondale: Southern Illinois University Press, 2013.

———. "A Good Person Speaking Well: *Eloquentia Perfecta* in U.S. Colleges: A Brief Genealogy." *Conversations on Jesuit Higher Education* 43 (2013): 10–13.

Mariani, Paul. *Thirty Days: On Retreat with the Exercises of St. Ignatius*. New York: Compass, 2003.

Mathieu, Paula. "Composing Mindful Teachers and Community Partners." Presentation at Boston Rhetoric and Writing Network (BRAWN) Conference, Boston, May 30, 2014.

McInnes, William C. "The Current State of the Jesuit Philosophy of Education." In *Jesuit Higher Education*, ed. Bonachea.

———. *Jesuit Higher Education in the United States*. Boston: Boston College Press, 1982.

McDonough, Peter. *Men Astutely Trained*. New York: Free Press, 1992.

McKevitt,Gerald. S.J., "Jesuit Schools in the U.S.A., 1814–c. 1970." In *The Cambridge Companion to the Jesuits*, ed. Worcester.

Murphy, James, J. ed. *A Short History of Writing Instruction from Ancient Greece to Contemporary America*. 3rd ed. New York and London: Routledge, 2012.

O'Hare, Joseph. "Jesuit Education in America." In *The Jesuit Tradition in Education*, ed. Christopher Chapple. Scranton: University of Scranton Press, 2005.

O'Neill, Peggy, and Cinthia Gannett, eds. *A Guide to Writing in All the Disciplines for Students of Loyola College*. In *A Writer's Reference*, ed. Diana Hacker. 6th ed. Boston: Bedford St. Martin's Press, 2007.

O'Malley, John W. *The First Jesuits*. Cambridge, Mass.: Harvard University Press, 1993.

———. "Eloquentia." *America* (May 16, 2011). Accessed June 4, 2014.

———. "The Historiography of the Society of Jesus: Where Does It Stand Today?" In *The Jesuits II: Cultures, Sciences, and the Arts, 1540–1773*, ed. O'Malley et al. Toronto: University of Toronto Press, 1999.

———. "How the Jesuits First Became Involved in Education," 56–74. In *The Jesuit Ratio Studiorum*, ed. Diminuco.

———. "Not for Ourselves Alone: Rhetorical Education in the Jesuit Mode with Five Bullet Points for Today." *Conversations on Jesuit Higher Education* 43 (2013): 3–5.

Owen, Diana "Eloquentia Perfecta and the New Media Landscape." *Conversations on Jesuit Higher Education* 43 (2013): 26–28.

Parmach, Robert J. "*Eloquentia Perfecta*: A Way of Proceeding." *Conversations on Jesuit Higher Education* 40 (2014).

Pavur, Claude. *The Ratio Studiorum: The Official Plan for Jesuit Education*. St. Louis: Institute of Jesuit Sources, 2005

Reitmeyer, Morgan. "*Eloquentia Perfecta* as Critical Engagement: Restructuring Regis' First Year and Beyond." New Orleans: Heartland Delta Faculty Conversations, Loyola University, February 2013.

Rock, Judith. *Terpsichore at Louis-le-Grand: Baroque Dance on the Jesuit Stage in Paris*. St. Louis: Institute of Jesuit Sources, 1996.

Rowntree, Stephen C. "Ten Theses on Jesuit Higher Education." *America* (May 1994): 6–7.

Sauvé, James W. "Jesuit Higher Education Worldwide," in *Jesuit Higher Education*, ed. Bonachea.

Schroth, Raymond A. *The American Jesuits: A History*. New York: New York University Press, 2007.

"Seven Characteristics of Jesuit Colleges and Universities: A Self Evaluation Instrument." *Conversations on Jesuit Higher Education* 42 (2012): 39

Society of Jesus, General Curia of. "The Characteristics of Jesuit Education, 1986," 161–230. In *The Jesuit Ratio Studiorum*, ed. Diminuco.

Toulmin, Stephen. *Cosmopolis: The Hidden Agenda of Modernity*. Chicago: University of Chicago Press, 1990

Traub, George W. *Do you Speak Ignatian? A Glossary of Terms Used in Ignatian and Jesuit Circles*. Cincinnati: Division of Mission and Identity, Xavier University, 2006.

Traub, George W., ed. *A Jesuit Education Reader*. Chicago: Loyola Press, 2008

Tripole, Martin R., ed. *Promise Renewed: Jesuit Higher Education for a New Millennium*. Chicago: Loyola Press, 1999.

Turkle, Sherry. *Alone Together: Why We Expect More from Technology and Less from Each Other*. New York: Basic Books, 2013.

———. *Life on the Screen: Identity in the Age of the Internet*. New York: Simon and Schuster, 1997

Walvoord, Barbara A., and H. Fil Dowling Jr., with John Breihan, Virginia Johnson Gazzam, Carl E. Henderson, Gertrude B. Hopkins, Barbara Mallonee, and Sally McNelis. "The Baltimore Area Consortium." In *Programs that Work: Models and Methods for Writing Across the Curriculum*, ed. Toby Fulwiler and Art Young, 273–86. Portsmouth, N.H.: Boynton-Cook.

Warren, James Perrin. *Culture of Eloquence: Oratory and Reform in Antebellum America*. University Park: Penn State University Press, 1999.

Welch, Kathleen E. *The Contemporary Reception of Classical Rhetoric: Appropriations of Ancient Discourse*. Hillsdale, N.J.: Lawrence Erlbaum Associates, 1990.

Whall, Helen M. "Once upon a Time, There Was a Jesuit College without a Core . . ." *Conversations on Jesuit Higher Education* 38 (2010): 10–11.

Worcester, Thomas W., S.J., "The Core: A Musty Relic or a Gift to 21st-Century Students?" *Conversations on Jesuit Higher Education* 38 (2010): 6–8.

Worcester, Thomas W., ed. *The Cambridge Companion to the Jesuits*. Cambridge: Cambridge University Press, 2008

Yancey, Kathleen Blake. *Reflection in the Writing Classroom*. Logan: Utah State University Press, 1998.

THE NEW *ELOQUENTIA PERFECTA* CURRICULUM AT FORDHAM

Anne E. Fernald and Kate M. Nash

In November 2003, Joseph McShane, S.J,. was installed as the thirty-second president of Fordham University, a private, Jesuit university in New York City with an undergraduate enrollment of approximately 8,000. Shortly thereafter, a strategic plan for the future of Fordham was underway. This plan, "Toward 2016," was prepared by the faculty on the Core Curriculum Development Committee and begins with a restatement of Fordham University's mission and a discussion of the role of the core curriculum within that mission.

The new four-course *eloquentia perfecta* requirement, as a central piece of the new core curriculum, emerged in the context of this university-wide curricular self-study, initiated by the administration and carried out by the faculty. Despite the hierarchical origins of the overall change to the core curriculum within the College of Arts and Sciences, support for a stronger and more consistent presence for rhetoric emerged quickly as a common goal, shared by faculty and administration alike, regardless of other disagreements on the overall shape of the curriculum. This chapter describes the aspirations and implementation of the new *eloquentia perfecta* (EP) distributive requirement at Fordham, within the context of a major revision to the core curriculum, with special attention to the development of the curriculum, the role of training, and the function of the syllabus-vetting committee (properly known as the EP Subcommittee of the Core Curriculum Committee).

Fordham University was founded in 1841. It currently enrolls over 15,000 students in ten schools. The *eloquentia perfecta* curriculum applies to students in the College of Arts and Sciences, which is housed on two campuses: Rose Hill in the Bronx, with over 3,600 undergraduates, and Lincoln Center in Manhattan with nearly 1,800 undergraduates. Fordham students in the second decade of the twenty-first century are nearly 53 percent women, and nearly 30 percent of Fordham students are from traditionally underrepresented populations; the largest single minority group at Fordham is Hispanics, who account for 14 percent of the student body (Fordham Facts).

In "Toward 2016," the goals of a Fordham education are divided into five sections (education for: intellectual excellence, freedom, others and respect of difference, leadership, and wisdom). *Eloquentia perfecta*—codified in the *Ratio Studiorum* in 1599—emerges as a central part of the first aspect of the core, education for intellectual excellence:

One purpose of the Fordham University liberal arts core is to enable students to go beyond mere proficiency and achieve a level of excellence in the essential skills of literacy. Excellence in the expressive skills of writing and speaking with logical clarity, that is, *eloquentia perfecta*, is founded on the arts of reading, listening, observing, thinking, and mastery and thorough understanding of the topic under consideration. The first task of the student of the liberal arts is listening and observation for the sake of understanding. Such observation and listening is not, in essence, passive but rather a supremely active engagement of the mind in a genuine conversation.

—Core Curriculum

The Jesuit principle of *eloquentia perfecta* is not new to Fordham University, but a core curriculum with a consistent emphasis on rhetorical training is. Also new is a distributive requirement that ensures that every graduate will take four *eloquentia perfecta* courses over the course of four years, with EP 1 required for all first-years and EP 4 open only to seniors. The old core (the one immediately prior to this 2008 revision) had a major flaw that the new *eloquentia perfecta* curriculum corrects: Despite required courses in composition and rhetoric and two courses each in theology, philosophy, history, and English, it was possible for a student to choose sections with only a limited writing and speaking component. With the new *eloquentia perfecta* curriculum, students cannot avoid active and substantial rhetorical training. Richard Gyug, who served as co-chair of the Core Curriculum Development Committee (CCDC), explains it this way:

> Rhetorical proficiency was a goal of the old core, witness the freshmen seminar. And individual majors had capstones with advanced presentations and writing requirements, which meant that the overall undergrad goal was rhetorical proficiency, but the core was not such a prominent means of achieving that goal. In hindsight . . . intro lectures were probably not a good way to enhance rhetorical skills, and the new core moves to make many of those classes either EP or advanced.

Because instruction in rhetoric has always been an emphasis of the university, the new core is not a reimposition of rhetoric; rather, the new core provides structure around already existing goals. Nonetheless, things have changed substantially since the "three grammar classes" of Fordham's nineteenth-century core (Taaffe, 73).

From the start, the president and administration urged the faculty to consider the university's mission and Jesuit identity in designing the best possible core curriculum for Fordham University.[1] Since faculty have widely varying commitments to the university's "Jesuit-ness," the very request to consider mission and Jesuit identity in reimagining the core raised the widest possible range of responses, from enthusiasm to resistance. One faculty member bluntly stated, "No one in the history department cares about the Jesuit-ness. In fact, no one in the university, except the Jesuits, does" (Ben-Atar). His is a minority view. In practice, most faculty members seem to appreciate the intellectual heritage of Jesuit pedagogy, particularly the focus on writing and rhetoric, some adopting its terms pragmatically, others adopting them out of a sustained intellectual commitment. Mission remained a key term of praise among administrators; by contrast, the principles of an *eloquentia perfecta* curriculum emerged among faculty as a pragmatic, concrete set of principles from which to draw guidelines for our courses.

The first step in revising the core was the selection of members for the Core Curriculum Development Committee (CCDC). The CCDC consisted of the deans of the Rose Hill and Lincoln Center campuses and ten tenured faculty members; it met most intensively during the 2006–7 academic year. Faculty voted on and approved the new curriculum in February 2008, and implementation began in 2009.

While the mandate for reexamination came from the administration, there was substantive faculty participation throughout the revision process. The Core Curriculum Development Committee encouraged responses, both formal and informal, from all department and program chairs as well as individual faculty members, held fora for students on both campuses, met with members of the Jesuit community, and surveyed seniors on their experience of the core. The committee compiled summary documents and made them available to all faculty on a secure blackboard website (where they still reside). From the start, this was a wholesale revision of the entire core curriculum, of which *eloquentia perfecta* previously had been only one part, albeit a substantial one.

FINDINGS OF THE CORE CURRICULUM DEVELOPMENT COMMITTEE

If the administration's primary mandate was to rethink the curriculum in light of the university's mission, the primary concerns that emerged from faculty and students revolved not around mission but around the size of the core and its flexibility. Seventeen departments and programs responded to a survey in the winter of 2005–6. That survey indicated wide (but not universal) consensus that the core as it then stood was too large and inflexible (Winter–Spring Summary of Responses). The requirement-heavy first two years made it difficult for students to explore new fields and discover their intellectual strengths and passions. Respondents raised the possibility of a more even distribution of requirements and greater cohesion across the core. The summary report to the CCDC also noted that "the most commonly mentioned deficiencies are in writing skills and critical thinking" (Winter–Spring Summary Report). This feedback regarding writing, thinking, and speaking, in particular, was pivotal in subsequent discussions about the new core. Once again, in difficult, even contentious discussions, *eloquentia perfecta* appeared a likely site for consensus.

In its outreach to faculty, the CCDC affirmed the desire to promote cohesion across the core by uniting courses in the common goal of *eloquentia perfecta*:

> We will focus the Core Curriculum more sharply on the primacy of the Ignatian tradition in concrete ways such as fully integrating the preparation of students in *eloquentia perfecta*: right reason expressed effectively, responsibly, and gracefully. The renewed core will be smaller, more focused, a true Core. . . . In conjunction with renewing the Core, we will ensure that our broader undergraduate curriculum will be enriched by the opportunities and challenges of New York City with its international heritage and destiny.

In the language surrounding the proposed core, the word *rhetoric* is not especially prominent, nor did the committee often use terms (such as *WAC* and *WID*) current in composition studies. By contrast, the phrase *eloquentia perfecta* was prominent from the start, as was the desire for clearer and more rigorous writing and speaking requirements.

Similarly, in its study of other core curricula, the faculty on the committee paid special attention to how other universities implemented writing requirements. Thus, while rhetoric was not an explicit focus, traditional rhetorical principles, especially those associated with Jesuit education, stood at the heart of what the committee sought to find reflected when it looked elsewhere. While it was clear that the principles of *eloquentia perfecta* should be emphasized across the curriculum, the question remained as to its implementation. To glean information about core curricula on other campuses, peer and aspirant research was conducted. The blackboard website on the core curriculum, a site on which all faculty were included as participants, houses a compilation of documents summarizing the core curriculum at other Jesuit institutions as well as twenty-one other institutions of higher education nationwide, both peer and aspirant. This list of twenty-one included private secular, private Catholic (non-Jesuit), and public colleges and universities including, for example, Amherst, St. John's, Wellesley, and the University of California, Santa Cruz.

In February 2007, the CCDC also distributed a questionnaire to gather information from faculty regarding the direction of the new core. In that survey, one question was included regarding the merits of an interdisciplinary versus disciplinary core, using Harvard, Columbia, Yale, Princeton, Alverno, the University of Dallas, and Providence College as primary examples. While faculty were split as to whether a disciplinary or interdisciplinary core would be most effective, the survey responses yielded new questions regarding the desired outcomes of the core revision. One faculty member noted that the survey itself was framed in terms of process rather than outcomes, writing, "We want someone who can reason clearly and communicate well in English" and "every student meets a standard competency level that can be reached in lots of ways (e.g., courses in literature, logic, rhetoric, writing skills, speech) . . . not to be measured in terms of seat time, but in terms of achievement" (Individual Faculty Responses, 3). Another faculty member noted that above all else "students should be able to read, write, and argue effectively. They should be able to analyze and problem solve complex scientific or social issues. They should have a strong sense of ethics and social justice" (Individual Faculty Responses, 23). Such comments regarding outcomes weighed prominently in the crafting of the new core. If one goal was excellence in writing, then writing should be emphasized across the curriculum. If another goal was to close the gap between those students who may have had training in public speaking in high school versus those who did not, then speaking should be emphasized across the curriculum. In accordance with *eloquentia perfecta*, both would have to be pursued in an active and public manner.

In subsequent debates regarding core structure, various proposals were considered. One initial proposal included a three-part year-long sequence based on the classical trivium in which logic and rhetoric were taught as separate courses in the philosophy department, with grammar taught as a third course by the English department. Another proposal included a four-course sequence in the Catholic intellectual tradition for a more interdisciplinary approach. Those proposals were ultimately eschewed in favor of continuing the composition and rhetoric requirement (and adding Composition One, for our least-prepared students, on the Rose Hill campus) and replacing the two required English classes with a four-course *eloquentia perfecta* requirement, spreading writing instruction across the departments and throughout the entire four years of a college degree.

What had been, from the beginning, a powerful desire to see that all Fordham College graduates emerge with the ability to express themselves, orally and in print, with power and clarity, became a very practical four-semester sequence: four courses, four opportunities to hone the skills of *eloquentia perfecta*, within and outside the major. In their April 2007 report, the CCDC outlined its proposed revision to the core. The goals of the core for "Responsible Freedom in the 21st Century" included providing "students with basic academic skills, a breadth of knowledge, exposure to great works, considerable flexibility and choice, and lasting habits of learning that will make for a good life after graduation," with an emphasis on "highly reflective, integrative habits of learning that together form a wisdom that will grow in students' lives well into the 21st century" (April Report, 11). Upper-level courses would provide "Transitions to Wisdom," preparing students for postgraduate life by "engendering 'big picture thinking' guided by the faculty's teaching of their highest intellectual, world transformative and social values" to engender social responsibility (April Report, 11). The proposed EP sequence charted a movement from entering the conversation, to writing within the disciplines, to interdisciplinary work.

As is evident, continued conversations between departments and across the university and debates within the CCDC culminated in a new core with the principle of *eloquentia perfecta* at its heart. Beyond establishing mere proficiency, these core courses would promote observation, critical thinking, reflection, and oral and written expression.

THE NEW CORE: THE *ELOQUENTIA PERFECTA* SEQUENCE

Since the beginning of the 2009–10 academic year, all students have been required to take four *eloquentia perfecta* (or EP) seminars, spread across their four years, each one limited to nineteen students and each requiring speaking, fifteen pages of final-draft writing, and 20 percent of class time devoted to a pedagogy that fosters student speaking, writing, and critical thinking. Students in these courses spend more time preparing and giving reports, working on writing assignments, and receiving feedback from their instructors and their peers than in other courses. And instructors have the chance to get to know students and provide that feedback because EP classes are restricted to nineteen students. The revised core served to make the implicit explicit. The resulting four *eloquentia perfecta* (EP) seminars are:

EP 1: First-year seminar
EP 2: Texts and Contexts
EP 3: Designated sections of the core, major, or elective requirements
EP 4: Values seminar

In addition to these four courses, students also take a course in composition and rhetoric. Achieving an internal cohesion and creating an appropriate sequence was one main goal of the CCDC. EP 1 introduces students to college-level speaking, writing, and critical thinking; EP 2, primarily taught by English-department instructors, continues the development of written and oral expression and emphasizes social awareness through the study of literature in context. The subsequent EP 3 course is an upper-level seminar, enriched by special attention to writing and speaking, and the final, EP 4 course, always also a course in values and ethics, encourages students to look outward, recognizing interrelationships among ways of knowing in the world. Because these courses come from across the university and are distributed across the undergraduate experience, the *eloquentia perfecta* sequence enacts both writing across the curriculum and writing in the disciplines, with an end goal of erudition in speaking and writing directed towards the common good. As students move through the curriculum, their critical-thinking skills are engaged to develop moral discernment and social responsibility. In particular, the capstone Values Seminar, EP 4, challenges students to use these skills to tackle contemporary moral issues.

The CCDC surveys not only helped to craft the current EP core but also shaped its internal structure. In a January 2007 email survey of seniors, which yielded twenty-seven responses, a common thread was a desire for a smaller, more flexible core. One student's response that students should have a choice among sections of English core classes became a powerful influence in the development of Texts and Contexts, or EP 2. Sections of this course in literary analysis, housed in the English department (with occasional sections taught by instructors in classics, literary studies, and modern languages), are now listed with subtitles such as "The Afterlife of Austen," "The Phenomenon of Oprah's Book Club," and "Minding the Body." It took the department a few years to get this right: A new online registration system, the course's frequent reliance on adjunct and graduate-student teachers who may get their teaching assignments after registration, and faculty overburdened by administration conspired to mean that, for a while, the subtitles were invisible to students. Now that students register for specific topics, the associate chairs hear loud complaints when an instructor (and therefore a topic) changes at the last moment: Such complaints may be our clearest indicator of how powerfully students like having this small measure of choice.

ONGOING IMPLEMENTATION AND THE DEVELOPMENT OF STUDENT AND FACULTY RESOURCES

In this new core, a faculty committee reviews each EP syllabus, and each EP course must devote a minimum of 20 percent of classroom time to speaking, writing, and critical thinking, including a minimum of fifteen pages of final-draft writing. The writing requirement was designed to emphasize the writing process, particularly revision, and to ensure that students wrote a minimum of two graded papers in each EP class, thereby giving each student a chance to learn from (and improve on) at least one prior graded assignment from that instructor. Fifteen pages was deemed sufficient to count as writing-intensive while respecting the challenges of writing longer papers in non-writing intensive disciplines (such as mathematics) and without overburdening faculty. Students *must* take four EP classes—meeting the faculty's desire for rigor. EP 1, 3, and 4 classes run across the curriculum, and EP 2 classes, mostly taught by the English department, are topics-based—offering undergraduates some of the flexibility they desire.

One important support mechanism for faculty teaching the EP curriculum was the Center for Teaching Excellence (CTE). Its role in training has shifted significantly since the core was first implemented a few short years ago. When the core was initially rolled out, the CTE offered a series of workshops for faculty to explore and share innovative methods of teaching speaking and writing in EP courses, mostly led by the writing director for Lincoln Center on the Lincoln Center campus (Fernald) and by the director of the Center for Teaching Excellence on the main, Rose Hill campus (then the associate director, Erick Kelemen). However, from the beginning, there was disagreement as to whether faculty ought to be required, or only encouraged, to attend the workshops. At the same time, there was a strong support for requiring doctoral students to attend workshops before teaching an EP class. The English department refused mandatory participation outright, on two grounds: first, that the pedagogical techniques of EP courses were central to the department's pedagogy, and second, on the grounds of academic freedom. Nonetheless, faculty participation at the CTE workshops was strong in the first year of the core. As faculty members have become more familiar with the core, the CTE has adapted by offering individual consultations rather than large-scale workshops. More recently, the CTE has begun offering hour-long teaching seminars to advanced doctoral students who will be teaching *eloquentia perfecta* courses. These seminars, offered within individual departments, combined with individual consultations, particularly for incoming faculty, look to be the primary mode for transmitting the principles of *eloquentia perfecta* moving forward. Unfortunately, the provost disbanded the CTE in spring 2014. It is impossible to know what—or if—a new pedagogy center will support *eloquentia perfecta*.

On the administrative side, all teaching faculty, regardless of rank, are now required to submit their EP syllabi to the EP Subcommittee of the Core Curriculum Committee for vetting. This, too, has met with some resistance from our most fervent advocates of academic freedom. The committee confers via email, with two faculty members commenting on every syllabus. In the first few years of the new core, the committee read an average of ten syllabi each semester. These were, almost without exception, thoughtful, detailed, well-conceived syllabi with creative and dynamic approaches to fulfilling the EP requirements. As full implementation of the core began, however, it became necessary for all existing senior Values Seminars to obtain the EP 4 designation. This resulted in a deluge of submitted syllabi in the fall of 2011.

Whereas in prior semesters the committee had seen, at most, a dozen syllabi, the EP Subcommittee read 114 syllabi submitted during the summer and fall of 2011. The small subcommittee expanded to double its original size (from four to eight) to account for the one-time increased workload. Unfortunately, our failure to anticipate this inevitability was only made worse by a patchwork of technology: Syllabi came in via paper and email, sometimes to a dean, or her assistant, or a prior chair of the subcommittee. Nonetheless, the committee performed its work with great goodwill and, in the end, approved 83 courses outright. Courses that needed revision or received a split decision from the committee were *not* approved. Many courses were approved on the condition that the instructor follow one or more suggestions as explained by committee members in the individual evaluations. These latter proposals, marked "yes with revision," were sufficiently strong to give the committee confidence that the instructor could easily make the small changes. In approving syllabi, the committee took the minimum requirements for an EP class (20 percent of class time devoted to writing, speaking, and critical thinking, fifteen pages of final-draft writing) very seriously and the majority of rejected syllabi failed to meet these minimum requirements (or, in the case of papers with varied length requirements, made it possible for a lazy student to shirk the minimum). Thus, syllabi were rejected for the following reasons:

> Syllabi that did not give a chance for revision on at least some short papers were sent back for revision. Not every single response paper needs to be revised, but there should be a strong message about revision running through the course.
>
> Courses that assigned a single fifteen-page paper were seen as not within the spirit of an EP course, even with substantial process deadlines.
>
> "Discussion" was not judged sufficient to fulfill the speaking requirement, as all EP courses are seminar-style: We looked for, at a minimum, one formal speaking occasion for each student. (This was an issue especially for EP 4 classes.)
>
> Cover sheets that did not show us how critical thinking was happening, even allowing for a wide range of methodologies across disciplines, were sent back for revision. In particular, syllabi that had only one type of writing assignment (especially if that was summary- or report-style writing) or relied on a single textbook, or only on artistic texts without any critical ones, were, in some cases, sent back for revision.

Faculty whose courses were rejected often reacted with good grace, but occasionally with anger and frustration. One objected, "If you 'script' a syllabus as thoroughly as the EP Committee wanted, you leave no room for the kind of spontaneity which I have always made room for in my pedagogy" (Naison). Sometimes, a faculty member would make clear that he or she genuinely did not understand the reasons for requiring drafts of papers, and such conversations became an occasion for explaining basic principles of writing pedagogy.

Because some EP 1 and EP 2 courses are taught by doctoral students, the Teaching Practicum, cotaught by Fernald and Moshe Gold, the writing director at Rose Hill, focuses on tangible methods of facilitating speaking and writing in classes. The Practicum begins with an analysis of the classical trivium and the way in which logic, rhetoric, and grammar are inextricably linked. When teaching composition, these doctoral students are encouraged to assign shorter essays at the beginning of the semester, to allow students to explore logical techniques and hone rhetorical moves, all while refining their grammar. In accordance with *eloquentia perfecta*'s goal of fostering the common good, longer essay assignments at the end of the semester include crafting a creative solution to a contemporary problem of social injustice and researching an aspect of New York City's history.

Teaching a section of EP 2 has become a wonderful opportunity for Fordham's PhD candidates in English, most of whom fulfill the obligations of their fellowship and receive their pedagogical training by teaching composition and rhetoric. The English department now tries to give each doctoral student at least one semester of EP 2 so that students will have had the experience teaching literature. Still, most full-time faculty fulfill their obligation to contribute to the core through EP 2; nonetheless, about 30 percent of composition and rhetoric classes are taught by full-time faculty on each campus. At Rose Hill, where graduate students are based, they teach half of the composition and rhetoric classes, with adjuncts teaching the remainder; the proportions are inverted in writer-rich Manhattan, with adjuncts (often independent scholars or young poets with prestigious MFAs and a passion for teaching) teaching about half of composition and rhetoric. Like many institutions, composition and EP 2 are, by far, our most adjunct- and graduate-student-dependent courses, but the proportions described here, if not ideal, do make for a rich range of sections and a diverse and dynamic community of teachers.

The Jesuit Pedagogy Seminar, an interdisciplinary colloquium, is yet another opportunity for graduate students to explore Jesuit pedagogy and employ it in the courses that they teach. Each graduate student who participates in the seminar is mentored by a faculty member from a different discipline in the School of Arts and Sciences. This kind of cross-disciplinary pairing and opportunity for collaboration fosters an exploration of the way in which Jesuit principles can be found across the university. At the conclusion of the seminar, each graduate student presents on an aspect of Jesuit pedagogy and discusses how it has been applied in the course that he or she has been teaching that semester.

The CTE supported faculty and graduate students; the Practicum and the Jesuit Pedagogy Seminar offer further support to graduate students. Undergraduates, too, have additional opportunities to work on their rhetorical skills. One is the Matteo Ricci Seminar, launched in 2010–11 at the Lincoln Center campus. Faculty members nominate high-achieving sophomores and juniors for participation in a biweekly seminar where they discuss and debate issues in the contemporary world and the creation of a more just society. While the focus of the first semester is on dialogue and continued excellence in rhetoric, the goal of the second semester is to connect students with research opportunities and fellowship programs. This seminar provides Fordham students, many of whom have great intellectual ability but lack the economic advantages of some of their peers, a chance to acquire the final intellectual skills—of both polish and depth—that will allow them to excel in the most competitive settings.

Because many of these programs and the Core itself have been newly developed, their assessment is ongoing. For each EP course, essays have been selected for evaluation, with the end goal of tracking improvements in writing over time. Fernald developed a rubric for assessing EP 1 and EP 2, using five learning goals from the university's *eloquentia perfecta* documents: (1) distinctness, quality, and development of thesis, (2) analysis of evidence and critical thinking; use of evidence to support claims and thesis, (3) writing organization: global, (4) writing organization: paragraph. Learning goal 5 for EP 1 is grammar and mechanics; for EP 2, Texts and Contexts, it is the use of a contextual source to meaningfully enrich a reading of a literary text. Unfortunately, the dissolution of the CTE and an overworked assessment officer have delayed the process of assessing what we have collected.

ELOQUENTIA PERFECTA AT FORDHAM IN THE TWENTY-FIRST CENTURY

Eloquentia perfecta is certainly the end goal of a Fordham education, but excellence in writing and speaking can be developed only over time. In a Jesuit education, activity is demanded of students, with an insistence "placed on the genuine formation of human faculties rather than the amassing and learning of facts" (Farrell, 402). The *eloquentia perfecta* distributive requirement at Fordham serves to do just that, in an ongoing manner. As more students move through the new curriculum, we continue to assess its efficacy, with the end goal of creating expressive and socially conscious men and women for others.

NOTE

1. Anne Fernald participated in such a discussion, facilitated by a senior member in the philosophy department, at new faculty orientation on August 26, 2004. In that meeting, the facilitator distributed a copy of Fordham's mission statement to a small group of new faculty members, of varying ages and from across the university's divisions, and we were asked to discuss it.

WORKS CITED

Ben-Atar, Doron. "Re: EP History Question." Email to Anne Fernald. March 5, 2012.
"Core Curriculum." Undergraduate Bulletin: 2014–2016. Fordham University, Accessed February 25, 2015.
Core Curriculum Development Committee. April Core Report. April 16, 2007.
———. Individual Faculty Responses. 2007.
———. Outreach to Faculty Members. Fall 2006.
———. A Summary of Emails to Corerevision@Fordham.edu From Seniors. January 7, 2007.
———. Toward 2016—Fordham's Liberal Arts Core Curriculum. 2008.
———. Winter 2005–Spring 2006 Core Questionnaire Summary Report to CCDC.
———. Winter 2005–Spring 2006 Core Questionnaire Summary of Responses.
Farrell, Allan P. *The Jesuit Code of Liberal Education: Development and Scope of the Ratio Studiorum.* Milwakee: Bruce, 1938.

Fernald, Anne. Report of Summer 2011 and Fall 2011 EP Syllabus Submissions. February 6, 2012.

Fordham Facts. www.fordham.edu. Accessed September 3, 2012.

Grimes, Dean Robert. Personal interview. 14 Mar. 2012.

Gyug, Richard. Re: EP History Question. Email to Anne Fernald. March 5, 2012.

Naison, Mark. "The EP Subcommittee and My Affirmative Action Seminar—How Scripted Curricula Stifle Creative Teaching." *With a Brooklyn Accent.* Mark Naison. Accessed April 25, 2012.

Taaffe, Thomas Gaffney. *A History of St. John's College, Fordham, N.Y.* New York: The Catholic Publication Society, 1891.

JESUIT RHETORIC AND THE CORE CURRICULUM AT LOYOLA MARYMOUNT UNIVERSITY

K. J. Peters

In March 2011, the Loyola Marymount University faculty voted for a new core curriculum, the prescribed set of courses every LMU student must take.[1] During one of the last meetings of the Core Curriculum Committee before the vote, members considered final responses to the new core courses that had been posted on a discussion board. The first concerned *Eloquentia Perfecta*, or the EP course, the proposed replacement for ENGL 110 "College English." One faculty member quipped, "*Eloquentia Perfecta* sounds like something taught at Hogwarts."

After the laughter died down, the committee started tossing around alternative titles. Rhetorical Arts won the day. There was no discussion of the fact that the title was a response to the perceived need to return to Jesuit tradition, a need for a return that had initiated the core revision. There was no recall that the title *Eloquentia Perfecta* was drawn directly from the *Ratio Studiorum*. After five years of debate on many aspects of the new core, arguing over a course title was clearly inopportune. The joke that shifted *Eloquentia Perfecta* to "Rhetorical Arts" may seem a small thing.[2] The joke was funny, it fell easily to hand, and it had the persuasive force to reduce the Jesuit rhetorical tradition to a fantasy-literature nerd check. Looking back, I now understand that much more was at play.

From 2008 until 2012, I was an ex offico member of the Core Curriculum Committee (CCC), appointed by the chief academic officer to consult on the topic of college writing.[3] To aid in my recollection of the story of *Eloquentia Perfecta* and the fate of the EP course, I rely on the published CCC minutes, reports, internal committee emails, and my own memory and notes of committee discussions, and I triangulate these sources of information with the memory of my fellow faculty member Steven Mailloux, appointed to the CCC in the fall of 2010.[4]

The Hogwarts joke was one of the final moments in a long process. Yet, I now see it as a distillation of worrying conditions and trends that, while allowing Jesuit educational principles to persist as ideals, attenuates them during curricular revisions. The first condition concerns the process itself. If contemporary curricular revision is a product of faculty debate and a transparent process, the resulting curriculum will be shaped by disciplinary thinking, departmental ambition, and individual dispositions that can speak in the moment.

The most disturbing trend concerns the voices that do not or cannot respond to the call for a new Core. First among these quiet voices are the rhetoric and humanities professors dispersed long ago when *studia humanitatis* splintered into the isolated disciplines of rhetoric, communication, philosophy, and literature (the rudiments of *eloquentia perfecta*). As a result, there is no single discipline or department that can promote, claim, or protect *eloquentia perfecta* as its turf. In addition, the ever shrinking Jesuit presence means that there are fewer who can argue with authority from the Jesuit tradition or history. Finally, the great horde of contingent instructors, who often carry the larger burden of the Core, have no standing in core-curriculum discussions.

Having observed the revision process at LMU, I am convinced that Jesuit principles of higher education will persist mainly as curricular aspirations and as phrases used in executive summaries. I am equally convinced that the hurly-burly of curricular debate will be shaped not by relevant research, discernment, and a serious contemplation of what formation means for a contemporary university. Rather, the qualities of a new Core will be determined by the rush to meet the call for a new Core by those who can and want to reimagine Core education. As the Hogwarts joke demonstrates, the initial motive that drives a revision of Core education at a Jesuit university can become archaically charming and irrelevant compared with the disciplinary, departmental, and individual perspectives that animate committee discussions.

1993–2011: DISCOVERING WHAT HAS BEEN LOST

Curricula are always under construction. Jesuit curricula have been revised in subtle and important ways for four hundred years. In the past twenty-five years, LMU has tried to revise its core three times: in 1988, 1993, and 2011. Our new Core is a significant revision, initiated in 2003 owing to external and internal concerns. During the accreditation process, the Western Association of Schools and Colleges asked the CCC to "address how directed student learning outcomes [student work products] are used as a basis for assessing effectiveness of the core" (CCC, "Summary"). Internal concerns with the Core had been voiced for a number of years, eventually moving the CCC to sample campus opinions.

Over the following few years, the CCC and the office of LMU Assessment began to gather internal perceptions of the current Core through interviews of graduating seniors (2003), faculty, and staff (2004). After three more years of conversations and small group interviews, the CCC compiled its findings in two documents, a detailed report spanning 2003–5 and a one-page summary of findings spanning 2003–7.[5]

Both reports described consistent and wide-ranging dissatisfaction with the current Core. The topics of concern ranged from questions of diversity to technology. However, both reports framed the range of topics and questions with a single theme—mission failure.

> The core curriculum does not adequately embody the mission, goals, and objectives of Loyola Marymount University, including but not limited to the following: education grounded in critical discernment, a faith that does justice, education of the whole person, education that values the person as individual, and a life of learning and service.
>
> —Core Curriculum Committee, "Improving," 1–2

The disconnect between the mission of the university and the curriculum of the university was voiced by every sector of the community surveyed.

With significant fidelity, these complaints and the implicit desire for a clear curricular embodiment of our mission echo the goals of the early Jesuit educators as defined in the *Ratio Studiorum* and as articulated in the principles of *eloquentia perfecta*. In this volume, David Leigh, S.J., explains that the primary goal of an early Jesuit education was to develop individuals intellectually, morally, and religiously prepared to do justice and serve their community as leaders (Part I). Not all members of the LMU community may have been as well versed in Jesuit ideals as the reports suggest. Nevertheless, the clarity with which the reports' findings reflect Jesuit principles of education and student formation demonstrates that an understanding of these principles was not only present but also the primary argument for core revision.

In 2008, the CCC drafted the "Philosophy and Goals" statement for the core. Soon after, faculty were asked to develop, individually or in teams, visions of the Core and to present those visions during an open forum. In the fall of 2009, the CCC created two working groups charged with developing Core models based on the four most popular core visions. A third working group was formed to explore first-year seminars (FYS), as these seminars were common in the Core visions and popular among the faculty.

The working groups' membership reflected the wide-ranging dissatisfaction with the old Core. Significantly, the membership of the working groups also reflected a growing desire within the larger CCC for a truly interdisciplinary Core. The interdisciplinary argument gained traction among the CCC membership and eventually was reduced to an oft-repeated catchphrase—"no one owns the Core." The CCC moved that the working groups would represent each college and school equitably. The deans and the vice president for mission and ministry developed a roster of potential members, and the CCC in consultation with the faculty senate established the final membership (CCC, "Minutes 8.26.09"). An existing member of the CCC chaired each working group.

ELOQUENTIA PERFECTA BECOMES RHETORICAL ARTS

Eloquentia perfecta emerged as a potential guiding concept and structural armature for the new Core in February 2010, during what I now see as the closing of the aspirational stage of Core revision. Mailloux proposed that "*Eloquentia Perfecta* and the Jesuit *Spiritual Exercises* could create the 'through-line' from the first year through the core to capstone courses" (CCC, "Minutes 2.11.10"). Following his suggestion, the CCC charged the working groups with addressing how "they can include and articulate the Ignatian Tradition" (CCC, "Minutes 2.11.10").

The need for an Ignatian "through-line" understood in terms of *eloquentia perfecta* and the *Spiritual Exercises* resonated with the working groups.[6] By April 2010, the CCC working groups had completed a majority of their work and presented their drafts to the CCC. Both of the proposed models made use of a three-part structure inspired by the *Spiritual Exercises*, and both referenced *eloquentia perfecta*.[7] During the CCC meeting of April 11, 2010, the first motion on the floor was to approve a fall semester FYS taught by tenure-track professors with the assistance of writing instructors. The motion passed. The second motion that passed that day approved a spring semester *Eloquentia Perfecta* course linked to the preceding FYS course. The final successful motion of the meeting was to approve the "Foundations," "Explorations," and "Integrations" structure of the Core (CCC, "Minutes 4.11.10"). Significantly, none of the working groups proposed a specific course entitled *Eloquentia Perfecta*, and yet the larger CCC approved an EP course, still undefined, as part of the new Core.[8]

As rhetoricians interested in Jesuit rhetorical and educational history, Mailloux and I were thrilled by the *Eloquentia Perfecta* course. However, we failed to recognize that the ideal of *eloquentia perfecta*, and its vision of intellectual, moral, and religious formation of presumptive community leaders, had shifted from an armature framing the entire Core to a single course. Even the phrase *eloquentia perfecta* was reduced, once the course was approved, to the phonetically more comfortable "EP" course.

Soon we were asking ourselves, how should we actually understand *eloquentia perfecta*, past and present? More urgently, how would we transpose the Jesuit's rhetorical way of proceeding for contemporary, first-year students in one of the most diverse private universities in the United States? Looking back, I now find it odd that after 2007 the CCC did no further investigation of the failings of the existing Core and that the CCC made no attempt to further research the Jesuit tradition and mission or initiate new members into the history of the ongoing revision. During my interview with Mailloux, he could not recall any discussion of the old Core or its failings (Mailloux).[9] Our resistance to reviewing the intentions and failings of the 1993 Core may be explained by the common belief that its shortcomings were well understood. As for a formal investigation into the history or contemporary articulations of Jesuit higher education, I cannot say why the CCC was hesitant other than that we were very busy building the new Core.

Still, what does it mean to base a curriculum on invocations of lightly grasped principles? For example, one of the emphases in our "Philosophy and Goals" states the Core will fulfill LMU's "special role in creating men and women who will be discerning and active members of diverse communities, local and global" (CCC, "New," 1). However, the CCC did not define "discernment" historically or define it in the current nomenclature of contemporary Jesuit colleges and universities. And the committee did not explore the idea of "formation" and the difficult questions it raises concerning agency, academic freedom, ideological acculturation, and the ethics of the asymmetric student–teacher relationship.

Even if the CCC wanted to incorporate *eloquentia perfecta,* a bigger challenge would have been waiting—defining it. And defining *eloquentia perfecta* is difficult. Clearly, it is not just a set of skills or a determined content, but more like the development of a disposition and sensibility that is informed by texts, content, and codified practices that instill rhetorical skills and acumen. At the time, the understanding that Mailloux and I relied on was informed both by the written history of Jesuit rhetorical education (the *Ratio Studiorum* and *Constitutions*) as well as the practices (*Spiritual Exercises* and casuistry) of sixteenth- and seventeenth-century Jesuit educators.

Within four days of the CCC vote that established the course, we drafted a one-page pedagogical description for the CCC's consideration. Our proposal described a course pedagogy founded on three principles: eloquence, erudition, and moral discernment. As is clear in the first draft of our proposal below, we were still wrestling with a definitive pedagogy that would characterize an *eloquentia perfecta* based first-year writing and rhetoric course.

Eloquentia Perfecta

Jesuit education in general and *eloquentia perfecta* more specifically "moves the learning experience beyond rote knowledge to the development of the more complex learning skills of understanding, application, analysis, synthesis, and evaluation." *Eloquentia perfecta* refers to an integrated set of skills, competencies, and knowledges that enable students to engage in public debate with persuasive force and stylistic excellence.

Emerging out of Renaissance humanistic rhetoric, *eloquentia perfecta* developed the Ciceronian ideal of the good person writing and speaking well for the public good. This Jesuit rhetoric holds that the teaching of eloquence should be combined with moral discernment, and thus *eloquentia perfecta* constantly focuses on ethics and communication, virtue and authority, knowledge and social obligation. Traces of Ciceronian rhetoric are most clearly seen in *eloquentia perfecta*'s examination of the practical, social effects of effective articulate expression.

A pedagogy of *eloquentia perfecta* is also informed by the principle of *Tantum Quantum*—continual improvement guided by practical, proven methods and the replacement of ineffective approaches. This pedagogy creatively combines the traditional and the innovative within the rhetorical tradition. For this reason, *eloquentia perfecta* also draws upon modern composition studies and contemporary rhetorical theory.

Outcome objectives for an *eloquentia perfecta* Course can be developed through the conceptual principles of the Spiritual Exercises. The Exercises are intended to result in a perspective and understanding that is incarnational, transforming, and culturally embedded.

INCARNATIONAL: An engagement with otherness and the sublime that is disorienting as it calls into question previous understandings and preconceived ideas.

TRANSFORMATIVE: A movement from a preoccupation with the personal to an awareness of social obligations fulfilled through service, participation, and leadership within public discourse.

EMBEDDED: An understanding that all expressions and acts are culturally embedded and socially significant necessitating a constant examination of the historical context of one's personal beliefs and a consideration of the relationship of the just and the expedient in human action.

—Peters

Our pedagogical description was intended to serve as a point of departure for the ongoing development of the EP course. We did not, however, notice that the moment to explore and implement *eloquentia perfecta* in the new Core had passed.

When the working groups returned a few months later with their models of the Core and a model of a FYS, a different set of concerns rang in our ears. The CCC was behind schedule because the working groups took longer than expected. Unlike the working groups, which had the luxury of debating Core visions with the authors of those visions absent, the CCC was now confronted with two models created by members of the CCC. In addition, rumors about the shape of the future Core had circulated and caused a great deal of interest, entrenchment, and lobbying. The concerns that occupied the CCC during the late spring of 2010 no longer reflected the crisis of the 1993 Core and the perceived disconnect with the Jesuit tradition and our own mission. Rather, we on the CCC were desperate to respond to an increasingly contested debate, a short timeline, and urgent practicalities.

ASPIRATIONS GIVE WAY TO PRACTICALITIES

Three practicalities determined the fate of the EP course. First, the revision process opened the entire Core for reconsideration. As a result, groups that saw the Core as impinging on specific schools and majors joined the debate. Second, the desire for disciplinary representation displaced more holistic aspirations for the Core. Finally, fearful that small groups would militate against the entire Core if they did not achieve concessions, the CCC's attention shifted to accommodation for the sake of a passing vote rather than curricular aspirations for a Jesuit Core.

The first site of contention was the size of a Core curriculum. Professional schools explicitly saw the Core not as a unifying curricular experience and foundation, but as a competitor for hours or credits required by their majors. Since 1993, the Core was composed of fourteen to sixteen courses. For years, the Seaver College of Science and Engineering chafed from what seemed excessive Core requirements and the requirements of its major. Over time, they had successfully reduced the engineering students' Core requirement to nine to ten courses. Early in the Core revision process, the Seaver College administration expressed concern with the size of any proposed Core. Further, it became clear that a majority of the faculty of Seaver College would oppose any Core that was the same size or larger than the existing Core. As Steven Mailloux recalls, "This was a big deal, the discussion went on and on but we eventually had to make this concession; otherwise, there would be no Core. We finally realized we could not get 13 courses, even with a small Core, that everyone would take."

In writing about the Core revision at the University of Detroit Mercy (UDM), D. R. Koukal noted the same pressure exerted by professional programs to reduce the Core or create a "'derivative' Core tailored to their [the professional schools'] own programmatic needs" (53). Koukal argued that derivative curricula marked some students as unworthy of the "broadening function of the general education promised by the Jesuits" (54). At LMU, the reverse appears to have been the case. Biased arguments posed by the administration and faculty of the Seaver College of Science and Engineering cast the Core as an intrusion. As at UDM, the size conflict was resolved, not by reference to the Jesuit tradition, to the practices of other Jesuit universities, or to our mission to educate the whole person, but to the threatened scuttling of the revision process. The new Core would be composed of only thirteen courses, and as in the old Core, there would not be a universally required set of courses because only a twelve-course Core would be required of engineering students. At the time, no courses had yet been proposed and the votes that created the three-part structure, FYS, and the EP course had not happened. And yet at this early point in the revision process, it became clear that a smaller Core created a land rush for the curricular space remaining. And as with any land rush, there would be winners and losers.

Some departments and programs that had purchase in the 1993 Core would lose their stake, and, as "no one owns the Core," other departments saw an opportunity to compete for increasingly contested space. For example, a long-desired requirement of two semesters of a foreign language lost momentum after the smaller, twelve- to thirteen-course Core was established by the CCC. Members of the philosophy department, on the other hand, argued strenuously to retain a very explicit element of the Core. And, as Mailloux recalls, communication studies, not represented in the 1993 Core, "made a concerted effort to make sure its field was represented in a way the English Department did not do" (Mailloux). The study of literature, which had a one-semester presence in the 1993 Core, is not present in the new Core.

Why philosophy demanded to hold on to its seat at the Core table, when English and literature walked away, and why communication studies demanded a new role, is explained in part by the splintering of *studia humanitatis*. United under a humanist dream of the Renaissance, philosophers could speak for eloquence, rhetoricians for aesthetics and style, and literature professors for logic and form. Divided, they are isolated departments competing for scarce resources. The divergent responses of these three departments are also explained by their different levels of participation in the old Core.

After the English department, the philosophy department had the greatest commitment to Core education under the 1993 Core. When making their case to remain a part of the new Core, the philosophy professorate argued from the long tradition of philosophy within Jesuit higher education. It is also true that the philosophy department's participation in the Core, a participation of mostly tenure-track and tenured professors, contributes to the large size of their department and adds weight to arguments for tenure lines and other resources.

In contrast, tenure-track and tenured English professors at LMU have consistently been excused from teaching in the two first-year Core courses, College English and Introduction to Fiction/Poetry/Drama. For some time, part-time instructors have taught Core English courses, leaving English professors to focus on upper-division literature courses. As a result, literature professors saw no need to stake a claim on courses they rarely instructed.

Professors of literature can take this position because English as a departmentally sustained study has become highly specialized and disconnected from rhetoric and composition.[10] No argument was made about the central role of literary studies as a foundation for humanistic education, because there was no such need and no perceived crisis of literature's absence from the new Core. Communication studies was not a required element of the existing Core. However, the department fought hard and successfully to secure such a place. Its path into the Core was the EP course developing during the spring of 2010.

When we drafted the EP pedagogy description and talked about the Jesuit rhetorical tradition with the members of the CCC, Mailloux and I emphasized that EP was a concept emerging from the Jesuit rhetorical tradition, Renaissance humanism, and Ciceronian ideals—the "good man speaking well." The *Ratio Studiorum* of 1599 defines *eloquentia perfecta* as arts of oratory and poetry. However, we initially developed an EP course that emphasized eloquence, erudition, and moral discernment in writing only. We simply did not anticipate that speaking would be a significant component of the new EP course. Communication studies, however, saw in the EP description our reference to the "Ciceronian ideal of the good person writing and speaking well" (Peters) and started lobbying the CCC as an organized group. In the end, we could find no justification for excluding speech from the EP course other than the observation that every hour spent teaching speech was one less hour teaching written composition and moral discernment.

Our position was less than persuasive, primarily because our earlier arguments introducing and defining the concept of *eloquentia perfecta* had already set the terms of the debate. On this occasion, our own practical concerns and disciplinary ambitions reintroduced in EP an essential element that we had intentionally excluded. Though I argued against what I saw as an intrusion, I now see that an EP course must include the teaching of oral eloquence. The question is, Why did I not see it before? As I said above, I was invited to participate in the Core discussion to represent the interest and expertise of composition and rhetoric. As the WPA for LMU, I had long heard the unfounded complaints commonly tossed at writing programs—"Why can't our students write?" It goes without saying, but the external questions and internal concerns that haunt my discipline are very different from those of the communication-studies faculty. I was not thinking *eloquentia perfecta* and formation when I spoke against oral skills in the first year. The crisis I was responding to concerned the need to increase, not reduce, the classroom presence of writing and rhetoric.

By the same measure, communication studies was not purely motivated by a desire to reinvigorate *eloquentia perfecta* and return to its Renaissance roots. The debate was also driven by practical desires. Oral communication as part of the Core claims a place in the consciousness of first-year students looking for majors. In addition, communication studies wanted to be able to make the same argument for resources and tenure lines that had expanded the philosophy department. It is not that the Jesuit educational tradition was not important to either side of the debate, merely that the argument from tradition enabled both communication studies and I to speak to the concerns that arise from our own disciplinary interests and departmental ambitions.

This paper is an attempt to understand what happened to *eloquentia perfecta* at LMU, but it was motivated by embarrassment. I am embarrassed to have tried to define a contemporary *eloquentia perfecta* course and teach moral discernment while ignoring oral skills. I have spent some time wondering why I would attend to the crisis (a lack of respect and accusation of ineffective pedagogy) that had distracted composition studies and WPAs for years, and I believe that the desire for a return to Jesuit educational principles could be satisfied with such a limited understanding. My fear is that the disciplinary training and research interests of the contemporary professorate works against larger, curricular ideals. My fears are mostly borne out by the development of the FYS as a place for individual passions and pursuits.

As stated above, one of the first articulations of the new Core by the CCC was the approval of the FYS course to be offered in the fall of the year followed by the EP course in the spring. Though the FYS course objectives had yet to be developed during the spring of 2010, from the very beginning FYS was perceived as a place where professors would share their research passion with first-year students. The course is also "aimed at improving students' written and oral communication skills"; however, these outcomes are the concern of the attached writing instructor (CCC, "New," 5–6).

The bifurcated FYS course was the least contested and most popular proposed course of the new Core for many reasons. First, FYS courses are limited to nineteen students. Also, the writing instructor provides the discipline professor a great deal of freedom. The new Core document states that FYS professors are to "share the example of life-long commitment to intellectual life and creative activity by developing topics of compelling interest that grow from their own work" (CCC, "New," 6). Beyond that, the Core document is intentionally vague in the hope that open course objectives and prescribed freedoms would make recruitment of FYS professors easier.

Individually, the FYS and EP courses were a significant departure from the existing Core,[11] and, as Mailloux recalls, "the CCC felt pretty good about the structure of the FYS and the EP course with the through-line of the writing instructor and it was thought very innovative" (Mailloux). Ideally, part of the orientation courses and workshops for the FYS professor would include how the seminar would be related to the Jesuit tradition, LMU, and the subsequent EP course.

It is more likely that the writing instructors are the ones receiving training in the Jesuit tradition, since such training can be required of part-time instructors. With the part-time writing instructors serving as the link between the two first-year courses and holding the responsibility for articulating the principles of *eloquentia perfecta*, the pool of potential FYS professors increased beyond those willing to sit for training in the Jesuit educational tradition.

The FYS *EP* sequence is innovative and remains popular. And yet it is also an example of how curricular aspirations can be washed away by disciplinary interests, departmental ambitions, and individual perspectives. If curricular coherence is essential to the multiple sections of FYS and subsequent EP courses, a pliable part-time instructor pool more easily serves the needs of the first-year sequence. However, the CCC's initial understanding of what gave the curriculum coherence was *eloquentia perfecta* and the *Spiritual Exercises* as expressions of the larger Jesuit educational tradition. In addition, a primary driver of the FYS was the sense that first year students were being taught by too many part-time instructors. The "Summary and Reflections" of the CCC in 2007 spoke plainly when it came to part-time instructors. It stated that "overall, it is believed that too many part-time faculty teach in the Core, and there appears to be no system to ensure quality control of these instructors" (CCC, "Improving," 5). Local opinions of the part-time pool of instructors did not change from 2007 to 2011. The concerns that drove Core revision did change. During the spring 2014 semester, 74 sections of "Rhetorical Arts" were offered. Of that number, five were taught by tenured or tenure-line faculty.

There would be no comedy without juxtaposition, and juxtaposition is why the Hogwarts joke broke up the room. It was funny because what was once thought of as a guiding principle in the revision process and structural armature of the new Core seemed, in the moment, as practical as a "Transfiguration" course where young wizards learn Latinate spells. And admittedly, it was funny because it made a space for solidarity in a room that had seen little harmony in the preceding months.

Eloquentia perfecta was an answer to a concern that occupied the CCC in the early stages of Core revision. However, it became a comically inapt response for the very different concerns that occupied the CCC during the final days before the vote.

CONCLUSION

What happened in 1988 and 1993 speaks to what happened to *eloquentia perfecta* in 2011. Our history shows that when entering the Core revision process, the first instinct for CCC members was to be impelled to action by what appears to be a rising tide of faculty discontent. The second instinct was to recall the Catholic and Jesuit foundation of the university. It is easy to rally around Jesuit principles of higher education, in part because they are often generally drawn and perhaps more generally understood by the professorate. However, as earlier Core revision committees moved from aspirations to objectives to structures and then to courses, the Jesuit principles that had earlier appeared so essential remain abstract principles. It is as if the Jesuit tradition and principles of higher education can only haunt the Core wars; they appear, they impel action and unanimity for a time, but they do not materialize.

At one time, rhetoric was the imprimatur of a Jesuit education. As O'Malley explains us in his foreword to this volume, "rhetoric in the humanistic tradition was not simply a discipline, not simply the culminating discipline, but the discipline that imbued the whole system with its *finality* and gave it a life-shaping force" (my emphasis). The "finality," O'Malley reminds us, of the Jesuit system of education was informed by Cicero's words in *On Duties*: "We are not born for ourselves alone . . . but men are born for the sake of men, so that they may be able to assist one another" (10). As my own arguments for a writing-based EP course demonstrate, my disciplinary concerns and my own experience determined my understanding of rhetoric and my understanding of my duty. Yes, we need to solve practical problems as deadlines loom, and, yes, we must speak for the competencies and knowledge of our disciplines. But who will speak for *eloquentia perfecta*? Who will take the time to define it in all its historical manifestations and potential contemporary, curricular deployments?

The Hogwarts joke was easy, just as it was easy to use *eloquentia perfecta* to rally a committee. On a Jesuit campus, other arguments do not fall as easily to hand. The argument that rhetoric is trans-disciplinary and a foundation of Jesuit education, the argument that *eloquentia perfecta* has a place within the contested space of the contemporary university curriculum, and the argument that the Jesuit "finality" (men and women serving others) should shape Jesuit curriculum—all these are arguments that should be suited to curricular-revision debates on Jesuit campuses. Instead, such arguments haunt curricular revision, but do not materialize; or at least not yet.

I am convinced that the new Core of LMU is innovative and impelled by a desire to invoke our mission in the classroom, and I know that our faculty will rigorously inhabit what is now a collection of documents and descriptions with dynamic teaching, passion, and a principled search for knowledge. However, I also believe the story of *eloquentia perfecta* and the proposed EP course at LMU illustrates the difficulties of bringing aspiration into articulation through core-curriculum revision.

NOTES

1. The faculty voted overwhelmingly to adopt and implement a new Core curriculum for our undergraduate students. Approximately 82 percent of eligible faculty members voted and, of those, approximately 76 percent endorsed the new core.

2. Kevin Clarke, associate editor of *America*, echoed the joke describing *eloquentia perfecta* as "one of the more benign spells cast by Hermione Granger" (Clarke, 13). To be fair, Clarke used this line to start an essay arguing for the continued relevance of *eloquentia perfecta*.

3. I was ex officio because the CCC membership is divided among our colleges, and the seat representing the college of liberal arts was already filled.

4. Steven Mailloux was appointed when the previous liberal-arts college representative stepped down. Mailloux's memories and insights provide a great deal of information as well as texture to the recollections that follow. In addition, the same skills and qualities that made him the perfect appointment to the CCC also make him an excellent source for the recovery of CCC deliberations. Steven Mailloux has my thanks for his contributions to this paper, which are extensive, and my thanks for his support.

5. The longer report was entitled "The Core Curriculum at Loyola Marymount University. Improving the Core: Summary and Reflections," and the single-page summary was entitled "Summary of Key Findings, 2003–2007." The long report, "Improving the Core," established four areas of necessary improvement: alignment with mission, content, infrastructure, and pedagogy and advising.

6. Foundations, Explorations, and Integrations also structure the core curriculum at Santa Clara University, a Jesuit university often identified as a peer competitor of LMU. The Santa Clara core influenced our own discussions, as did the Fordham curriculum and their emphasis on *eloquentia perfecta*. For more on the educational impact of the *Spiritual Exercises*, see Robert R. Newton, "Reflections on the Educational Principles of the Spiritual Exercises" (Denver: Regis University, 1994). http://www .seattleu.edu/uploadedfiles/core/jesuit_education/exercises.pdf. Also, see Ann E. Fernald's and Kate M. Nash's analysis of the Fordham curriculum and *eloquentia perfecta* in Part III of this volume.

7. The three-part architecture of the new core is defined by "Foundation" courses, "Explorations" courses, and "Integration" courses. As the name implies, the six Foundation courses are envisioned as the bedrock of the new core and are intended to provide skills and competencies necessary to the specialized and interdisciplinary approaches that are to inform the Exploration and Integration courses. Four Exploration courses are to build on the skills and competencies developed in the first year and "serve the education of the whole person by inviting students to engage in a critical examination of self, society, and the world through a variety of disciplinary perspectives" (CCC, "New," 9). The three courses that compose the Integrations set are Faith and Reason, Ethics and Justice, and Interdisciplinary Connections.

8. Hereafter *eloquentia perfecta* will refer to the Jesuit ideals of communication informed by moral discernment. *EP* will refer to the short-lived first-year writing course that became the Rhetorical Arts course.

9. The existing 1993 core was posted on the internal LMU Blackboard website and was also described for students in the university catalog/bulletin. In addition, small working groups did circulate papers they found useful, and many members of the CCC investigated the websites of other Jesuit universities, looking for best practices. Still, there was no organized, in-depth historical analysis of what constitutes a Jesuit education.

10. Specialization was made possible in part by the diminution of comprehensive Rhetoric of the nineteenth century.

11. The existing 1993 Core required a sequence of two writing courses of all first-year students. The first writing course was the ENGL 110 College Writing course. The second course of the sequence, typically taken in the spring, was one of three options selected by the student: ENGL 130 Introduction to Poetry, ENGL 140 Introduction to Fiction, and ENGL 150 Introduction to Drama. These were courses designed to develop competencies for making evidence-based arguments while studying style and aesthetics through the literary arts.

WORKS CITED

Clarke, Kevin. "How to Build a Better Student." *America* 204, no. 16 (May 2011): 13–17.
Cicero. *On Duties*. Edited by Miriam Griffin. Translated Margaret Atkins. Cambridge: Cambridge University Press, 2000.
Core Curriculum Committee. "The Core Curriculum at Loyola Marymount University. Improving the Core: Summary and Reflections." Los Angeles: Loyola Marymount University, October 2007.

———. "Minutes 8.26.09." Los Angeles: Loyola Marymount University, February 11, 2010.

———. "Minutes 2.11.10." Los Angeles: Loyola Marymount University, February 11, 2010.

———. "Minutes 4.11.10." Los Angeles: Loyola Marymount University, April 11, 2010.

———. "New University Core Curriculum." Los Angeles: Loyola Marymount University, February 2011.

———. "Preliminary Statement of Goals and Objectives of the Core Curriculum." 3rd draft. Los Angeles, Loyola Marymount University, April 30, 1991.

———. "Summary of Key Findings, 2003–2007." Los Angeles: Loyola Marymount University, October 2007.

Koukal, D. R. "Dishonesty of 'Course Lite': The Battle for a Truly Common Core." *Conversations on Jesuit Higher Education* 39, no. 1 (2011). Accessed February 1, 2011.

Mailloux, Steven. Interview, March 8, 2012.

Peters, K. J. "*Eloquentia Perfecta*: Pedagogical Description." Personal document. Loyola Marymount University, Los Angeles. April 15, 2010.

JESUIT ETHOS, FACULTY-OWNED ASSESSMENT, AND THE ORGANIC DEVELOPMENT OF RHETORIC ACROSS THE CURRICULUM AT SEATTLE UNIVERSITY

John C. Bean, Larry C. Nichols, and Jeffrey S. Philpott

> Jesuit education systematically incorporates methods from a variety of sources which better contribute to the intellectual, social, moral, and religious formation of the whole person. . . . [T]hat which may work better is adopted and assessed while that which is proven ineffective is discarded.
> —Peter-Hans Kolvenbach, S.J., "Jesuit Education and Ignatian Pedagogy," September 2005

Building on a tradition of writing across the curriculum established in the 1980s, Seattle University has strived to develop a multilayered approach for teaching *eloquentia perfecta* within our undergraduate curriculum. Our approach has developed organically over the arc of the past twenty-five years through a variety of related initiatives, with individual elements falling into place either through serendipity or through intentional planning. At several stages in this process, our general-education program (the University Core) has played a key role, including the development of writing across the curriculum in the 1980s and the institution of strategies to reduce dependence on part-time faculty in the late 1990s. In 2013, a new outcomes-focused version of the University Core came online integrating writing, speaking, and rhetorical numeracy across its vertically sequenced modules. Meanwhile, a writing-in-the-majors initiative leading to senior capstone projects has helped integrate rhetorical knowledge and skills across the curriculum of most undergraduate majors. Rhetorical education in both the Core and the majors is also supported by peer tutoring at our large Writing Center. Finally, in recent years our particular approach to outcomes assessment—emphasizing embedded assignments and backward design of the curriculum—has strengthened pedagogical practices related to rhetorical education at Seattle University.

At every stage of its development, rhetoric across the curriculum has been influenced by our institution's Jesuit ethos. Our goal in this chapter is to unpack this Jesuit influence, which is explicitly visible in our Core and university learning outcomes but also emerges implicitly through our campus culture, our awareness of mission, our commitment to service, and our approach to teaching the "whole person." The coauthors of this chapter have all been directly involved in this work and are all rhetoricians: John Bean, consulting professor for writing and assessment, came to Seattle University in 1986 as a specialist in writing across the curriculum; Larry Nichols, a leader in our regional writing-centers community, has been director of the Seattle University Writing Center since 1993; and Jeff Philpott, a rhetoric scholar in communication studies, has been director of our current University Core curriculum since 2005 and has guided the university toward the newly designed, outcomes-focused core that we will describe in detail later in this chapter. For convenience, we will divide our analysis into chronologically arranged subsections beginning with Seattle University's inauguration of an innovative, award-winning Core curriculum in 1986. (For the rest of this chapter, we will call this 1986 core the "old Core," which was replaced by the outcomes-focused "new Core" in 2013.) This historical perspective is important because Jesuit influence is particularly manifest at certain transformative moments in the evolution of our curriculum and teaching practices.

LAYING FOUNDATIONS: BEGINNINGS–1995

Seattle University, as it is now known, was founded in 1891 as a parish school, which became Seattle College in 1898. In its early history, the university offered a curriculum based on the *Ratio Studiorum*, emphasizing English, history, mathematics, theology, philosophy, Latin, and Greek. Renamed Seattle University in 1948, it developed a Core curriculum that was built on a distribution model, along with a required minor in philosophy. That curriculum included courses in both writing and speech. The 1948 curriculum was replaced in 1965 with a narrower Core that emphasized philosophy, theology, English, science, mathematics, and social science. Speech and the classical languages were dropped from this curriculum, and, with the exception of the English courses, an emphasis on rhetoric was no longer visible within the requirements.

In 1986, after several years of grant-supported faculty discussion, Seattle University launched a completely revised, progressive Core curriculum that included required Core courses in each of a student's four undergraduate years, culminating with a senior synthesis course that linked the Core and the major. The development of rhetorical skills was an important goal for the faculty designers of the 1986 Core, who purposely decided to require "a substantial amount of writing" in every core course rather than to create writing-intensive or "W" courses to fulfill a writing requirement. Particular linkages were established between first-year composition and first-year courses in philosophy and literature. Each of these courses was rhetorically rich, shaped by the Jesuit and Catholic intellectual tradition that valued both philosophic inquiry into the nature of the human person and the aesthetic, illuminating power of literature. To help institute this writing-across-the-curriculum mandate, the university hired John Bean, a coauthor of this chapter, to create and sustain the necessary faculty conversations.

WRITING ACROSS THE CURRICULUM AND THE *RATIO STUDIORUM*

During the early years of the 1986 Core, the university used a grant from the Consortium for the Advancement of Private Higher Education to fund writing and critical-thinking workshops for Core teachers and provide released time for Bean to write an in-house book that would serve as a writing-across-the-curriculum guide for teachers in the new Core. Reproduced locally for all faculty, this book featured examples of assignments and critical-thinking exercises from Seattle University faculty and later became the first draft of his widely used Jossey-Bass book *Engaging Ideas: The Professor's Guide to Integrating Writing, Critical Thinking, and Active Learning in the Classroom* (1996; 2nd edition, 2011). In the foreword for this in-house book, Fr. William J. Sullivan, S.J., president of Seattle University, noted:

> In a Jesuit university, the teaching of writing is among the most important things we do. The long history of Jesuit education is characterized by written interpretation of thoughts, facts, events, and ideas. We attempt to pass on to students not only our own and others' interpretations, but also the tools they will need to develop their own. Writing is an active and fundamental tool: through writing, rethinking, and revising, students come to apprehend knowledge and to develop a complex system of personal values.

In writing this book, Bean had numerous conversations with Seattle University Core faculty, many of whom noted similarities between the "active learning" movement in the late twentieth century and the emphasis on student engagement in the *Ratio Studiorum*. In the preface to his in-house book, Bean quoted Superior General Luis Martin, S.J., in his 1893 address to Jesuit students in Holland. Martin insists that the spirit of the *Ratio* is not contained in specific curricular content but in its insistence "first, that activity be demanded of the student, and secondly, that insistence be placed on the genuine formation of the human faculties rather than on the amassing and learning of facts" (quoted in Farrell, 402). This distinction between "genuine formation of the human faculties" and "amassing and learning of facts" seems analogous to the distinction between "deep learning" and "surface learning" in the current pedagogical literature where "deep learning" implies the learner's ability to integrate knowledge with meaningful personal experience, to retrieve the knowledge from long-term memory, and to apply that knowledge to new problems within complex settings (see Bransford, Brown, and Cocking; Nelson, Shoup, Kuh, and Schwarz; Willingham). Bean's preface, as summarized in the accompanying table, pointed to further connections between the *Ratio* and the pedagogical practices underlying writing and critical thinking across the curriculum. This resonance between the *Ratio Studiorium* and "active learning" as promoted in the 1980s pedagogical literature provided a persuasive rhetorical trope for establishing our infusion model of writing across the curriculum in the early years of the 1986 Core.

Principles from the Ratio Studiorum	Active Learning and WAC Pedagogy
"Clear-cut organization of successive objectives to be attained by the student."	Establishing of outcome goals; scaffolding; sequencing of assignments; Hillock's "environmental mode" of instruction
"The use of objection and discussion and, within proper limits, of emulation, as essential parts of the teaching technique, in order to guard against an attitude of passivity or mere absorption of classified information."	Elbow's "believing and doubting game"; in-class debates; imitation exercises; small-group problem-solving; critical-thinking tasks focused on evaluation of alternative solutions
"Making provision for a variety of class exercises, written and oral, to keep interest aroused and to demand of the student evidence of mastery."	Low-stakes writing assignments; class-preparation activities; in-class debates, small-group work, or Socratic discussion; seminar presentations; rigorous standards
"Stimulating at every stage of development of the power of written and oral expression in accordance with the highest ideals of the intellectual and moral order."	All forms of writing or communication activities across the curriculum; focus on argumentation as seeking "best solutions" rather than winning
"Personal interest in and contact with the student for the purpose of inspiring and encouraging him to achieve distinction in both learning and virtue."	Establishing class as a safe place; reducing fear as motivation; promoting personal engagement; teaching to the whole person; creating a peer-tutoring writing center

ESTABLISHING THE WRITING CENTER: A CRUCIAL ELEMENT OF STUDENT LEARNING AND SERVICE IN SEATTLE'S WRITING-ACROSS-THE-CURRICULUM PROGRAM

Our infusion model of writing across the curriculum would not have been feasible without a strong peer-tutoring writing center. The Seattle University Writing Center was started in 1987 through the same grant that sponsored the workshops in writing-across-the-curriculum. In 1993, Larry Nichols, a coauthor of this chapter, was hired as its first full-time director. Each year from its inception until 2009, the Writing Center employed seventeen to twenty-five undergraduate writing consultants who conducted a yearly average of two thousand five hundred one-hour sessions. In 2010, with increased undergraduate enrollment and the Writing Center's move to a new home in the Lemieux Library and McGoldrick Learning Commons, demand for Writing Center services rose dramatically. The center hired a half-time assistant director and increased the number of peer consultants in order to conduct roughly three thousand sessions per year. As part of a very diverse campus, each year the center serves clients from over thirty-five different first languages, with nonnative speakers of English constituting about one-third of its clients.

Becoming a Writing Center consultant is a very selective process. Each year the center selects ten to fifteen new undergraduate consultants from a pool of promising candidates nominated by faculty across the curriculum. Considered professionals in training, new consultants enroll in a tutor-training course during their first fall quarter on staff. This five-credit course, taught by the Writing Center director, engages consultants in the professional literature of rhetoric and composition as a basis for learning and reflecting on their own peer-tutoring practice. As a capstone to the course, consultants conduct a research project aimed at furthering their rhetorical education and knowledge of Writing Center practice. Beyond the course, ongoing observations, discussions, staff meetings, and further research enliven the Writing Center community.

Operating from the belief that effective writing often emerges from dialogic conversation, the Center offers hour-long sessions designed to help students negotiate all phases of the writing process. Consultants work collaboratively with clients to invite and stimulate creative and critical thinking, making the Writing Center a lively crucible for learning—both for consultants and for clients. Additionally, working in the Center affords consultants sustained practice in the Jesuit tradition of combining engaged learning with service. In drawing their clients into conversation, listening empathically, and taking their clients' ideas seriously, consultants help create an intellectual environment that values the "whole person" while contributing to their clients' long-term growth as writers and thinkers. Throughout our history, Seattle University writing consultants have participated in professional organizations; some have had their research published in professional journals, and several have moved on to graduate work in rhetoric and composition. Regardless of their career trajectory, however, most consultants find the intellectual and interpersonal skills they learn in the center to be instrumental in their professional formation.

FALLOWNESS AND REVIVAL, 1995–2008

By the early 1990s, the faculty communities built during the early years of the 1986 Core began to dissipate through faculty turnover and changes in the university culture. No mechanisms had been established to continue writing-across-the-curriculum workshops for new faculty nor to maintain curricular linkages between English and philosophy or other Core disciplines. Moreover, the constitution of the Core faculty changed dramatically in response to new institutional demands for faculty scholarship.

Starting in the early 1990s, Seattle University moved rapidly toward increased publication demands for promotion and tenure. To encourage faculty scholarship, the College of Arts and Sciences reduced teaching loads for tenure-line faculty from seven courses per year to six (quarter system) and instituted a sabbatical program funded by using part-time adjuncts for sabbatical replacements. Whereas the 1986 Core was originally taught almost exclusively by full-time tenure-track faculty, by the late 1990s the Core was taught primarily by part-time faculty most of whom worked for low wages without benefits and without long-term attachment to the university. The early, heady days of writing-across-the-curriculum were now ten years in the past. The early spirit of pedagogical innovation went fallow, and the numerous adjunct teachers hired for the Core had little connection with the university's Jesuit heritage or mission. The next sections tell how we revived some of the old spirit.

THE SOCIAL-JUSTICE MISSION: PROFESSIONALIZING COMPOSITION FACULTY AND INSTITUTING A THEME-BASED FIRST-YEAR WRITING COURSE WITH A JUSTICE FOCUS

To ameliorate the problems caused by a high turnover of adjunct faculty, the College of Arts and Sciences, starting in 1999, began creating full-time Core lecturers with renewable contracts—initially to staff the first-year composition course and then increasingly to staff other Core courses. Although not tenure-track, Core lecturers nevertheless received better pay, full benefits, a measure of job security, and increased status as vital Core teachers welcomed into the long-term university community. In both overt and covert ways, the decision to hire full-time Core lecturers was influenced by the university's Jesuit-inspired mission to create "leaders for a just and humane world." Proponents of Core lectureships used social-justice arguments to make their case to the university administration. They pointed out the unjust working conditions of short-term adjuncts, arguing that teachers of Core courses should receive living wages, full benefits, and reasonable job security within a supportive community that valued their work. While the creation of the Core-lecturer position has not succeeded in addressing all of the issues of equity associated with a tiered faculty system, it has certainly helped elevate both the status and the compensation for a large number of faculty members who provide valuable service to the university.

For its first-year composition program, the English department hired Core lecturers for mission—faculty with strong backgrounds in rhetoric and composition, exemplary pedagogical skills, commitment to the university's mission, and enthusiasm for teaching in the Core. By professionalizing its composition staff, the English department was once again able to create a coherent composition program, which is now influenced by recent scholarship in genre and rhetorical theory and ready to commit to the progressive learning outcomes for first-year composition advocated on a national level by the Council of Writing Program Administrators (WPA). Composition faculty redesigned the first-year writing course as a theme-based seminar, each section of which would emphasize civic issues with a justice dimension such as food politics, immigration, war theory, environment, global poverty, educational policy, and issues of class and gender. This approach is firmly rooted in what composition scholar Richard Fulkerson calls the "rhetorical tradition" within composition studies (in contrast to the expressivist tradition, the formalist tradition, or the "cultural studies" tradition). Typical assignments for the course ask students to enter civic debates, research policy issues, and make persuasive arguments to different audiences in different genres. The course's rhetorically focused pedagogy uses the classical appeals of *logos, ethos,* and *pathos* to teach rhetorical reading, ethical argument, and responsible use of evidence, aligning the program, we feel, with the Jesuit rhetorical tradition of the responsible citizen—the Ciceronian orator-philosopher in the public forum, where rhetorical practice serves the common good.

OUTCOMES ASSESSMENT AND REVITALIZING WRITING ACROSS THE CURRICULUM

As we explained earlier, the early spirit of writing across the curriculum stimulated by the 1986 Core went fallow in the 1990s. What revived it, quite serendipitously, was our particular "embedded assignment" approach to outcomes assessment, which restarted faculty conversations about writing. Although Seattle University was an early national leader in writing across the curriculum, it came late to assessment, not establishing systematic assessment procedures across campus until mandated to do so by external accreditation (gently in 2000 and then forcefully in 2010). Given fierce faculty resistance to assessment in the early 2000s, our provost hired as an outside consultant Barbara Walvoord, whose assessment work was rooted in writing across the curriculum. (Much of her early work was done at Loyola Maryland, another Jesuit institution.)

The assessment process recommended by Walvoord uses faculty-graded assignments already embedded in courses as a means of assessing specified learning outcomes. According to Walvoord, the foundational assessment act is an instructor's grading of a student's performance—an approach that validates an instructor's expertise and allows grades to be used productively for assessments so long as the grades are justified by reference to shareable criteria, usually through a rubric (see Walvoord; see also Walvoord and Anderson,

151–71). Using this approach, an instructor grades an embedded assignment chosen for its focus on a particular learning outcome and reports patterns of student strengths and weaknesses to a community of stakeholder faculty, who then, through a process of backward design, plan ways to ameliorate student weaknesses by improving instructional methods, assignments, or curricular design upstream from the assignment.

Once we began applying Walvoord's approach to students' written work, campus conversations about writing began to change. Departments began to ask how well their seniors could produce "expert insider prose" (a phrase we have adopted from Susan Peck Macdonald) as evidenced in some kind of capstone or capstone-like project. As shown in the work of Anne Beaufort, expert insider prose requires a complex integration of different kinds of knowledge and skills: subject-matter knowledge (both conceptual and procedural), genre knowledge, discourse community knowledge, rhetorical knowledge, and writing-process knowledge. Thus an assessment of expert insider prose is more than an assessment of writing; it is an assessment of a student's integrative ability to do the intellectual work of his or her discipline—in short, to think and write like a historian, economist, chemist, political scientist, or nurse.

Starting in the early years of the first decade of this century, several departments began doing intensive assessment projects focused on disciplinary writing (particularly history, English, finance, economics, and chemistry). In all these departments, assessment projects led to rich faculty discussions that sometimes resulted in significant restructuring of the curriculum to help students move from novice to expert as disciplinary thinkers and writers. Some of these projects resulted in peer-reviewed publications (Alaimo, Bean, Langenhan, and Nichols; Bean, "Backward Design"; Bean and Iyers; Bean, Carrithers, and Earenfight; Carrithers and Bean; Carrithers, Ling, and Bean). Additionally, our approach to assessment began receiving national attention in the pedagogical literature (Walvoord and Anderson, 173–78; Adler-Kassner and O'Neill, 124–29). Seattle University is also featured in the "assessment gallery" of the "NCTE-WPA White Paper on Writing Assessment in Colleges and Universities" (http://wpacouncil.org/whitepaper).

Despite the success of these projects, they represented only the work of isolated departments rather than reflecting a systematic approach to assessment across the whole university. The processes we have taken to scale up our model to all undergraduate majors and to adapt it to our Core curriculum are described in the final sections of this chapter.

COMMUNITIES OF ASSESSMENT: *ELOQUENTIA PERFECTA* ACROSS THE CORE AND THE MAJORS, 2008–2012, WITH A VISION FOR THE FUTURE

To help us scale up our use of embedded assignment assessment projects, the university received a major Teagle Foundation grant aimed at developing "communities of assessment" within the majors and the Core. Like the previous grants, the Teagle funding helped the university develop capabilities and expertise that would then infuse work supported by normal university funding. In our Teagle grant proposal, we defined a "community of assessment" as a group of stakeholder faculty who are committed to the learning outcomes they set for students and who have the time, the support, and the power to design and improve curricula and teaching methods to help students achieve the outcomes. We recognized from the start that it is easier to create such communities within the majors, where faculty clearly own the curriculum and are committed to disciplinary learning outcomes for students, than in the Core, where outcomes are broader, cut across many different disciplines, and often don't feel owned by identifiable faculty.

We'll turn first to the way that we addressed this problem in the Core curriculum.

RHETORIC IN THE NEW OUTCOMES-FOCUSED CORE CURRICULUM

Our new Core curriculum is designed to address two essential problems in our old 1986 Core: First, despite its innovative design, the old Core was only loosely tied to specified learning outcomes, and second, its required courses were housed within—and effectively controlled by—individual departments rather than by the faculty as a whole or by the University Core leadership. Thus the math department owned the required Core math course, the English department owned the composition and literature courses, and so forth. The lack of clearly specified Core outcomes, combined with a weak Core governance structure, meant that there were no effective mechanisms for coordinating instruction across Core courses; neither were there stakeholder faculty who identified with the Core rather than with their individual departments. We needed to create a new Core structure that was designed around learning outcomes rather than around individual courses and that provided governing mechanisms for coordinating the courses to achieve the outcomes.[1]

This crucial difference can be illustrated with mathematics. The old Core specified that all students take a single math course higher than high-school algebra; the Core did not provide any additional details regarding the objectives of this course. In contrast, the new Core identifies "quantitative literacy" as a Core learning outcome. We have defined quantitative literacy as students' ability to understand quantitative information; make sound mathematical arguments;

interpret, evaluate, and create probability-based claims; read and create graphs and tables; and apply mathematical knowledge in non-mathematics courses. Embedded in this definition is a desire for our students to learn to approach numbers rhetorically. The new Core still includes a required math course, but this course has been newly designed to focus explicitly on these quantitative literacy skills. In addition, the Core also has two other courses in the curriculum that require interpretation of quantitative data and the effective use of numbers. Students' quantitative literacy will be assessed so that the University Core leadership and stakeholder faculty committed to quantitative literacy will be able to use those results to make "closing the loop" recommendations for refining learning objectives or improving course modules, assignment design, or pedagogy.

To be sure, developing this new Core involved a lengthy and often politically charged process that is still unfolding. Our objective was to design a Core that achieved specified outcomes, that incorporated best practices based on current research in higher education, and that remained true to the university's Jesuit Catholic character. Eighteen months of design work, with broad participation by faculty, students, and staff, led to the development of learning outcomes and a curriculum design that were endorsed in 2011 by a majority of faculty and approved by both the university's academic assembly and board of trustees. The new Core was fully implemented by fall of 2013.

Our Jesuit, Catholic heritage insured that incorporating rhetorical knowledge and skills in the new Core was a priority from the beginning. Whereas the writing-in-the-majors initiative focuses primarily on "expert insider prose" in students' academic disciplines, we wanted to set broader rhetorical goals for the Core, and a key to doing so was to develop learning outcomes that explicitly identified rhetorical knowledge, skills, and values. Thus, "effective communication" became one of the four broad learning outcomes for the new core, calling for students to develop a broad set of rhetorical *knowledge, skills,* and *values.* For rhetorical *knowledge,* students develop an understanding of the relationships among the rhetorical variables of "situation, author or source, intention or goal, audience, message, reception or effect, and medium." A variety of communication *skills* are identified, including the ability to write with "clarity and elegance" and develop "advocacy skills." The skills outcome also focuses on developing students' rhetorical flexibility, including the "ability to write in multiple genres with emphasis on persuasion, argumentation, and reflection; [the] ability to suit form of communication to content; [and the] ability to communicate in different rhetorical contexts." The *values* objective calls for students to appreciate "the importance of communication in everyday life." In short, we've attempted to integrate key elements of *eloquentia perfecta* into the pedagogical design of the new curriculum.

Individual courses in the new Core are being designed to ensure that students receive systematic instruction and practice in developing these skills, knowledge, and values. As in the previous 1986 Core, we have continued with an infusion model of writing across the curriculum, which we can now more properly call "rhetoric across the curriculum." In our new Core, writing and rhetorical instruction remain anchored in a one-quarter composition course (retitled the "Academic Writing Seminar") focused on an engaging issue that provides the subject matter for students' development of reading and writing skills.

Building from this introductory course, all Core courses require writing. Some of these explicitly build on the knowledge and skills learning in the Academic Writing Seminar, including more complex use of genres learned in the seminar, the introduction of new genres (for example, writing and speaking for civic contexts), or more extensive and sophisticated use of research. As mentioned previously, the new Core also features a strong quantitative literacy focus with some assignments explicitly asking students to analyze quantitative material, create data-based arguments, and create and interpret graphs and tables. Finally, selected courses throughout the Core require reflective writing assignments—which focus on wrestling with complex questions, synthesis of previous learning, and discernment.

While a number of faculty believe that a Jesuit core curriculum should include at least one course on oral rhetoric (including the analysis of important historical speeches), it was not possible to include this requirement in the new Core curriculum. However, oral presentations are built into four of the new courses, including several in the freshman year.

A strong feature of the new Core curriculum is that it includes mechanisms to support faculty efforts to teach rhetorical knowledge and skill. Because very few faculty across the curriculum have significant training in rhetoric (either composition or rhetorical theory) or in teaching oral communication, the new Core has a budget for ongoing faculty workshops. Given our infusion model of rhetoric across the curriculum, faculty from a wide variety of disciplines will have direct responsibility for incorporating rhetorical education into their courses. Faculty development workshops will focus on key principles of rhetoric and help teachers design effective pedagogy, assignments, and grading rubrics. These workshops will also help Core teachers coordinate with the Writing Center to maximize students' engagement with course assignments. Our goal is to make rhetorical thinking and practice a common feature across the university Core experience.

SUSTAINING THE WRITING IN THE MAJORS INITIATIVE THROUGH UNIVERSITY OUTCOMES ASSESSMENT

Beyond the Core curriculum, *eloquentia perfecta* is further promoted in our writing in the majors initiative, which is sustained through systematic outcomes assessment. The Teagle grant that funded discussions for the new Core also helped us institute embedded assignment assessment projects within most disciplines on campus. Over four years of Teagle grant funding (2008–11), Bean and Nichols, coauthors of this chapter, joined with reference librarians to conduct two-day "writing in the major" workshops for faculty in twenty-two different undergraduate majors. (For a detailed description of the theory and practice of these workshops, see Bean, "Backward Design.") Workshop faculty identified the skills and knowledge needed for seniors in their majors to produce "expert insider prose" and, through the process of backward design, began developing instructional modules and assignment sequences needed earlier in the major to prepare students for capstone work. The workshops helped faculty abandon the myth that learning the "research paper" in first-year composition transfers effectively to research writing in a discipline. Rather, subject-matter faculty themselves took on the task of teaching new majors how to do disciplinary thinking, writing, and research. They developed strategies to teach disciplinary uses of evidence; they also designed strategies to teach the information literacy and rhetorical reading skills needed for posing disciplinary problems, reviewing the discipline's scholarly literature, and staking out disciplinary claims or hypotheses.

The experience gained in these workshops has led to procedures now required by the University Assessment Committee for each major's annual assessment project and report. From 2010 to 2012, almost every undergraduate major in the College of Arts and Sciences and in most disciplines in other colleges used embedded writing assignments (or speaking assignments) as direct evidence of student learning for a variety of disciplinary learning outcomes. (Those that didn't use embedded writing assignments were the performance disciplines focused on performance projects—visual arts, music, or theater—but even these often included reflective writing as part of the assessment.) In some cases, a disciplinary assessment project focused directly on a writing or communication skill. For example, the English department assessed the quality of researched interpretive papers written for capstone senior literature seminars while faculty in art history assessed the quality of students' researched oral presentations (aimed at an informed museum audience) on a chosen painter. Other departments used embedded writing assignments to assess content outcomes within the discipline. For example, the history faculty used an assigned formal essay to assess students' ability to look at a historical phenomenon through a theoretical lens—in this case, to apply feminist theory to a nineteenth-century travel document written by a woman. In a similar way, faculty in women's studies used an essay exam question to assess students' transfer of learning about "intersectionality." This use of embedded assignments has strongly encouraged faculty to think about their discipline from a rhetorical perspective, helping them recognize the value of having students write in more than one genre and increasing faculty focus on the quality and sequencing of writing or speaking assignments throughout the curriculum.

Combined with the Core's emphasis on writing and speaking, the writing in the majors initiative has helped students develop strong basic writing skills and then expand their rhetorical flexibility in order to be able to communicate effectively in a variety of contexts: professional, personal, and civic.

CONCLUSION

Inspired by our Jesuit ethos and by the long history of ancient rhetorical instruction coded into the *Ratio Studiorum,* Seattle University's work in curriculum design, writing instruction, hiring for mission, and outcomes assessment has helped create important faculty conversations about the role of rhetoric in our students' education. As those conversations have proceeded over the past quarter century, our conscious awareness of our Jesuit character has nurtured a growing emphasis on a rhetorical education rooted in the key principles of *eloquentia perfecta*: the thoughtful application of specific rhetorical principles and skills to unique situational demands, the inexorable connection between critical thinking and communication, and a profound appreciation for the role of communication as a vehicle for leadership and positive social change. While rhetoric and *"eloquentia perfecta"* have not always been highlighted in either the university's public image or internal culture, the organic and sometimes serendipitous character of our path has resulted in a quietly strong and pervasive emphasis on rhetorical education, and that path may be instructive for other institutions. By maintaining a focus on our Jesuit identity and the role of rhetorical education in that tradition, we've made substantial progress in connecting what could have been discrete and separate initiatives into a more coherent and purpose-driven whole.

NOTE

1. Key elements in improving the governance of the new University Core include establishing clear and agreed-on guidelines and objectives for each Core course, using a curriculum committee composed of faculty members from a wide range of disciplines to review and approve courses for inclusion in the curriculum, and designating all Core courses with a common departmental code (UCOR, for University Core). A broadly representative faculty Core governance body is also being created.

WORKS CITED

Adler-Kassner, Linda, and Peggy O'Neill. *Reframing Writing Assessment to Improve Teaching and Learning.* Logan: Utah State University Press, 2010.

Alaimo, Peter J., John C. Bean, Joseph Langenhan, and Larry Nichols. "Eliminating Lab Reports: A Rhetorical Approach for Teaching the Scientific Paper in Sophomore Organic Chemistry." *WAC Journal* 20 (2009): 17–32.

Bean, John C. "Backward Design: Towards an Effective Model of Staff Development in Writing in the Disciplines," 215–36. In *Writing in the Disciplines*, ed. Mary Dean and Peter O'Neill. London: Palgrave, 2011.

————. *Engaging Ideas: The Professor's Guide to Integrating Writing, Critical Thinking, and Active Learning in the Classroom.* 2nd ed. San Francisco: Jossey-Bass, 2011.

Bean, John C., David Carrithers, and Theresa Earenfight. "Transforming WAC through a Discourse-Based Approach to University Outcomes Assessment." *WAC Journal* 16 (2005): 5–21.

Bean, John C., and Nalini Iyer. "'I Couldn't Find an Article That Answered My Question': Teaching the Construction of Meaning in Undergraduate Literary Research," 22–40. In *Teaching Literary Research*, ed. Kathleen A. Johnson and Steven R. Harris. Chicago: Association of College and Research Libraries, 2009.

Beaufort, Anne. *College Writing and Beyond: A New Framework for University Writing Instruction.* Logan: Utah State University Press, 2007.

Bransford, John D., Ann L. Brown, and Rodney R. Cocking, eds. *How People Learn: Brain, Mind, Experience, and School.* Expanded ed. Washington, D.C.: National Academy Press, 2000.

Carrithers. David, John C, Bean, and Teresa Ling. "Messy Problems and Lay Audiences: Teaching Critical Thinking Within the Finance Curriculum." *Business Communication Quarterly* 71, no. 2 (2008): 152–70.

Carrithers, David and John C. Bean. "Using a Client Memo to Assess Critical Thinking of Finance Majors." *Business Communication Quarterly,* 71, no. 1 (2008): 10–26.

Council of Writing Program Administrators. "WPA Outcomes Statements for First Year Composition." Council of Writing Program Adminstrators, 2000. Accessed July 5, 2012.

Elbow, Peter. *Writing Without Teachers.* New York: Oxford University Press, 1973.

Farrell, Allan P. *The Jesuit Code of Liberal Education: Development and Scope of the "Ratio Studiorum."* Milwaukee: Bruce, 1938.

Fulkerson, Richard. "Composition at the Turn of the Twenty-First Century." *College Composition and Communication* 56, no. 4 (2005): 654–87.

Hillocks, George. *Research on Written Composition: New Directions for Teaching.* Urbana, Ill.: ERIC Clearinghouse on Reading and Communication Skills and the National Conference on Research in English, 1986.

Kolvenbach, Peter-Hans, S.J. "Jesuit Education and Ignatian Pedagogy." Association of Jesuit Schools and Colleges, September 2005. http://business.fordham.edu/faculty_resources/documents/Jesuit-Education-and-Ignatian-Pedagogy.pdf. Accessed April 22, 2012.

MacDonald, Susan. P. *Professional Writing in the Humanities and Social Sciences.* Carbondale: Southern Illinois University Press, 1994.

Nelson Laird, F. Thomas, Rick Shoup, George D. Kuh, and Michael J. Schwarz. "The Effects of Discipline on Deep Approaches to Student Learning and College Outcomes. *Research in Higher Education* 49 (2008): 469–94.

Walvoord, Barbara E. *Assessment Clear and Simple: A Practical Guide for Institutions, Departments, and General Education.* San Francisco: Jossey-Bass, 2004.

Walvoord, Barbara. E., and Virginia. J. Anderson. *Effective Grading: A Tool for Learning and Assessment in College.* 2nd ed. San Francisco: Jossey-Bass, 2010.

Willingham, Daniel T. *Why Don't Students Like School? A Cognitive Scientist Answers Questions about How the Mind Works and What It Means for the Classroom.* San Francisco: Jossey-Bass, 2009.

CURA PERSONALIS IN PRACTICE: RHETORIC'S MODERN LEGACY

Karen Surman Paley

In *The Catholic University as Promise and Project: Reflections in a Jesuit Idiom*, Michael J. Buckley, S.J., takes to task the mission statements of three unidentified Catholic universities. He finds them bland and formulaic, so generalized that they could as well apply to secular schools. I find it surprising that in his book on the Jesuit university, Buckley makes no mention of the presence or absence of a specific Jesuit value, *cura personalis*, or the education of the whole person.

The mission statement for Loyola Marymount University (LMU), updated May 2010, cites "the encouragement of learning, the education of the whole person, and the service of faith and promotion of justice." From LMU's perspective, the education of the whole person means "the simultaneous process of information, formation, and transformation." Such an education "encourages personal integration of the student's thinking, feeling, choosing, evolving self. *It does this by fostering not only academic and professional development but also physical, social, psychological, moral, cultural, and religious/spiritual growth*" (emphasis added).

It is this idea of education of the whole person, or *cura personalis*, that is my focus here, and how it serves as a Jesuit phrase for rhetoric itself. *Cura personalis*, like rhetoric, has as its goal the transformation and development of character. Enacted as part of a writing pedagogy per se, *cura personalis* is a process that leads to engaged writing, a specific form of what David Leigh in this volume calls "self-active," a pedagogy in which students are required to reflect on the way in which course reading and concepts pertain to them. Using ethnographic case studies on writing across the curriculum at a Jesuit school, I explore how the reflective teaching and learning in two classes demonstrates an engagement with *cura personalis*, which is consistent with the notion of Jesuit rhetoric as a means not only of developing intellectual knowledge but also of cultivating both personal understanding and a sense of community identity and responsibility. I describe writing assignments in a philosophy class taught at LMU by department chair Sr. Mary Beth Ingham[1] and a theology class with Tom Powers, S.J.[2]

Looking first at a definitional overlap between rhetoric and *cura personalis*, I will briefly provide an etymology of the phrase, how it developed from a concept about the relationship between the director and novice Jesuit, or between an instructor and retreatant about to experience the *Spiritual Exercises*, into a more contemporary educational value and practice that connects with rhetorical goals and practices in writing pedagogies. While several other contributors to this volume also discuss curricula or programs (Leigh, Bizzell, Adams, and Peters), I describe specific courses, as embodied rhetorical encounters with specific curricular and narrative sequences, as typical of the genre of ethnography. The intent is to help the reader see examples of the modern legacies of a nearly five-hundred-year heritage of Jesuit education and to see specifically how formal rhetorical training as intellectual and public work (for the class and for the society) and as reflection (inner-focused language) work to discern the written expression of emotional and spiritual understandings across the disciplines.

WHAT IS RHETORIC?

If we take the word *rhetoric* to pertain in part to formation of mind, knowledge, and character, as do Quintilian, Richard Lanham, and David Fleming, then my two ethnographic sites, Ingham's philosophy and Powers's theology class, were courses in rhetoric as well the heart of Jesuit education. Drawing on the 1934 work of Francis Donnelly, Patricia Bizzell argues that "a major component of the Jesuit educational mission has been, and is, education in rhetoric." Or, as Gabriel Codina, S.J., puts it in his analysis of four hundred years of the application of the *Ratio Studiorum*, the goal of education was the classical man who had reached "perfect eloquence 'eloquentia perfecta' . . . which meant not only being able to speak, to write, and to communicate one's own ideas with facility and elegance, but also having the capacity to reason, to feel, to express oneself and to act, harmonizing virtue with learning" (8).

David Fleming's preferred definition of the word *rhetoric* is "the study of speaking and writing well, a historically prominent and remarkable program of instruction involving both theory and practice and aimed at the moral and intellectual development of the student" (172). Further, according to Fleming, the purpose of the study of rhetoric is "the development of a certain kind of person: engaged, articulate, resourceful, civil—a person trained in, conditioned by, and devoted to what was once called *eloquence*" (172–73). In other words it matches the Jesuit construct of *cura personalis*, which is "to promote formation of character and values, meaning and purpose" (LMU Mission Statement). Finally, in his study of the Jesuit practice of liberal arts education and rhetoric, David Leigh writes that the Jesuit goal in *eloquentia perfecta* is the development of "eloquent and mature" students "who are intellectually, morally, and religiously integrated and responsible to become public leaders in a well-governed state."

THE SEARCH FOR *CURA PERSONALIS*

Cura personalis has had three different denotations. First, historically it is a description of the way in which novices to the Society of Jesus and retreatants in the *Spiritual Exercises* are trained. Here it addresses the *pedagogy and character* of the director or instructor. Second, it refers to the *relationship* between the spiritual director or teacher and the learner. Lastly, it is an *attitude* cultivated in the learner and to be carried into a larger community.

While the phrase *cura personalis* is frequently used among Jesuit educators at many of the twenty-eight Jesuit colleges and universities in the United States today, it is a multifaceted concept that is not referenced explicitly in the foundational texts of the Society, the *Constitutions* of the Society of Jesus or the *Spiritual Exercises* of Saint Ignatius (*SE*) (Padburg, Gray, Hewitt). However, Howard Gray, S.J., sees the seeds of the desirable relationship between instructor and retreatant or student in all of these texts, indicating that the sentiment for *cura personalis* derives from St. Ignatius of Loyola:

> In terms of the trust for personal experience, the need to adapt any code or process to the reality of the person in front of you, the careful processing of interviews for candidates to the Jesuits, etc., it is clear that Ignatius gave a priority to the care for persons.
>
> —personal communication

Gray points to sections 250 and 263 in part 3 of the *Constitutions*, where he sees the core teaching on *cura personalis* as pedagogy and relationship because of "the overall concern for the individual." In section 250 there is very specific advice to the novice to take care of his eyes, ears, and tongue, to be humble, and to know when to speak and when to be silent. The Jesuit is to "show *devotion*, signifying the divine nature within any reality (the 'finding God in all things')" (Gray). The relationships cultivated in the training of a Jesuit are normative in their future ministries; the treatment of the novice is to be carried out in a future community. In section 263 of part 3 of the *Constitutions* we learn of the necessary qualities of the instructor, "a person whom all those in probation may love and to whom they may . . . open themselves with confidence" (Ganss, 159). Such an instructor must be quite trustworthy to be privy to this knowledge of the individual.

Peter-Hans Kolvenbach, the superior general of the Jesuits, finds evidence of *cura personalis* as relationship and pedagogy also in the annotations that precede the *SE*. "In essence, 'cura personalis' is simply help, from person to person, so that God and man may really meet" (15). The teacher is essentially a companion who chooses words simply and not "in the scholastic manner . . . to find something that will make it a little more meaningful for [the exercitant] or touch him more deeply" (16). This adaptation to the individual is a theme that runs through the annotations and parallels that we see in part 3 of the *Constitutions*. It is a characteristic of Jesuit spirituality, which Leigh refers to as "historically embedded." When the individual is going through turbulent times, the one giving the Exercises should ask "encouraging" questions without being "harsh or severe," so as to "shed light on everything that the good and the bad spirit may provoke in a person's heart" (Kolvenbach, 13). Kolvenbach also sees in the *Ratio Studiorum* (1599) the importance of the character of the instructor and of attention to the individual. He writes that what affects the "formation of students" in this curriculum more than the words of their teachers is "the example of their personal lives" (16).[3]

TEXTUAL MANIFESTATIONS OF *CURA PERSONALIS*

The first printed reference to *cura personalis* is the essay "Personalis Alumnorum Cura" (1956) by Robert A. Hewitt, S.J., which derives from the Instructions on Studies and Teaching for the American Assistancy (1948) by the "Very Rev. Father General," who would have been Jean-Baptiste Janssens (35). Hewitt quotes parts of article 7 in the Instructions; the goal of education is "not merely erudition, but the *formation of the whole man* with all his faculties" (36). Hewitt calls for school guidance programs to avoid having to expel students who "with proper personal attention could have been saved" (40). The calls for attending to the whole student led to the creation of the Jesuit Association of Student Personnel Administration (JASPA) in 1958 (Thon, 10).

Two decades after Hewitt's essay, there begin to be many more references to *cura personalis* in the literature. The reason may be found in the decline in the number of Jesuits after 1964 and the subsequent search for an identity particular to the Jesuit college and university, the result of the anti-institutional movements of the 1960s, which, according to William C. McInnes, S.J., "rolled across the Society of Jesus, rocking it from top to bottom" (30). The decade of the '70s focused on the Jesuit "search for identity—specifically religious" that resulted in the formation of the Association of Jesuit Colleges and Universities (AJCU) to develop a statement on the nature of Jesuit distinctiveness (McInnes, 31–36). I think that in this search for identity, the Jesuits returned to their roots in the spirit of St. Ignatius and published a series of essays that name *cura personalis* as one of its several manifestations (pedagogy and the character of the teacher, the relationship between student and teacher, and students' relationship to the larger community). The combination of the spirit of the concept in the foundational texts and these essays led to *cura personalis* as praxis in the two classroom ethnographies that follow.[4]

CURA PERSONALIS IN THE
TWENTY-FIRST-CENTURY CLASSROOM

During the year and a half period in which I directed freshman English and began to develop a writing-across-the-curriculum (WAC) at LMU, I was able to conduct two semester-long observations of classes and student–teacher conferences as well as examine student essays with teacher comments.[5] I offer these ethnographies as modern legacies of the nearly five-hundred-year heritage of Jesuit education, beginning with the foundational texts as noted above, and linking formal rhetorical work and rhetorical discernment in the education of the whole student.

Will It "Absolutely Change Your Life"?
The Philosophy of Human Nature

I met Sr. Mary Beth Ingham while conducting a WAC needs assessment survey through informal interviews at LMU. She told me of her philosophy-of-life writing assignment in the course Philosophy of Human Nature, which I observed in the spring of 2000. Later, one of her students would tell me, "I felt that this paper really made me think about who I am and what I want to become as I get older." The assignment is a principled example of how the teaching of rhetoric can help to form the personality. It required self-examination and enabled some students to make positive behavioral changes.

The philosophy-of-life assignment is a three-step writing sequence. Each phase builds on the one before it, as students proceed from "mere 'belief' (the conviction that something is true based solely on the sincere conviction of the believer)" to reasoned argument, anticipation of and response to objections, self-evaluation, and predictions for the future (Soccio, 11).

The preliminary stage of the assignment is not graded and is done "prior to any formal study of philosophy." In two to three pages, students write out their "tentative philosophy of life or an explanation of [their] goal in life." For the next draft, students present a reasoned argument for their goal in life or philosophy of life. The directions call for attention to rhetorical strategies. "You will clarify any assumptions which are the basis for your position; offer three good reasons why your position is a sound one; raise two possible objections against your own argument; and respond to the objections."

In the final stage, students revise the paper based on their instructor's written comments and on discussion in an optional conference. Additionally, they are asked to speculate about what philosophy means in practice. The last stage is thus in accord with one of the manifestations of *cura personalis*, extension of care for the individual to the world in which he or she lives. They are to address several questions, such as "What if everyone held your position? What kind of society or world would there be?" "What will you be like in ten years if you continue to follow this philosophy of life?" "Are there any values related to your position which have come to light in the course of writing this paper?"

Ingham made a big claim for the assignment on the first day: "If you take it seriously, it will *absolutely* change your life." As the semester and the assignment sequence progressed, she would frequently use words like *transformation*. Although she told me she does not consciously think about *cura personalis* in her teaching, this assignment is evidence that she does care about more than having her students memorize and repeat back in essays and exams what they have heard her say in class or read in books. (Of course, the exams do require that students be quite familiar with the course content.) She cares about having students think for themselves and about having them think about the impact of their philosophy of life on others.

Did the assignment "absolutely change lives"? Yes, some students did, in fact, report change. To determine what changes students experienced, I distributed an optional questionnaire at the end of the semester. It included the statement "While it may be too soon to tell if the writing process [for this assignment] affected you in any major way, I would like to hear about any possible changes to date." Twenty-three out of twenty-nine students responded, and seven voluntarily signed their names. Many students reported that there were no observable changes, but there was much evidence of discernment, of the inner-focused language work as they moved toward greater spiritual and emotional understandings. "The paper did start directing me and made me think how I would like to live the rest of my life." While no major transformations were reported, a few respondents did acknowledge some changes in the way they think or live. "It allowed for a lot of personal reflection, which I don't think I would have done otherwise." "I began to doubt some of my previous convictions and saw flaws in my character that needed changing. For example, I am too dependent on other people. . . . I have made a conscious effort to change that."

Juan, June, and Chris

Let me illustrate the effect of this assignment on three students. The impact on Juan was immediate as he came to see himself as a hypocrite. On the one hand, his philosophy was the golden rule: Do unto others as you would have done unto you. However, he began to notice how frequently he made personal insults about such things as a person's weight. Because the paper had inspired self-examination, he reported discontinuing the offensive behavior. "And you directly attribute [stopping the personal insults] to thinking through this paper?" "Definitely, because this paper helped me sit back and view how my life, how I really wanted to live my life."

A returning student, June really struggled with the directions for the paper and the submission guidelines, became antagonistic toward Ingham, and dropped the class for fear of lowering her GPA. Although still holding a grudge toward Ingham, she had something positive to say about the assignment. "The paper, though I almost killed myself doing it and making sure I got it in on time . . . proved to be more beneficial than I ever could have imagined. . . . I have spent the past several weeks narrowing [my thesis] down to what I actually want to do in life."

Finally, I was able to obtain a retrospective point of view from Chris, a student who had taken the class several years before and was now doing an ob/gyn rotation as part of his medical training.[6] When I contacted him in August 2000, he was quite pleased with the results from his "med boards" and had just delivered his first baby. The philosophy he had argued for in Ingham's class was that each person should achieve his or her true potential: "Everyone is capable of so much and so many people settle for less. Be the best you can be. Do everything you can to make yourself grow, and when you reach your full potential, you will want to help others." He said that the paper was very important to him at the time, as it prodded him to come up with a principle to live by. "I had to think where do I really stand?" Realizing that there was an underlying theme to his life surprised him. "Whether or not the assignment had an impact, it is the way I have been living my life ever since. I used it to study for my exams [medical boards] and I use it on my rotations."

When Chris started college, he had plans to go to medical school but did not work very hard the first two years. "My grades were so-so. Maybe 3.3 [GPA]. I knew I had to do better." In the summer after his sophomore year, he volunteered in the emergency room of a hospital in South Central Los Angeles. "This was it," he said. "This was what I wanted to do with my life. It was how I had wanted to live my life before that [taking Philosophy of Human Nature], but I made a conscious decision beginning my junior year to strive every day. I took 18 science credits and got my first 4.0 that semester."

I think it would be overstating the case to say that Chris completed Philosophy 160 in the spring of his sophomore year (earning an A–) and then turned his life around. Chris used the word *coincidence*, whereas I might say "confluence." He was experiencing internal dissatisfaction with the way school was going. "I was unmotivated," he said. During the period of dissatisfaction, he took Ingham's class to fill a core requirement for graduation. Ferreting out his philosophy of life, realizing he had one, and seeing that he was not living by it was a fortuitous series of cognitive events that prodded him to try to get more out of his education.

Ingham's writing pedagogy demonstrates that a rhetorical assignment based on philosophical reasoning can lead to changes on a personal level. Her sequence begins as a writing-to-learn assignment in which students tentatively discover their philosophy of life. That evolves into a disciplinary discourse; students learn strategies of reasoned argumentation by practicing them as they examine their own lives for flaws and self-initiate change for the better. For some students at least, it is a moral exercise, a rhetorical education that helps to form strong and ethical character.

Liberation Theology: Transforming Attitudes toward Poverty

Have the course be a way to learn how to live your life.

—Tom Powers, S.J.

Allowing room for people to offer personal reflection created a more intimate class setting. . . . I think many times our educational system does not allow us time to make the connection between our school work and our personal experiences. In doing so, we're allowed to grow more as human beings, while ultimately preparing us for the world beyond the university.

—Student evaluation

In this example, I draw on a student's essay and dialogue in a conference with her professor to demonstrate the manifestation of *cura personalis* as both relationship and care for a larger community and to demonstrate how rhetorical assignments in the discipline of theology can contribute to discernment and a change of attitude. I observed the class Liberation: Bible, Church, and Theology taught by Tom Powers, S.J., then director of the Center for Ignatian Spirituality at LMU, in the spring of 2001. Powers initially contacted me after reading in a campus newspaper about my research on *cura personalis* in Ingham's philosophy class and invited me to write about his course.

Each student was to write six three-page papers on some aspect of the assigned reading.[7] The instructions request that each paper include "a brief analysis of the material, your own interpretation of what the author[s] is/are saying, and *an explanation of how this applies to your life*" (my emphasis). The combination of analysis, interpretation, and self-reflection was decidedly Jesuit and, consequently, rhetorical but not easy for the students to implement. Eight of the twenty-nine students in class gave me copies of their papers with Powers's comments. The papers revealed difficulty in carrying out all three requirements. Any given paper could offer summary and analysis sans commentary on what the reading meant personally or a solely personal reflection with no interpretation or analysis.

What Is Liberation Theology?

Early in the semester, Powers asked the class, "Were any of you raised to ask, 'Is this the way Christianity should be and, if not, what are you going to do to change things?' What did Christ do consistently to challenge the systems that oppressed people, to raise up people who had been oppressed? Isn't it interesting that that scares most Christians today?" (January 24, 2001). Liberation theology questions oppressive systems and motivates people to stand up against them. In one course text, *The New Catholicity: Theology between the Global and the Local*, Robert Schreiter identifies liberation theology as one of several "contextual theologies" that began to appear in the 1970s in Latin America in opposition to "universalizing theologies that extended the results of their reflections beyond their own contexts to other settings, usually without an awareness of the rootedness of their theologies within their own contexts" (2). Thus liberation theology is consistent with the Ignatian concern for adaptation of any program to the individual and the place.

Another element of liberation theology, according to Schreiter, is resistance. What I observed, especially early on, was a lot of resistance to the course and to Powers himself. Annette, who identified herself as Roman Catholic and Native American, challenged Powers in class on March 7. "Any time anyone says 'in the name of God,' I am afraid," she said, "because a lot of murders have been committed in the name of God. Other people do good things but don't say they are doing it in the name of God." Celia, who said she was taking the class because her husband wanted her to be more of a feminist, challenged Powers's request not to identify God with a gender. Then there was Carey, who revealed an unabashed opposition to liberation theology's "preferential option for the poor" and the struggle against the oppression of ethnic minorities. She writes in her first paper:

> And I have, in all honesty, become agitated by and a bit tired of the constant attention drawn to such injustice. . . . I begin to ask "What about my poverty?" . . . I am alienated from Biblical texts through time-honored interpretations that have become meaningless. I am alienated from the Mass, the so-called celebration that often feels more like a funeral than anything else.

Three months later Carey publicly reexamined these beliefs. In an oral presentation on the novel *The Tortilla Curtain* by T. Coraghessan Boyle, she told the class, "*I have not suffered*" (my emphasis). Soon she would turn in her fourth and fifth papers on Boyle's novel. The novel uses a point-and-counterpoint structure between two parallel plots involving an undocumented Mexican couple (Cándido and América Rincón) and an upper-middle-class white couple (Delaney and Kyra Mossbacher), whose lives intertwine in Topanga Canyon, California. Carey writes"

> The *Tortilla Curtain* hits home. It hits home because it is practically home. . . . I never think about the families that may be living in a ditch—or on the other side of the border—or the struggle for their lives to make it here. . . . I tell myself, "There are Mexicans in my family. My cousins are Mexican. . . . I can't be racist. I have no prejudices. . . . What will it take to help me see that *poverty needs no qualifications*, but is worthy enough on its own to elicit help? . . . If I really think being alienated from a Catholic Mass is comparable to being homeless, jobless and deathly ill, I am seriously mistaken." [My emphasis]

What transpired during the three months of the course to give Carey pause? When I asked Powers over a decade later how he had employed *cura personalis* in this course, he told me: care for the subject matter, care for the students who were absorbing the subject matter, and the inherent challenge that *students reexamine what they think* (February 16, 2012, my emphasis). I think Carey's attitude changed because Powers challenged her indifference to the poor in conferences. Her transformation was also the result of rhetorical examination of a novel, which takes place in her own community, enabling her to see that material deprivation is much more immediate and desperate than discontent with the practice of her religion.

Powers and his student met on February 7. Although I thought his demeanor was gentle but earnest, later she would tell me she felt he was trying "to force his opinion on her." He told her, "I am not saying that your life has to be a tragedy for someone to understand liberation theology, but you are called to at least be able to open your heart enough to understand that." He moved easily from pathos to logos, from emotional to strictly rhetorical concerns, asking for more support for her opinions. He read aloud from her paper: "I believe what Gustavo Gutiérrez [a liberation theologian] says about the process of liberation being a necessary and intrinsic part of Christianity" (Hennelly, 21). He then read his own comment aloud to her, "Because?" In fact, at several points in the conference, returning to the problem that she did not explain the reason for her points, Powers said that theology is about understanding. He felt that Carey was writing too much from "her head" and not her "heart." "But you see," he explained, "it's not just thinking, it's connecting the heart, too." He wanted the educational process to engage the whole person and wanted Carey to work to transform her own understanding and moral character by developing compassion for others. His voice was soft, and he spoke slowly: "I'm not demanding that you be a Christian. I'm not demanding that you be a believer, but you have to think in terms of understanding." Yet Carey kept resisting. "I'm a senior. I don't know . . . Mexican American, Asian, and it's like, well, what about me? . . . I don't have extreme economic poverty."

Carey brought up this conference with me in an email after the course ended, denying it any turning-point status. "I didn't think that Fr. Powers really understood where I was coming from at the time, and I felt like he was forcing his opinion onto me. . . . Nothing I could have said would have helped him 'diagnose' me—it's something time, exploration and experience with him and the class needed to do. My last paper is the result of all those things. I now consider Fr. Powers one of my absolute favorite college professors. Furthermore, he is among the few I enjoy 'mingling' with, and the only one I would really consider as a friend" (May 27, 2001).

Her final paper continues the exploration of class and takes up another counterargument she made against the option for the poor and the course reading from Luke:

> When I side with the poor, must I hate the rich? . . . Can I honestly look at wealthy people and say that God does not love them. Hatred will just continue the cycle of prejudice—when will it end? It's so easy to switch hands and say that the last are now first and the first now last. But will not the hands switch over time and time again? . . . How unconditional is God's love for all God's children?

I think that Carey was moved by the Boyle novel, coming at the end of a whole semester's reading, writing, and discussing the issues, especially through the self-reflection required in each writing assignment. She came into the class angry at the way the rich are punished in the afterlife in the Bible, perhaps because of her own presence in a more well-to-do class. Cándido's rescue of the wealthy man who tried to murder him at the end of *The Tortilla Curtain* is clearly in line with Carey's conception of a Catholicism that does not condemn the rich per se. Also, because the novel's setting is so close to the school and the students' home communities, the literary text makes a strong case for liberation theology. As Powers said to me, "Sometimes it takes literature to see ourselves"—a point very important to rhetoric through the ages and certainly critical to Jesuit notions of rhetorical study (July 24, 2001).

CONCLUSION

Powers cares about how books affect his students as people, and he encouraged them to relate course material to their lives. Although he occasionally became frustrated by students' not coming to class prepared, his kindness and caring for the whole person were prevalent. It is telling that when students who are "pissed off" (to use Powers's words) at a professor are able to communicate that to him directly instead of complaining to others. Despite being wary of consequences, Carey could risk expressing her disenchantment with the focus on poor ethnic minorities, because she trusted Powers to understand. The attention to the individual in conferences, in the context of compelling reading, achieved a key goal of rhetoric: transformation of the person—in this case, from being a woman indifferent to and judgmental of economic deprivation to being aware and compassionate.

From the sixteenth century, when Ignatius lived, to the twenty-first century, and from care for the Jesuit novice or for the retreatant to care for the student, we come to see a single aim—caring for the individual becomes care for the larger community. *Cura personalis* is the effective mechanism behind Jesuit rhetorical education that leads to transformation of character.

NOTES

1. As of spring 2012, Ingham is professor emerita at LMU and teaching at the Franciscan School of Theology in Berkeley.

2. Powers is currently the executive director of the Jesuit Retreat Center of Los Altos, California, but no longer a member of the Society of Jesus.

3. A fourth expression of the concept of *cura personalis* before the phrase came into print occurs in the book *Principles of Jesuit Education in Practice* (1934), by Francis Donnelly, S.J., as he describes the encouraging teacher who is aware of the feelings of his students and their need for balance between critique and praise. He writes in Latin,

"Laudare denique si quid apte perfectum sit" (104). In short, with praising, a person will be complete.

4. There are a few important early publications that use the phrase *cura personalis*. The Jesuit Secondary Association (JSEA) published *Reflections on the Educational Principles of the Spiritual Exercises* by Robert R. Newton, S.J., in 1977. Newton's focus is on pedagogy and relationship. Each student paper should be a "highly personal experience" (25). Students are to be allowed to discover some matters by themselves rather than be flooded with explanation from teachers (18).

In 1986 JSEA published *Go Forth and Teach: The Characteristics of Jesuit Education*. *Cura personalis* is manifested in terms of relationship, as educators ought always to be "ready to listen to their students' cares and concerns" (21). Of note regarding recommended pedagogy is the similarity to that of feminist philosopher Nel Noddings, who wrote in 1984 that "the student is infinitely more important than the subject" (20). The JSEA writes that "the curriculum is centered on the person rather than the material to be covered" (21).

Beginning in the 1980s, much Jesuit commentary focuses on the third denotation of *cura personalis*, care for the a larger community in the form of attention to social issues, one of the aims of rhetoric itself (McInnes, Haschka, O'Hare, Lucey). As Joseph O'Hare writes, "our graduates should not simply be careerists, but also responsible citizens, concerned especially for the poor and the marginalized" (145). Brad, a student in Mary Beth Ingham's class, notes, "My true self is in actuality only part of the greater self known as humanity, and it lies within every man and woman on this planet."

5. Space does not permit a full discussion, but I want to acknowledge the teacher research described by Theresa Kappus and Kelley O'Brian Jenks, librarians at Gonzaga University in Spokane, Washington. Training provided by JesuitNet, an online course offered by Association of Jesuit Colleges and Universities, enabled them to bring *cura personalis* into their own course in library instruction for the online graduate program in the School of Professional Studies. The pedagogy is recognizably Jesuit in its attention to the individual and the use of inner-directed language: "[We] would like our students to be *transformed* as researchers. We would like them to be bold in the face of their fears and inadequacies surrounding technologies used by libraries and resources provided by libraries. . . . We would like them to see librarians as gatekeepers, who are willing to address their most difficult concerns" (741). One self-active method included, at the end of each module, responding to self-reflective questions such as, "Were you mostly excited and amazed or confused and frustrated?" "Have your feelings changed about doing research?" "Do you feel more prepared to do research?" "Have you surprised yourself?"

6. I am grateful to Deb Wilson, the former director of Health Services at LMU, for referring me to this student.

7. The texts included *Liberation Theologies: The Global Pursuit of Justice*, by Alfred Hennelly; *Christian Feminist Theology: A Constructive Interpretation*, by Denise Carmody; *Called for Freedom: The Changing Context of Liberation Theology*, by José Comblin; *The New Catholicity: Theology Between the Global and the Local*, by Robert Schreiter; and the novel *The Tortilla Curtain*, by T. Coraghessan Boyle.

WORKS CITED

Bizzell, Patricia. "Historical Notes on Rhetoric in Jesuit Education." In *Traditions of Eloquence*, ed. Gannett and Brereton, 39–59.

Boyle, T. Coraghessan. *The Tortilla Curtain*. New York: Penguin, 1995.

"Brad." Unpublished paper. Philosophy 160. April 2000.

Buckley, Michael. *The Catholic University as Promise and Project: Reflections in a Jesuit Idiom*. Washington D.C.: Georgetown University Press, 1998.

Carmody, Denise L. *Christian Feminist Theology*. Cambridge: Blackwell, 1995.

Codina, Gabriel. "'Our Way of Proceeding' in Education: The Ratio Studiorum." *Educatio S.J.* 1 (May 1999): 1–15. www.marquette.edu/umi/ratio2.html

Comblin, Jose. *Called for Freedom: The Changing Context of Liberation Theology*. Maryknoll, New York: Orbis, 1998.

Donnelly, Francis P. *Principles of Jesuit Education in Practice*. New York: P. J. Kenedy and Sons, 1934.

Fleming, David. "Rhetoric as a Course of Study." *CE* 61, no. 2 (November 1998): 169–91.

Gannett, Cinthia, and John Brereton, eds. *Traditions of Eloquence: The Jesuits and Rhetorical Studies*. New York: Fordham University Press, 2013.

Ganss, George E., ed. and trans. *The Constitutions of the Society of Jesus*. St. Louis: Institute for Jesuit Resources, 1970.

Gray, Howard. Personal communication. February 8, 2012.

———. Personal communication. October 27, 1999.

Haschka, David. "The International Commission on the Apostolate of Jesuit Education: Characteristics of a Jesuit Education, a Summary." Presentation at JAWPA (Jesuit Association of Writing Program Administrators) conference. Milwaukee: Marquette University, December 10, 1987.

Hennelly, Alfred T. *Liberation Theologies: The Global Pursuit of Justice*. Mystic, Conn.: Twenty-Third Publications, 1997.

Hewitt, Robert A. "Personalis Alumnorum Cura." *Jesuit Educational Quarterly* 19, no.1 (June 1956): 35–41.

Ignatius Loyola. *The Spiritual Exercises of St. Ignatius*. Translated by Anthony Mottola. New York: Image/Doubleday, 1964.

Ingham, Mary Elizabeth. Personal communication. April 2000.

———. Personal communication. October 4, 2000.

———. "Paper Assignment–Spring 2000."

Jesuit Secondary Education Association (JSEA). *Go Forth and Teach: The Characteristics of Jesuit Education*. Washington, D.C.: JSEA: 1987.

"Juan." Personal communication. April 11, 2000.

"June." Personal communication. May 21, 2000.

Kappus, Theresa, and Kelly O'Brien Jenks. "Angels and Demons: Online Library Instruction the Jesuit Way." *Journal of Library Administration* 50 (2010): 737–46.

Kolvenbach, Peter-Hans. "*Cura Personalis*." *Review of Ignatian Spirituality* 114 (2007): 9–17.

Lampe, Chris. Personal communication. August 16, 2000.

———. Personal communication. September 1, 2000.

Leigh, David. "The Changing Practice of Liberal Education and Rhetoric in Jesuit Education: 1600–2000." In *Traditions of Eloquence*, ed. Gannett and Brereton, 125–40.

Loyola Marymount Mission (LMU) Statement. May 2010. www.lmu.edu. Accessed January 15, 2012.

Lucey, Gregory. *"Cura personalis": Roots and New Growth.* JASPA '95 Summer Workshop: *Cura personalis.*" VHS. Milwaukee, 1995.

McInnes, William C. "The Current State of the Jesuit Philosophy of Education." In *Jesuit Higher Education: Essays on an American Tradition of Excellence,* ed. Rolando E. Bonachea, 26–45. Pittsburgh: Duquesne University Press, 1989.

Newton, Robert R. *Reflections on the Educational Principles of "The Spiritual Exercises."* Washington, D.C.: JSEA, 1977.

Noddings, Nel. *Caring: A Feminine Approach to Ethics and Moral Education,* Berkeley: University of California PRess, 1984.

O'Hare, Joseph A. "Jesuit Education in America." In *The Jesuit Tradition and Missions: A 450-Year Perspective,* ed. Christopher Chapple, 143–53. Scranton, Pa.: University of Scranton Press, 1993.

Padberg, John W. Personal communication. November 19, 1999.

Powers, Tom. Personal communication. May 15, 2000.

———. Personal communication. September 7, 2000.

———. Personal communication. February 16, 2012.

Schreiter, Robert J. *The New Catholicity: Theology from the Global and the Local.* Maryknoll, New York: Orbis, 1999.

Soccio, Douglas J. *How to Get the Most out of Philosophy.* Belmont, Calif.: Wadsworth, 1998.

Thon, Andrew J. *The Ignatian Perspective: The Role of Student Affairs in Higher Education.* JASPA: December 1989.

Wilson, Debbie. Personal communication. June 26, 2000

SERVICE LEARNING AND DISCERNMENT: REALITY WORKING THROUGH RESISTANCE

Ann E. Green

> Each of us has our own little world of immediacy, but all such worlds are just min-
> ute strips within a far larger world, a world construed by imagination and intelli-
> gence, mediated by words, and based largely upon belief.
> —Bernard Lonergan, S.J., as quoted in Denk

At Jesuit universities, service learning is often marketed as a corner-stone of the Jesuit commitment to social justice. Rhetorically, the phrase *service learning* sounds great. It's hard to argue that stu-dents serving in the community—feeding the homeless, repairing houses, tutoring children—is not for the greater good, and service-learning programs are often used to market our universities to parents and students. As a teacher of service learning, however, I am often frustrated by the overuse of the term for projects that are one-time only, that engage students in tasks that are not relevant to their coursework, or that do not ask students to criti-cally reflect on issues of social justice or civic engagement. Experience itself does not automatically mean that students become better critical thinkers or advocates for the poor. Conflating experientially based learning that might be more accurately called "volunteering" or "internships" with service learning undercuts the power of service learning as a transformational pedagogy.[1] "Ser-vice learning," as I am using the term, involves intentional, relationship-based experiences that fulfill a real need for a community partner and that serve as another text for the course.[2]

In the context of U.S. Jesuit education, it's useful to consider who our stu-dents are. In the summer of 2011, the U.S. Department of Education created a website called the College Affordability and Transparency Center. It provides various ways of analyzing college costs. Of the schools with the highest net prices, three Jesuit schools are in the top thirty (my own, Saint Joseph's, is num-ber eleven in net cost, and the most expensive university in Pennsylvania).[3] Dean Brackley, S.J., writes, "Today, this kind of experience [such as service learning] is a necessary part of education for the middle-class 'tribe,' to which most of the population of Catholic colleges and universities belongs" ("Higher Standards," 191). While I appreciate Brackley's enthusiasm for students to have transformative experiences, I wonder about the word *necessary*. Why "neces-sary"? It seems to me that for our students to become effective advocates and rhetors for social justice, they must first recognize their privilege, and not every student will be able or ready, some for very good reasons, for a transformative service-learning experience during their four years of Jesuit education. For service learning to be effective, the need at the service site must be real and the student must discern that she or he is ready for the service experience. While most of our students might be white and middle-class, some are not, and class discussions about discernment and privilege must account for these differences. By engaging students in the Jesuit practice of discernment, we can help them think through rhetorical strategies that effectively promote social justice.

While all writing classes at my university list the engagement of students in "thoughtful, imaginative, and well-organized language (*eloquentia perfecta*)" as a goal, the particular, long-term goal of the service-learning and writing class is to help them articulate and advocate for social justice to a broader public. What I hope is that the writing and speaking that students engage in during their service-learning course prepares them to advocate for justice throughout their careers as lawyers, social workers, teachers, librarians, pharmacists, physicians, and managers in the corporate world. It is not enough to simply have the experience of service, but one must be able to reflect on it, internalize it, and speak about it. One of my colleagues long ago said that service-learning students were the most vocal advocates for affirmative action on our campus, and I often reflect on this comment and consider how service-learning courses can teach students to speak effectively to their peers about controversial issues, but I also want them to take their effective, graceful speech further, into their lives beyond our campus.

Teaching service learning is a complicated pedagogical endeavor, and incorporating effective reflection strategies that lead to a consideration of social justice includes, in many contexts, teaching middle-class, often white, students a language for reflection and discernment that critiques what Adolfo Nicolás, S.J., calls "the globalization of superficiality" (1).[4] The Ignatian practice of reflection, action, reflection is a useful tool when incorporated into a service-learning course (Martin, 322). Terms from the *Spiritual Exercises*, particularly those relating to the language of discernment, can be useful rhetorical strategies for teaching students to dig deeper into their experience of service learning and for encouraging them to become "ruined for life" (in the language of the Jesuit Volunteer Corp) by considering the power and privilege that create the conditions for service learning. For example, in their first writing about service, I often ask students to describe, in the third person, their service site. By asking students for concrete, specific details, I try to avoid the "my service site is in a bad neighborhood" truisms that can often emerge in initial writing about service. Once these field notes are written, however, I ask students to return to them to think about how a client from the service site might feel about the description and how the client might describe the site. As we discuss these field notes, students begin a pattern of reflection, writing, and reflection that enables them to consider audience, purpose, and their own position as a rhetor in describing service.

If our students are middle class, they may be unfamiliar with the struggles that impoverished people face and hold stereotypical notions of the causes of poverty. The language that they employ to describe poverty can draw heavily on the commonplaces embedded in popular culture: Students at the service site may not "care" about school the way middle-class students do; parents might be absent and therefore uncaring as well; and the site might be too "disorganized" if it doesn't match middle class students' notions of propriety. If our students are white and they are performing service in communities that are predominantly of color, service can reinforce negative stereotypes about race and poverty, and the language that African American teachers use when speaking to African American children can be perceived as harsh, while to African American service-learning students the language may be familiar.[5] To ensure that our service-learning pedagogy doesn't become what Mitchell et al. call a "pedagogy of whiteness," we need to model language that creates space for reflection on systemic issues. If our students come from the communities that they serve, they may experience a different kind of disorientation as both insiders and outsiders to the service sites. By using oral reflection on service during class discussion, students can achieve a deeper understanding of systemic injustice. By incorporating the practice of discernment and language from the *Spiritual Exercises* into service-learning courses, we can help students reflect on their own positioning in, and responsibility to, "the faith that does justice."

Dean Brackley, S.J., writes that "reality is often much worse than it appears at first. It takes effort to observe and listen carefully to uncover how bad things are. The truth has to work its way through our internal resistance" (*Call to Discernment*, 25). Ignatius's exercises are particularly helpful in providing the retreatant with the ability to name his or her experience. Terms such as *desolation, consolation*, and *indifference* give the retreatant a way to articulate a particular moment in relationship with God. Similarly, the terms that Ignatius uses can help students name their experiences an,d by naming them, have power over them. Providing students with a language for reflection, whether drawing directly from Ignatius's terms or not, can assist them in the process of discernment. A typical problem in the service-learning experience is that, because "helping" is supposed to feel good, when it does not, students have difficulty naming why it is not working, and they often place the blame squarely on the service partners or the clients at the site. By explaining to students that a period of desolation might simply be part of the pattern of the service experience, they have a way of naming their experience and reflecting on their inscription in culture. Students can then deepen their understanding of service and bring that experience back to the world. Especially in the contemporary moment when we are all bombarded with information and action steps, with Facebook and email, creating space in the classroom for students to reflect and slow down is useful for inducing them to think deeply about complex ideas rather than rejecting the difficult out of hand. Engaging students in a variety of different kinds of reflection—both oral and written—helps them to consider audience and purpose and to make connections between the service experience and larger issues of justice and injustice. Discernment involves both self-reflection and an increasing awareness of self in relation to others— including a willingness to revise one's sense of self and one's understanding of audience.

One of the first steps in the process of discernment is "indifference." James Martin, S.J., defines this as "freedom" (306). Rather than approach a particular situation with an idea of the outcome, those who are beginning the process of discernment should strive for middle ground, a place where they are not influenced by their preconceived notions of what is the best decision. In the case of service learning, what I often want students to do is put aside their assumptions about the service site, about poverty and race and class, and about what the clients at the site "need." To model indifference, rather than writing journals about their service (which can quickly devolve into how good or bad a particular student feels about "helping"), I ask students to write "field notes," participant-observer descriptive notes modeled on anthropological field notes. While there are many ways to use journaling effectively in the service-learning classroom, by naming students' weekly writing "field notes," I have had success in encouraging "indifference" in their writing. The language that teachers model for students helps them shift their thinking; because many students come to us with previous experiences of writing about service that may not include critical reflection on systemic issues, I have found that naming informal writing "field notes" encourages them to think about the audience for their writing and the purpose of it. I want to encourage students to consider how their writing and serving is in relationship with the clients at the service site; while they are writing reflectively, they are also always considering the implications of power in their writing about service. Students are sometimes given prompts that ask them to observe aspects of their service experience, such the language used at the sites ("What words are unfamiliar to you?"). By asking students to play with indifference through their field notes, I am hoping that they have a space for reflection that does not reinforce their previous biases concerning the poor.

Students receive responses to their field notes in several ways. When I comment on the notes, I often ask students questions that encourage them to reflect on systemic injustices and to relate them to individual experiences. Field notes are often shared with classmates so we can all engage in thinking about our collective experience. Eventually, the field notes become the basis for a final paper, in which I often ask students to think about addressing an issue from their service site for a real audience, for their community partner or a larger public. Field notes begin as public writing for an audience of the class but then are revised for more specific purposes and audiences that, ideally, push toward advocacy.

In addition to field notes, students complete weekly "Critical Incident Questionnaires" (Brookfield) that ask them to reflect, anonymously, what about the service or the course has been engaging and troubling for them during the previous week. These CIQs (see appendix) enable me to gauge where students are in the stages of discernment—whether they are in "desolation" or "consolation." The CIQs ask students to reflect on when they have been distanced, engaged, and surprised during a particular week of a course, but it does not assign value per se to this distancing, engagement, and surprise. At the end of the semester, students review their copies of the CIQ (they fill out duplicate forms, anonymously, every week) and reflect on any patterns they see in them. This is a way to create a pause, a note of rest, in the noise of the work of the classroom and the service site. This pause gives students a chance to step back and reflect on their experience, and to have a space where discernment can happen. Let me illustrate how this can take place around the issue of race in service learning.

WORKING THROUGH RESISTANCE

Everyone goes through stages of racial-identity development, although these stages differ according to what race(s) you are and your location. In the United States, whites are often slower to recognize the significance of race or racism, and, because whites are often in positions of power or privilege, they can remain unaware of race and racism for long periods of time. In my service-learning classroom, white students often are asked to think about race, and whiteness, consciously for the first time, and they can find this experience discomforting. In "Is White a Race? Expressions of White Racial Identity," psychologist Robert T. Carter describes stages of white racial-identity development. White people move from the idea that white is not a race and the stance that "race doesn't matter" or "I don't see race, I just see people" through a series of steps that, if completed, assist them in developing an anti-racist racial identity.

The first stages of white racial-identity development represent the recognition of racism and the movement away from unconscious racism embedded in most of the dominant white culture (Carter, 200). The first stages involve the experience of, in Ignatian terms, a kind of "desolation." As whites recognize their own positioning as racial beings, they often experience anger and despair at the recognition that the playing field that they assumed was level is not. This recognition that "inequality is not a defect of the system; it is the system" (Brackley 26) causes a great deal of internal conflict and questioning.

For example, Terri, a self-identified feminist and a white student in Writing through Race, Class, and Gender, wrote in her mid-semester evaluation about how angry she was, in general, about her experience of race at the service site and about how uncomfortable it is for her to recognize her own race, or whiteness. During our mid-semester conference, I talked with Terri about how her anger is a normal part of her racial-identity development and about how many white people, when first recognizing their race, experience a period of anger. Terri seems relieved to know that her anger is normal and also, probably, temporary. During one of our next classes, she explains to the class that recognizing her anger as a stage in her racial-identity development has been helpful for her. In terms of rhetoric: After speaking with me, Terri was able to refine her thinking and make her comments to her classmates, who were in various stages of racial-identity development themselves. As Terri articulated her state of racial-identity development, her audience, the class, was able to move forward in its collective knowledge of racial-identity development. Because she was able to name the experience she was having, she was able to reflect on it and communicate it orally to her audience. By semester's end, she reported that she had moved from a period of desolation into a period of consolation, as she had considered and reflected on race at the service site and was also talking about race with clients there. Since white students often find silence the only "safe" option when the subject of race comes up, I was humbled by Terri's courage in speaking about it.

Another white student, Randy, expresses similar distress at conversations about race. When asked to write about his own cultural background, he expressed anger and frustration that he had "nothing to write about" because he is just a white, middle-class man with no culture (and some of the readings from the course made him feel shame at being both white and middle class). Randy seemed troubled by the recognition that many writers assumed that their the typical reader was white; making whiteness visible as a construct disturbed him. During a conference, we talked about ways that his experience was not typical of a white middle-class man, and about how, even when aspects of his experience were typical, they might be worth writing about and making visible as inflected by race and class. In responding to our conference afterward, Randy expressed relief that he did have experiences to write about, and that it was good to have a conversation about what he was struggling with and to think about his audience for his writing. The first assignment did not ask students to address conditions at their service site but to look at their own race, class, gender, sexuality, and moments of difference; this assignment deliberately asks students to consider their own position and how they present that position rhetorically in order to bring those considerations to the service site.

Finally, Christina, an African American student, expressed hope that our class had been able to discuss race. While she was sometimes amazed and taken aback by some students' comments (for example, during a discussion of the Trayvon Martin case, one student said, "Yes, I don't see why you need a gun in a subdivision of Florida, but in West Philly . . . ," and we spent some time in class unpacking that), she also wrote about her experiences of racism on our campus, to address white privilege. By semester's end, Christina and a friend had organized Informed Students on the Basis of Race, a multiracial discussion group on racism on our campus. By engaging in a process of discernment, Christina had taken her experiences from the service-learning site and class-room discussions and used them to address structures of racism on campus. She modeled the experience, reflection, and action of the *Spiritual Exercises*. Since then, Christina has used her rhetorical acumen to organize a protest against larger class sizes at Saint Joseph's.

THE TEACHER DISCERNS

Each service-learning class is a new opportunity for growth and learning on the part of the teacher as well as of the students. Over years of teaching service-learning classes, I have found that weaving discussions of race, class, gender, and sexuality throughout the course rather than addressing them in particular classes works more effectively to encourage discernment and deep thinking, and I have had to learn, too, that discernment takes quiet and time, that it is a process, not a goal. Earlier in my teaching, I would be more likely to meet anger, particularly from white students, head-on. For example, when white students responding to readings by bell hooks described her as angry, I would ask them to look for particular moments in the text when hooks's rhetoric was angry. The response usually was "I can't find a particular passage, but I just know she is," and the student would often retreat to silence rather than continue to ar-gue with me. Now I sometimes approach this issue more indirectly by having students read hooks later in the semester, after writing about their own experi-ences with race, class, gender and sexuality. Rather than using hooks as a model, I try to bring out students' thinking and give them space for reflection and opportunities to revise their thoughts rather than allow them to become more entrenched. The more often I teach hooks, the more I think that she might be upsetting for middle-class white students because of her construction of audi-ence. Rather than assume that her readers are whites or intellectuals, she delib-erately writes without footnotes for a broader audience and writes polemically about controversial issues. In asking students to reflect on hooks' audience and purpose, we can consider the challenges of writing about race (or class, gender, or sexuality) for hostile or uninformed audiences.

Sometimes, after a particular reading about race, I ask students to write about the question of what whiteness is. This question generally takes students of all races aback, momentarily. By approaching questions about race, class, gender, and sexuality in ways that consider "God in all things," by asking stu-dents to think through the implications of whiteness, there can be an opening up, a broader consideration of other worldviews, and a chance to reflect. When I ask a question about what whiteness is and ask students to write about it, I don't have a particular answer in mind, and, when I am my best self, I write, too. I am trying to model discernment as well as teach it. Being able to ask the question at all is part of my growing awareness of audience. I have learned what a predominantly white, middle-class, Catholic student body responds to in gauging the kinds of questions I ask in service-learning courses.

Introduced to the process of discernment, especially around issues of race and class, students are better positioned to let "gritty reality" (as Kolvenbach writes) into their lives and learn to speak and write effectively about challenging and difficult topics. In my service-learning courses, I have found that some activities that mirror the stages of discernment in the *Spiritual Exercises* are useful tools for students as they engage in *eloquentia perfecta*. Students can gain a greater understanding of systemic injustice, and deepen their understanding of how their own experiences shape their vision and responses to inequality, by engaging in the kind of reflection, speech, and writing that has long been part of our Jesuit tradition.

APPENDIX: CRITICAL-INCIDENT QUESTIONNAIRE

A Place to Reflect on Your Learning

1. At what moment in class this week did you feel most engaged with what was happening?
2. At what moment in class this week did you feel most distanced from what was happening?
3. What action that anyone (teacher or student) took this week did you find most affirming and helpful?
4. What action that anyone (teacher or student) took this week did you find most troubling or confusing?
5. What about the class this week surprised you the most? (This could be something about your own reactions to what went on, or something that someone did, or anything else that occurs to you.)

NOTES

Thank you to Ann Marie Jursca Keffer, M.S.W, the associate director of the Saint Joseph's University Faith-Justice Institute, for her insights and contributions to this piece. And thank you to all of the staff in the Faith-Justice Institute who so seamlessly and generously facilitate, mediate, and create our service-learning program. Thank you to Melissa Goldthwaite, PhD, Saint Joseph's University, and the many other readers of this chapter for their helpful advice. Many service-learning students over the years have pushed my thinking about issues of justice, and I need to thank them as well. This article began as a conference paper for the 2005 Commitment to Justice in Jesuit Higher Education Conference in Cleveland. Thank you to Thomas Brennan, S.J., PhD, and Peter Norberg, PhD, for presenting with me and reading early drafts of this paper.

1. See Cuban and Anderson for a helpful definition of continuum-of-service learning.

2. Jeffrey Howard in *Service-Learning Course Design Workbook* provides useful definitions of the differences between service-learning, internships and volunteering. "Service as Text: Making the Metaphor Meaningful" by Lori Varlotta is a useful for thinking about how service functions in the classroom.

3. See also *The Philadelphia Inquirer*, April 15, 2012.

4. For more on the complexity of teaching service learning, see Davi et al., "Feminist Ways" and "Exploring Difference," and Green, "Difficult Stories" and "But You Aren't White."

5. See Delpit for more on language.

WORKS CITED

Brackley, Dean. *The Call to Discernment in Troubled Times: New Perspectives on the Transformative Wisdom of Ignatius of Loyola*. New York: Crossroad, 1994.

———. "Higher Standards." In *A Jesuit Education Reader*, ed. Traub, 189–94. Chicago: Loyola Press, 2008.

Brookfield, Stephen. *Becoming a Critically Reflective Teacher*. San Francisco: Jossey-Bass, 1995.

Carter, Robert T. "Is White a Race? Expressions of White Racial Identity." In *Off White: Readings on Race, Power, and Society*, ed. by Michelle Fine, Lois Wise, Linda C. Powell, and L. Mun Wong, 198–209. New York: Routledge, 1997.

College Affordability and Transparency Center. U.S. Department of Education. Accessed June 22, 2012.

Cuban, Sondra, and Jeffrey B. Anderson. "Where's the Justice in Service-Learning? Institutionalizing Service-Learning from a Social Justice Perspective at a Jesuit University." *Equity and Excellence in Education*. 40 (2007): 144–55.

Davi, Angelique, Michelle Dunlap, and Ann E. Green. "Exploring Difference in the Service-Learning Classroom: Three Teachers Write about Anger, Sexuality, and Teaching for Justice." *Reflections: A Journal of Writing, Service-Learning, and Community Literacy*. 4, no. 1 (Spring 2007): 41–66. Reprinted in *Writing and Community Engagement: A Critical Sourcebook*, ed. Thomas Deans, Barbara Roswell, and Adrian Wurr. New York: Bedford / St. Martins.

———. "Feminist Ways of Seeing: Preparing Students for Service Learning." In *Handbook on Service-Learning in Women's Studies, Interdisciplinary Studies, and the Disciplines*, 14–25, 91–92 Institute for Teaching and Research on Women. (ITROW). 2007.

Delpit, Lisa. *Other People's Children: Cultural Conflict in the Classroom*. New York: New Press, 1995.

Denk, Kurt M. "Making Connections, Finding Meaning, Engaging the World: Theory and Techniques for Ignatian Reflection on Service for and with Others." Justice Web: A Resource for Jesuit Colleges and Universities: Ignatian Spirituality Resources. Loyola University, Maryland.

Green, Ann E. "'But You Aren't White': Racial Perceptions and Service-Learning." *Michigan Journal of Community Service-Learning* 8, no. 1 (2001): 18–26.

———. "Difficult Stories: Service-Learning, Race, Class, and Whiteness." *College Composition and Communication* 56, no. 2 (2003): 276–301.

Howard, Jeffrey. *Service-Learning Course Design Workbook*. Ann Arbor, Mich.: University of Michigan Office of Community Service Learning Press, 2001.

Kolvenbach, Peter Hans. "The Service of Faith and the Promotion of Justice in American Jesuit Higher Education." In *A Jesuit Education Reader*, ed. Traub, 163–76. Chicago: Loyola Press, 2008.

Martin, James. *The Jesuit Guide to Almost Everything: Spirituality for Real Life*. New York: HarperCollins, 2010.

Mitchell, Tania D., David M. Donahue and Courtney Young-Law. "Service Learning as a Pedagogy of Whiteness." *Equity and Excellence in Education* 45, no. 4 (November 2012): 612–29.

Nicolás, Adolfo. "Challenges to Jesuit Higher Education Today." *Conversations on Jesuit Higher Education Today* 40, no. 5: 6–9.

Traub, George W., ed. *A Jesuit Education Reader: Contemporary Writing on the Jesuit Mission in Education, Principles, the Issue of Catholic Identity, Practical Applications of the Ignatian Way, and More*. Chicago: Loyola Press, 2008.

Varlotta, Lori. "Service as Text: Making the Metaphor Meaningful." *Michigan Journal of Community Service Learning* (Fall 2000): 76–84.

NETWORKING RHETORIC FOR JESUIT
EDUCATION IN A NEW WORLD

Jenn Fishman and Rebecca S. Nowacek

> The Society eagerly undertakes secondary and higher education so that Jesuits can be properly instructed both in doctrine and in the other matters that contribute to helping souls, and so they can share with their neighbors what they themselves have learned.
>
> —*Ratio atque Institutio Studiorum*

> That word, "networking," so often used these days, is, in fact, typical, of the "new world" in which we live—a world which has as its "principal new feature," what Pope Benedict XVI calls "the explosion of worldwide interdependence, commonly known as globalization."
>
> —Adolfo Nicolás, S.J., "Depth, Universality, and Learned Ministry: Challenges to Jesuit Higher Education Today"

Historically, rhetoric has had pride of place in Jesuit higher education. During the sixteenth and seventeenth centuries, as the first Jesuit schools were established across Europe and elsewhere, rhetoric was the crown jewel of the Jesuit trivium or "lower studies," which also included humanities and grammar. Distinguished from basic reading and writing instruction, rhetorical study was defined as "education in perfect eloquence," or what the *Ratio atque Institutio Studiorum* describes as "mastery of rules for speaking, rules for style, and [rules] for scholarly learning" (155). In the curriculum ruled by the *Ratio*, every day begins with exercises in memorization and rhetorical precepts followed by close examination of Greco-Roman exemplars in oratory, poetry, and drama. In addition, the *Ratio* prescribes composition exercises and the publication or performance of students' work. Of course, the curriculum invoked by any textbook is not necessarily the curriculum taught. In the case of the *Ratio*, which provincials tested in their schools prior to its 1599 publication, the text was simplified both for the sake of brevity and to accommodate application over time across highly varied educational settings. Thus, while contemporary readers may be alternately baffled and bemused by some of the *Ratio*'s recommendations, including bans against swords and swearing (199), they should also recognize extended lines of connection between past and present pedagogical practices, from prompts to place annual book orders on time to strategies for cultivating the kind of personal relationships between students and teachers that prepare young people for lives of justice and service to others (*Characteristics*, 180–81).

Readers of the *Ratio* should also recognize a familiar triangulation of rhetorical education, available technology, and far-flung community. Indeed, the first edition of the *Ratio*, as an artifact of early book culture, bears witness to a Jesuit legacy of new media integration for the purposes of geographically widespread communication. From this point of view, the *Ratio* is not only a handbook for novice educators and a treatise on the relevance of the *studia humanitatis* to Christian education (Padberg, O'Malley); it is also a record of rhetoric at the crossroads of early modern education change and evolving literacy. Examined in this light, the identification of speech, style, and scholarship as a keystone in Jesuit schooling reinscribes the complex amalgam of orality and literacy characteristic of the time. Thus while the "Rules for Professors of Rhetoric" are rich with oral residue, which Walter J. Ong defines as habits of mind and practices "tracing back to preliterate situations . . . or deriving from the dominance of the oral as a medium" ("Oral Residue," 146), they also exhibit ways of thinking and modes of expression associated with both writing and print. Accordingly, the *Ratio* asserts that "daily exercise of the memory" is "necessary for the rhetorician" (157), and it underscores the importance of "rather frequent solo delivery from a podium in the auditorium, the church, and the classroom." At the same time the *Ratio* encourages students to "post their own signed poetic compositions publicly" on a regular basis (165–6), and, more generally, to prepare themselves for lives in which direct ministry is increasingly augmented by books, pamphlets, and engravings.

In this essay, where our main interest is the role of rhetoric in the present—and future—of Jesuit higher education, we locate our work at the current juncture of education change and literacy evolution. Specifically, we query *eloquentia perfecta* in what Ong refers to as "our electronic age." In *Interfaces of the Word: Studies in the Evolution of Consciousness and Culture*, Ong defines this era in relation to "a new kind of orality," secondary orality, which is paradoxically dependent on the closed logics of writing and print and yet endemic to "cultures very much drawn to openness and in particular to open-system models for conceptual representations" (305). At least in the late 1970s, when *Interfaces* was published, television "manifest[ed] perhaps most clearly, and certainly most massively and deeply," the impact of secondary orality: namely, "the breaking up of the closed systems associated with the verbal art forms generated by writing and print" (315). Likewise, "ecological concern" represented for Ong "the ultimate in open-system awareness," exemplifying the human ability to conceive individuals as "inextricably related to the other, the outside, the 'environment'" (324, 325). Today, the Internet may provide even greater challenges to literacy, while "networks" may best capture our sense of the systems that identify and divide us. Certainly, networks now preoccupy Jesuit educators, including participants in the 2010 conference where Superior

General Father Adolfo Nicolás identified global and technological concerns associated with networking as paramount. While Fr. Nicolás urged his international audience to apply themselves to three goals—"promoting depth of thought and imagination," "re-discovering and implementing [Jesuit] 'universality,'" and "renewing the Jesuit commitment to learned ministry" (2)—on this occasion we ask how can and should rhetoric contribute?

We pose this question against the backdrop of Jesuit education represented by this anthology as well as against the larger setting of historical rhetorics, which portrays rhetorical education as a perpetual push–pull of prescriptiveness and accommodationism. For our part, we do not anticipate that the answers will be best articulated through new rulebooks or compulsory curricula, and we do not expect rhetoric's contribution to be only in general, supporting roles. Instead, attentive to the triangulation of Jesuit education, new media, and global networking, we believe that rhetoric can contribute most when it is understood and taught as a productive architectonic art. That is to say, with Richard McKeon, we embrace the idea that rhetoric is epistemic, and as teachers we believe it is our goal to help students realize their potential as rhetor-*architectons*, or master builders responsible for the fundamental work of "producing subject matters and organizing them in relation to each other and to the problems to be solved" (McKeon 48). Architectonic productive rhetoric operates—or has the potential to operate—within open systems to produce both knowledge and relationships across networks of time and space as well as disciplines, campuses, and communities. Interested in what *this* rhetoric can and should contribute to post-secondary Jesuit education, we turn to two examples from our own campus: Who Counts? and the Social Innovation Initiative. While neither is part of Marquette's regular rhetoric curriculum, which includes first-year English, the writing-intensive English major, and regular writing-center programming, both initiatives foster rhetorical praxes we believe are exemplary. Specifically, Who Counts? and Social Innovation engage students in global, multimodal writing for reflection and social action, and in doing so they model some of the ways in which *eloquentia perfecta* not only can but also already does contribute to Jesuit education in a networked age.

TAKING INITIATIVE

Over the last ten years, Marquette University has supported a variety of curricular and co-curricular initiatives, including Who Counts? Math Across the Curriculum for Global Learning (2007–10), and the Social Innovation Initiative (2010–present). On the surface, math instruction and social entrepreneurship appear to have little in common and little to do with rhetoric. Who Counts? was designed to strengthen students' quantitative-reasoning abilities and confidence through direct instruction in non-STEM courses, while the Social Innovation Initiative aims to "leverag[e] institutional identity for innovation" by "integrating social entrepreneurship into Marquette's curriculum" and "position[ing] the university as a regional convener for social entrepreneurship" ("Marquette University"). At root, however, both initiatives share a substantial commitment to connecting Jesuit education with networked concerns. Who Counts? developed in relation to Marquette's participation in an Association of American Colleges and Universities initiative for global learning and social responsibility, which was "built on the assumption that we live in an interdependent but unequal world and that higher education can prepare students to not only thrive in such a world, but to creatively and responsibly remedy its inequities and problems" ("Shared Futures"). Similarly, the Social Innovation Initiative developed in conjunction with Marquette's designation as an Ashoka Changemaker Campus. Ashoka is the premier global organization for social entrepreneurs, or individuals seeking system-changing solutions to social problems, and its Changemaker Campus Program recognizes and supports "institutions [that] share the vision for higher education to become the next global driver of social change by transforming the educational experience into a world-changing experience" ("Changemaker"). Putting these aspirational statements to the test, faculty and students undertook curricular and co-curricular activities spanning courses, contests, and conferences. Engaged directly in math education and social innovation, they were also reinventing *eloquentia perfecta* for a networked age.

Over the three years that Who Counts? was supported by a grant from the Fund for the Improvement of Postsecondary Education (FIPSE), participants amassed a virtual primer for contemporary Jesuit rhetoric. Indeed, the Who Counts? corpus provides a basic guide to *eloquentia perfecta* as a means of effectively identifying and engaging global concerns. As project director and professor of English Christine L. Krueger explains, "global" in this context refers not to world geography or cosmography but to an attitude that "include[s] any [pedagogical] approach which addresses the interdependence of human experience across local, national, international, and/or transnational contexts" ("Call"). Ultimately, more than two thousand students enrolled in courses offered by faculty from seventeen departments. Teaching students how quantitative reasoning informs everything from project management to health economics to quests for God, the Who Counts? curriculum illuminated the rhetorical nature of mathematical data, and, at the same time, it brought reflection to the fore. In particular, the mathematical-reasoning assignments (MRAs) that anchored Who Counts? instruction called attention to reflection as a "formative and liberating" or architectonic productive process ("Ignatian Pedagogy," in Duminuco, 248). As such, Who Counts? demonstrated in practical terms one of the most powerful ways in which rhetorical learning might be integral to networked Jesuit education.

For example, in Literatures of Migration and Transnational Justice, taught by John Su, mathematical-reasoning assignments asked students to investigate claims such as "Illegal immigrants are stealing jobs from Americans" and "Britain is becoming an Islamic state." To complete these assignments, students had to find and work with relevant data, creating visual representations, predicting future outcomes, and formulating their own responses. As much mathematical rhetoric assignments as reasoning assignments, Su's MRAs compelled students to become active consumers as well as producers of quantitative data-based arguments. Su's MRAs also helped students discover, hands-on, how quantitative rhetorics inform both literary production and interpretation; in conjunction with subsequent encyclopedia-entry and research-essay assignments, his MRAs also encouraged students to gain a new understanding of literary study as inquiry into open systems of texts. Ultimately, Literatures of Migration encouraged students to gain new perspectives on reflection by reflecting on subject matter and engaging in self-reflection. To do so, Su steadily engaged students in deliberate acts of invention, inquiry, and both verbal and visual interpretation, teaching them the basics of classical rhetorical learning alongside literature and quantitative reasoning. In this way, Who Counts? transposes reflection into a new, networked key, helping students to connect knowledge and build relationships across disciplinary as well as global communities. As Su's course demonstrates, by taking a global approach, professors of various subjects become professors of rhetoric, working to help students first perceive and then reflect on their relationship to contemporary consciousness and culture.

Social Innovation also positions Jesuit education globally, acting as an academic GPS that invites students, faculty, and staff to participate in a kind of JesEd 2.0. Invoking the second-generation designation, which names emergent online applications and the principles behind them (O'Reilly), the version of Jesuit instruction that Social Innovation encourages is an aggregate of recent and ongoing developments. Laying important groundwork for next-generation developments, *The Characteristics of Jesuit Education* (1986) connects the "total formation of each individual within community" with not only the sound intellectual formation gained through "mastery of basic humanistic and scientific disciplines" but also through "a careful and critical study of technology" (176–77). *Characteristics* also promotes "effective communication skills," including "traditional skills in speaking and writing" and "facility with modern instruments of communication such as film and video" (177). Of course, fully realized *eloquentia perfecta* in a networked age includes not only individual media skills but also the multimodal savvy necessary for activating rhetoric as an architectonic productive art. At the Annual Social Innovation Design Contest, for example, students work in pairs or teams, pitching solutions to social problems. Like the competitions described in the *Ratio*, sponsored "to feed an honorable rivalry" among students and "to spur studies" (148), the Social Innovation Design Contest emphasizes idea generation, problem solving, systems thinking, and team building. The contest also emphasizes the importance of multimodal rhetoric, and students argue their designs via Power-point and Prezi presentations that integrate the spoken and written word with word art, still images, charts and graphs, video clips, and more.

As the Design Contest demonstrates, Marquette's Social Innovation Initiative facilitates networked Jesuit education through its global orientation and the priority it places on multimodal communication. Social Innovation also performs a bridging role, between campus and community, that is characteristic of JesEd 2.0. Jesuit educators have historically examined injustice within their curricula, "aware of and involved in the serious issues" of the day (*Characteristics*, 191, 192). What Social Innovation contributes is a tangible bridge between the preparatory, consciousness-raising work of the classroom and actual works of justice. Students respond with designs for projects that address water shortages in African countries, hunger and poverty in neighborhoods adjacent to campus, youth education, prisoner reintegration, and more. While some Design Contest presentations are progymnasmatic, more rudimentary exercises than fully mature proposals for feasible resolutions to complex social problems, the contest nevertheless creates an opportunity for winning participants to implement their ideas. At Marquette, Social Entrepreneurs in Residence such as Ashoka Fellow Greg Van Kirk models this kind of networking. His MicroConsignment initiative leads health, education, economic, and energy efforts in rural, isolated communities across Latin America. Closer to home, Marquette Faculty Champions from every college serve as mentors to the Social Innovation and Entrepreneurship Student Organization. The co- and extracurricular instruction that these educators provide is distinct from service learning and other efforts to scaffold experiential learning in relation to specific courses and disciplinary content. Operating with centrifugal rather than centripetal force, Social Innovation affirms Jesuit education as both formative and performative. That is to say, it prepares students for lives as changemakers by enabling them to enact social change as students and to "be the difference" during as well as after their college years.

To summarize our observations: We recognize Who Counts? and Social Innovation as representative examples of campus initiatives across the Associatoin of Jesuit Colleges and Universities. We also recognize them as drivers of contemporary education and education reform that underscore the exigency for reconsidering the objectives and scope of *eloquentia perfecta* in and for a networked world. Who Counts? was part of a larger effort to "galvanize Marquette's next stage of general education reform" by "integrating our general education curriculum into our mission," better connecting it to "diversity, service-learning, and justice education initiatives," and "creating structures for faculty to . . . develop interdisciplinary opportunities for students" ("Shared Futures"). Similarly, Social Innovation stands to galvanize the campus community. At the 2012 Ashoka U Exchange Conference, colleagues from New York University and Tulane described how their social-innovation programs helped their institutions revitalize in the wake of 9/11 and Hurricane Katrina, respectively. At Marquette, where recent incidents of sexual violence and intolerance signaled an urgent need to reconsider diversity from multiple standpoints, the Social Innovation Initiative is poised to contribute powerfully, not least because of its capacity to foster the development and use of *eloquentia perfecta* as a tool for multimodal reflection and social action in response to the pressing, global concerns of a networked age.

IN LIEU OF RULES

We opened this essay with epigraphs from texts that span the technologizing of the word in Jesuit higher education. Positioned at the start of this tradition and at the onset of print, the *Ratio* counsels professors of rhetoric and other academic personnel to "energetically devote their efforts to making sure that what is prescribed . . . is put into effect in a smooth and trouble-free manner" (6). Conversely, Fr. Nicolás enumerates the challenges that Jesuit educators face in a "new world" of networking and secondary orality. As professors of rhetoric in this context, we conclude this essay not with new rules but with recommendations, which we intend especially for readers who are stewards of *eloquentia perfecta* in the present day.

1. We recommend collaboration across the curriculum and across curricular, co-curricular, and extracurricular boundaries. Our examples—Marquette's Who Counts? program and its Social Innovation Initiative—show how the province of *eloquentia perfecta* continues to encompass the full range of Jesuit educational activities, reaching beyond a single class or department. And so colleagues across campus—in other departments and colleges, in the Center for Teaching and Learning, in Student Life, in the President's office and elsewhere—are partners in ensuring that rhetoric reaches its potential as an architectonic productive art clearly linked to the mission of the university in ways that prove profoundly meaningful.

2. We advocate visibility. In both Who Counts? and the Social Innovation Initiative, rhetorical teaching and learning may have been everywhere in evidence, but instruction was often tacit, and as a result the rigors of rhetorical learning were unacknowledged while the histories, theories, and purposes of rhetorical praxes were unexplored. Research in rhetoric and composition, especially studies informed by educational psychology and cognitive theory, illuminate the value of making tacit knowledge explicit. To do so in the context of Jesuit education, everyone involved in designated rhetoric curricula—first-year composition, undergraduate writing courses, graduate pedagogy courses, and rhetoric graduate programs—has a special responsibility to make *eloquentia perfecta* known to its practitioners, while making its history as well as its contemporary study both accessible and germane to overarching educational aims.

3. We encourage sustainable change. Recognizing that this is perhaps our most challenging recommendation, we urge colleagues seeking new opportunities for *eloquentia perfecta*, whether through special initiatives or curriculum reviews, to plan programs and create courses that can be sustained over time. The very strengths of programs that embody architectonic productive rhetoric—their multidisciplinary, co-curricular nature, forging relationships and connections across time and space, disciplines and communities—can also make them particularly vulnerable. Despite the success of Who Counts?, for example, which documented positive changes in students' attitudes toward quantitative reasoning, no amount of data could generate funds equal to the program's initial FIPSE grant. As a result, Who Counts? program leaders have sought new partners in the university libraries and writing center, and individual faculty continue to design and assign mathematical-reasoning assignments to their students. Similarly, the future of the Social Innovation Initiative is uncertain. The same extensive energy that draws participants to it also works against the intensive nature of university life, including the narrow tracks of most degree programs, the structural constraints of department and college budget lines, and the entrenched nature of hierarchical organizational practices. In this context, it remains to be seen whether and how an inter- and extra-disciplinary initiative such as Social Innovation will be able to reach its full potential for changemaking over time.

Despite these and other challenges, we remain hopeful about the future of networking rhetoric for Jesuit higher education in a "new world." In making this admission, we see ourselves as neither Mirandas, regarding the territory ahead as a brave new world ripe for our discovery, nor as doomsayers who greet new means of networking and mediation as harbingers of humanity's end. Instead, we are encouraged as educators by the steadfast commitment of the Jesuit tradition to instruction that teaches students to triangulate reflection, experience, and social action, and we appreciate the role rhetoric is poised to play. Celebrating the four hundredth anniversary of the *Ratio* in 1999, Vincent J. Duminuco, S.J., called for "*a framework of inquiry that encourages the process of wrestling with significant issues and complex values of life, and professors capable and willing to guide that inquiry*" (156, his emphasis). We see rhetoric and specifically the Jesuit rhetorical tradition embodied by *eloquentia perfecta* as ready to help engineer this framework, especially as we continue working with one another and with our students to foster global attitudes and multimodal ways of expressing them.

WORKS CITED

"Call for Proposals: "Who Counts? Math Across the Curriculum for Global Learning." For Faculty and Staff: Core Documents for Faculty. Marquette University.

http://www.marquette.edu/coreinfo/documents/Who%20Counts%20Call%20
for%20Proposals%20AY%202009-10.pdf. Accessed June 16, 2012.

"Changemaker Campus." Ashoka U. Askoka, 2011. http://ashokau.org/changemaker
-campus/. Accessed June 16, 2012.

Characteristics of Jesuit Education. Rome: Jesuit Curia, 1986.

Duminuco, Vincent J. "A New *Ratio* for a New Millennium?" *The Jesuit Ratio
Studiorum: 400th Anniversary Perspectives*, ed. Vincent J. Duminuco, 145–61.
New York: Fordham University Press, 2000.

Kreuger, Christine L. "Who Counts: Math Across the Curriculum for Global
Learning." September 24, 2010. http://www.youtube.com/watch?v=htpoRDsnua4.
Accessed May 29, 2012.

Marquette University. *Ahsoka U.* Ashoka, 2011. http://ashokau.org/marquette
-university/. Accesed June 18, 2012.

McKeon, Richard. "The Uses of Rhetoric in a Technological Age: Architectonic
Productive Arts." In *The Prospect of Rhetoric*, ed. Lloyd F. Bitzer and Edwin Black.
Englewood Cliffs, N.J.: Prentice Hall, 1971.

Nicolás, Adolfo. "Depth, Universality, and Learned Ministry: Challenges to Jesuit
Higher Education Today." *Networking Jesuit Higher Education: Shaping the Future
for a Humane, Just, Sustainable Globe.* Mexico City, April 23, 2010. *AJCUnet.edu*,
16 June 16, 2010. Association of Jesuit Colleges and Universities. http://www
.ajcunet.edu/ajcunet/files/ccLibraryFiles/Filename/000000000595/NicolasSJ.pdf.
Accessed April 8, 2012.

O'Malley, John W. "From the 1599 *Ratio Studiorum* to the Present: A Humanist
Tradition?" In *The Jesuit Ratio Studiorum: 400th Anniversary Perspectives*, ed.
Duminuco, 127–44.

Ong, Walter. *Interfaces of the Word: Studies in the Evolution of Consciousness and
Culture.* Ithaca, N.Y.: Cornell University Press, 1977.

———. "Oral Residue in Tudor Prose Style." *Publications of the Modern Language
Association* 80, no. 3 (June 1965): 145–54.

O'Reilly, Tim. "What Is 2.0: Design Patterns and Business Models for the Next
Generation of Software." O'Reilly.com. September 30, 2005. Accessed June 19,
2012.

Padburg, "Development of the *Ratio Studiorum.*" *The Jesuit Ratio Studiorum: 400th
Anniversary Perspectives*, ed. Duminuco, 80–100.

The Ratio Studiorum: The Official Plan for Jesuit Education. Translated by Claude
Pavur. St. Louis: Institute of Jesuit Sources, 2005.

"Shared Futures: Global Learning and Social Responsibility." Association of
American Colleges and Universities. http://www.aacu.org/SharedFutures/index
.cfm. Accesed May 29, 2012.

Social Innovation Design Contest. Social Innovation Initiative at Marquette University. Marquette University. 2012. http://www.marquette.edu/social-innovation/
contest.shtml. Accessed April 25, 2012.

Su, John. Literatures of Migration and Transnational Justice. Syllabus. The Center for
Transnational Justice, Marquette University. http://www.marquette.edu/ctj/
documents/Su.pdf. Accessed June 16, 2012.

WHAT WE TALK ABOUT WHEN WE TALK ABOUT VOICE: REINTEGRATING THE ORAL IN THE CURRENT WRITING CLASSROOM

Vincent Casaregola

PART I: "IS THERE A VOICE IN THIS CLASS?"

Over thirty years ago, Stanley Fish wrote a book asking, "Is there a text in this class?" A different but parallel question echoes in my mind today: "Is there a *voice* in this class?" During any particular week in the semester, as I look out over a class about to begin, I witness students absorbed in a variety of texts and images appearing on the screens of their electronic notebooks, tablets, smartphones, and other devices. As I listen, I seem to I hear fewer words being spoken, the pre-class buzz of many voices increasingly replaced by what, to me, is reminiscent of the sound of a telegrapher's key—the incessant sound of fingers clicking away at the machine.[1] Sometimes the interactions suggest a resistance to direct speech, individually or collectively, as if the attempt to make actual conversation were more effort than it was worth. While it may be idiosyncratic, I cannot help but trust my sense that something is missing—the simple and, to me, quite reassuring sound of human voices in casual conversation.

My students are perfectly willing to try to attend to the class, and a number are also willing to dispense with, for a short time at least, some elements of their constant connectivity, although doing so appears to make them restless. Indeed, they show signs of a kind of electronic dependency, almost as if, for a new generation of human beings, full consciousness itself is dependent on being somehow plugged in. For many, that which is unmediated seems to have a strange unreality about it, like the experience of Binx Bolling, the main character in Walker Percy's *The Moviegoer*, for whom no place is quite real unless he has experienced it on film. (Binx also demonstrates an awkward emotional distance from actual human beings—a kind of mild, media-enhanced, affective disorder.)

These contemporary students are, of course, "digital natives," a title that some openly claim and most others would likely accept. Born into the world of the Web, many, even in early schooling, have been acclimated to digital environments as a significant (or possibly primary) mode of communication. There is nothing wrong with such developmental experience per se: these students have become quite efficient at maneuvering through the world of digital environments, achieving a high level of "digital literacy" (which I prefer to call "digital *mediacy*.") They know the basic skill sets and how to manage the skills to communicate through a variety of new digital media. This is not only desirable but actually necessary, given the ubiquitous nature of digital media and their still expanding influence on communication and culture.

As I watch these students, their messages move swiftly from device to device, brief texts that flash across the screens and across consciousness, their words both exciting and expendable at once. Whether these communications enhance to or create distraction from the classroom experience is an open question. They probably provide both, depending on the behavior of individual students, circumstances of specific classes and even classroom spaces. Like other media technologies (including books), these devices certainly provide opportunities for increased attention as well as access to a wide range of useful information for class discussion, but they also offer many silent temptations that disrupt work of the class and the flow of that discussion (and perhaps the sense of the class as a community).[2]

Often messages like these satisfy the transactional informational needs of personal or professional relationships (e.g., checking times and places of meetings, confirming the fulfillment of an obligation, noting a prescription to be picked up, or a bill to be paid). Many times, however, the meaning is ephemeral, digital small talk or "phatic" communication. Yet where actual oral small talk in a face-to-face situation brings with it a host of additional nonverbal elements, most of those are lost in the digital version (a loss not fully compensated by iconic elements such as emoticons and texting abbreviations). Moreover, face-to-face small talk reinforces the sense of relationship with one person (or a few people) in a particular setting, amplifying the sense of "presence" in the holistic experience of sound.[3] For digital phatic messages, however, the dominant purpose can seem the very act of connectivity itself—reemphasizing that each individual is still "alive" in the network, as if the network and the technology were a significant or primary audience. For some people, it is as if to be even temporarily cut off from this evolving textual process would be stressful and isolating. In her recent book *Alone Together: Why We Expect More from Technology and Less from Each Other* (2011), social psychologist and new media scholar Sherry Turkle explores these problems in depth. And problems they are: For example, I recently asked one student, "What would happen if something went wrong with the network and you could not text anyone?" She candidly replied, "Well, it would be hard for a while to get used to it. It is kind of like a drug. I guess I would have to go through withdrawal."

Now, before it appears that I am a technophobe, evoking dystopic images of "The Borg" from *Star Trek* or the machine-based demons from *The Matrix*, I should emphasize that I do not oppose the deployment of these new media either in academic and scholarly discourse or in more common popular settings. Indeed, these new media have provided truly wonderful opportunities to expand our teaching and our research, as well as to expand the cultural experiences of our students. But it's important to acknowledge that every new educational technology must be assessed, and careful assessment has not always been possible in the rapidly developing environments of new media. All new technologies have opportunity costs. Where I see these costs most evident, at present, is in what appears to be a gradual erosion of spoken discourse (both interpersonal and public), and I believe that the extent to which the new media have come to dominate our activities as teachers or students (as well as the rapid increase of their overall influence) has led to some specific unanticipated consequences that we should consider as we proceed to incorporate them in our pedagogies. Much has been written on the current and future benefits of these technologies (see Fishman and Nowacek, Part III), but I wish to examine these particular costs and how to mitigate them, sometimes through alternative applications of the very same media.

Of course, new communication media have always brought challenges throughout the long history of written discourse. Writing and then printing, which broadened and deepened the impact of the written word across time and place, were once new technologies as well, and the advent of writing and printing caused far-reaching cultural changes. Indeed, as Walter J. Ong noted, writing is a technology that "restructures consciousness." Writing when radio and then television were the shockingly new and seemingly frightening media, Ong reminds us that any and all media interact both with individual brains and minds and with cultural communities and organizations, eventually shaping cultural epistemology in many ways, both obvious and subtle (*Orality and Literacy*, 78–83; see also Lauer Rice, Part II). His teacher and friend Marshall McLuhan—a media guru, whose posthumous reputation, having spent its decades in the wilderness, has come now round once again with authority—argued that all technologies, media included, both extend the human body and mind and also serve to "amputate" or eliminate elements of the human person, figuratively at least.[4] When we think of the relationships between technology and language, we realize that the issues are not only about electronics.[5]

So in this second decade of the twenty-first century, standing before that very representative class of the perpetually plugged-in before class starts, I ask myself, what (in McLuhan's terms) has been amputated here? As you will have guessed, it seems to be the active, self-sponsored exercise of the voice. Several signs suggest this to be the case, not the least of which is the often clipped, chirped, guttural, or chiming speech—almost always too rapid and frequently indecipherable—left on my voicemail. These messages originate with voices, yes, and human ones, indeed, but they seem at times so altered by habits of speech that might be useful within peer groups where the contexts are already shared but almost insufficient to the needs of more public communication. In fact, these voices sometimes seem to emanate from a state of mind that perceives little or no need for a listener to understand what is said, merely to be an auditory witness to the sound. In my more pessimistic moments, I fear that the ability and willingness to speak and listen carefully in a variety of discourse communities seems to be diminishing year by year, being replaced by the ability to produce and consume a wider multiplicity of sounds (and images). That cornucopia of sounds may engage the consuming listener at some level, and satisfy the producing speaker (both of whom may be multitasking in the process), but such interactions do not necessarily lead to genuine, caring dialogue and communion. The *I* and the *thou* of any relationship can be lost, drowned in noise.

Indeed, I find that these discourse habits not only impact casual conversation but also seem increasingly evident in writing. As I read my students' writing, in both critical and creative modes, I find that they demonstrate a decreasing comfort with and understanding of the basic rhythmic potential of language. In part, this rhythm is achieved through consciously careful syntactic construction and semantic selection, and yet on another level, there is a "felt sense" of language rhythm that comes from frequent, active engagement in speaking that is also rooted in careful, active listening. I worry that that some students are developing a "tin ear" in their writing because they seem less and less attuned to the potential music of language, spoken or written, poetry or prose, in part because of their increasing dependence on mediated speech and on written forms so cryptic, coded, and iconic as to return almost to pictograms. Such forms, often quite efficient and not without artfulness, militate against more rhythmic language structures, because of their often clipped and fragmentary nature. Decreased attention to the potential learned artfulness of everyday speech results in speaking and listening habits that have consequences for the writing. Writing in new media environments places a high value on a kind of rapid verbal shorthand that often pays little attention to speech rhythms and nuances, eroding some of the useful connections between the spoken and written word. This is not necessarily a new problem, nor is it attributable exclusively to the extensive and intensive use of new media. Still, I would argue that the loss of longer and more rhythmic constructions can deteriorate the sense of "voice" in writing, a sense that is fundamental to building the essential relationship between reader and writer.

Voice, that profound and problematic concept in writing, is linked inexorably with our experience of sound, and sound, as Ong was so fond of reminding his listeners as well as his readers, leads us to the experience of "presence." While much ink has been spilled over both terms—*voice* and *presence*—I believe both essential for the understanding of language in all its forms. Ong reminds us that the experience of language is a complex human one, rooted in the body and the "sensorium." For Ong, speech is the occasion when the literal presence of sound is experienced by both the one who utters it and the one who hears it. And it is a multisensory experience because sound impacts not only the ear but the whole body.

Consciously directed at the sense of hearing, the waves of sound produced are not only heard by the ear but felt by the body. Unconsciously, our skin feels the touch of utterance, the potential caress of language, the sense of it enveloping us, whether as a gesture of love or of anger. Sound encompasses us in the moment, in time and place and the acoustics of life. This is what Ong means by the "human sensorium," and this is what he means by "presence." This latter term refers not to some linguistic abstraction about speech versus writing but to the fundamental fact that we bodily experience speech in time and place in ways that we do not experience writing. Presence points to the immediacy of interpersonal interaction that is experienced through this comprehensive sensory and psychological event. Our sense of relatedness to others is intricately interwoven with our experience of speech, of dialogue, of language embodied in what Ong refers to as "the human life world." In short, while all language, written or spoken, can "touch" us metaphorically, only direct speech literally causes sound to touch our bodies, a subtle but undeniable sensory experience that adds an underlying element to the emotional texture of direct speech.

Of course, communicative technologies are not foreign to human nature and human culture; indeed, they are integral to all aspects of human life, since the earliest human communities of hunters and gatherers shared their experiences through rituals we can now recall only from their cave paintings and other artifacts. At the same time, as many years of environmental science and ecological studies have also taught us, technologies are not necessarily benign in their impacts on either the biosphere or the human communities in that biosphere. As with all forms of technology, it is not a question of the very fact of its artificiality but of its effects, good or bad. That is why those who develop or deploy new technologies have an obligation to engage in rigorous testing and technology assessment. McLuhan's endlessly quoted and frequently misapplied dictum that "the medium is the message" refers to the fact that broadly adopted technologies, by virtue of their very existence and constant use, deliver the ontological message of their own structure and function to the minds and bodies of the users. In the case of media technologies, that means that widely adopted new media change the users through the action of the use—physiologically, psychologically, and culturally. We should know, as best we can, before broadly deploying a technology, that it will accomplish its goals as well as or better than what we currently use to meet such needs, and that it will do so with fewer negative side effects. These are the rules we now use for assessing industrial, energy, transportation, medical, and other technologies, and asking communication technologies, new or old, to abide by such rules seems quite just and useful. In the case of new media technologies, as with the others, deployment preceded analysis because of the dominance of power on the supply side of economic activity. For most of the past three decades, the electronics industry in general, and its computer and communication sectors more specifically, have driven the process. Consumers have been propelled into an accelerating process of technological change without much time to evaluate the consequences. Since the industry has been large and powerful enough, it can leverage the adoption of these new technologies in business, government, education, and organizational settings. Consumers have had little choice but to follow along. Of course, there have been many and varied benefits as a result. Yet as we saw with the automotive industry in the first half of the twentieth century, only after more than half a century did we really begin to see the negative consequences of the aggressive deployment of this transportation technology. We are now in the fourth decade of the developments of micro- or personal computing and in the third decade of web technologies, and we have yet to do much thorough assessment because we have been too busy trying to keep up with each new generation of products. Thus, new media technologies, deployed either with the general public or in academic settings, have therefore not been subjected to this basic and important kind of technology assessment.[6]

It is impossible, of course, to reverse time and it is unrealistic to expect that we can keep ahead of an industry so supply-side in its fundamental economics and so powerful in its influence. Obviously, we need to find ways of "embracing" the new technologies while making sure that, when they "hug back," they do not crush us. We can, I believe, receive the multiple benefits of various new media technologies (academically and otherwise) while we compensate for the inevitable "amputations" they create. This requires a great deal of work and patience. And for the teaching of rhetoric and composition in this moment, I think it calls for a re-exploration of the dynamics of voice.

THE PROBLEM OF VOICE: LET'S NOT LOOK INTO IT—LET'S LISTEN INSTEAD

Walter Ong was fond of writing (and saying) that spoken language is deeply embodied, both as we listen and as we speak. Counterintuitively, but accurately, our experience of spoken language begins not with the sense of hearing but with the sense of touch, and our bodies feel sound before they hear it (feel it, even if they do not hear it in the traditional sense).[7] Sound is kinetic energy first and foremost, carried on waves through the medium of air, washing up against and over the body even before entering the ear, whose complex mechanical and neurological structures convert kinetic energy to the electrochemical energy carried by the nerves into our brain (and so into our consciousness). Our bodies also feel sound before we utter it, feel it in the subtle movements of the structures of the larynx and the motion of breath through the lungs and up across vocal structures. Speech is tactile before it is sonic. Over sixty years ago, the poet Charles Olson captured something of the relationship between the bodily production of sound and the breath-based nature of poetic rhythm with his concept of "projective verse," connecting the poetic line to the dynamics of breathing. That is just one more modern instance where the literal embodiment of language has been recognized as fundamental to its nature.

Sound also subtly but surely helps us understand our sense of placement in physical space, as the acoustic qualities of a room shape our experience of the sounds within it. Thus, our bodies in space and in time, experience sound and speech in a complex and multisensory, multimodal form. Indeed, the first true "media" technology for language may have been architectural rather than textual, in the form of an altered or built environment that is consciously designed to optimize the potential of sound. Ong accurately perceived the complex nature of speech, and he held that often the most important components of speech, though not the most frequently analyzed, have to do with the experience of the human sensorium—how when we speak to one another we sense a common presence in space and time that is distinctive and unique. We really do touch each other when we talk to one another face to face, in the same physical space, and, as noted earlier, this is not a metaphor but a fact of physics and biology.

Even in writing and reading, our sense of the spoken continues, not merely because what we write can be uttered aloud or because what we hear we can transcribe. Indeed, contemporary neuroscience research suggests that even during the act of silent reading and writing we trigger the speech centers in the brain along with our other language centers.[8] As we read or write in silence, activating no part of the speech or hearing mechanisms other than our breathing, still the nerves in the larynx and auditory areas are lighting up. Language, even in its most silent and visual forms, also comes up as speech on our internal radar. We are hardwired to sense the voice in the text, and we are evolved to this kind of synesthesia. That being said, we also engage in numerous practices, some unconscious but some highly artificial, by which we construct in writing elements of the spoken and the sonic. This includes everything from the obvious sonic effects of onomatopoeia in literal sound words like *buzz* or *bang* to the intricate prosody of the many formal and informal kinds of verse, and to the equally subtle, complex rhythms of carefully written prose. The vocal qualities of language influence our choices as we compose, often leading us to emulate speech patterns, accents, and dialectic differences in the syntactic construction of our sentences. Likewise, we consciously compose structures that create overt sound and sense patterns that integrate the conceptual with the rhythmic.

That written language often evokes, consciously and unconsciously, the experience of spoken words, can be widely agreed upon, but when we begin to examine in detail the nature of what we call "voice" in writing, much confusion can ensue. When experienced directly, voices seem concrete and identifiable, but we also specifically deploy the term *voice* in analysis and interpretation of prose and poetry, using it in a variety of metaphorical and analogic ways to get at something difficult to define—our complex sense of ourselves in relationship to the text we are reading. The complexity of what the term can represent often leads to uncertainty and disagreement. The term takes on meaning from its literal use to describe the idiosyncratic features of a particular individual's familiar speech that make it characteristic and identifiable, so much so that even if the person were hidden from us in all other ways, we would often recognize him or her from the unique qualities of the voice (as when a parent can, from across a crowded park or playground, pick out the specific cry of his or her own child's distress). Yet our individual sense of such experiences is itself particular and idiosyncratic, dependent on a range of issues in the psychology of perception, and making the concept of voice difficult to pin down. At the same time, we are reluctant to depart from this controlling metaphor as one of our primary means of analyzing our writing and reading, because, despite its complexities (or perhaps because of them), it evokes something essential in our experience of language.

Some might say that *voice* is merely another term for *style*, but I believe that style can be more easily reduced to specific patterns of syntax, semantics, and pragmatics. While conscious and unconscious stylistic choices in composing texts reflect habits of usage and patterns of vocalization, the term *voice* carries more weight than that in our discussions of writing. Indeed, as a term of art in of writing, *voice* has come to represent far more than simply stylistic choices; rather, it is the very personality and character of the writer as we experience that in the words themselves. For me, these qualities make the definition of voice echo Aristotle's description of the rhetorical concept of "ethos" in speech— "the character of the speaker" as "created in the speech" (not based on our prior knowledge of the speaker).[9] For Aristotle, this artful construction of character through language was the fundamental basis for the trust the audience would place in both the speaker and the speech. Likewise, the relationship between writer and reader, the potential intimacy between them, is intricately bound up in the subtle vocal nature of language.

In writing, therefore, voice serves as an obvious analogy for the relatedness of writer and reader, a way of the writer's evoking a sense of relationship to which the reader may respond and so be co-participant in the construction of the text (a shared effort of writer and reader). Writers attempt to suggest aspects of personality and relationship that the reader may recognize and interact with, allowing writing and reading to become a dialogue. At the same time, the term *voice* is not merely an analogy but also a window into how we experience our personalities and those of others; it is a textual echo of our oral verbal relatedness. Writers must be sensitive to the sound of language in order to write well, and no effective writing can ignore its sonic components. Awkwardly constructed sentences, with uneven rhythms or ill-chosen words, often keep us from fully appreciating what is being written because the implicit sound is cacophonous. With good reason and sometimes good results, writing teachers endlessly coach their students to read drafts aloud to determine if the writing is fluent and graceful. These terms reflect a metaphorical connection with the flow of sound through the language, the inherent potential for language to be musical, be it poetry or prose. Thus, voice in writing reflects both the evocation and the reception of personality in the text and also the musical power of language that makes it so memorable and effective in speech or writing. Failure to attend to such issues frequently produces writing that is leaden and difficult, weight without measure. Only through the experience of the spoken language, the sonic element, do we fully and effectively develop these qualities as writers. For writing instruction, then, we need to rediscover the means of bringing the "lost voice" back into the classroom.

COMPOSING AS PERFORMANCE / PRODUCING WHAT WE COMPOSE—SOME LESSONS FROM JESUIT EDUCATIONAL TRADITIONS FOR A CONTEMPORARY PEDAGOGY

"OK, can we get back to that classroom now?" Yes—all this analysis of the nature of voice in human communication may be fine, but how do such interests directly impact the pedagogical issues of constructing and teaching writing courses in a contemporary university? How can I begin to bring back to this room of gently clicking keys the additional sound of multiple human voices in more active performance of the spoken word?

Fortunately, I would say that the teaching of "voice" literally echoes through my academic setting. Working as I do in a Jesuit institution (indeed, in the very university where Walter Ong himself devoted his life to teaching, scholarship, and service), I am continually made aware of the multifaceted and robust educational traditions of the Jesuit order—whether in formal faculty symposia and workshops or in informal daily interchanges with colleagues and students. Here I can find both inspiration and precedent for evoking the human voice in the pedagogy of discourse, both oral and written. In the *Ratio Studiorum* itself, as in many of the other early Jesuit tracts on educational purpose and practice, we can find many examples of how to integrate the spoken word with the written text, the oral performance with the written discourse. Indeed, for the Jesuit order, both in its origins and in the present, the rhetorical act of teaching itself, so essential to the order's mission, is at least as much an oral art form as a written one. Additionally, it is a matter not merely of teachers preaching to the listening mass of students but, more importantly, of encouraging both individual students and groups to engage in open oral expression in the classroom and in public performances.

Thus, the traditions of voice come alive in countless ways for me, and for this, I am quite grateful. Many of these traditions are rooted in the long history of rhetorical education that goes as far back as Isocrates, a curricular model later evoked and redeveloped by Renaissance humanists from the fourteenth through the sixteenth centuries. These humanists, coming in the centuries immediately before the founding of the Jesuit order, and in many cases still contemporary with the first several generations of Jesuit educators, provided a Christian variation on the classical rhetorical tradition. This humanist model was also one that Jesuits admired and adopted as part, though certainly not all, of their educational program. It cannot be stated too strongly that the Jesuit mission has always been fundamentally to transform the order's deep commitment and devotion to the Catholic faith into an intricate and intensive pattern of combined spiritual, intellectual, and social action in the world. Thus, its focus on education was not only to develop and maintain a system to train each new generation of Jesuits but also to educate as many as possible of the laity as well, spreading the faith throughout communities wherever it established schools (O'Malley, 133–38).

So a spiritually driven but still intellectually robust educational agenda has always been central to the Jesuit mission. As the Jesuit historian John W. O'Malley has noted, in pursuing these ambitious goals, the early Jesuits drew on a range of cultural and religious influences, the first of these naturally being the Christian scriptures themselves (understood, of course, in the apostolic tradition of Roman Catholic theology and doctrine), in addition to a longstanding pattern of integrating Greco-Roman philosophy with Christian beliefs.[10] Central to this latter part of the project was the importance of the *Summa* of Thomas Aquinas and the tradition of scholastic philosophy and theology—all still fundamental elements of the Jesuit order and its educational program today.[11] Despite this strong foundation in scholasticism, however, the Jesuits were also heavily influenced by the intellectual and educational projects of Renaissance humanism and its strong ties to ancient Greco-Roman rhetoric. Founding both their order and their first schools during an intellectual period so shaped by the humanist agenda, the Jesuits turned to this influential tradition to help form the basic structure of their institutions, and this structure persisted far beyond the general decline of humanist thought in the seventeenth century (Attebury, 26). Additionally, the word *basic* is the key here, for it is at the lower but most foundational levels of education that rhetorical arts, with their concomitant emphasis on oral performance, were most important.

O'Malley emphasizes that, while Jesuits saw theological and philosophical studies as the pinnacle of their educational system—the essence of the higher levels of university learning—both the university arts curriculum and, especially, the curriculum of the secondary schools were devoted largely to the discourse arts of the trivium: grammar, rhetoric, and logic, with rhetorical performance being at the heart of pedagogy (O'Malley, 133–39). In organizing the rules for "lower studies," the *Ratio* also specifically puts great emphasis on the need, in rhetorical education, for oral declamations and disputations, both in the classroom itself and in monthly public performances and in specially organized academies (*Ratio Studiorum*, trans. Pavur, 124–25, 202, 212–13). Of course, it can be argued that, since these are the "lower studies," they are given less value and therefore have less importance. Certainly, that can be true in a technical way, since rhetorical performance is nowhere near the top of the Jesuit educational pyramid when one examines both the *Ratio* itself and other documents. At the same time, accepting the stated programs as the complete facts of the educational practice may be deceiving. O'Malley cautions that the facts of educational circumstances often belie the full stated agenda for two main reasons: First, most Jesuit educational activity was in the secondary schools whose curriculum was largely a rhetorical one; second, for practical reasons many Jesuit institutions implemented only a "truncated" curriculum, one that concentrated on achieving first the goals of the lower order curriculum, even if the higher order goals could not be part of that school's individual curriculum (138). Thus, the fundamental education in discourse arts—in rhetoric—often proved not only the most basic and fundamental but also often the most common form of Jesuit education (138–39).

In addition to their emphasis on rhetorical training, the Jesuit schools and colleges put great store in musical and dramatic performances (and in dramatic musical performances) that, while rooted in liturgical celebrations and other devotions, expanded into a range of other subjects. Within the Jesuit schools themselves, as well as within the communities served by those schools, the Jesuit scholars and students took every opportunity to engage in dramatic performances as a means of reaching a still wider audience with the spiritual message that motivated all the order attempted (Kennedy, 17–18). As with all else the Jesuits found in the world around them, they sought passionately to understand it as a manifestation of the divine and as possible means of working for "the greater honor and glory of God." Just as they incorporated humanist rhetorical education into their expanding portfolio of mission-driven activities, they also embraced dramatic performance as another compelling means of persuasion at a time when the dramatic arts were flowering all across Europe. Thus, for Jesuit education, the experience of oral performance was in no way limited to the traditions of classroom and public demonstrations of the overtly rhetorical arts but enthusiastically included the multivocal experience of theatrical performance. Indeed, O'Malley claims that the Jesuit schools presented theatrical productions "in such number and with such exuberance and excellence that they must be considered an integral part of those schools' self-definition" (139). So whether through the clearly rhetorical education in discourse or in other venues such as theater, Jesuit education has traditionally sought every opportunity to emphasize the discourse arts and, in that emphasis, to integrate active oral performance with their equally strong efforts in written composition. For the Jesuits involved in discourse education, the oral and the written have always been complementary voices in the chorus of educational action.

Therefore, with such august and active voices ringing in my own imagination, mediated always by the scholarly efforts of Walter Ong, I am inspired to try integrating the use of voice and new media into the current writing classroom, a problem I have been struggling with for some time, and still not an easy one to resolve. After all, constructing college writing courses is always intellectually and pedagogically demanding, and with so many issues to confront and skill sets to be mastered, writing curricula can often seem crowded with tasks and resistant to new material. How and when do I fit in a new emphasis on this complex issue of voice and also integrate into the course structure these oral performance experiences? Likewise, not being a "digital native" myself, and being only a "guest worker" in the "digital nation," I find it difficult and time consuming to deploy new media in my classroom. It requires a lot of startup time and assistance, and sometimes, after I have expended such time and effort, the university will change platforms or applications, requiring a whole new effort on my part. Nevertheless, I do see real opportunities for integrating work with direct speech and mediated discourse in my courses, enough so that I think the extra effort is worthwhile.

To begin the process, it occurred to me not too long ago that, lying within my usual syllabus, like some long-forgotten and rarely enforced zoning ordinance, is the "class participation" clause. Like many instructors, while using this as an evaluation of effort in class discussion, I have also tended to leave this category vaguely defined to allow me to give some credit for demonstrable commitment to the course and personal effort to do one's best—a kind of academic "good conduct medal." Now, however, I have begun to see this as an opportunity for challenging both myself and my students to do something more with the spoken side of language, at least besides informal discussion (not that such discussion is without value—quite the contrary, but more is needed). Therefore, I have now changed this to a participation/performance category in my writing courses, and I am requiring that students not only write but also perform that writing. Like students in a music class, who must do more than read and discuss the notes on the page but actually play the music—and play it so an audience would want to hear it—my students are now asked to perform at least some of their texts, and to perform them in a way that "delights" as well as "instructs."

As noted in detail above, this concept of performance can be found in the underlying traditions of Jesuit education, going all the way back to the originating educational program of the *Ratio Studiorum*. I can find longstanding roots for the educational potential of integrating oral performance with writing pedagogy, even if I do teach in an English department and not a communication department.[12] As a starting point for this new approach, and as an attempt to integrate both mediated and direct performance of discourse, I have chosen the broadcast technology of radio as a site from which to garner "texts" for study and possible imitation. Specifically, I have selected my local public radio station (KWMU, 90.7 FM in St. Louis) for one of the course requirements.[13] This is simple and cost-effective, as broadcasts are available in real time and online as archives, along with other audio formats (e.g., podcasts).

I am aided in this endeavor by the fact that about 90 percent of the programming on this particular station is in the "talk" format. While radio waves abound with "talk," much of it on AM (not to mention the endless possibilities offered by vast online sources), I naturally prefer the non-commercial and less strident forms found in the usually balanced and consistently reliable efforts of public radio.[14] In the midst of all the energy devoted to new media, radio often seems the forgotten stepchild in the history of recent media technologies. (It is, after all, less than a century old, and that is not much time in the history of recorded human discourse.) Of course, a vast range of radio is available in both synchronous and asynchronous forms through new-media outlets, and I do suggest these as further options, but I believe that the immediacy of the local public radio station has a particular value. Additionally, I think that it is useful to encourage students to understand and appreciate the public service provided by this venue in creating a sense of community through the spoken word.

The specific shows that I prefer to use include *This American Life*, with its richly textured engagement with the specifics of both everyday life and unusual experience, and *Snap Judgment*, with its focus on concentrated oral narratives that revolve around a common weekly theme. Additionally, I suggest the StoryCorps pieces, usually part of NPR's *Morning Edition*, as excellent specific examples of reflection and dialogue that can be imitated by students restricted to a brief time frame. By making regular listening to these broadcasts a part of the course requirements, I can help students to appreciate once more the richness of oral performance, while also leading them to consider the limits, demands, and opportunities created by a specific technological medium. I also suggest other shows that can help exemplify various aspects of discourse, such as the interview techniques deployed by Terry Gross in *Fresh Air* or the way call-in hosts such as Diane Rehm or those for *Talk of the Nation* moderate discussion, debate, and dissension among various speakers. Each of these shows, along with a number of others, can provide examples of oral discourse that demonstrates the qualities of "voice" that might be considered in written examples as well (for I have certainly not abandoned written texts for study in the writing class, be they sometimes in print and sometimes electronic). The overall goal is to immerse students in the oral-performance environment, with a variety of different kinds of discourse, each of which can be studied and analyzed as well as imitated. Fortunately, new media can also offer the opportunity to bring asynchronous broadcasts into the classroom environment for the same kind of detailed and careful examination as has traditionally been applied to written work (though written work continues to be examined in this way in class). Thus, throughout the semester, oral performance becomes not an add-on but an integral part of the discourse being studied.

Students' own work with oral performance must start early in the semester, with oral reading of short pieces, mostly brief exercises, but then this builds

toward the second half of the semester, during which a great deal more attention is given to workshopping of texts. In each case, the text in question must
be performed before it is analyzed and critiqued. Thus, the course structure is
itself guided more by the movement to performance competence before an
audience than merely by the movement from one strategy or form of writing
to another. Obviously, for some longer pieces, only segments may be performed
in order to have time to allow for full responses, but all students must engage
in oral performance. The course culminates, then, with some kind of presentation event covering a sequence of classes during the concluding weeks.
Throughout the course, perhaps every third or fourth session, a certain amount
of time is devoted to an "open mic" event, in which students can try out developing material of various kinds, even what is not being prepared for our specific class. The open-mic environment breaks down barriers to performance,
and it encourages experimentation with discourse. Also, just as class time (and
personal-conference time) is devoted to reading and responding to draft material, and additional class time is given to analyzing stylistic and formal concerns, so time must be devoted to workshopping oral performance and its
technical and stylistic features.

Certainly, you say, this is not really a new pattern at all—so many writing
courses have concluded with the oral presentation of research projects (or other
kinds of writing, depending on the course). Yet, despite such presentations being common, often little emphasis is placed on the actual vocal performance,
the oral art of language. And far too often, the end of such courses is measured
out, not with Prufrock's "coffee spoons," but with PowerPoint slides of equal
futility, and the oral component recedes into the background. In the course
I am devising, however, the goal is for students to gain an active appreciation
for the sound and rhythm of language, the power of the utterance as its own
kind of music. Indeed, for some of the performances, musical accompaniment is one option, a different kind of media technology in the classroom.
The point is that, by the course's end, students should be far more aware of the
complex interactions between speech and writing, and far more capable of
deploying in their writing a wide range of explicit and implicit sonic elements
that, in the aggregate, constitute what we experience as voice in the first sense,
as well as understanding the many stylistic and rhetorical subtleties that constitute voice in the second, more metaphorical sense.

"But didn't you say something about embracing new media?" Yes, and that
is the other component of the process. Encouraged by the excellent example of
several younger colleagues and by a number of graduate student instructors,
I have begun requiring that, along with the "live" performances, students
must also submit "mediated" performances. Given my relative inexperience
in this area, even compared to many first- and second-year undergraduates, this requirement is in part an opportunity for students to teach me,
among others, the technical skills of how to plan, design, construct, and produce

a multimedia/multimodal presentation. Students are asked to explore how to integrate audio, textual, visual, and other components into a balanced and unified presentation. The end result can take many forms, everything from a hypothetical political advertisement to a brief instructional video, and these may integrate multiple arts, including music, movement, theatrical performance, visual art and design, and others. Students can be divided into teams, each of which has members more and less sophisticated in the use of these media and the development and production of such mediated performances. I call upon the assistance, as well, of other instructors who are much more knowledgeable than I in these techniques to help lead introductory workshops about the media (a real opportunity for my students to witness my listening and not talking so much, as well as to see me in their role as just one more neophyte—indeed, likely more of a neophyte than they).

I admit that these mediated-performance assignments are something very new to my teaching, and I am still exploring the best ways to use them. I am convinced, however, that they are useful not only because they help students negotiate media environments that will be essential in other situations, especially in future career settings, but also because such performance activity allows them to engage the problem of voice in a new way, witnessing the changes in the experience as one moves from live to mediated speech (not just what they witness in the productions of outsiders but in their own productions and those of their familiar classmates). The ultimate goal is to celebrate neither the presence or the absence of technology but to provide new opportunities, both mediated and live, through which students may explore the nature of voice in both writing and speaking.

My recent experiments with this kind of blended pedagogy, using a combination of direct and mediated discourse, have proved successful enough for me to continue them and even to expand on them. I have made discoveries in the process, particularly about what allows students to experience breakthroughs in either the direct or mediated forms. For example, an exercise in which students are asked to speak from the perspective of a different person (someone whose life experience, personality, and identity are significantly different from their own) generated unexpected success in students' beginning to sense how the nuances of the spoken word (and of voice in the written word) convey so many subtle aspects of character that an audience picks up through inference.

Conversely, allowing students to perform through new-media applications has demonstrated that such mediation could be quite liberating, creating whole new perspectives on how they might reach an audience on a variety of levels at once.[15] These are merely two of a number of examples, and my pedagogical experiments are still developing, but this experience has made it evident to me that the oral and the mediated are not in opposition. In fact, the more the study of oral discourse is integrated with both writing and other forms of mediated discourse, the richer and more comprehensive the students' understanding of the fundamentals of rhetoric and of the practical demands of successful discourse. Such integration is itself inherent in the long tradition of rhetorical education, as well as in the fundamental principles of Jesuit pedagogy. While our cultural obsession with new media may have led us, for a time, to forget some of the elements that the oral must contribute to our study of the written and the otherwise mediated forms of discourse, reintegration of oral performance study with the study of writing, especially as enhanced by the use of new media, offers genuine opportunities for new achievements in a richer, more balanced rhetorical pedagogy.

For me, it still begins and concludes in the sense of voice. As I have noted earlier, voice is not a superficial characteristic that accessorizes writing. Rather, it is at the core of the fundamental elements of rhetorical theory and practice, at the center of the vital connection between the person engaged in expression and the person towards whom that expression is directed. It is in the physical experience of voice as sound, as well as voice in its many layers of metaphorical and analogical meaning, that we most intensely experience what truly engages us in writing and other media. What is that? It is the sense of another person seeking to join us in a common space at a particular moment, touching us with sound. And that sound is far more than mere "sound and fury," far more than mere "sounding brass" and "tinkling cymbals"; rather, it is embodied language whose energy we sense and whose meaning we experience all the more deeply because of that sense.

NOTES

This essay grew, in part, from a paper presented at the 2012 CCCC (Conference on College Composition and Communication) convention, "Orality, 'Literally': Re-Embodying the Voice as Oral Performance in the Writing Classroom."

1. I do not recall the sound of actual telegrapher's keys, only those representations of those keys I have heard in countless Hollywood films. In one sense, the telegram was an earlier form of the contemporary text message.

2. I should note that a number of my colleagues, some younger and some older, have incorporated these new digital processes into the fabric of their courses, and with some success. I have no problem with that approach, and I can acknowledge that it does provide some advantages and achieve some gains. At the same time, it also has "opportunity costs" that impact other aspects of learning and discourse. I have tried a different approach, asking students to turn off all such devices, as if they were passengers on an airliner about to take off (what I call classroom "electronic decorum"). Only when the class is asked to use the devices for something specific as part of the classroom work are they to be turned on.

3. This kind of experience, the all-encompassing nature of the sound of human voices shared in actual physical space, is something that Walter J. Ong spent a great deal of time exploring and considering in a number of his works, such as *The Presence of the Word*, and while deeply valuing the many contributions of all media, he never

forgot the rich emotional nuances, so important to relationships, that were evoked in direct speech.

4. See *Understanding Media*, especially chapter 1, "Medium is the Message." Also see *The Mechanical Bride*.

5. I have noted that those who declare themselves to be "digital natives"—declaring this often with an almost ethnic identification and nationalistic fervor—may suggest something even more extensive than McLuhan's concepts of technological extensions and amputations, perhaps more than even Ong's restructuring of consciousness. Perhaps we witness here the declaration of new nation of people whose fundamental shared identity is technological at heart. This seems evident in the recent *Frontline*/PBS documentary *Digital Nation*.

6. I discuss the issue of technology assessment of new media and writing pedagogy extensively in "The Text Is Always a Technology: Assessing New Technologies as Environments for Literacy," in *TnT: Text and Technology*, ed. Ollie Oviedo and Janice Walker (N.Y.: Hampton Press, 2003. 205–39).

7. It should be noted that even the deaf can experience sound and their communication and expression can be affected by it. They cannot hear sound but can feel rhythm and can physically produce rhythm though bodily motion—the deaf can dance, and their signing hands and expressive faces create kinetic songs.

8. There is an increasing body of research literature in the field of speech-language pathology about the possible "shared neural substrate" of both silent and vocalized language use, referred to as "silent and overt speech." One sample of that kind of research is "Comparing Cortical Activations for Silent and Overt Speech Using Event-Related fMRI" in *Human Brain Mapping*.

9. As Aristotle states in *Rhetoric*, "The character of the speaker is a cause of persuasion when the speech is so uttered as to make him worthy of belief. . . . This trust, however, should be created by the speech itself, and not left to depend upon an antecedent impression that the speaker is this or that kind of man" (trans. Lane Cooper, 8–9). I first explored the issues of voice in regard to Aristotle's definition of ethos in my dissertation, "Inventions for Voice: Experiments in Elizabethan Prose Fiction" (University of Iowa, 1989).

10. See O'Malley's excellent article, "From the 1599 *Ratio Studiorum* to the Present: A Humanistic Tradition?" in *The Jesuit Ratio Studiorum: 400th Anniversary Perspectives*.

11. Indeed, at my own university, there is an annual "Sumathon"—a marathon reading of portions of Aquinas' magnum opus, just one more reminder of the essential role played by scholasticism in Jesuit education.

12. I often think it shameful that we have for so long (over a century now) separated departments of Communication and English, a separation now codified into disciplinary custom and practice. I see in the advent of new media a cultural site from which, eventually, these two separate realms of discourse scholarship and teaching might be re-united.

13. While there are many sources for oral performance, not the least of which is You-Tube, I find that, for pedagogical purposes, the NPR format of my local station is an effective means of provided widely varied content that has still been vetted by responsible journalists and programmers.

14. I have now chosen to donate a specific dollar amount, per student, for my NPR station's annual fund drive ($5 or $10 depending on the size of the class), and I invite each student in the class to make a matching donation. It is a great deal less expensive than buying an additional textbook.

15. I should note that the class also spends time looking at additional forms of mediated performance that blend audio, visual, video, and other possible elements.

WORKS CITED

Aristotle. *Rhetoric*. Trans. Lane Cooper. Englewood, NJ: Prentice-Hall, 1933

Attebury, John. "Humanities and Rhetoric." In *Ratio Studiorum: Jesuit Education, 1540–1773*, ed. John Attebury and John Russell, 24–27. Boston: John J. Burns Library, Boston College, 1999–2000.

Casaregola, Vincent. "The Exact Location of the Voice: Walter Ong and the Embodiment of Discourse." *Proceedings of the 10th Annual Media Ecology Association Convention*, June 19–21, 2009. http://www.media-ecology.org/publications/MEA_proceedings/v10/index.html.

———. "Inventions for Voice: Humanist Rhetoric and the Experiments of Elizabethan Prose Fiction." PhD diss., University of Iowa, 1989.

———. "The Text Is Always a Technology: Assessing New Technologies as Environments for Literacy." *TnT: Text and Technology*, ed. Ollie Oviedo and Janice Walker, 205–39. N.Y.: Hampton Press, 2003.

Huang, Jie, Thomas H. Carr, and Yue Cao. "Comparing Cortical Activation for Silent and Overt Speech Using Event-Related fMRI." *Human Brain Mapping* 15 (2001): 39–53.

Kennedy, T. Frank. "Drama and Music." In *Ratio Studiorum: Jesuit Education, 1540–1773*, ed. John Attebury and John Russell, 16–19. Boston: John J. Burns Library, Boston College, 1999–2000.

McLuhan, Marshall. *The Mechanical Bride: The Folklore of Industrial Man*. Boston: Beacon Press, 1951.

———. *Understanding Media: The Extensions of Man*. New York: McGraw-Hill, 1964.

O'Malley, John W. "From the 1599 *Ratio Studiorum* to the Present: A Humanistic Tradition?" In *The Jesuit Ratio Studiorum: 400th Anniversary Perspectives*, ed. Vincent J. Duminuco, 127–44. New York: Fordham University Press, 2000.

Ong, Walter J., SJ. *Orality and Literacy: The Technologizing of the Word*. London: Methuen, 1982.

Percy, Walker. *The Moviegoer*. New York: Alfred A. Knopf, 1961.

The Ratio Studiorum: The Official Plan for Jesuit Education. Translated by Claude Pavur. St. Louis: Institute for Jesuit Sources, 2005.

Turkel, Sherry. *Alone Together: Why We Expect More from Technology and Less from Each Other*. New York: Basic Books, 2011.

REFLECTION: ECHOES OF JESUIT PRINCIPLES IN RHETORICAL THEORIES, PEDAGOGIES, AND PRAXES

Krista Ratcliffe

Marquette is a Jesuit university in Milwaukee, Wisconsin, whose mission is the production of transformative knowledge via research and pedagogy, with an emphasis on the four pillars of excellence, faith, leadership, and service. Marquette University High School is also the alma mater of Edward P. J. Corbett, who was my rhetoric professor in graduate school, and it happens to be the university where I now work, serving as chair of the English department. Because I grew up attending Quaker meetings, when I studied with Corbett at the Ohio State University in the 1980s, the Jesuit resonances in rhetoric theories and praxes and even in his pedagogy were not audible to me. Now, however, after spending eighteen years working at Marquette, I can hear the echoes of Jesuit principles in my rhetoric training and also more generally in the rhetoric theories, pedagogies, and praxes that constitute the discipline of rhetoric and composition studies.

Jesuit principle 1: Defending faith through education (critical thinking). I first encountered this Jesuit principle in 1993 when I interviewed for a tenure-track faculty position in the English department at Marquette. At various meetings during my on-campus visit, faculty and administrators kept asking me, "Why do you want to be at a Jesuit institution?" At my exit interview, I turned the question around and asked the interview committee, "Why do you want me, someone who studies feminist rhetoric, at a Jesuit institution?" The response I got was twofold. First, I was told that traditional rhetoric had a long and significant place within Jesuit pedagogy, and thanks to Mr. Corbett's training, I was conversant in traditional rhetoricians from Corax to Kenneth Burke; second, I was told that feminist rhetorics, such as those of Virginia Woolf, Mary Daly, and Adrienne Rich, on which I was then focused, provided a critical lens through which to evaluate how cultural discourses work in the world and that, when passed along to students, such a lens would allow students to challenge their beliefs in order to strengthen them and even to revise them if necessary. At that point, I realized that the Jesuit principle of defending the faith through education was tied to genuine critical thinking about the world and that, in terms of Jesuit rhetoric education, such critical thinking had real stakes in the world. This idea of stakes meshed nicely with my own beliefs about teaching rhetoric. But the link between Jesuit principles and the discipline of rhetoric and composition studies is more complicated than a mere focus on critical thinking; other Jesuit principles intersect with critical thinking to inform rhetoric theories, pedagogies, and praxes.

Jesuit principle 2: Service. Like the discipline of rhetoric and composition studies, Jesuit rhetorical pedagogy insists on the intersection of rhetoric theory and praxes, of critical thinking and action. But within Jesuit pedagogy, such praxes and action are always inflected with service. And such service has a definite purpose: working toward social justice for everyone, a perspective often conceived by putting the poor at the center of any analysis. Many Marquette students in rhetorical theory and composition classes humble me with their commitment to social justice and service, not as a line on a résumé but as a way of being in the world. What this embodiment means is that service is viewed not simply as two hours a week spent at an assigned service venue or a week spent in Haiti where "others" are helped. Rather, taking a note from Mary Daly, who claims that pronouns are our most troublesome words, many Marquette students learn how to move from viewing "others" as objects (i.e., as *them*) to seeing people as subjects with individual names and identities who may offer the students doing the service as much if not more than the students give. Moreover, many students begin to view service more generally as all their actions in the world, whether those actions occur at an assigned service venue or in the classroom, on the job, with friends and family, or anywhere else. To reinforce this expansive notion of service, students in rhetoric and composition classes study cultural scripts, such as gender, race, class, and sexuality, that are encoded within our cultural discourses; this study of discursive cultural scripts, in turn, provides students a site for both thinking critically and grounding their service and actions.

Jesuit principle 3: Growth via discernment (transformative education). Like the pedagogy of rhetoric and composition studies, Jesuit pedagogy insists that the end of its rhetorical education, which includes service, should be the transformation of students. Transformative education changes students and provides them with knowledge and skills that they may transfer from classroom to classroom and from university to nonacademic settings. Such transformative, transferable education means asking students (and ourselves as teachers) to engage in discernment: i.e., to imagine beyond our comfort levels, to listen to others, and then to reflect (prayerfully if one wishes) on how our imaginings and our hearings affect our thinking and acting in the world. Marquette has influenced not only my interactions with students but also my interactions with myself. From listening to my colleague Ron Bieganowski, S.J., speak at teaching-assistant orientation about Jesuit education, I learned, among other things, to reflect daily on gratitude and on the justness of my daily actions for all concerned. Marquette has even transformed my scholarly focus. I remember having coffee several years ago with my former colleague Paula Gillespie and describing to her my feminist, antiracist research project that would eventually become *Rhetorical Listening*. As we spoke, I suddenly recognized another connection and said to her, "I think I'm channeling the Jesuits." We both laughed. But we laughed because we both recognized, in part, the truth of that statement in terms of how listening is linked with growth through discernment.

Jesuit principle 4: Development of character via modeling. As Quintilian notes in his *Institutio Oratio,* modeling is a cornerstone of classical rhetorical pedagogy. Jesuit education echoes the idea of rhetorical modeling, too, in terms of linking seeing and doing with becoming. Although modeling in the classical sense of translation or transliteration is not common in writing classrooms these days, other types of modeling remain, and they invoke the idea of seeing/doing/becoming. For example, when we ask students to identify discourse conventions of a certain community and to adapt their ideas to those conventions in order to increase their chances of being heard within that community, then we are teaching a type of modeling as a way of becoming a member of that community. And when we teach students to identify cultural scripts in discourses and ask them to reflect on which scripts to perform and which ones to revise, we are also teaching a kind of modeling performance. With this pedagogy of modeling performance, rhetoric teachers echo Aristotle's link between rhetoric and ethics as well as Judith Butler's link between discourse and performance, both of which help students make visible to themselves the development of their own characters and the degree of agency that they have in the formation of these characters. In addition, this pedagogy not only helps students understand how and why they may (or may not) model cultural scripts but also how and why they may (or may not) embrace leadership positions and then model for others actions that lead to social justice.

Jesuit principle 5: Cura personalis. The Jesuit principle of care of the whole person informs rhetorical education in that it coincides with Plato's notion of rhetoric's being present from the dinner table to the public courtroom, with Kenneth Burke's notion of rhetoric as a socializing process, and with Adrienne Rich's argument that the personal is the political. This "whole person" view of education in general and of rhetorical education in particular helps students imagine and understand how the rhetoric of overlapping discourses not only affects their communication (reading, writing, speaking, and listening) but also shapes their thinking, informs their identities, and provides both means and limits to their agencies. With these realizations, students learn to see rhetoric everywhere and to take responsibility for their participation in its performance, perpetuating, revising, and/or interrupting it.

Jesuit principles 6 and 7: Collaboration and magis. The intersection of collaboration and *magis* (the more) results in rhetoric teachers and students working together to educate students (and teachers) as men and women for others. Collaboration reinforces the notion that no one person possesses either a totality of knowledge or a capacity to change the world on her or his own; collaboration also gives rhetoric students a concrete sense of audience. *Magis* reinforces for students the idea of giving more, of taking the extra step, to achieve social justice: For some students, *magis* is grounded in giving more to God or Christ; for some students, it is grounded in giving to other people; for some students, it is both. Regardless, the intersections of collaboration and *magis* result in students working together—i.e., going out into the world and networking (in the best sense)—to create forces for a more just world. And to invoke Corbett for a moment, it is important to approach such actions with an Isocratean intellect that is both creative and analytic and to grace that intellect with an open hand, not a closed fist.

A final thought. In a much-discussed keynote address at the international Jesuit higher-education conference in Mexico City in 2010, the superior general of the order reinforced the idea that Jesuit principles continue to resonate with the study of rhetoric. In his talk, Adolfo Nicolás, S.J., named as one of the main educational problems today the "globalization of superficiality," and he asks what Jesuit universities should look like in the twenty-first century if they are to counter it.[1] One possible response, he suggests, is that

> creativity might be one of the most needed things in present times—real creativity, not merely following slogans or repeating what we have heard or what we have seen in Wikipedia. Real creativity is an active, dynamic process of finding responses to real questions, finding alternatives to an unhappy world that seems to go in directions that nobody can control.

The operative word in that last sentence is *seems*. Fr. Nicolás encourages students and teachers to see beyond what only *seems* to be. To encourage students and teachers to become rhetorical agents who can counter superficiality as well as the prevailing sense of lack of control, Fr. Nicolás offers one solution: Jesuit education. Specifically, he suggests a Jesuit education that cultivates a depth of thought *and* imagination (thanks to Mr. Corbett, I hear Isocrates here), because a deeper understanding of ourselves and of others may foster a more productive acting together (thanks to Mr. Corbett, I hear Kenneth Burke). The superior general's ideas echo discussions in rhetoric and composition studies about critical thinking, agency, stases (posing questions), identification, consubstantiality (acting together), and, yes, even rhetorical listening. For this reason, as we move more deeply into the twenty-first-century study of rhetoric, I encourage us all to continue pondering how Jesuit principles may inform rhetorical theories, pedagogies, and praxes . . . and also, of course, questioning how they may not.

NOTE

1. Aldopho Nicolás, "Depth, Universality, and Learned Ministry: Challenges to Jesuit Higher Education Today," April 23 2010, http://www.sjweb.info/documents/ansj/100423_Mexico%20City_Higher%20Education%20Today_ENG.pdf (accessed July 20, 2012).

AFTERWORD: TECHNOLOGY, DIVERSITY, AND THE IMPRESSION OF MISSION

Joseph Janangelo

> In some ways our schools are less Catholic and less Jesuit than they used to be.
> —Harry R. Dammer, "Obstacles to Excellence"

M*ission* is a word that echoes with considerable reverberation. As such, it embraces a range of meanings. One suggests conscription: "a specific task or duty assigned to a person or group of people." A second describes intent: "often in the phrase mission in life." A third bespeaks community: "a group of persons sent by a church to carry on religious work, especially evangelization in foreign lands, and often to establish schools, hospitals, etc." (Dictionary.com). The specific *etc.* discussed here is the work of composition instruction at Jesuit colleges and universities as it relates to mission.

At Jesuit institutions, mission provides a core identity and legacy that guide pedagogical practice. Whether volitional or assigned, that identity can become a key presence and force in our writing programs. Situated at a nexus of interdisciplinary (e.g., composition as a service course) and institutional concerns (e.g., teaching *eloquentia perfecta*) composition programs can advance a school's mission by helping students become accomplished and ethical rhetors. They can also further our institutions' promise of pedagogical excellence as we work to deliver high-quality instruction that inspires stellar student performance.

This work is not uncomplicated by millennial interests and concerns. Nor is it untouched by a host of contemporary issues that imbue higher education. To me, the worthy project is not to feign or retain untouched status. Rather it is to engage thoughtfully with twenty-first-century literacy practices, some of which may appear to signal important tensions between the pedagogical work of Jesuit institutions and the writing that contemporary students are doing here and now in our classrooms and writing centers.

This productive tension between tradition and innovation sparks passionate debate among scholars who ask what it means to honor the past while engaging in contemporary pedagogical practice. This chapter examines aspects of one such conversation. My goal is to offer a reading that outlines the conundrum of moving forward while honoring valuable, venerable traditions. This chapter has two parts. Part one engages a published discussion of perceived obstacles to achieving excellence; part two poses questions about the impediments and incentives involved in defining what it means to "move forward."

A TASTE OF TECHNOLOGY

I wish to discuss a provocative article that appeared in the spring 2011 issue of *Conversations on Jesuit Higher Education*. The issue asks an important question: "Excellence: Where Is It?" and discusses good work being done at Jesuit colleges and universities. In "Obstacles to Excellence," a fine contribution to the conversation, Professor Harry R. Dammer, a member of the National Seminar on Jesuit Higher Education, explains how mission can drive institutional practice. Dammer begins by bringing key tension points into sharp focus "This issue of *Conversations* contains many examples of excellence at our 28 Jesuit institutions. However, we are called to do better and more." He adds, "So with appreciation for what we have accomplished, here are some challenges that face us." He begins with an acknowledgement: "These ideas are not novel, nor are they necessarily special to Catholic or Jesuit universities. But our purpose here is simply to jumpstart a 'conversation' about the pursuit of excellence" (1).

Dammer lists "five obstacles to excellence": the explosion in the use of technology, the costs of a Jesuit education, the issue of rigor, diversity as a challenge to mission, and obstinacy to change (1). While all of these topics are important, I wish to discuss technology and diversity because they are so incendiary and represent important tensions between historical notions of Jesuit educational mission and current interests and innovations in Rhetoric and Composition. I quote Dammer's first paragraph:

> Technology is not inherently bad. Those of us in the trenches, however, are aware of the difficulty of getting students to focus and/or even read a challenging text. Why? Research reflects lower reading and math scores for those that have more technology and fewer books around the house while growing up. Students cannot concentrate and cannot focus on one thing for longer than fifteen minutes.
>
> —Dammer, 1

While Dammer does not shy away from assertion, some teachers may identify with the problems he pinpoints. It can be challenging vying for in-class attention with students' seemingly omnipresent social networking and entertainment devices in continuous play.

Echoing the idea that we teach in "the age of distraction" (Babauta) Dammer explains how technology has become a pedagogical problem. He argues that

> the inability to concentrate leads directly to their inability to think deeply and later express themselves clearly in written or oral forms (*eloquentia perfecta*). Further, can students under the influence of electronic stimulation ever truly focus on context, experience, reflection, action, and evaluation or deal with the key issues of life—'who am I, and for whom shall I serve?' Superior General Fr. Adolfo Nicolás, S.J., has referred to this expanding problem of technology as the "globalization of superficiality." He argues with

authority that new technologies, along with the influences of moral relativism and consumerism, are shaping the interior worlds of young people in ways that limit their ability to respond to their own "intellectual, moral and spiritual healing."

—Dammer, 1

Not content to merely outline the problem, Dammer offer us three "possible solutions." He says we should "include context, experience, reflection and self-evaluation components in all classes" and "bring back quiet hours to library and dorms." He urges us to "prohibit cell phones or computer use in class," adding "and less *power point* would help too!" (1).

Dammer's argument is compelling; the idea of engaging in sustained quiet reflection has articulate admirers like Randy Bomer and Peter Elbow. Dammer also highlights a host of tension points pertinent to twenty-first-century teaching and learning. In this scenario, technology (a presumed enhancement) is portrayed as an impediment that can keep teachers from doing our best work for our students. Such arguments find strong voice in such works as Mark Bauerlein's *The Dumbest Generation*. Yet depicting technology as pernicious devices of temptation and distraction—ones which herald a watering down of education and undermine human interaction (Turkle)—may prove dissonant with scholarly visions of contemporary communication and composition (Selfe).

For example, some of Dammer's ideas may be perceived as being at odds with theories of visual and aural rhetoric whose adherents contend that writing is intrinsically mediated (Haas) and that students should be composing and critiquing online texts (Ball). For well over ten years, multimodal composition has found scholarly purchase in Rhetoric and Composition as a theoretical and pedagogical activity. Along with the longstanding journal *Computers and Composition*, examples include Diana George's influential "From Analysis to Design: Visual Communication in the Teaching of Writing" and, more recently, Bump Halbritter's *Mics, Cameras, Symbolic Action: Audio-Visual Rhetoric for Writing Teachers*. In concert with contemporary academe, the work of delivering effective online composition courses has inspired Scott Warnock's *Teaching Writing Online: How and Why* and the 2013 CCCC *Position Statement of Principles and Example Effective Practices for Online Writing Instruction*. This work continues as the Committee for Effective Practices in Online Instruction is charged with sharing effective practices in March 2016.

Multimodal composition is also present in the first-year college composition curriculum. In terms of best practices, the Council of Writing Program Administrators' *WPA Outcomes Statement for First-Year Composition* (3.0), challenges students to "match the capacities of different environments (e.g., print and electronic) to varying rhetorical situations" and to find "ways to make informed decisions about intellectual property issues connected to common genres and modalities in their fields." At course level, Kristin L. Arola, Jennifer

Sheppard, and Cheryl E. Ball's *Writer/Designer: A Guide to Making Multi-modal Projects* invites students to participate in the rich spectrum of multimodal composition. For example, it teaches students to compose threshold assignments (e.g., analysis of a website's rhetorical elements) to designing born-digital work such as webtexts and researched arguments with embedded video. Examples of such innovative projects can be found in "(Re)mediating the Conversation: Undergraduate Scholars in Writing and Rhetoric," special issue 16, no. 1, of the peer-reviewed online journal *Kairos: A Journal of Rhetoric, Technology, and Pedagogy*. Such inquiry and [best] practice signifies an interest in multimodal composition that transcends the desire to be au courant or to characterize technology as just another on-trend curricular possibility. It offers academic hospitality (Phipps and Barnett) to multimodal composition as a vital knowledge-making activity that helps millennial rhetors, including students and scholars, do serious and valuable intellectual work.

Just as some scholars have reframed multimodal composition as an enhancement to, rather than diminution of, academic literacy traditional notions of what constitutes paying attention have also received articulate scrutiny. For example, in *The Pleasure of Reading in an Age of Distraction* Alan Jacobs suggests that distraction can play a contributory role in strengthening reading comprehension. In *Now You See It: How the Brain Science of Attention Will Transform the Way We Live, Work, and Learn* and "What Do We Mean By Attention, Distraction, and Mutlitasking? #FutureEd," Cathy Davidson describes distraction and multitasking as valuable pavers to meaningful, creative learning. Davidson's ideas, which celebrate paying divided attention to a given subject while toggling among other intellectual tasks, comport with those suggested by HASTAC—the Humanities, Arts, Science and Technology Alliance and Collaboratory—of which she is a member. The value of connected, interactive learning also aligns with George D. Kuh's influential description of high-impact educational practices, especially "collaborative assignments and projects" and "service learning, community-based learning."

Some may argue that contemporary composition, and therefore contemporary composition instruction, involves helping writers compose in online environments and to frame and respond to quick and quixotic digital texts—e.g., Facebook and Twitter. Still another complication is that in business-writing courses, for example, PowerPoint is not just a method of information delivery but a subject of rhetoric, a writing assignment, and an occasion for peer review. Composing effective PowerPoints, much like document and web design and other activities companies use to maintain their social media presence, are ones that writers must practice and refine in order to participate, communicate, and thrive in professional settings.

Another potential tension point is that the author may be assuming that face-to-face instruction is the sine qua non. To this, some composition instructors might ask, what about distance learning and online course delivery (Warnock)? What constitutes presence in those contexts? My point is that these assumed pedagogical irritants have become, for many teachers, central pedagogical responsibilities. Some of us may see it as a vital project to help students compose effectively and collaboratively in online environments. Technology, then, may not be an enhancement, but a necessity in our classrooms however virtually and physically constellated. This notion is supported by documents that identify composition studies' best practices such as the *Conference on College Composition and Communication Position Statement on Teaching, Learning, and Assessing Writing in Digital Environments* and the *Council of Writing Program Administrators' Outcomes Statement for First-Year Composition (3.0)*. These statements of best practice are, in turn, reified by accrediting agencies (e.g., Collegiate Learning Assessment, the Higher Learning Commission, North Central Association Commission on Accreditation and School Improvement, and the Southern Association of Colleges and Schools, to name a few) and the National Survey of Student Satisfaction (NSSE), which seek to assess how well institutions of higher learning are meeting contemporary educational goals in terms of quality control, professional development, student satisfaction, student retention, and time to degree (Bowen et al., 224).

For me the larger question—and I write as someone simultaneously skeptical and appreciative of the dramatic characterization of "students under the influence of electronic stimulation" (1)—is how might Jesuit institutions of higher learning help students and faculty rigorously engage current and evolving technologies as tools and objects of study? Relevant to mission, it strikes me that delivering credible and responsible education can involve more than celebrating blogging per se. It can mean extending mission's remit to help students become effective and ethical rhetors whose rhetorical sophistication helps them use technology to make intellectual and civic interventions. Such work, I suggest, is endemic to contemporary Jesuit institutions and should not be dismissed as the dubious or lesser province of secular schools. Here technological innovation invites mission to expand its purview. We might ask:

Which changes shall we *celebrate and cherish as* "improvements" to our discipline and work?

Which changes shall we *castigate or merely countenance* as "impediments" to the work of supporting the academic and social literacies of all of our students?

A BITE OF DIVERSITY

In outlining the challenges to mission presented by technology, Professor Dammer shows himself to be a prescient scholar. In detailing the challenges diversity portends, he shows himself to be a brave one. Here is the beginning of his discussion of "diversity as a challenge to mission:"

At the risk of sounding un-PC, I think it is important to mention a major challenge to mission that has developed quickly over the last twenty-five or so years—diversity. No one would argue that diversity is a bad thing. But emphasis on diversity creates challenges from three sources: students, faculty, and ideas. Our current students differ more than in religion and skin color. They are also more likely to be from single parent families, foreign countries, have learning disabilities or psychological disorders, and are less likely to have attended Catholic secondary schools.

—Dammer, 2

Appreciative of Dammer's insights, and especially the candor with which he shares them, I confess to seeing the opening as something of a salvo. For example, one might take issue and even umbrage at the tacit description of diversity as threat and deficit. Dammer cites several problems. For example, current students are said to present major pedagogical challenges, to differ from their better-prepared predecessors, and to sometimes be from single-parent families. Moreover, "they" sometimes have learning disabilities or psychological disorders.

This deficit characterization is stigmatizing in that it presents contemporary students as inadvertent and somehow insidious troublemakers whose presence and ideas complicate the noble and well-intentioned pedagogical work of Jesuit institutions. To me, this runs close to sounding like an idea of institutional entitlement that is out of line with the increased focus on social justice in Jesuit education and important scholarship on diversity in Rhetoric and Composition (Butler, Condon, Garza). For example, here are some ways that eloquence and diversity interact:

Personal writing taught in college-level rhetoric courses is enriched by students' varied perspectives and experiences. Across individual texts and in "capstone courses and projects" (Kuh) such as course and learning portfolios, students may use words, images and sounds in ways that contest and expand received notions of eloquence. While eloquence may still be a subject of imitation and emulation, it can also be an expression of resistance and critique.

Peer review is an activity where intercultural communication occurs as learners are asked to listen to others, advocate for their ideas, and reflect on their own assumptions.

Students' self-sponsored literate activities, including their posts on Twitter, Facebook and YouTube, often express rhetorical acumen and a sophisticated sense of multiple audiences and their particular, and possibly conflicting, needs.

Some composition programs are evolving to serve the abilities and needs of students who are in active military service or are veterans (Valentino).

The Jesuit tradition, which has always been international, welcomes students and teachers from all language and national backgrounds. With sensitive stewarding, identity politics and perceptions of one's gender assignment (e.g., trans- and cisgender) become valuable tools for open communication, intellectual development and identity formation. Louise Rosenblatt offered us this lesson in 1938 when, in *Literature as Exploration*, she explained how individual readers use their diverse experiences and creativity to perceive and assign textual meaning.

Most important, international students and English-language learners are increasingly regarded as enriching the classroom, campus, and curriculum with their presence and work (Fox; Kirklighter, Cardenas, and Wolff Murphy; Ritter and Matsuda, and Severino, Guerra, and Butler). Regarding linguistic and social diversity, Ilona Leki's *Understanding ESL Writers: A Guide for Teachers* (1992) helps us understand some of the strengths, motivations, and interests of English-language learners. More recently, Asao B. Inoue and Mya C. Poe's *Race and Writing Assessment*—winner of the 2014 CCCC book award for an edited collection—offers ways of reading student work without dwelling on, or looking for, errors. Moreover, writing across the curriculum, with its international focus, helps us recognize the presence and writing of English language learners as vital to our classrooms. Such work includes *WAC and Second-Language Writers: Research Towards Linguistically and Culturally Inclusive Programs and Practices*, edited by Terry Myers Zawacki and Michelle Cox, and Michelle Cox's "WAC: Closing Doors or Opening Doors for Second Language Writers?" Moreover, the study "Do Gays Get Better Grades?" (2009) further undermines sedimented surfeit and deficit models of diversity in academe.

I share these sources to show that in Rhetoric and Composition the idea of eloquence itself is being redefined and becoming more expansive. It is no secret that print literacy and undivided attention are simply *those* practices whose time and reputation as unequivocal good things are receiving challenge and critique. The relatively encapsulated and cellular discourse pertinent to some digital writing (e.g., texting, tweeting) and oral presentations (e.g., delivering TED talks and elevator pitches) offers alternative definitions of, and poses powerful challenges to, traditional print-based notions of eloquence and rhetorical ability.

Given these capacious definitions of eloquence, I find Professor Dammer a bit too ready to equate diversity with students' being underprepared or unreceptive. I would like to hear more discussion of how international students, students of color, and those from different religious traditions (or none), students with various nuclear-family structures, such as single-parent families, and students with different learning styles and predispositions bring vital and varied perspectives to reading activities, physical and online class discussions, collaborative learning, peer review, writing-center conferences, and writing projects. For example, the depiction of students who come from "foreign countries" differs from descriptions of affluence and cultural/rhetorical sophistication discussed by other scholars such as Ilona Leki (2007), Paul Kei Matsuda, and Tony Silva. This kind of critique suggests that institutional mission might have sailed unassailed had it not been for these newcomers.

The challenges diversity poses include both the faculty and the content of the curriculum. As Dammer describes the problem:

> Our faculties are even more diverse than our students. At my medium-size university I have colleagues who have attended universities in twenty-one countries and I have met those who are who are Buddhist, Jewish, Muslim, Hindu, Wiccan, atheist, and agnostic. Ideas that are brought forth in the classroom, the laboratory and at public lectures are also much different from those only twenty-five years ago. The science of stem cell research, the sociology of post-modernism, and the discussion about GLBTQ issues, cause consternation for presidents and bishops across the country.
>
> —Dammer, 2

To the concern that "faculties are even more diverse than our students," some readers may remember when institutions made it a point of pride and equity to recruit and retain diverse faculty members. Regarding "GLBTQ issues," did this particular diversity really occur "only twenty-five years ago" or were earlier faculty members more self-censoring and self-silencing lest news of their identities and lives yield undesired personal and institutional consequences? Perhaps the "consternation" is not caused by these peoples' presence but by their honest, vocal, and unapologetic pedagogy and scholarship which may question traditional teachings (see Butler, Denny, Sedgwick, and the U.S. Department of Education's recent announcement that Title IX protects transgender students).

Yet the consternation—"feeling of alarm, confusion, or dismay, often caused by something unexpected" is eminently understandable (definition from Bing .com). Matters intensify when institutions are centuries old and have venerable traditions. They become even more complicated when a religious order's mission statement underwrites an individual institution's own mission. Any perceived loss of control can catalyze enduring disagreements, resulting in perceived threats of secularization and allegations that serious, radical change can lead to an irretrievable lapse in standards.

IMPRESSING MISSION

Dammer continues outlining causes of consternation when he writes that "in some ways our schools are less Catholic and less Jesuit than they used to be" (2). This assumption, which seems to evoke a pre–Vatican II sensibility, begets major challenges:

The impact is visible in the short term and problematic for the long term survival of our institutions. Students with poor academic backgrounds are challenged by the rigors of philosophy and theology as well as other liberal arts courses. What percentage of students and faculty are Catholic or attend campus-held Masses? Students who have serious psychological issues may find it difficult to handle the stress of rigorous study.

—Dammer, 2

I confess that here is where I most appreciate the important project of debating and protecting mission. On the one hand, diversity is still described as a deficit model, further embroidered with a comment about "students who have serious psychological issues," as though that happened less often when our students were less diverse. I also detect strains of empire thinking (Dobrin) and a nostalgia for cleaner, simpler times when the operations of mission could proceed unguarded, uninterrupted or at least unchallenged by the "new" including its technologies, exemplars, and advocates.

Yet there are at least two important causes for celebration here. The first is the care for the whole person, the *cura personalis*, and the striving, which Dammer evinces, for students' well-being and success. Such care is a catalyzing hallmark of Jesuit education and its adherents. The second cause is represented in the fifth obstacle to excellence, one Dammer calls "obstinacy to change." Here I am pleased to quote from his conclusion:

Recent books . . . stress the need for thinking more creatively, about the way we do our business of education. All four of the "obstacles" discussed here feed directly into this point. They will be addressed only if we are willing to "think outside the box" about how Jesuit and Catholic education is administered.

—Dammer, 2

This focus on the intellectual work of doing "our business of education"—the emphasis put on being continually reflective, creative, exploratory, occasionally contentious, and always self-critical—lies at the heart and in the mind of Jesuit higher education. It shows the impression of mission, which is both the marks we make and the legacies we inscribe and communicate.

PROVOCATIONS AND POSSIBILITIES

The authors in this section, in their discussions of technology, new media, diversity and service learning, have given specific accounts of the work they do to help their students at Jesuit colleges and universities. To encourage further thinking, I will conclude by posing some questions intended to help us engage the important work of providing instruction that is conversant with disciplinary standards, professional best practices, contemporary learners and teachers, and evolving technologies—and that aspires to evince *cura personalis* and embrace the whole person and their needs whether they be undergraduate or graduate student, staff, adjunct instructor, full professor, writing-center director, writing-across-the curriculum director, or designated writing-program administrator (WPA). Having briefly sketched some of the interest and stakes that rhetoric and composition has in technology and diversity, I offer the following questions to stimulate thought about how composition programs can interact more fully with the project of keeping mission *at* work *in* our work.

How might writing programs address the important concepts as mission and service in our curricular and pedagogical/professional development activities?

How might we explore the creative, and occassionally taxing, tensions between tradition and innovation in pedagogical work being done (and not done) at Jesuit colleges and universities?

What are the pertinent, challenging, and rewarding pedagogical and administrative issues facing us?

What are the salient equity and labor issues regarding tuition cost and the use of contingent faculty? How do they relate to social justice?

How do writing programs relate to other academic and service units such as writing-across the curriculum, writing centers, experiential learning, and first-year experience seminars? How does the work connect with advising activities and retention initiatives?

How do we bring our Jesuit-centered curricular and pedagogical work into conversation with the discipline of Rhetoric and Composition/ Writing Studies?

How do we bring our pedagogical and administrative work into close conversation with best practices (such as those voiced by the Conference on College Composition and Communication, the Council of Writing Program Administrators and the International Writing Centers Association), national mandates (e.g., assessment), evolving technologies, diverse learners, as well as ongoing core redesign and renewal?

How do composition scholars working at religious institutions connect their work to "secular" research and theory? What are the major constraints and opportunities? What professional development opportunities currently exist, or could exist, for these individuals?

How does mission intersect with programmatic, unit, and institutional branding and rebranding?

In terms of graduate-student preparation, what are the key professional development innovations and achievements that mission, and mission awareness, provide? How might we assess and learn from them?

I do not wish to foresee or forestall the future. With neither barometers to explain nor bromides to extol, I think that, given the unlikely resumption of belletristic literacy, undivided attention or deferent diversity, a nostalgia that champions a nobler past may not be the most effective way of envisioning, achieving, and sustaining future excellence. As I see it, there is warrant and opportunity for concern *and* celebration. At times, the many competing voices of the millennial classroom (some of which are online) may appear, and perhaps are, more cacophonic than harmonious. But that, I suggest, *is* a good thing, because we have a big, complicated, and important project—with many portals of activity and risk—to give us purpose and fuel our creativity.

As we move purposefully forward, we can remain mindful of valuable legacies and lessons. Aligning our programs with institutional mission and higher education's evolving goals challenges us to develop capacious and thoughtful criteria for discerning meaningful innovations from mere trending topics. In pursuing and reflecting on our work, we might remember Dammer's good advice that "for sure there are many reasons why each of these ideas is impractical or politically uncomfortable. But they all are ideas that will be part of the 'conversations' within Jesuit circles in this century—if we like it or not" (2). Personally and professionally, I value the creative tension that this enduring conundrum inspires and fuels. As this book's authors have eloquently shown, relating mission to our work is an ongoing and worthy project. That is why the ideas are worth engaging again and anew.

NOTE

I am grateful to Yola C. Janangelo, Farrell J. Webb, and the editors for their encouragement and advice.

WORKS CITED

A Position Statement of Principles and Example Effective Practices for Online Writing Instruction (OWL). Conference on College Composition and Communication, March 2013. http://www.ncte.org/cccc/resources/positions/owiprinciples. Accessed January 1, 2015.

Arola, Kristin L., Jennifer Sheppard, and Cheryl E. Ball. *Writer/Designer: A Guide to Making Multimodal Projects*. Boston: Bedford / St. Martin's, 2014.

Babauta, Leo. *Focus: A Simplicity Manifesto in the Age of Distraction*. West Valley City, Utah: Waking Lion Press, 2011.

Ball, Cheryl E. "Assessing Scholarly Multimedia: A Rhetorical Genre Studies Approach." *Technical Communication Quarterly* 21, no.1 (2012): 1–17.

Bauerlein, Mark. *The Dumbest Generation: How the Digital Age Stupefies Young Americans and Jeopardizes Our Future (Or, Don't Trust Anyone under 30)*. New York: Tarcher, 2009.

Bomer, Randy. *Time for Meaning: Crafting Literate Lives in Middle and High School*. Portsmouth, N.H.: Heinemann, 1995.

Bowen, William C., Matthew M. Chingos, and Michael S. McPherson. *Crossing the Finish Line*. Committee for Effective Practices in Online Instruction. Conference on College Composition and Communication, March 2016. http://www.ncte.org/cccc/committees/owi. Accessed May 20, 2015.

Butler, Judith. *Gender Trouble: Feminism and the Subversion of Identity*. New York: Routledge, 2006.

Completing College at America's Public Universities. Princeton, N.J.: Princeton University Press, 2009.

Condon, Frankie. *I Hope I Join the Band: Narrative, Affiliation, and Antiracist Rhetoric*. Logan: Utah State University Press, 2012.

Conference on College Composition and Communication Statement on Teaching, Learning, and Assessing Writing in Digital Environments. February 2004. http://www.ncte.org/cccc/resources/positions/digitalenvironments. Accessed January 1, 2015.

Craig, Collin Lamont, and Staci Maree Perryman-Clark. "Troubling the Boundaries: (De)Constructing WPA Identities at the Intersections of Race and Gender." *WPA: Writing Program Administration* 34, no. 2 (2011): 37–58.

Dammer, Harry R. "Obstacles to Excellence," *Conversations on Jesuit Higher Education* 39 (2011) 1–2. http://epublications.marquette.edu/conversations/vol39/iss1/8. Accessed May 20, 2015.

Davidson, Cathy. "What Do We Mean By Attention, Distraction, and Mutlitasking? #FutureEd." HASTAC, February 8, 2014. https://www.hastac.org/blogs/cathy-davidson/2014/02/08/what-do-we-mean-attention-distraction-and-multitasking-futureed. Accessed January 1, 2015.

Davidson, Cathy. *Now You See It: How the Brain Science of Attention Will Transform the Way We Live, Work, and Learn*. New York: Viking Adult, 2011.

Denny, Harry C. *Facing the Center: Toward an Identity Politics of One-to-One Mentoring*. Logan: Utah State University Press, 2010.

Dobrin, Sidney I. *Postcomposition*. Carbondale: Southern Illinois University Press, 2011.

Elbow, Peter. *Writing without Teachers*. 2nd ed. New York: Oxford University Press, 1998.

Fox, Tom. *Defending Access: A Critique of Standards in Higher Education*. Portsmouth, N.H.: Heinemann, 1999.

Geekgirl in Social. "Do Gays Get Better Grades?" July 15, 2009. http://lgbtlatestscience.wordpress.com/2009/07/15/do-gays-get-better-grades/. January 1, 2015.

George, Diana "From Analysis to Design: Visual Communication in the Teaching of Writing." *College Composition and Communication*. 54, no. 1 (2002): 11–39.

Haas, Christina. *Writing Technology: Studies on the Materiality of Literacy*. New York: Routledge, 1995.

Halbritter, Bump. *Mics, Cameras, Symbolic Action: Audio-Visual Rhetoric for Writing Teachers*. Anderson, S.C.: Parlor Press, 2012.

Humanities, Arts, Science and Technology Alliance and Collaboratory. https://www.hastac.org/. January 1, 2015.

Inoue, Asao, and Mya C. Poe. Eds. *Race and Writing Assessment*. Peter Lang , New York: 2012.

Jacobs, Alan. *The Pleasures of Reading in an Age of Distraction*. New York: Oxford University Press, 2011.

Kirklighter, Christina, Diana Cardenas, and Susan Wolff Murphy, eds. *Teaching Writing with Latino/a Students: Lessons Learned at Hispanic-Serving Institutions.* Albany: State University of New York Press, 2007.

Kuh, George D. *High-Impact Educational Practices: What They Are, Who Has Access to Them, and Why They Matter.* Washington, D.C.: Association of American Colleges and Universities: 2008.

Leki, Ilona. *Undergraduates in a Second Language: Challenges and Complexities of Academic Literacy Development.* New York: Routledge, 2007.

———. *Understanding ESL Writers: A Guide for Teachers.* Portsmouth, N.H.: Boynton/Cook, 1992.

"MILESTONE: US Dept. of Education. Announces Title IX Protects Transgender Students." National Center for Transgender Equality. April 29, 2014. http://transequality.org/news.html#DepartmentofEducationClarification. Accessed January 1, 2015.

Phipps, Alison and Ronald Barnett. "Academic Hospitality." *Arts and Humanities in Higher Education* 6, no. 3 (2007): 237–54. http://ahh.sagepub.com/content/6/3/237.short. January 1, 2015.

"(Re)mediating the Conversation: Undergraduate Scholars in Writing and Rhetoric," ed. Shannon Carter. Special issue, *Kairos: A Journal of Rhetoric, Technology, and Pedagogy* 6, no, 1 (2011).

Ritter, Kelly, and Paul Kei Matsuda, eds. *Exploring Composition Studies: Sites, Issues, Perspectives.* Logan: Utah State University Press, 2012.

Rosenblatt, Louise. *Literature as Exploration.* New York: D. Appleton-Century, 1938.

Sedgwick, Eve Kosofsky. *Epistemology of the Closet: Updated with a New Preface.* 2nd ed. Berkeley: University of California Press, 2008.

Severino, Carol, Juan C. Guerra, and Johnnella E. Butler ed. *Writing in Multicultural Settings (Research and Scholarship in Composition).* New York: Modern Language Association, 1997.

Silva, Tony, and Paul Kei Matsuda, eds. *Practicing Theory in Second Language Writing.* Anderson, S.C.: Parlor Press: 2010.

TED Talks. Technology, Entertainment and Design. https://www.ted.com/talks/browse. December 8, 2014.

Turkle, Sherry. *Alone Together: Why We Expect More from Technology and Less from Each Other.* New York: Basic Books, 2011.

Warnock, Scott. *Teaching Writing Online: How and Why.* Urbana, Ill.: National Council of Teachers of English, 2009.

WPA Outcomes Statement for First-Year Composition (3.0).Adopted by the Council of Writing Program Administrators (CWPA) July 17, 2014. http://wpacouncil.org/positions/outcomes.html. January 1, 2015

Zawacki, Terry Myers, and Michelle Cox, eds. *WAC and Second-Language Writers: Research towards Linguistically and Culturally Inclusive Programs and Practices.* Anderson, S.C.: Parlor Press, 2014.

ACKNOWLEDGMENTS

This book is a true collaboration. It began as a project of the Jesuit Conference on Rhetoric and Composition, a group of scholars and teachers at Jesuit colleges who felt the need for sharing teaching approaches and scholarship. Cinthia agreed to help coordinate and commission chapters from scholars among the group, and she and John, her husband, ultimately agreed to serve as editors of the volume, but many members of the group helped shape and develop the collection, and many other scholars, interested in Jesuit educational history and Jesuit rhetoric, joined us along the way. We're pleased to report that our contributors represent faculty from sixteen different Jesuit and at least eleven secular universities. Patricia Bizzell at the College of the Holy Cross wrote and presented an early inquiry on Jesuit rhetorical history that circulated informally for years and served as a prompt for the entire JCRC. Peggy O'Neill at Loyola University of Maryland, Cinthia's former colleague, was instrumental to the formal creation of the JCRC, and Virginia Chappelle from Marquette University for many years hosted the listserv we all used to build our original community of scholars.

John traces part of his interest to a conversation he had with Bob Connors at a Conference on College Composition and Communication meeting in the mid-1980s. He and Bob were talking about areas of rhetorical history that had been overlooked by historians of composition. John said "the Jesuits," and Bob, after a moment's consideration, nodded his agreement. This volume is a long-delayed follow-up to that conversation and a tribute to Bob's memory.

We both want to acknowledge the enthusiastic reception we found from a whole series of scholars who led us to wonderful sources, both human and textual. We owe a special debt to the Jesuits who were willing to share their knowledge and provide us with feedback. Among them are John Padberg, who spent an afternoon with us in his St. Louis office, helping set us on our path with rich bibliographical materials; John O'Malley, the dean of Jesuit historians, who helped shape our thinking early on and set us straight more than once; and Paul Fitzgerald, who believes in eloquence. French Jesuits Patrick Goujon and Marc Rastoin welcomed us to the Jesuit house on rue Blomet in Paris and explained much of the tangled history of the Jesuits in France. We also owe a huge debt to the entire Jesuit community at Campion Hall at Oxford, where we spent an extraordinary week, a visit facilitated through the good offices of Fairfield University's James Bowler, S.J., then a visiting fellow at Oxford, and Fairfield University's president, Jeffrey von Arx, S.J. At the University of London our good friend Mary Scott introduced us to Paddy Walsh, a great source of information about the Jesuits in England.

One of the pleasures of doing a book like this is the conversations it leads one to have with colleagues. We have benefited greatly from such conversations with Isabelle Delcambre of the University of Lille; Sylvie Plane of the Sorbonne, and her husband, Bruno, himself educated by Jesuits; Martine Jey and Delphine Denis of the Sorbonne; Louise Wetherbee Phelps of Old Dominion University; and Susan Jarratt of the University of California, Irvine. Their generosity and helpful interest in the project gratified us to no end.

Excellent colleagues at both Loyola Maryland and Fairfield, where Cinthia has worked, have provided critical support and advice ("Just finish!") and patiently endured her frequent impromptu expostulations on the place and promise of Jesuit *eloquentia perfecta*. A research sabbatical from Fairfield provided needed time and space for such an unwieldy project to be assembled, and our visits to Fordham University, Loyola Marymount University to work with Dorothea Herreiner, John Carroll University to work with Tom Pace, and Loyola University of New Orleans to work with Kate Adams and Stephen Rowntree, S.J., provoked our thinking and fostered our work along the way. We thank our community of contributors for their many versions and revisions; one piece that came in near the end identified itself as "Draft 23." And Cinthia wants to remember Bob Connors, who loved a juicy story about rhetorical history; Don Murray, who reminded her to write in all the nooks and crannies of a day; and Tom Newkirk, who helps her to care about big odd questions.

We owe special thanks to our astute reviewers, James Murphy of the University of California, Davis; Deborah Holdstein at Columbia College, Chicago; and one anonymous reviewer, all of whom provided us with important suggestions for improvement. At Fordham University Press, Fred Nachbaur, Eric Newman, and Will Cerbone have been highly supportive editors, the kind every author hopes to have. And Fordham's astute copy editor Nicholas Frankovich has skillfully shepherded our complex manuscript through a long and tedious process.

Our cover comes from one of our favorite galleries, London's Wallace Collection. It represents one way the Renaissance appropriated classical learning, with young Cicero, dressed in Renaissance garb, anachronistically reading a book, not a scroll, with a pile of books next to him. Foppa's fifteenth-century fresco at once idealizes classicism and makes it approachable, just as the Jesuits would do when they were founded in the next century.

Of course, apologies to our families. Books take too long.

CONTRIBUTORS

KATHERINE ADAMS is the William and Audrey Hutchinson Distinguished Professor of English at Loyola University New Orleans. With Michael L. Keene, her book publications include *Women of the American Circus, 1880–1940*; *After the Vote Was Won: The Later Achievements of Fifteen Suffragists*; *Alice Paul and the American Suffrage Campaign*; *Seeing the American Woman, 1880–1920: The Social Impact of the Visual Media Explosion*; *Controlling Representations: Depictions of Women in a Mainstream Newspaper, 1900–1950*; *Easy Access: The Reference Handbook for Writers*, and *Instant Access: The Pocket Handbook for Writers*. She is also the author of *A Group of Their Own: College Writing Courses and American Women Writers, 1880–1940*; *A History of Professional Writing Instruction in American Colleges*; *Progressive Politics and the Training of America's Persuaders*; *Teaching Advanced Composition: Why and How*; and *The Accomplished Writer*.

JOHN C. BEAN, emeritus professor of English at Seattle University, is the author of *Engaging Ideas: The Professor's Guide to Writing, Critical Thinking, and Active Learning in the Classroom*, 2nd edition (Jossey-Bass, 2011) and co-author of three composition textbooks—*Writing Arguments*, *The Allyn and Bacon Guide to Writing*, and *Reading Rhetorically*. He has also published numerous articles on writing pedagogy and, earlier in his career, on literary subjects including Shakespeare and Spenser. In 2010 his article "Messy Problems and Lay Audiences: Teaching Critical Thinking within the Finance Curriculum" (co-authored with colleagues from finance and economics) won the 2009 McGraw-Hill—Magna Publications Award for the year's best "scholarly work on teaching and learning."

PATRICIA BIZZELL is Distinguished Professor of English at the College of the Holy Cross, where she has taught since 1978, regularly offering courses in academic writing and in rhetoric theory and practice. Among her publications is *The Rhetorical Tradition*, co-authored with Bruce Herzberg, which won the National Council of Teachers of English Outstanding Book Award in 1992. She was given the Exemplar Award by the Conference on College Composition and Communication in 2008. Her recent projects include helping to set up a writing-across-the-curriculum program at Sogang, the Jesuit university in Seoul, South Korea, and writing a book about the experiences and opinions of expat English teachers there. She earned a master's degree in Jewish studies at Hebrew College in 2013 and continues to study and publish on Moses ben Nachman, a.k.a. Nachmanides, an important medieval rabbi.

JOHN C. BRERETON is professor emeritus of English at the University of Massachusetts Boston. He has also taught at the City University of New York, Wayne State University, Brandeis University, and Harvard University. Among his books are *The Origins of Composition Studies in the American College, 1875–1925*, which won the Outstanding Book Award from the Conference on College Composition and Communication; *The Norton Reader*; *Living Literature*; and *A Plan for Writing*. In 2012–15 he served on the executive board of the Conference on College Composition and Communication; he now serves on the executive board of the Division of the History and Theory of Rhetoric of the Modern Language Association.

VINCENT CASAREGOLA received his doctorate in English at the University of Iowa in 1989. He is a professor of English and film studies at Saint Louis University, where he also served as writing-program director in 1994–2007. His areas of interest include film and media studies, rhetorical studies, and American cultural studies. He has published numerous academic articles, along with poetry and creative nonfiction. In his book *Theaters of War* he examines the American representation of the Second World War, in literature and on film, from the war itself up to the twenty-first century.

FRANK D'ANGELO is professor emeritus of English at Arizona State University. He has served as chair of the Conference on College Composition and Communication and on the board of the Rhetoric Society of America, the MLA Division on the Teaching of Writing, and on the executive committee of the National Council of Teachers of English. He won the Braddock Award for the best article in *College Composition and Communication*. His many publications include *A Conceptual Theory of Rhetoric* and many articles and book chapters on rhetoric and composition studies.

THOMAS DEANS teaches, directs the writing center, and leads a writing-across-the-curriculum program at the University of Connecticut. He is the author of *Writing Partnerships: Service-Learning in Composition* and *Writing and Community Action: A Service-Learning Rhetoric and Reader*; he is also co-editor of *Writing and Community Engagement: A Critical Sourcebook* and series co-editor for the Oxford Brief Guides to Writing in the Disciplines. While most of his research focuses on contemporary writing instruction, he also does some work on early modern literacy practices. His engagement with the Jesuit tradition emerged during his studies at Georgetown and a year with the Jesuit Volunteer Corps.

ANNE FERNALD is associate professor of English and director of Writing and Composition at the Lincoln Center campus of Fordham University. She has taught composition courses at Yale (where she received her doctorate) and at Fordham. She is the author of *Virginia Woolf: Feminism and the Reader*, the editor of a textual edition of *Mrs. Dalloway*, and an editor of *The Norton Reader*.

JENN FISHMAN, associate professor of English at Marquette University, is the author of scholarship that has appeared in *Composition Studies, Composition Forum, College Composition and Communication, The WAC Journal*, and several edited collections. Her editorial work includes special issues of *CCC Online* and *Peitho* as well as of *REx: The Research Exchange Index*. Her long-term research extends from the Stanford Study of Writing and the Embodied Literacies Project to Kenyon Writes, an Andrew W. Mellon–funded study of writing at Kenyon College in Gambier, Ohio.

MAUREEN A. J. FITZSIMMONS holds a bachelor's and a master's degree in English from Loyola Marymount University in Los Angeles. She is currently working on a doctorate in English at the University of California, Irvine, focusing on rhetoric and composition. She has served as vice chair of the Jesuit Conference on Rhetoric and Composition and as co-president of the UCI Rhetoric and Composition Graduate Collective and has been appointed a UCI Regent's Fellow and a fellow in the Lilly Fellows Program in the Humanities and the Arts. Her scholarly interests include composition historiography, composition pedagogy in all its manifestations, and media ecologies.

CINTHIA GANNETT is associate professor of English and director of Core Writing at Fairfield University. She is the author of *Gender and the Journal* and many professional articles in the United States and abroad. Previously she directed the writing center at Loyola College of Maryland and at the University of New Hampshire. She has served on the executive board of the Rhetoric Society of America and in 2012–15 served as president of the Jesuit Conference on Composition and Rhetoric.

ANN E. GREEN is professor of English at St. Joseph's University. Her many publications include "'The Quality of Light': Using Narrative in a Peer Tutoring Class," in *Writing Centers and the New Racism*, edited by Laura Greenfield and Karen Rowan; "Local Politics and Voice: Speaking to be Heard," in *Academic Cultures: Professional Preparation and the Teaching Life*, edited by Sean P. Murphy; and "Diversity Work and the WPA: Feminist and Activist Writing Center Work Prior to Tenure," in *Promise and Peril of Writing Program Administration*, edited by Theresa Enos and Sean Borrowman. In 2015 she was elected president of the Jesuit Conference on Composition and Rhetoric.

MICHAEL HALLORAN is professor emeritus of English at Rensselaer Polytechnic Institute. He is the co-author, with Gregory Clark, of *Oratorical Culture in Nineteenth-Century America: Essays on the Transformation of Rhetoric*, and has published many articles and book chapters on the history of American rhetoric. In 1992–93 he served as president of the Rhetoric Society of America.

GERARD HAUSER is professor emeritus of Communication at the University of Colorado, Boulder. Among his many publications are *Introduction to Rhetorical Theory*, *Vernacular Voices: The Rhetoric of Publics and Public Spheres*; *Prisoners of Conscience: Moral Vernaculars of Political Agency*, and numerous research articles on the subject of rhetorical theory and criticism. He is a Distinguished Scholar of the National Communication Association (NCA) and a fellow of the Rhetoric Society of America (RSA). He is recipient of NCA's Marie Hochmuth Nichols Book Award, RSA's Charles Kneupper Outstanding Article Award, and RSA's George E. Yoos Distinguished Service Award.

JOSEPH JANANGELO is past president of the Council of Writing Program Administrators and associate professor of English at Loyola University Chicago. His publications include *Resituating Writing: Constructing and Administering Writing Programs* (with Kristine Hansen) and *Theoretical and Critical Perspectives on Teacher Change*. His work has appeared in *College Composition and Communication*, *College English*, *Computers and Composition*, *Journal of Teaching Writing*, *The Writing Center Journal*, *WPA: Writing Program Administration*, and *Kairos: A Journal of Rhetoric, Technology, and Pedagogy*, *Rhetoric Review*.

DAVID LEIGH, S.J., was ordained a priest in 1968 and completed his doctorate in English at Yale University in 1972. He has taught English at Gonzaga University (1972–83) and at Seattle University (1983–present). He has also served as English Department chair and as director of the University Core Curriculum at Seattle University. His publications include *Circuitous Journeys: Modern Spiritual Autobiography* and *Apocalyptic Patterns in Twentieth-Century Fiction*, as well as dozens of articles on British literature.

STEVEN MAILLOUX is President's Professor of Rhetoric at Loyola Marymount University. Previously, he taught rhetoric, critical theory, and nineteenth-century U.S. cultural studies at the University of California, Irvine. His books include *Interpretive Conventions: The Reader in the Study of American Fiction*; *Rhetorical Power*; *Reception Histories: Rhetoric, Pragmatism, and American Cultural Politics*; and *Disciplinary Identities: Rhetorical Paths of English, Speech, and Composition*.

ROBERT MARYKS is associate professor of history at Boston College. He has published on various aspects of the history of the Jesuits, including *Saint Cicero and the Jesuits*; *The Jesuit Order as a Synagogue of Jews*; *Pouring Jewish Water into Fascist Wine*; *"The Tragic Couple": Encounters Between Jews and Jesuits* (co-edited with James Bernauer); *A Companion to Ignatius of Loyola*; and *Jesuit Survival and Restoration* (co-edited with Jonathan Wright). He is associate director of the Institute for Advanced Jesuit Studies at Boston College, editor-in-chief of the *Journal of Jesuit Studies* and of the book series Jesuit Studies, and general editor of *The New Sommervogel: Boston College Jesuit Bibliography*.

PAULA MATTHIEU is associate professor of English and director of the writing program at Boston College. She is the author of *Tactics of Hope: The Public Turn in English Composition*; *Writing Places* (with George Grattan, Tim Lindgren, and Staci Shultz) and "Questions of Time: Publishing and Group Identity in the StreetWise Writers Group," in *Writing Groups Inside and Outside the Classroom*. She is co-editor, with David Downing and Claude Mark Hurlburt, of *Beyond English, Inc.: Curricular Reform for a Global Economy*.

CAROL MATTINGLY, retired professor of English, taught rhetoric, writing, and literature and administered writing programs at a variety of institutions, including Louisiana State University and the University of Louisville. Her publications include *Well-Tempered Women: Nineteenth-Century Temperance Rhetoric* and *Appropriate[ing] Dress: Women's Rhetorical Style in Nineteenth-Century America*.

GINA M. MERYS earned her doctorate in rhetoric and composition at Saint Louis University. After serving as the director of composition and assistant professor of English at Creighton University, she returned to Saint Louis University, where she serves as the associate director of the Paul C. Reinert, S.J., Center for Transformative Teaching and Learning. Her scholarship focuses on Ignatian pedagogy, discourse practices, literacy issues, digital technology, and postcolonial and gender studies. Her peer-reviewed publications have appeared in edited collections as well as scholarly journals.

KATE M. NASH is a doctoral candidate at the Rose Hill campus of Fordham University. She has taught rhetoric and composition as well as modern Irish literature.

GERALD NELMS received his doctorate in English, specializing in rhetoric and composition, from Ohio State University, where he studied under Edward P. J. Corbett and Andrea Lunsford. For twenty years, Jerry was on the faculty at Southern Illinois University Carbondale, where he directed the communication-across-the-curriculum program in addition to holding other administrative posts as well as teaching. He began his scholarly work as a historian of rhetoric and composition, focusing on the development of modern composition studies and the influence of classical rhetoric in particular. He has also published and presented papers on historiography, writing across the curriculum, plagiarism, writing and learning assessment, journal writing, active learning, knowledge transfer, student learning, and teaching researched writing. Nelms is currently a visiting instructional consultant at the University Center for the Advancement of Teaching at Ohio State University and is involved in studies on bridging rhetoric and composition and faculty development.

LARRY C. NICHOLS has wrestled for over forty years with questions and teaching strategies based on two core beliefs: that anyone can write well and that any piece of writing can become effective. As director of the Seattle University Writing Center from 1993 to 2015, he applied those beliefs in teaching over two hundred undergraduate writing consultants learn skillful means of helping students successfully negotiate all sorts of writing tasks. For over twenty years, Larry collaborated closely with John Bean and other faculty colleagues to create and sustain a dynamic writing program at Seattle University. Invested in bringing writing-center colleagues into meaningful dialogue, he has served as founding treasurer and president of the Pacific Northwest Writing Centers Association. Now retired from Seattle University, Larry continues to teach writing and serve writers as a writing coach and editor. More information about that work is available at larrycnichols.com.

REBECCA NOWACEK is associate professor of English and director of the Norman H. Ott Memorial Writing Center at Marquette University. Her books include *Agents of Integration: Understanding Transfer as a Rhetorical Act*, *Literacy, Economy, and Power* (co-edited with Julie Christoph, John Duffy, Eli Goldblatt, Nelson Graff, and Bryan Trabold) and *Citizenship Across the Curriculum* (co-edited with Michael B. Smith and Jeffrey L. Bernstein). She is co-author, with Susan Mountin, of "Reflection in Action: A Signature Ignatian Pedagogy for the 21st Century," in *Exploring More Signature Pedagogies*, edited by Nancy Chick, Aeron Haynie, and Regan Gurung.

JOHN O'MALLEY, S.J., is University Professor in the theology department at Georgetown University. His specialty is the religious culture of early modern Europe, especially Renaissance humanism. His most important work dealing with rhetoric is *Praise and Blame in Renaissance Rome*, which won the Marraro Prize from the American Historical Association in 1979. He has written extensively on the early history of the Society of Jesus and on the Jesuit tradition of education, including its rhetorical aspects. He is a fellow of the American Academy of Arts and Sciences, elected in 1996, and of the American Philosophical Society, elected 1997, and has received many other honors and awards for his scholarship.

THOMAS PACE is associate professor of English and director of Core Writing at John Carroll University, where he teaches a variety of writing and literature courses. He also directs the English department's Professional Writing Track. His areas of interest include style, the history of writing instruction, and popular culture. He has published articles on style and audience and is the co-editor of *Refiguring Prose Style: Possibilities for Writing Pedagogy*. More recently, he has published on the rhetoric of Generation X in such television shows as *Mad Men* and *Girls*.

KAREN PALEY taught literature and writing over a twenty-year period at institutions including Boston College and Loyola Marymount University, where she directed the freshman English program. She is the author of *I-Writing: The Politics and Practice of Teaching First-Person Writing* and "Impaired Faculty: Tenure: Treatment, or Termination?" Paley is currently a financial representative for John Hancock in Warwick, Rhode Island, with special interests in socially responsible investing and long-term health care.

K. J. PETERS is an associate professor of rhetoric and critical theory in the Department of English at Loyola Marymount University. Among his publications are articles addressing the thematics of Hemingway, the rhetoric of privacy, Levinasian phenomenology, and academic freedom. His current research includes the rhetorical tradition of Jesuit education and a reimagining of classical rhetorical concepts for the contemporary multimedia classroom. He currently serves as the director of the freshman English program at LMU.

JEFFREY S. PHILPOTT is a rhetorician in the Department of Communication at Seattle University. His work in rhetorical theory and criticism focuses on public epistemology, particularly on how shared meanings of major events are constructed and transformed in news and political discourse. He currently serves as director of the Seattle University Core Curriculum, where he has been guiding a major revision of the general-education program, which includes the infusion of rhetorical skills throughout the curriculum.

PAUL RANIERI teaches first-year writing, rhetoric, and the humanities at Ball State University. He has been an educator for more than forty years and credits his learning experiences at Xavier University (Ohio), Trinity University (Texas), and the University of Texas at Austin with challenging him to ask the "big" questions, the ones that seek to integrate human knowledge and practical wisdom. He is currently working on two major projects: a pair of multimodal, digital textbooks for first-year composition, and a monograph on liberal education in the twenty-first century. Both projects are rooted in classical rhetoric, a contemporary understanding of cognition, and the resulting demand for integrating classical and digital approaches to learning and assessment.

KRISTA RATCLIFFE became chair of the English department at Purdue University in 2015. Her publications include *Rhetorical Listening: Identification, Gender, Whiteness* (winner of the Outstanding Book Award from the Conference on College Composition and Communication), *Anglo-American Feminist Challenges to the Rhetorical Traditions: Virginia Woolf, Mary Daly, and Adrienne Rich*, and many articles and book chapters. In 2012 she served as president of the Rhetoric Society of America. She has also served as president of the Coalition of Women Scholars in the History of Rhetoric and Composition, as a member of MLA's Division on Teaching Writing, and on the advisory board of *PMLA*.

JANICE LAUER RICE is professor emerita of English at Purdue University. She has been Reece McGee Distinguished Professor of English at Purdue University, where she founded and directed a doctoral program in rhetoric and composition. In 1998 she received the Exemplar Award from the Conference on College Composition and Communication. For thirteen summers she directed a two-week international rhetoric seminar. She has served on the executive committees of CCCC, the National Council of Teachers of English, the Rhetoric Society of America, and the Discussion Group in the History and Theory of Rhetoric of the Modern Language Association; she has coordinated the Consortium of Doctoral Programs in Rhetoric and Composition. Her publications include *Four Worlds of Writing: Inquiry and Action in Context*; *Composition Research: Empirical Designs*; *New Perspectives on Rhetorical Invention*; and *Rhetorical Invention in Rhetoric and Composition*, as well as essays on invention, disciplinarity, writing as inquiry, composition pedagogy, historical rhetoric, and empirical research.

MIKE ROSE is research professor at the UCLA Graduate School of Education and Information Studies. He has received a Guggenheim Fellowship, the Mina P. Shaughnessy Prize from the Modern Language Association for Outstanding Research Publication in the Teaching of English Language and Literature, and the Outstanding Book Award from the Conference on College Composition and Communication. Among his many publications are *Lives on the Boundary*; *Why School?: Reclaiming Education for All of Us*; *An Open Language: Selected Writing on Literacy, Learning, and Opportunity*; *Possible Lives: The Promise of Public Education in America*; *The Mind at Work: Valuing the Intelligence of the American Worker*, and many articles and book chapters on language and literacy in America. He has been elected to the National Academy of Education.

THOMAS WORCESTER, S.J., is professor of history at the College of the Holy Cross; he is a specialist in the religious and cultural history of early modern France and Italy and the author of *Seventeenth-Century Cultural Discourse: France and the Preaching of Bishop Camus*. He has published articles in journals including *Seventeenth-Century French Studies*, *Sixteenth Century Journal*, and *French Colonial History*. Editor of *The Cambridge Companion to the Jesuits*, he is also co-editor of four books, including *From Rome to Eternity: Catholicism and the Arts in Italy, ca. 1550–1650*, co-edited with Pamela Jones, and *The Papacy since 1500: From Italian Prince to Universal Pastor*, co-edited with James Corkery, S.J. He is general editor of the *Cambridge Encyclopedia of the Jesuits*, scheduled for publication in 2017.

INDEX